THE
FAQS
FREQUENTLY ASKED QUESTIONS
OF
LIFE

THE
FAQS
FREQUENTLY ASKED QUESTIONS
OF
LIFE

EDITED BY CAMILLE N. CLINE

CADER BOOKS • NEW YORK

**Andrews McMeel
Publishing**

Kansas City

THANK YOU for buying this Cader Book—we hope you enjoy it. And thanks as well to the store that sold you this, and the hardworking sales rep who sold it to them. It takes a lot of people to make a book. Here are some of the many who were instrumental:

EDITORIAL: Jake Morrissey, Dorothy O'Brien, Nora Donaghy
DESIGN: Charles Kreloff and Orit Mardkha-Tenzer
COPY EDITING/PROOFING/INDEXING: Ann Adelman, Roland Ottewell, Joan Jackson
PRODUCTION: Polly Blair, Carol Coe
LEGAL: Renee Schwartz, Esq.
WRITING/RESEARCH: Jenny Bent, Adam B. Bernstein, Genevieve Field, Alfred Glossbrenner, Emily Glossbrenner, Amy Lemley, Fabienne Marsh, Timothy A. Meis, Tanya Mohn, Jennifer Nauss, Michael O'Halloran, Eileen Smith, David Wall, Deborah E. Yeh
ADDITIONAL HELP: Jesse Wann, Rhonda Wills

If you would like to share any thoughts about this book, or are interested in other books by us, please write to:
Cader Books
38 E. 29th Street
New York, NY 10016
Or visit our Web site:
http://www.caderbooks.com

Library of Congress Cataloging-in-Publication Data

The FAQs of life: over 2,500 of the most frequently asked questions and their answers on every topic imaginable. —1st ed.
p.   cm.
ISBN 0-8362-3574-6 (pbk.)
1. Questions and answers.   I. Cader Books.
AG195.F37   1997
031.02—dc21   97-27469
                                                                          CIP

November 1997
First Edition
10 9 8 7 6 5 4 3 2 1

Attention: Schools and Businesses
Andrews McMeel Publishing books are available at quantity discounts with bulk purchase for educational, business, or sales promotional use. For information, please write to: Special Sales Department, Andrews McMeel Publishing, 4520 Main Street, Kansas City, MO 64111.

Contents

Introduction

For those of you unfamiliar with the term, FAQs are the helpful lists of frequently asked questions and answers invented on the Internet to help newcomers and browsers alike resolve common queries. *The FAQs of Life* reinvents this handy convention and takes it to the next level—by presenting FAQs on all manner of subjects, from questions on home decorating to answers on pipe smoking. Many of our entries come from authorities who routinely provide answers to questions about their fields. Other lists were specially created by experts who have been asked for years about what they do. Not only will you find out the most-sought information, but you'll also discover which entertaining and compelling questions keep us up at night (like "Whatever happened to New Coke?" and "How much should I spend on an engagement ring?").

Every chapter in this book is filled with great information—the answers either complete your search about a specific issue or subject, or serve as a springboard for further research. The source notes at the end of each Q&A often give you other reference points, including publication names, telephone and fax numbers, mailing addresses, and Web sites or e-mail addresses.

The FAQs of Life was long in the making, and many of our sources were contacted or contacted us numerous times to update the time-sensitive data. Their generosity with their time, resources, and expertise is readily apparent in the quality of the information. All court cases, technological breakthroughs, and government findings are current up to this writing. It is impossible to detail the special kindnesses and enthusiasm of our source contacts, but I wish to thank them all for their help.

I also wish to thank the researchers and writers who worked many long hours to put together these chapters, some of which were not included because our page count would have been pushed to an unmanageable size. Some of these researchers worked on this project for more than two years, and their dedication and professionalism toward this endeavor were enormously helpful to me.

Special thanks also to Deborah Yeh, who came in at a critical point in the organization of the project; Cathe Giffuni, who fact-checked many of our FAQs; and the Larchmont Public Library Reference Desk and all the other people who got us moving in the right direction.

—CAMILLE N. CLINE,
Editor

Abbreviations

AA	Alcoholics Anonymous
AAP	American Academy of Pediatrics
AARP	American Association of Retired Persons
ACLU	American Civil Liberties Union
ADD	Attention Deficit Disorder
AFDC	Aid to Families with Dependent Children
AIA	American Institute of Architects
AIDS	Acquired immunodeficiency syndrome
AI	Amnesty International
ANSI	American National Standards Institute
AOL	America Online
ASL	American Sign Language
ASTM	American Society for Testing and Materials
ATM	Automated Teller Machine
AZT	azidothymidine
CAT	computerized axial tomography
CD	certificate of deposit; compact disk
CDC	Centers for Disease Control and Prevention
CFS	chronic fatigue syndrome
COM	computer output microfilm
CPA	certified public accountant
CPR	cardiopulmonary resuscitation
CPS	cycles per second
CPSC	Computer Product Safety Commission
CPU	central processing unit
D/ART	Depression Awareness, Recognition, and Treatment
DEA	Drug Enforcement Agency
DNA	deoxyribonucleic acid
EBV	Epstein-Barr virus
ECG	electrocardiogram
ECT	electroconvulsive therapy
EEO	equal employment opportunity
EEOC	Equal Employment Opportunity Commission
EKG	electrocardiogram; electrocardiograph
EMTALA	Emergency Medical Treatment and Active Labor Act
EPA	Environmental Protection Agency
ERT	estrogen replacement therapy
FAA	Federal Aviation Administration
FBI	Federal Bureau of Investigation
FCC	Federal Communications Commission
FDA	Food and Drug Administration
FDIC	Federal Deposit Insurance Corporation

FICA	Federal Insurance Contributions Act
FOIA	Freedom of Information Act
FRB	Federal Reserve Board
FSLIC	Federal Savings and Loan Insurance Corporation
FTC	Federal Trade Commission
GAO	General Accounting Office
GATT	General Agreement on Tariffs and Trade
HBV	hepatitis B virus
HIV	human immunodeficiency virus
HMO	health maintenance organization
HRT	hormone replacement therapy
INS	Immigration and Naturalization Service
IRA	individual retirement account
IRS	Internal Revenue Service
ISP	Internet service provider
IUD	intrauterine device
IVF	*in vitro* fertilization
MS	multiple sclerosis
NAIC	National Association of Investors Corporation
NAMI	National Alliance for the Mentally Ill
NARA	National Archives and Records Administration
NASA	National Aeronautics and Space Administration
NAV	net asset value
NHTSA	National Organization of Circumcision Information Resource Centers
NIMH	National Institute for Mental Health
NORML	National Organization for the Reform of Marijuana Laws
NOW	National Organization of Women
NPA	National Peliculosis Association
OCD	obsessive-compulsive disorder
OSHA	Occupational Safety and Health Administration
PMS	premenstrual syndrome
PVC	polyvinyl chloride
S&Ls	savings and loans
SRI	seritonin reuptake inhibitor
STD	sexually transmitted disease
STI	sexually transmitted infection
TD	traveler's diarrhea
UFO	unidentified flying object
WHO	World Health Organization
www	World Wide Web

HOME

———◇———

Architects and Contractors

What does an architect do?

An architect can guide you through the entire design and construction process, starting with helping you define what you want to build. Whether you are remodeling, adding on, or building from scratch, an architect can help. Working with contractors and other construction professionals, the architect should enable you to end up with a well-designed project that meets your needs, budget, and time frame.

A well-conceived project can be built efficiently and economically. An architect can design a building to maximize heating from the sun and let in natural light, thus reducing your heating, cooling, and electric bills. She will help you choose materials and finishes that are durable as well as aesthetically pleasing. Architects also stay up to date on advances in roofing, brickwork, floor tiling, paint finishes, and more.

The architect will help you select appropriate materials and construction at a fair price. She will look out for your interests and try to find ways to make the building process go smoothly. If your project requires engineering or other design services, the architect can coordinate this team of experts for you. The architect will sort out building codes and zoning laws, help you find qualified construction contractors, and visit the construction site to verify that the project is being built according to plans and specifications.

How do I work with an architect?

Most projects start with a want or need. The architect works with you to translate that want or need into square feet and three-dimensional space.

Your first step is to think carefully about your goals. Do you need more space? Who will use the space? What activities will be housed in the space? How much can you spend on the project? How will you finance the project? Where will it be located? Do you plan to do some of the work yourself? Don't worry if you don't have all the answers. The architect can help you clarify all this. As your ideas evolve, so does the building plan. The architect's thorough drawings and specifications enable you to get accurate bids from contractors and help the contractor to build the project.

Another cost-effective building and remodeling trend is the growing number of architects who design *and* build projects, which gives homeowners flexibility in both design and construction. With this approach, the architect assumes sole responsibility for developing the design, establishing the construction budget, and hiring and supervising the labor, within a guaranteed maximum price. An architect can help determine whether this is an appropriate option for either new construction or a remodeling project.

Designing a building is an exciting, creative challenge. The process can be fun, satisfying, and positive; it can also be hard work. The best projects are created when client and architect work together as a team. You should take an active role. If at any time in the design process you are uncomfortable about something, discuss it with your architect. You don't want to feel that the building is no longer yours. But you also want to be careful not to restrict the architect so much that you don't get your money's worth in terms of design creativity.

How do I find the right architect?

Architects vary in their style, approach to design, and methods of work, so it's important to find one who understands your style and needs. Start by building a list of potential names. Find out who designed projects in your community that you like. Get recommendations from friends, relatives, or acquaintances. Check to see if the architect is a member of the American Institute of Architects (AIA); such membership in the AIA means that the architect subscribes to a professional code of ethics and has access to professional and technical resources. Contact your local AIA chapter; many have lists of member-owned architecture firms and their areas of specialization. Another option is to have a look at the listings in the AIA Web site: http://www.aiaonline.com.

Call each firm on your list. Describe your project and ask if they are available to take it on. If they are, request literature outlining the firm's qualifications and experience. (If they can't take on your project, they may be able to suggest another firm.) In reply, you might receive a letter, brochures, fact sheets, photos of past work, and biographical material about key personnel. Try to determine which firms have the right experience and capabilities for you. At this point, you should be able to narrow your list to two or three. Some architects charge for an interview, so ask up front if there is a fee. An interview is important, because you will be working with the architect for a long time; allow at least an hour. The meeting might take place at the architect's office, so you can see where the work will be done; or it could be at your home or office, which is helpful if the architect can learn more about the project that way. The architect may show you slides or photographs of past work.

Ask questions: How busy is the firm? Does it have the capacity to take on your work? Who will handle the job? Insist on meeting the person who will actually design your project. What is the firm's design philosophy? How does the architect intend to approach your project? How interested is the firm in your job? Talk about your budget and find out the range of fees the architect anticipates. If during the discussion you don't understand something, ask the architect for clarification. If you feel intimidated, or if the architect doesn't explain things in a way that you can understand, then that person may not be right for you. Before making a final decision, have the architect take you to a completed project. It is proper to ask your architect for references from past clients. These references are invaluable.

Once you have found your architect, you are ready to put in writing the terms of your agreement on the scope of the work, services, schedule, construction budget, and architect's compensation. This written agreement can take many forms. The AIA has developed a variety of standard contract forms that are used industrywide.

How do architects get paid?

How architects charge for their services can be confusing because there is no set fee for a particular type of project. Fees are established in a number of ways, depending on the sort of project and the amount and nature of the services.

Some projects are best done at hourly rates; others are best done for a stipulated sum per unit, based on what is to be built—for example, the number of square feet, or the number of apartments or rooms. Some architects charge a fixed fee; some charge a percentage of construction costs.

Discuss with the architect how she would expect to establish the fee. The architect may suggest a combination of the above methods. The basis for the fee, the amount, and the payment schedule are all issues for you to work out together.

What are "schematics"?

An architect's rough sketches are known as "schematic" designs. These show you the general arrangement of rooms and the site. If you have difficulty understanding the schematic designs—and many people do—ask the architect to explain. Some architects will also make models of the design so you can visualize it. The schematic designs are not finished construction documents; they are meant to show possible approaches for you to consider.

What does the contractor do?

The general contractor, or builder, is responsible for construction methods, techniques, schedules, and procedures. Using the project drawings and specifications prepared by your architect, the contractor creates the actual building. The contractor is the person who buys the materials and assembles the work teams. Although your architect will periodically observe the construction, the contractor is the person who supervises and directs the day-to-day work and bears the responsibility for its completion.

How do I choose a contractor?

There are a number of ways. Your architect may make recommendations. You can also ask neighbors and friends about contractors they have worked with. If you already know of someone you want to work with, you could send the construction documents to that contractor and negotiate fees and costs. Frequently, contractors are selected through a bidding process. The architect will help you prepare the bidding documents, which consist of the drawings and specifications for the project. These are sent to several contractors, along with a letter inviting them to bid. Within a stated period of time, the contractors then submit bids. The lowest bidder is often selected to do the work, but not always.

The architect can recommend contractors and assist you in the selection process, but the final choice is up to you. Some people prefer to act as their own general contractor or do part or all of the construction themselves. These methods can save you money initially but can also add problems and costs later on. Discuss the pros and cons with your architect, who can help you decide what will work best.

Source: The American Institute of Architects, 1735 New York Ave., NW, Washington, DC 20006; phone: (202) 626-7300; Web site: www.aiaonline.com.

Barrier-Free Living

What do people mean by "barrier-free living" and "universal design"?

"Barrier-free living" and "universal design" are two concepts of designing an environment for maximum use by all people. Everyday examples of barrier-free elements range from ramps and curb cuts to levered door handles. Universal design applies to far more than people who use wheelchairs. Strobe-equipped fire alarms tell people who are deaf and hearing-impaired that there is an emergency. Traffic signals with audible chimes let people who are blind know it's safe to cross the street. "Talking" signs help people with learning disabilities read maps and directions. The "universal" in universal design means exactly that—the design should help everybody.

I don't have a disability. How does universal design help me?

Have you ever pushed a stroller or shopping cart? Think of how much easier that is to do when a curb cut allows you to roll the stroller or cart along a slight incline and you don't have to struggle up and down a curb. Have you ever cursed to yourself as you tried to shop in a store where the merchandise racks were crammed together and the lighting was so poor you couldn't read the tags? The wider aisles and brighter lighting mandated by the Americans with Disabilities Act of 1991 have made everyone's shopping more pleasant. Do you use an ergonomic keyboard or a soft-grip pen or pencil at work? If so, you are using aids to daily living initially designed for people with disabilities.

If you are planning outdoor activities, is your yard accessible? Many wheelchair users will have no problem with a yard; but uneven terrain, wooded areas, or transitions between paving, decks, and lawns can be a problem. Go to your friend and explain the situation. "Mary, we're having a Super Bowl party and I'd love for you to come. There's a one-inch threshold to get into the house, but otherwise the living room is completely accessible. Our bathroom is small, though, and there aren't any grab bars." Mary now has the information she needs to make an informed decision.

Won't adding universal design to my house make it ugly and hard to resell?

No! Well-planned design elements such as wider doors and hallways will make your house seem brighter and more spacious. Raised electrical outlets appeal to parents of young children as well as to older people who don't want to stoop. Kitchen modifications such as dual-height countertops (to be used standing or seated) also appeal to parents with young children who want to help. Spacious bathrooms with larger tubs, roll-in showers, and roll-around storage units are considered a luxury in many homes and are invaluable to new parents who may need to install changing tables or store toys for bath-time play. Levered door handles come in many attractive styles and are especially welcomed by people with armfuls of groceries. These features all add to the value of your home.

Someone told me I'll have to rip out all my carpeting to make my home barrier-free. Is this true?

Not necessarily. It is true that shag or deep pile carpeting is hard to negotiate for people with mobility impairments or people who use wheelchairs. Area rugs that are not secure are a definite hazard and should be avoided by anyone with mobility, balance, or vision impairments. Carpeting may be harder to clean than bare floors. In many situations, however, low pile or loop carpeting is not a problem and may be beneficial. Carpets can cushion falls and provide needed shock absorption for people who must stand for long periods.

My father can't climb stairs anymore, but otherwise he is fine. Will he have to move out of his two-story house?

Lifts of various kinds can be installed on existing stairways; even narrow staircases often can accommodate a lift. If a lift is determined to be medically necessary, part of the cost may be assumed by Medicare or private insurance companies. Your father's bedroom, though, should be located on the first floor so that if there is a fire at night he can leave the house quickly even if electricity is out. Lifts are powered by electricity.

My mother, who lives with us, is losing her eyesight. How can I help reduce her chance of injury?

One thing you can do is remember to pick up after yourselves. This applies to everyone in the family. If you have small children who tend to leave toys and other items lying about, confine the toys to the children's bedrooms or a special area. Do not move furniture around. Put night-lights in hallways, the bathroom, and your mother's bedroom. Consider special night-lights that will continue to shine even if power is out. They do not cost much more than the more standard night-lights, and they can be a lifesaver in an emergency.

Remember that a loss of vision may engender other hazards. Be sure that easily confused medications, lotions, etc., are not stored together. If your mother is taking several medications that are similar in size and shape, consider dispensing them yourself into a day-by-day pill reminder so that she does not inadvertently take the wrong dose.

How do I get information about making my home more accessible?

The American Association of Retired Persons (AARP), (202) 434-2277, publishes a brochure and resource guide called *The Perfect Fit: Creative Ideas for a Safe and Livable Home*. This common-sense guide is in large print, with full-page pictures that illustrate modifications suitable for any home, with little or no remodeling. For people who are remodeling or building a new home, AARP also publishes *The Do-Able Renewable Home*, which offers more detailed advice but is written for the layperson.

You may also want to visit your local public library or bookstore. Many excellent books deal with making homes, gardens, and the workplace accessible. Modern books often contain sections on homes designed for accessibility. Another source of information is NARIC, the National Rehabilitation Information

Center, which is the library of the National Institute on Disability and Rehabilitation Research (NIDRR). NARIC keeps a database of research and literature related to almost every aspect of disability, including universal design. You can visit the Web site at www.naric.com/naric. The Web site also has links to other disability-related organizations that may provide help or information on design and funding. If you are doing in-depth research, a NARIC information specialist can send you copies of most articles held by NARIC.

Source: National Rehabilitation Information Center; call toll-free, (800) 346-2742. NARIC is funded by the National Institute on Disability and Rehabilitation Research (NIDRR), under contract number HN970020, and operated by KRA Corporation of Silver Spring, MD.

Bathrooms

How much water do you use during the average shower versus a soak in the average bathtub?

Unless you're a teenager whose hair is your crowning glory, the average shower lasts 7 minutes. Using a showerhead that delivers 2.5 gallons of water per minute, you'll use 17.5 gallons during that time. This compares with 43 gallons, which is the capacity of the average 5-foot bathtub.

What should I look for when buying a faucet?

Make sure the sink or lavatory you're installing it on has a compatible number of holes. Check spout length to ensure adequate reach into the basin. Levers or lever handles are easiest to use if you have physical limitations. For a coordinated look, use accessories—towel bars and rings, paper holders, glass shelves, and soap dishes—that match or complement your faucets. In the kitchen, consider a faucet with a high-arch spout to make it easy to fill tall containers or large pots.

What is the most popular faucet finish?

Polished chrome accounts for approximately 83 percent of the faucets sold in the United States, followed by 9 percent polished brass. Other specialty finishes, including color, make up the remaining 8 percent.

What can I do to keep my fixtures and faucets looking their best?

No matter what materials your fixtures are made of—cast iron, vitreous china, stainless steel—rinse and dry them after each use. Avoid any abrasive cleaners that may eventually scratch and ruin the surface of a fixture. In kitchen sinks, avoid soaking dishes for long periods of time, and refrain from leaving coffee grounds, tea bags, and pottery with rough bottoms in the sink. For toilets, do not use in-the-tank cleaners that contain chlorine (calcium hypochlorite), which can affect the working parts of a flush valve.

Mild soap and water is usually all that is necessary to keep faucets and metal shower door frames clean. Wipe completely dry with a clean soft cloth. On metal and glass finishes you may also use cleaners like Windex, Glass Plus, and Lime Away. Avoid cleaners with chemicals like ammonia, which could adversely affect metal finishes.

What causes my toilet to sweat, and is there a way to stop it?

The "sweat" that forms on the outside of your toilet tank is condensation. Condensation forms when warm, moist air in the bathroom contacts the cool surface of the tank. The tank is cooled by the cold water inside. You may see the same thing happen to your kitchen or bathroom windows on a cold day. You can eliminate this by insulating the cool tank surface from the warm, moist air. Many toilet manufacturers offer a factory-installed foam lining that is inexpensive and will last for the life of the tank.

What's the lowdown on low-flow toilets?

The 1992 Energy Policy Act mandated that toilets produced after January 1, 1994, use no more than 1.6 gallons of water per flush. Toilets produced prior to that date use about 3.5 gallons per flush or more. Manufacturers have responded with stylish new designs and flushing technology that makes the most of this reduced amount of water.

What is a *bidet*?

Europeans have long known about the comfort and effectiveness of the bidet for personal hygiene. The bidet, usually installed next to the toilet along the same wall, is actually a sit-down wash basin used for partial bathing.

What should I look for when buying a whirlpool?

Look for a design with ergonomic body-supporting headrests and lumbar contours; fingertip controls should be within easy reach from a reclining position. An integral heater keeps water temperature where you want it during an extended soak. Consider a 6-foot whirlpool with a generous bathing basin to accommodate two people. For a truly personal massage, make sure the whirlpool jets are independently adjustable. Neck, back, and foot jets placed appropriately pinpoint hydro relief where you need it most. If you choose a cast-iron whirlpool—the premium material for bathtubs and whirlpools—look for a slip-resistant finish. And make sure your whirlpool is UL-listed for safety.

How do I clean a whirlpool system?

Whirlpool bath systems should be cleaned at least twice a month. Adjust the jets so there is no air induction. Fill your bath with hot water to a level above the highest jets. Add 2 teaspoons of low-foaming dishwasher detergent, such as

Calgonite or Cascade, and 4 ounces of household bleach to the water. Run the unit for 10 to 15 minutes, then drain the bath. Fill the bath with cold water to 2 to 3 inches above the highest jets. Run the unit another 5 to 10 minutes, then drain. Wipe dry with a soft cloth.

How do I make my bathroom more accessible?

To promote accessibility, include properly installed grab bars adjacent to the toilet and inside the shower and tub. The shower should have no sill or other obstruction to step over. A handheld shower attached to a wall bracket will accommodate users of varying heights and abilities. Provide wrist blade or lever handles on faucets for the sink and bathtub. Light switches and ventilation controls should be at a height that children or a person in a wheelchair can reach. These steps are part of "universal design," which is space planning that seeks to make independent living a reality for all.

Source: The Kohler Company, 444 Highland Drive, Kohler, WI 53044; (414) 457-4441.

Carpets and Rugs

Is there any difference between a carpet and a rug?

Both are used fuzzy-side-up, but a carpet is usually attached at the walls onto a tack strip that keeps it stretched and smooth. Rugs, even if room-size, are loose-laid—that is, unfastened.

What do I need to know when I buy a carpet?

Before purchasing carpet or rugs, you need to answer the following questions: How is the room going to be used—will it have heavy or light traffic? Will the room be the center of activity for family and entertaining? Is there direct access from outside, or will the carpet be away from entrances?

To determine the approximate quantity of carpet you will need, multiply the length of the room by its width, measured in feet. Carpet is sold in square feet or square yards (square feet = square yards x 9) and is usually made in 12-foot widths. A percentage must be added to account for room irregularities and rooms with widths greater than 12 feet. It is best to have your retailer or installer make final measurements, to ensure that you purchase the correct amount. Professionals know how to include hallways and closets, match patterns, and plan seams.

How many different kinds of pile are there, and why is the pile of a carpet important?

Pile reflects a carpet's construction. The carpet construction—how the yarn is "tufted" or locked into a backing—affects its texture and ultimately its long-term durability and appearance. *Level-loop pile*—loops of equal height—generally offers long-lasting wear for high-traffic areas. Many of the popular Berbers are level-loop. *Multilevel loop pile,* with two or three different loop heights, creates pattern effects and provides good durability.

Cut pile, in which the loops are cut, leaving individual yarn tufts, is still popular. Its durability is achieved with factors that include the type of fiber, density of tufts, and the amount of twist in the yarn. *Cut and loop pile* is a combination of cut and looped yarns, which provides a variety of surface textures and sculptured effects.

How do I know which fiber to choose?

There are five basic types of carpet pile fibers:

1. Nylon is wear-resistant and resilient. It withstands the weight and movement of furniture and provides brilliant color. It has the ability to conceal and resist soils and stains, and it is generally good for all traffic areas.
2. Olefin (polypropylene) is strong, resists wear and permanent stains, and is easily cleaned. It resists static electricity and is often used in both indoor and outdoor installations.
3. Polyester is noted for its luxurious, soft "hand" when used in thick, cut pile. It has excellent color clarity and retention, is easily cleaned, and is resistant to water-soluble spills.
4. Acrylic has low static level and is moisture- and mildew-resistant.
5. Wool is noted for its luxury and performance. It has soft, high bulk.

How do I choose a reputable retailer when buying a rug or carpet?

The better stores will have a knowledgeable staff to answer your questions. Choose a carpet dealer who has a wide selection of samples, stands behind the installation, and can help you with maintenance questions. Your friends and neighbors can be a good source. Look for a retailer who displays the CRI (Carpet and Rug Institute) Seal of Approval, showing that the retailer is committed to customer service and satisfaction.

What should I expect when I have wall-to-wall carpet installed?

Have a clear understanding of the services the retailer will provide and those you must handle. For example, who will move the furniture, take out the existing carpet and cushion, and be responsible for disposal? Ask that seams be placed in less visible areas, and request that the installer follow the instructions from the carpet manufacturer or those described in the CRI 105 Residential Installation Standard, the accepted industry standard. Carpet should be power-stretched to minimize wrinkles and ripples. It is your responsibility to provide an adequate supply of fresh air during installation.

Why do people say Persian rugs are the best?

Persian or oriental rugs have been made from wool for centuries with very small knots individually tied through a canvas. Because they are very dense and well made, they are durable. Antique ones are particularly desirable.

Do I really need a separate layer of padding under my carpets?

Yes, unless the carpet is glued down. A firm, resilient carpet cushion, no more than $7/16$ inch thick, is necessary to form a good foundation, increasing comfort and extending the carpet's life by absorbing the impact of foot traffic. A cushion also adds insulation and reduces noise.

How can I keep my area rugs from sliding?

Underlays, or cushions, are made especially for area rugs that are to be placed over hard surfaces or over carpet. These cushions will lessen foot impact and prevent the rugs from creeping or wrinkling.

Do you have any decorating advice for using small area rugs on top of my wall-to-wall carpet?

Rugs can add pizzazz to an otherwise plain floor and can draw attention to specific areas, such as a dining table or a seating group around a coffee table. Choose a style or design that complements colors and patterns drawn from fabrics or paintings in the room. The variety of rugs is endless—oriental, ethnic, regional, geometric, bold, subtle, simple, intricate, or contemporary. The added benefit of an area rug is the use of that same rug when you move to another house or move that furniture to another room.

I want to hang a rug on my wall like a tapestry. How do I do that?

Rugs that are to be hung should be attached to a rod or board across the entire width of the rug. Then that support structure can be attached to the wall.

Can I harm my carpet by vacuuming too much?

Not at all. Carpet is protected from abrasive soil and looks better longer if vacuuming is done consistently. In areas of high use, vacuum often—several times a week; in other areas, vacuum once a week. Use a well-functioning vacuum cleaner with adjustable brushes, good air flow, and an enclosed, high-efficiency filtration bag.

What can I do to keep my carpet in good condition?

Proper maintenance will extend the carpet's life span and keep its fresh appearance. You should vacuum properly, remove spills, and provide long-term care and deep cleaning. To retain its luster and beauty, your carpet should be deep-cleaned before it appears soiled, every 12 to 18 months, either by you or by a professional cleaning service. See the manufacturer's recommendations in your carpet warranty to select the best cleaning method.

What will remove food spills from my carpet?

Use a clean, white cloth or paper towel and pretest a small, inconspicuous area to ensure that the cleaning solution will not damage the carpet or its dyes. Gently work in the cleaning solution from the edges of the spot to the center. Blot thoroughly and repeat until the spill no longer transfers to the cleaning cloth.

First try a detergent solution that is a mixture of 1 cup of water and ¼ teaspoon of a mild, nonbleach dishwashing liquid without lanolin. If the spot remains, an ammonia solution of 2 tablespoons of household ammonia and 1 cup of water can be used, following the same procedures. Lukewarm tap water can follow as a third method. If the spot is still there, then it is time to call a professional cleaner.

How can I fix a cigarette burn in my wall-to-wall carpet?

If the burn has only singed the tops of the fibers, simply clip off the burned tips with scissors, shaping the surrounding fibers. If the burn has melted fibers to the backing, the only remedy may be to remove the section and replace it with a scrap of the carpet.

Source: The Carpet and Rug Institute, Box 2048, Dalton, GA 30722; (706) 278-3176.

Cleaning

How does *detergent* differ from *soap*?

Soap is made by treating fats and oils, or their fatty acids, with an alkali. Detergents are made from a variety of petrochemicals (derived from petroleum) and oleochemicals (derived from fats and oils). Sodium and potassium hydroxide are alkalis used to make both soaps and detergents. Because of their chemical makeup, detergents are less sensitive to water hardness minerals and therefore less likely than soaps to form a film or scum.

Does it make any difference if I use a powder detergent or a liquid detergent?

Both powder and liquid laundry detergents are suitable for all washable fabrics and are formulated to remove a wide variety of soils and stains under varying water and temperature conditions. Liquids are especially effective for oily soils and for pretreating soils and stains; powders for lifting out clay and ground-in dirt.

Aren't all soaps antibacterial?

No; many soaps do not contain an antibacterial ingredient. However, washing hands thoroughly with any soap and warm water will remove many of the bacteria that can cause skin infections, intestinal illnesses, and other commonly transmitted diseases. Soaps that contain an antibacterial ingredient can actually kill microorganisms and therefore further reduce bacteria on the skin, either immediately upon use or through residual activity.

Antibacterial soaps are specifically formulated to help reduce the number of germs transferred by hands during everyday tasks, such as changing diapers, caring for ill family members, playing with pets, and preparing meals.

I have very sensitive skin, due to allergies. Which soap or detergent is best for me to use?

The simplest answer is, if you know the ingredient you're sensitive to, look for a product that does not contain it. You can call the manufacturer to find out if a product contains a specific ingredient. Some people are sensitive to fragrances, so you may want to try an unscented product.

If the care label on my garment says "Dry Clean Only," can I safely wash it?

No. Garment manufacturers have a specific reason for recommending dry cleaning. The fabric may shrink or colors may bleed in the washer. Additionally, the garment may have trims, buttons, or interfacing that cannot be washed. The reason for the recommendation may not always be obvious, so the safest way to protect your garment is to follow the manufacturer's cleaning instructions, which usually appear on a sewn-in label inside the garment.

Why do some care labels in garments state: "Use a nonchlorine bleach"?

The dyes in the garment may not be stable enough for sodium hypochlorite (chlorine) bleach. An oxygen (color-safe) bleach is gentler and is safe for all colored washables. If the care label states "No Bleach," avoid using any bleach, even an oxygen one.

When I'm doing laundry, how can I tell if bleach will harm a fabric or not?

Read the garment label; it should tell you if a garment cannot be bleached. Sodium hypochlorite bleach (also called chlorine or liquid household bleach) can be used on washable, colorfast natural fibers (cotton, linen), except protein fibers like wool. It is also safe on washable synthetic and permanent press fabrics, except spandex. Oxygen bleach (also called all-fabric bleach) is safe for most colored washable fabrics. However, if the care label states "No Bleach," don't use any bleach. To determine if a color is bleach-safe, test for color fastness in an inconspicuous area, following instructions on the bleach package.

What will clean those oily stains from collars and cuffs?

Pretreat collars and cuffs with a prewash stain remover, liquid laundry detergent, or a paste of powder detergent and water.

There are greasy-looking spots on some of my garments after they've been washed. What causes these spots and how can I remove them?

If undiluted fabric softener comes in contact with fabric during the rinse cycle, it can cause greasy-looking spots. These spots do not harm the fabric and can be easily removed by dampening the fabric and then rubbing the spots with hand soap. Rewash the fabric in the usual manner. To prevent this spotting from occurring, be sure to follow the manufacturer's instructions and dilute the fabric softener before adding it to the rinse water. This can be done by using the fabric softener dispenser on the washer or by manually diluting the softener before adding it to the wash load.

What will remove ink stains?

Some inks may be impossible to remove. Laundering may set some types of inks. Try pretreating using a prewash stain remover, then launder. Or you could try denatured alcohol or cleaning fluid. Sponge the area around the stain with the alcohol or cleaning fluid before applying it directly on the stain. Place the stain facedown on clean paper towels. Rinse thoroughly, then launder. An alternate method, using denatured alcohol or cleaning fluid, is to place the stain over the mouth of a jar or glass. Hold the fabric taut. Drip the alcohol or cleaning fluid through the stain, so the ink will drop into the container as it is being removed. Rinse thoroughly, then launder.

How do I remove paint from fabrics?

The treatment depends on whether the paint is water-based or oil-based. For water-based paints, rinse the soiled area in warm water, then launder. Removal must be done while the paint is still wet. When dry, water-based paints become permanent.

For oil-based paints, check the paint can label, then use the same solvent that you see recommended as a paint thinner. If there is no label, use turpentine. Whatever solvent you use, always test it on an inconspicuous area of the garment first before trying to treat a larger area. After treating the paint stain with the solvent, rinse the garment. Then pretreat with a prewash stain remover, bar soap, or laundry detergent. Rinse again, then launder.

My friend suggested putting tennis balls in the dryer with my comforter to keep the filling from clumping. Is this a good idea?

The tennis balls would help distribute the filling while the comforter is drying. However, this practice is not recommended for three reasons:

1. The rubber in the tennis balls may not be able to withstand the heat;
2. The dye may transfer from the neon-color balls to the garments being dried;

3. The balls could become wedged between the dryer baffle and the bulkhead, which might require a service call to repair.

There is an alternative. To help keep the filling evenly distributed while drying a comforter or something with similar stuffing, periodically stop the dryer, remove the comforter or garment, and shake it vigorously. If you can't spend that much time revisiting the dryer, you can add clean, dry towels to the load. The towels will help distribute the filling and will avoid possible problems caused by tennis balls.

What's the best way to clean silverware or silverplate?

Check the manufacturer's instructions on dishwashing silver or silverplate. If it can be placed in the dishwasher, place silverware and stainless-steel flatware in the silverware basket so they do not touch. Avoid spilling or pouring the detergent directly on flatware. Older, hollow-handled flatware may have glued handles that could be loosened by heat from the dishwasher. It should be washed by hand.

I live in a humid climate and have mold and mildew in my shower. How can I get rid of it?

Many products on the market today remove mold and mildew. Read the labels on cleaning products to find a tub and tile cleaner or other bathroom cleaner that states it removes mold or mildew. Then follow the label directions. To help prevent mildew buildup, wipe down shower walls after showering. Keep the shower area well ventilated and as dry as possible.

How do I clean my good wood furniture, or should I just polish it?

Wood furniture, like any household surface, should be cleaned to remove dirt and dust that can scratch the surface. A furniture cleaner, cleaner polish, or polish can be used to remove dust and stains and add shine and protection. Apply the product to the surface and then wipe, being sure to use a clean, soft cloth.

Source: The Soap and Detergent Association, New York, NY; (212) 725-1262; www.sdahq.org.

Fences

What are the basic fencing materials or types?

Basic fencing for residential use includes tubular iron in square or round shapes; steel wire fences with a steel or wood frame; wood panel and rail fences; aluminum fencing available with wire mesh, panel, or glass inserts; and the new polyvinyl chloride fences.

What should I tell a contractor who is going to build a fence for me?

Once you have decided to install a fence, you should be prepared to discuss the following points:

- The purpose of the fence
- The exact location of the fence
- What type of design features you want (height, style, material, and color)
- Approximate budget

How long will my fence last?

Many factors affect the life of a fence—local climate, soil conditions, and the materials used, to name a few. You can expect a properly installed fence to last a long time, if it is appropriately maintained. Your contractor should be able to help you decide which type will serve you best.

Fence contractors are most often willing to give 10- to 20-year warranties on hot-dipped, galvanized chain-link fences. Polyvinyl chloride (PVC) fences would likely come with warranties for 20 years or more. Wood fences are likely to last from two to ten years, depending on the proximity to dry rot, powder post beetles, and termites.

How deep do fence posts have to be set into the ground?

This depends on many factors, including the climatic conditions in your area (for example, snow loads, frost level, wind velocities), and the height and style of the fence. It's a good idea to consult with an experienced local fence contractor familiar with the specifications and standards associated with fence installations in your area.

Do I have to put a protective coating of some sort on wood fence posts before I set them into the ground?

No, you don't. Untreated redwood is durable. The California Department of Transportation rates untreated redwood equal to pressure-treated Douglas Fir for guardrail posts. Use of the Penta preservatives is limited to pest control companies and is not available to installers. We have not found other types of paint or sealers to be effective against termites or dry rot. One thing you can do to help protect the wood is to keep the soil around the fence posts as dry as possible.

What kind of fence will keep my dog confined but won't block my view?

A chain-link fence with black vinyl fabric and a black frame and fittings is generally considered the best to see through. Flat black is better than gloss for this purpose.

I'd like an old-fashioned picket fence, but how can I avoid painting it every year?

I have never seen a wooden picket fence that looked good unpainted. Tom Sawyer started a trend. A picket fence made of PVC is the best solution. No painting is needed, it can be cleaned easily, and some manufacturers of PVC fencing provide a lifetime guarantee.

I have an old rusted and flaking wrought-iron fence around my house. How can I restore it?

You could either sandblast or wire-brush the fence to remove all rust. After that, you would apply a zinc-enriched primer, allow that to dry, then apply one or two coats of finish, preferably with a rust-inhibitor additive. Just as you do for your car, you can enhance the life of an iron fence simply by cleaning and polishing with a good automotive wax. You can do that for your fence when you do your car.

What sort of fence will keep animals out of my vegetable patch?

Damage from grazing animals like cows, sheep, goats, and horses will require a fence of sufficient height to keep them from getting their heads through and over. The fence must also be strong enough to withstand their weight. To control smaller animals like rabbits, try chain-link fencing with a 1.5-inch mesh. Fencing has not been successful in stopping burrowing animals like gophers, moles, and prairie dogs. However, you can try burying part of the fence by digging a trench around the area where you garden, setting in the fence, and then putting back the dirt. If you have a problem with snakes, try using hardware cloth along the bottom portion of the fence.

How do I select a good fence contractor?

The American Fence Association (AFA) recommends that you do your homework before you select a contractor. Interview a few different contractors before you make a decision. Some questions to ask are:

- Does your company hold liability and workers' compensation insurance?
- Can you supply me with a sample of your contract and products?
- What guarantees and warranties come with my fence?
- Do you belong to your national or local trade association?

Fence contractors who belong to the AFA abide by a strict code of ethics governing quality workmanship and business practices. However, this does not imply that nonmembers are not reputable companies. The American Society for Testing and Materials (ASTM) develops and publishes standards for thousands of products, including fences. A knowledgeable, well-trained fence contractor will be versed in ASTM standards for fence products and installation. Members of the American Fence Association are regularly supplied with an updated ASTM manual for fence products.

Source: John B. Clark, Jr., member of the American Fence Association and chairman of the San Diego Fence Co., Inc., San Diego, CA 92111.

Furniture

What are the different styles of furniture?

There are really only two basic styles of furniture: contemporary and tradi-tional. Contemporary got started about 1920 or 1925. Styles before that are considered traditional—for example, American Country, or eighteenth-century reproductions. The newer contemporary styling would include Mission and other more modern styles.

Is the Mission style of furniture the same thing as the Arts and Crafts style?

Mission and Arts and Crafts are very similar. Mission is considered an American style, as is Arts and Crafts. However, the Arts and Crafts movement was initiated in Great Britain by William Morris, the artist and designer, as an aftermath of Art Nouveau. It was not a significant style, though, and didn't gain popularity with the masses. Frank Lloyd Wright was the icon of that era; if not for him, the Arts and Crafts style might not have had much presence in America.

How do I know if a piece of furniture is well-made?

A better question is: What do I want a piece of furniture to do? A park bench is well-made. But if we want something delicate and lovely, it won't last like a park bench. The issue is like the question: What is beauty? We all have a dif-ferent concept of what "well-made" means. Some of us associate it with dura-bility; at the other end are those who think it means how aesthetically beautiful something is. Somewhere on that continuum, you make your choice.

What should I look for in a sofa?

The buzzword of the 1990s is "comfort." The second thing you would look for in a sofa is a fabric that pleases you.

What's the difference between a *sofa* and a *settee*?

A settee is fairly delicate-looking—in fact, some people think of it as a flimsy two-seater. Nobody uses a settee or that word anymore. We seem to have lumped everything into sofa or loveseat. A loveseat is a two-cushion, smaller version of a sofa. Another distinction is that a settee generally is not upholstered all over; the wooden frame is more exposed than you would find for a sofa.

What are the standard upholstery fabrics used for most furniture?

The most popular upholstery fabrics are combinations of cotton and polyester. Rayon is also used. Almost all upholstery fabrics today are a blend, unless you are buying at the very high end of the market and creating a formal atmos-phere. But most of us don't live that way. Today, most upholstery fabrics are made for durability and beauty.

I want my living room to seem bright and airy. What sort of furniture should I consider?

Rather than thinking in terms of furniture styles, you could consider light colors. However, the style could have an uncluttered look and be rather streamlined. Within each style there are uncluttered looks. The eighteenth century, for example, runs from fairly simple all the way to the rococo look. Ornamentations like ball-and-claw feet and decorative carving would be cluttered. Uncluttered eighteenth century would be the basic American Colonial, or the provincial look that is called American Country. America was creating more simple interpretations of the eighteenth-century look originating in Europe. The colonies were more simplistic in design, and the craftspeople of the Midwest didn't have the talent or machinery to make ornate reproductions.

Contemporary is a good choice because of its usually uncluttered designs. Within each style you should be able to find simplicity as well as ornateness, except within the modern styles, like Danish modern. But generally speaking, you can run the gamut from simple to ornate.

What style of furniture will give my formal sitting room an elegant look?

French Regency is a logical choice—this is a style from the reign of Louis XV, which has a very elaborate look. Most elaborate reproductions would fit the bill. French styles from the various Louis eras (e.g., Louis XIV, the Sun King) are generally very ornate and formal-looking. These elegant furnishings are also called the High Court look.

What style of furniture will suit the modern look of my new house?

Any contemporary styling will work. Look for furniture designed after 1920 or 1925.

How do I take care of my furniture?

People always despise the answer to this question. For upholstered furniture, you should vacuum every single week. That's what you ought to do. Weekly vacuuming will keep it clean. If you ever look at dust particles under a microscope, you will see that most of them have sharp edges. As we sit on upholstered furniture and move around—which everyone does—we work those sharp-edged particles into the fabric. This not only embeds the dirt, but it breaks down the fibers in the fabric. The best way to keep dirt from building up is to vacuum every week.

Turn the cushions on your sofa and chairs every week if you have loose cushions. Purchase upholstered furniture with loose cushions so you can turn them, because you will get twice the wear from your furniture that way.

Another step is to have your upholstered furniture professionally cleaned. High-traffic areas (e.g., where three kids and a dog spend a lot of time) might need cleaning really often. However, if some pieces of furniture receive only light use, you may never have to have them cleaned.

How can I protect tabletops from scratches and other damage?

Consider buying Formica or glass-topped furniture. People often can't tell the latest Formica products from real wood. If you want a wood surface, though, be willing to take care of it. Use coasters and hotpads to protect the surface from moisture and heat. Clean up spills immediately. Be respectful of your furniture. Some people have a compulsion to cover their wood tabletop with vinyl cloth. Don't do this. For a short time, like a picnic, it is okay, but don't leave a vinyl cover on wood furniture longer. The wood can't breathe, and moisture will be trapped by the vinyl and ruin the wood.

What can I do if I get a scratch or stain on my table or other wood furniture?

The best advice is, don't make a scratch. If you do get a tiny nick, use shoe polish the same color as the wood and blend it in. Shoe polish is just wax, so it fills in. If you have a water ring, you can use some toothpaste applied with a clean cloth if the stain hasn't set a long time. Speed is of the essence with any scratch or spill on wood or upholstery.

In the winter my chairs get loose and wobbly. What can I do to keep them in one piece?

Buy a humidifier and use it. Your body will thank you for it, too. Wood never dries. Although it is kiln-dried, it doesn't have all the moisture removed; if it did, you'd have just a stack of toothpicks. Moisture keeps wood together. Furniture is manufactured to tolerate what moisture levels should be in our homes. Information about moisture levels usually can be found on the side of any humidifier that you buy.

Source: The American Furniture Manufacturers Association, High Point, NC 27261; (910) 884-5000.

Home Climate

What options do I have for heating my house?

Gas and oil furnaces warm your house by circulating heated air through ducts. Boilers heat your home by circulating steam or heated water through a system of pipes and baseboard or radiator heat exchangers that heat room air. Another option is the electric heat pump, a forced-air system that provides not only heating but central air-conditioning. Heat pumps are a good choice if electricity is the most economical energy option in your area.

Furnace efficiency is measured by the AFUE (annual fuel utilization efficiency) rating. The government's minimum standard for gas furnaces is an AFUE rating of 78; high-efficiency furnaces may have AFUE ratings as high as 96.6. Usually, the higher the AFUE of the furnace, the more it will cost to buy but the less fuel it will use to heat your home, so the cost is paid back through lower utility bills. In a cold climate, you could see a payback in a few years. If you live in a moderate climate, it might make more sense to purchase a lower AFUE furnace. Your heating contractor can use heating data from your area to help you determine what is the best system for you.

How does a heat pump work?

Heat pumps look a lot like air conditioners. During the heating season, a heat pump takes heat out of the outside air and moves it inside the house, where it is transferred to the air circulating through your home. Even at cold temperatures, like zero degrees, the outside air contains a great deal of heat. Heat pumps are often installed with backup electric resistance heat or a furnace to handle heating requirements when more heat is needed than the pump can supply.

The heat pump's HSPF (heating season performance factor) rating indicates its efficiency. The higher the HSPF, the less electricity the unit will use to heat your home. The government's minimum standard for new heat pumps is 6.8 HSPF. An HSPF of 7.5 or higher is considered high efficiency; the maximum available is 10 HSPF. Cooling efficiency is indicated by a SEER (seasonal energy efficiency ratio) rating. The higher the number, the greater the efficiency. The minimum standard for new homes is 10 SEER. When replacing an existing system, make sure the indoor and outdoor units are the right match, or you may not get the stated SEER or HSPF rating, and the system may not perform properly.

Can you explain the thermostat to me?

The thermostat is a device that regulates temperature by comparing the thermometer reading of a room's temperature to the desired temperature you selected on the thermostat. Then it gives a "start" or "stop" command to the heating or cooling system.

Newer electronic thermostats contain a microprocessor. Programmable thermostats let you customize your heating and cooling system. You can enter different temperature settings for different times of the day, and different settings for weekdays and weekends. For example, the programmable thermostat will automatically turn down the heat setting at your usual bedtime, and turn it up in the morning so the house warms up before you get out of bed.

Check your thermostat settings. If you want heat, the system switch should be on "Heat" or "Auto." The "Fan" switch should be set at "On" for continuous blower operation, or "Auto" if you want the blower to function only while the unit is operating. If you want cooling, the system switch should be on "Cool" or "Auto."

How often should I change my furnace filter?

At least every three months. And have your whole heating or cooling system inspected annually, before the heating or cooling season begins.

Are air conditioners bad for the environment?

Air conditioners aren't, but some refrigerants are. Refrigerants that contain compounds called CFCs *(chlorofluorocarbons)* can cause damage to the ozone layer if they accidentally escape from an aging system. The culprit is a chlorine atom that reacts with ozone in the upper atmosphere and destroys it. However, non-CFC refrigerants have been developed and are available in the more recent air conditioners.

When buying central air-conditioning, what should I look for?

Keep in mind three factors: efficiency, sound levels, and comfort. Cooling efficiency is measured by the SEER rating. The higher the number, the greater the efficiency. The government's minimum standard for new units is 10 SEER; the maximum available is about 17 SEER. A high-efficiency unit will cost more to buy but less to operate.

A noisy outdoor unit can ruin your backyard peace and quiet, so compare sound levels when looking at systems. The sound level of outdoor condensers is measured in bels on a scale from 0 (barely perceptible sound) to 13 (the threshold of pain). Most A/C units operate at 8 to 9 bels, but some are as low as 6.8 bels. That may not sound like a wide range, but keep in mind that 9 bels sound about ten times louder than 8 bels.

Look at comfort features as well. Two-speed units can run on energy-saving low speed up to 80 percent of the time, so they operate more quietly and run for longer periods at a time than single-speed models. This means fewer on/off cycles, fewer drafts, and much smaller temperature swings—only 2 or 3 degrees instead of 4 degrees. You also get better air circulation, which breaks up stratification when warm air rises to the ceiling and cold air settles to the floor.

What do I need to know about the humidity inside my house?

Humidity is the moisture in the air. Controlling humidity in your home can affect how comfortable you feel, and can save you money. We feel heat as a combination of temperature and humidity—the more humid the air, the warmer it feels. If you add humidity to dry, heated air in winter, you can feel warmer at a lower thermostat setting.

Added moisture helps prevent dry, cracked skin, makes it easier to breathe, and can make you less susceptible to sore throats and colds in winter. Increased humidity helps your furnishings, too. In dry, heated air, wood furniture can splinter and crack, and carpets and upholstery are more vulnerable to wear. Also, the wood in the framing around your doors and windows can shrink, which can break the weathertight seal in your home. Dry air can increase static electricity in your house. Those shocks are not only annoying and painful, but can actually damage computer disks.

In summer, you want to keep humidity down inside your home. Air-conditioning can take care of excess humidity. If humidity is low, you can keep the thermostat setting higher, still feel comfortable—and still save money on your utility bill. Here's a tip for even greater comfort: control the amount of humidity you create inside your home by using an exhaust system in areas like the kitchen, bathroom, and laundry room. That moves the moist air outside.

Should I change the thermostat setting at night, or leave it at a steady temperature around the clock?

Setting the thermostat lower on winter nights or higher on summer nights can help you save on heating and cooling costs. You can save even more by using a programmable thermostat that automatically adjusts the setting when your family is at work or school or on vacation.

What can I do to improve the air quality in my house?

Air pollution isn't just an outdoor concern. Dirt, dust, grease and smoke particles, pet dander, pollen, mold, and gasses are present inside your home, and because a home is a fairly sealed environment, most of these particles are recirculated over and over. If someone in your family has allergies or breathing problems, the effects can be very irritating. Furnishings and expensive electronic equipment can also suffer.

The particles you see in a beam of afternoon sunlight streaming through the window represent only about 1 percent of the millions of particles in your indoor air. Standard air filters trap about 15 percent of these particles. Mechanical and electronic air cleaners can trap a higher percentage—some up to 95 percent. Electronic air cleaners give a small electrical charge to particles so they are attracted like magnets to metal plates.

The easiest way to get fresh air into your home is to open a window. This, however, affects indoor air that you may have paid to heat or cool. An alternative is a ventilating system that brings in fresh air and extracts stale indoor air without adversely affecting your heating or cooling efforts.

How can I have an ideal indoor environment while conserving energy?

Here are some tips to save energy. Because 25 percent of your heating or cooling can be lost through windows, use caulking and weatherstripping to stop heated or cooled air from escaping, and replace single-thickness windows with energy-efficient windows. Install storm doors. Install extra insulation in your attic ceiling.

Some adjustments in lighting can save energy. Consider replacing incandescent bulbs with fluorescent ones, which use a quarter of the wattage while providing the same amount of light. In small areas like hallways and vestibules, use lower-wattage bulbs. Remember to turn out the lights when you leave a room.

Usually, the biggest user of energy in your home is the heating and cooling system. One of the simplest things you can do to conserve energy is to wear clothing appropriate for the season: lightweight clothing in summer, warmer clothing in winter. Then you won't have to cool or heat the indoor air as much. Consider upgrading older, less efficient equipment with higher-efficiency equipment. Also, make sure that your heating and cooling equipment is properly sized for your home. A heating and air-conditioning contractor can help you determine the best size.

Install electric ceiling fans to increase air circulation and comfort in summer and winter. When you shop for a new furnace, heat pump, or air conditioner, check the efficiency ratings. Ratings are displayed on the yellow hangtag required by law on each new unit sold. Buy the most efficient unit you can afford. Remember, you may pay more to buy a more efficient unit, but it will be cheaper to operate.

What's "zoning"?

"Zoning" means thinking of your house as a collection of areas with different energy needs. You heat or cool the zones in the home that most need it. A zoning system lets you turn off heating and cooling in a room the same way you can turn a light on and off.

Source: Adapted from information presented in the Carrier Corporation Web site, www.carrier.com.

Home Office

Do you have any general advice for creating a home office?

Yes. Some general rules you want to follow when setting up your office at home include:

1. Stay away from "built-in" furniture and equipment; look for furniture that is modular and adjustable. You should always allow for changes in business focus as well as the growth of your business. For example, when thinking about shelving, instead of having shelves built into the wall, look at buying bookcases with holes drilled up and down on both sides. This gives you the option of changing the height of each individual shelf, which may not seem important now, but if you find yourself storing everything in binders two years hence, you will want shelves that can accommodate the binders. Further, buying a bookcase instead of having the shelving built in gives you added flexibility. You may think you need shelving on the south wall, but after you've been in your office for six months you may decide that shelving on the north wall works better for you. You can move a bookcase. Try to purchase flexible furniture and equipment because you want to be able to rearrange, add, and remove furniture as your office needs change.

2. Invest in a good-quality chair. Your chair is probably the most important piece of furniture you can buy; make sure it fits you. Insist on taking the chair home for a trial run, because it's difficult to tell if a chair will work for you just by sitting in it in a store. If you have back problems or will spend 75 percent of your time seated, it is worth your while to shop at a specialty store. Regardless of the type of chair you choose, it should have adjustments both up and down, as well as forward and back. This is especially important if more than one person will be using the chair. Also be sure you can make these adjustments to the chair while sitting in it; the days of turning the chair over on the floor and spinning the legs are gone. Good-quality chairs have levers you can push/pull while seated to raise and lower the seat.

3. Don't buy a cheap filing cabinet. While a chair is the most important piece of furniture you can buy, a filing cabinet is the most important piece of *equipment* you can buy; don't go cheap. It is much better to work out of boxes until you can afford a good-quality cabinet than to buy a cheap one right away. A good cabinet will be weighted: you won't be able to open more than one drawer at a time; consequently it won't tip over. It will also have ball-bearing guides, which means it will consistently open quietly and easily. Don't ignore used cabinets. There are good, used, commercial-grade filing cabinets available that are great buys; for the price of a low-quality new cabinet you can get a good-quality used one.

How do I decide where to put my office? I have a basement, an attic, a garage, and a spare bedroom as options.

You need to take several things into consideration. What type of space do you need for your work? Do you stay seated, or do you walk around? Do you see clients at your office? Do you want to be part of the household activity, or do you want to be isolated? Are you willing to give up or share the basement, attic, garage, or spare bedroom? Each room has its positives and negatives. The key is to find the option that works best for both you and your family.

When looking at basement, attic, and garage, be sure to consider ventilation and lighting. Will those areas be cool enough in the summer and warm enough in the winter? Will there be adequate natural lighting? If the answers to those questions are yes, then they are good places to start looking. If you need to meet with clients at your office, you also need to consider accessibility. Can clients and guests get to your basement, attic, or garage without undue exertion?

A drawback to having your office in a basement, attic, or garage is the isolation factor. Many people who work at home deal with isolation from the business world, and putting your office physically away from the rest of the household serves to isolate you further. If you need to be around the household activity to remain stimulated, you probably don't want to be off in a completely separate area. In my opinion, a spare bedroom is the best space to put a home office. It typically has enough room for the furniture and equipment you need, as well as adequate lighting and ventilation. It is also separated from the hub of the house, yet not isolated. If you need to meet with clients, however, a drawback can be its location. Do you want your clients traipsing through several rooms to get to your office?

How do I keep my family from interrupting me all the time?

Communication is the key. Your family must understand that this room is now an office—a place of business and a place where money is made. It is no longer a spare bedroom or closet or dining room. You need to create both physical and nonphysical boundaries for your family and enforce them. For example, if you don't have the luxury of being in a separate room, you can create "walls" and "doors" with plants, office furniture, and room dividers. You can even create imaginary walls with rugs; everything that's on this side of the throw rug is in my office; everything that's on that side of the rug is in the dining room.

You can set nonphysical boundaries by telling your family that you are not to be interrupted from 10:00 A.M. to 2 P.M., for example, and when they do interrupt you, remind them that you are at work and are, in effect, gone, and they will have to wait to talk to you. Then go back to work. With small children, you can set a timer and tell them that when the timer goes off, you can play, and that when it goes off again, you have to go back to work. This gives them the anticipation of spending time with you, yet it is structured and allows you the freedom to enjoy your time with your child without feeling guilty. It is difficult for a family when one member begins working in a home office, but it can be done successfully once the family members understand that this is not a hobby or a pastime, but real work.

Can I turn a closet into a home office?

Depending on the size and configuration of the closet and the type of workspace you need, absolutely. Because home offices are so prevalent, most furniture stores now have departments devoted specifically to office furniture, and there are typically three or four "office in a box" options. An "office in a box" is designed to hold everything a professional needs in one piece of furniture. Typically, they can house a computer, a printer, a fax, a phone, and have the same amount of storage space for supplies as a desk. Some have drawers that can hold files, some don't. The beauty of the "office in a box" is that you have not ruined the integrity of the closet; if you decide you need the closet back, you simply move the "office" to another room or closet. Depending on the size of the closet, you can either store your chair in the closet along with the "office," or you can keep it elsewhere and simply roll it in when you need it. The major disadvantage of working out of a closet is that you are typically in a small space, so if you are the least bit claustrophobic this is probably not the best solution for you.

What's the difference between legal- and letter-sized files, and lateral and vertical files, and how do I know when to use which one?

Legal-sized files measure 8½ by 14 inches and are referred to as "legal-sized" because most legal documents are that size. Letter-sized files are 8½ by 11 inches. The rule to use when deciding which size is best is the "over 60 percent rule": if over 60 percent of your files are one size or the other, use that size. Keep in mind that legal-sized supplies (folders and hanging folders) cost approximately 25–30 percent more than letter-sized supplies, and take up more space.

Vertical cabinets hold files front to back; lateral cabinets hold files side to side. Vertical cabinets don't take up as much floor space but can require up to 2 additional feet to allow for the opening of the drawers, while lateral files only require 1 foot. One benefit to lateral files is they also provide an alternative work surface, so if you need lots of space to spread things out, this equipment can double as a piece of furniture. Vertical, letter-sized cabinets are typically recommended for most home offices, but lateral cabinets will work just as well if the space will accommodate them.

My desk has limited drawer space. Where else can I keep things?

First, since your desk has limited space, be sure you are only storing there what you need to do your job, things you are using at a minimum of once a day; any less than that and they can be stored elsewhere. If you need more file space you can purchase rolling file carts that accommodate the equivalent of two desk drawers. These can be rolled next to your desk when you need them, then rolled into a corner of the room or a closet when you are finished. They come in a large variety of colors, sizes, and finishes.

If you need to store office supplies or other small "widgets," you have a number of options—be creative. Jewelry and shoe organizers that hang from a closet rod are great solutions. Make sure you buy organizers that have clear pockets so you can always see what is in each pocket. You can also buy clear plastic shoe boxes, store unusually sized items in those boxes, and then stack them. Make sure you label the outside of each box, since once they're stacked you won't be able to see into them clearly. Another alternative is the product designed to hold towels in a bathroom. It can hang from the hinges of your door and has a pocket accessory that you can add; again, you can store separate items in each clear pocket.

All these products use vertical space, which is normally the most wasted space in any office. Look through the bathroom and kitchen sections of household catalogs and see if there are products in those sections you can adapt to your office. Many bathroom and kitchen items attach to the walls.

Is there an ideal configuration for office furniture and equipment, and for what I should keep on my desk?

The ideal configuration is the one that works for you. There are no cookie-cutter rules about what goes onto a desk or in an office and what doesn't. There is, however, a basic principle of organization you can keep in mind: Put the things closest to you that you use the most. If, for example, you use an adding machine every day, it needs to be close and accessible. However, if you only use an adding machine periodically, you can eliminate it from your desktop and use a handheld calculator that you can keep in your desk drawer, or you can simply use the calculator function on your computer.

Use your desk file drawer for "Active" or "Project" files, not "Reference" files. Many people keep "Reference"-type files in the desk drawer, but "Active" or "Project" files are a better use of the space. The "Active" files are files that are looked at or referred to frequently, so they belong in a drawer that is close at hand. If you refer to many files, keep your filing cabinet handy so you can drop files in there and they won't accumulate on your desk or elsewhere in your office.

If you spend a great deal of time on your computer, it should occupy a prominent space on your desktop. If you conduct your business largely by phone, it should be easily reached, and not behind you. There is no rule that says you have to have a stapler, tape, and pen set on your desk; those items only need to be there if you use them frequently. The one thing that should have a home on your desktop is your calendar or planner system.

The same principle holds true for your office furniture: Put the furniture closest to you that you'll use the most. If you spend lots of time sending or receiving faxes, put the fax machine close to your chair so you don't have to get up each time you address the machine. Ideally, everything you need to do your job should be within arm's reach and between your chest and your knees, both in front of you and behind you.

Source: Holly Uverity, Office Organizers®, Box 692005, Houston, TX 77269.

Home Tools

What basic tools do I need to keep my house in good repair?

The most important consideration when doing a job is using the right tool. But even a limited set of basic tools can tackle most of the general home repair tasks you're likely to encounter. A basic set might include: a 16-ounce claw hammer, a retractable utility knife, a tape rule, a crosscut handsaw, a push drill, slip-joint pliers, 6 inch and 8-inch adjustable wrenches, a small level, a combination square, and an assortment of standard and Phillips head screwdrivers. Keep in mind that quality is key. A well-designed hand tool can last a lifetime, while cheaper tools are less efficient and will have to be replaced numerous times.

What are the different kinds of hammers, and what is each kind used for?

Nail hammers, the most common type of hammer, are available with either curved claws for pulling nails or straight claws for ripping apart pieces of wood that have been nailed together. Handles come in a variety of materials: fiberglass, graphite, steel, and wood. Jacketed graphite or fiberglass handles offer superior overstrike protection compared to fiberglass-filament handles.

Framing hammers are simply heavier versions of nail hammers, with longer handles for better leverage, and an optional checkered face for a better grip on the nail head. A cushioned grip is essential on a nonwood handle.

Among the other types are the small, lightweight tack hammers (often with magnetic heads for holding tacks); ball-peen hammers for striking cold chisels and punches, rounding rivets, or forming unhardened metal; soft-face hammers and mallets for jobs where steel would damage a surface; and sledgehammers for heavy jobs where great force is required.

Are all saws pretty much the same?

Saws come in quite a variety. The most popular general-use saw is the crosscut saw, which is used to cut across the grain of lumber (or in any direction with plywood); aggressive tooth versions will cut on both push and pull strokes. Another kind of saw is the ripsaw, which has large, chisel-shaped teeth designed for cutting along the lumber grain rather than across it. Ripsaws have a more jagged cut and are not suitable for smooth finish work.

There are a number of more specialized saws. For example, miter and backsaws are designed for fine cuts in finish work. Compass and keyhole saws are used for cutting along irregular and curved lines. Coping saws are used for curved and intricate cuts in wood and plastics that are less than three-quarters of an inch thick. Drywall and wallboard saws will cut into plasterboard without clogging or dulling. Finally, hacksaws are used for cutting metals and other materials harder than wood.

What sort of pliers do I need?

It depends on the particular job you are doing. Slip-joint pliers are the best for general use; these feature jaws that can be adjusted between two positions, or widths, of maximum opening. For larger gripping jobs, you could use groove-joint pliers, which have angled heads and multiple positions for gripping. Locking pliers enable objects to be held in a viselike grip. Long-nose pliers are used to reach into tight spaces to hold, bend, or cut wire. Diagonal cutting pliers cut wire and other narrow metal objects.

What are the different kinds of wrenches?

The two basic types of wrenches are adjustable and fixed. Adjustable wrenches have one fixed and one movable jaw that you tighten against the fastener (a nut or bolt), using the wrench's adjusting mechanism. Fixed wrenches are not adjustable but they provide a tighter fit on the head of the object they are holding or turning. They are often sold in sets. Fixed models include open-end wrenches, which have different sizes of C-shaped jaws on either end; another fixed type are box wrenches, which have closed ends of different sizes that fit over hexagonal-shaped fasteners. There are also combination wrenches with open jaws on one end and box jaws on the other.

Socket wrenches are extremely versatile fixed wrenches used broadly for both automotive and general household use. They can be fitted with various extensions and handles and come in individual sizes or in sets to fit standard nut and bolt heads.

What is the most important factor in ensuring the success of any home project?

The most important factor is careful measuring and layout. As the old saying, "Measure twice, cut once," suggests, big mistakes are avoidable. By making use of a variety of measuring and layout tools, you reduce the chances of costly errors and you increase accuracy.

Aside from a quality, retractable, locking tape rule, combination and carpenter's squares are also a must for accuracy. The combination square is the most versatile layout tool. It can be used as a try or miter square to check and mark angles, as a marking gauge, or a depth gauge. A built-in level indicates plumb and level surfaces. The carpenter's square is intended for large layout and framing jobs, and is usually used for marking 45-degree and 90-degree angles.

Other important layout tools include bevels for marking angles of any degree, and levels for checking level and plumb surfaces. Common carpenter's levels have three vials. (You know a surface is level when the bubble of air aligns with markers on the vial.) Chalkline and plumb bobs are for marking long, straight lines and establishing horizontal and vertical alignments.

Source: Stanley Tools, a division of The Stanley Works, 1000 Stanley Dr., New Britain, CT 06053; (860) 225-5111.

Insulation

Why should I insulate my house, and how does insulation work?

Insulation lowers utility bills, increases sound control, increases resale value, and adds comfort for your family. All insulation materials work on a single basic principle: Heat moves from warmer to cooler areas. On cold days, heat from inside the home seeks to get out; on warmer days, the heat from outside the home seeks to get inside. Insulation is the material that slows this process.

Can you explain what "R-values" are?

Insulation has tiny pockets of trapped air. These pockets resist the transfer of heat. The ability of the insulation to slow the transfer of heat is measured in R-values. An R-value is a measure of insulating power. The higher the R-value, the better the insulation material's ability to resist the flow of heat through it.

What types of insulation are available?

The two broad types of fiberglass insulation are batts and loose fill. Batt insulation offers faced (that is, lined with a vapor barrier) and unfaced, with R-values ranging from 11 to 38. Insulation can be installed in attics, cathedral and flat ceilings, exterior walls, basements and crawl spaces, interior walls, and floors.

Loose-fill insulation is a viable alternative to batts in difficult areas such as truss attics or closed wall cavities. It is also widely used in conventional attics. Loose-fill insulation requires using a blowing machine for installation. Professional contractors are trained to install it to the proper level to insulate your home effectively.

How do I know how much insulation to buy?

To calculate the amount of insulation you will need, first measure the length and width of the area to be insulated (the dimensions of the walls, ceiling, or floor area). Then multiply the two numbers to determine total square footage. Next, measure the distance between studs or joists to determine the correct insulation width for the job. Lastly, divide the square footage to be insulated by the square footage per package of insulation to determine the number of packages needed for the job.

Be sure to choose the appropriate recommended insulation product, or R-value, for your project. To find out what R-values the Department of Energy recommends, call the Owens Corning information line, (800) GET-PINK.

What is a *vapor retarder*?

A vapor retarder, or vapor barrier, is a material that slows the passage or movement of water vapor. It helps control the amount of moisture passing through the insulation and collecting inside exterior walls, ceilings, and floors. To be classified as a vapor retarder, the material must have a *perm rating* of 1 or less. The perm is a measure of the flow of water vapor through a material.

What are the different kinds of vapor retarders?

There are three types of vapor retarders or barriers: Kraft paper-faced, foil-faced, and polyethylene. A Kraft paper-faced vapor retarder is created by coating Kraft paper with a layer of asphalt adhesive. The paper is then applied to the unfaced insulation material. The asphalt adhesive bonds the Kraft paper and the insulation together. Kraft paper-faced retarders look like brown paper bags.

A foil-faced vapor retarder is created by coating foil-backed paper with a thin layer of asphalt adhesive. The coated side of the paper is then applied to the unfaced insulation material, and the asphalt adhesive bonds them together. Foil-faced insulation looks like the thin foil that's wrapped around gum. In certain applications when installing unfaced insulation, a separate vapor retarder will be used. This separate retarder is called *polyethylene*. Polyethylene looks like the the plastic freezer bag you probably use for leftovers, but it is in fact a much thicker plastic that retards the moisture. Polyethylene covers the insulation and is stapled to the wood studs.

Whatever vapor retarder you choose, remember this important rule of thumb: When installing a vapor retarder, always put the vapor retarder toward the warm-in-winter side or living area of the house (in cold weather climates). Do not leave them exposed because they are flammable. Be sure to follow manufacturer's directions on the packaging for the installation of all vapor retarders.

What is *condensation,* and why is it bad for houses?

Moisture is carried in the air as a vapor. When vapor comes into contact with a cold surface, such as a can of soda, it will reach its dew point, and condensation is formed—the soda can will be covered with water drops. Showers, cooking, washing, and just breathing can put a surprising amount of moisture into the air in a typical home, 5 to 10 pounds a day. If you wash and dry clothes indoors, you may be adding another 30 pounds.

Without the use of a vapor barrier, this moisture can collect in the exterior walls, ceilings, and floors. In the winter, any moisture that passes through these surfaces can accumulate and condense on the cold inner sides of exterior surfaces. The first signs of condensation problems are mold, mildew, and musty odors. Eventually this condensation may blister the paint inside and outside the home, form stains, or even damage the house structure.

How do I avoid a condensation problem?

Proper ventilation and a vapor retarder are the best methods. When a house has been properly ventilated and vapor-retarded, a positive air flow is created, which allows the house to breathe and helps prevent moisture buildup. Vapor retarders and proper ventilation will reduce the amount of condensation in the house. Talk with an insulation contractor or builder for best recommendations on vapor retarders.

How can I repair a tear in a vapor retarder?

Patch rips or tears in vapor retarders before installing the interior finish.

Are there any areas of my house that I shouldn't insulate?

Insulation must be kept 3 inches away from recessed lighting fixtures unless the fixture is marked "I.C."—which means insulated ceiling, designed for direct insulation contact. Because insulation does its job in retaining heat, it is not recommended to place insulation in spaces surrounding metal chimneys, fireplaces, or flues. Follow the fireplace manufacturer's recommendation for proper clearance.

Source: Sandy Brunt, Owens Corning Product Specialist Technician, Building Materials Technical Services, 1 Owens Corning Parkway, Toledo, OH 43680; (419) 248-8000.

Interior Design

How can I attractively accessorize my room?

Consider your style first—are the pieces you have Country, Contemporary, Traditional, or early Salvation Army? Take an inventory of everything you have and start thinking creatively about what you could set out or hang. Perhaps your pictures are too small to work well over the sofa, so plan an arrangement. Lay them on the floor first and try to square out a particular space. You may want to add a shelf with something on it—even some good-looking books would work, or a vase, sconce, or beautiful plate. Use your imagination and be bold. Keep moving the accessories around until they fit the space you've squared off.

I have an elaborately woven rug and want to match it with a floral print. Do I need to get rid of one or the other?

Consider the rug a piece of art, which is what it is. You can certainly combine large floral prints and complicated rugs, such as orientals, in the same room. The key is your use of colors, which should be married together like two different but complementary people. If you have a burgundy and navy oriental, do not buy a sofa with a seafoam green and peach print. Consider the way the colors will "get along."

Everyone tells me I have too much beige and off-white, but I am afraid of color. How can I add color?

One thing you can always do is add an oriental rug, out of which you pick the colors that you could live with as accessories. For instance, if the rug is burgundy and navy, gather some lovely velvet and tapestry pillows in burgundy and gold. Leave out some colors for the winter season, and then in spring bring out shades of blue in large checks and plaids and, instead of a gold accent, add a touch of sunny yellow between the plaids and checks. Yes, you can mix plaids and checks. Again, the rule is to marry the colors. Be adventurous. By bringing color into the room with accessories, you can change the season or your mood.

I live in an apartment in the city and I crave light, but I don't have a very nice view. What can I do?

Today, there are wonderful pleated shades that open from top or bottom. If you want light to come in, you could pull the shade down from the top or up from the bottom, at the same time blocking out the less-than-great view.

My living room is very large, and it's hard to arrange the furniture around the fireplace to make it cozy. If I stand the furniture at the center, I can't have my lamps connected. What to do?

First, bring the furniture into a comfortable arrangement around the fireplace and bring your lamps and tables into the area as you like it. The key here is to use your imagination. Place a rug (oriental, needlepoint, or simple border rug) and then run an extension cord under the sofas or the loveseat and under the rug, bringing it closer to the outlet. If there is still cord exposed, find a beautiful container (basket, brass, or ceramic) to place next to or over it and in which you can put a large plant.

How high should I hang my pictures? Shouldn't they be at eye level?

No. People come in all sizes and what is eye level for one may not be for someone else. Pictures should be hung in relation to what they complement. For example, if you were hanging a picture over a sofa, the bottom of the picture should be about 9 to 10 inches above the piece.

My property is quite wooded, so I've left the windows bare. However, when the leaves fall my windows are exposed to the sun. What can I do to filter out those bright rays?

If you have a beautiful view, you'll want to enjoy it all year round. However, country or city, the sun can be a problem. A good solution in both cases is the silhouette shade, a Venetian blind system that incorporates sheets of fabric. In the open positions, these shades cut down on the sun's brightness without obstructing the view. When they are closed, they provide complete privacy. Additionally, they can be matched to any decor.

Source: Terry Womelsdorf, Interior Design Society, American Society of Interior Designers Allied, 631 Fairfax Drive, Ramsey, NJ 07446; (201) 236-0530.

Kitchens

How much will it cost to remodel my kitchen?

The price for a new kitchen will be affected by (1) where you buy it; (2) what features it includes; and (3) the brands and models you select. Pricing can range from $5,000 or so (if you do some work yourself) to as much as $150,000 and higher. On average, a kitchen will cost from $15,000 to $21,000, including design, products, and installation. The cost will be lower or higher depending on what you are looking for.

What makes a kitchen more or less expensive?

Cabinets account for about half the total cost of the project and will have the greatest impact on your budget. They range in price considerably, based on quality, the type of material used, and whether they are stock (ready-made in specific sizes) or custom (produced specifically for your kitchen in whatever sizes are needed). The material you choose for surfaces—including counters, backsplashes, and floors—can also account for variations in price.

Other key elements that factor into the equation are talent and skill. In the remodeling business, you tend to get what you pay for. An accomplished designer and an expert installation crew may cost you more. However, you'll appreciate their ability every time you use your kitchen.

How much cabinet space is needed in a kitchen?

It depends on the size of the kitchen. If the room is over 150 square feet, it should include at least 192 inches of base cabinets, with cabinets at least 21 inches deep. You should also have at least 186 inches of wall cabinets. This should provide adequate storage. A kitchen under 150 square feet needs at least 156 inches of base cabinets and at least 144 inches of wall cabinets.

How high should kitchen counters be?

Ideally, you should have at least two work-counter heights in your kitchen. One should be 28 to 36 inches above the finished floor; the other should be 36 to 45 inches above the finished floor. Having two different heights makes good sense because of the different people who may be using the kitchen. Families come in mixed sizes. Age can make a difference, too—children, young adults, and middle-aged and older adults all may have different needs. Also, different counter heights add to a kitchen's accessibility whether you work standing up, sitting on a stool, or sitting in a wheelchair.

Installing counter heights should not be haphazard. Plan out the work areas. Think of the individual uses of a particular work center, and then think about who may be using the area. Plan for the future as well as the present, and for resale value as well as your own needs.

What is the kitchen "work triangle," and why is it considered important?

The work triangle is the kitchen area from the refrigerator to the main cooking area to the main sink. Connect the three with imaginary lines and they should form a triangle—unless you have a "one-wall" kitchen. The triangle is important because all the key activities—food preparation, cooking, and cleanup—occur at or immediately adjacent to the triangle's points. The work triangle helps to ensure that your kitchen will be functional. It keeps cooking activities centered in one area with all the necessities close at hand.

Where's the best place to put a microwave?

Like most things in your kitchen, it depends on how you and your family use the appliance. From a safety and accessibility standpoint, the microwave should be positioned so that the bottom is 24 to 48 inches above the floor. You could consult with a kitchen designer about the best place to locate it.

What is "GFCI" and do I need it?

GFCI stands for ground fault circuit interrupter—a safety device for electrical wiring. The GFCI monitors the balance of electrical current moving through a home's circuit (your home's electrical system consists of a number of circuits; each circuit usually controls several outlets). If an imbalance occurs, the GFCI cuts off the electricity. Its purpose is to prevent fatal electrical shocks. As you probably know, water and electricity are a deadly combination. Because both are necessary in kitchens and bathrooms, all switches, sockets, breakers, and circuits for those rooms should be GFCI-protected for your family's safety.

Source: Nick Geragi, Director of Education and Product Development, National Kitchen and Bath Association, 687 Willow Grove St., Hackettstown, NJ 07840; (908) 852-0033.

Lighting

What are *lumens*?

Lumens are a measure of the quantity of light. For example, a common 100-watt household incandescent bulb produces 1,700 to 1,800 lumens, while a flashlight bulb produces about 5 to 10 lumens.

What's the difference between *spotlighting* and *floodlighting*?

These are general terms for describing a beam of light. *Spotlighting* usually refers to narrow, well-defined beams; *floodlighting* refers to beams that are wider and less well defined. However, there are no strict limits, and the interpretation depends on the application.

How can I eliminate glare when watching TV?

Do not have bright lights such as uncovered windows or light fixtures in the background where they can be seen along with the TV screen. And avoid bright lights located where they will reflect from the screen. However, it is undesirable for the room to be dark; there should be at least a low level of light so that the TV screen is not seen as a bright source amid dark surroundings.

Should I use the same kind of lighting for working at my computer that I use for watching TV?

The same rules apply for controlling glare. But often, other visual tasks are done at the same time as using a computer—such as referring to printed material. Adequate lighting for these other tasks is important.

I like to work in natural light. What artificial lighting comes closest to natural light?

Natural light is extremely variable in light level, directionality, and color quality. The choices depend on the use of the light. For example, artists often prefer a reasonably shadowless, blue-tinted light such as what comes through a large, north-facing skylight. A more typical color quality would be that for which daylight color film is balanced—that is, a mix of sunlight and skylight. Several fluorescent bulbs are similar to this color balance and are technically described as having a color temperature of about 5,000–5,500 kelvin, and a color rendering index of about 90. Examples of such fluorescent lighting are the Design 50™ and the Octron® 950 colors or their equivalents. (Note that the Daylight color fluorescent bulb does not have the color balance of outdoor daylight.)

Aren't halogen bulbs a problem because they get very hot?

Halogen bulbs do get hotter than ordinary incandescent bulbs and can be a hazard if not properly used. The type with a single glass envelope surrounding the filament should be used only in light fixtures that are specifically designed for halogen bulbs. These fixtures should have a suitable protective cover to keep materials from coming into contact with the hot bulb and to contain the hot particles of glass if something ever breaks the bulb.

There is another type of halogen bulb with a second, outer glass envelope (a bulb within a bulb). This does not have to be used in special enclosed fixtures because the outer envelope serves as the protective cover. The outer glass envelope may be frosted or may be reflector shaped with a lens, such as the PAR lamp that often is used to light driveways and yards. An example of this second type of halogen bulb goes by the trade name of Capsylite®.

How do energy-saver bulbs produce the same light as higher wattages?

A variety of techniques are used. For example, the gas fill in the bulb or its electrical characteristics may be changed. Some bulbs with reflectors, such as the incandescent PAR lamp that often is used to light driveways and yards, may be designed with more efficient reflectors.

What are the pros and cons of fluorescent, incandescent, and halogen lights?

Incandescent bulbs are less expensive to buy than fluorescent bulbs. However, for the same amount of light, fluorescent bulbs use much less energy and therefore are less expensive to operate. Fluorescent bulbs are typically four to six times more efficient than incandescent bulbs. Energy and operating costs are less important issues if a bulb is used infrequently.

Other factors can be significant; physical size, for example, or the fact that incandescent bulbs make more effective spotlights. Halogen is a type of incandescent bulb in which the efficiency and life are increased (but still well below fluorescent bulbs) and the light is somewhat whiter.

Can I use a dimmer switch with any kind of fixture?

No. Generally, incandescent bulbs can be used on dimmer switches. Not all types of fluorescent bulbs can be dimmed. Those that can require a special type of dimmer switch and ballast (the device that controls the electric current in the fluorescent bulb).

Is spotlighting the same as accent lighting?

Spotlighting is a general term for when lighting is directed to a particular location. *Accent lighting* is when additional light over and above that in the general area is used to highlight or accent some object or location. Accent lighting is commonly accomplished by spotlighting.

Where should I use recessed lighting?

This is a design issue. Should the light fixtures be inconspicuous or an element of the architecture? What is to be accomplished by recessing the lighting? How should the light be distributed through the space? Don't forget practical issues such as available space above the ceiling in which to recess the fixtures.

What is track lighting best for?

The advantages of track lighting are that it provides freedom in positioning lighting fixtures, allows their adjustment to direct light to specific locations, and permits easy changes whenever desired.

Can you help me decide between dusk-to-dawn and motion-sensitive exterior lighting?

There are no firm rules. Motion-sensitive lighting is desirable when light is needed at specific locations for convenience or safety only when someone is present. Examples would be at a door, on a driveway, or at a set of stairs. Dusk-to-dawn lighting generally covers larger areas and, in addition to convenience and safety, may include the functions of providing ambiance and of deterring intrusion.

What's the best lighting for reading in bed?

Most important is that the light should fall on the reading material. Generally, this means that the light fixture needs to be near the head of the bed. If there is general room lighting, bright light sources should not be directly visible as you are reading.

How do I know the right wattage for different activities, like reading, doing needlework, watching TV, working at a computer, relaxing?

For these decisions, the amount of light on the task is more important than the amount of light produced by the bulb. The light on the task depends not only on the bulb but also on the type and placement of the light fixtures. As a generalization, tasks involving fine detail and critical seeing require more light than is needed for casual and relaxing activities.

If lighting in an area seems acceptable to you, then replacement bulbs of the same type should be of the same wattage. If the type of bulb is changed—for example, replacing an incandescent bulb with a compact fluorescent bulb—then a bulb of approximately the same lumen rating should be used. For more complete recommendations, see *Design Criteria for Lighting Interior Living Spaces*, RP-11-95, published by the Illuminating Engineering Society of North America, 120 Wall Street (17th Floor), New York, NY 10005.

Source: Corporate Communications, Osram Sylvania Corporation, Danvers, MA; (508) 777-1900.

Moving

Is it really worth it to hire professional movers?

This depends upon how much you value the possessions you want moved. If you are moving pieces that aren't counted among the family heirlooms, the cost of professional movers might be over the top. However, the fact of the matter is that delicate or precious pieces should be handled by people who know what they're doing and have the proper equipment. Damage will be minimal and big companies offer (often require) additional valuation, which makes it much easier to deal with damaged items. The delicious luxury of seeing someone else break their back hefting your household goods around should be experienced at least once in life—especially if you've experienced moving "the other way" more than once before.

How much can one expect to pay for a professional move?

This depends on three factors: what you want moved; where you're moving it from and to; and whether there are any big obstacles in the way. Labor is the greatest cost and this can run high if the origin or destination lacks an elevator, ready access, etc. Long-distance moves are more expensive, the bill being figured by both mileage and the weight of the goods. In general, jobs are figured in one of two ways, *binding* or *estimated,* the former being most likely to score the bargain. In all cases, a representative of the moving company will survey the possessions to be moved in order to make the most realistic estimate possible. Getting an estimate over the phone is unreasonable.

Is it better to pack yourself or have it done by a professional?

Again, this is a question of how much you value your possessions. Professionals know how to pack delicate items so that they'll survive a move. Movers can handle items best when they have been packed well; therefore, if you're planning to use a professional mover, getting your stuff packed professionally ensures extra care. Furthermore, professional packers enforce a certain amount of organization among your possessions as they tend to box things room by room, area by area. This will add a structure to your move and unpacking that might not otherwise exist. Some companies insist upon packing materials that you insure with them. In most cases, you will have no claim if your possessions are damaged but the cartons into which *you* packed them are undamaged.

How does one go about moving a larger and/or more awkward item?

These sorts of pieces, such as a chandelier or a large mirror, must be crated and often partially disassembled, which needs extra planning. Some moving companies won't crate everything; some companies refuse to disassemble items; most will move anything once it's been crated and/or disassembled. Thankfully, there are companies that specialize in moving odd items, such as pianos, and will crate anything. Items of particular value should be handled by a professional and should be insured.

Are there places into which large items simply cannot be moved?

As the old expression goes, where there's a will, there's a way—and also a price. Through various configurations of hoists and rigs almost any piece can be lifted through a window or up a stairwell. These operations are seldom handled by moving companies, but by separate hoisting and rigging firms. This sort of work is dangerous, rather precise, and should not be attempted by the nonprofessional. Most big moving companies will be able to recommend a firm to handle such items.

Source: Mayflower Movers, 5620 First Ave, Brooklyn, NY 11220; phone: (718) 439-1500; fax: (718) 439-3767; contact Susan Ramos.

Paint

What are the different kinds of paints and what are they each used for?

There are almost as many different kinds of paint as painting situations. To help generalize, consider the following types and their uses:

> *Alkyds:* Best for new or bare wood because they penetrate deeply for better adhesion
> *Latex:* Great for color and gloss retention, flexibility, and can be used in almost any situation

Stains: For beautifying and enhancing the natural look of wood
Enamels: For higher-wear areas

Can I use exterior paint indoors?

The answer to this may vary with the manufacturer. Exterior coatings usually take longer to dry, and the pigments in them are less finely ground, which may not look quite so decorative. Also, many contain mildewcides and other ingredients necessary for exterior conditions. Indoors, these may or may not be harmful, depending on the individual paint and the material used. Try to stick with the manufacturer's intended use.

When should I use a brush, a roller, a pad painter, or a sprayer?

Use a brush for hard-to-reach areas and for small jobs such as cutting-in. "Cutting-in" refers to applying paint to a limited area by a different method than that used over the greater surface—use a brush for the area of the wall along a molding strip or where the wall meets the ceiling, because a roller wouldn't give you the control you need.

Paint rollers are best for wide-area jobs such as walls and ceilings. A paint pad is best for working with stains. Spraying is the fastest method of application and best for larger jobs, where a minimum amount of masking is needed to protect other surfaces.

Can you give me any information about disposable brushes?

Disposable brushes can be an economical way to get the job done; use for small touch-ups or where a less decorative finish is acceptable. These brushes tend to lose bristles easily. If this happens, remove the bristles from the surface before the paint dries.

Do you have any advice about painting ceilings?

When painting ceilings, try not to excessively cut in the edges in narrow strips. A wider, even coat will blend better and prevent the problem of "hatbanding"—the difference in color where the walls meet the ceiling (or where the walls meet in a corner).

When I painted the living room, the corner areas were lighter than the rest of the walls. What happened?

This is called "hatbanding"—strips that don't match the rest of the wall or ceiling. Hatbanding can be caused by variations in color texture where roller surfaces join work cut in with a brush. To correct the problem, apply a heavier wet film or an additional coat of paint. Hatbanding is also caused by applying a wet coat onto areas that are already dry. Avoid this by reducing the amount of cut-in area so that a wet edge can be maintained. Another measure is to use a short nap sleeve ($\frac{3}{8}$ to

¼ inch) when rolling on smooth walls, which minimizes the different textures produced by a roller and a brush. The "sleeve" is the fuzzy pad that slips onto the frame of the roller. A "short" nap means that the pad is less fuzzy than you'd find on a long nap sleeve.

Can I paint over wall covering?

Yes, but make sure that the wall covering is securely attached to the wall. Also, glossier surfaces may benefit from a high-adhesion primer. Consult a professional for advice on painting any exotic or specialty wall coverings. Test an inconspicuous area to see if the dyes or glues are sensitive to the paint. Some dyes and pastes may be water-sensitive, others solvent-sensitive, so colors may bleed or the wall covering may loosen or wrinkle.

Usually it is best to remove the wall covering, remove all paste residue, and paint the properly cleaned and prepared substrate below.

Is it true you should use only a glossy paint on woodwork?

Many people like to use glossy paints on woodwork and trim for the practical reason that these coatings tend to be easier to clean and have greater mar resistance. But if your woodwork is plain and you don't want to highlight it in any way, then go ahead and use the same finish (eggshell, satin, and so forth) that you use on the walls.

How do I paint concrete?

First, make sure that new concrete is fully cured. Latex paints are generally the rule for coating this kind of surface because they don't react with the alkalinity the cured coating usually contains. If the concrete is a floor, it must be etched after it's cured and before it's painted.

To paint paneling, do I have to prepare the surface in any way?

Paneling with a smooth or shiny surface should be evenly sanded with a fine-grit sandpaper. An acrylic primer formulated with enhanced adhesion qualities will also be helpful.

I touched up a small area of the wall, but the color is slightly different from the rest. Why?

You may have used a different tool to apply the touch-up than you used for the original paint job. This can leave a different texture on the surface, which reflects light differently and appears to be a variation in the color. Also, the temperature of the air and surface when the original paint dried, as compared with those conditions during touch-up, can affect color. Another possibility is that you used a different batch from the original. Even if manufactured by the same company under the same standards, there can be a slight difference in color between batches.

When I painted my bathroom, the paint blistered and peeled. What can I do?

Not an easy answer, because blistering and peeling can occur for many reasons. You may have moisture problems, wallpaper paste residue, the wrong type of paint for the previously painted surface, or the wall surface wasn't adequately cleaned before the paint was applied. Assuming a perfect world where the blistering and peeling occurred by chance, you may be able to correct the problem if you sand the surface smooth, then clean the area and reapply the paint.

Do you have any tips for cleanup and for storing paint?

Always follow the manufacturer's recommendation for cleanups; substitutions may not produce the same results. Paint should be stored in a tightly closed container equal to the amount to be stored. For example, if you use 4 gallons from a 5-gallon container, store the remainder in a 1-gallon container. This leaves less room for air, which can cause the paint to form a thick skin.

Never dispose of paint down the drain. Recycle unused material, or share it with a friend who may need a little paint to complete small projects around the house. Generally, old paint cans should contain a minimum amount of material, which can be left open to dry. In most areas, this may be acceptable for disposal. Check with local authorities to be sure.

Source: Benjamin Moore Paints, 51 Chestnut Ridge Rd., Montvale, NJ 07646; (201) 573-9600.

Roofs

Why are some roofs sloped and others flat?

The additional time and material required to build an attic is saved if the roof has a very low slope or is flat. Some designers specifically choose a flat roof because they consider the look more modern.

Different shapes have been developed over the years for sloped roofs. The reasons for the slopes have to do with the materials used and the local weather conditions. For example, the slope carries rain off the roof. The mansard and the gambrel (a barnlike roof) developed because local taxes were based on the number of floors in a building. If the roof was almost vertical, you gained a floor but paid taxes as if you had one less floor.

How does a flat roof work?

A "flat" roof actually should have some slope so that rain can drain off. The idea is to have a waterproof layer that extends wall to wall. Where pipes and air conditioners come through, the roof is attached to them so that the whole assembly is still waterproof. For roofs that have walls built up around them, drainage is accomplished through interior drains. In case the drains plug up, the walls have holes in them, called *scuppers,* to let water drain off so the roof doesn't fill up and collapse the building.

Why do roofs have gutters?

Gutters catch water coming off the roof and direct it toward downspouts that take it to the ground. The gutters prevent the water from falling off the building and eroding the ground under the edge of the roof. Without gutters, every time you walked under the edge of a building you would get very wet. Gutters are sometimes omitted, however, in areas where heavy snow loads are expected.

Why do roofers put felt under shingles?

Felt is an extra layer of protection in case the shingles don't stop water. The layer of felt is also a way for the contractor to get the building protected while putting the shingles on the roof. In some roofing systems, the felt protects the roof in cases where wind-driven rain could get under the primary protection, as with tile or slate.

Why do some roofs have a pattern of melted snow that looks like claws near the edge?

Heat inside a building can escape up into the attic. When the attic gets above freezing, the snow on the roof melts. The edge of the roof is cold because it overhangs the walls, so the water from the melting snow refreezes in this area. This ice can build up until it dams the water so deeply that it backs up under the shingles and gets into the house.

Homeowners can fix the problem by sealing their ceilings and insulating the attic. As an expediency, some homeowners place heating cables on the roof. These cables melt the forming ice dam so the water doesn't back up. As the heat from the cable melts the snow above it, a zigzag pattern usually forms along the edge of the roof.

What are the eagles and other funny-shaped things that I see on some roofs?

These are probably snow guards. They keep snow from sliding down the roof and falling onto people or things near the side of the building. There are a variety of designs, and the snow guards can be made from copper, brass, or aluminum. In heavy snow areas, small fences are used to stabilize the snow and limit the potential for a slide.

Why are some shingles called asphalt and some fiberglass when they look much the same?

Shingles are made from a reinforcing material that has been soaked with asphalt. Asphalt is used because of its water resistance. But it needs a reinforcement to give it strength. The reinforcement used to be made from recycled rags and recycled cardboard, called "organic reinforcement." Fiberglass is a more recent reinforcement, and it changed the shingle. The original shingles are still called "organic shingles" in some circles, but to the average person they are "asphalt shingles." In either case, the shingle is covered with granules to protect the asphalt from the effects of the sun and to give it colors to suit the design of the house.

Why do some people put tin roofs on their houses?

Very few people put on actual tin roofs anymore; what most people put on today is painted steel. The metal roofing panels of earlier times shed water and snow very nicely and were an inexpensive way to get good protection. The metal could be stamped to provide attractive profiles and give a home a unique look. Today, metal is popular because it can add nostalgia or a very modern look, depending on what is desired.

What is the best roof?

That's like asking, What is the best car? There is no one answer for every situation. Roofs that last a long time can cost more. Some buildings need a certain type of roof to provide the right appearance. There are literally thousands of different roofing materials and ways to put a roof together. The one that is best for you is going to depend on the look you want to achieve, your budget, and how long you want the roof to last. There are more factors, but these three are the most important to most people.

We know of stone roofs over 1,000 years old. Copper roofs over 700 years old are also documented. Lead on cathedrals in England has lasted 400 years. So choose one of those if longevity is important.

How much overhang should I have on my roof?

In some climates a large overhang helps to shelter the walls from the sun, which can keep the house cooler. Overhangs also help throw the snow or rain farther out from the sides of the building, which can reduce erosion or problems with expansive soils. Some architectural styles are partially defined by the amount of overhang, so period styles are locked into certain overhangs. Roof styles are often based on local weather conditions. The Cape Cod in New England was a compact design and had a roof that deflected the wind. The Southern styles, with high ceilings and large overhangs, encouraged air movement and kept the occupant cooler when the temperatures climbed. For practical purposes today, some overhang is desirable to encourage ventilation of the attic space and to keep any runoff from running down the walls of the building.

Why do roofs always leak?

Most designers design buildings to have a useful life of between 50 and 100 years. There are very few roofing materials that can last that long, so at some point in the building's life the roof is going to leak. One of the most common reasons that flat roofs leak is because the roof is not maintained. Roofs need to be maintained in order for them to last as long as possible. Most often, roof maintenance involves little more than keeping gutters and valleys (where two roof areas meet and form an angle) clean and clear of debris. Flashings (metal strips used to create a waterproof barrier) should be checked, as well as any chimneys or walls that could let water in around the flashing.

What are the advantages and disadvantages of a tile roof?

The tile roof has been in use for hundreds of years, and in some markets it is the predominant roofing system. The reasons people like tile include the look, the longevity, and the fire resistance. The problems with tile generally begin with the cost. Tile is not inexpensive, and the home needs to be constructed to carry the weight. Also, tile can be damaged if you try to walk around on it.

Tile earned a bad reputation in Hurricane Andrew. The technique to install it in Florida was to put down a paddie of mortar. A *paddie* looks like a thick "cow pie" and is a blob or plop of mortar. Hurricane Andrew peeled off tiles that had not been set in large enough mortar paddies, and those tiles broke tiles on other roofs, which continued the process.

Is tar paper really made with tar?

Not very often. Tar paper used to be paper that was soaked with coal-tar pitch. Today, most of the material that people call tar paper is asphalt-saturated organic felt. It is used under shingles and in rare cases as part of a built-up roof, which is constructed of alternating layers of asphalt and reinforcing felt. The built-up roof is sometimes referred to as a "tar and gravel roof," even though most don't use tar anymore. Only about 6 to 10 percent actually use tar. Most flat roofs use asphalt, or a synthetic sheet material.

How do I replace a missing shingle?

First, be careful when going onto a roof. If your roof has too much slope, or if the surface is slippery, the chance of falling makes a do-it-yourself repair a poor investment.

Often, what looks like a missing shingle is really a missing tab. The *tab* is the piece approximately 12 by 6 inches that gives the roof its overlapping pattern. If the tab is missing, the area where it lay is still protected by the shingle underneath it. If the tab is lost but the rest of the roof is still intact, then the process is easier than for more serious damage. A tab can be replaced by cutting another tab off a new or spare shingle and then gluing it in place of the one that was lost, using tab adhesive or plastic roofing cement.

If there is more severe damage, the old shingle can be removed and replaced. This involves breaking loose the sealed tabs and then carefully removing the old shingle. The old nails can be driven down, using a thin ripping bar. The new shingle is slid into place and nailed down under carefully bent-back tabs of the shingle above. The tabs are then resecured, using tab adhesive or plastic roofing cement.

Source: Roofing Industry Educational Institute, Englewood, CO; (303) 790-7200.

Security

How can I make sure my front door is burglar-proof?

Make sure every door to the outside has a sturdy, well-installed deadbolt lock. A *deadbolt* is a bolt that is retracted by means of turning a key, as opposed to a *spring bolt,* which is retracted when you simply turn the doorknob. The spring-bolt lock, even if secured with a key or a button on the doorknob, is not enough.

Remember, a lock on a flimsy door is about as effective as locking your car door but leaving the window down. All outside doors should be metal or solid wood. If your doors don't fit tightly in their frames, install weatherstripping around them. Install a peephole or wide-angle viewer in all entry doors so you can see who is outside without opening the door. Door chains break easily and don't keep out intruders.

Don't hide keys around the outside of your home. Instead, give an extra key to a neighbor you trust. Whenever you move into a new place, have all the locks changed.

I have sliding glass doors opening onto a backyard patio. What's the best way to secure them?

Sliding glass doors can offer easy access if they aren't properly secured. Secure them by installing commercially available bar or frame locks or by putting a broomstick or dowel in the inside track to jam the door. To prevent the door from being lifted off the track, drill a hole through the sliding door frame and the fixed frame. Then insert a pin in the hole.

What are the best ways to keep windows secure?

Lock double-hung windows with key locks. Another method is to drill a small hole at an angle through the two thicknesses of the window frame where the top of the inner window frame overlaps the bottom of the outer window frame. Insert a sturdy nail or dowel that you can easily remove when you want to open the window. For basement windows, consider installing grilles or grates. Be sure they have quick-release mechanisms on the inside.

When I go on a trip, what should I do to make sure everything stays safe back home?

Create the illusion that you're home by getting some timers that will turn lights on and off in different areas of your house throughout the evening. Lights burning 24 hours a day signal that the house is empty. Leave shades, blinds, and curtains in normal positions. Don't let your mail or newspapers pile up. Either stop delivery, or ask a neighbor to collect them for you. Never leave a message on your answering machine that indicates you may be away. Rather than saying, "I'm not at home right now," say, "We're not available right now."

What can I do to increase security outside my home?

Walk around the outside of your house and do a safety check. Thieves hate bright lights, so install outside lights and keep them on at night. Keep your yard clean. Prune back shrubbery so it doesn't hide doors or windows from view. Cut back tree limbs that someone could use to climb to an upper-level window. Clearly display your house number so police and other emergency vehicles can find your home quickly. Join a Neighborhood Watch group.

How do I start a Neighborhood Watch group?

Work with your local police or sheriff's department; they will be your partners. A Neighborhood Watch (or Block Watch, Town Watch, or Crime Watch) is one of the most effective and least costly answers to crime, and many law enforcement agencies across the country report substantial decreases in crime and fear due to such local prevention efforts. The basic goal is to build your community into a safer, friendlier, and more caring place in which to live.

One of the first steps is to organize a meeting for neighbors from your street, block, or apartment house. Arrange with your local law enforcement agency for a crime prevention officer to attend the meeting. Select a meeting place that is accessible to people with disabilities. Publicize your meeting at least one week in advance with door-to-door fliers, and make follow-up phone calls the day before. Translate your announcement into any languages needed by non-English speakers in your community. Stress that a Watch group is an association of neighbors who look out for each other's families and property, alert the police to any suspicious activities or crime in progress, and work together to make their community safer and better.

At the meeting, focus on home security and build neighborhood cohesion. Then move into other areas, such as educating residents about child protection, drug-abuse victim services, and domestic violence. Explore circumstances in the community that might contribute to crime—the physical design of buildings, traffic patterns, drug trafficking, too few jobs or recreational opportunities for teens, lack of affordable housing. Look for long-range solutions.

Some Watch groups start a block parent program or McGruff House to help children cope with emergencies while walking to and from school or playing. Some groups work with small businesses to repair run-down storefronts, clean up streets, and create jobs. Some sponsor seminars for the elderly and others on how to avoid becoming victims of con games and fraud. Some establish a buddy system for the elderly and people with disabilities so that someone checks by phone with them daily. Some groups turn a vacant lot into a park, playing field, or community garden.

Link your Watch group with efforts promoted by other groups: drug prevention, child protection, antivandalism projects, arson prevention, neighborhood cleanup, recycling. Share resources and promote each other's activities. Invite guest speakers to Watch group meetings.

Get youth organizations to work with senior citizen groups. Young people can help the elderly enhance home security, or go to the store for them; seniors can tutor youths or help with recreational projects, oral histories, or cooking classes. Recruit utility workers, cab drivers, and other people with two-way radios or cellular phones to extend your Watch network. Publicize your program and its successes in the local media.

What should I know about alarm systems?

Alarms can be a good investment, especially if you have many valuables in your home or live in an isolated area or one with a history of break-ins. Check with several companies before you buy, so you can decide what level of security fits your needs. Do business with an established company and check references before signing a contract. Learn how to use your system properly. Don't set off false alarms: people will stop paying attention, and you could be fined.

Some less expensive options are available. You can buy a sound-detecting socket that plugs into a light fixture and makes the light flash when it detects certain noises. Motion-sensing outdoor lights turn on when someone approaches. Lights with photo cells turn on when it's dark and off when it's light.

Lots of people are safety-conscious when it comes to keeping out intruders, but what about weird phone calls?

Your best protection when you get any kind of suspicious call is to just hang up the phone. If the calls are personally threatening, call your local phone company and the police. If the calls are sales pitches and you aren't interested, then tell the caller politely that you don't want to waste time. You can also tell them to please not call back. Then hang up. If you are dealing with telemarketers and you tell them not to call back, they are breaking the law if they call you again.

There are other legal lines that can't be crossed. If the caller says you have won a prize, you cannot be asked to pay anything for it; you can't even be required to pay shipping charges. You cannot be asked to pay in advance for acquiring a prize or for some other service; you pay for services only if you ordered them and they are actually delivered. Don't give telemarketers your credit card number, bank account number, Social Security number, or other personal information. And don't authorize bank drafts. If you suspect fraud, call the police and the National Fraud Information Center at 1-800-876-7060.

Source: National Crime Prevention Council, Washington, DC; (202) 466-6272.

Wall Covering

Is wall covering the same thing as wallpaper?

Because the product known as "wallpaper" is available in a variety of materials, the name "wall covering" was coined. However, in recent years, the industry has begun to use "wallpaper" again, recognizing it is more commonly used. In reality, wall covering may be constructed of the following materials:

1. Paper: plain paper or strippable (removable) paper
2. Paper-backed vinyl, also referred to as solid vinyl
3. Fabric-backed vinyl, with either a polyester/cotton scrim (woven fabric), or nonwoven material backing

4. Various synthetics, such as polyolefin, for different functional purposes, including acoustical control

5. Various textiles and natural fibers such as grasses, jutes, strings, and rayon, with paper backing

Do I always have to soak wallpaper before I hang it?

Not always, but usually. An inherent characteristic of paper is that it expands. Once wet, if not allowed to expand prior to hanging, it will expand on the wall, creating long vertical bubbles, known as "expansion bubbles." These will not go away when the strip dries. The recommendation is to wet the prepasted strip (or paste the unpasted strip), then book-fold, roll, and allow to rest (expand) for a specified time prior to hanging.

The correct method of book-folding is: Fold each end of the strip toward the middle, pasted sides together, aligning the edges carefully so they do not dry out. Roll the folded strip as you would a loose newspaper, again being careful to keep the edges aligned. The length of booking time that is needed will vary with the construction (paper, vinyl, etc.) and should be indicated in the hanging instructions accompanying the particular wall covering.

What is "liner paper"?

Liner paper is a plain, nondecorative sheet made of polyester cellulose and chemical additives to provide body, rigidity, and smoothness. It is used over rough, paneled, or cinder-block surfaces, under decorative wallpaper. Liners are available in different weights to camouflage varying degrees of surface irregularity. The coverage specifications of each liner must be coordinated with the surface to be covered.

It is important to note that liners should be installed horizontally to prevent the seams from falling in the same place as the decorative wallpaper seams. Also, the surface being covered must be primed with a wall-covering primer prior to installing liner paper, and then again over the liner before installing the decorative wallpaper.

How do I figure out how much wall covering to buy?

There are various methods to calculate the number of rolls you will need. Some factors to consider are: the width and length, or square foot coverage, of the roll or bolt; the pattern match; and the design repeat of the specific item you have selected. You will also need to know the measurements of the area to be covered, taking into account the number and size of windows, doors, etc. The safest thing to do is to provide all of the information to your decorator, retailer, or wallpaper installer, who can help estimate your needs.

Remember, it is always better to overestimate than to run out. If you don't have enough to complete the job, when you reorder, the same run number or dye lot may not be available. Also, if you have extra, it will be available later if you need to replace a damaged area. This is particularly important in high-traffic areas, or in homes where small children reside.

What do I need if I'm going to put up wall covering myself?

In addition to the wall covering itself, and adequate lighting, you will need the following:

large table, or smooth, flat working surface
paint roller and paint tray, or paste brush (for unpasted paper)
water trough (for prepasted paper)
plastic smoother or smoothing brush
clean, soft sponges
water bucket
pencil
level
scissors
razor knife, with a good supply of blades
measuring tape or ruler
broad knife
straight edge
drop cloth
ladder or step-up stool
good-quality wallpaper primer
good-quality premixed adhesive, appropriate to the wallpaper being hung

How can I be sure to do a good job when I hang wallpaper?

The key to a successful installation is surface preparation. Always be sure the walls are smooth, clean, and free of mildew, grease, and stains. Apply a good-quality wallpaper primer appropriate for the surface you are working with and the wallpaper you are installing. Important note: Be sure the label says "wallpaper primer." This product is different from a paint primer; they are not interchangeable. Most of today's good-quality wallpaper primers are appropriate for almost all surfaces and wallpapers.

Allow the primer to dry overnight. Then follow the hanging instructions enclosed with the wallpaper carefully, paying particular attention to the times recommended for soaking and booking, and the proper adhesive to use. If there are no instructions in the rolls, ask your retailer or decorator for advice, or call the manufacturer.

Is it okay to put new wall covering on top of old?

Only if the existing wallpaper is well-bonded to the wall. You must first apply a pigmented wallpaper primer, to prevent the design of the original wallpaper from showing through the new. If the wallpaper bubbles, you must stop and remove it thoroughly before proceeding. Recently, several removal products have been introduced that make this an easier, neater job than in the past.

How can I refasten wallpaper that is pulling away from the wall at the top?

Using a vinyl over vinyl (VOV) adhesive, apply a small amount to the back of the wallpaper. Allow it to dry slightly so it is tacky to the touch. Smooth firmly with a smoothing tool or damp sponge, being careful not to squeeze out the adhesive.

To apply a decorative border, do I paste it over the wall covering, or shouldn't they be layered like that?

If the border is being installed at the same time as the wallpaper, it is best to "inlay" the border adjacent to, rather than over, the wallpaper. You will get a smoother seam and avoid the sidewall design showing through the border. If the sidewall has already been hung, you may layer a border over it by following these steps:

1. Apply a pigmented wallpaper primer to prevent the design of the wallpaper from showing through the border.

2. If hanging over paper wall covering, install the border according to the hanging instructions enclosed with it when you bought it.

3. If hanging over vinyl wall covering, use vinyl over vinyl adhesive. If the border is prepasted, wet the prepaste, apply the VOV, and hang according to the hanging instructions enclosed with the border.

How can I tell from a sample if a pattern will really suit a room?

Whenever possible, bring the sample book or larger sample of the wallpaper to the actual environment where it will be hung. Be sure the colors and pattern suit the lighting and other major decorative elements in the room. Remember, this is only a sample; when you receive your actual wallpaper, differences in dye lots may cause a slight variation. It should be acceptable to match carpeting and other coordinating items from the samples, but if you plan to cover items such as bedspreads, draperies, and so on, with matching fabrics, you should have both the actual wallpaper and fabric in your possession before proceeding with either installing the wallpaper or fabric-covering the accessories.

Generally, large-scale prints will work better in large areas and small patterns in smaller areas. Many different prints can work together in one area if they are balanced in scale and coordinated in color. Color can have a major impact in an area. Bright colors tend to make an area appear smaller; soft colors will tend to make it feel larger. Blues and greens will create a relaxed atmosphere, reds and yellows a more vibrant one. Wall covering sample books usually are arranged to show a variety of patterns, textures, sidewalls, and borders of one "color story" that can work together. Many have coordinated or matching fabrics and decorative accessories. Refer to them, and ask your retailer for help in planning and coordinating a professional decorator look for your home.

Can I use any kind of wall covering in my kitchen, or are there some I should stay away from?

Any wallpaper used in a kitchen (or any area that may be prone to splatters and stains) should be easy to clean. Wallpaper that is labeled "washable," or even better, "scrubbable," would be the best choices. These can be cleaned with mild soap and water, and will hold up best to the high traffic of most kitchens.

Source: Marcy Graham, Quality Assurance, Waverly Fabrics, FSC Wallcoverings, a division of F. Schumacher & Co., 79 Madison Ave., New York, NY 10016; (212) 213-7900.

Walls and Ceilings

What is a *load-bearing wall*?

A load-bearing wall bears the load, or weight, of a building's other structural and nonstructural elements or assemblies. For example, a load-bearing wall might support the roof or upper floors of a home. Inadvertently removing a load-bearing wall during remodeling is a prescription for trouble.

When buying a house, what do I need to know about walls?

Nontextured walls should be reasonably smooth, free of excessive cracks and pits, and should be installed perpendicular to the floor. If the house was finished using drywall, the nails or screws used for attachment should not be protruding from the wall surface. Stains on walls may be a sign of water-intrusion problems or plumbing malfunctions. Look for areas of excessive repair that may indicate a hidden problem. Although cracks in walls are not necessarily a cause for concern, an excessive number of large cracks may be an indicator of serious structural movement.

Will a new house have basically the same kinds of walls that an old house has?

If the old house is more than 40 or 50 years old, probably not. Gypsum wallboard (drywall construction) was not widely used as a residential interior construction wall finishing until immediately after World War II. Before then, most interior partitions were finished using plaster. Plaster is applied as a wet compound over an underlying framework called a *lath*, which is typically constructed of narrow wood strips or mesh.

Can you give me some tips about fastening mirrors and other heavy things on my walls?

Wherever possible, have the fastening device—the nail, screw, or other fastener—attach directly into a building element such as a stud or joist. If that's not possible, use a hollow-wall fastener or a toggle bolt large enough to accommodate the weight of the item to be hung. Make sure that the wall can support the weight of the item you intend to hang on it. A ½ inch sheet of drywall, for example, can typically support an item that weighs up to 30 pounds hung from a toggle bolt that has a ⅛ inch diameter. For anything heavier, you should use an alternative fastener or have supplemental support installed in the partition.

How do I remove mollies and similar hollow-wall fasteners?

You don't want to pull out such fasteners, because that often causes the wallboard or plaster to stress and crack or break, which can create a big hole. Instead, my favorite method is to force the unwanted fastener into the wall cavity and then patch the resulting hole with joint compound or plaster. If it's a hollow-wall fastener installed in drywall, you can generally keep torquing (with a screwdriver, twisting with force) the hanging screw until the flat head of the fastener breaks through the drywall and falls back into the wall cavity. This usually leaves a hole no more than about ½ inch in diameter.

Another method that is also one of my favorites is to leave the old fastener in place and hang a new picture or mirror over it, although this is generally frowned upon by most interior decorators.

Are there different types of ceilings?

Absolutely. Just as walls are constructed of a variety of materials, so are ceilings. Generally, in most houses, the ceilings are constructed using the same facing material as the walls. If the walls are plaster, so are the ceilings. You will also find ceiling options such as ceiling tiles or molded tin. You can easily mix and combine different ceiling materials throughout a home to obtain a variety of different looks.

Can I buy fake molded-tin or molded-plaster ceilings?

Faux-tin ceiling products are manufactured by a number of different ceiling tile manufacturing companies. Most are manufactured for the restaurant and hospitality industry and are perfectly adaptable for home use. Real tin ceilings are also still manufactured by a few companies. Plaster molding—either genuine or made to look genuine—is readily available for use in residential dwellings.

I painted over a brown stain in one corner of my ceiling, but the spot is back. How do I get rid of it?

First, make sure that the source of the stain has been eliminated. Then determine the composition of both the stain (rusty water, mildew, etc.) and the stained surface (drywall, plaster, paneling, etc.). Take your information to a reputable paint store—preferably one that services the professional painting industry. They should be able to recommend a product that will seal the stained area and prevent the stain from bleeding through the fresh paint.

We just moved into our house, and the movers punched a hole about the size of a basketball in our wall. How do we fix it?

Assuming that the wall is drywall, first cut a square area around the hole back to the studs that support the wall and remove the damaged drywall. Then take a new piece of drywall that is cut to the size of the square, and set this into the opening you've created. Attach the new drywall to the studs, and finish the joints around the patch with joint compound. You may want to paint the entire wall to minimize the patched appearance of the repaired area.

When I had an old built-in air conditioner removed, the mason blocked up the opening, but how do I fix the interior wall?

If the interior wall is bare masonry with no surface covering, you probably are looking at an area where the blocks don't match the original construction.

From a performance standpoint, the repaired masonry is acceptable. However, it probably looks awful. One solution is to completely cover the interior wall surface, choosing between either a paint-type material with a thick, dense texture or a product such as drywall that completely covers the affected area.

Avoid thin materials such as nontextured paint, because they will cover only the surface of the wall and you will still be able to read the imperfections in the mismatched masonry. If you use a textured material to cover up the new masonry, be prepared to coat the entire wall surface. Coating just the affected area will result in a wall that will look just as bad as an uncoated, mismatched surface.

I'm finishing off my basement. Should I install the drywall parallel or perpendicular to the studs?

You should always install the board to minimize the quantity of joints that will have to be finished. A good general rule is, if the ceiling height is less than two board-widths high, install the drywall perpendicular to the studs (that is, horizontally across the vertical studs). However, every project is different, so a bit of planning can save you some extra work.

Source: Michael Gardner, Technical Director, Association of Wall and Ceiling Industries, 307 E. Annandale Rd., Falls Church, VA 22042; (703) 534-8300.

GARDENING

Backyard Habitats

Bulbs • Compost • Flowers

Fruit Growing

Garden Pests and Beneficials

Garden Tools

Greenhouses and Coldframes

Ground Covers

Heirloom Plants • Herbs

Hydroponics

Indoor Gardening and Houseplants

Landscaping • Lawns

Pest Solutions

Propagation

Rock Gardens

Seeds • Shrubs • Soil

Vegetables

Window Boxes

Xeriscaping

Backyard Habitats

If I set up a bird feeder, is that a backyard habitat?

Just barely. For a backyard habitat, you want to attract a variety of wildlife—birds as well as butterflies, toads, crickets, and others. Bird feeders are a good start, but try planting shrubs and vines that produce berries, too. You can also leave the seedheads on flowers during the winter. Think about the natural plantings that can attract wildlife

How can I start a backyard habitat?

You need to think about the needs of various wildlife—for example, food, shelter, water, and nesting sites. Then make a list of appropriate plants for these purposes. Draw a design of your garden that includes these various components. Your local garden center or nursery may have suggestions.

What sort of plants do I need for a backyard habitat?

A variety of plantings is important, as is a mixture of food types, so that you have a year-round cycle of flowering and fruiting. One study listed the ten most valuable hardwood plants as oak, blackberry, cherry, dogwood, grape, pine, blueberry, maple, sumac, and beech.

Which plants provide the best cover for birds?

Evergreen trees and shrubs such as yew provide good places for birds to retreat to. Hollow trees also provide areas of shelter. Other good covers are tall grasses, briar patches, and shrubs such as barberry.

Won't wildlife become too dependent on what I provide?

They will if you provide only supplementary sources, such as seed at bird feeders and sugar water at hummingbird feeders. If you incorporate plantings that feed animals naturally, you will create a more sustainable habitat. Never start feeding wildlife unless you can continue through the season.

Do I have to provide water in my backyard habitat?

Yes, definitely. Water is one of the most important elements. It can be a birdbath, a small pool or pond, or very simply a saucer sunk into the ground.

Are any gardening practices harmful to wildlife and do any enhance wildlife?

The more chemicals you use, the less wildlife you will have. Most pesticides kill insects indiscriminately. If you use them, you will destroy the source of food for young birds. Most garden insects are not detrimental. Many are helpful, such as ladybugs, syrphid flies, and green lacewings. You will have a more nature-filled garden if you work without harmful chemicals. It will be safer for people, too!

Some research indicates that using too much commercial fertilizer can destroy microorganisms in the soil. Composting and other organic gardening methods enhance the soil and keep alive the microorganisms that are an important part of the natural food chain. The wildlife of the soil can be one of the most interesting aspects of gardening, especially for children. Robins will love it as well.

What are some flowers that attract butterflies?

Butterflies are fond of the aptly named butterfly bush. They also like monarda, day lilies, echinacea (purple coneflower), rudbeckia (coneflower, black-eyed Susan), and Joe Pye weed. Butterflies and caterpillars—which are going to turn into butterflies—like butterfly weed.

There are lots of cats in my neighborhood. Won't they prey on the birds that are drawn to my backyard?

Yes! If you want to keep cats away, use citrus peelings in your mulch. If you know the areas where cats like to lie, you can put thorny shrub cuttings in those areas to make them less inviting.

Can my vegetable garden coexist with my backyard habitat, or will the birds and other animals eat my crops?

This may be a problem whether or not you have a backyard habitat. If you have a lot of wildlife, you will probably need to protect your vegetable garden with fencing.

My neighbors have a wild, overgrown backyard, but I hate messy things. Can a backyard habitat look neat?

Yes, but you need to allow some of your shrubs to take on a more natural shape, rather than the sheared look. Perhaps you could plan for some less visible areas of the garden to have a less than immaculate look. Birds and other wildlife love flowers that have gone to seed, bogs, dead logs, brush piles, and tall grasses.

Where can I get more information about backyard habitats?

Two helpful handbooks are *Butterfly Gardens* and *Going Native: Biodiversity in Our Own Backyards*. Each is available for $9.95 plus a $4.00 shipping fee from Brooklyn Botanic Garden, 1000 Washington Ave., Brooklyn, NY 11225.

Source: Ellen Kirby, director of Brooklyn Greenbridge, the community horticulture program of the Brooklyn Botanic Garden, Brooklyn, NY. For more information, call the National Wildlife Federation toll-free at (800) 477-5560. The Federation's Backyard Wildlife Habitat Program has been going since 1973. They have an information packet and guide for planting, along with a certificate program for applicants who qualify for creating and maintaining their own backyard habitat. The packet (which includes a 75-page booklet) costs $4.95 plus a shipping charge.

Bulbs

How deep should I plant bulbs?

For spring bulbs (which are planted in the fall), plant them two and a half to three times the height of the bulb. Larger bulbs such as tulips or daffodils will be planted about 8 inches deep, while smaller bulbs might be about 3 to 4 inches.

HINT: How quickly the soil warms up affects the growth of the bulb. Bulbs planted in full sun will start to grow and bloom sooner than the same bulbs planted in a shady spot. Likewise, bulbs planted next to each other with about 1 inch difference in planted depth will start to grow and bloom at different times. Don't be afraid to experiment.

Do I have to dig up my bulbs in the fall and replant them in the spring?

Check with your local nursery or garden center. Depending on their hardiness (their ability to survive winter freezes), some bulbs can be left in the ground and some will need to be lifted and stored.

Do I have to divide bulbs every few years to prevent overcrowding?

Maybe, maybe not. It's better to watch for the quality of flowering. For example, daffodils and some tulips can go on *naturalizing* (remaining in the ground and multiplying) for many years before the flowering starts to taper off. It's at this time that the bulbs should be lifted and divided.

Do bulbs have to be fertilized?

Yes. When planting fall flowering bulbs, mix 5-10-5 fertilizer into the soil where the bulbs will be planted, using ¼ cup per square foot. Bonemeal also works well. These fertilizers are high in phosphorus, which is good for bulb production. Do not fertilize after they have started to grow.

Summer flowering bulbs can be fertilized with a 10-10-10 soluble fertilizer at the rate of 5 tablespoons per 10 square feet as soon as the shoots break through in the spring.

I know not to cut back the leaves of my bulbs after the flowers die, but how can I make the plants look less messy?

The best way to keep the bulb foliage from looking messy is to plant the bulbs among perennials that will quickly grow up around the mess and hide it. Day lilies are an example. Another method practiced by many gardeners, but not encouraged by horticulturists, is to loosely tie the foliage into bundles with rubberbands. This method prevents all the leaves from doing their job, which is to photosynthesize and replenish the bulb. It will take many years, however, for bulbs to suffer after cutting the leaves, and by that time you may have moved.

How can I force bulbs to bloom indoors during winter?

Forcing bulbs indoors involves gently reproducing nature's treatment of bulbs as if they had been planted outdoors. Spring bulbs require a cooling-off period; that's why they are planted in the fall. The entire process, in short, requires potting the bulbs, cooling them, and making sure the soil stays moist throughout. Avoid using the refrigerator because ripe fruit releases a gas that may prevent flower formation.

Different bulbs need different cooling periods. Some, such as paperweight narcissus and amaryllis, need none. It's best to talk with your local nursery for more details.

What are the easiest bulbs to grow and what are the most difficult?

Daffodils are the easiest bulbs to grow. They have no pest problems, grow just about anywhere (except in wet soil), and naturalize beautifully. Amaryllis are the hardest to grow. They have very strange eating and resting habits that make them less frustrating and more enjoyable if purchased each year as a plant from your local nursery. Their habits are so strange that I wonder where their natural habitat is, because I'm not sure I'd want to go there.

How can I protect my bulbs from animals that eat them below the ground?

Some bulbs, such as fritillaria and alliums, are foul-smelling, and when planted around yummy bulbs can repel pesty underground rodents. For top-feeding rodents, a netting placed on the soil where the bulbs are planted works well. Or try cats; they work pretty well too.

I planted lots of different kinds of bulbs, but only the daffodils came up. What happened?

Where should we start…Were the bulbs hardy in your area? Was the soil too wet? How about the planting depth? Do you need a cat? (Daffodils are poisonous bulbs; that's why the rodents don't eat them.) These are just a few of the questions to ask in the investigation process. I recommend waiting until winter to consult with your local nursery or garden center. They will be starved for company and more than willing to discuss any gardening questions you may have.

One last word: Gardening is like boiling noodles. The box has very specific directions, but does anyone actually follow them? When one understands the concept, the directions are ignored and the noodles turn out great anyway. (For most of us, I hope!)

Source: Rachel Williams, Horticulturist, Chicago Botanic Gardens, Chicago, IL.

Compost

Do I need a bin for my compost, or can I just pile it on the ground in a corner of my garden?

Loose piling is all right for a compost pile, and it allows easy access, but it may appear messy. Keep the compost lightly covered with leaves or straw and it will look better.

What is the best sort of bin for compost?

You want a compost bin that allows good airflow and ease of access. Lattice wood bins are very nice, and the most natural kind of bin, and they can self-compost over three to four years. Many people like plastic bins, which are durable, but be careful about the kind of plastic. Bins made from recycled plastic can fall apart over time because of exposure to the sun. Very promising is a plastic insulated bin that is being developed in Switzerland. It has air pockets in the walls to help hold in more heat.

Why is heat important for compost, and won't lots of airflow cool it down too much?

Heat and airflow can work against each other to some extent, but both are necessary for the composting process. If there is no airflow, the compost pile cools off. Microbes—the organisms that help turn those kitchen scraps and grass clippings into compost—need air or they will die. A freestanding bin with lots of air coming in would not be too much air.

Heat makes microbes happy. Mixing your compost pile well is good for its heat level. So is moisture from the fresh materials you put in. Fill the bin as quickly as you can. Get it all in there—branches, grass clippings, leaves. That's not hard to do in summer and fall. Volume promotes heat.

Why should I turn my compost pile, and how often should I do so?

Turning helps to homogenize the materials. The idea is to remix the layers. Don't just stir the contents around; get what is at the bottom of the pile and move it up. Stir the compost loosely every six weeks, and try to turn it completely every two to three months.

What do people mean when they talk about "green" and "brown" compost?

These terms reflect the material's freshness. Green would be any fresh vegetative matter, like new grass clippings or vegetable scraps left over from dinner. Brown materials would be somewhat dry, like old leaves or hay—anything not fresh. You can't always go by color. Manure, despite its color, is a green material.

What should I put in my compost pile and what should I leave out?

Almost any organic material is fine. You want to keep control of the various ingredients, however. Balance green and brown materials. Balance loose materials with compact ones; loose material would be anything highly porous. Brown materials are usually porous and therefore loose materials. Compact materials would be very wet or heavy; soil, for example, is compact but not wet.

Soil is a traditional ingredient for the compost pile, but it isn't needed. Some people think you shouldn't add meat scraps, but they are okay. Pine needles are also okay, though they don't break down well. You can use a little bit, however. Be careful about pet feces—dog and cat feces can spread communicable diseases. The feces of rabbits and hamsters should be okay.

How long does compost usually have to decompose before I can use it?

Probably about a year. The material you add this summer and fall will be just about ready next spring.

When is the compost ready for my garden, and how do I use it?

The compost should have a loose and crumbly look, no odor, and no obvious pieces of food scraps or grass clippings. You can spread this well-stabilized compost on top of the soil and just leave it there, or you can lightly work it into the soil. Anywhere from ½ to 2 inches is a good thickness, depending on the kind of compost. Use less of a manure compost, since that contains too many nutrients.

Should I water my compost pile?

Always. Keep it moist, but don't overdo it. If it looks like a mudball, your compost pile is too wet. If it's too wet, mix in some dry material like hay or leaves.

If I put weeds in my compost pile, won't they sprout and spread the weeds when I put the compost on my garden?

Compost can spread weeds. To avoid that, let the compost decompose a really long time, and turn it several times. Any weed seeds will germinate and die. They cannot grow inside compost as they die from the heat and moisture.

Don't compost piles smell bad?

They shouldn't. Turn your compost pile, and keep it moist. Then it should be fine.

Source: Will Brinton, Woods End Research Laboratory, compost consulting and agricultural and environmental research, Mount Vernon, ME.

Flowers

Are *annuals* and *perennials* basically the same?

Yes and no. Annuals and perennials have different growth habits. Annuals have the ability to grow from a seed into a mature, profusely flowering plant during a single growing season. Perennials, on the other hand, have the ability to remain in the ground year after year and, depending on their hardiness, reemerge each year to produce flowers or decorative vegetation. During their first year or two, perennials may seem disappointing. They need a few years to become established, and then will produce more blooms.

Annuals and perennials respond similarly to proper location and growing conditions—for example, appropriate sun or shade, good soil preparation, and proper watering.

What's a *biennial* and does it need any special treatment?

Biennials are plants that grow from a seed, produce root systems and vegetation above ground during the first growing season, and then reemerge the second season to produce flowers. These flowers produce the seeds that start the next two-year cycle. Biennials, like all other flowers, require proper location in sun or shade. Like perennials, biennials need a space that will be undisturbed from one year to the next. They may also need mulch for freeze/thaw protection, depending on your hardiness zone.

How can I make sure my flowers have enough water?

Sufficient water varies widely, depending on the type of plant. Experience and daily observation are important factors. Plants will naturally wilt to tell you when to water. It isn't so easy to tell when you are overwatering—unless it is too late and the plant rots and dies. Generally, it is better to underwater than overwater.

A full 1 inch of natural rainfall per week will sustain most plants. Supplemental watering during hot summer months is often necessary. A soaker hose is the premier way to water your flowers; hand-watering one plant at a time is the next best method. Or use a slow-flowing hose around the base of the plant; this reduces erosion and gets right to the plant. Sprinkler hoses that spray a fine mist are another option. But never water roses with a spray or sprinkler; instead, water them close to the ground, so the leaves stay as dry as possible. Finally, don't water your flowers too late in the day because the plants need time to dry off before the colder night temperatures set in, otherwise fungus can develop.

How can I make my flowers have many blooms that last a long time?

Abundant flowering can usually be achieved by pinching early growth, and by deadheading spent flowers and stems. However, some flowers naturally produce blossoms over a long period of time, and others bloom one day and are gone the next.

Deadheading is the removal of spent flowers so that the plant's energy is not wasted on developing seeds but rather goes to produce more flowers. Better plant appearance is also a consideration—especially with bearded iris, hostas, hollyhocks, day lilies, and delphiniums. Pinching helps a plant get over the shock of transplant. A plant puts a lot of energy into a flower bud. If the bud is removed, the plant will put its energy into developing the root system or branches.

When my plants start to die, should I pull them out?

It depends. Most annual plants tend to live out the summer season if they have had sufficient water. At the end of the summer, you could pull up the dead plants. Some people leave these in place during winter because the dried plants add contrast to a snowy landscape.

If your annuals start to die in midsummer, there could be a problem. They could have a disease, and if so, these affected plants should be removed to help prevent the spread of disease. On the other hand, some perennials tend to blossom early, then die back and disappear. Put a marker by such plants so the area is not disturbed. Late planting of annuals in such bare spots is sometimes done, so long as the crown and roots of the perennial are not injured.

What is the best way to control weeds?

Careful cultivation and mulching will control weeds. Of course, you can also pull them out by hand, one by one. *Cultivation* means scratching the soil around the plants with a hoe or 3-fingered weeder, but not too close or too deep. This scratches out newly emerging weeds. If the weeds get too big, hand-pull them. If a weed is too close to the plant, you should also pull it out by hand so you don't damage the plant. When you cultivate, don't get within 3 inches of the plant, or more than 2 to 3 inches deep into the soil.

Mulch also controls weeds. You can use grass clippings, ground leaves, or well-decomposed compost. Wood chips are sold as mulch, and they are fine, but wood chips usually include some large pieces that take a long time to break down. They can get in the way of your next planting. Cocoa-bean hulls make a good mulch—and when it rains, your garden will smell like hot chocolate. Debris left over from cotton milling works well because of its fine consistency. Wood chips from tree-trimming services are usually free, but make sure they are dried chips from trees trimmed during the winter. Summer trimmings aren't good for mulching because they contain green leaves and sap, which get too hot as they decompose. Let fresh trimmings age before you use them.

Apply mulch about 2 inches deep around your plants—1 inch is too meager, 3 inches a bit much. Tuck the mulch up around the plants. Weeds won't germinate where you have covered the soil with mulch, and the mulch holds in moisture for the plant.

There are preemergent weed preventers on the market that can be applied at planting time. But be sure to follow the directions on the package. Chemical treatment is not recommended (for environmental reasons) once your garden plants are maturing. Also, chemical controls may not be selective enough—they can damage flowering plants as well as kill weeds.

What flowers are good for hanging planters or flower boxes, and what sort of soil should I use?

Annuals like marigolds, geraniums, and impatiens are popular for hanging baskets and window boxes. Begonias in the whisky or vodka series, with bronze leaves, have flowers that keep coming and coming. An attractive plant is dusty miller, which doesn't blossom but has light gray foliage that provides a nice accent or contrast among the flowers. Asparagus fern has a very fine leaf that also provides a different texture.

You can buy hanging baskets that are already planted and blooming. These always look beautiful when you buy them. The growers use a soilless mix to start the plants, and in the greenhouse they control light and fertilizer, so the baskets turn out fine. But when you bring them home, remember to water them almost every day and feed them with liquid fertilizer at least once a week. If you don't, your hanging basket will dry up and not do well.

A good soil mix for your planter is one part topsoil; one part compost or manure, for nutrients; one part perlite, which is porous and keeps the soil from compacting so it drains well; and one part milled sphagnum moss, which contributes organic material, is a soil conditioner, and helps hold in moisture. Sphagnum moss holds four times its weight in water; even small pieces in the mixture help retain moisture.

Prune hanging baskets periodically so the hang isn't more than 8 to 10 inches over the side of the planter. Pruning promotes additional growth and more flowers.

Why didn't the peonies I transplanted last year do well this year?

Peonies take a long while to establish, so give them time, and make sure they have full sun. You also need a big enough hole—a ten-dollar hole, not a two-bit one. You can help the hole with compost and sphagnum moss. Divide and transplant peonies in the fall; cut their tops off close to the soil. When you dig up the corm (the root), you will see the red buds that are next year's leaves. Peonies are particular about how deep you plant them: they should be no more than 2 inches below the finished surface of the soil. One inch is better than 3, but 2 inches is the optimum.

Full sun is important. The vegetation must flourish even after the flowers are gone. If you want large flower heads, pinch off side buds near the leaf nodes so the main bud gets bigger. Pinch the buds off close to the stem. You will have fewer blossoms, but they will be big and showy. And don't worry about those ants on your peonies. They eat the sweetness around the bud and do no harm.

How should I cut back my rosebushes?

Basically, you want to cut off any black wood and leave the green wood around the core. Cut your roses back in spring. Roses are hardy, so you don't have to wait until after the last frost; any time in April seems good. You want to see where the new growth is and where there is no new growth. New growth is where the new blossoms will appear. In the fall, you won't know what will grow, so wait till you see green in the spring, and then do your cutting back. Cut at a 45-degree angle, using a sharp shearing knife, not a crushing or anvil-type pruner. When cutting roses to bring into the house, cut back to a five-leaf branch or node, not a three-leaf one. Make your cut about ¼ inch above the five-leaf branch.

Are there any low-growing flowers I can plant among the stones of my walkway?

Phlox subulata is low-growing, about 2 or 3 inches tall, with white, pink, or purple flowers; one plant can cover an area about 12 to 18 inches. The flowers appear in the spring, and then you would have the green foliage for the rest of the growing season.

Source: Richard D. Peterson, Master Gardener, Gardeners of America, Johnston, IA.

Fruit Growing

I have several acres of land and would like to grow fruit. What do I need to know?

Save yourself time and money by planning ahead. Fruit plants grow best if you give a lot of thought to locating the right site. Full sunlight and a well-drained soil are critical. You'll need to do a soil test and prepare the site accordingly, which may require modifying it with certain fertilizers and other amendments. Coming up with a good planting design, choosing right varieties, and planting correctly are important, too. It's well worth your time to read as much as you can before you begin.

Can I grow fruits organically?

Yes, but some fruits are easier to grow organically than others. Blueberries, for example, are easier than tree fruits such as apple and peach, which have a much larger number of insect and disease problems. A good source of information about what is easiest to grow is your county cooperative extension. Each county has one of these offices, and you'll find it listed in your phone book in the White or Blue Pages. Look up your county name, followed by "Cooperative Extension" or "Extension Service."

What's a good fruit to start with if you've never grown fruit before?

A small number of strawberries—perhaps just twenty-five plants—would be a great choice. They take up little space, have few rigorous requirements if you plan ahead and choose the site and varieties correctly, and of course are incredibly satisfying. Care requirements vary somewhat depending on where you live, so ask a local resource, such as an extension agent, for advice about variety choices, site preparation, and maintenance needs.

I live in the northern part of the country. Will varieties that are sold from southern nurseries be less hardy?

Nope. A variety will be true to its individual characteristics, no matter where it originates. However, be kind to your local neighbors and order from them if you can, wherever you live.

What kinds of fruit can I grow in my high-rise apartment, which has limited light?

Better stick with another crop, or go with a houseplant suited to low light levels. Nearly all fruits require full sunlight and need space to grow. The time and money invested in grow lights and other materials could be spent at your favorite local market.

Why won't my fruit trees bear fruit?

Fruit trees fail to produce fruit for many reasons. Blooms may be sparse or lacking. You may have varieties that aren't sufficiently cold hardy for your region. A late spring frost, a disease, poor plant nutrition, or not having a sufficient number of varieties for cross-pollination can all affect fruit set. Look closely at your planting throughout the season. Becoming intimately attuned to what's happening in your home orchard will help you pinpoint problem spots.

How come my strawberries produce only nubby, seedy little button berries instead of fat red fruits?

Your strawberry blossoms are probably being infested by an insect called the *tarnished plant bug,* which sucks the juices in the bud and injects toxic substances that kill the surrounding tissues. The berries remain small, with a woody texture, and fail to mature. For gorgeous fruit, get rid of the pests while the plant is blossoming.

Will I get fruit if I plant just one blueberry variety?

You will, but you will get larger fruit if you plant two varieties. A little-known fact about blueberries: planting just one variety yields small fruit, but planting two or more produces larger berries.

How would I transplant wild blueberry bushes from my friends' woods to my suburban garden?

Choose the smallest plants possible, dig up as much root as you can, and cut the plants back at planting. Do this in the spring only, to give the plants a chance to get established while the weather is cool. Summer transplanting would stress them out. Be sure the site you have selected is ready for the plants. They prefer an acid, sandy loam with good drainage, yet also with good moisture-holding capacity. But first: Are these the varieties you really want? You could purchase varieties selected for excellent flavor, size, cold hardiness, and other qualities.

How would I go about selling my fruit, and how much fruit would I have to produce?

Selling your fruit requires not just knowledge of growing the crops well but skills in marketing, too. Before getting in over your head, you need to ask some questions. Is there a market for this type of fruit? How will you deal with the problem of seasonality? Grocery stores, for example, often avoid purchasing from small growers because the supply is more inconsistent than from larger growers in regions with long growing seasons. Where will you market the fruit? What are the costs involved? What type of quality do your markets require? Can you offer fruit of top quality, or will problems of disease and insects make this a formidable challenge? Are you willing to work long hours and on weekends? What if the restaurants in your area need a steady supply of fresh fruit daily?

Talk to local growers and local markets. Visit your county cooperative extension service. As you might guess, there is a lot more to marketing fruit than meets the eye.

Source: Marcia Eames-Sheavly, Horticulture Educator, Fruit and Vegetable Science Department, Cornell University, Ithaca, NY.

Garden Pests and Beneficials

How can I keep rabbits out of my garden?

One method is to alter your landscape to get rid of the sort of habitat that rabbits like. Rabbits usually live in brush or thickets; you'll also find them in the spaces between rocks, and in the burrows of other animals. Rabbits like grassy or weedy conditions, too, where they can create a ground nest. To make your landscape less hospitable, you want to remove brush piles, weedy thickets, stone piles, and junk piles.

Fencing is an option. Get chicken wire with a 1-inch mesh. You want a fence that's at least 2 feet high after the bottom 3 inches are buried in the ground. You can also try ¼ inch hardware cloth, which is good around fruit trees or favored shrubs. Bury this at least 3 inches in the ground.

Some chemical repellents with the fungicide thiram may discourage rabbits. Remember that repellents have to be applied again after a heavy rain.

Are there any garden plants that rabbits won't eat?

Although sometimes rabbits seem insatiable, there actually are plants they don't favor. Butterfly bush, azaleas, bush cinquefoil, sumac, and yew are fairly safe shrubs. Trumpet vine is usually successful. Reports vary widely on clematis. Perennials least favored by rabbits include lily-of-the-valley, peony, sedum, day lily, hollyhock, bleeding heart, tickseed, columbine, bee balm, foxglove, lady's mantle, forget-me-not, cardinal flower, and Stokes aster. Hyacinth, daffodil, and allium also do well. Ornamental grasses are successful, too. Annuals you might try would be pot marigold, vinca, begonia, spiderflower, geranium, and ageratum.

Safe vegetables would be onions, leeks, squash, tomatoes, potatoes, asparagus, and rhubarb. If you like fresh fruit, try grapes, currants, or gooseberries. Rabbits are usually merciful toward herbs, so try mint, tarragon, chives, marjoram, oregano, basil, parsley, and savory.

How can I keep birds from eating my fruits and berries?

The answer is netting—the only consistently effective option for a homeowner to use on fruit plants. Try a 1-inch mesh of nylon or plastic netting. Garden centers, hardware stores, and gardening catalogues sell netting that is specifically designed for protecting fruit crops.

What shrubs can I plant that will be safe from deer?

Among the shrubs least favored by deer are barberry, paper birch, boxwood, Russian olive, pieris, holly, and leucothoe. Others with a fairly good record are white birch, forsythia, bittersweet, dogwood, inkberry, lilac, mountain laurel, beautybush, and flowering cherry.

Can I use the same pesticides on my food plants that I use on my ornamentals?

Not necessarily. You want to be very careful here or you can do harm to yourself or your plants. Each pesticide is specifically labeled for the pests and plants that it can be used on. You must follow the label exactly.

What does the phrase *integrated pest management* mean?

Integrated pest management (IPM) refers to combining multiple strategies for pest control into a unified program. Generally, chemical pesticides are only a small component of the management program. Habitat and cultural controls are the big alternative; attracting beneficial insects is second; using pesticides is the last alternative. As the word "management" reflects, the idea is not to eradicate all pests but to limit their development and numbers.

Can I really control harmful insects without using synthetic chemicals?

Yes. The two basic ways are by using cultural and biological methods. *Cultural control* involves manipulating the pest's environment. You can change habitat conditions (such as water, temperature, and space) to reduce insect populations. For example, you can rake up leaves and dethatch your lawn to remove insect breeding and hiding grounds. Rototill the garden in the fall to expose pests to adverse elements. Another cultural alternative comes from what you decide to plant in your garden. Use plant varieties that are bred for their resistance to pests.

Another cultural method is crushing the insects one by one between your fingers, or stepping on them. You can also find large industrial vacuums that will suck them up. Some insects can be kept from plants with row covers or other barriers.

Biological methods get us into the area of "beneficials"—the good insects or organisms that can control the bad ones. There are three types of biological controls: predators, parasites, and pathogens. To be effective, a beneficial has to keep up with a pest's high reproduction rate. You also want it to be host-specific: it should go after the organism that is a pest, but leave other organisms alone. And the beneficial also must be able to tolerate any cultural or chemical controls you are using.

Predators will capture and eat the pest that is bothering your garden. Although the praying mantis is frequently sold as a biological control, it isn't satisfactory from the reproductive angle, it isn't host-specific, and it won't tolerate other controls well. The larvae of the green lacewing are useful predators of aphids, scales, and mites. You can buy green lacewing eggs that you apply where the insects have been a problem; when the larvae emerge, they will feast. Syrphid flies, or hover flies, also like aphids. They lay eggs in aphid colonies, and the eggs hatch into maggots that eat the aphids.

Parasites are insects whose larvae feed on the inside of the pest. An example is the trichogramma wasp, or egg parasite wasp, which lays eggs in the eggs of other insects. Ichneumonid and brachonid wasps lay eggs inside caterpillars. The larvae emerge from the eggs, feed on the caterpillar's insides, and the caterpillar dies.

Pathogens are diseases. Insects are as susceptible as humans are to bacteria, virus, fungi, and protozoa. Pathogens are very good biological controls because they are very host-specific, so you and your pets are safe, as are the beneficial insects in your garden. A good example of pathogens available for use in home gardens are the *Bacillus thuringiensis*. Several strains are useful against caterpillars, mosquitoes, and some beetle larvae.

Source: Jane C. Martin, Horticulture Extension Agent, Ohio State University and Franklin County Extension Service, Columbus, OH.

Garden Tools

I'm just beginning to garden, so what tools do I need?

A beginning gardener needs the basics: fork, spade, shovel, and trowel. It makes good sense, especially for those just starting out, to purchase the best-quality tools possible; the glow of a bargain tool will quickly turn to a glower when it breaks and needs replacement. With the proper investment of quality and care, your tools will become old friends. Another useful tool comes in the form of knowledge. Read up on what you think you'll be doing. A beginner's book on gardening, such as Rodale's *Organic Gardening*, offers a wealth of information on a variety of subjects.

How many different kinds of hoes are there, and what do they do?

Hoes come in many different varieties, and each offers its own special talents. For instance, a narrow, flat-bladed hoe is great for weeding small spaces; larger-headed hoes can mound earth and build raised beds; a smaller, pointed hoe acts like a finger to poke into the smallest spots. However, any hoe left lying on the ground can become a weapon and handle-smack an unsuspecting gardener in the face. (Rakes can do the same trick.) To avoid this, put these sneaky critters away when finished with them.

What should I look for in a pruner?

Look for quality. Remember that fancy bells and whistles may not always mean better. Simpler tools made of drop-forged, heat-treated steel are built to last and are a good bet for longevity. One feature not to overlook is a safety lock. Another useful feature is Teflon-coated blades. Teflon-coated blades stay cleaner longer and help prevent sap buildup. Nevertheless, pruner maintenance is necessary; cleaning and sharpening the blades improve their effectiveness and extend the life of your pruner.

Pay attention, too, to the comfort factor in a pruner. You may find yourself using it for long stretches at a time. It is important that a pruning tool fit your hands, arms, and body strength; like a favorite pair of shoes, you'll like to use it if it's comfortable. Do not purchase tools you have to stretch to grip.

Be aware of what you want to use pruners for; different pruners perform certain tasks better than others. For example, don't attempt to use pruning shears on big branches; bigger loppers are designed for heavy cutting.

Will I get more use out of a pointy-end spade or a flat-edge shovel?

Different tools do different jobs: you will get the most out of a tool when you match it to the task it is designed to perform. A pointed shovel is good for digging in gravel or moving lots of soil; flat-edge shovels are great for digging holes, slicing and moving sod, or dividing perennials. When using shovels and spades, be aware of your physical strength. Don't overdo it by lifting heavy loads, or by digging for a long period of time.

How can I keep my shovel in good condition?

Don't leave a shovel or any tool out of doors, or it will weather and rust. Make a habit of cleaning off dirt and mud. Plunging a shovel in a bucket of sand mixed with used motor oil is an excellent way of cleaning and oiling it in one step. You can also spray a tool with WD-40 as a good preventative measure.

Treat wooden shovel handles with linseed oil or Thompson's Water Seal. Sand the handles to prevent painful splinters. If a handle breaks, don't throw out the shovel; broken handles can often be replaced. It is also good maintenance to check the connection between the metal head and handle to make sure it is tight.

How can I keep cutting tools sharp?

You can keep your tools on the cutting edge by sharpening them frequently, using special "pruner-sharpening" files. These files keep pruners (and other tools) at their best, making quicker work of pruning tasks while reducing plant and personal injury.

How can I stop my hose from leaking where it joins the faucet?

Preventing water from going AWOL may be easier than you think. A drippy hose usually needs a new washer. These washers are very inexpensive and can be installed quickly and easily by anyone. Another tip: Try wrapping Teflon tape over the threads on the end of the faucet.

What hand tool works best for weeding?

Again, the task defines the tool. Small forks are good for rooting out stubborn weeds, while weeding knives work well on others. A Cape Cod weeder is another effective weeding tool. Weeding doesn't mean being on your knees all the time; stand up and use a sharp, narrow hoe (Swan Neck or Collincar) or a steel-tine rake. Narrow hoes dig weeds out of tight spots, while steel-tine rakes can attack larger areas. As far as hand tools are concerned, those made of solid one-piece construction work best for weeding because they won't break or bend. Keep the comfort factor in mind as well.

Does it make a difference if my leaf rake has bamboo, plastic, or metal tines?

Good lawn rakes are lightweight, sturdy, and able to collect debris without damaging the grass. So far as bamboo, plastic, or metal tines are concerned, all are lightweight and lawn-friendly. Durable plastic rakes are inexpensive, and they won't rot or rust; however, you may like bamboo rakes for the width of their tines. Another option is an adjustable-tine rake, which allows one rake to have multiple personalities; this type can be sized to dive into tight spots or to sweep across broad areas. It boils down to a matter of personal preference.

What's the difference between a garden cart and a wheelbarrow?

The difference is in the physics. A wheelbarrow puts most of the weight of the load on your arms and back when you lift it. A garden cart spreads the load, and balances it for easier transport. Wheelbarrows can maneuver into tight spots more easily than a garden cart. If possible, have both on hand.

Is a sprinkler better than a soaker hose for most gardening?

Sprinklers cover wide areas indiscriminately, saturating a lawn or an entire garden with equal amounts of water. Soaker hoses leak slowly, directing water to the roots of plants where needed, and supplying it at a much slower rate. Irrigation technology for the home gardener is much easier than most people imagine. A small investment in drip hoses and emitters can yield huge savings in water use—and healthier, happier plants.

Source: Jennifer Mayott, Gardener's Supply Company, Burlington, VT; (802) 660-3500.

Greenhouses and Coldframes

What is the difference between a *greenhouse* and a *coldframe?*

A coldframe usually consists of a small unheated frame with a glass or plastic cover that is either hinged or slides to open. It is used to protect seedlings and tender plants from frost. In many instances, a greenhouse is a glorified cold-frame. The greenhouse is a larger structure, frequently heated, that allows a wide variety of plants to be grown and propagated in various microclimates. The greenhouse itself provides a microclimate different from the one outside, but you can also have different microclimates within the greenhouse, depending on how close to the heating or cooling elements an area is. You can tailor your greenhouse's microclimates to the different plants you want to grow.

Usually, neither the greenhouse nor the coldframe has a floor. They may be only temporary structures that you take apart in the winter, so you wouldn't want a permanent foundation.

Do greenhouses need electricity and running water?

Although having these utilities is very helpful, they aren't necessary. Vents can be opened manually to provide air circulation and ventilation. Some vents are activated mechanically by thermal expansion. Water can be brought in from an outside source by hose, watering can, or other means. Having running water available makes watering, fertilizing, cleanup, and humidifying much easier. In fact, both hot- and cold-water connections are advisable where possible. Electricity in a greenhouse allows the use of electric fans, swamp or evaporative coolers, powered vents, heating mats, humidifiers, lighting, and various automated controls.

How do I regulate the temperature in my greenhouse or coldframe?

Temperature is controlled by ventilation, shading, heat, and insulation. Both greenhouses and coldframes require adequate ventilation for cooling, and fresh air to provide a healthy environment for plants. In a greenhouse, this ventilation may include ceiling and floor-level vents as well as fans. Coldframes are ventilated by opening the top either manually or mechanically with the use of a thermal vent opener.

Covering the greenhouse or coldframe glazing with special paint or shade cloth can help to moderate the temperature during hot weather. Misting systems and evaporative coolers, or swamp coolers, can provide cooling in greenhouses. The basic idea of the swamp cooler is to cool the air by drawing it through a wet sheet, usually with the help of a pump and fan. Swamp coolers are more typically used in hot climates than in milder growing areas.

Heat can be provided in a greenhouse with thermostatically controlled electric or gas heaters or woodstoves. Solar greenhouses may be heated entirely by the sun. Coldframes also depend on the sun for heat. Thermal coverings can be added at night.

Some coldframes have been heated with manure. Dig out an area, add a layer of manure, an optional layer of straw, and a top layer of soil. Set in your plants. The decomposing organic matter generates heat. Or you can line the north wall of the coldframe with several rows of bricks, which will store heat during the day and release it at night.

What is the best location for my greenhouse or coldframe?

Choose a relatively level site if possible, or plan to make it level. Generally, a south or southeast exposure is best for a lean-to greenhouse or a coldframe, although more easterly or westerly exposures are possible. The orientation of a freestanding greenhouse is not as critical because it receives light from all sides; however, most authorities recommend that the ridge (the roof peak) run from east to west. Both greenhouses and coldframes should be located where the light is not unduly obstructed by trees or buildings. They need a minimum of six hours of direct sunlight a day.

Is it easy to build a greenhouse or coldframe?

Most greenhouse or coldframe kits can be assembled by anyone handy with tools, although you may want one or two friends to help you with larger structures. Complete instructions are generally included. You don't absolutely need a kit, but building a greenhouse from scratch is more difficult because few plans are available, and greater skill and technical expertise are required. Coldframes, on the other hand, can be easily built from plans found in many gardening books.

What is the best-size greenhouse to buy?

The largest one you can! No greenhouse gardener ever has enough room for all of the plants grown or acquired. Fortunately, some greenhouses can be expanded with additional sections.

What types of glazing and framing materials are available for a greenhouse or coldframe?

We use the term *glazing* in a general sense; it doesn't refer specifically to glass. To let in the light, greenhouses and coldframes may be glazed with polyethylene film, fiberglass, acrylic panels, polycarbonate panels, or glass. Glazing is usually a matter of preference and expense: plastics can yellow and deteriorate after a few years, so you will have to replace them. Glass lasts longer but is easier to break. Soft plastic films are relatively inexpensive, but so are scrap windows that someone might want to get rid of.

Coldframes usually are framed from wood. Greenhouses may use wood, steel plate, aluminum extrusion, or flexible plastic piping.

Can I find a greenhouse that matches the architecture of my home?

Yes, there are greenhouses to match almost every style of home, be it modern, colonial, Victorian, or rustic. The more elaborate greenhouses are often referred to as "conservatories" and combine a living area with growing plants.

Are there any greenhouses for very small gardens?

There are walk-in greenhouses as small as 6 by 8 feet; some of these are free-standing. Lean-to models, which are attached to an existing structure, can conserve space. Various mini-greenhouses, which are a variation on the cold-frame concept, are also available. Apartment dwellers might consider a balcony greenhouse. Another possibility is a window greenhouse, which fits over an existing window area to make use of vertical space.

When should I move the plants from the greenhouse or coldframe into my garden?

Unless they are cold hardy (like broccoli and cabbage), plants should not be moved into the garden until all danger of frost in your area is past. Remember to protect new transplants from excessive sunlight and drying out. You can buy paper caps made specifically for this, or save your empty plastic gallon containers, old screens, or anything that will shade your transplants slightly.

Is a greenhouse very time-consuming?

It depends on what you are growing, where you are growing it, and how much automation you have in the greenhouse. Some plants require more time and care; others less. Cacti and succulents, for example, won't demand lots of watering. Temperature-sensitive plants like the gesneriads (African violets or gloxinia)—or generally any plants with fuzzy leaves, and any tropicals—may keep you busy opening and closing vents.

How much daily attention a greenhouse needs often depends on the climate and the season. With automated venting, humidifying, watering, and heating, a greenhouse requires only a few hours a week to maintain.

What is the best way to select a greenhouse or coldframe?

First, decide what plants you want to grow and find out their requirements. Next, determine where you can locate a greenhouse or coldframe and what size it should be. Then, read as much information as you can, talk to neighbors and friends with greenhouses, visit showrooms, and contact greenhouse manufacturers for their literature. A directory of U.S. and Canadian manufacturers of hobby greenhouses, solariums, sunrooms, and window greenhouses is available for $2.50 from the nonprofit Hobby Greenhouse Association, 8 Glen Terrace, Bedford, MA 01730-2048.

Source: Janice L. Hale, Editor, Hobby Greenhouse Association, Bedford, MA.

Ground Covers

What exactly is a *ground cover*?

Generally *ground cover* is used to mean any low-growing, spreading plant that forms a dense carpet over soil. Often the term refers to woody shrubs or shrublets that spread by creeping stems or root suckers and don't get any taller than a foot or so. But anything can be a ground cover—vines, herbaceous perennials, larger shrubs, even trees if they have branches close to the ground.

The ideal ground cover has attractive evergreen foliage for year-round effect; grows densely and vigorously to choke out weeds; has a neat, spreading habit; and is an easy plant to grow, requiring little maintenance to look good. Another important criterion is attractive blooms or colorful leaves. Why settle for dull green when you can have some jazzy color?

Why are most ground covers evergreens?

So they look good in winter.

What should I plant on a very steep bank?

Especially if it's in hot sun, you want vigorous plants that can take heat and dry soil well. Dense-growing, easy perennials like day lilies or *Hypericum* (St. John's wort) do a great job. So do low-growing shrubs like junipers, cotoneaster, and potentilla.

What ground cover will grow over a rocky area?

There are lots of choices depending on what part of the country you live in. *Arctostaphylos uva-ursi* (bearberry), *Genista* (broom), *Phlox subulata* (moss pink), verbena, dianthus (pinks), gaillardia (blanket flower), lavender, delosperma (hardy ice plant), and yucca come to mind.

What ground cover makes a good lawn alternative that can take regular foot traffic?

The answer for most parts of the country is none. If you live in Southern California, you can plant that wonderfully invasive weed *Dichondra*. And there are a few plants that can take infrequent light steps and recover quickly (two delightful scented herbs are creeping thyme and chamomile). But if you want something living you can really walk on often, you're going to have to plant grass. However, smart gardeners realize that the area they really need to walk on is actually quite limited—certainly less than the expansive sheets of wet, squishy grass most suburbanites labor over. You can greatly cut down on yard work by transforming most of that useless expanse—the parts you don't need to walk on—into colorful, blooming ground covers.

Should I ever mow a ground cover?

It depends on what it is. Some plants respond well to occasional mowing by developing more side branches and shoots (hence denser growth, and often more flowers and foliage), and by staying neater and lower. But why would you want to plant a ground cover that needs mowing? If you want to spend tons of time and money getting all sweaty, why not have a huge lawn?

Nothing grows underneath my maple tree. What ground cover should I try?

Even if you live in a wet climate, because maple roots are so greedy, you want a ground cover that can tolerate dry shade. Some good choices are epimedium, vancouveria, *Tiarella* (foamflower), *Heuchera* (coralbells), and *Polygonatum* (Solomon's seal).

Do violets make a good ground cover?

Yes, they are lovely and trouble-free plants for shade or part shade, ideal under hostas and shrubs in rich moist soil. Be sure you plant the perennial kinds, not pansies (both are in the genus *Viola*). There are some spectacular new perennial violas on the market, and many bear wonderfully fragrant flowers. The most fragrant of all, of course, are the old-fashioned *Viola odorata*.

I like the look of creeping phlox, but will it grow in shade?

Phlox stolonifera and *Phlox divaricata,* both sometimes called creeping phlox, are woodland plants with charming blue flowers in spring. They should be grown in at least part shade and moist soil high in organic matter, where they make very pretty and fuss-free deciduous ground covers.

Is there any way to control the spread of English ivy?

Other than by pruning, none that I know of. But pruning works, as long as you stay ahead of it. Sometimes this is hard—I'd swear if you slowed down a bit when you walked past, it would start growing up your leg. The biggest pain is when it grows 40 feet up tree trunks to make giant masses of foliage that weigh as much as a house, and you have to pull it down with a crane. It's soooo much simpler to trim back those delicate little shoots before they get out of reach.

How do I get rid of pachysandra?

A nuclear bomb does a pretty good job. But you might have to repeat it a couple of times. Seriously, probably the only way is to use a foliar-spray herbicide, applied repeatedly and thoroughly to attack every bit of growth you can find.

Both of these last questions make an excellent point: Beware of hypervigorous ground covers like pachysandra. Others that deserve caution include bamboo, *Aegopodium* (bishop's weed), *Houttuynia*, liriope (lily turf), lamium (dead nettle), *Lysimachia nummularia* (moneywort), *Coronilla* (crown vetch),

Hypericum calycinum (St. John's wort), and many vines such as *Hedera helix* (English ivy) and *Lonicera* (honeysuckle). And really watch out for that weediest weed of all: lawn grass of just about any kind. Nothing's worse than trying to rid a bed of Kentucky bluegrass.

Of course, all these are fine plants as long as you use them where you can let them romp, and contain them appropriately from where you don't want them to go. A weed is simply a plant out of place.

Source: Michael McKinley, horticultural writer for Wayside Gardens, Hodges, SC; (800) 845-1124.

Heirloom Plants

What makes a plant an *heirloom*?

An heirloom plant is one that has been around since 1950 or earlier and is open-pollinated (which means it is not done by scientific manipulation). Also, heirloom implies that the plant carries a history with it—it may have significance for a family or a culture.

What is the difference between an *open-pollinated* plant and a *hybrid*?

An open-pollinated plant hasn't been deliberately crossed with any other variety. "Open" means that the pollination is open to the forces of nature, not done scientifically with predicted end results. Hybrids are deliberate crosses—two different parent plants are manually cross-pollinated to create a plant with desired characteristics. A hybrid is a contrived crop.

If you keep the seeds from an open-pollinated plant, and the plant didn't accidentally cross-pollinate with another variety, they will breed true. That means their genetic makeup will remain unchanged, so the plants you grow from these seeds will be like their parent plants.

Seeds saved from hybrids do not produce plants like their parent plants. They may be sterile, or they may revert back to the ancestral strains and display characteristics that are usually undesirable.

Why do people grow heirloom plants?

Heirlooms have been saved because they are so good! They are superior in taste, disease resistance, or regional adaptability. They have stood the test of time because people have known their value and handed them down in their families.

Aren't modern hybrids more disease-resistant than heirlooms?

Some are, some aren't, depending on which plant is grown where. Some hybrids can be more disease-resistant but require a specific fertilizer, fungicide, or pesticide to perform well.

Do I have to protect my heirloom vegetable plants from cross-pollination to make sure the crop is true to type?

Yes, if you intend to save the seeds from this year's seed crop so you can plant the vegetable again next year. Open pollination, because it is open to nature, may result in accidental cross-pollination. Two plants in the same species but different varieties can cross, and their seeds would be genetically somewhere in the middle.

To maintain an heirloom's genetic makeup, you want to avoid cross-pollination. One way to do this is to isolate one variety from other varieties with the same Latin name. Distance is the easiest method: don't plant related varieties near each other. Time also works. For example, plant one variety of corn really early, a different one later, so they don't flower at the same time. You can also use physical barriers, like bags or cages.

If you just want to eat the produce but not save the seed, cross-pollination doesn't matter. One exception, however, is corn, because the kernels that you eat are in fact the seeds. Sometimes cross-pollination of corn can result in an interesting crop.

If black corn and white corn cross-pollinate, you may get black and white kernels together, and it's still a good crop; some crosses may give a different texture to the kernels and lessen your enjoyment of the corn.

How do I save the seeds of heirlooms to grow them again next year?

This is a very complex question with many variables. It depends on the particular plant. The best resource is a book by Suzanne Ashworth, *Seed to Seed* (Decorah, Iowa: Seed Savers Exchange, Inc., 1995).

How can I save heirloom tomato seeds?

First, be sure the tomato variety was isolated from other varieties by 10 feet or more while growing. Use only ripe tomatoes for seed saving, and work with only one variety at a time. Cut across the middle of each tomato, then squeeze out the seed and gel into a glass container. Do this with each ripe tomato. Add a bit of water to barely cover, and put the container in a warm place. You want mold to develop, so it's best not to cover the container. And you probably don't want to put this in your kitchen, because it smells awful.

Stir the contents of the container once or twice a day for three to five days. When the surface of the water is covered with mold, the fermentation process is complete. Pour all this into a strainer and rinse several times until the seeds are clean. Fill up a container with the clean seeds and water, and let this settle a few minutes. Viable seeds will sink, so pour off and discard the light, floating seeds and water. Spread the seeds in a single layer to dry in a glass dish, like a glass baking pan, and put this somewhere warm (70° to 85°F) but out of the sun. Stir occasionally to dry all sides. When the seeds are dry, store them in a container in a dry, cool, dark place. The seeds will last for four to ten years.

What are some heirloom tomatoes I can grow?

If you live where summers are long and hot, one of the best heirloom tomatoes is Brandywine. Others are Amish Paste, Andrew Rahart's, and Old Brooks. For tomatoes in cooler summer areas, try Stupice, Chadwick's Cherry, Pruden's Purple, Yellow Pear, Earliana, and German Gold.

Where can I find heirloom seeds?

Several places sell heirloom seeds. Three good sources are Abundant Life Seed Foundation, P.O. Box 772, Port Townsend, Wash. 98368; Seed Savers Exchange, Route 3, Box 239, Decorah, Iowa 52101; and Seed Dreams, 231 Fair Avenue, Santa Cruz, Calif. 95060.

Are some heirloom varieties disappearing?

Yes! The Seed Savers Exchange found that of the 5,000 open-pollinated vegetable varieties commercially available in 1984, two-thirds had been dropped by 1994. Many of these were delicious heirloom varieties that were available from only one source. Small seed companies are going out of business, or being bought up by large companies that have little interest in heirlooms. Keeping heirlooms alive in our own backyards may be the best chance we have to keep them around for future generations to enjoy.

Source: Tessa Gowans, Seed Coordinator, Abundant Life Seed Foundation, Port Townsend, WA.

Herbs

What kind of soil and nutrients do herbs need?

The notion that all herbs prefer desert conditions and a starvation diet has led many a gardener to failure. Most herbs must have well-drained soil, since they resent soggy roots, and they prefer a fairly lean soil. Mints, oregano, parsley, basil, chervil, chives, dill, and lovage prefer moist soil as long as the drainage is good. Some herbs, such as thyme, prefer alkaline soil.

Beyond that, they all need water and at least an annual dose of nutrients, such as compost or composted manure. Some herbs, like parsley, enjoy liquid fish emulsion several times during the year. Overfertilizing causes rapid growth and less flavorful leaves, but *no* fertilizing causes weak, sickly plants, especially if your herbs are in pots.

What herbs can I grow in shade?

No herb will be happy in really dense shade, but several will flourish with only a few hours of sunlight each day. Chervil, chives, lovage, the mints, parsley, and sorrel will all do well in light or partial shade. Even basil, thyme, and tarragon grow quite nicely with only morning sun.

How can I keep mint from spreading?

Gardeners have tried almost everything to restrain the invasive mint family: The surest way is to grow your mint in pots. If you prefer, you can grow mint in a bottomless pot—such as a terra-cotta chimney flue—either sitting on top of the ground or partially buried. Don't bury it too deep, though, or the roots will simply run down the length of the pot and head out on their own. You will have to divide and repot the plants every few years. It will be clear the time has come when the center of the plant starts to die out.

What's the best way to harvest and store herbs?

Many herbs dry well, either in the microwave or hung in bunches in a dark, dust-free, well-ventilated environment like a cellar, attic, or spare room. Pick them at the time of year when their oils and resins are at peak concentration, which will vary from herb to herb. The best time of day to harvest is midmorning of a sunny, dry day. If you dry the herbs by hanging them up in bunches, check them every couple of days. You'll know they're dry when the leaves crumble easily. Store the leaves in glass jars in a cool, dark, dry cabinet.

What's the best way to preserve cilantro and chervil?

Neither of these herbs dries well; they tend to lose most of their flavor and wind up tasting musty and dusty. To preserve cilantro and chervil, chop them in a food processor, blending in enough olive oil to make a thick paste. Freeze in dollops on a cookie sheet. Once the dollops have frozen, put them in a freezer bag. Then add them as needed to soups, stews, salsas, vegetables, and other dishes.

What are *fines herbes*?

Translated from French into English, they are literally "fine herbs." Fines herbes (pronounced "feen airb") are a mixture of equal amounts of finely chopped chervil, tarragon, chives, and parsley. Each herb should be chopped separately so the amount can be measured. Don't prepare the fines herbes too far in advance of using them, as they are all delicate herbs that dry out quickly. Add them just before your dish has finished cooking, otherwise their delicate flavor will be destroyed. Fines herbes are great in egg dishes, salads, mashed potatoes, or on roast chicken.

How do I grow basil indoors?

The most common mistakes with indoor basil are too much water and too little sun. Indoors, the minimum is at least six hours a day of sun. Too much water often results in even adult plants damping off, or wilting and dying. If you don't have a really sunny window, you can grow basil under plant lights, or choose a variety that needs less sun. African blue basil gets along with less light than the more common basils, so it would be a good choice for indoor growing.

What's the best way to start new sage plants?

Sage is easy to propagate either by layering or taking cuttings, and since sage plants need to be replaced every four or five years, it's a good idea to have new plants coming along. To layer a plant, just bend a branch to the ground, pin it down about 4 inches below the tip so it is in contact with the soil, and wait for it to develop roots. Then cut it from the branch and transplant it.

Or you can take cuttings from the tips of branches. Strip off the lower leaves. Dip the cut ends in rooting hormone. Then stick the cuttings into sterile sand or vermiculite. In about six weeks, you will have plants ready to move into pots, then later into the garden.

Source: Mary Morgan, Editor, *Kitchen Garden* magazine, Newtown, CT.

Hydroponics

What is *hydroponics?*

Hydroponics is a method of growing plants in which the roots are immersed in water plus nutrients in the form of inorganic salts. Scientists use the term *solution culture,* which is synonymous with hydroponics but more descriptive. By either term, the supplies needed for plant growth are reduced to their simplest form (water, nutrients, and oxygen), but management is complex.

What are the basic methods used for hydroponics?

There are three basic systems. The simplest is a container to hold the nutrient solution, generally 1 to 2 gallons for a single plant. The oxygen level must be maintained by pumping air through the solution. Where a large number of plants are grown, aeration of the solution is maintained by recirculation from a reservoir through a series of containers or troughs. This is called *trough* or *flow culture,* and is often used for commercial-size plantings.

Another common type of commercial system uses pea gravel contained in a trough several inches deep. The gravel provides support for the plants' root system and retains a surface coating of water and nutrients from the solution, which is recirculated through the bed periodically from a nearby reservoir. A modification of this system uses sand as the rooting medium, with nutrient solution applied periodically to the surface.

What can I grow hydroponically?

Any plant can be grown by hydroponics. The most commonly grown commercially are vegetables such as tomatoes, cucumbers, and peppers, but fruit trees, various ornamentals, and even grass plants can be grown hydroponically. The only requirements are to provide the proper environment, the nutrient balance needed by the plant, and adequate support for the plant to develop.

Is it true that hydroponic gardening requires fewer chemical sprays and fertilizers?

Plants can be attacked by insects or diseases regardless of the method of culture, and these must be controlled to maintain the health of the plants. Open-air hydroponic systems are subject to the same organisms as soil-grown plants. A greenhouse environment provides a certain amount of physical protection from some organisms, but the more humid climate may make plants more susceptible to other organisms. Thus, there should be no expectation that pest-control requirements will be reduced.

The fertilizer requirements for hydroponics are different from gardening in soil. Fertilizer sources must be in the form of inorganic chemicals in order to provide the nutrients in ionic form for uptake by the plants. Organic materials will not supply nutrients in the proper balance for hydroponics.

What are the basic nutrients that my hydroponic plants can't do without?

There are 16 elements known to be essential for the growth of horticultural plants. Of these, the ones required in larger amounts—the *macronutrients*—are carbon, hydrogen, oxygen, nitrogen, phosphorus, potassium, sulfur, calcium, and magnesium. The first three are constituents of the water and air, and thus do not need to be supplied by the horticulturist. The elements required in lesser amounts—the *micronutrients*—are iron, manganese, copper, zinc, molybdenum, boron, and chlorine. In soil culture, the micronutrients are generally available in adequate amounts from soil minerals or as impurities in fertilizer materials. In hydroponics, however, all of the elements must be supplied, and in proper proportions. A number of published formulas have been developed for this purpose. Some soluble fertilizer mixtures available at garden stores contain all of the elements and are useful for home hydroponic gardening.

Which costs more, hydroponic or regular gardening?

The physical equipment required for hydroponics (containers, reservoirs, and pumps) and the complete nutrient-solution constituents make hydroponics much more expensive than regular gardening in soil.

Can hydroponic gardening be done indoors and outdoors?

Yes, but special lighting and climatic-control equipment will add to the cost indoors. Plants require a specific light spectrum and duration for growth and development, which is provided by natural sunlight outdoors. Indoors, a similar spectrum can be provided artificially by special lightbulbs. Each plant species has its own requirements of temperature and humidity for proper development, so heating and humidity-control equipment are required for climate control indoors.

Is the quality of my local water supply important to successful hydroponics?

Local water supplies can contain some elements in excess of the amounts required by plants, or they may be high in total soluble salts. While acceptable for human consumption, these excesses can have adverse effects on plant growth, and under some conditions can be toxic. It is therefore important to investigate local water quality for levels of total salts and the concentrations of such elements as boron, chlorine, and fluoride in terms of the tolerance levels of the plants you want to grow.

Are there any advantages to growing seedling plants hydroponically to plant later in the garden?

Transplants for the garden can be grown very easily in small containers using a good potting soil available at most garden stores. Good plants can also be grown hydroponically, but will require greater input in terms of management and equipment.

Can seedlings grown in the garden be used in my hydroponic system?

Yes they can, but at some risk of contaminating the hydroponic equipment and the nutrient solution by organisms from the garden soil.

How does the quality of fruits and vegetables grown hydroponically compare with those grown in soil?

Fruit and vegetable quality is determined by the environmental conditions under which they are grown, including nutrition, light, and climate. Each species has its own requirements for best performance. Assuming these conditions are met in both soil and hydroponic systems, the mature quality should be essentially identical.

What is the best method for small-scale hydroponic gardening?

A plastic 2-gallon pail is sufficient for one or possibly two plants, depending on the type of plant and its ultimate size. An aquarium pump with a small plastic hose and an air stone will aerate the solution. A fairly good nutrient solution can be prepared from one of the garden store's soluble fertilizer mixes that contains all of the elements. Make a dilute solution based on the label directions, approximately 1 tablespoon per gallon. Change the solution weekly.

Some method of supporting the plant at the top of the container will be needed. If the system is to be used indoors, light will have to be supplied either artificially or by outside sunlight through a window.

Source: Hunter Johnson Jr., Extension Specialist Emeritus, University of California, Riverside, CA.

Indoor Gardening and Houseplants

What should I look for when purchasing a new houseplant?

First, look at all the plants available for purchase. They should appear healthy, with lots of lush green foliage. If not, shop elsewhere; but let's assume they look great. Grasp an individual plant at its base and pull gently. It should be well anchored in the pot. This is a good sign that the roots are vigorous and healthy. Now look carefully at the top and bottom of the leaves. Avoid plants that have any visible pests or whose leaves have yellow flecks and curled edges. These can be signs of uninvited guests on the plant.

What can I do to help my new plant once I get it home?

Give your plant a bath. Modern greenhouses are in the business of producing plants. This involves high rates of fertilizer and possibly some chemicals for insect control. Such excess should be removed. Begin by placing the plant in a sink or tub and allow water to run through the soil for several minutes. This flushes away excess fertilizer. Continue the bath by wetting the foliage and wiping the leaves gently with a soft rag. Place the plant in a shady spot for a few days, then gradually move it to the appropriate brightness. It is common for a plant to drop some leaves as it becomes acquainted with its new home.

Which are better, clay pots or plastic pots?

Neither is better; they both have advantages and disadvantages. Clay can be heavy and fragile compared to plastic. Extra care and strength are needed when moving the pots around to avoid injuring your back or the pot. Clay also allows the soil to dry faster, because clay is more porous than plastic, so more frequent watering may be needed. Aesthetically, many people prefer clay pots. They say a healthy plant in a clay pot just looks right. The decision is yours.

How do I know when to repot my plant?

It is easy to tell when a plant needs to be repotted. Here are a couple of good signs to confirm your suspicions. First, look for roots growing out of the drainage holes at the bottom, or circling around the top of the pot. A second sign is the soil's inability to hold water. You will know this because the water you pour in will pour out just as fast, usually making a wet mess. Garden centers and most home discount stores carry a full line of products necessary for repotting plants.

Will my plants be okay while I'm on vacation?

Yes, but some planning is necessary. If you plan to be gone a week or less, water well, and move them to a cooler, dimmer location. If you will be away longer than a week, have a friend water them, or build a wick water system. To do this, cut a cotton-based fabric such as an old T-shirt into strips. Push one end several inches into the soil and place the other end in a large bucket of water. Again, plants should be moved to a cooler, dimmer location. These methods are not as good as a thorough watering, but your plants will survive.

How often should I water my plants?

A good question with a vague answer: As often as they need it. Experience can help here, but if you're uncertain, stick your index finger about 1 inch into the soil. If it feels moist, wait before you water.

My plant's leaves are yellowing. What should I do?

Yellowing leaves can be a sign of many different problems. Therefore, we need to decide which problem is most likely. Has the plant been moved to a new location? Changes in its environment can cause some yellowing and normal leaf drop. A move to very bright light can cause a bleached look. Try a more gradual change. Has the plant been kept too wet or too dry? Both conditions will cause leaves to droop and turn yellow. Has the plant been fertilized? Yellowing, particularly of the older leaves, indicates the need for an all-purpose fertilizer. Follow the directions on the label and never exceed the listed amounts—more is not better.

Is air-conditioning bad for my plants?

The actual cooling of the air is not bad for plants. Generally, if you are comfortable with the temperature, your plants will be too. But there is a catch. Most air conditioners remove moisture from the air. Most plants don't like dry air and can develop brown, crisp edges as a result.

What can I do to keep the edges of leaves from turning brown and crisp?

The condition you describe is most likely caused by low humidity. This is a common problem, thanks to our modern heating and cooling systems. Here are a few suggestions that may help. Purchase a mist bottle or a humidifier; both add moisture to the air (the latter is more efficient, but expensive). An easier way is to purchase large plastic saucers (clay is permeable), fill them with pea gravel, and add water. Set your plant pots on the gravel, making sure the base of each pot is not into the water or root rot is likely to occur. The water evaporates, helping the plants maintain lustrous, green foliage. You now have a catch basin for runoff when you water.

What are those bugs, and how do I get rid of them?

Here are the five most common insects that can affect houseplants:

1. *Aphids*—small, fleshy, green or black suckers focusing on new growth
2. *Mealybugs*—small, furry, white suckers
3. *Spider mites*—very small mites; webs visible
4. *Scale*—small, hard, round; brown dots
5. *Whiteflies*—whiteflies that gather under leaves and fly when disturbed

The best way to keep your plant insect-free is to use routine screening. Inspect the plant carefully each time you water. If you discover insects, isolate the plant. Try washing them off with water or use a Q-Tip and rubbing alcohol. It may take several tries to get them under control, but it is worth avoiding chemical sprays if at all possible.

Insecticidal soap is another way to get the upper hand. Often a combination of two or more techniques works best. If all this fails, consider using organic insecticides sold as rotenone and pyrethrum. These are powerful insecticides but are quickly broken down into harmless organic chains. Before doing any spraying, consult your local garden center for assistance.

Source: Mark Zimmerman, Horticulturist, Department of Botany, University of Georgia, Athens, GA.

Landscaping

How can I best plan landscaping for my home?

Whether you are landscaping your present property or studying a possible site for a new home, you need a landscape plan on paper with which to work. This is a map of your land, showing property lines, all buildings, walks, drives, utility poles and lines, fences, and walls. It should indicate all existing trees and shrubs, including variety as well as neighboring trees and shade. When filling in your plan, keep in mind the following general guidelines: An unbroken lawn, bordered with shrubs and flowers, gives a good appearance; scattered shrubs of various kinds look unplanned and messy. *Foundation plantings* (deciduous and evergreen shrubs planted near the house foundation) keep a home from appearing naked; they look best when taller plants are used to soften corner lines and smaller plants are placed near the main entrance. When placing a tree, remember to keep in mind the mature size of the variety and not its size at planting; the most important guide is where you want shading.

What inexpensive landscaping is suggested for a new home on a bare lot?

Shade trees come first. Next, buy foundation plantings for the front, beginning with small, less expensive plants. Add other shrubs and plantings as you can afford them. Not only does this spread your costs, but if you plant carefully and buy slowly, you can evaluate and modify your plan as you see how things are coming along.

Is it better to select a landscape architect to design your property?

You may decide to hire a landscape architect or designer to advise you in plant selection. This person can make all the decisions for you, based on your description of hoped-for results. He or she may even purchase and plant your shrubs and trees and start to revive a lawn. This, of course, can be expensive, sometimes leaving you with little more satisfaction than writing a check.

I've always wanted to grow fruit trees. What is the best advice for a beginner?

The best choice for an amateur gardener is to develop dwarf trees. When choosing varieties, consider the pollination habits of each. Some fruit trees, such as peaches and apricots, are *self-compatible,* which means they can make use of their own pollen in order to bear fruit. Others, such as many apples, sweet cherries, and pears, require another variety of the same fruit to be blossoming nearby at the same time. Lay your orchard out in a sunny, well-drained area with rich soil and be sure to have a program for pruning and spraying that you can accomplish regularly.

When is the best time to plant trees and shrubs?

Planting time isn't that critical. While spring and fall are best for most plants, many of them, especially balled-and-burlapped or container-grown stock, can be planted during most of the growing season, since their roots will not be disturbed during planting. Bare-root plants, however, should go into the ground in the early spring while they are still dormant.

Source: Adapted from *The Gardener's Complete Q & A,* Garden Way Publishing Editors, Storey Communications, Inc., Schoolhouse Rd., Pownal, VT 05261; phone: (802) 823-5819; fax: (802) 823-5200. ©1995 by Doubleday Books and Music Clubs, Inc.

Lawns

How can I best choose a grass for my lawn?

The difference between individual grass varieties (*cultivars*) is mostly a matter of preferred color, texture, or growth habit. Care is less of a consideration. Seed firms provide helpful information about their products, and responsible houses use quality components in their weed mixtures that you can accept on faith. The new cultivars have exhibited at least some superior characteristics. They are chosen for reasonable resistance to the usual lawn diseases, for comparatively low rather than tall growth, and for their attractive appearance.

What is the best sort of grass to plant for a lawn that is given less than constant care?

Look for some of the old-fashioned, self-reliant cultivars so well adapted to the casual care of yesteryear. Among the Kentucky bluegrasses are Arboretum (Missouri) and Kenblue (Kentucky) strains for the southern portions of the bluegrass belt, and Park (Minnesota) for northern and western zones of the country. They are best mowed fairly tall, with at least 2-inch clipping height. Some of the newer cultivars, such as Birka and Plush, are similar. The better recent cultivars, such as Rugby, Parade, and Baron, though finest when well cared for, do reasonably well under some neglect.

How often should a lawn be watered?

The needs of a well-kept lawn do not vary greatly from species to species, although certain grasses, such as buffalo grass, are more able to endure prolonged drought. At the height of the growing season, any flourishing lawn needs about 1 inch of water per week. This must be provided by rainfall, irrigation, or stored moisture in the soil.

Location in part determines this need. Soil types, too, have an influence. The top foot of heavy soil, such as clay, can hold 3 inches of moisture, while a sandy soil will hold perhaps only ½ inch. When watering, keep this difference in mind. Sprinkling a sandy soil with more than a ½ inch of water will be a waste, whereas clay should be watered for a prolonged time until 2 to 3 inches of water have saturated the soil to the root zone. A cursory, nightly after-dinner sprinkling with the hose may relax the person sprinkling, but it does little to improve the lawn.

What kind of mower should I buy?

Most equipment dealers today recommend small tractors. If you have a very large lawn, they are fine, but buy a mower that matches your lawn size. For a small lawn, a hand-push, unmotorized mower is perfectly adequate. The reel versus rotary mower question has been pretty well settled in favor of the latter. Reel mowers have the advantage of cutting with a scissorlike action against a fixed bed and are highly recommended for low-mowed turfs that are well tended. These mowers are also somewhat safer than other types. But rotary mowers are less expensive and easier to sharpen, adjust, and maintain than reels. They are also more versatile—able to get closer to walls and other obstructions.

Does it make a difference in which direction I mow?

Not too much. Purists mow parallel to the street, so that the mowing lines are not seen by passersby. Specialists also recommend mowing in different directions in subsequent mowings, saying that this will avoid the tendency of the grass to lean to one side.

Are there any natural controls for lawn weeds?

There are. Much weed management is based on an understanding of weed growth. For instance, many weeds grow in infertile soil, overacid or overalkaline soil, or poorly drained or hardpan soil. Rid your lawn of these weeds by improving the soil. However, the surest way to avoid weeds is to create a good lawn from the beginning. Close-growing grass will crowd out most weeds. Organic gardeners thus have a rule for weed control in lawns: If weeds threaten, add fertilizer. They also warn against mowing too closely and excessive watering.

What makes a lawn look good?

Good looks are due mainly to density, uniformity, and rich color of the grass plants. Planting improved cultivars helps greatly, but you must also mow regularly and eliminate weeds. Proper fertilizing will help achieve a deep color and keep the grass vigorous to help you fight weeds. Lawns must be mowed—as often as once weekly when the grass is determined to grow. They must be fertilized and they must be watered in dry seasons, or allowed to go dormant and brown. Finally, they must be watched, to see that none of the typical lawn problems reaches unmanageable proportions.

Source: Adapted from *The Gardener's Complete Q & A,* Garden Way Publishing Editors, Storey Communications, Inc., Schoolhouse Rd., Pownal, VT 05261; phone: (802) 823-5819; fax: (802) 823-5200. ©1995 by Doubleday Books and Music Clubs, Inc.

Pest Solutions

What kinds of safe botanical insecticides are available?

Pyrethrum is made from dried chrsyanthemums, which are toxic to pests but not to people. On contact, it kills aphids, leafhoppers, thrips, and whiteflies. *Rotenone* is derived from the derris root. It wards off aphids, harlequin bugs, chinch bugs, spittle bugs, spider mites, pea weevils, and houseflies. From the roots and stems of *Ryania* comes a dust or spray that doesn't kill but incapacitates many bugs and beetles. Oil and water sprays, when used correctly, will deter chewing and sucking insects from orchard trees before the buds open, and from some shrubs and plants. The mixture creates a film over insect eggs that live through the winter on trees. The eggs suffocate and die before hatching, but so do good insects—use sparingly. Commercial oil and water mixtures can be bought at garden stores or made at home.

Is there something on my premises that needlessly invites pest infestations?

The following common-sense steps help to modify pest habitats:

1. *Remove water sources.* All pests need water for survival. Fix leaky plumbing and do not let water accumulate anywhere in your home.
2. *Remove food sources* (if the pest's food is anything other than the plant or animal you are trying to protect). Store your food in sealed glass or plastic containers; place your refuse in tightly covered, heavy-gauge garbage cans, and avoid leaving your pet's food out for extended periods of time.
3. *Remove or destroy pest shelters.* Caulk cracks and crevices to control cockroaches; remove piles of wood to avoid attracting termites; remove and destroy diseased plants, tree prunings, and fallen fruit that might attract pests.
4. *Remove breeding sites.* The presence of pet manure attracts flies; litter encourages rodents; and standing water provides a perfect breeding place for mosquitoes.
5. *Remove sources of preventable stress to plants.* Use mulch to reduce weed competition.

How can I put "good" insects to work in my garden?

Although it requires some work and the results are not immediate, biological treatments really work. Populating gardens with predators such as purple martins, praying mantises, and ladybugs, pathogens such as bacteria, viruses (generally not available to homeowners), and other microorganisms like *Bacillus thuringiensis* and milky spore disease greatly reduces pest infestation. Although there is no way to be certain how long predators will stay in target areas, biological treatments are generally effective for longer periods of time and are unequivocally safer than chemical treatment.

How do I dispose of excess pesticides?

The best way to dispose of a small, excess amount of pesticide is to use it—apply it—according to the directions on the product label. If all the pesticide cannot be used, check with your local health department to determine whether your community has a household hazardous waste collection program. If no program exists, follow the label directions for how to dispose of the container.

Do not pour leftover pesticides down the sink or into the toilet. Additionally, an empty pesticide container can be as hazardous as a full one because of residue. Never reuse such a container.

If I use pesticides, how do I know they are safe?

Products containing pesticides include herbicides, rat baits, and insecticides. The labels indicate the pests that the chemical is approved to control, the situations it should be used in, and safety restrictions and first-aid directions.

How do I choose a pest-control company?

Research the company's track record, and don't rely on the company salesperson to help form your opinion. Call the Better Business Bureau or local consumer office and check if the company has a record. Check if the company is insured, and if so, what type of insurance it carries. Contractor's general liability insurance gives the homeowner a certain degree of protection should an accident occur during pesticide spraying. Contractor's workmens' compensation insurance can also protect you should an employee of the contractor be injured while working in your home.

Check if the company is licensed and affiliated with a professional pest-control association. Selecting a pest-control service is just as important as selecting any other professional service. Look for the same high degree of competence you would expect from a doctor or a lawyer.

Source: Adapted from *Citizen's Guide to Pesticides* by the Environmental Protection Agency. For more information, contact the EPA Headquarters: (202) 382-4454; 401 M Street SW, Washington, DC 20460.

Propagation

What is *propagation?*

Plant propagation is the multiplication of plants, primarily by seed (*sexual* propagation) or by divisions or cuttings (*asexual* propagation).

How many different ways can I propagate plants?

There are two basic types of propagation—sexual and asexual. Sexual plant propagation requires that the reproductive parts of the plants make spores or seeds. Asexual plant propagation includes cuttings, division, layering, suckers, runners, and grafting and budding. Some plants also reproduce by spores, which is asexual reproduction. Other more advanced methods include tissue culture.

The most common methods for the average gardener would be propagation by cuttings, division, layering, and seed. Cuttings are done by taking a piece of the plant, usually part of a leaf, a stem shoot, or a leaf bud. This piece is then set into a rooting medium to develop roots. Division is frequently used for plants that grow from bulbs, corms, or tubers. The plant is dug up; any off-shoots are separated from the main part of the bulb or corm, and any clumps of roots are divided into two or more groups. Then everything is replanted, allowing sufficient space for each plant to mature.

Layering is done by bending down a branch still attached to a growing plant and keeping part of it in contact with the soil until it roots. When the roots are established, this new plant can be cut from the parent plant. Then it can be moved to a new permanent location. You can save the seeds of your favorite annuals, perennials, and vegetables to grow new plants. However, keep in mind that if the plant is a hybrid, the seedlings you grow may not be the same color, size, or shape as the parent plant.

Does it matter which method of propagation I use?

Yes. Not all plants can be propagated by division or cuttings, and must be propagated by seeds. Others do not produce seed and would most easily be propagated by division, cuttings, or one of the other techniques.

What plants can I propagate from leaf cuttings?

Begonia, sedum, crassula, peperomia, African violets, sanseveria, and some lilies can be propagated by leaf cuttings.

When should I take cuttings for rooting?

Stem cuttings can be taken from houseplants almost any time. Outdoor plants require more precise timing so that cuttings are taken when the stems are at just the right stage of maturity. In either case, cuttings should not be taken when the plant is under stress—for example, during the hottest part of the day, or when in heavy flower.

Will plants root as well in water as they do in soil?

All plant parts require oxygen for proper growth. Although many plants will readily form roots when placed in water, the roots will not be as strong and healthy as they would be in other rooting media.

Can I propagate ferns by taking cuttings?

No. Ferns are propagated by spores, divisions, or tissue culture. They will not grow from cuttings.

Can I propagate a palm tree from a cutting?

Palm trees are *monocots* and have only one *meristem* (growing point) per plant. This growing point is destroyed if a cutting is taken. Palms are propagated by tissue culture, seed, and in some cases division.

Can hybrid tea roses be propagated from a cutting?

Roses can be grown from cuttings, but most hybrid tea roses are grafted to rootstock of a species rose for stronger root growth and better plant hardiness. Any cuttings you grow would not have the grafted rootstock and would probably not perform as well as the original plant.

Source: Nick Snakenberg, Plant Propagator, Denver Botanic Gardens, Denver, CO.

Rock Gardens

How do I start a rock garden?

First, some questions. What type of rock garden do you want: naturalistic, formal, planted wall, planted terrace, or patio? What site do you have: sunny, shady? What is the background: freestanding, against a building, on a natural slope? What type of plants would you like to grow? Will you do everything yourself or will you have some help (free or paid)?

If you have a slope too steep to grow and cut grass, if you have so many stones that it is impossible to plant tomatoes or rosebushes, rock gardening is not necessarily the answer to your problem. Before you touch the first stone, do some planning and a little studying. Try to see some existing gardens, either public (nurseries or botanical gardens) or private. This is the best way to get ideas, see what you like and don't like, what seems to work and what doesn't. Pay a couple of visits to local garden clubs; this will give you access to private gardens and to the gardeners and their experience. And please, don't be too ambitious at the beginning. You can always increase the size or redo your rock garden later. Start with the easy rock plants.

Just one word of general practical advice: When you build your rock garden, the first step is to make sure that all the weeds and bushes preexisting on the site have been killed. If you don't, they will grow, take over, and destroy your new rock garden within a year.

What are some easy plants to grow in a rock garden?

Some of the easy plants to start out with are *Aquilegia flabellata* (columbine), *Campanula* (bellflower), *Aubrieta deltoides* (rock cress), *Dianthus deltoides* (pink), *Gentiana scabra* (gentian), *Geranium dalmaticum* (cranesbill), *Iberis sempervirens* (candytuft), *Penstemon hirsutus* (beardtongue), *Phlox subulata* (ground pink), *Sedum* (stonecrop), and thyme. Most rock plants are known by their botanical name because many of them have no common name. There would be no common English name, for example, for a plant native to the high Swiss Alps or the Himalayas.

What makes a plant a "rock plant"?

The late Lincoln Foster said, "A rock garden plant is what I say it is"—meaning that there is no generally accepted definition. If you think it looks good in your rock garden, then it is a rock plant. But most people will agree that it shouldn't be tall. Rock plants tend to be less than 1 foot, yet there are dwarf conifers and other exceptions. Rock plants are mainly low-growing perennials and shrubs. Annuals are not often used because of the work to replace them every year, and because they tend to grow and grow, threatening their neighbors.

Rock plants are not rampant or invasive. A nice rock garden has a great many different plants. You do not want one or two that smother all the rest. Ivy is not a rock plant, nor is pachysandra.

What are *alpines?*

"Alpine" basically means "living on high mountains," very often above the timberline. It has to do with a set of conditions frequently met on high mountains: lots of light, very good air circulation, good snow cover in winter, cool in summer. Rock gardens were created (at least in Europe and North America) to grow alpines. But there are alpines that you would not use in a rock garden— for example, plants that thrive in snow melt. Also, many rock gardens contain plants that are not alpines, but they have the shape, size, growth, and flowering habits of alpines.

Does a rock garden need much attention?

Rock gardens don't require much maintenance. The most labor goes into the initial construction. You will have to do thorough weeding. Careful watering is needed during the growing season. You must remove dead plants and dead leaves. Add a little gravel in very early spring. Fertilizing is minimal.

Can I use any kind of rock?

Yes. Rocks are a matter of taste and functionality. If you want a naturalistic rock garden, try to imitate what you see in the mountains. The rocks are all of the same type. Mixing shapes, colors, and textures works for plants, but not for rocks. It is difficult to do anything with round stones and glacial boulders. In any case, they should be buried deep (80%) into the ground, otherwise they won't be stable.

If you build and plant a wall, use whatever stones are suitable for the wall, but leave small spaces filled with soil between the stones. If you build a raised bed type of rock garden, you do not need stones at all, although you can use a few just for decorative effect, because some plants look better when they grow at the base of a rock. The stone also provides some shade or a cool run for the roots of a plant.

How much soil does a rock garden need?

It is not so much a question of how much soil as what *type* of soil. The answer depends on what type of plants you want to grow and where your garden is located. Some plants have very long taproots. Many have long roots that will travel far in crevices and between rocks to get moisture.

It is more important to know whether the plants prefer acid soil or need lime. Most are happy in a neutral soil, but some have definite requirements. Some rock plants need quite a bit of organic matter or humus, but many like lean mixtures, even in pure sand.

How do I get good drainage in my rock garden?

Use a lot of coarse sand in the soil. If you do not build on a natural slope, at least do not build at the bottom of a depression. But if that is all you have, build a raised bed on it. One foot above the normal ground surface is plenty. That will let you grow even many of the demanding rock plants that need special care if far from their natural location.

Do rock gardens need full sun, or is a shady spot okay?

Some require full sun, but more precisely, they like a lot of light. Full sun might be too hot at low altitude (many rock garden plants are alpines, which normally grow at higher altitudes where it is cooler). A few hours of sun are required to get the plants to bloom. Yet many successful rock gardens do not get all that much sun—on the north side of a tall building, for example. And there are beautiful naturalistic rock gardens planted with woodland (shade-loving) plants.

Source: North American Rock Garden Society, Millwood, NY; http://www.nargs.org.

Seeds

Does it make any difference if I start seeds indoors or sow them directly in the garden?

Yes it does, depending on the particular type of seed. Vegetables such as beans, corn, melon, and squash have large seeds that can be easily planted directly into the garden. Vegetables with smaller seeds, such as tomatoes, peppers, and eggplants, require temperatures around 70°F for germination, and are best started indoors where this temperature can be maintained. They also grow more slowly and take six to eight weeks to reach transplant size.

For flower seeds, the easiest to start outdoors are large seeds like sunflowers, zinnias, marigolds, cosmos, sweet peas, and nasturtiums. Smaller seeds that need very warm temperatures for germination, such as petunias, impatiens, begonias, and geraniums, should be started indoors.

What kind of soil mix do I need to start seeds indoors?

A packaged potting soil is best for starting seeds indoors. Most well-known brands (Hyponex, Peters, Fafard, Pro Mix) are suitable for medium and large seeds. For very tiny seeds, such as petunias, impatiens, and begonias, look for a special fine-textured mix such as Jiffy Mix, which works best with these small, dustlike seeds.

How early can I plant seeds?

Consult your local cooperative extension service for planting dates for your area. Seed catalogues and packets will often explain the number of weeks a particular type of seed needs to reach transplant size, or whether it can be directly seeded into the garden.

Do I have to plant my seeds in neat rows, or can I scatter them instead?

You can cultivate vegetables more easily if they are planted in rows. Flowers often look better if they are scattered in groups around the garden. It all depends on what effect the gardener is trying to achieve.

How can I sow very fine seed like lettuce evenly?

Mix small seeds with an equal amount of sand, then scatter this over the planting area. An added advantage is that the sand is a lighter color than the soil, so you can see where the seeds are going.

My seeds stayed in my mailbox all day in 20°F weather. Are they still good?

Yes, they are fine. Cold temperatures will not harm seed viability. In fact, the National Seed Storage Laboratory at Colorado State University has a long-term storage facility that holds seeds at -10° to -15°F.

Can I use old seeds in this year's garden?

Only if they were stored in a cool, dry area and aren't more than two or three years old. Seeds exposed to extreme heat or moisture for any length of time lose their viability quickly and usually yield less than a 50 percent germination rate.

How can I store seeds?

Seeds must be kept cool and dry. The easiest way is to place them in a sealable plastic bag or a jar with a tight-fitting lid and keep them in the refrigerator. A small packet of silica gel can be added to the container (but is not absolutely necessary) to absorb excess moisture.

Why didn't my seeds sprout?

The most common reasons are the wrong temperature range or too much water. Seed packets usually give the best temperature range for each type of seed. Try to stay within 5° above or below that temperature for best results. Seeds that need a 55°F night temperature will not germinate if the room temperature remains at 70°F.

Keep the soil mix moist but not overly wet. An easy way to monitor the moisture level is to cover the seed tray with clear plastic wrap. If you see a heavy condensation of water droplets under the plastic during the day, the soil is too wet. Remove the plastic for about an hour to let the soil dry, and check the tray again later in the day.

Why do my seedlings grow tall, thin, and leggy?

They may be too wet or are not receiving enough sun. Keep the soil moist but not overly wet. If you are bottom-watering, don't let the seedlings sit in a tray of water for more than an hour at a time. If you aren't sure whether you need to water on a given day, you probably don't. Wait a few hours, and if the soil is beginning to dry, then water.

Source: Wanda Sorrells, Senior Staff Horticulturist, Park Seed Co., Greenwood, SC; phone: (800) 845-3369; fax: (800) 275-9941.

Shrubs

Why should I plant shrubs?

Shrubs are the backbone of a garden. They are the intermediate structure between trees and the annuals and perennials of the flower bed. Many shrubs make a good background for a perennial border. They give form to a landscape, and they provide structure in winter. They also provide wildlife with a refuge and food. If you don't have room for trees, you do have room for shrubs.

What is the difference between a *shrub* and a *tree*?

The main difference is size. Shrubs are woody plants with a height range up to about 15 feet, although some shrubs are no more than 1 or 2 feet in height. In fact, some shrubs are ground covers (e.g., some of the cotoneasters and junipers). Trees typically reach heights greater than 15 feet. Another distinction is that shrubs usually are multistemmed—their branches form at ground level. Trees usually are single-stemmed—their branches form higher up on a main trunk.

When should I plant shrubs?

Shrubs that may be marginally hardy in a particular area are usually best planted in the spring, which gives them time to become established before the harsher conditions set in. Bare-root shrubs are usually planted in the fall, which is their dormant period. Container shrubs can be planted almost any time during the growing season, provided you give them adequate care and water.

How do I plant shrubs?

When planting shrubs, it is recommended that you dig the hole as wide as possible, to loosen the soil. But don't dig the hole any deeper than the rootball. You don't want the base of the stem to be below the soil line.

Also, don't amend the soil. If you add fertilizer or organic matter, the roots won't be encouraged to grow beyond that enriched area.

Which shrubs make the best hedges?

Good choices for hedges are yew, holly, firethorn, boxwood, arborvitae, juniper, some euonymus, and some barberry. Privet, however, is not recommended for hedges because it has been listed as an invasive exotic. Whether or not a particular shrub is a good candidate for a hedge depends on several factors. The shrubs shouldn't mind shearing—the kind of cutting that gives a hedge straight lines. The shrubs shouldn't look bad if sheared. Also important is that the shrubs have a uniform growth pattern and a dense branching structure.

Do I have to prune my shrubs?

Only if you want to. It is much better to purchase a shrub that will mature into the space you have, rather than trim back a shrub to confine it in a space it was not naturally intended to be in. Hedges, however, should always be pruned so they are wider at the bottom than the top. You might have noticed that some older shrubs have a top-heavy look and are very sparse at the bottom. That's because sunlight didn't make it to the bottom branches. The lower branches can get shaded out, or crowded out, by upper branches that are healthier because of more access to sunlight. Prune hedges to allow the lower foliage more sunlight. Then they will remain bushy and green and stay on the plant.

How do I prune shrubs?

Certain shrubs grow more rapidly than others and may need pruning more than once a year. Some produce their flowers on year-old wood; some produce their flowers on new wood. So you must be careful what you cut. Fortunately, many gardening books discuss pruning and are geared to the home gardener. Consult one before you do any pruning.

My garden is shaded by trees. Which shrubs are good for shady locations?

Abelia will tolerate shade, as will redbud. Camellia and some euonymus do well in partial shade. Fothergilla prefers partial shade. Mountain laurel, spicebush, azalea, and rhododendron all thrive in partial shade. Other choices for shady locations are Japanese andromeda, hydrangea, leucothoe, and viburnum.

Which shrubs will add color and interest to my landscape in winter?

You could try viburnum, crape myrtle, stewartia, witch hazel, winter sweet, cotoneaster, red-twigged or yellow-twigged dogwood, and holly. Any evergreen will provide color and mass.

Are any shrubs a good food source for birds or other wildlife?

Good sources of food for wildlife are viburnum, holly, firethorn, blueberry, spicebush, and juniper. (Deer will eat almost anything, of course!)

Source: Ruth Dix, Horticulturist, and Janet Walker, Education and Visitors Services Leader, U.S. National Arboretum, Washington, DC.

Soil

What are the different types of soil, and why should I know about them?

There are thousands of different types of soils. Several common characteristics are used to distinguish the different types and to determine their potential uses. A soil's *texture*, for example, is the distribution of particle sizes in the soil. Soils range from coarse-textured sandy soils to very fine-textured heavy clay soils. Between these extremes are the more desirable loam-type soils—a mixture of sand, silt, and clay particles. Texture can indicate the soil's nutrient-holding capacity, strength, and drainage, which are important to know before you try to grow any plants.

The depth of soil to *bedrock* (the solid rock under the soil) will determine the volume of soil available for root growth, and thus nutrient and water uptake. The drainage of a soil is critical. Roots require oxygen, which can be limited if the soil is saturated with water. Excessively well drained soils, however, can only hold a limited amount of water, and thus tend to be droughty. The color of a soil can be an indication of the types of minerals in the soil and the presence of organic matter. High-organic-matter soils tend to be darker in color.

Soil survey reports provide information on an area's soil types and their characteristics. These reports include maps of the soil types on aerial photographs, so you can determine the major differences in soil type for your garden. For a soil survey report, contact your county's cooperative extension office or extension service, listed in the phone book.

Do I have the same kind of soil everywhere in my garden?

Soils vary considerably. However, in a small area such as a garden it is unlikely that the soil properties would vary significantly. The factor that might vary the most is soil depth. In areas where the bedrock is near the soil surface, soil depth can vary quite a bit in short distances.

How do I get my soil tested, and what will the test show?

Soil tests are available from many sources. In addition to commercial soil-testing labs, most states have a university soil-testing lab. You need to contact the lab for information on how to submit samples of your soil for testing. Information about university labs can usually be obtained through the county cooperative extension service.

It is important to use a soil-testing lab that uses procedures and recommendations adapted for your local area. The types of tests and the recommendations will vary based on the soil, crop, and climatic conditions for a given area. Be sure to follow all of the instructions carefully for how to take a proper soil sample.

A soil test will show your soil's pH and lime requirements. It will also show levels of phosphorus, potassium, calcium, and magnesium. Based on the test results, the report will make recommendations for what you want to grow. Some labs run tests of micronutrients such as iron, manganese, zinc, copper, boron, and sulfur. High pH soils in the western United States have lots of problems with micronutrients, as do some sandy soils. But the average gardener doesn't need information about micronutrients.

How can I improve the soil in my garden?

Many things can contribute to high-quality soil in your garden. In areas with acid soils, applying limestone to obtain the optimum soil pH is critical. A soil test will determine if your soil is too acidic and how much limestone you need to add for balance. Applying the correct balance of nutrients as fertilizer or from other sources such as manures or composts is also important. The proper amounts of nutrients can be determined from a soil test. Apply nutrients at the recommended rates. Sometimes overapplication and the resulting nutrient imbalances can be as much of a problem as not adding enough of a nutrient.

The physical and chemical properties of many soils can be improved by adding organic matter such as manure, compost, or plant residues to the soil. Plant residues are whatever is left over from the plants in the garden—for example, the foliage and stalks. Turn back into the soil anything that isn't harvested.

Don't abuse the soil. For example, don't work in the soil when it is wet because this can result in serious harm to the soil structure due to compaction.

What causes poor drainage, and how can I improve the drainage in my garden?

Some soils are naturally poor drainers: they are heavy and don't have a good structure. Clay soils usually are poor drainers, although some clay soils have a good porous structure. Your location on the landscape will also affect drainage. On a hilltop, you can usually expect good drainage. But in some locations, water tends to come out close to the surface. You might be sitting right on the water table.

In general, you need to focus on maintaining good soil structure so that there are adequate pores to drain water from the soil. You can do this by maintaining good organic-matter levels in the garden and by avoiding overtillage (overplowing) and compaction. In some cases, it may be possible to install artificial drainage to remove excess water from a poorly drained soil. You can dig a ditch and put in a perforated drainpipe. Usually this would be done on a big scale in fields, but it could be done in a garden. Also, you may be able to overcome poor drainage by using raised beds in the garden.

What is *rototilling,* and does my garden need it?

Rototilling is a method of tillage (plowing). A rototiller uses rotating tines to cut through and mix the soil. Tillage has several benefits: It helps eliminate weeds; it incorporates plant residues; it mixes lime and fertilizer with the soil; and it prepares a uniform seedbed for planting. Actually, plants can be grown without tillage. In fact, many farmers now grow crops with little or no tillage. But when tillage is eliminated, its functions must be handled in other ways. For example, without tillage, weeds may have to be controlled by chemicals or with plastic mulches (sheets of black plastic).

A common mistake made by many gardeners is to overtill, which can cause many physical, chemical, and biological problems in garden soil. The most noticeable problem is the physical one. Good soil has good aggregates. Overtilling makes the particles too fine, and then they settle down into one big mass. This powder cements together, and it crusts when it rains, so plants can't get through it. Pea- to gravel-size aggregates are best. The main chemical and biological problem is that compaction and crusting reduce the oxygen supply in the soil, which is not good for roots—or for microbes, which need oxygen too.

What sort of winter crop would improve the soil in my vegetable garden, or should the soil rest over the winter?

Growing a *cover crop* in the garden during the off-season can help protect the soil and conserve nutrients. Cover crops also provide a source of fresh organic matter when they are tilled into the soil next year as *green manure.* Green manure is simply a cover crop that is tilled into the soil. Cover crops are grown not for harvest but to protect the soil; green manure is turned in to enrich the soil.

Probably the most common cover crops are winter grains such as wheat or rye. These crops will grow in the fall and then again in the spring before it is time to till and plant the garden. Legumes (peas, beans, clovers) can be used as cover crops to achieve the same benefits. In addition, legumes will contribute valuable nitrogen to the soil for the next season. Before you plant legumes, though, you need to check which ones are adapted to your winter conditions.

Is there a difference between *topsoil* and *humus*?

Topsoil usually refers to the soil that we influence with our management. It is the soil we work with, the zone we have the most impact on with our tillage, planting, and other efforts. Topsoil is usually darker in color than the subsoil (the soil below topsoil and above bedrock) because of additions of organic matter.

Humus is the end result of the breakdown of organic matter. Plant residues, green manures, and other organic materials are broken down by microbes. Something fresh like green manure begins to break down rapidly, but the whole process takes time. The final stable product is called *humus*. If you see pieces of leaf or stem in the soil, it isn't humus yet. Humus is a component of topsoil—the organic component. Minerals are the other material.

What makes some soils red?

The principal factor is weathering. Some soils have weathered a lot, so not much organic matter remains. In warmer, wetter climates, organic matter breaks down quickly. You will see red soils in the southern states, for example. Also, red soils will have weathered down to iron-based minerals. The iron gives the soil the red color.

I've been told that onions grow best in muck. Is there really a kind of soil called "muck"?

Muck is a real term in the study of soils. Muck is soft and fluffy, so the bulb of an onion would probably find it easy to develop in those conditions. And mucks are extremely high in organic matter. Normal soil may be 1 percent to 2 percent organic matter. Muck could be 20 percent organic matter, which is why muck soils are so dark.

I know earthworms help aerate the soil, but do animals like moles, voles, and gophers contribute anything?

Burrowing animals do contribute to aeration, but only in the localized area where their burrows are. The tillage they do just by digging around in the soil also helps.

Why does soil need to be aerated, and does walking in those special spiked shoes really work to aerate the soil?

Aeration simply means getting air into the soil. Roots and microbes in the soil need oxygen just as we do. Drainage benefits as well because aeration helps open pores. Anything that makes holes will help. But spikes can actually work against aeration. The hole is there, but soil compacts around the spike. The best aerator should core out, not just push in the soil. You can buy appropriate corers that take out plugs of soil. This makes a mess for a little while because the core is popped out on top of the soil, but these plugs break up after a couple of rains.

Tillage and spading also aerate. Anything you do to loosen up the soil creates pores. But don't overdo it.

Source: Douglas Beegle, Professor of Agronomy, Penn State University, University Park, PA.

Vegetables

What kind of soil do vegetables need?

Vegetables do best in loose, rich loam soil. Clay soils are too heavy, and sandy soils lose nutrients too quickly. Loam retains moisture so that roots can feed, yet it also provides good drainage. However, almost any garden soil amended with organic matter (*humus*) will do.

Should I fertilize my vegetables?

If a soil test shows inadequacies in nutrients, then you might think about enriching your vegetable patch with fertilizer and organic matter before you plant. At transplant time, you could apply a low-level fertilizer like a 5-10-5 or 5-10-10—but don't let it touch the roots. You can repeat the application at blossom time, and again later when the plants are producing their fruit.

Be careful about fertilizing, though. Most soils need nitrogen, which depletes year after year. But too much phosphorus or potassium can make your plants sick. In fact, overfertilized plants can look as if they need more fertilizer. A soil test is important for checking the levels of potassium and phosphorus. Some soils have high levels, so you wouldn't want to add more. That is why low-level fertilizers are safest. That string of three numbers on the fertilizer package, like 5-10-5, tells you its makeup. The first number is for nitrogen, the second is for phosphorus, and the third is for potassium. You probably don't want a mix that is 15-30-15.

Which vegetables should I grow if I have only a small garden?

Size is relative. For some, a 20'-by-20' vegetable patch is a large garden; for others, it's too small. If your space is limited, grow only your favorites. It does no good to grow small plants if you don't really like some of them. Also, check out "bush" varieties, which don't require a lot of space. There are bush cucumber types, determinate tomato types, and bush squash and bush melon varieties.

Growing vertically is another way to make good use of a small space. Try peas and pole beans. Pole beans take up less space than bush beans.

How can I grow vegetables in containers?

Start with large containers that you set in the sun. Fill them with loose, rich loam soil. Choose bush varieties or those specifically intended for container gardening. Container plants will need more fertilization than plants growing in a regular plot. More water is needed too, since containers generally dry out.

Can I grow vegetables indoors?

Herbs can be grown successfully indoors, but not most vegetables. Try lettuce and spinach in a bright sunny window.

Why shouldn't certain vegetables be planted in the same spot year after year?

Planting the same crop in the same place year after year will deplete the area of the same nutrients each year. It also leaves diseases and pests in the soil that will attack the next year's crop. To avoid these problems, vary the kinds of vegetables you plant and where you plant them from year to year.

It helps to divide your vegetable patch into four quarters. Think of them as plots A, B, C, and D. In plot A, you would plant tomatoes, peppers, and eggplant, which are all in the same class. The second year, use plot A for leafy things like lettuce and spinach. Meanwhile, plot B could take those tomatoes, peppers, and eggplant. The third year in plot A, plant vine crops like cucumber, melon, and squash. (Plot B in this third year would take the leafy vegetables, and plot C would have the tomatoes, etc.) In the fourth year, plant plot A with cold crops like broccoli, cabbages, and brussels sprouts. After the fourth year, you would start the rotation cycle all over again.

Don't forget that you can double up crops within a block. Root crops, for example, can go in with leafy crops—plant lettuce in the spring, carrots later. Beans can be planted in the cabbage and broccoli block.

How often should I water my vegetables, and what's the best way to water them?

Vegetables grow best with at least 1 to 3 inches of water a week. Water is how plants soak up nutrients. You don't want to water every day, however, except maybe for container plants. Water deeply. After watering, check the moisture depth by digging down with a trowel, or use a can as a rain gauge. Watering only the root zone is best, if possible. Sprinklers can splash muddy water onto the leaves, which can spread disease. Dry leaves keep disease in check.

Try to water your plants early in the morning. Plants use water through the day; at night, they rest. The earlier you water, the more the plants will gain from the water. But water any time during the day rather than not at all.

Which vegetables can I plant really early in the spring?

Try hardy, cool weather crops, like onions, leeks, beets, spinach, cabbage, and broccoli. Plant them as early as the ground can be worked, or after the last

FAQS OF LIFE

killing frost date of your area. But pay attention to weather forecasts so you can protect your plants in case there is a late frost.

How should I harvest and store winter crops like turnips and other root vegetables?

Harvest the vegetables when they are ripe; brush off the soil; then store them in a root cellar or other cool, humid area. Don't store them in plastic bags, which will create too moist an environment. You want a humid air temperature, but the crops shouldn't be wet.

You can dry root crops a bit after you harvest them by spreading them on a table or other raised surface. You want to lift them off the ground; you also want to protect them from the sun. Try a garage or other protected area. In some regions, you can leave root crops in the ground and harvest them as needed. But this is iffy. Do some research first. Know your area. Storing root crops in the ground is an art, not just a procedure to follow.

Do any vegetables like shade?

Some vegetables that do well in partial shade are lettuce, beets, spinach, cabbage, radishes, arugula, and asparagus. But they should have four or five hours of sun daily.

Source: Sharon Kaszan, Trials Manager, W. Atlee Burpee & Co., Warminster, PA; (215) 674-4900.

Window Boxes

What are the general guidelines for the selection of window boxes?

Use a high-quality grade of lumber, such as redwood, cedar, or pressure-treated pine, that will be resistant to water and weather. Wooden boxes are preferable to plastic ones as they insulate the potting soil, keeping it cool and moist. The boxes should be at least 8 inches wide and 8 inches deep. The length depends on the length of the window. Several smaller boxes are easier to handle than one large one.

What type of plants should I use in a window box?

Choose plants that are compact and have a long season of bloom. Place taller flowers such as geraniums, salvia, marigolds, or zinnias in the back. Petunias, ageratum, and nasturtium can fill out the center; and ivy geranium, lobelia, or sweet alyssum can cascade over the front. Be sure to plant so that your window boxes look attractive from the inside of the house as well as the outside.

Should I plant flowers directly into wooden flower boxes?

As long as the box has drainage holes, you can, or you can plant the flowers in a metal or plastic liner available at garden centers. For small boxes, place individual flowerpots in the box. Then, if one of the plants should fail, it is easy to replace.

How do I plant my window box?

Be sure there are drainage holes in the box, and cover the holes on the inside with window screening, pieces of broken crock, or gravel. Fill the box to within 1 inch of the top with soilless growing medium. Space plants somewhat closer together than you would if they were in the ground; strive for a full effect. Water well and place the box in the shade for a few days until the roots have a chance to establish.

How much should my window boxes be watered?

That depends on the size of the box. Smaller ones will need to be watered more often than large ones. Check every day to be sure. When it is very hot or windy, you may need to water daily, or sometimes even twice a day. In rainy weather, less watering is in order.

How much and how often should I fertilize my window boxes?

Window boxes, because they are watered more frequently, will leach out fertilizer very quickly; that is, as the water percolates down through the soil, it washes out the nutrients. Therefore, feed lightly but more often than you would fertilize the same annuals in the ground.

Source: Adapted from *The Gardener's Complete Q & A*, Garden Way Publishing Editors, Storey Communications, Inc., Schoolhouse Rd., Pownal, VT 05261; phone: (802) 823-5819; fax: (802) 823-5200. ©1995 by Doubleday Books and Music Clubs, Inc.

Xeriscaping

What is *xeriscaping?*

Xeriscape (pronounced "ZEER-i-scape") is a term coined in Denver, Colorado, for a landscape that conserves water and protects the environment. Water utilities and landscape professionals are promoting xeriscape landscaping, which helps preserve our water supplies while producing beautiful, high-quality landscapes.

Xeriscape, which comes from the Greek word *xeros*, meaning "dry," is an alternative to conventional landscapes that have high water requirements. In many urban areas, residential and commercial landscapes use more than 25 percent of the total water consumed. This percentage can be cut in half by incorporating xeriscape principles into home or commercial landscapes.

Xeriscape landscapes utilize seven basic principles to save water and provide an environmentally sensitive landscape:

1. planning and design
2. soil analysis and improvement
3. appropriate plant selection
4. practical turf areas
5. efficient irrigation
6. use of mulches
7. appropriate maintenance

By using these seven principles, you can help preserve our most precious natural resource—water.

Is a xeriscape made up of cactus and rock gardening?

No. Every plant in the nursery or garden center truly has a place in a xeriscape landscape. You can have green landscapes full of beautiful plants that are maintained with water-efficient practices. The same green landscapes we are accustomed to can be achieved and still conserve water.

How is xeriscaping done?

One of the basic elements of xeriscaping is not which plants you use but where you put them. Three different plant zones can be incorporated into a xeriscape landscape: regular watering zones; occasional watering zones; and natural rainfall zones. By zoning your plants according to their water requirements, you prevent the situation of having to overwater one plant to meet the need of another.

Established plants in the regular watering zone would require watering once every week or more in the absence of rain. Established plants in the occasional watering zone would require watering once every two or three weeks in the absence of rain. Established plants in the natural rainfall zone would rely on natural rainfall; you would not water these plants. Remember that these guidelines come into play after the plants have become established in your garden. Until your plants are established, you would probably give them more water.

In every region, you can choose from a palette of plants that are adapted to the soil, temperature extremes, and pest problems of the area. The challenge for the gardener is to categorize the plants based on expected water requirements. Most gardeners can place the plants from their regions into the three water-use zones. For example, in areas with 30 or more inches of rainfall a year, the regular watering zone would probably include turfgrass and annual flowers. The occasional watering zone would include perennial flowers and tender woody shrubs and vines. The natural rainfall zone would include tough woody shrubs and vines and all trees.

How can I make my lawn more water-wise?

You can implement a number of strategies to reduce the amount of water you use on your lawn while still reaping the many benefits of a cool, green lawn. Start by dividing the lawn into irrigation zones based on water requirements, so you can water the lawn separately from other landscape plantings. Select turf species and varieties that are adapted for lower water demand.

Divide the lawn into irrigated and nonirrigated areas. Let the nonirrigated lawn go off-color. The irrigated lawn should provide a function: recreation, foot traffic, dust and noise abatement, glare reduction, temperature mitigation, and aesthetic appearance. Irrigate for the lawn's true water needs, not the calendar. Increase mowing heights to decrease the lawn's water use and stress. Decrease fertilizer rates, and properly schedule fertilizations.

What should I do for my landscape during a drought?

Maintenance practices such as mulching, mowing, and fertilizing greatly affect the landscape's water requirements, as well as its ability to survive a drought. Mulch everything in sight. Mow the lawn as high as is acceptable to your spouse and neighbors. Be very frugal with your fertilizer. And get out there and pull those water-guzzling weeds!

What watering methods are used in xeriscaping?

Two types of irrigation are used—*sprinkler* irrigation and *drip* irrigation. Within a xeriscape, use a combination of these two systems in watering lawns, trees, shrubs, ground covers, and flowers. The goal of an irrigation system is to give the plants a sufficient amount of water without waste. Sprinkler irrigation is the most commonly used method of watering lawns. But the most efficient way to water the landscape plants, other than the lawn, is with a properly designed and well-maintained drip irrigation system.

Drip irrigation slowly applies water to soil—the water flows under low pressure through emitters laid alongside the plants. Water applied by drip irrigation has little chance of waste through evaporation or runoff; the water is applied directly to the plant's root zone. This also eliminates waste because the water is applied only to your planted areas, not to unplanted or weedy areas.

How do I water my landscape properly?

Probably the most important concept in xeriscape landscaping is proper watering. Knowing when to water, and for how long, is fundamental to maintaining a quality landscape that is water-efficient. Of the tremendous amounts of water usually applied to lawns and gardens, much is never absorbed by the plants and put to use. Some water is lost to runoff by being applied faster than the soil can absorb it, and some water evaporates from exposed, unmulched soil before it can be used by the plant. Yet the greatest waste of water is when too much is applied too often. More plants are killed by too much water than by too little.

Most lawns receive twice as much water as they require for a healthy appearance. It is best to not water by the calendar. You don't want to automatically water once a week; better to water when the plant needs watering. Most gardeners can readily recognize lawn stresses due to lack of water, such as wilting and yellowing. The key to watering lawns is to apply the water as infrequently as possible, yet thoroughly.

Trees and shrubs also should be watered as infrequently as possible, yet thoroughly. Most established trees and shrubs will benefit from a twice-a-month thorough watering during the growing season in the absence of adequate rain. Normal lawn watering is not a substitute for thorough tree and shrub watering. Newly planted trees and shrubs will need more frequent watering from the planting time until they are well rooted. During this establishment period, plants can be gradually weaned to a smaller amount of water. Proper weaning develops deep roots and makes plants drought-enduring.

Source: Douglas F. Welsh, Associate Professor and Extension Horticulturist, Texas A&M University, College Station, TX; phone: (409) 845-7800; fax: (409) 845-8906.

COMPUTERS

Buying a Computer

Where to Buy a PC

Backing Up

Ergonomics

Getting Help

Buying the Right Printer

Using the
World Wide Web

The Internet and the
World Wide Web

"Netiquette"

Newsgroups and Internet
Mailing Lists

Computer Viruses

Shareware

Ten Most Frequently Asked
Tech Questions

Getting the Best Performance

Buying a Computer

What's the best computer to buy?

There is no single answer, but the first thing to decide is whether you want an Apple Macintosh or a "Wintel" machine, so called because it uses an Intel processor chip and runs Microsoft Windows. Macintoshes have long had a reputation for being easier to use than Wintel machines, but with the release of Microsoft's Windows 95 and Windows NT 4.x, the gap has narrowed considerably. However, Macintoshes are still preferred by graphic designers, typesetters, desktop publishers, and similar professionals.

Okay, so what's the best Wintel machine to buy?

Buy the most powerful machine you can afford. That means the most powerful CPU (central processing unit, the chip at the heart of the computer), the most RAM (random access memory), the biggest hard disk drive, and so on. The more powerful your machine, the more satisfied you will be with it in the long run.

Historically, the general rule of thumb is that a solid machine capable of doing real work always costs about $2,500. But, of course, you get even more power and features for your money at each point.

The good news is that you can now get a Pentium 166 MHz system, including 16 megabytes (MB) of RAM, a 33.6 data/fax modem, an 8x CD-ROM drive, a floppy disk drive, a 2-gigabyte (GB) hard drive, a wavetable sound card, and speakers for under $1,000. Add $300 for a monitor, and $200 for a basic printer, and you'll have a complete system for about $1,500.

Can you be more specific on the CPU?

To be well-positioned for years to come, make sure you get an Intel Pentium MMX, a Pentium II (a Pentium Pro with MMX), or a compatible clone (Cyrix and AMD are the leading Pentium clone makers). These chips include features specifically designed to improve sound quality and to speed up graphics and video. They are also particularly well suited to running programs written in the Java language popular among Internet developers.

For technical reasons, MMX chips boost the performance of all programs by about 10 percent. But when you run sound, video, and graphics programs that have been specifically written to take advantage of MMX, the performance boost can be as high as 60 percent.

If I don't have the money right now, can I upgrade later?

PCs are almost infinitely upgradable; so, if funds are tight, you can always add more memory, a second hard drive, a larger monitor, and other peripherals in the future. Still, at less than $10 a megabyte, memory is cheap. Ideally, you should have 32 MB for a Pentium MMX and 64 MB for a Pentium II. Don't bother with in-between combinations like 24 MB or 48 MB.

And speaking of memory, don't overlook the VRAM, or video RAM. The more VRAM you have, the more colors you'll be able to display at higher resolutions. Be sure to get a video card populated with at least 2 MB of VRAM, or more if you can afford it.

As for your hard disk, 2 gigabytes (GB) is pretty much the minimum these days for anyone in business or anyone who spends much time on the Internet. If you plan to scan images or do serious desktop publishing, a 4-GB or even a 6-GB hard drive is not out of the question.

I've heard a lot about multimedia. Can you tell me about the hardware?

There is hardly a PC sold today that does not include the three components essential for multimedia: a CD-ROM drive, a sound card, and a set of speakers. Depending on where you buy your system, you may or may not have the option of changing the "package" by requesting different components.

Speakers are easy. Start with the cheapest models available. You can always upgrade to a more expensive set if you find that you need truly superior sound. If your computer comes with "3-D" sound, it contains a special "surround sound" chip and a third "subwoofer" speaker. You can always add a subwoofer and 3-D sound chip later.

You will want at least an 8x CD-ROM drive. The 8x is pronounced "eight times," and it refers to a speed that is eight times faster than the speed required to play an audio CD. Some systems come with 16x CD drives.

What about sound?

There are three ways PCs can generate sound. They can use digital audio to play back previously recorded sounds, as with audio CDs and .WAV files in Windows. The drawback is that about 10 MB of disk space is required for one minute of high-quality sound. Or they can use FM (frequency modulation) chips to synthesize sound using the instructions contained in a small file. Unfortunately, FM sound is not all that good.

Or they can use MIDI wavetable synthesis (MIDI stands for musical instrument digital interface). A *wavetable* consists of recorded, digitized sounds of actual instruments. It's not unusual for a wavetable sound card to contain 4 MB of ROM (read only memory) holding sound samples of nearly 700 musical instrument "voices" and drum sets. Because of this, a wavetable sound file need only contain instructions as to which sampled sounds to play and when. Such files use just 10K per minute of music to produce sound as realistic as digital audio, giving you the best of both worlds.

I know I'll need a *modem* to connect with the Internet. How much do I need to know about modems?

Not much, actually. Virtually every computer sold today includes an internal modem (short for modulator/demodulator) that lets you connect the machine to the phone jack as if it were a telephone. There are just a few details you need to know.

Modem speed is measured in kilobits per second (Kbps). The top speeds are 33.6 Kbps and 56 Kpbs. Unfortunately, to achieve those speeds, the modem attached to the computer you call must also support them. It may even have to be made by the same company. In any case, you'll only achieve those speeds on an exceptionally clean phone line. In the real world, you will probably find you do most of your communicating at 28.8 Kbps or at 14.4 Kbps.

All modems sold today can handle both data and fax communications. Your computer will almost certainly come with some kind of fax software. Indeed, a fax capability is built into Windows 95. Software may also be included to let you use your modem and part of your hard disk to set up an answering machine or voicemail system.

"Monitor not included"? Now what do I do?

Sad to say, it is standard procedure in the computer industry to run an ad that shows a system unit, keyboard, speakers, mouse, and monitor with a big, splashy starburst reading "Only $999!" Then in teeny-tiny type you see: "Monitor sold separately."

Another decision to make. Yes, but it is not a tough decision. There are just a few specifications to consider. You want a noninterlaced, 0.28 mm dot or Sony "stripe" pitch, a refresh rate of 75 Hz or higher at a resolution of 1024 x 768 pixels. The only variable is the size. Measured diagonally in inches, popular sizes include 14, 15, 17, 20, and 21.

That pretty much answers it for a desktop system, but what do I do if I'm on the road—or in the air—and need a laptop or notebook computer?

The first thing to ask yourself is just exactly what computer-based tasks you want to be able to perform while on the road. If you need to write memos, letters, and reports with a word-processing program, and to send and receive electronic mail or connect with the Internet, then just about any laptop or notebook computer will do. (A notebook is a laptop computer that weighs 5 to 7 pounds.)

Your primary considerations should be whether the unit has a keyboard/glide-pad/trackball or mouse interface that you find comfortable and easy to use; whether the display is easy to read; and whether the hard drive has the capacity to hold both the programs you are most likely to use and the data you are most likely to generate.

You will also need to think about battery life. The typical notebook computer contains internal batteries that last between two and four hours on a full charge. But longer-life batteries are available. Check the current magazine reviews for specifics.

Okay, but couldn't I use my notebook computer and an office-based docking system to cut costs and increase convenience?

Sure you could. But it would not make good sense. What happens if your notebook computer, with its hard disk drive containing all your files, gets stolen while you're waiting for a plane?

Think of a notebook PC as a real notebook—a sketchpad and pen you can use to communicate with the office. Or as a device you can load up for doing after-hours work at home.

It is important to know that nearly every notebook or laptop computer made uses proprietary designs, which means you'll be locked into buying memory and other internal parts made by the notebook maker. Also, since you always pay more for the miniaturization of any component, it makes the most sense to buy the least expensive notebook computer capable of serving your needs.

How can I get the most current information when I'm ready to buy?

When it comes to personal computing, change is a permanent part of the landscape. The general outline of the answers offered here will not change much over time, but the specific details certainly will. Don't forget, both Microsoft and Intel, the two most important companies in the field, depend on periodically persuading everyone to buy their latest and greatest.

Then, too, there is Moore's Law. In 1964, Intel co-founder Gordon Moore stated that the number of transistors on a microprocessor—which is to say, the power of a CPU—doubles every 18 months. And, as others have noted, the price of computing power drops by half. This has proved to be the case for nearly 25 years and is expected to continue for the next decade.

When you're ready to buy, pick up a copy of *PC magazine* or a similar publication. Use the information you've gained here to get a sense of the market. Then call your local reference librarian and ask if the library subscribes to the *Computer Select* CD-ROM product from Information Access Company. This monthly CD contains the full text of articles from the previous 12 months of all the leading computer magazines. The built-in software makes it easy to call up the latest hardware and software reviews and buying guides.

Source: Alfred Glossbrenner, author of over 40 books, including *The Complete Handbook of Personal Computer Communications* (New York: St. Martin's Press), published in 1983, more than a decade before the current online and Internet craze appeared. He has also written numerous books and articles about hard disk drives, computers, DOS, Windows, and computer software, not to mention nearly a dozen books about the Internet, the Web, and online services. He can be reached at gloss@gloss.com.

Where to Buy a PC

What's the best way to buy computers, hardware, and software?

Studies have shown that the vast majority of first-time PC buyers buy from retail stores, while a huge proportion of second-time buyers buy from a mail-order firm. You'll pay a little extra buying from a store, but it can be worth it, particularly if you are an absolute novice and need the kind of support and "hand holding" a good local dealer can provide.

Mail-order firms offer support, too, via the phone. But you may find yourself on hold for lengthy periods, and the call probably won't be toll-free. On the other hand, the mail-order computer business is extremely competitive, so you usually get a lot for your money. Mail-order firms can offer lower prices because of low overhead, and because they either build the machines themselves, as with Dell and Gateway, or they get big-volume discounts from Compaq, IBM, and others.

Saving money via mail order is great, but what about warranties?

There's an old saying about personal computer equipment: If it works for the first 90 days, it'll work forever. That's largely true, and it is certainly one reason to avoid buying the "extended warranty protection" salespeople will try to push on you. It is also a good reason to make a point of testing every hardware component in your system thoroughly during the first three months, since any piece of equipment you buy from a reputable source will be warranted for at least 90 days.

As for standard warranties, a one-year parts and labor warranty is typical for computers bought from a store, while a three-year warranty is common among mail-order firms. Not all three-year warranties, or any other warranties for that matter, are equal. Some cover parts and labor for the first year but only parts for the second and third years.

If I go with a mail-order firm, how will I get my computer serviced if something goes wrong?

Mail-order houses provide service and repair in one of two ways. Some ask you to mail your system back to their service center. Others have contracted with a national service firm like General Electric to provide either on-site service at your location or carry-in service at authorized local repair centers. Local stores may use the same repair centers.

Service just isn't a huge issue anymore when dealing with a leading mail-order firm. And get this: Most retail store warranties offer nothing in the way of free telephone tech support. But mail-order firms like PC/Mac Connection ([800] 800-5555) say, "Enjoy free technical support on products purchased from us. We offer factory-authorized warranty and post-warranty repair service for most major manufacturers, usually repaired and returned to you within 24 to 48 hours."

Leading computer mail-order firms are every bit as good as L.L. Bean, Lands' End, Williams-Sonoma, or any other leading direct merchant.

What about sales tax, shipping charges, and delivery times?

State sales tax laws vary. But in practice, if you order something from a company that has no retail outlets in your state, you are normally not charged sales tax. You may be required by state law to pay the applicable tax on your own. But that's between you and your state government.

The point is that state sales taxes can add up. On a $2,500 computer, for example, a sales tax of 6 percent comes to $150. But might not your tax savings be eaten up by shipping costs? It's possible. All really top-drawer mail-order firms will be able to tell you what your shipping costs will be for a given item.

Okay, I'm sold. I'll give the mail-order option serious consideration. But how can I find reputable mail-order firms?

You're right to be skeptical. The fact is that almost anyone with some basic technical knowledge can acquire and assemble the necessary parts into a PC and offer it at a bargain-basement price. Still, it's hard to see how you could go wrong with many mail-order firms. One way to find a list of firms is to go to the library and read the articles in computer magazines about buying equipment through the mail. The reference librarian will be able to point you toward the right resources. The other way is to contact your local user group.

"User group." What's that?

User groups are one of the great unknown treasures of the personal computing universe. They are nonprofit organizations made up of computer users of every degree of experience who meet regularly to share information. These are folks who routinely spend one Saturday a month attending a user group meeting. They are just the sort of people to ask for recommendations on which mail-order vendors to patronize and which to avoid.

There are lots of ways to locate local user groups. You can start with the computer or online editor at your newspaper. If there is a computer/software store or repair shop in your area, call and ask for the back-room technician. He may well be plugged into the local user group scene.

Suppose I've identified five reputable mail-order firms. I've done my product research and have a pretty good idea of what I want, need, and can afford. Now what?

Now you begin playing one mail-order firm off against another. For better or worse, buying computer equipment of any sort—whether from a retail store or a mail-order firm—is more like buying a car than purchasing a book or a video. Which is to say there is almost always room for negotiation. Margins are so thin on a $1,000 system that it is probably a waste of time to push for much. But on a $2,500 system, well, "we can talk." And there are all kinds of talking points: free shipping, bonus software, steep discounts on add-on features like more memory or a joystick—it all depends on the mail-order firm and how eager it is to make a sale. It also depends on how hot a given item is at the moment.

Get one firm's deal, then call a competitor and ask if it can offer you something better. The only crucial point is that you be in a position to say, "If you can give me this deal, I'm prepared to buy today." No salesperson is going to really sharpen her pencil for a casual tire-kicker.

Let's say I've done my homework and made the calls. I know what I want to buy and from whom. I've settled on an offer. What are the last-minute details?

There are seven points to check:

1. *Clarify the terms:* Manufacturer, model number, make, size, and all component parts or extras you expect. Verify product compatibility and confirm all warranties.
2. *New or used?:* Be clear on whether the product is new or reconditioned, and state specifically whether you will accept a reconditioned product if a new one is not available.
3. *"Net 30 or nothing":* Buy only from companies offering a 30-day, no-questions-asked money-back guarantee.

4. *Tech support:* Make sure the vendor provides tech support for everything you buy.

5. *Credit cards only:* Always use a credit card to make your purchase. Credit cards are your only protection against fraud. And make sure that there is no surcharge or "service fee" imposed by the vendor for using a credit card. If such a fee is imposed—usually about 6 percent—see if you can talk the salesperson out of it.

6. *Keep copies of everything:* This applies to any mail-order or phone transaction.

7. *No refund, no return:* When you are in the middle of a dispute with a vendor (or product return of any kind), do not send the product back until the vendor instructs you to do so. The vendor will give you a return authorization number. Write it down for yourself and write it in large numbers on the package.

What about buying a used computer?

A used computer may not offer the latest technology, and it probably won't come with a warranty. But it can offer savings of as much as 40 percent compared to a new machine, and may be almost as good. Computer user groups are good places to find individuals who want to sell their current machines. But there is also a well-developed used computer marketplace.

Used computer brokers specialize in bringing together buyers and sellers from all over the country. Typically, you send the money to the broker, and the broker notifies the seller to ship the equipment. You take delivery, test the machine, and if everything is fine, notify the broker to release the money. The broker does so, less a small commission.

For more information and current equipment prices, contact one or more of the brokers listed below:

American Computer Exchange	(800) 786-0717
Boston Computer Exchange (BoCoEx)	(617) 542-4414
The Computer Exchange	(800) 304-4639
United Computer Exchange	(800) 755-3033

Some computer makers, like Compaq, sell refurbished models from factory outlet stores (call the Compaq Works outlet at (800) 318-6919 for more information). IBM Credit Corporation ([800] 426-5440) sells equipment that has come off lease. Other firms offer reconditioned items from all leading manufacturers. Computer Renaissance operates a chain of used PC stores in 30 states (call [800] 433-2540 for the location of a store in your area). Two of the largest companies offering used equipment by mail are Rumarson Technologies ([800] 929-0029) in Kenilworth, NJ, and Micro Exchange ([800] 284-1200) in Nutley, NJ.

Source: Alan Freedman, author of *The Computer Glossary and Computer Desktop Encyclopedia* (AMACOM), the premier references of computer terms, concepts, and important products. Annual subscriptions to the *Encyclopedia* on CD-ROM are $64 (four CDs per year, requires Windows). The Computer Language Company, Inc.; phone: (215) 297-8082; fax: (215) 297-8424; e-mail: sales@computerlanguage.com; Web site: www.computerlanguage.com. To locate a computer user group, if you have access to the World Wide Web, point your browser at www.ugconnection.org to reach the User Group Connection, a site with over 2,400 Macintosh and 1,600 PC user groups in its searchable database. Also, try the Association of Personal Computer User Groups (APCUG) at www.apcug.org. Or call them at (914) 876-6678. The recorded information system will let you search for a group by area code, state, or ZIP code.

Backing Up

I see references to "backing up your system" in computer magazines and newsletters. Just what does that mean?

Making a backup means making a copy. And it is important because, as the old saying in the personal computer industry goes, it's not a question of "if" your hard disk drive will fail, it's a question of "when." Making a backup copy is like taking out an insurance policy against such a disaster.

But even if your drive doesn't fail, as we all know, "stuff happens." Your home or office could catch fire. A freak power surge could fry your system. Thieves could break in and cart off your computer. Floods, earthquakes, plagues of locusts—just name your disaster.

Wait a minute. I've got a 2-gigabyte hard drive. Do you mean I have to copy everything to a floppy disk? That'd take all week.

No, no. You definitely don't have to routinely copy everything, and you don't have to use floppy disks. Remember, if one of the programs on your hard drive gets zapped, you can reinstall it using the original distribution disks. That can be a nuisance, but it's not a tragedy.

The tragedy is having your data files get wiped out. Your Quicken financial records, your MS Word correspondence, your proposals, the report you just finished, and anything else that you have created. Data of this sort is all but irreplaceable, and the thought of losing it is the strongest incentive for backing up on a regular basis. The software supplied with most backup hardware will let you specify the kinds of files (data, program, etc.) you want to copy. But here's a time-saving tip: Make a separate directory or folder and use it to store all of your data files. That way you can simply tell your backup software to back up that entire directory or folder. This frees you from having to specify individual files or file types.

Okay, let's suppose I've made a complete backup of my system. Is there something I should be doing every day?

Absolutely. Make a habit of frequently saving your work to your hard disk as you use a program. Then, whenever you finish a work session, make a habit of copying the files you have created to a floppy disk. Think of it as a bit of extra insurance.

Also, remember that the likelihood that you'll need a given data file diminishes with time. Certainly your financial records need to be preserved in their entirety. But if the file containing a report you created six months ago suddenly gets trashed due to hard drive problems, it may not matter. The report is old news, after all.

On the other hand, if you were to finish this quarter's report tonight, go to bed, and discover that your hard drive was dead in the morning, you could be in big trouble. That's why it's a great idea to copy to floppy disk any data files you have created before ending your current work session. It only takes a minute, and it can save you hours and hours of work. (For still more peace of mind, print out a hard copy of every file you've created at the end of the day, even if you are still working on some of them.)

What about a complete system backup?

Everyone should have at least one complete backup containing every file on the hard disk. The reason is sheer convenience. If you've got floppy disk copies of all your data files and floppy or CD-ROM copies of all your program files, you have all the elements needed to re-create your dead hard drive.

Is one complete backup enough?

Technically, no. People who are really serious about backing up their systems think in terms of "grandfather, father, and son." Start by making two complete backups. Take one set home or out to the garage or to some other off-site location. That will become the "grandfather." Leave the second copy near your computer as a convenience. It will become the "father."

The next complete backup you make in the normal course of things becomes the "son." When that third copy is made, it is time to rotate the generations. The "father" is taken off-site, the "grandfather" comes back to the office for recycling, and the "son" is parked near the computer where the "father" used to be. The next time you back up, use the "grandfather" media, and rotate the generations again.

This isn't as complicated as it sounds. The benefit is that if you back up every week, and your office is destroyed, you will never lose more than one week's worth of data, thanks to the off-site "grandfather" backup.

That makes sense. But what hardware options should I be looking at?

As hard drive capacities have grown, so too have the hardware options for backing them up. We'll steer clear of the exotic and concentrate on the basics, which means tape-based or disk-based systems.

First, tape drives. At prices ranging from about $120 to $450, tape drives and tape cartridges ($30 to $40 apiece) are cheap. "Travan" drives are the industry standard and are capable of storing 800 MB to 8 GB of data, depending on the drive you buy. Drives are made by 3M, Hewlett-Packard's Colorado Memory Systems division, and other industry leaders. Such drives can read tapes created under the former QIC or "Quarter Inch Cartridge" standard.

Okay, but what about "disk-based" random access options?

Although the technology may not matter to you, the disks used in backup systems may be *magnetic* (like tape, floppies, and hard drives) or they may be *optical* (like CD-ROM drives and disks). All of them offer you random access akin to that available from an audio CD or a CD-ROM.

On the magnetic side, the leaders are Syquest's SyJet and EZFlyer lines and Iomega's Zip and Jaz units. The SyQuest products are basically removable cartridges that use the same technology found in every hard drive. That makes them very fast. Drives sell for between $235 and $500; cartridges are $25 to $125 apiece. Capacities range from 230 MB to 1.5 GB.

Iomega's Zip and Jaz lines use the same kind of medium found in floppy disks. Prices start at $200 for a Zip drive capable of storing 100 MB of data on a single $20 cartridge. And, as a bonus, Zip drives can both read and write 720K and 1.44 MB 3.5-inch floppies. Iomega Jaz drives use a different technology, sell for $500, and can store 1 GB on a single $130 cartridge. Both types of drives are fast enough to be used as an extra floppy disk drive.

Now for the optical side of things. Optical drives sell for between $400 and $2,000 and create a CD-ROM disk that will safely preserve data for 30 years. Disks can be erased and reused. Capacities range from 460 MB to 4.6 GB and cost between $50 and $170 per disk. Some units can also operate as conventional quad-speed CD-ROM drives.

There are so many options. What should I do?

Everyone has different needs, of course. So here's the quick take on your options. Tape drives and tapes are cheap, but you'll have to do a lot of "fast-forwarding" whenever you want to restore a given file. Optical drives offer long-term data security, but they're expensive and relatively slow. On the other hand, you can use some models for both backup and as a conventional CD and CD-ROM player.

SyQuest's SyJet and EZ units and Iomega's Zip and Jaz drives appear to offer the best of both worlds. The drawback is that you've got to buy only SyQuest or Iomega Zip/Jaz media. But the Iomega products can also be used as a second 3.5-inch floppy drive, which can be a convenience when you want to copy a disk. And the SyQuest equipment can be used as an add-on hard disk drive.

If cost is the major consideration, go with a tape system. If long-term durability of the media is the main focus, go with a magneto-optical system. Otherwise, you will probably be happiest with an Iomega Zip or Jaz drive or a SyQuest product.

Of course there is another possibility: Buy a second hard disk drive and use it as your backup system. You can get a 1.6 GB drive for about $200. Add backup software, and you'll be all set—provided you remember to make the backup and provided your computer doesn't get stolen or damaged.

Any final words of wisdom?

But of course. The two most important considerations for most people are cost per megabyte and convenience. When comparing backup hardware options, add up the cost of the drive and the cartridge and divide it into the number of megabytes that cartridge can hold. That's your cost for backing up a single megabyte of data, and it is an excellent way to compare the true cost of storage options.

Second, opt for the solution that makes it as painless as possible for you to back up your system. If you have to pay a little more to get a disk drive or tape drive that can back up your entire hard drive in one fell swoop, do so. Why? Because you will then be able to "set it and forget it" when backing up your system. Let the thing run overnight or during your lunch break. You'll get a complete backup without having to return to your computer to insert one or more fresh cartridges. That means that you will be inclined to make backups more often, which is really the point. The ease with which you can make a backup is far more important than the speed with which you can restore a given file.

Source: Alfred and Emily Glossbrenner have written over 40 books in the last 20 years, racking up sales of close to 1 million copies. Glossbrenner's *Hard Disk Handbook* and *File and Disk Management,* both from Osborne/McGraw-Hill, are considered classics in their fields. But whether the topic is QIC or Zip drives, making money on the Internet, or even baseball (as in *The Art of Hitting .300,* written with the late Charlie Lau), the Glossbrenners have a reputation for providing clear explanations of complex topics that are both easy to understand and fun to read. They can be reached at gloss@gloss.com.

Ergonomics

Why should I use a wrist rest?

When positioned correctly, a wrist rest helps encourage a neutral wrist position in which the forearms, wrists, and hands are in a straight line. Some experts recommend keying or typing with the wrists elevated off the rest, and resting the wrists and palms on the rest during pauses. People who don't have a wrist rest often rest their wrists on a sharp desk edge or the hard edge of a keyboard tray. This can actually create pressure points that aggravate hand and wrist problems.

Do I need to sit in the same perfect posture all day?

Actually, no. You should try to vary your activities and position during the day to stimulate circulation and rest overworked muscles. Find a couple of low-risk positions that offer support and comfort, and shift between them. If you plan to do a repetitive task that involves working at your desk for an extended period, many experts feel you should take frequent mini-breaks of a few minutes each hour. During these breaks you could do different work like file, sort your mail, stretch, tidy up your office, or walk to the copier and make copies.

What is the best way to organize my workstation?

You should keep the most frequently used items within easy arm's reach and on the side of your dominant hand. For instance, if you spend a lot of time on the phone and are right-handed, you should have your phone within reach on the same side of your workstation as the arm you use to hold the phone. Avoid awkward reaching, bending, or stretching to reach frequently used items.

How do I know if I need a footrest?

If your chair is adjusted to the proper height and your feet aren't supported, you should use a footrest. Footrests can also help individuals who have problems with their lower back to keep positioned against the backrest of their chair. That way the chairback, instead of their lower back muscles, is providing the support they need.

How do I know if I need an office air cleaner?

If you are one of the estimated 20 percent of the population who suffers from allergy problems or you are concerned about the indoor air quality in your area, an office air cleaner can help reduce the concentrations of allergy-aggravating particles, like dust and pollen, as well as many other indoor pollutants in your office air.

My monitor is too high (or too low) according to the ergonomic guidelines. What can I do?

If you are the only one using your equipment, you can raise the monitor by using telephone books, monitor blocks, or reams of paper. If you share your equipment, you should consider using an articulated monitor arm that easily adjusts the position to meet each person's requirements. People who need to lower their monitors typically have them sitting on top of their computers. Placing the monitor directly on the work surface usually solves that problem.

How do I know if I need lumbar support?

Everyone should have lumbar support. The *lumbar region* of your back is the area just above your waistline where your spine gently curves inward (sometimes called the small of the back or the lower back). If the backrest of your chair doesn't support this area, you should consider adding an auxiliary lumbar support.

If I work at a computer, how often should I have my eyes checked?

A minimum of once every two years. When you make an appointment with your eye-care professionals, you should mention that you work at a computer and ask if they need any further information. They may want to know how much time you spend at the computer and how far your monitor is from your eyes. If you are a heavy computer user, they may offer you glasses that are optimized for computer work.

Source: 3M Company. Contact: Tom Albin, P.E., C.P.E., 3M ergonomics specialist (612) 733-9711.

Getting Help

I paid over $2,500 for my computer, and a couple hundred more for various programs. The manuals are either so thin they're worthless, or so packed with jargon they might as well be written in a foreign language. What can I do?

There are at least two reasons why this situation exists. First, customers tend to be unwilling to pay extra for support. Given the opportunity, most people will go for the cheapest price. Hardware and software makers thus make low prices their major goal and keep their support costs and services as low as possible.

Second, there are programs that you simply have to buy because they are industry standards. These include Windows, Lotus Notes, possibly Microsoft Office, and so on. Since you have to buy the product anyhow, there is no advantage to such firms in offering great customer support. Doing so wouldn't get them any more sales and would merely cut into their profit margins.

So what do I do?

First, you relax in the certainty that the information you need is out there someplace. You're not stranded. Next, you consider your options. These include telephone support from the company, of course. That's the obvious option, but the call may not be toll-free, and you may be put on hold for half an hour or more. In most cases, there are far better and faster ways to get the information you need. These include:

- Books and magazine articles
- Company-created Web sites
- Company-sponsored forums on CompuServe, America Online (AOL), and Prodigy
- Customer support bulletin board systems (BBSs)
- Independent Internet newsgroups
- Local and national user groups and associations

Books and magazines make sense. What should I start with?

First, books are great supplements or even replacements for hardware and software manuals. As for magazine articles, call the reference librarian at your local library and ask if a CD-ROM product called *Computer Select* is available anywhere in the library system. Issued each month, this product contains the full text of over 150 computer publications published during the last 12 months. Key in your topic, hardware or software product, or keywords, and you will almost certainly get the information and answers you seek.

As for Web sites, these days, nearly every high-tech company has one. Of course, they vary in quality. But the good sites will contain help information, answers to frequently asked questions, patches to upgrade the version of the software you are currently using, and much more. To find a given Web site, point your browser at www.altavista.digital.com and search on the company name.

What about CompuServe, AOL, BBSs, newsgroups, and those other online options?

The fact is that many companies have established "forums" on systems like these for the sole purpose of offering customer support. Online forums let you post questions, read the questions and answers other users have provided, and download updates, fixes, templates, and other software related to a given product. To locate a forum of interest on AOL, do a Control-K and search for a keyword (like the name of the company). On CompuServe, do a GO INDEX to search for the same kind of thing.

Some companies also maintain bulletin board systems (BBSs) that offer the same sort of information. Check your product literature for BBS numbers. The one catch is that you will have to use a communications program like Windows Terminal or ProComm to dial up such systems. Netscape and other Web browsers will not work.

As for newsgroups—those free-flowing discussion groups on the Internet—your best bet is to point your browser at www.dejanews.com and search for newsgroups devoted to your product or company. Once you've found the right group, you can easily search for answers or post queries of your own.

One group you should be sure to check is comp.sys.ibm.pc.hardware.video. Look for the "PC Hardware FAQ"—a continuously updated posting prepared by Ralph Valentino. It contains great stuff. On a flyer, you might also check in with *TechHelper: The Virtual Helpdesk* from CMP Publications. Point your browser at www.techhelper.com and prepare to be amazed.

Okay, I happen to be on the Net, so I can tap into these things. But what about someone who doesn't even own a modem?

Online support options are fun, fast, and effective. But the real jewel in the computer support crown consists of local and national user groups. User groups are all about pooling knowledge, needs, and experience. Most are non-profit organizations staffed and run by volunteers. Membership dues are typically about $35 a year; and people of every level of knowledge are welcome. Indeed, most computer user groups place special emphasis on bringing in absolute beginners.

If you're a Macintosh user, you can simply pick up the phone and dial (800) 538-9696, ext. 500. This Apple Computer–sponsored service will then direct you to the nearest user group based on your ZIP code. You can also find Macintosh user groups at Apple's home page (www.apple.com/documents/usergroups.html).

If you don't have a computer or do not yet have access to the Internet and other online systems, one of the best ways to locate a local user group is to ask a computer-using friend or two. If that doesn't work, try asking at CompUSA, Radio Shack, or any other place that sells computers. If you can, ask to speak to the "techies" in the back, the people who repair computers, since they are even more likely to be tapped in than the sales staff.

But what if I'm a Microsoft user?

To reach the Web home page of the Microsoft user group program, point your browser at www.microsoft.com/mindshare. Microsoft started its Mindshare User Group program in 1987. It now lists over 1,500 independent groups worldwide. These are Macintosh and PC user groups, and special interest groups devoted to one or more Microsoft products. There is a monthly Mindshare newsletter, as well as a tremendous amount of help for user group leaders and for anyone thinking of starting a new group.

But what most people will find most interesting is the site's locator service. You start by clicking on a list of user group types (PC, Macintosh, Excel, etc.). Then you click on a list of regions of the world or of the United States. You can then click on the Search button, and a list of the groups matching your criteria will appear on your screen.

That's not all. Microsoft's Mindshare does a nice job, but it really doesn't cover the entire user group universe. It may be that no one can do that. But certainly the User Group Connection (UGC) at www.ugconnection.org comes close. This organization's database includes approximately 2,400 Macintosh user groups and 1,600 PC-oriented user groups in the United States and Canada, for a total of over 4,000 groups in all.

User groups and online sites sound like incredible resources. But surely, with the need for computer help so great, there must be third-party companies who offer help for—*gulp*—a fee?

There certainly are. And the fees are not that scary, particularly when you consider that the alternative may be waiting on hold for half the day as you call the company that made your hardware or software. Compaq Computer, for example, began charging customers for answers to all questions that aren't the direct result of a product defect. The cost is $35 per question. This trend of charging for support has spawned a brand-new industry, two good examples of which are:

> *HelpNet*—Run by KnowledgeBroker, Inc., HelpNet offers 24-hour support for nearly any PC hardware or software problem. Toll-free calls to (800) 927-4524 are billed at a flat rate of $16.95; and (900) number calls to (900) 289-4357 are billed at $1.95 per minute. The company also handles queries via the Internet at www.kbi.com.

> *Software Support, Inc.*—This company also operates round the clock. Its experts offer help with some 150 PC and Mac software titles. Infrequent users can call (800) 277-1435 for a $25 credit card charge or (900) 454-4435 for a $2.95-per-minute phone bill charge. There is also a subscription program for either 90 days or one year of toll-free help. The company claims that it resolves 93 percent of the queries it receives, completing most calls within ten minutes. Call (800) 756-4463 for more information.

In the end, the answers you need *are* available. The challenge for all computer users is to find the sources of those answers as quickly, efficiently, and cheaply as possible. Would that it were otherwise, but this is simply one of the realities faced by all PC users today. Hopefully, the answers provided here will greatly shorten or short-circuit the process.

Source: Emily Glossbrenner spent nearly a decade as an IBM marketing representative and manager for *Fortune* 500 accounts before leaving to write books about the burgeoning computer industry. To date, she has authored or co-authored nearly a dozen titles dealing with computers and the Internet, including *The Computer Sourcebook* from Random House, a rich, highly browsable compendium of information that every computer user needs—containing hundreds of customer support numbers and Web sites. She can be reached at gloss@gloss.com.

Buying the Right Printer

What kinds of printers are available?

There are three main printing technologies: *dot-matrix, inkjet,* and *laser.*

Dot-matrix printers operate by literally hammering ink from a ribbon onto paper. The printhead is rectangular and consists of a single vertical column of tiny wires or pins. The pins can be pushed forward or withdrawn. When a pin is in its forward position and the printhead is hit with a tiny hammer, the pin is forced into the ribbon, creating a dot of ink on the paper.

Inkjet printers (or "Bubble Jet," as Canon likes to call them) take a similar dot-based approach. However, they literally spray droplets of ink on the page through 50 to 64 tiny nozzles, each about half the diameter of a human hair. The ink is forced into a nozzle by a heated wire. When the wire gets hot, an ink bubble is formed, and as the bubble grows it passes through the nozzle and onto the page. The process repeats an astounding 3,600 times a second for each nozzle. Because the ink droplet dots are so tiny—25 of them are needed to create the dot of a lowercase letter "i"—the output can be nearly as crisp as that of a laser printer.

What makes laser printers different?

Laser printers also form letters with dots. But lasers use toner instead of ink and operate on the same principle as photocopiers. A laser beam is focused on a rotating drum that is designed to produce a charge of static electricity wherever the laser hits it. Particles of toner, which carry an opposite charge, are attracted to those locations on the drum. When a piece of ordinary paper is passed over an arrangement of corona wires in the machine, it too becomes charged. When this paper is pressed against the drum, the particles of toner are transferred. Heat is then applied to permanently fuse the toner to the paper. (That's why, if you ever get toner on your hands or clothes, you should be sure to wash with cold water, not hot.)

What performance considerations are the most important when choosing a printer?

There are two main measurements of any printer's performance: *resolution* and *speed.* Resolution is measured in dots per inch, or "dpi." These days, just about every printer sold can produce 300 dpi output, sometimes expressed as 300 x 300 dpi to indicate that the printer can print that many dots vertically and horizontally. A resolution of 300 dpi is perfectly acceptable for just about every application outside of typesetting. Most printers now tout an ability to do 600 dpi, which is nice to have, but not necessary for most business applications.

Dot-matrix printer speed is measured in characters per second (cps), and a speed of 120 cps in letter-quality mode is considered quite good. The speed of inkjets and lasers is measured in pages per minute (ppm). Black-and-white printing is faster, so you will see speeds ranging from 4 through 12 pages, with some high-end lasers clocking in at 24 ppm.

If you're buying a printer for home use, it is probably not going to be worth paying extra for a laser printer that produces black-and-white pages faster. But it can definitely be worth paying more for a faster color inkjet. The least expensive color inkjets take about two minutes to produce a page when printing in color. For just a bit more money you can get a model that produces four pages a minute in color.

How important is the memory a printer comes with?

Memory is an important feature for laser printers. Laser printers are essentially specialized computers, and all computers need memory. And as is always the case, the more memory the better.

Laser printers use memory as a "print buffer" to hold information that is about to be printed as it comes in from the computer. The bigger the print buffer, the sooner your computer can pump the print job to the printer and return its attention to you. Memory is also important when you're printing graphic images. To be able to print an entire image, you will need a printer with at least 1 MB of RAM.

Why would anyone buy a dot-matrix printer?

Two words: multipart forms. Carbonless multipart forms like the airbills you fill out for overnight delivery services must be completed either by hand, by typewriter, or by a dot-matrix printer. Lasers and inkjets literally have no impact on such forms. The original dot-matrix machines had printheads with nine pins. Those sold today have 24 pins and produce much higher quality. Today's units also have built-in typefaces, optional color kits, and other whistles and bells. Expect to pay $300 to $450 for a name-brand model.

I've noticed that you can get an inkjet or a laser printer for about the same price. Which one should I choose?

The main consideration is whether or not you want to be able to print in color. If you have kids, you'll definitely want a color printer. You can also use color for business brochures and flyers. (Or you can print a master and have a copy shop run off a quantity with a color photocopier.) But if you are going to be producing business output, pay particular attention to how crisply the printer does text.

You see, less expensive color inkjets use a cartridge holding cyan, magenta, and yellow inks. They lay these colors down on top of each other to produce their printed color. Since there's no black ink, however, black must be simulated, and the results are never as crisp as when real black ink is used. You can replace the color cartridge with a black ink cartridge when you want to print just text, but that's a nuisance. And it means that you can never do genuine black text with color images.

Better models include black ink as well as cyan, magenta, and yellow (CMY). And here's an important tip: Make sure that your inkjet uses *separate* cartridges for each ink color. That way you won't have to throw away still-usable cyan and magenta ink, for example, after running out of yellow.

Insist on up-to-date software drivers for your printer—a driver that's not only compatible with your operating system, but takes full advantage of the printer's features. This is particularly important for color inkjets, whose latest drivers provide sophisticated options for color management.

What about paper? Is there anything I should consider?

Yes, there is. The first point is capacity: How many sheets can the printer hold? Nothing is more aggravating than to set your system to printing, only to return later to discover the job isn't finished because the printer didn't have enough paper. A paper tray able to accommodate 100 to 250 pages is fairly standard. More expensive laser printers may include trays for both letter- and legal-size pages for a total capacity of 350 sheets.

There's also the matter of coated paper. All inkjets produce superior graphics if you feed them specially coated paper that lets their ink bond more precisely to the page with less smearing. Indeed, using coated paper is the only way to achieve 600 or 720 dpi color output.

Speaking of special paper reminds me, is there a way to save money on printing supplies?

There are several ways, in fact. The easiest is to see if your printer has a print density or darkness dial. Experiment by printing the same text page at ever lower settings until you reach the lowest setting that produces acceptable quality. The factory setting for these dials is rarely the most economical. New ink/printhead cartridges typically cost about $30. Fortunately, you can refill most empty cartridges about ten times before you have to buy a new one. Refill kits sell for about $15 and are available at most office supply stores and computer-oriented mail-order houses. It's important to be aware, however, that some cartridges are easier to refill than others.

How do I go about refilling and recharging inkjet and laser cartridges?

For step-by-step instructions on the leading cartridges, point your Web browser at www.image-control.com. Image Control Corporation, (416) 694-7929, manufactures its own refill kits for inkjets and remanufactures laser printer cartridges. You might also contact Computer Friends, (800) 547-3303, and Renewable Resources, (800) 734-6548.

Laser printer cartridges can also be recharged, usually at about half the price of buying a new one. Contact the companies listed for inkjet refills. Or try The Laser Group, (800) 527-3712, one of the long-established firms in the field. You will probably want to sell your old, spent cartridge to the recharging company for $5 to $7 and buy a new cartridge from them that is specifically designed to be refilled. You will eventually need two cartridges, one for your printer and one to be sent out to be refilled. By recharging your cartridges, you can save literally thousands of dollars over the years. Or months, if you do a lot of printing.

Source: Alfred Glossbrenner began the computer life in 1979 with an 8080-based CPT word processor that was equipped with 8-inch floppy disks and a Radio Shack Daisy II printer (total equipment cost: $13,000). The printer made so much noise that Alfred Glossbrenner had to leave the room during a long print job. But it produced countless books, articles, scripts, and corporate communications pieces with unprecedented ease. To learn more about Mr. Glossbrenner's books, point your browser at www.amazon.com and do an author search. Or e-mail him at books@mailback.com.

Using the World Wide Web

I've been on the Internet, and it seems awfully hit-or-miss. Surely there must be a better way to find things on the Web.

Today, your best bet is to use one of the many *search engines* that are available on the Internet. Search engines are a relatively recent phenomenon that gives you powerful tools for finding what you want. Most search engines operate by launching *spider programs* that prowl the World Wide Web. The spiders are designed to automatically follow the links they find on any given Web page and to make sure that the text of all the pages they visit gets saved to disk back at their search engine headquarters. That text is the guts of the database you search when you use an automated search engine.

But that isn't the only approach. Yahoo!, probably the most famous search engine, consists of a directory of Internet resources prepared by human beings.

What are the leading search engines and where can I find them?

Here's a list of the most popular search engines and their locations on the Web:

AltaVista	www.altavista.digital.com
Excite	www.excite.com
HotBot	www.hotbot.com
Infoseek	www.infoseek.com
Lycos	www.lycos.com
OpenText	www.opentext.com
Yahoo!	www.yahoo.com

Most of these search engines let you search both the World Wide Web and newsgroups. There are also search engines that specialize in e-mail and land addresses and phone numbers. "White Pages" directories like Four11 (www.four11.com) serve as national phone books for individuals. "Yellow Pages" services like Big Book (www.bigbook.com) will help you find companies, stores, and the like. If you are running the Netscape browser, you can get a comprehensive list of search engines by clicking on Directory on the toolbar and then on Internet Search.

What do I need to know to be able to use these search engines effectively?

The *full-text* searches offered by most search engines are the most challenging search of all, even for professional online searchers. Small wonder that most people end up being overwhelmed with hundreds or even thousands of "hits" when they do an online search.

Search engines vary, but many offer advanced tools and techniques for sharpening the focus of your search. If you do a lot of searching, you'll want to explore these tools. They may take a while to master, but they'll save you huge amounts of time and frustration in the end. If you're a more casual searcher, you can improve your results enormously if you just stop and think before you key in a search term.

What do you mean?

The trick is to think of the most unique word or name relevant to the information you seek. Suppose you're looking for the date of the Battle of Trafalgar for a homework assignment. "Trafalgar" is an unusual word, and if you searched on it, you would find all the Web pages that contain the date of the battle. But you would also find hundreds of irrelevant Web sites, including one put up by the Trafalgar Estates housing development.

Back to the drawing board for a second trick. And that is to think of a series of words that would absolutely have to be on the kind of page you seek. So, you key in "Battle-of-Trafalgar" on AltaVista, where joining words with hyphens means they must appear as a phrase. This time, you're down to about 100 sites. But one of the first ones turns out to be some Englishman's personal list of favorite pubs, one of which is the Battle of Trafalgar (Guildford Road, Brighton, UK).

Back once again for a third search. This time, remembering the name of the admiral who won the battle (but lost his life as the battle ended), you include the word "Nelson" as a search term. That proves to be the charm. Your first list of results even includes a Web site created in 1996 to celebrate the 190th anniversary of the famous battle.

Are there other resources besides search engines that I should know about?

If you are really serious about a topic, there's at least one other place you should consider. It's called the Argus Clearinghouse for Internet Resource Guides (www.clearinghouse.net). Right now, more than 600 guides are available for download, and more are being added all the time.

Clearinghouse guides are prepared by longtime Internet users, university students, and others who "have an interest in repackaging the Internet's information in ever more useful ways, and in sharing their labors with you." Most are on the order of 20 pages or more of single-spaced text. And each typically covers all the Internet resources related to a particular topic: Web sites, newsgroups, mailing lists, Gopher menus, Telnet sites, files you can download via FTP—the works!

Source: Emily Glossbrenner is the author of *Search Engines for the World Wide Web: Visual QuickStart Guide,* from Peachpit Press. This is a book for anyone who has ever been frustrated by the task of finding information on the World Wide Web or the Internet as a whole. In clear, straightforward language, laced with lots of screen shots, Ms. Glossbrenner shows you how to take control of the Internet's leading search engines and make them find what you want. She can be reached at gloss@gloss.com.

The Internet and the World Wide Web

I see references to the Internet and World Wide Web everywhere, but I don't really know what they are. Is this something I should be interested in?

It depends on your other interests. I've yet to meet someone whose life hasn't been enriched by using the Net. But let's back up and define a few terms. Specifically, the Internet, the World Wide Web, and Web browser software.

First, the Internet itself is nothing more than the collection of wires, switches, and software that make it possible for computers all over the world to "talk" to each other on the phone. It's like the whole physical infrastructure used to bring TV or radio signals to your home. But what good are signals if they don't carry any TV shows or radio programs? Well, the World Wide Web contains the "shows" you can "watch" using Web browser programs like Netscape's Navigator or Microsoft's Internet Explorer.

Is there anything "on" that I would want to "tune in" to?

Almost certainly. The Web has grown so fast with so many sites that, regardless of your interests or needs, you'll find a "home page" that can help. A Web site, incidentally, is what you reach when you tell your browser program to take you to an address like www.caderbooks.com. The home page is like the site's welcome mat. It explains what the site offers, who created it and why, and so on.

As for items of interest, how about tax forms and publications—all of them—from the IRS to your specific state forms? There is an official IRS site, but you might like www.1040.com better since it covers both federal and state forms. Find the form you want, click with your mouse to tell the site to send you the form as a computer file, and almost instantly you'll have a copy of the form on your hard disk.

Print the form with your PostScript printer or with Adobe Acrobat (available free of charge from the site), and you're all set. No more racing around at the last minute trying to get the forms you need from the post office. No more sitting down on the night of April 15 only to realize that you're missing a crucial form. You can get any form you need in seconds, thanks to the World Wide Web.

What about the fun stuff?

Okay. How about movies? Located at us.imdb.com (and also at uk.imdb.com), the Internet Movie Database includes biographies and filmographies on hundreds of thousands of actors, actresses, directors, craftpeople, and reviews. And it is searchable. So you can discover all the movies a given actor, composer, director, or screenwriter has worked on in seconds.

Want the latest sports scores? Go to the *USA Today* site at www.usatoday.com/sports/sfront.htm and click on Scores. Need a ZIP code? Go to www.usps.gov, a site that lets you key in the target address and then presents you with the correct "ZIP+4" code.

In addition, nearly every leading museum, orchestra, and college or university has a Web site. So it's easy to find out about special exhibits, performance schedules, or course offerings. This information has always been available, to be sure, but now it is *instantly* available to you at any time of day or night. That's the big difference that the Web makes.

I'm sold. I want to "surf the Net" and "browse the Web." What do I do next?

Tapping into the Internet has never been simpler. All you need is a computer, a device called a *modem*, a communications software package, and, of course, a telephone line.

Most computers these days come with a built-in modem. If you have yet to buy your computer, however, I recommend getting an external modem that can sit on your desktop. With an external modem, you'll be able to look at the lights to see if you're connected. And you'll be able to turn the unit off easily should you get hung up. Look for a "33.6" or 56K modem.

You also need an account on a system that offers Internet access. There are two main types of systems: Value-added companies like America Online (AOL), CompuServe, and Prodigy, that offer Internet and World Wide Web access in addition to many other proprietary, "home-grown" features. The alternative: Netcom, AT&T WorldNet, Earthlink, Voicenet, and many small local firms that offer just a plain connection. Both typically charge about $20 a month for unlimited access.

Another way to get hooked up is to find a local Internet service provider or ISP. ISPs will give you the software you need (Navigator or Internet Explorer, Trumpet Winsock, etc.) free of charge. You'll be able to make a local phone call, and for $20 a month or less, you'll have unlimited Internet/Web access.

Check the newspapers, particularly any local computer-related newspapers or magazines, ask at local computer stores, or ask a friend to recommend a local ISP. If you have a friend who already has an AOL, CompuServe, Prodigy, or other account, ask them to send an e-mail message to the address info@celestin.com. The message can be blank or contain "Please send information." Celestin will automatically e-mail a response telling you how to get the latest list of Providers of Commercial Internet Access, the POCIA list. Or have your friend visit the online ISP directory operated by *Boardwatch* magazine at www.boardwatch.com/isp/usisp.htm.

All right. I've got my account with a local ISP. I've got Navigator or Internet Explorer installed. Now what?

Now you run the programs as instructed. Your service provider will tell you the actual addresses and other settings you'll need to key in. Once the connection is made and your browser (Navigator or Explorer) has appeared, you'll be ready to "surf."

Probably the software will be set to take you automatically to the Netscape or Microsoft home page. You can change that by clicking on the Options button on the toolbar. You can tell your browser software to start you off with any home page you like. One particularly useful option is to start with a search engine like Digital Equipment Corporation's Alta Vista (www.altavista.digital. com) or Yahoo! (www.yahoo.com).

Let's assume that I've successfully logged onto the Internet. I'm sitting here at the Yahoo! or Alta Vista home page. Now what?

The key to moving around the Web and the Net is "addresses" or "locations." In Web parlance, they're called URLs, or uniform resource locators. They're very much like the telephone numbers of all the different phones on the global network.

Look at the top of your Web browser for a single-line box that contains "http://" followed by something like "www.netscape.com." Whenever you want to browse another area, just key in a new address in that box. Key in "http://www.1040.com" and you'll be taken to the tax form site mentioned earlier. Depending on your browser, you may even be able to key in just "1040" instead of the full character string.

Start shopping online: Go to www.internetmall.com, learn more about birds of prey at www.raptorworld.com, or have a good chuckle at www.hardy-harhar.com. That's how Web browsers work. You start off with some page, and then you go someplace else. You can tell your browser software which page you want to start with by changing your preferences. When you encounter a page you may want to come back to in the future, you use your browser's "bookmark" option. When you "bookmark" a page, you tell your browser to record its address on a list. To return to a given page, you simply call up your list of bookmarks and click on the desired location. No need to remember or key in the site address in the location box.

The locations given here are great places to start. All of them contain "links" to other pages, making it possible to cruise the Net by simply clicking on the link or button. When you want to return to a page, click on your browser's Back button near the top of the screen. You'll be surfing the Web in no time.

Have fun!

Source: Dave Taylor, Ms.Ed., is president of the interface design firm Intuitive Systems. He is author of numerous best-selling books on Internet and Web topics, including *Creating Cool HTML 3.2 Web Pages,* from IDG Books. Mr. Taylor is also a weekly columnist for *InfoWorld* and a frequent contributor to other national publications. You can reach him via e-mail at taylor@intuitive.com, or start your online surfing by visiting Intuitive Systems at http://www.intuitive.com.

"Netiquette"

I read an article the other day about e-mail, and it used the word "netiquette." Just what is netiquette, and why is it important?

Netiquette is nothing more than good manners online. The essence of the Internet is people, and wherever people are concerned, politeness, courtesy, and consideration for others is crucial. The reason the term is used in more and more magazine articles is that there has been a noticeable decline in Internet netiquette in recent years due the huge influx of "newbies."

Remember, for over 20 years the Internet was a very exclusive community, made up of defense contractors, university people, and military types. These initial Internet users were the ones who more or less decided "how we do things around here." When the cold war ended, the Net was opened to the world, and in came millions of people who had bought their first modem only a week ago. They didn't have a clue.

So what kind of mistakes do new users typically make?

A good example is the use of capital letters in e-mail messages. Whatever you put in caps comes across as SHOUTING. It's unpleasant to read and visually distracting. The correct way to emphasize a word is to frame it with asterisks like *this.* This is a convention that has evolved over more than two decades on the Net, on bulletin board systems, and on systems like CompuServe. The problem is that most new users today have no way of knowing this.

Are there other e-mail netiquette points?

There are indeed. First, always begin an e-mail letter with a salutation, as in "Dear John" or "Elizabeth—". It is just plain rude to begin your letter without a salutation. Second, make sure your correspondent knows what you're talking about. Don't assume that she will automatically remember the details of the last letter you sent. So be sure to include something like, "As you know from my last letter, we're reviewing the Perkins account with an eye to…"

Third is the matter of quoted text. Mail programs and browsers let you attach a letter someone sent you to your reply. That's often helpful. Less helpful is the feature that lets you reply to individual lines in the original message. Doing so makes things easy for you, but it may result in a message your correspondent will find difficult to decipher.

What about attachments and postings?

If you're sending a message, be sure to include a subject line that is truly informative, not just "stuff" or "comments." Don't attach a large file to the message unless the person has asked for it. When you do attach a file, tell your correspondent what kind of file it is and the format it uses. If it is a ZIP or SIT (StuffIt) file, say so. And don't assume that the entire world uses your word processor. If the file is in MS Word or ZyWrite or WordPerfect format, for heaven's sake, say so.

The same goes for Internet newsgroups, except that with newsgroups you are dealing with a complete micro-community. Don't just barge in. Take the time to read the postings and to get to know the group, its interests, even the names of its leaders. When you do make your first "post," be brief, and make sure that it relates to the topic the group was created to discuss. (You'll find a complete FAQ on newsgroup netiquette at www.pccomputing.com.)

What is "flaming"?

"Flaming" is an odd phenomenon you might call "unpoliteness in the extreme." A flame is a violent, verbal, and often personal attack on someone for the ideas or opinions he has expressed by posting a message to some online system or Internet newsgroup. Flames have nothing to do with "witty repartee" and everything to do with unchecked anger and emotion, feelings that are sanctioned by the anonymity of computer communications.

For example, you post your opinion on the latest best-selling book or top-of-the-charts movie to an Internet newsgroup. Someone, somewhere, reads your note and disagrees, so he or she decides to flame you with a highly emotional message, posted for all to see. If you respond in kind, a "flame war" may ensue. Others may join in, and a good time may be had by all. Or hurtful words may be exchanged by people who enjoy this kind of thing.

In general, a spirited, well-informed discussion among people of opposing ideas is one of the great benefits of being online, while a down-and-dirty flame war is simply disgusting.

Are there any other points to remember?

First, be sure to include your name at the end of any message: Which is to say, sign your mail and postings. Better still, take the time to create a "sig file" (signature file). This is a small text file that your browser program can automatically attach to all your outgoing messages. The file can contain anything you want, but it should probably contain the same information found in your company or personal letterhead (land address, fax and voice phone numbers, e-mail address, etc.). Many users also include a favorite quotation at the end of their sig files.

You may find it helpful to use "smilies." Sometimes called "emoticons," these combinations of letters and punctuation symbols are designed to convey a facial expression or emotion in e-mail messages, newsgroup postings, and in chat rooms. The only catch is that you have to turn your head to the left before they make sense. Internet users have created literally thousands of smilies, but most people use just these three:

:-) Smile

;-) Wink

:-(Frown

Finally, as in life "offline," you can't go wrong if you make a point of being considerate of the other person. This requires some effort on your part since it involves putting yourself in the other person's shoes.

Source: Janet Attard, author of *The Home Office and Small Business Answer Book* (New York: Henry Holt & Co., 1993). Ms. Attard is president of Attard Communications, which runs the Business Strategies Forum on America Online, the Business Know-How Forum on the Microsoft Network, and the Business Know-How Web site at www.businessknowhow.com. Ms. Attard also manages the Web site for the U.S. Air Force Office of Small and Disadvantaged Business Utilization at www.safsb.hq.af.mil.

Newsgroups and Internet Mailing Lists

I was thumbing through an Internet magazine the other day and caught references to "USENET newsgroups." What in blazes are they? I thought the Internet was the World Wide Web.

It's true that most of the buzz about the Internet centers on the World Wide Web. But the Web is actually a relative newcomer to the Net. Long before there were "browsers," there were newsgroups—or "netnews," as this feature is often called.

Netnews is transmitted by a server program called Usenet. It was set up in 1979 to automatically distribute news about various aspects of the UNIX operating system to all who were interested. But the topics covered have grown considerably since then. In fact, there are now an astounding 25,000 newsgroups devoted to every subject you can imagine (and some you'd rather not): everything from the TV shows *Beavis and Butt-head* and *The Rockford Files* to tips on brewing your own beer or improving your sex life.

Okay, so what does a newsgroup contain?

There are two things you need to know about the contents of newsgroups. First, each consists of what might be thought of as huge player-piano rolls of messages, or "postings." Postings, or "articles," are rather like open e-mail letters. They pose questions, they make comments, they answer questions or provide advice, and so on. Basically, a given newsgroup lets people converse about specific topics over time.

The second thing you need to know is that anyone anywhere in the world can post to a given newsgroup. "Well, sure," you say, "that's a given." It is, but think about what this means: Tens of millions of people with Internet access and tens of thousands of newsgroup topics. If you have a question about anything, there's a very good chance that someone, somewhere, has had the same question, posted it to the relevant newsgroup, and had the question answered by someone else.

Internet newsgroups are nothing less than what someone once called the collected consciousness of the world. But you can think of it as an incredibly broad and deep advice column, drawing on the wisdom and experiences of millions of people worldwide.

So how do I tap into this resource?

Newsgroups are incredibly significant. And they offer something you simply cannot find on the World Wide Web. Fortunately, all browser programs (Netscape, Explorer, etc.) can be used to read newsgroup postings. You know how you key in "http://" followed by the address of a Web page in your browser's location box? Well, to read the latest postings to a given newsgroup, key in "news:" followed by the newsgroup name. Like this: news:news.answers.

There is a catch, however. Usenet is set up to transmit the postings to any and all newsgroups to servers who want them across the Internet. But the administrators who oversee these servers control which newsgroups their systems will carry. To put it another way, the newsgroups you'll have access to are governed by the company providing you your Internet connection, be it CompuServe, AOL, or Joe's Internet Services down the street.

Is that a problem, and if it is, how can I get a list of all of the newsgroups that are out there?

Yes, it could be a problem. In general, the plain text of most newsgroup postings does not require much hard disk space to store. But there are so many groups and so many postings that many Internet service providers (ISPs) limit the number of newsgroups they carry. And most delete postings that are older than about two weeks.

As for obtaining a comprehensive list of all the newsgroups that exist, you can do so by pointing your browser at news:news.lists or news:news.groups. The "Lawrence List," created and maintained by David C. Lawrence, is regularly posted to these groups. It offers the group name and a witty one-line description of what it covers. Frankly, though, most new users will be better off checking Deja News.

"Deja News"? What's that?

Deja News is a Web site (www.dejanews.com) that provides the key to making full use of Usenet newsgroups. The company's goal is to offer a searchable database consisting of every posting anyone ever made to a newsgroup from the beginning of Usenet to the present day. This means that you do not have to worry about whether your Internet service provider carries a given group or whether postings get deleted every two weeks. And you don't need to worry about obtaining a comprehensive list of all newsgroups in existence.

When you have a question—a question about anything you can think of—point your Web browser at www.dejanews.com and search the database of newsgroup postings. The best approach is to think big and simply assume that the answers you seek are out there, no matter how obscure they may seem to you. If woodpeckers are pounding the heck out of your house or trying to build a nest, for example, search on "woodpeckers and home and damage." Chances are you'll locate numerous messages advising you on how to deal with this problem. (The most effective solution: Hang a plastic owl near the site.)

You have to try it to believe it, but Deja News is one of the most remarkable features on the Internet. Think of a question about absolutely anything, go to the site and give it a shot. There are no guarantees, but you will most likely be amazed at the results.

You said there are over 25,000 newsgroups. How are they organized?

Newsgroups are organized by hierarchies, and the longer the name of a group, the more specific its focus. There are over 15 top-level categories, or "domains," including biz (business), k12 (kindergarten through grade 12), rec (recreation), comp (computer topics), and alt (alternative).

So a group called alt.music might be formed to discuss all aspects and types of music. But a subgroup called alt.music.baroque might be formed to narrow the focus. A group called alt.music.jazz.hampton might be devoted to the music of Lionel Hampton. Newsgroup names can get painfully specific. But it's all in the good cause of organization, and now that you've got the hang of it you won't have much trouble.

That same magazine piece that mentioned newsgroups talked about "mailing lists." What are they?

Along with newsgroups, mailing lists are another major feature. They exist because in the early days a subnetwork called Bitnet, which is now a part of the Internet, couldn't handle newsgroups. Since Bitnet served mainly colleges and universities, Internet mailing lists tend to have a rather scholarly and academic focus.

For example, the FWAKE-L@IRLEARN.UCD.IE list is devoted to the discussion of the James Joyce novel *Finnegan's Wake*. The ALLERGY mailing list is devoted to the discussion of all types of human allergies. And so on. Once you "join" or "subscribe" to a list, all the postings of all other list members will be sent to your e-mail address.

It does sound scholarly, but, just in case, how do I get a list of Internet mailing lists?

The most comprehensive file is the one maintained by Vivian Neou. This is sometimes called the SRI List of Lists. To get a copy, mouse up to the location box at the top of your browser screen and key in "ftp://sri.com". Once you reach the SRI site, click on the netinfo directory and download the file interest-groups.txt. If you want to search for mailing lists of interest, point your browser at Liszt (www.liszt.com).

Okay, I've found a list I want to be part of. Now what?

All Internet mailing lists have two e-mail addresses. There is one address you have to use to ask to be added or removed from the list. And there is another address to use when you yourself want to post an article that will be delivered to all members of the list. The write-ups you will find in the SRI List list and the results of your Liszt search will tell you which address to use for which purpose.

Note that you subscribe to most lists by sending a simple e-mail message to the subscription address. But you may have to include some special word or phrase in your subscription request. (Many requests are handled automatically by computers, not human beings.) So it's important to pay attention to the requirements set forth in the list descriptions.

Are newsgroups and Internet mailing lists ever going to replace the World Wide Web?

No. The World Wide Web will be a dominating factor in online computing from now on. But the newsgroups and Internet mailing lists offer unique features that the Web lacks and is likely to lack for some time to come. Many Web users aren't even aware that these other features exist.

Web pages tend to be very self-centered: "Here's what *I* think, here's what *my* company offers, here's why you should buy what *I'm* selling." Newsgroups and mailing lists, in contrast, take the approach of, "Okay, here's a topic of interest. What does everybody think? And what does everybody else think about the comments made so far?" They're discussions, not monologues.

No sponsors. No click-through advertisements. Just a free-flowing, global sharing of thoughts, ideas, advice, opinions, and every other element in the discourse soup. The Web is great, but it would be a mistake to overlook newsgroups and mailing lists.

Source: Kevin Savetz is America Online's Internet AnswerMan (at keyword ANSWERMAN). He maintains AOL's Net.Help forum, is co-author of the *Official America Online Internet Guide* and editor of the *1996–97 Microsoft Bookshelf Internet Directory*. He is a regular contributor to *Netguide, Computer Shopper,* and other publications. Mr. Savetz lives is Northern California with his wife, their dog, five cats, and four Macs.

Computer Viruses

What are *computer viruses,* and should I worry about them?

A computer virus is a program that can infect other computer programs by modifying them in such a way as to include a copy of itself. If you recall your high school biology, you'll remember that viruses, unlike bacteria, invade living cells and take over their machinery to produce copies of themselves. That's why the term is so appropriate here.

Computer viruses are also designed to spread unseen. For example, you might have a virus on your hard drive tucked away in a hidden file or, worse yet, tacked onto a crucial program file. Such a virus will almost certainly be programmed to check each floppy disk you place in a drive to see if it has been infected. If the floppy is clean, the virus will do its best to copy itself onto the disk so that it can spread to the next computer that uses that floppy. It's kind of like the movie *Invasion of the Body Snatchers.*

Notice, however, that being designed to delete or corrupt files or do other damage is not part of the definition. Some people create viruses just to show how clever they are. Such "benign" viruses might do nothing more than stop your computer and pop up the word "Surprise!" on a given date. But even they can be harmful. Imagine if that happened to a computer used for life support in a hospital. So, yes, you should be concerned about viruses of any sort.

What kinds of viruses are there and how do machines get infected?

Virus experts have developed multiple categories and terms to classify various types of viruses. But there's no need to get that technical. It is helpful to know, however, about so-called Trojan Horse programs and Microsoft Word "macros," even though they are technically not viruses and thus do not replicate themselves.

A Trojan Horse is a program that is almost always malicious and that always masquerades as something else. The classic case is the one where a shareware program available for download via an online system is said to improve your video dramatically. You download it, run it, and it distracts you with some colorful graphics while it is systematically wiping out your hard disk.

More recently, the nation's sociopaths have found ways to turn Microsoft Word macros into engines of destruction. A "macro" is a recorded list of keystrokes that can be replayed by entering a single key combination. The feature was created to make it easy to automate frequently repeated word-processing tasks, including the erasing of files. So you download a Word macro that promises to completely automate a task like printing, you run it, and only later discover that it has not only printed garbage but has also wiped out all of your disk files.

How can I tell if I have a virus on my computer?

Should you see unusual messages, music, or graphical displays...should pieces of text files be missing or even the files themselves...should you suddenly be out of RAM, you may have a virus.

What should I do if I think I have a virus?

If you're a relatively new user, your first step should be to contact someone with more experience. Ask the person to look at your system and advise you. The next step is to say to yourself, "Don't panic!" The worst that can happen is that you have lost important text, graphic, and other data files you have created. And presumably you have backups of them.

The disk can be reformatted, all of your operating system and program files can be reinstalled, and there are even data recovery services that can bring back files that have been erased and overwritten. So what you've got is a major inconvenience, not a tragedy.

Next, run a good virus scanner program to locate the virus. One technique such programs use is to search the files on your disk for virus "signatures," patterns of bytes that are unique to a given virus. However, since new viruses are constantly being introduced, it is crucial to use the latest version of a scanner program available.

A good place to start is with the shareware SCAN program made available by McAfee Associates, one of the leaders in the antivirus field. Point your Web browser at www.mcafee.com to pick up with the latest copy.

What happens after a virus scanner detects a virus?

Different programs work in different ways. But typically a scan is done to locate the virus. This can take several minutes since your entire hard disk must be checked. Then you have the opportunity to run a "clean" program to actually remove the virus.

No one who offers virus-scanning software claims that their products can't deliver a "false-positive." It may be that some perfectly innocent, clean program on your disk just happens to contain a series of bytes that matches a known virus signature. You wouldn't want to have the SCAN program automatically delete such a file.

Once the virus has been removed, the danger isn't over. If you did indeed make backup files, they too may be infected. If the virus has nibbled away at or otherwise affected specific files, do not blindly restore them from your backup media. If a data file is involved, you are probably safe in restoring it. But if a program file needs to be copied back onto your hard disk, don't use your backup tape. Instead, use the original program distribution disks that you got with the package.

Next, make a complete backup up of your now clean system. And delete all of your previous backup tapes or disks. This is a nuisance, but it's the only way to make sure that you don't reinfect your system from your own backups.

How can I guard against infection in the first place?

The simple answer: Don't run any program or macro that you are not certain came from a reliable source. For example, the people who supervise forums and other online features offering downloadable files on CompuServe and America Online are required by contract to check each file for virus infection before making it available for download. Any reputable provider of such files on the Internet and World Wide Web will have a similar policy and will announce it to all visitors.

Yes, but what if the policy isn't as vigorous as it should be? What can I do on my own that doesn't depend on some other person or system?

First, no system offering downloadable software can afford to have a "virus scandal." Word would spread like wildfire, and in a few days no one would sign on to such a system. So the incentives to be "virus-free" are enormous.

Second, the best thing you can do to avoid infection is never to run any program or load any floppy disk from any unknown source. So if a coworker hands you a disk and says, "You've got to run this game," don't do it. You don't want to give your coworker the third degree, but you also don't want to run a program of uncertain origins.

How do I protect myself against viruses in programs I cannot avoid running?

Automatically load a virus-monitoring program each time you turn on your computer. Think about it: There is no way a virus can have any permanent effect on your computer if it cannot mess with your hard disk, deleting files or parts of files, scrambling disk file directories, and so on. If you load a program that is specifically designed to prevent unauthorized disk activity in memory each time you boot up, you can pretty much pull the teeth of any virus.

Not all, of course. The battle between virus creators and virus killers is never-ending. But if yours is a computer used by many people, or if you frequently run programs downloaded from an online source or loaded from someone's floppy disk, then a virus SHIELD program is essential. (We're not selling here. SHIELD is available free of charge from McAfee Associates and its online venues cited earlier.)

What's the bottom line? Should I be worried or not?

The bottom line is that you should be aware of the problem and that you should be cautious. Viruses are not a plague. Should your system become infected, cures are available. It is not a death sentence. If you've made regular backups, a virus infection is not much more than a huge nuisance.

Still, if you want to minimize the chances of your personal or company computers becoming infected, install virus-monitoring software, and do your best to make sure that no one runs a program or a macro that hasn't first been checked by your on-staff computer person.

Source: Alan Freedman, author of *The Computer Glossary and Computer Desktop Encyclopedia* (AMACOM), the premier references of computer terms, concepts, and important products. Annual subscriptions to the *Encyclopedia* on CD-ROM are $64 (four CDs per year, requires Windows). Contact: The Computer Language Company, Inc.; phone: (215) 297-8082; fax: (215) 297-8424; e-mail: sales @computerlanguage.com; Web site: www.computerlanguage.com.

Shareware

What is *shareware*?

Shareware is actually a marketing method for commercial software. Unlike software marketed through normal retail channels, which you buy before ever using, shareware lets you try a program for a period of time before purchasing it. If, at the end of a trial period (typically 30 days), you decide to keep using the program, you simply send the program's author the fee he has set for the program. Popular titles that made their debuts as shareware include DOOM and Procomm.

What happens if I don't pay for the program?

Your computer won't blow up, but your program will generally remind you that your trial period has expired. Some shareware programs have a built-in expiration feature that disables the software if it hasn't been registered within the trial period.

Why should I pay for and register the program if I continue to use it?

For one, because it's the honest thing to do. Shareware is commercial software, fully protected by copyright laws. Like other business owners, shareware authors expect to earn money for making their programs available. Even if you purchase shareware (a nominal charge) through a catalogue, from a computer show, or at a retail outlet, you should pay for and register the program if you decide to keep on using it. None of the money you paid to the vendor goes to the author. If you pay up and register, this not only properly rewards the program's author, but lets him know that there is a need for this type of program, which will ensure program improvements and updates.

What percentage of users actually end up paying for and registering their shareware?

Because there are so many methods of distributing shareware, this is a hard number to pin down. Industry sources put the figure near 30 percent.

Besides the trial period, how does shareware differ from other kinds of software?

1. *Price:* In general, shareware costs less than software distributed through other channels. Prices range from as little as $5 to $50.

2. *Support:* As a rule, shareware technical support doesn't run to huge staffs. On the other hand, shareware users often end up talking to the person who actually wrote the program, so feedback can be quickly incorporated into the next version of the program.

Otherwise, all types of games, word processing, programs on real estate, personal finance, graphics, education, utilities, and a host of others are available as shareware. In fact, due to lower development and distribution costs, there is a dizzying variety of shareware around, from programs that duplicate and even extend the capabilities of retail software to those that perform functions that can't be found in retail stores.

Does using shareware increase my chances of introducing a virus into my computer?

Shareware authors and bulletin board and online service operators thoroughly check shareware programs for viruses before making them available to consumers. In fact, one of the most popular antivirus programs, from McAfee Associates, is available as shareware.

Where can I find shareware?

Shareware can be found on electronic bulletin boards; at online services such as CompuServe and America Online; at Web sites such as http:// shareware.com; and in department stores, discount outlets, and even supermarkets.

Why do developers market programs through shareware?

Marketing through shareware means lower marketing, packaging, and advertising costs, all of which pay off in lower prices. Shareware also allows developers to maintain complete control over their product, rather than cede it to their employers.

Source: The Association of Shareware Professionals (ASP), an international trade organization consisting of over 1,500 shareware authors, vendors, and online providers. Its members agree to uphold high standards of professionalism, and to deal fairly and courteously with customers. The ASP places its logo only on products that have complete documentation and that have been produced, tested, and evaluated by an ASP member. For more information, contact: ASP, Bob Ostrander, President, 5437 Honey Manor Dr., Indianapolis, IN 46221; http://www.asp-shareware.org; 76635.1670@compuserve.com.

Ten Most Frequently Asked Tech Questions

Why won't my system boot?

The problem is always found in the last place you look. So start simple. Check both ends of the power cord to make sure they are firmly seated in their respective sockets. While you're at it, make sure the keyboard cord, monitor cable, modem cable and power connection, and all other connections are also attached securely.

If your computer beeps several times and then stops working, the problem may be more serious. Much more serious: Anything from your motherboard to your hard disk drive may have failed. On the other hand, sometimes one of our computers goes into a fugue, beeping madly and refusing to boot. We have no idea why, but we know that the only solution is to shut it off and wait for two or three minutes (one minute is not enough) before turning it on again. After which everything works fine.

The key thing to remember is "Don't Panic!" The only component that really matters is your hard disk drive. That's where all your data is stored, after all. And even if the problem lies with the drive, there are companies that specialize in retrieving data from dead drives.

Why is my system so slow?

In a word, you probably don't have enough RAM. Whether you're a Windows or a Mac user, 8 MB of RAM is just about the minimum these days, and the time is rapidly approaching when 16 megabytes will be the minimum.

It is an oversimplification, but there is hardly a performance problem that cannot be solved or improved by adding more memory. Got an old, slow hard drive? Add more RAM and install a disk cache like Microsoft's SmartDrive, giving it plenty of RAM to use for storage. (SmartDrive comes with DOS and Windows, and the current version compares quite well with commercial counterparts.)

Why is my computer out of memory?

As central as RAM-based memory is to personal computing, "managing" said memory remains largely a black art. One of the most important things you need to know is that regardless of how much RAM you have, DOS can only see 1 megabyte of it. And most DOS programs were written to run within the first 640K of that megabyte.

The more small programs, drivers, and the like you can load into the 360K of memory addresses that lie above the 640K line, the more of that 640K of "conventional memory" your programs will have to work with. That's what the LOADHIGH and DEVICEHIGH commands are designed to do.

Windows actively manages memory. But even Windows can do little if a program fails to release the memory it used when you close it. Still, if you're out of memory in Windows, the thing to do is to start closing programs. Also, make sure that you have told Windows to use a "permanent swap file." Enter this setting in the Enhanced Virtual Memory dialog box, reached via Control Panel.

How do I get my data from a crashed hard disk?

If your disk has truly crashed and you need the data it contains, you might start by calling the disk manufacturer and asking for suggestions. More than likely you will be directed to a firm that specializes in data recovery.

Of course the way to minimize the impact of a dead disk is to *back up!, back up!, back up!* Every day, if you have to. The secret is to get a tape drive or disk-based backup unit that makes backing up your drive so easy you'll do it more often.

Why is my display blank or distorted?

Check the power cord and the cable that connects the monitor to your system. Then check the controls on the monitor itself, either on the front panel or at its back. Make sure that the "brightness" knob has not accidentally been turned down to make the screen black. (Great practical joke on the part of your coworkers, that.)

If the monitor worked before when using the same program, then there are just a few possibilities:

1. the monitor itself has gone bad;
2. the video card into which the monitor plugs has gone bad; or
3. the video driver software that translates software commands into a form the video card can understand has been trashed (or Windows has somehow forgotten about it).

The best first step: Reinstall the video driver software. If a hardware component has worked for 90 days, it is likely to work practically forever. It is much more likely that the software side of things has been corrupted.

Why can't I print a document?

Check all cables—all of them—and then check the paper supply. If you have no joy, turn everything off and wait for three minutes. Then start again.

If the printer worked when it was installed and has continued to work, then the fault may lie with either the printer driver or the board or port into which the printer cable has been plugged. And, by the way, make sure that your printer is "online." Look for a light and a button on the printer itself that indicates whether it is "online" or "offline."

Why did my peripherals stop working when I installed a new card?

Unfortunately, if you are among the vast majority of PC users, it is your responsibility to tell your computer how it should communicate with a specific peripheral without interfering with equipment that's already installed. This means specifying interrupt numbers (IRQs) and DMA (direct memory access) channels for many individual peripherals.

Macintosh users have not really had to face this problem, even though it exists in the Mac as in any computer. Microsoft's Windows 95 with its "Plug and Play" standard is designed to eliminate such problems.

Why doesn't my modem respond?

The best way to check things out is to load a communications program—anything from Windows Terminal to Procomm or something else—key in "AT" and hit Enter. If "OK" then appears on your screen, you will know that you do not have a hardware problem. The "OK" comes from the modem itself, so clearly your terminal and modem are communicating.

If you do not get an "OK," then you should check your cable and electrical power connections. That may mean turning off your computer, opening it up, and unseating and then reseating the card into which your modem plugs, or the internal modem card itself. Another possibility is that your modem is set to use one communications port while your program is set to use another.

Modem communications ports are set with a jumper on either your serial communications card or your internal modem card. Software ports are set by configuring your program.

Why do I lose my modem connection when I'm online?

Sometimes an online system will hang up on you for no apparent reason. It may be because it hasn't received any keystrokes from you for the last several minutes and has thus automatically logged you out.

Perhaps the biggest culprit, however, is your failure to disable call waiting. If your modem line has call waiting, add the following line to the beginning of your logon script: atdt*70. That will dial *70 and tell the modem to pause for two moments. Call waiting will be disabled for the duration of the call.

Why does my notebook battery last only 15 minutes?

Most laptops use nickel-cadmium (NiCad) batteries. These batteries work best when they are recharged only after they have been completely run down. If you recharge such batteries before they have been completely drained, the battery will eventually develop a "charge memory" that will cause it to lose its ability to hold a complete charge.

The solution is to do a deep discharge of your current battery. Use the DOS EDIT program to create an endlessly looping batch file called DRAIN. BAT that contains these lines:

```
dir c:
chkdsk c:
drain.bat
```

When you run DRAIN.BAT, the system will do a directory, run the DOS check-disk program, and then run DRAIN.BAT again. When the battery is drained, recharge it. You may have to repeat this process several times to restore the battery's ability to take a full charge.

Source: Jack Nimersheim has written over 35 books and more than 1,000 magazine articles on computer-related topics and has been a columnist and contributing editor for a number of popular computer magazines, including *Home Office Computing, Mobile Office* magazine, and *PC/Computing*. Mr. Nimersheim is also an award-nominated science fiction author. His newest book, a collection of short stories entitled *Grafitti from the Subways of My Mind,* is available from Farthest Star Books (www.abooks.com/nims/grafitti).

Getting the Best Performance

How can I get greater performance from my current system, so I won't have to buy a new one?

First, the march of technology is relentless. So at some undefined point in the future (three years, five years, ten years) you will have to replace your current computer setup. The trick is to put off that day for as long as you possibly can without undergoing any inconvenience.

So start by improving the performance of your current system. Optimize what you have first, and live and work with it until you cannot make it do what must be done anymore. That means considering your CPU, memory, hard disk, and video.

Let's start with the CPU, the chip at the heart of your system. It sounds dumb, but it has happened to all of us: Check the "turbo" switch on the front of your computer to make sure that your CPU is running at its highest speed. Sometimes these switches get stuck and are set to your chip's lower speed. If the position of the turbo switch doesn't seem to affect the system's speed, check its connection to the motherboard. Some motherboards default to the nonturbo settings if the switch is accidentally disconnected.

Next, check your BIOS settings. BIOS stands for Basic Input/Output System, but there's no need to worry about that. Instead, see if your computer doesn't tell you that you can change settings by hitting the Del or some other key right as it is starting to boot. Do so, and you will probably see a menu, one or more items of which will concern CPU caches. Make sure that "internal" or "Level-1" cache is enabled. Then do the same for "external" or "Level-2" cache if possible. Make sure you save your settings. Then tell the system to reboot.

Also, if you're running Windows 95 you may want to disable its Auto Play CD drive feature. That's because the feature polls your CD drive every second or so to see if a new CD has been inserted, which is largely a waste of CPU power. Run Control Panel/System/Device Manager, then select your CD-ROM drive and click on Properties. Uncheck the Auto Insert Notification option.

What about tuning my system's memory?

Don't waste time on this step if you don't have at least 8 MB of RAM installed. This applies whether you run Windows 3.1x or Windows 95. And resist the siren song of so-called RAM compression programs. They are no substitute for real RAM, and they often introduce side effects and incompatibilities without increasing performance.

As for memory management software, if you run only Windows 95 or NT and only 32-bit applications, you don't need it. Windows will manage everything itself. If you run Windows 3.1x or DOS programs, however, a memory manager may be able to squeeze out extra kilobytes. However, you should start with MemMaker, a program first supplied with MS-DOS 6. It is also on the Win 95 CD in the Other\OldMSDOS directory. Copy MEMMAKER.EXE, CHKSTATE.SYS, and SIZER.EXE into your Windows directory. Then reboot in DOS mode, change to the Windows directory, and run MEMMAKER from the DOS prompt.

What about my hard disk?

The hard disk is quite literally where you "live" on your computer. It holds everything of value, and your computer accesses it almost constantly. The faster your hard disk, the faster your system will perform.

There are two important, no-cost steps to take to boost the speed of your current hard disk. First, use the DEFRAG program supplied with DOS 6.x, Windows 3.1x, and Windows 95. When DEFRAG is finished, all the "clusters" that contain the sequential pieces of your files will be arranged in order, cheek-by-jowl. That means the read/write head of your drive will be able to scoop and shovel up all the clusters in one continuous operation.

For technical reasons, prior to running DEFRAG, there's a good chance that your read/write head would have had to move all over the disk "cherry-picking" clusters from their widespread locations. So, make a practice of running DE-FRAG against your disk drive at least once a week. And don't worry if the first time you do it takes a while. Once DEFRAG gets your disk in order, far less time will be required to tune it up in the future.

The second thing you can do is to make sure you are using a disk-caching program. Disk-caching programs are designed to deliver data stored on your hard drive with the speed of RAM. They perform this magic by storing the data you most recently requested from your hard disk in a RAM cache on the theory that you will probably want it again. In which case, your cache program can deliver it almost instantly from RAM since it does not have to pull it off your hard drive or your CD-ROM drive.

Many such programs also make an educated guess about the next chunk of data you will want and automatically read that into RAM from your drive before you actually call for it. As it happens, the good people at Microsoft have supplied you with just the tool you need: SMARTDrive. Give SMARTDrive 1 MB or more of RAM to serve as its cache, and you are likely to see dramatic improvements in your system's performance.

And the last component is my video. What do I do there?

The way to dramatically boost your video performance is probably to buy a faster, more powerful video card. We'll get to that in a moment. Right now you should know that video performance depends primarily on four things: the speed of the video board; the speed of the CPU; the bandwidth (the diameter of the "pipe") between the CPU and the video board; and the efficiency of the video driver software.

The video driver software is typically the only thing you can change without a hardware upgrade. Most vendors regularly provide updates to their video drivers. These updates fix bugs and sometimes add features or performance enhancements. You can look for drivers and updates at a vendor's World Wide Web site. Many vendors also have support forums on CompuServe and America Online.

If video performance still has you down, try using a lower color depth or resolution. On most video boards and applications, high-color 16-bit graphics are just about as good as true color 32-bit graphics—and they are much faster. The lower the video resolution, the fewer pixels Windows has to move, so the faster the response.

What if I do all of these things and the performance still is not acceptable?

Well, then it's time either to replace your entire system or to selectively upgrade your hardware. This is where things get complicated because they tend to veer off into endless cost-benefit considerations. In general, however, if your current system is anything less than a Pentium 133 or its equivalent, you probably should not be adding new hardware or additional memory. You are likely to be better off "swapping out" your current motherboard and replacing it with a newer board sporting a faster Pentium- or Pentium II–level chip or an equivalent.

The motherboard is the main circuit board, the board into which everything else plugs. Replacing your motherboard while leaving all your other equipment alone is one of the cheapest, easiest ways to increase the performance of your computer dramatically. But this concerns more than the CPU; newer motherboards feature local business graphics connections, which can dramatically boost the performance of your video hardware.

If you already have a Pentium 133 MHz system or better, your best option is likely to be adding RAM. If you've got 16 MB, taking your system to 32 MB can make a huge difference. You can never have too much RAM. The easiest way to increase your RAM is to carry your system into a trusted retailer. However, you can save some money by buying RAM from a mail-order house such as PC Connection or Micro Warehouse, and the sales reps there will help you determine what you need.

There are so many options. I'm confused. Can you straighten things out?

It is impossible to offer generalities, but basically, if you want to hold on to your current system, the best thing you can do is to try the free optimizing fixes suggested above. If they don't deliver the improvements you seek, add RAM. More RAM can make your hard drive and CD-ROM drive seem faster, thanks to caching programs. Additional RAM can improve the performance of any Windows program. If you have a few bucks more, buy a faster video card with more VRAM (video RAM) than your current installation, since that, too, will deliver dramatic speed improvements.

If you're computer savvy (and current in your knowledge) or if you have a really good computer service person, you might consider replacing your present motherboard. This is the cheapest way to give yourself a "new computer," but you really do need to know what you're doing.

Finally, it is easy to upgrade individual components. You have a 2x CD-ROM drive that you want to replace with a 12x drive. You have a 750 MB hard drive, and you'd like to add a faster 2-GB drive. And so on. There's nothing wrong with such "incremental upgrades."

But we all must be aware of the costs and benefits of the "package deals" offered by mail-order and other firms. Some of these deals are so good that it may actually be cheaper for you to donate your current computer to your local school system and buy a brand-new system with all the latest trimmings than to try to upgrade and replace individual components.

Source: John F. Mosier, president of Technology Enterprises Corporation. Since 1985, Mr. Mosier has operated a regional (PA, NJ, DE) computer maintenance and support business, providing a variety of computer products and services. These include custom-configured computer systems, system upgrades, system maintenance, and repairs. In keeping with technological demands, Mr. Mosier's business has also expanded to incorporate Internet Web site design, publication, and support services in a global environment. He can be reached at mosier@tec-2000.com or at the Technology Enterprises Corporation Web site: www.tec-2000.com.

RAISING CHILDREN

—◇—

Attention Deficit Disorder (ADD)
Baby Names • Child Abuse
Children and Religion
Children and TV
Choosing a Baby-Sitter
Choosing a Child-Care Program
Choosing an In-home Caregiver
Discipline • Divorce
The Dreaded Sex Talk
Children's Parties
Head Lice • Sibling Rivalry
Special Needs
Programs for the Gifted
Talking to Your Terrible Teen
Selecting a College

Attention Deficit Disorder (ADD)

What is *attention deficit disorder?*

ADD is a neurobiological disability that interferes with a person's ability to sustain attention or focus on a task and to delay impulsive behavior. It is characterized by attention skills that are developmentally inappropriate; impulsivity; and, in some cases, by hyperactivity.

What causes ADD?

ADD is one of the most studied childhood disorders. Research exploring the hereditary nature of the disorder, brain-imaging studies, studies of twins, and the recent identification of a possible genetic marker for ADD have led researchers and clinicians to conclude overwhelmingly that ADD is a neurobiological disorder.

How do I know if my child has ADD?

Determining if a child has ADD is a multifaceted process. Many biological and psychological problems can contribute to symptoms similar to those exhibited by children with ADD. For example, anxiety, depression, and certain types of learning disabilities may cause similar symptoms. A comprehensive evaluation is necessary to establish a diagnosis, rule out other causes, and determine the presence or absence of co-occurring conditions.

Such an evaluation will often include intelligence testing plus the assessment of academic, social, and emotional functioning and developmental abilities. Measures of attention span and impulsivity will also be used, as well as parent and teacher rating scales. A medical exam by a physician is also important.

At what age does ADD manifest itself?

ADD characteristics often arise in early childhood. The disorder is marked by behaviors that are chronic, lasting at least six months with onset before age seven.

What do I look for in determining if my child has ADD?

Characteristics of children with ADD can include:

- fidgeting with hands or feet
- difficulty remaining seated
- difficulty following through on instructions
- shifting from one uncompleted task to another
- difficulty playing quietly
- interrupting conversations and intruding into other children's games
- appearing not to listen to what is being said
- doing things that are dangerous without thinking about the consequences

How common is ADD?

In this country, ADD affects up to 5 percent of all school-age children.

Is it ever misdiagnosed?

A significant percentage of children with ADD are never properly diagnosed. Until recently, ADD was misunderstood by many people—children and adults with ADD were often wrongly labeled "a behavior problem," "unmotivated," or "not intelligent enough," and many clinicians and educators knew little about ADD. Today, ADD is recognized as a treatable, yet potentially serious, disorder.

What happens if it isn't treated properly?

Without early identification and proper treatment, ADD can have serious consequences. Children with ADD are at risk for school failure and dropout, academic underachievement, depression, and behavior disorders. Social and emotional adjustments are also often difficult probably because ADD makes children vulnerable to failure in the two most important arenas for developmental mastery: school and peer relations. However, with early identification and treatment, these children can succeed.

Does ADD ever go away?

Until recently, it was believed that ADD symptoms disappeared in adolescence. It is now known that many symptoms continue into adulthood for as many as two-thirds of all individuals with ADD.

Is ADD a learning disability?

No. Add is often inaccurately portrayed as a type of specific learning disability (SLD). It is not. Children with ADD are not unable to learn, but they have difficulty performing in school due to poor organization, impulsivity, and inattention. However, some children with ADD also have a learning disability, further complicating identification and treatment.

What is the appropriate treatment?

Treating ADD in children requires effective parenting, an appropriate educational program, and, when needed, individual and family counseling and medication. Parents should work closely with other members of the treatment team, including your child's pediatrician, psychologist, and/or psychiatrist, to develop an appropriate treatment plan.

What kinds of medications are used in treating ADD?

Psychostimulants are the most widely used medication for the management of ADD-related symptoms. Between 70 and 80 percent of children with ADD respond positively to such medications. Psychostimulants decrease impulsivity and hyperactivity, increase attention, and, in some children, decrease aggression.

Source: Children and Adults with Attention Deficit Disorders (CHADD), the national organization dedicated to helping children and adults with ADD succeed, 499 NW 70th Avenue, Suite 101, Plantation, FL 33317; (800) 233-4050.

Baby Names

Which is better: a popular or an uncommon name?

It's a lot easier to answer this question if you consider some of the advantages and disadvantages of popular and uncommon names. Popular names are very familiar. They tend to have positive images. They tend to be easy to spell and pronounce. On the other hand, there may well be several boys named Michael or girls named Ashley in each classroom. Your child may not like sharing a name with other friends. More unusual names are often more difficult to spell and pronounce. They tend to have weird or flaky images. But your child is unlikely to have to share the name.

I often find that grown-ups who were given unusual names were uncomfortable with those names through childhood, when they were subjected to teasing. Many people dropped their names, switching to their middle name or a nickname. However, many of the people who kept their unusual names tend to enjoy them now that they are adults.

I've heard that a name can be an important factor in a child's self-image and self-esteem. Is that true?

There have been a number of studies done about the impact of names on people. The impact works in two ways: It affects what other people think about a person and also the way a person thinks about himself or herself. Consider the fact that names create pictures in people's minds. When you think about Adolf, does Adolf Hitler immediately come to mind? When you think about Elvis, does Elvis Presley immediately come to mind?

I commissioned a survey to test people's impressions of 1,400 names. What I discovered was that most common names have stereotypes. These images affect the way a person is perceived by both others and by himself/herself. For example, most people would expect a boy named David to be intelligent and a boy named Elmer to be dumb. And most people would expect a girl named Lucy to be funny and a girl named Bertha to be fat and ugly.

A study of sixth graders in New Orleans by S. Gray Garwood concluded that students with names that were popular with teachers scored higher on skills tests and were better adjusted than students with names that were unpopular with teachers. A San Diego study concluded that essays written by students with popular names received higher scores than the same essays written by students with unpopular names.

That's why I recommend that parents make a list of the names they like best and then ask their friends what images each name calls to mind. One quick way to check the "personality profile" of common names is to refer to *The Baby Name Personality Survey,* a book I wrote based on a survey of 75,000 people conducted by Barry Sinrod.

How do I make up a brand-new name?

It is getting harder and harder to come up with a unique name because there are so many names in circulation. I recently published *35,000 Baby Names,* and though most people will find their own name in that book, it does not contain every possible name. One reason is that many people make up their own unique name, starting from scratch.

Making up a new name is kind of fun. You can take a common name and simply find a new way to spell it, like Cindeigh instead of Cindy or Cindee. Or you can throw in a new syllable, like Jonishah instead of Joan or Joni. If giving your baby a unique name is important to you, you probably ought to refer to a name book with lots of entries in it so you can see what names other people have used.

How important are gender considerations in naming a child?

I think gender is a more important consideration when naming boys than when naming girls. Boys with names that are thought to be feminine, like Caroll or Leslie, are likely to be teased during childhood. (The song "A Boy Named Sue," popularized by Johnny Cash, tells how difficult it can be for a boy to have a feminine name.) But girls can thrive with names like Pat, Chris, Robin, or Dana, which are commonly used for both boys and girls. In fact, these names often convey an image of competence when given to girls. Think about it. If you ran a newspaper, who would you rather have selling ads or doing an undercover investigative report: a woman named Chris or a woman named Priscilla?

Source: Bruce Lansky, author of *35,000 Baby Names* and co-author of *The Baby Name Personality Survey* (Meadowbrook Press, distributed by Simon & Schuster).

Child Abuse

How many children are victims of child abuse?

On average, every 10 seconds of every day, one child is being abused or neglected in the United States. In a recent year, over 3 million cases of child abuse and neglect were reported, although several studies suggest that even more children suffer than are reported through official statistics.

Who are the victims?

Most child-abuse reports were made for children under the age of one. In a recent year, about 51 percent were 7 years old or younger, and 26 percent were less than 4 years old. Just over half the victims were female, but girls were twice as likely as boys to be sexually abused. For victims younger than 12, males were more likely than females to be physically abused, but victims of physical abuse who were 12 and older were more likely to be female. Of children runaways, 70 percent are fleeing an abusive home environment.

Who are the abusers?

About 95 percent of victims know their perpetrators. Children are most often maltreated by parents or other family members. Recent data from 40 states show that 77 percent of the perpetrators were the victims' parents, and an additional 12 percent were other relatives.

The relationship of the perpetrator to the victim varies, depending on the type of abuse. A recent study found that while neglect and physical abuse were most often perpetrated by a natural parent, other adults and parent substitutes accounted for nearly half the perpetrators of sexual abuse. Research states that stepdaughters are six times more likely to be sexually abused than daughters who live with a natural father, and are more likely to be sexually abused by other men, especially friends of their parents.

The gender of the perpetrator also varied with the type of maltreatment. Neglect was more often perpetrated by females, and physical and sexual abuse by males. The typical child sex offender molests an average of 117 children, most of whom do not report the offense.

How many children are sexually abused?

Research shows that as many as 38 percent of all women and 20 percent of all men have been sexually abused during their childhood.

What are the most common types of abuse?

Neglect is the most common type of maltreatment among children. In a recent year, data from substantiated reports show that about 54 percent of the victims suffered neglect, another 25 percent suffered physical abuse, 11 percent were sexually abused, 3 percent suffered emotional abuse, and 6 percent, other forms of maltreatment. Some children were victims of more than one type of maltreatment.

Do children die frequently from abuse?

On average, more than 5 children die each day from child abuse, based on an estimated minimum of 2,000 children dying annually, although the National Research Council suggests that the actual number of fatalities may be much higher. Child abuse is the leading killer of children under four years of age.

How do the deaths occur?

Head trauma is the leading cause of child-abuse deaths. Shaken baby syndrome is so lethal that up to 25 percent of its victims die and most survivors suffer brain damage. Near-fatal abuse and neglect leave another 18,000 children permanently disabled each year, and an additional 141,000 are seriously injured. In the last several years, most deaths occured to children under five years old.

Is there any evidence linking alcohol or other drug use to child abuse?

A recent study by the U.S. Department of Health and Human Services found that 65 percent of the children maltreated by substance-abusing perpetrators were abused or neglected while the perpetrator was under the influence of alcohol or other drugs. In addition, children in alcohol-abusing families were nearly four times more likely to be maltreated overall, almost five times more likely to be physically neglected, and ten times more likely to be emotionally neglected than children in non-alcohol-abusing families. Approximately 25 percent of the deaths caused by child maltreatment involved parental substance abuse.

Who makes the reports?

More than half of all reports alleging maltreatment come from professionals, including educators, law enforcement and justice officials, medical professionals, social service professionals, and child-care providers. About 18 percent of reports come from persons related to the victim or from the victim herself. Approximately 10 percent of all reports are from anonymous or unknown sources.

Is corporal punishment legal in schools?

At present, over 50 percent of states continue to allow the use of corporal punishment in the classroom.

What effect does child abuse have long term?

Adults who viewed domestic violence in the home as children have a greater difficulty in holding jobs or maintaining relationships with their peers, and have a higher risk of developing mental health disorders.

Long-term effects of child abuse include fear, anxiety, depression, anger, hostility, inappropriate sexual behavior, poor self-esteem, tendency toward substance abuse, and difficulty with close relationships.

Sources: David S. Kurtz, Ph.D., Director of Childhelp USA, and the National Clearinghouse on Child Abuse and Neglect Information. Both provided information based on a synthesis from many different sources. For more information, call the Childhelp USA/IOF Foresters National Child Abuse Hotline toll-free at (800) 422-4453. Or contact: National Clearinghouse on Child Abuse and Neglect Information, P.O. Box 1182, Washington, DC 20013-1182; (800) FYI-3366.

Children and Religion

How do I respond to my children's questions about religion, which seem so hard to answer?

Children are known to ask tough questions, and some of the toughest can be about religion. Sometimes these questions are tough because parents may be in the process of redefining their own perspectives and may not have clear answers for themselves, let alone their children. Some may relate to religious behavior; others may relate more to spirituality, or to the internal experience of ultimate realities in the world. As with all tough questions, parents can keep their responses simple, appropriate to the age level of the child, and limited to what was actually asked. Philosophical or theological lectures are not necessary; honesty and authenticity are.

What should I say when they ask, "Why isn't everybody our religion?"

The developmental context here is the child's ability to notice the difference and the subsequent concern about whether "different" is "wrong." Differences can be explained by helping children understand that growing up in a particular family or cultural group makes it more likely we will share that family's or group's beliefs, at least initially. A child's concern about those differences can be addressed by acknowledging that we tend to think that what is not familiar is "wrong." Cognitive and faith development both require the ability to acknowledge multiple perspectives. Responding, parents can teach and model respect for other people, even those with whom we disagree.

And when they ask about why we practice rituals (like Lent, Passover, baptism, Ramadan)?

Rituals serve a number of functions within a family or religious community—such as defining membership, providing emotional healing and support, celebrating transitions, and expressing beliefs and values. As parents, you can give examples of times when rituals have been important to you or to others in the family or community. In addition, you may want to consider developing or modifying some rituals to make them more personal and significant for your own family. For example, a family with young children may make Christmas more significant by baking a birthday cake for Jesus; or a busy dual-career family may buy ready-made cookie dough for Hanukkah cookies.

This question is most likely to be difficult for parents who are themselves not sure about the history or meaning of such rituals. Parents need not be embarrassed to say that they are unsure of the symbolism, and can seek the answer along with the child. Clergy persons, elders in the faith tradition, or the local library might be resources for you to explore with your child.

"Do I have to go to church/synagogue/mosque?"

This question is perhaps asked most commonly by teenagers, since they are shifting their point of reference toward peers and exploring ways they may be different from their families. It is a healthy part of faith development, since it enables the teenager eventually to make an individual commitment to a belief system. In responding, parents can emphasize the value of community and a supportive network of those who share our beliefs. Parents may want to consider allowing the teenager some leeway in making personal choices about religion (for example, how often she joins in religious practices, or the freedom to experiment with other traditions).

My children ask so many questions about God, and life and death...how should I best answer them?

Questions about spirituality may include those about God (or an ultimate spiritual being), such as "Is there a God?" "If there is, what is God like?" "Does God know who I am?" "Where is God? "Why doesn't God answer all my prayers?" Often questions about life and death seem quite philosophical, as in, "What happens when we die?" "Where is heaven?" "Is there a hell?" "Why do bad things happen?" What children are really asking in these questions may be, "Am I cared for? Is the world a good place to be? Can I trust the people around me?"

Parents can respond by citing examples of times when the child or family has been cared for, when the parent has protected the child, or people have acted in dependable ways. Sometimes, parents live the answers to these difficult questions even when they cannot verbalize them. Conceptually, children will shape their ideas about God on the basis of their experience with their parents or other caregivers. The most important element here is to affirm that these are good questions, questions people have asked since the beginning of time and that many parents have also thought about.

What if I don't have specific answers ready for my child?

Don't feel embarrassed or incompetent if you do not have specific answers readily available. Families can talk and consult others (such as clergy persons, pastoral counselors, members of faith communities, funeral directors, or written materials). Parents know their own children best and will be able to ascertain whether a storybook, a video, or personal examples are most effective in communicating the family's values.

Do children need religion?

Research suggests that one of the characteristics of strong families is spiritual well-being, which incorporates a family's ability to deal with questions about ultimate realities (death, Supreme Being, responsibilities to others). Religious belief systems can provide a number of positive, enriching experiences, including a framework for meaning. When religious traditions are integrated into the family in positive, life-affirming ways, children are more likely to develop a sense of identity, connectedness, and purpose.

What happens to children who have no religious orientation or upbringing?

Humans seem to share a desire to understand the ultimate realities of life. While a religious framework is not necessary for understanding the ultimate realities or for nurturing spiritual well-being, it does provide training both in the content of beliefs and values and the process of applying these beliefs and values to life. When a religious framework has been absent from a family's experience, or has been applied with coercion and manipulation, children may need to work harder as they mature to develop a belief system that helps them understand and relate to the world.

What are some of the effects of interfaith marriages on children?

The core question here is how well the parents resolve their own religious differences. When parents and extended family respect the different practices and beliefs of each faith, children have the opportunity to feel connected to two communities and share a broader perspective for interpreting the world. They observe a model for valuing and respecting different traditions, and for finding areas of commonality and shared meaning. If, however, parents and extended family cannot resolve their differences, religion can be used to undermine the other parent's faith or to employ the children as pawns in a larger power struggle. Children then may experience conflicted loyalties and confusion over faith and family.

How can I make religion a good experience for my child?

Research suggests that families who are able to talk about these important questions in open, nonjudgmental ways are families whose experience of religion and spirituality is positive and enriching.

Sources: Judy Watson Tiesel, Ph.D., is chair of the National Council on Family Relations—Religion and Family Life Section; she is also a practicing family therapist and psychologist, Adjunct Assistant Professor at Saint Mary's University, Minneapolis, Minnesota, and Faculty Associate at Bethel Theological Seminary, St. Paul, Minnesota. Carla M. Dahl, Ph.D., is Associate Professor of Marriage and Family Studies, director of marriage and family therapy training programs at Bethel Theological Seminary, St. Paul, Minnesota, and vice chair of the Religion and Family Life section of the National Council on Family Relations.

Children and TV

How much TV does the average child watch?

According to researchers at the A. C. Nielsen Company, the people who pay close attention to this stuff, kids 2 to 11 watch about 22 hours of television each week. There are two really interesting things about this statistic. The first is that this figure is down from about 26 hours a week a few years ago, and getting lower. The reason it's getting lower is because kids now spend a lot more of their time watching videos and playing video games. In fact, if those two things were together on one TV network, it would be the number one network among children 2 to 11, by a mile.

The second interesting thing about this statistic is that parents generally average more TV viewing—about 28 hours per week—than their kids do. That's because parents, even more than their children, are apt to turn on the set and use it for background noise. Among other things, this means that a lot of the TV programming children see is really not intended for them but for adults.

So, there are two lessons here. The first is that if you're concerned about how much TV your children watch, think about the totality of their media use, and ask yourself if and how they benefit by it. Second, examine your own TV viewing habits and see if there isn't room for improvement. You can't beat the power of a good example.

So, what's wrong with children's TV?

Remember, whenever you turn on your TV set, you're turning your kids over to strangers whose only objective, at least on commercial channels, is to sell them to advertisers. If a stranger came to your door and asked if he could come inside and play with your children for 30 minutes while you made dinner, would you let him in? Look at your television with the same skepticism.

If you do, you'll notice a lot of unpleasant strangers. They're there because children's TV is ruled by economics. Children are a small audience and hard to make profitable. During peak children's viewing hours, for example on Saturday morning or about 7 P.M. on weeknights, the total child audience is never bigger than about 10 million. Even on Saturday mornings, when the concentration of children in the audience is greatest, there is still only one child watching TV for every five adults. The math is simple: In order to succeed, a children's television program has to be inexpensive to make, and it has to draw a big enough audience that advertisers will support it.

The result is predictable: Entertaining but educational programs get pushed off the air in favor of other programs that are cheaper to make and draw higher ratings. In 1995, for example, the ABC network pulled the plug on *Cro,* a critically acclaimed Saturday morning cartoon that illustrated basic principles of math and science, and put in its place an animated spin-off of the film *Dumb and Dumber. Cro* was watched by thousands of children—but not enough to keep it on the air.

In commercial broadcast television, the overriding issue isn't whether a program is good, or even whether millions of children watch it. Rather, the issue is whether any other program might make more money. That's why your children come home every day from school to see programs like *Jenny Jones* or *Inside Edition.* That is why one network, NBC, decided to get out of Saturday morning children's programming altogether and air news instead. And that is why so many of the remaining children's television programs aren't really programs at all, but commercials, programs based on existing toys whose primary purpose is to sell those toys.

What do some of the major studies tell us about the negative influence of TV on kids?

A lot. The influence of television viewing on children is perhaps the most studied social science question of the last 30 years, beginning in earnest with the 1972 Surgeon General's report ("TV Violence and the Child") that first linked violent programming to aggressive behavior in children. Since then, thousands of studies have sought to explore this link further, including most notably a

1982 study by the National Institutes for Mental Health and a 1992 study by the American Psychological Association.

For years the broadcast industry said these studies didn't prove anything, and in a sense they were right. If your Uncle Al smokes two packs of cigarettes for 30 years, then keels over dead one day with a heart attack, it's a good bet that smoking had something to do with it—but you can't prove it. After all, Uncle Al never exercised, and he ate steak and eggs for breakfast every morning.

Establishing this kind of definitive causality is equally impossible with television violence and social behavior, which is why researchers have gone to great pains to look at all kinds of children in all kinds of social settings. Several famous studies out of the University of Michigan have looked at cohorts of children over periods of 30 years or more. The result of all these studies is the same: Exposure to television violence does lead some children to behave more aggressively, and to become more aggressive adults. Often overlooked are the other effects of televised violence, namely, that it teaches children to accept violence as normal behavior and also that it leads many children to grow up with an overly fearful view of the world. Clearly, television violence is not the only cause of these behaviors, but it makes a significant contribution.

What can parents do to mitigate television's negative influences?

Here research confirms what common sense suggests: The most valuable thing you can do to ensure that your children benefit from television is to watch TV with them, or at least monitor what they watch. As obvious as this may seem, remarkably few parents actually do it.

There are two reasons why monitoring your child's viewing is important. The first, almost all researchers agree, is that children view television's messages much differently than adults do. Never assume that your child sees the same thing on the screen, and thinks about it in the same way, that you do. I once called out to my four-year-old from the kitchen, to ask what he was watching, and he responded, "Bill and Hillary." When I went into the family room to check it out, I discovered he was watching *The Beverly Hillbillies*.

The second reason to watch TV with your child is that when you do, you encourage him to become an active, critical viewer. You can teach your child to make interpretations, you can explain things she may find incomprehensible, and, most important, you have the immediate opportunity to tell your child why you object to something—whether it's sexist, racist, violent, tasteless, deceptive, unethical, unrealistic, or just plain dumb.

You also have the opportunity to discuss commercials with your child, and that's important. After all, the way that most television works is that when you turn on the TV set, you're the product; the real consumer is the advertiser, and the programs are just bait. This, too, is obvious, but it's amazing how many people don't quite grasp it. Make your kids wise to this little secret of the universe, and they will instantly achieve a level of media sophistication that eludes at least 98 percent of the adult population.

Can TV be good for kids?

Absolutely. Research by Children's Television Workshop (the outfit that produces *Sesame Street, Ghostwriter,* and other programs) and researchers like Harvard University's Gerald Lesser shows that programs with educational and pro-social objectives are measurably successful in realizing those goals. According to the U.S. Department of Education, for example, preschool children who watch *Sesame Street* are somewhat more likely to do better in school. Low-income children who watch the program are more likely to show literacy and numeracy skills. And in other Western democracies, most of which take educational children's television far more seriously than we do in the United States, research supports both the creation of good programs and a public policy that gets them on the air.

Sometimes, the benefits of quality kids' programs are unexpected ones. In the early 1980s, for example, researchers found that a PBS program called *The Electric Company* was particularly popular among children because it helped them with reading and writing skills in their homes, away from the pressure, and occasional humiliation, of the classroom.

Even commercial programming can be good for kids, provided that parents and children choose programs wisely and, whenever possible, watch them together. The key thing to remember is this: Your kid's brain is a lot more active than yours. By the age of 4, a child's brain is about twice as active as an adult's, and it stays that way through at least age 10, finally tapering off to adult activity levels at about age 16. That means your child's brain is literally soaking up information like a sponge. The better the stimuli, the better the brain development. Even the best television programming is inadequate stimulus by itself, and the worst television isn't anything you want your kid to soak up.

How much watching is considered okay?

There is no minimum or maximum. Some strong advocates of television rationing, such as pediatrician T. Berry Brazelton, recommend that children watch no more than an hour of TV on schooldays and two hours a day on weekends. But a more helpful question for every parent might be, Is there something better my child (or our family) could be doing with his/her time? Often as not, the answer to that question is yes. Sure there are times when for 30 minutes it's okay to turn on the tube; but like anything else, you don't want to make a habit of it.

How can a parent effectively monitor a child's viewing?

Ideally, the best way to monitor children's viewing is to watch television with them, as discussed above, and to encourage them to become critical viewers. When you do that, it's a lot easier, and more understandable to your child, when you try to set limits.

If you need more help, you can get it. By law, cable companies have to provide you with the ability to block out channels you don't want your kids to have access to. Plus, most electronics stores sell various kinds of lockout or TV timing devices you can use to control when and how much TV viewing your children do.

Soon other blocking technologies will be available. Under the Telecommunications Act of 1996, television manufacturers are supposed to install programmable computer chips in TV sets bigger than 13 inches. Known as the v-chip because it was conceived to limit kids' access to violent programming, this technology works only if the programmer rates its programs, and the major broadcast networks have said they will do that.

Has the TV children watch today gotten better or worse than a generation ago?

Children's programs themselves are probably not much better or worse, but the programming environment is certainly different. First, thanks to cable, there's a lot more children's programming available, much of it reruns of the stuff Mom and Dad watched growing up. There is some good programming on cable, on channels like Nickelodeon or Disney, but its quality is questionable and it's often heavily commercialized. On commercial broadcast TV, children's programming runs from abysmal to fair, depending mostly on whether and how hard the Federal Communications Commission is pushing broadcasters to use their publicly owned channels to serve children well, as the law requires. Public television offers some good programs for kids, but public broadcasting is starved for programming funds and, most experts think, will eventually lose all federal funding.

As far as the larger programming environment goes, children are exposed to a variety that Mom and Dad's generation never dreamed of. Again, thanks to cable, the competition for audiences leads programmers into previously taboo territory. Good or bad, much of that programming is definitely not for children. Today it is not at all uncommon, for example, to see a rape dramatized on prime-time television.

Are there any laws that protect children?

Not really. The First Amendment requires that children get special attention as listeners and speakers, and so, for example, the government still tries to regulate the broadcast of "indecent" programming. Also, the v-chip requirement is intended to protect children, but even in the best of circumstances it will require an attentive parent to be effective.

Another law—the 1990 Children's Television Act—is supposed to serve children, but it has not been very effective. The law requires broadcasters to air "some" "educational and informational" programming for children, but it doesn't say how much "some" is, when it should be on, or what the heck "educational and informational" means. As a result, it's easy for broadcasters to fill the letter of the law while trashing its spirit. Broadcasters often claim that programs like *Inside Edition, The Jetsons,* or *Leave It to Beaver* are educational. The Federal Communications Commission under Chairman Reed Hundt has been pushing hard to put some definitional backbone in the law, but so far without success.

How does the TV children watch in this country compare to that of other Western countries?

Actually, most other Western countries have strong children's television policies that provide children with high-quality noncommercial educational programs. One reason other countries have those policies is because they worry about the import of American programs, which they see as too violent and too commercial. As one British broadcaster told an American audience a few years ago, "You raise your children to be consumers. We raise ours to be citizens."

If you want to know where the information superhighway is going, follow the kids—everybody else is. Children are already one of the top target audiences for Internet providers, and while the Net is a fantastic resource for children, it is not a particularly child-friendly place.

The problem for kids is less pornography than games, advertising, and direct marketing. Having found little or no success with things like on-line banking, video-on-demand, or home shopping, many media companies have focused on services and programs for kids as the way into the American household. Some children's Internet sites are great, but many are not, and some are deceptive or just plain sleazy. From a marketer's perspective, the Internet is a great way to get your brand in front of young and predominantly well-off young people who have a lifetime of purchasing decisions ahead of them. The average age of Internet users today is 26; in four years it is expected to be 15.

It may be that the best rule of thumb for the future is the same rule of thumb that applies now: Look critically at what your children spend time doing, and whether and how they benefit by it.

Source: Craig LaMay, Assistant Professor, Medill School of Journalism, Northwestern University.

Choosing a Baby-Sitter

What references should I ask a baby-sitter for?

A minimum of two names, addresses, and telephone numbers should be made available to the parents at the interview. These names can include the baby-sitter's schoolteachers, scout leaders, guidance counselors, youth group leaders, or other parents he has baby-sat for.

What experience and qualifications should I look for?

The qualifications of a good baby-sitter should include an interest in young children, a sense of responsibility and honesty, and physical and emotional health. Also, the ability to supervise children's safety, carry out instructions, think clearly in emergencies, recognize safety hazards, provide first aid, prepare basic meals, play with children, and discuss job responsibilities and policies.

Are training courses available to become a qualified baby-sitter?

The American Red Cross offers a comprehensive baby-sitting course that can be taken by children 11 years and older. American Red Cross Community First Aid and Safety, Infant and Child CPR, and First Aid Progression are also recommended courses for young people interested in becoming baby-sitters.

What general house rules should be abided by?

The baby-sitter needs to be made aware of parent's expectations for his own conduct regarding visitors, TV, and snacks. The sitter should discuss with his employer policies on personal calls to friends and family.

How much should be reported on at the end of the evening?

The baby-sitter shouldn't needlessly tattle on children, but does need to make the parents aware of problems or concerns with behavior. The sitter should report good behavior and conduct as well.

What household responsibilities are considered the norm?

The baby-sitter should leave the house as orderly as he found it, which includes helping put away toys and tidying the kitchen after meals.

How much do I need to tell my baby-sitter about health issues?

Parents need to make the baby-sitter aware of any special health problems or allergies the children may have. The sitter will also need to know the types and quantities of medication that children may need to take while parents are away. If possible, the parent should administer medications prior to the sitter's arrival. The baby-sitter must be made aware of any serious symptoms—and remedies—for illnesses the children may have, such as diabetes or seizure disorder.

Should transportation to and from the job be provided?

Arrangements need to be made for the baby-sitter to arrive safely at the job, and to be escorted home at night, even if the distance is only two or three blocks away.

How can a fee be decided that will satisfy us both?

Wages should be negotiated by the baby-sitter with his employer prior to the job.

How much do I need to point out in my home?

A complete tour of the home should always be provided to the baby-sitter in order for him to become familiar with exits, door locks, light switches, fire alarms, telephones, fire extinguishers, flashlights, first-aid supplies, room arrangements, and play areas.

What contact numbers should be provided?

Parents need to provide the baby-sitter with information in case of an emergency, including the name, address, and telephone number where the parents can be reached; an alternate contact; emergency information such as 911 or the local emergency number; the telephone number of poison control; the family doctor's name and telephone number; and the telephone number, address, and nearest cross street of the actual home in which the sitter is working. This information should be kept with the sitter at all times.

What should be the rules on time of return or change of plans?

The baby-sitter should be made aware of the expected return time of parents, and parents should make a telephone call if these arrangements alter in any way. The sitter should know the whereabouts of parents at all times.

What emergency plans should be gone over with the baby-sitter?

All parents should have a plan that includes steps for safe evacuation in case of fire and that has been previously reviewed with the children. This plan should be discussed with the baby-sitter prior to taking on the job.

How much information do we need to give about a child's specific eating and sleeping habits?

The sitter should be made aware of appropriate foods for meals, mealtimes, nap times, and bedtimes of children he is caring for. This should include knowledge of bottle-feeding, burping, and preparing meals and snacks for toddlers and young children, as well as modeling good eating habits.

Should a baby-sitter answer the telephone?

Parents should inform the sitter of how they would like the telephone to be answered, or if they would simply prefer that calls be recorded by an answering machine. The baby-sitter should check with the parents before allowing young children to answer the telephone.

Source: American Red Cross, adapted from excerpts taken from a pamphlet, *Babysitting Instructor's Guide,* developed by the Badger Chapter, Madison, Wisconsin, © 1994 by The American National Red Cross.

Choosing a Child-Care Program

What's the best way to start looking for good-quality care?

A good place to begin a serious search is with your local child-care resource and referral agency. They know a lot about local choices, can refer you to specific programs and providers in your area, and can give you pointers about what to look for. Take time in choosing your child care. Look at several different programs, compare your choices, and ask plenty of questions. Talk to other parents about their experiences with the home or center you are considering.

How do I begin to evaluate programs?

Visit several child-care homes or centers, and plan to visit each program for at least an hour. On each visit, think about your first impression, but don't stop there. Keep in mind the best time to visit is in the morning. Try to include drop-off time in your observations so you can see how the children, parents, and caregivers interact. As part of your visit, make an appointment to talk with the caregiver for about 15 minutes after you've had time to observe the program. This may have to be during the children's nap time, with a follow-up conversation by telephone.

You should always visit a home or center more than once. And stay as long as possible so you can get a good feel for what the care will be like for your child. Even after you start using the child-care facility, continue to monitor and check out the care your child receives. The quality of a program can vary greatly over time, especially if there is staff turnover.

What specific things should I be looking for?

Does the place look safe and clean? Is the atmosphere bright and pleasant? Do the teachers enjoy talking and playing with the children? Do they get down and talk with each child at the child's eye level? Are there plenty of toys and learning materials within a child's reach? Is there a fenced-in outdoor play area with a variety of safe equipment? Can the caregivers see the entire playground at all times? Do the children sound happy and involved? Do the teachers speak in cheerful and patient tones? A place that's too quiet may mean not enough activity. A place that's too noisy may mean there's a lack of control. Are surprise visits by parents encouraged?

What should I know about the staff's training?

It's very important that the adults who care for your children have the knowledge and experience to give them the attention they need. Ask about the background and experience of all staff: the program director, caregivers, teachers, and any other adults who will have contact with your child in the home or center. Find out about the special training each one has had, as education and training have been found to be more important than experience and background. Providers who have special training in child development are more likely to be able to meet your child's individual needs at different ages, plan appropriate activities, and interact with children in warm and stimulating ways. They are also more likely to provide positive guidance for children rather than harsh discipline.

Is it important to ask about licensing and accreditation?

Yes. Licensing assures minimum health and safety standards have been met. Accredited homes and centers voluntarily measure up to national standards of quality that have been established by national child-care organizations, such as the National Association for the Education of Young Children (NAEYC) and the National Association for Family Child Care (NAFCC). They have gone beyond minimum licensing standards and have made a commitment to provide the kind of care, attention, and stimulating activities that you and your children require.

How much should I plan to spend?

Child care is often the second highest item in a family's budget. Parents pay an average of $3,500 a year for care, but experts estimate that good-quality care can cost up to $8,000 a year. Fees vary widely from area to area in the United States. The staff is an important factor in the quality of care, yet child-care teachers earn on average only $6.80 per hour. This causes high turnover, which affects the overall quality of a program and creates anxiety for children.

How important is group size and how many children should each caregiver be responsible for?

One of the most important factors contributing to the quality of a child-care program is the ratio of staff to children. Count the number of children in the group. Then count the number of staff members caring for them. Studies show that children benefit the most, socially and developmentally, from being in smaller groups: smaller sizes allow for more direct social interaction between children and caregivers.

Ask local experts about the best staff/child ratios for different age groups and types of care. A small number of children per adult is most important for babies and younger children.

Is being in child care good for kids?

Good-quality child care—in a safe environment, with trained, caring providers who offer stimulating activities appropriate to the child's age—helps a child to grow and thrive. Children in good child care are observed to feel more safe and secure, to have fewer behavioral problems, to be more proficient with language, and to display improved intellectual development. Recent research has raised alarms about the quality of care in the United States: Only 12 to 14 percent of children are in settings offering good-quality care. Another 12 to 21 percent of children—and 35 to 40 percent of the nation's infants and toddlers—are in settings potentially harmful to their growth.

Recent research also has shown that initiatives to improve the quality of care make a difference for children. Specifically, quality factors such as improved licensing regulations, provider training, improved education credentials, and fewer children per caregiver do significantly improve children's development.

How does child care in this country compare to that of other countries?

The United States is the only Western industrialized nation with no national policy or commitment to child care.

Source: Child Care Aware, 2116 Campus Drive SE, Rochester, MN 55904; (800) 424-2246 and Child Care Action Campaign, 330 Seventh Avenue (17th floor), New York, NY 10001; (212) 239-0138. To find your local child-care resource and referral agency for information on local programs in your community, tip sheets and information pamphlets, and checklists for checking out child-care programs, including after-school and summer programs, contact the Child Care Aware Information Hotline toll-free at (800) 424-2246.

Choosing an In-home Caregiver

What are the advantages of in-home versus out-of-home child care?

In-home caregivers offer many families an intimate and convenient arrangement, but on average cost more than other forms of child care, as one family pays the caregiver's entire salary. In-home caregivers are not regulated by states, and most of their interactions with your child will be unsupervised. Knowing that the caregiver you hire will become an important part of your family, your search must be thorough and careful.

Your most valuable assets in hiring an in-home caregiver are your instincts. Trust them. Do you feel comfortable with this person? What kind of "chemistry" exists among the candidate, you, and your children? If something about a potential caregiver is bothering you, eliminate that person from the search.

What are the different names for in-home caregivers, and how do their jobs differ?

- A *nanny* typically has some professional training, such as a college degree in child development or a certificate from a nanny school.
- An *au pair,* age 18 to 25, is someone from another part of the United States or a foreign country, who works for about a year in exchange for airfare, room and board, and a modest salary. Most au pair programs emphasize cultural exchange along with caregiving.
- A *baby-sitter* typically works fewer and more irregular hours than a nanny or an au pair and does not live in your home.
- A *housekeeper* may combine child care with substantial household chores several days per week.

How do I begin to look for an in-home caregiver?

You can find in-home caregivers through placement agencies, nanny-training programs, placing a classified ad, or referrals from relatives, friends, and coworkers. A good place to start is by consulting your Yellow Pages under "Child Care" and "Nanny." Your local resource and referral agency and national organizations can inform you of placement agencies serving your area. Nanny organizations also provide listings of training programs that place their graduates. These programs vary a great deal in the extent of training they give, ranging from a few weeks to a year. Ask about each program's curriculum to determine whether it is adequate to meet your needs.

How do you know if it is a good agency?

Ask to speak to families who have worked with the agency. Find out:

- How long has the agency been in business?
- How many placements does it make each year and what percentage of those placements last more than a year?
- What is the replacement/refund policy should a placement not work out?

- What professional standards does it maintain for its caregivers?
- Do the agency's background checks cover credit history, driving violations, and criminal records?
- Are its caregivers bonded (insured in case of theft)?
- Have complaints been filed against the agency with your local Better Business Bureau and/or Department of Consumer Affairs?

How can I search on my own?

Another option is to advertise in your local paper and on bulletin boards around town. At a minimum, your ad should specify your child's age, the hours of care needed, whether the position offered is live-in or live-out, the professional qualifications you require, and the benefits that you as an employer will offer.

What's the best way to prepare for the interview?

A caregiver is probably the most important employee you will ever hire, so set aside ample time to prepare for and conduct the interviews. If possible, interviews should be held in your home so your child can meet the candidate and you can observe how the candidate and your child get along with one another. Ask all candidates to bring the names and phone numbers of previous employers.

What specific issues should be discussed at the interview?

Before interviewing candidates, write a job description outlining what you think the caregiver's responsibilities should be. Think about a typical day in your home and how another person would fit in. Also consider how a caregiver's personal habits could affect your household.

- What are the days/hours the caregiver is needed?
- Will the caregiver live in or out?
- Does your child have special needs?
- Do you expect the caregiver to cook or clean or to drive your child to school or to visit friends?

You and the candidate should discuss and refine each responsibility listed on the job description. Encourage the candidate to ask questions.

What should I ask about the caregiver's personal background?

Review all of the candidate's education, training, and experience, and note the length of time she was involved in each activity. Discuss any gaps in the applicant's work history. Discuss the ages and gender of children with whom she has worked. Find out if the applicant has any training in first aid. Ask about the applicant's health, and make sure that there are no physical or mental conditions that would hinder her performance. Is the applicant energetic enough to engage your child?

What specific questions about child care should I ask?

Caregivers should know about child development and understand how children learn. They should be able to discuss activities that are appropriate for children of different ages. For example, ask what games she would play with an infant or how she would toilet-train a toddler. To assess the candidate's judgment, talk about how she would handle difficult problems.

Ask "what if" questions: What would she do if a child were injured, or how would she handle a child who wouldn't stop crying or misbehaved? Ask about the candidate's own upbringing and family life—people tend to raise children the way they themselves were raised.

How thoroughly should references be checked?

Never hire an in-home caregiver without checking references yourself—even if the placement agency claims to have screened the candidate's background. Talk to as many employers as possible, regardless of whether the job involved caring for children. Ask each employer what the candidate's responsibilities were, how long she worked there, whether she was dependable, what were her strong and weak points, why she left the position. If the work involved children, find out the children's ages and how they got along with the candidate.

Is it possible to observe the caregiver with my child before a decision to hire is made?

Once you have narrowed the field to one or two candidates, the potential caregiver should spend a day or two with your family and should be paid for her time. This observation period is the best way to learn whether both of you are comfortable working together.

Should we have a written agreement?

Once a caregiver is selected, it is important that both employer and caregiver are in agreement on all aspects of the job. Take the time to draw up a written agreement that includes: a comprehensive job description; salary and overtime policies; when and how salary will be paid; a probationary period; Social Security and income-tax deductions; sick leave, vacation, health insurance, and other benefits; giving notice; and rules regarding drinking, smoking, kitchen privileges, visitors, curfews, television, and telephone use. Also, make sure the caregiver has an up-to-date physical examination before starting work. (You may need to pay for this.)

What are my obligations as an employer?

When you hire an in-home caregiver for over 20 hours a week, you become an employer. As such, you must abide by state and federal fair labor practices and comply with IRS regulations for household workers. Check with the IRS, a tax adviser, or an accountant for up-to-date information on taxes, as well as any child-care benefits for which you may be eligible. Make sure you have the most recent

IRS booklet for household employers and employees. (Call the IRS at [800] 829-3676 to request its booklet on *Employment Taxes for Household Employees*.)

Source: Adapted from *Finding and Hiring a Qualified In-Home Caregiver,* Information Guide 20, Child Care Action Campaign. For more information on child-care resources and referrals in your community, and information pamphlets, call the Child Care Aware Information Hotline toll-free at (800) 424-2246. Or write: Child Care Action Campaign, 330 Seventh Avenue (17th Floor), New York, NY 10001; (212) 239-0138.

Discipline INTERVIEW WITH DR. LAWRENCE KUTNER

What are the fundamentals of discipline?

What's really important to understand is that *discipline* is different from *punishment*. Too many parents confuse the two. The word "discipline" has the same Latin root as the word "disciple": whenever you are disciplining a child, you are teaching the child. The question is, Are you teaching what you want to teach your child? If you haul off and swat a kid for misbehaving, you're probably teaching your child that big people can control little people with physical violence. That may not be the message you really want to get across.

How do you discipline effectively?

You not only have to point out what your kid's doing wrong, but you have to show your child what else she can do. A lot of times the things that annoy us about our kids are simply behaviors where they can't think of an alternative, especially young kids. If all of a sudden you get on the phone and the kid wasn't paying attention to you before, you become critically important. If you want your child to learn a better way or time to get your attention, you have to go beyond simply saying, "Don't do this, can't you see I'm busy right now?" You have to show them a different way of getting your attention. It's that teaching component that parents too often forget, and yet that's really the critical part of it.

What are some key ways to teach?

Acknowledge that your children want attention; they're not doing it to annoy you. Say, "Let me give you a hug. I have to stay on the phone. When I'm through, then I'll pay attention to you." If that doesn't work—and it probably will work with most kids—pay attention to them for just two seconds, and say, "Okay, you can stay right here by my feet, you can draw something for me." Give them something to do. That's very different from saying, "Why can't you just wait two minutes!" A young child can understand "I should wait" but can't think of "what I should do while I wait." You have to make that connection—make it more explicit for a young child.

How do you choose discipline that's right for your child?

You have to figure out what your goal is, what is really important. Safety is the number one concern for young kids because they just can't anticipate some of the dangers that they can get themselves into. Part of the key is understanding what your child can handle intellectually, and knowing what sorts of behaviors are appropriate for your child.

You can't have a three-year-old make his own bed. If you say, "You put these books over here and I'll put these blocks over here," *that* they can do. What you want your child to do is to have the opportunity to make appropriate decisions, to fail in safe areas, and to learn how to recover from those failures.

Is time-out effective?

Time-out is a wonderful technique, but one of the problems I've seen is people misapplying it; it doesn't work all of the time, and it doesn't work with every kid. I see parents say to their kid, "You're misbehaving, you spilled that milk, therefore go to your room, or go to the time-out chair for x number of minutes," and they will come up with a formula, one minute per year of age or something like that.

That is not what time-out is about. Time-out is a way of helping a child who's out of control to calm down, regain control, to chill out, and equally important, helping a *parent* regain a bit of control. You need to get your child out of the environment that is overstimulating him; this is where time-out really works. As far as helping the child learn how to calm himself down, the most effective use of time-out is to have it last as short a time as possible.

Why do kids have temper tantrums?

The child is emotionally overwhelmed and doesn't have the verbal skills to express that feeling. Temper tantrums are normal for two-, three-, four- and five-year-olds. They are so overwhelmed that they express it physically...they kick, they scream, they punch, they just fall apart. That's why it tends to disappear as kids get older, because they develop those verbal skills.

How do you handle temper tantrums?

Pay attention to the child without giving in to the behavior. First, physically pick up your child and move him, even if it's only two or three feet. That gives the message in a nonverbal way that you are really in control. Number two, you have to stay calm. Your child needs to borrow your emotional strength. If you fall apart and start screaming, it will just build up more and more, in a cycle. Talk your child calmly, helping him regain control.

You don't ever want to give in to the tantrum, because kids are smart, and if you give him the toy he's insisting on while he's having the tantrum, what's he going to do next time he wants something? Have a tantrum. Give the child another choice, of what tape you'll listen to in the car, or what book you'll read later.

Some parents will bite a child who repeatedly bites. Is that an effective means of discipling?

Absolutely not. Think of this as a teaching experience: What are you teaching your child? Look at why a child bites. Realize that a child is biting because she doesn't have the verbal skills to express intense emotions, the same as a temper tantrum. She is emotionally overwhelmed—and she bites.

What you want to do is help your child identify the emotion. "I can see that you are really angry that Billy took your toy." Let the child make that connection. And then you want to give your child alternatives. You need to show her a better way to show her frustration. There's a great Haim Ginott quote— that apples are for biting and sandwiches are for biting, but people are not for biting. That's a rule that a two-year-old can understand. But if you are really angry, and you need to show how angry you are, why don't we go over to the couch and you can punch a pillow. Biting her back gives exactly the wrong message.

Are bribery and rewarding effective?

As parents, we are really good at catching our kids being bad, but what we want to improve on is learning to catch them being good. We know that small rewards are much more powerful than big rewards. The problem with bribes is that they tend to be really inappropriate and they are for the wrong things. Let's take a kid studying for a spelling test. You say, "If you get an A on this spelling test, I'll give you a bicycle." The child can't control whether or not she gets an A and if the child feels she can't get an A, then why study? She's not going to get the bicycle.

Instead, ask yourself what your child can control. My child can control time spent studying and reviewing, so I'm going to reward that. "If you spend *x* amount of time studying, we'll go out for a slice of pizza."

What happens when parents have different discipline styles?

We all come from different backgrounds and have different assumptions about this. It is important to think about the critical issues, what it is that we really value as a couple in our kid's behaviors or upbringing. We have to work out compromises in our individual styles so that we are sharing that emphasis, so that the child knows that the message comes from both parents.

What if everything I try fails, and the kids just don't listen and don't do what I say?

Then you need an outside perspective and you need some help. People tend all too often think of going for help as an admission of defeat; it's actually an admission of intelligence. In other areas, we don't do that. If all of a sudden you started wheezing, would you have second thoughts about going to a physician? No.

There are multiple sources of help. One of the great things about parenting groups and parenting classes is that they give you a chance to see that you're not alone, to listen to other perspectives, and to hear other techniques.

What are some common mistakes parents make?

Parents fundamentally do a very good job. A lot of parents worry too much that if they make one mistake, their kid will be doomed forever, and that is simply not true. There are some things, like sexual abuse, that will have a major effect, but most kids are pretty resilient. Dr. Edward R. Christophersen, chief of behavioral pediatrics at Children's Mercy Hospital in Kansas City, Missouri, has a great saying—that God allows parents 10,000 mistakes before they have to apply for a refill.

Source: Lawrence Kutner, Ph.D. "Ask the Expert" columnist for *Parents* magazine, and author of many books on child development and parent-child communications, including the recent *Your School-Age Child* (New York: William Morrow, 1996). He wrote the internationally syndicated "Parent and Child" column for the *New York Times* from 1987 to 1994.

Divorce INTERVIEW WITH DR. STEPHEN P. HERMAN

What and how should we tell the children?

When it's clear to both parents that a divorce indeed is what's going to happen, and they've worked it through enough themselves first, in some families it's appropriate for both parents to tell the children at the same time. But in other situations it may be better and less tension-producing for everyone if each parent tells the child alone, pretty much within a close time frame, same day, and with a basically agreed-upon agenda. I think you have to be honest with your children; I think you have to tell them the truth in a way that's age-appropriate, but if there's a question about what or how much they should know, check it out with a counselor.

What reactions should the parents expect?

Children's reactions to divorce very often depend upon their developmental age, and parents should know a little bit about that. Everything from no reaction to complete and utter tears, anger, and tantrums depends on the age of the child, the personality of the child, and what the child has already gone through in terms of family experiences. You can get the full range of reactions in children of any age, from say three on, from no immediate reaction or just silent staring to the full gamut.

How do you tell if a child needs professional help?

Parents should expect that 100 percent of children develop symptoms when they experience their parents' divorce. There's no way to prevent a child from developing symptoms. The question is, Are the symptoms rising to a level that is interfering with the child's normal, everyday routine, either in terms of what a child is doing or how a child is feeling? And if there is any interference that's rendering the child unable to function or not function up to par, a parent should have it checked.

One of my criteria would be to check whether at least one parent is concerned enough to be asking the question, "Does my child need to see somebody?" And if a parent asks that question, it's worth checking with someone, because an ethical mental health professional is not going to sign up every child who comes to her for years and years of treatment.

Do you feel that most people in this situation could really benefit by having some counseling?

I think most people could really benefit from having *consultations* with mental health professionals familiar with divorce and the family. Absolutely. I'd love to see it required. "What should I be looking for? What should I be concerned about in myself, in my child; how do I know when to seek out ongoing help, if I need it?"

In some localities, there are court-mandated classes that parents have to attend prior to their divorce being adjudicated in court. And I think in Connecticut there are four different sessions, and one of them has to do with the emotional impact on the family, another has to do with finances. I think it is a good thing, if you get good people who are doing the teaching for parents, and making them sensitive to what's going on.

Will divorce leave scars that never heal?

Growing up in a loveless, sexless marriage leaves scars that never heal. And it's a question of parents coming to some kind of equanimity about the least detrimental plan for their children. While certainly divorce is a milestone event in the child's life, is never forgotten, and has lifelong repercussions, in fact, being scared doesn't render someone dysfunctional. Yes, there's hurt and trauma. But depending on how it's handled before, during, and after, the child can go on and live.

What steps can be taken to safeguard the child's best interests?

To allow as much as possible the child to have easy and frequent access with both parents, in which there is a reduction of tension and in which the child's needs are put ahead of each parent's needs. Whatever the custodial arrangement, whatever the living arrangement, whatever the legal arrangement, we know that children tend to do best after divorce if they have good solid relationships with both parents. Anything both parents can do to foster that is in the best interest of their child.

What inhibits the recovery from the traumas of divorce?

When one or both parents attempts for a variety of reasons to interfere with the child's easy access to the other parent. (I'm assuming that both parents are healthy and safe for the child. I'm talking about two basically normal parents who are divorcing.) If parents inhibit that, that's no good for a child. If one parent tries to ally the child against the other parent, that's no good for the child. If parents reverse the roles and seek the child out as a confidant and best friend to unload the parents' own heartbreak and anger, that's not good for the child.

How does battling over custody affect the children?

It magnifies a hundredfold or a thousandfold all of the pain and discomfort of a divorce, by putting the child in the middle of a tug-of-war where nobody is the winner, regardless of the legal outcome.

What are some alternatives to the custody battle?

No one alternative is right for all families. Some families need to go through the adversarial system for various reasons in order to reach some kind of denouement after the divorce. Other families could benefit from a mediated approach to custody. Mediation can work for some people, but the standards of the profession of mediation vary. Mediators come from many different professional backgrounds; there is no one way to mediate; and parents have to act as very smart consumers when they go for mediation, because a failed mediation can make a lousy divorce a truly horrible experience. Families have to be very careful about setting the boundaries of the mediation, who the mediators are, and what their goals are.

How would you like to see divorce handled better in this country?

I think any legal, constitutional means by which the government can track down fathers (mostly) who are obligated to pay and make them pay is important and helpful. Although, of course, fathers need to be worked with before it gets that far, so that children won't feel that they are being tossed away like trash because their fathers aren't paying.

We know that 90 percent of divorces end with the mother having custody of the children. That's about 1 million children a year in America who go through divorce, and 900,000 are them are going to end up living with their mother. And we also know that a woman's income tends to diminish significantly after divorce while a man's goes up. One of the forgotten parties to divorce is often the father. And this error is often made by mental health professionals. The correct way is for the mental health professional to say to the mother, "Look, whatever's gone on between you and your husband, these kids have two parents, and if I'm going to be helping your child or your children, I need to develop some kind of relationship with both parents. So I need to contact their dad, right from the start."

Source: Stephen P. Herman, M.D., a child and adolescent psychiatrist and pediatrician in private practice, who specializes in the medical-legal problems of children and their families. He is Associate Clinical Professor of Psychiatry at the Mount Sinai Medical Center in New York, and serves as a consultant to various courts in custody cases. Dr. Herman is the author of *Parent vs. Parent: How You and Your Child Can Survive the Custody Battle* (New York: Pantheon Books, 1990).

The Dreaded Sex Talk

Why do parents often dread talking to their children about sex?

Talking with your kids about sex is sometimes easy and sometimes difficult or uncomfortable, but it is always important. Sometimes we feel fine discussing sex with other adults, but when it comes to talking about it with kids, we may become

nervous—How will what I discuss with my kids affect them?
insecure—What if I don't know all the answers?
uncomfortable—Aren't my kids too young to know about sexuality?

These concerns are very common, and perfectly normal. But you're better equipped than you may think. In the long run, your kids will appreciate that you took the time to talk—and to *listen*—to them. By being accessible to your kids, you are giving them an invaluable gift, which they take with them through their teenage years and into adulthood.

What if I'm uncomfortable talking about sex?

Join the club. Most people are, and it's not surprising. Many people were taught that sex is too "dirty" to talk about. Some adults find it hard to admit that children are sexual. Some adults even find it hard to admit that *they* are sexual. Many of us fear the normal sexual feelings between our children and ourselves.

So, if you do feel uncomfortable talking about sex, you are certainly not alone. But you can still help your kids become comfortable with *their* sexuality. The best way to handle it is to be open with them about your feelings. When they ask questions—and sometimes they will and sometimes they won't—answer them honestly. If they don't ask questions, however, you should raise the issue yourself. If you're uncomfortable, let your kids know. Being "real" with them allows them to be "real" with you. You can start off by saying something like, "This is hard for me to talk about. My folks and I never discussed these things. But it's important that we do it differently."

Is it important that this information come from the parent?

Even though your child may not ask questions, or may be somewhat unresponsive when you bring it up, studies indicate that children *prefer* to get their information about sexuality from their parents.

Does talking to your children about sex prompt them to experiment?

Some parents are concerned that this is the case; however, the reverse is true. Young people who discuss sexuality, relationships, and values with their parents are actually more likely to postpone intercourse, and *less likely* to have unprotected intercourse, multiple sex partners, or to inject drugs. Teen girls whose mothers said they talked about sex with their daughters were *less likely* to have intercourse. And girls who said their mothers discussed birth control with them were *more likely* to use contraceptives effectively. It is never to early to begin these discussions—and it is important that your kids get *your* input.

How can you help your child avoid unhealthy sexual behavior?

We know that the best time to help youngsters avoid unhealthy sexual behaviors is *before* they ever have sex. So the time to talk is *now*. You may think (and your child may think) that they are getting enough information in school. However, fewer than 10 percent of American schoolchildren receive comprehensive sexuality education. Keep in mind that the world is a different place today from when you were growing up:

- 72% of boys and 66% of girls say they first learn about sex from someone other than their parents;
- 72% of *all* high school students have had sexual intercourse by the time they leave school;
- 3 million teenagers contract a sexually transmitted infection every year.

What do kids want to know about sexuality and when do they need to know it?

Youngsters learn about their sexuality from the day they are born. They learn an enormous amount about relationships, bodies, affection, and communication in the first year of life. By the time they are ten years old, youngsters have learned volumes from family, school, peers, television, books, advertising, and so on.

Young people want to know about their bodies, feelings, and how relationships work. It is important to help them feel good about their sexuality from the very beginning. This will make it easier for them to ask questions about sex throughout their lives. As they grow, we can give them useful information to help them make responsible, healthy decisions about their sexuality. What kids of all ages want most to know is that they're "normal." You can help them understand that *it is normal for everyone to be different.*

How do I explain the difference between love and sexuality?

Often, adults try to lessen the intensity of young adolescent feelings by using words like "crushes" or "puppy love." But to youngsters of all ages—and especially to those going through puberty—these emotional and sexual feelings are very real, and can be very strong. Parents need to respect this. Young people who understand their sexuality are better able to take charge of their lives and have loving relationships. They are also better able to cope with their feelings and with peer pressure. It is important to explain to children that there is a difference between love and sexual desire. Here is one way of explaining this difference: *Love* is a strong caring for someone else, and comes in many forms. There can be love for close friends, for parents and children, for a deity, and for humankind. *Sexual desire* is a strong physical excitement. Sometimes it is a fantasy, sometimes it is a heavy infatuation, and sometimes it is simply a flirtation.

Love can exist without sexual desire and sexual desire can exist without love. Many people are happiest when both love and sexual desire are shared by both partners. When it comes to love and sexual desire, however, it is normal for people to be different—in their feelings, needs, and behaviors. During puberty, your kids may begin to have strong feelings for different people in their lives. These can include friends, teachers, friends' brothers or sisters, etc. Sometimes, young people will have these feelings for someone of the same gender, and may wonder if this means they are homosexual. It is important to reassure them that these feelings are a normal part of growing up. They don't necessarily mean that someone is or will be gay, straight, or bisexual.

Where do my values fit in?

Basic values, beliefs, and attitudes about sexuality are established within the family structure. As a parent, you are your child's earliest and most important teacher about sexuality and values. You are not only a direct educator, but you also provide clues to what you think is right or wrong, without saying a word. For example, an adult who ignores or reacts negatively to a question about sex is implying that sex is bad, or that it shouldn't be discussed. Parents who answer their children's questions about sexuality openly and honestly send the message that sexuality is a normal part of life.

Values affect our behavior and the choices we make in our lives. As your children develop their decision-making skills and define their own values, it is important that you are clear about your own values. This will help you avoid confusing your kids when they have questions.

How can I explain without endorsing certain behavior?

It is important to explain the difference between facts and personal beliefs. You may believe that people should not have sexual intercourse until they are married. The fact is, however, that many people do have intercourse before marriage. Statements beginning with "I believe" or "We feel" will help your children understand the difference between your values and the factual information they need to make healthy decisions. Sometimes parents find it tricky to fit the subject of values into discussions about sexuality. It's hard to communicate your own values without dictating how your children should live their lives. At the same time, your kids need to know how you feel about sexual issues.

It can be helpful to talk through your values with your partner or spouse, religious counselor, or a close friend before you talk with your adolescent. Religion plays a role in many families and should be dealt with at home and in your religious communities. The issue of respect should be stressed: Your kids need to know that it is okay for them to disagree with someone who has different beliefs, but that that person has a right to her or his own beliefs.

Is there such a thing as too much information?

No. Information and education do not encourage young people to be sexually active. Kids make better decisions about sex when they have all the information they need and when there are no taboos on what they can talk about at home, and they are better at protecting themselves against pregnancy and disease once they do decide to have sex. It is not necessary to have a major conversation with your children each time they ask a question about sex. *Listen to them carefully.* Be sure that you are answering the question, rather than talking in general terms. Be sure they know they can ask follow-up questions. They may just want the answer to one question for the time being—and that's okay. Youngsters dislike hearing lectures when all they want is a simple answer to a specific question.

What should I tell my child about sex abuse?

The idea of sexual abuse can be very confusing for kids. They are told to respect adults, and to do what a parent or other family member tells them to do. It is important to make your child aware that there are some people who force others to have sexual intercourse or perform sexual acts against their will. You can help protect your kids by talking openly about what sexual abuse is, and the fact that they have the right to protect themselves. Make sure they know that

- No one ever has the right to touch them or make them do something sexually without permission, no matter who it is.
- People who have experienced sexual abuse are not responsible for what happened to them.
- Many kids are made to promise to keep sexual abuse a secret. But anyone who has been sexually abused should be encouraged to talk about it with a trusted parent, friend, teacher, or clergy member, who may be able to help stop the abuse.

How can I be frank about sexually transmitted infections and AIDS without frightening them?

Sexually transmitted infections can be very frightening, especially for youngsters. It's important to let your kids know that they can talk to you openly about their sexual health concerns. This can help ensure that they are diagnosed and treated if they become infected. It's also important to remind them that sexual relationships are a normal and healthy part of life. Sexually active people who practice safer sex can prevent infection if they have information and use it wisely.

AIDS can be a particularly sensitive subject. Chances are they have heard something about AIDS from friends or in the media, but they may not know the important basics. For example, do they know how AIDS is transmitted? Do they know that all sexually active people are at risk? Do they know that being young and straight is no protection?

The key to helping kids understand the basic facts about AIDS is to talk with them about it—often. Make sex and sexuality a relaxed and easy part of everyday conversation.

Source: Planned Parenthood® Federation of America, Inc., adapted with permission from *Talking About Sex: A Guide for Families,* ©1996 Planned Parenthood® Federation of America, Inc. All rights reserved. To order the *Talking About Sex* video, parent's guide, and workbook, call (800) 669-0156. To make an appointment at the Planned Parenthood health center nearest you, call (800) 230-PLAN.

Children's Parties

What kind of party does today's child want—an "at-home do-it-yourself" party or an "out-for-pizza/roller-skating" party?

The old-fashioned, less expensive home party is still a favorite among most kids today. Children are becoming increasingly tired of the generic prepackaged party that's not very original. Your personalized at-home party can be a piece of cake, with a little planning and some help from family and friends. It will also be memorable, since it will be tailored to your child's interests and needs. With a little imagination, the possibilities are endless, and the event can be easy, inexpensive, and much more fun. Check out the many kids' party books available, for ideas on easy-to-host homemade parties.

How do I plan for the party?

Work with your child to help develop plans. Divide the party into invitations, costumes, decorations, food, games, activities, and favors, for easy handling. Then begin preparing the invitations, which should go out two to three weeks beforehand, and decorations about a week before, tackling one or two projects each day with your child. Next, plan the games and activities that are age-appropriate, and check with your child to see which are the most popular. Save the food preparations for the day before, so everything will be fresh, and include a well-balanced diet, giving the treats silly names for fun. Buy or make inexpensive favors to send home, such as candy, stickers, comic books, or art supplies. When it's finally party day, everything will be ready to go!

Do I need a theme for the party?

A theme offers a focus, and provides guidance for the invitations, decorations, games, and food. You might ask your child for suggestions, or observe current interests and design a party around them. The theme might incorporate a favorite toy, a special movie, a sporting event, a storybook character, a superhero, a popular activity, or even your child's latest hobby. Once you've chosen the theme, the rest of the plans will fall easily into place.

Who—and how many—should I invite?

Have your child help you plan the guest list. Encourage limiting the invitations to good friends only, so you can manage the party size. If there are too many kids the event may turn to chaos. Many experts recommend that you invite the number of kids to match the child's age, so if your child is turning eight, invite eight kids. If you prefer a large group, ask a few of the parents to help out, or hire your usual baby-sitter, to keep things under control. Invite your guests through the mail or hand-deliver the invitations, but don't pass them out at school, so there are no hurt feelings.

How long should the party last?

A well-planned party begins and ends at specific times, clearly stated in the invitation. Two hours in the morning or afternoon is best, depending on your child's energy level during the day. As a general rule, hosting a two-hour party allows time for welcoming the guests, playing a number of games and activities, opening presents, sharing refreshments and cake, passing out favors, and saying farewells. A party that runs too long can make the kids restless and bored; too short may give the feeling of being rushed, with not enough time to satisfy anyone.

How am I going to keep the kids entertained for the length of the party?

Here's a rule of thumb: You can never have too many games! But you can have too few—and that can be disastrous if the kids run through them quickly or the party goes overtime. Celebrations turn to pandemonium when there's not enough to keep energetic kids busy. Plan quiet activities first, to help the guests warm up slowly in the beginning. Plan vigorous games—preferably outdoors—to help kids release that pent-up energy in the middle. End with a quiet game to calm down at the end of the party.

What about winners and losers?

Losing a game can take away the fun for some of the guests, so don't overemphasize winning, especially with younger kids. Losing often leads to disappointment, frustration, and tears. If your older guests appreciate competition, offer a few games that allow them the challenge, with group winners instead of individual winners. But try to offer enough games to give everyone a chance to win. For the losers, offer a consolation prize, or a funny booby prize, such as a rubber snake, oversized underwear, or a silly hat, so they have something to take home, too.

What do I serve a bunch of picky eaters?

Cake and ice cream are usually the highlight of a traditional party, and even though some kids don't like one or the other, they're expected. The cake can become part of the party fun if you let the kids help decorate it, or it can be a part of the decorations and atmosphere if made to incorporate the theme. The cake can even be healthy, if you use angel food or make a carrot cake and serve low-fat, low-sugar frozen yogurt on the side. You may want to limit other sweets and provide some healthy snacks, such as cheese and crackers, pieces of fruit, and cut-up veggies, so the kids won't overload on junk food.

What about the siblings of the guest of honor?

Often the brothers and sisters of the featured guest feel left out during these festivities. This can cause them to act out, cry, pull away, or just quietly feel hurt. You can help minimize this problem by having the siblings become involved in the party plans, give them special jobs to perform during the party, let them invite one friend, and incorporate them fully in the fun. Give the siblings a special gift before or after the party, to show your appreciation for their help.

What if the birthday guest of honor misbehaves?

Party time is often overwhelming, sometimes bringing out new emotions in the kids. Some kids who are made the center of attention just go wild and become out of control; others feel embarrassed at being the focus of the event and may prove unpleasant, ungrateful, or unhappy. Give your child time to relax before the party, to relieve the stress of all the excitement. Plan a few quiet activities or distractions both before and after the party.

Understand and acknowledge your child's moods and feelings, and help him find positive ways to enjoy this very exciting day. If your child needs a break in the middle of the party, ask him to help serve the food, set up a game, or do a special task. Keeping your child busy will help him enjoy the party and cope with being the star.

Source: Penny Warner, author of over 20 books, including *Kids' Pick-A-Party* (Deephaven, MN: Meadowbook Press, 1997), and *Kids' Party Games and Activities* (Deephaven, MN: Meadowbrook Press, 1993), both distributed by Simon & Schuster; and *Birthday Parties for Kids* (Rocklin, CA: Prima Publishing, 1995). She has written numerous articles and columns for magazines and newspapers, and is a college instructor in childhood development, special education, and sign language.

Head Lice

How common are head lice?

Head lice infestation continues to be a problem nationwide. It is not a reportable disease, therefore there are no official statistics, but estimates based on the sale of lice treatment products indicate there are up to 12 million cases a year.

Are head lice contagious?

Yes. Lice are highly communicable and difficult to prevent. In this country, with the exception of the common cold, lice is the most common of all communicable childhood diseases among school-age children.

What symptoms should I look for?

Watch for one of the most common signs of head lice: frequent scratching. Children seen scratching their heads repeatedly should be examined at once, as the itching occurs when lice inject histamines and suck blood from the scalp. Often red bitemarks or scratch marks can be seen on the scalp and neck.

What do lice look like?

Lice are small, wingless insects about the size of a sesame seed. They are usually light brown or reddish-brown but can vary in color. Lice eggs, called *nits*, are tiny, grayish-white or yellowish-white, always oval-shaped, and are glued at an angle to the side of the hair shaft. The way a nit is attached is its most distinguishing factor.

How do children get lice?

Lice cannot jump or fly. They are usually transmitted by direct contact with infested persons from head-to-head contact, but also from sharing hats, clothing, combs, or brushes. Children should be warned against sharing such personal items.

Can my children get lice from our cat or dog?

No. Household pets do not harbor head lice.

Do head lice have anything to do with poor hygiene?

Anyone can get head lice, which have been a parasite of humans since recorded time. Many people associate lice with unclean people or homes. This is not true in the case of head lice. Frequent bathing or shampooing will not prevent lice or eliminate them once they are established.

How do I look for lice?

Lice move quickly and shy away from the light, making them difficult to see. Identifying lice is generally done on the basis of finding nits, which can be seen much more easily and are visible to the naked eye in natural light. It used to be thought that nits would only live about ¼ inch from the scalp, but now evidence suggests that nits may be found at any distance from the scalp throughout the hair, but are most often located at the nape of the neck, behind the ears, and at the crown. Unlike lint or dandruff, they will not wash off or blow away. A magnifying glass and natural light may help when looking for them.

What do you do if you discover your child has lice?

Before treating your child, check to see if other family members are infested. Remember, all lice-killing products are pesticides. If you choose to purchase an over-the-counter treatment, it is important to follow the directions carefully and use with caution. Always have the child lean over the sink, not in the tub or shower, as this confines the lice product to the scalp and neck. Always keep the eyes covered with a towel or washcloth. The National Pediculosis Association (NPA) strongly discourages prescription treatments containing lindane. Since there are increasing reports of possible insect resistance on a national level to prescription treatments and some over-the-counter treatments, the NPA advises parents to discontinue their use at the earliest sign of failure. Manual removal is the best option whenever possible, especially when treatment products have failed.

Consult your pharmacist or physician before applying lice treatments when the person involved is pregnant, nursing, has allergies, asthma, epilepsy, a preexisting medical condition, or has lice or nits in the eyebrows or eyelashes. Never use a lice product on or near the eyes. Never use a lice product on your baby!

How do you remove the nits?

Separate the hair in sections and remove all attached nits either with a special lice comb designed for that purpose or with baby safety scissors or your fingernails.

Is it important to remove all the nits?

Yes. This assures total lice treatment, as lice products don't always kill all the eggs, which can then hatch into crawling lice within seven to ten days if they are not removed from the hair. Nit removal is also important in terms of appropriate public health standards.

Can lice be misdiagnosed?

Yes. Be sure to not confuse nits with hair debris such as bright white irregularly shaped clumps of dandruff stuck to the hair shaft, or elongated segments of dandruff encircling the hair shaft that are easily dislodged. If a parent has complied with necessary treatment guidelines but sees ongoing problems with nits without evidence of lice, it may be a misdiagnosis. Too often nits are confused with hair debris and children are treated unnecessarily. Lice treatment is not appropriate for hair debris.

How can I prevent lice from returning?

Machine-wash bedding and recently worn clothing in hot water and dry in a hot dryer. Combs and brushes may be soaked in hot (not boiling) water for 10 minutes. The National Pediculosis Association and the Centers for Disease Control and Prevention strongly discourage the use of lice sprays. They consider vacuuming the safest and best way to remove lice or fallen hairs with attached nits from upholstered furniture, rugs and carpeting, stuffed animals, and car seats.

Check all family members for lice and nits at least once a week for two to three weeks. This is the best way to protect your family and community. Regular checking and early detection is the best prevention. And when you find a case of lice, tell others! Call your child's school and child-care provider, and notify neighborhood parents.

Source: Adapted from *10 Steps to Help Keep Head Lice and Their Eggs Out of Your Child's Hair,* and other materials from the National Pediculosis Association, Inc. (www.headlice.org). For more information, send a self-addressed stamped envelope to: National Pediculosis Association, Inc., P.O. Box 610189, Newton, MA 02161-0189. Or call: (617) 449-NITS 24 hours a day to hear an educational message on head lice. To report outbreaks in your community, treatment failures, or adverse reactions to products, call (800) 446-4NPA. (This is a reporting line only.) The NPA also offers a state-of-the-art nit/lice removal comb, the LiceMeister. It retails for $14.95 plus shipping and is available by calling (617) 449-NITS, ext. 108.

Sibling Rivalry

What causes sibling rivalry?

At the root of sibling rivalry is each child's deep desire for the *exclusive* love of his parents. Why this craving to be the one and only? Because from Mother and Father, that wondrous source, flow all things the child needs to survive and thrive. It is parental love and encouragement that enables a child to grow in competence and slowly gain mastery over his environment. Why wouldn't the presence of other siblings cast a shadow upon his life? They threaten everything that is essential to his well-being. The mere existence of an additional child or children in the family could signify *less:* less time alone with parents, less attention for hurts and disappointments, less approval for accomplishments.

Why does sibling rivalry create so much tension in families?

Take any two kids in competition for their parents' love and attention. Add to that the envy one child feels for the accomplishments of the other, the resentment that each child feels for the privileges of the other, the personal frustrations that they don't dare let out on anyone else *but* a brother or sister, and it's not hard to understand why in families across the country, the sibling relationship contains enough emotional dynamite to set off rounds of daily explosions.

Is there anything about sibling rivalry that might be good for children?

A case can be made for the uses of some conflict between brothers and sisters: From their struggles to establish dominance over each other, siblings become tougher and more resilient. From their endless roughhousing, they develop speed and agility. From their verbal sparring, they learn the difference between being clever and being hurtful. From the normal irritations of living together, they learn how to assert themselves, defend themselves, compromise. And sometimes, from their envy of each other's special abilities, they become inspired to work harder, persist, and achieve.

What is the parents' role in the sibling relationship?

Parents need to find the ways to reassure each child that she is safe, special, beloved; they need to help the young antagonists discover the rewards of sharing and cooperation; they need to treat each child as an individual—not in relation to her sisters or brothers; they need to help their children express their savage feelings in civilized ways.

What can you do when one child says something hostile about another?

The very emotions that we want to close the door on and lock out need to be invited in and treated with respect. Children need to be able to air their feelings and wishes about their siblings, even the unsavory ones. It is important, however, to make a distinction between allowing *feelings* and allowing *actions*. All feelings are permitted; *hurtful behavior is not allowed*. For example, "I can see how mad you are at your brother, but I can't let you hurt him. Tell him what bothers you with words, not fists."

Is there anything parents should avoid doing?

- Resist the urge to compare, either favorably or unfavorably. The important thing is to stick with the issue of this one child's behavior; what her brother or sister is doing has nothing to do with her.
- Instead of worrying about treating the children equally, focus on each child's individual needs.
- Avoid the temptation to assign a different, mutually exclusive role to each child, e.g., the scholar, the athlete, the musician, etc. Every child should feel free to explore all of her potential.
- If one child attacks the other, don't give your attention to the aggressor; attend to the injured party instead.

What can you do when the kids fight?

If it's low-level bickering, you can ignore it. If you think the situation may be dangerous, ask: "Is this a play fight or a real fight? Play fights are permitted, real fights are not." If the children are about to hurt each other, you can say, "I see two children who are so angry they want to hurt each other. This is a very dangerous situation. We must have a cooling-off period. Quick—separate! You go to one part of the house, you to another."

Is there any way parents can help children resolve their differences?

We recommend a five-step approach:

1. *Acknowledge their anger.*
   "You two sound mad at each other!"
2. *Reflect each child's point of view.*
   "So, Sara, you want to keep on holding the puppy, because he's just settled down in your arms. And you, Billy, feel entitled to a turn too."
3. *Describe the problem with respect.*
   "That's a tough one: Two children and only one puppy."
4. *Express confidence in the children's ability to find their own solution.*
   "I have confidence that you two can work out a solution that's fair to each of you...and fair to the puppy."
5. *Leave the room.*

But what can you do if the children can't work out a solution that's fair to each of them?

You can tell them, "Children, this time I'll decide. And you may not be at all pleased with my decision. Right now, the puppy will come with me. But later, after dinner, we need to sit down together and work out some guidelines for what to do when you both want to hold your pet at the same time."

What can I do to make sure my children become friends?

Instead of worrying about your children becoming friends, think of using the natural friction that occurs between siblings to teach them the attitudes and skills they'll need in any relationship. For example, they need to know how to really listen to each other, how to move past who is right and who is wrong, and how to respect and resolve differences. Even if their personalities are such that they could never be close, at least they will have the power to make a friend and be a friend.

Source: Adele Faber and Elaine Mazlish, lecturers and authors of many best-selling books on child/adult communication, including *Siblings Without Rivalry: How to Help Your Children Live Together So You Can Live Too* (New York: W. W. Norton and Avon Books, 1987).

Special Needs INTERVIEW WITH DR. STANLEY D. KLEIN

When a newborn baby is diagnosed as having a disability, what happens to the parents?

It is shocking news to learn that a newborn baby has a disability. Hopefully, both parents are informed together by the physician who has made the diagnosis. However, even when the doctor is compassionate and demonstrates concern for the new parents, it is a normal, healthy reaction for parents to be very upset and to experience a wide range of emotions. Parents have endured a major loss: They have lost the healthy, normal baby they had anticipated. From an emotional or psychological perspective, they will undergo intense feelings very similar to those any person experiences when a loved one dies. At the same time, as the parents relate to the baby they actually have, they also undergo strong feelings of loving and caring. Accordingly, parents go through an extremely complicated emotional process of beginning to mourn the healthy baby they had expected, and beginning to love and bond with the newborn baby with a disability.

What can the parents do?

By contacting experienced parents of children with similar disabilities, new parents can ask questions that give them emotional support and a sense of hope. Emotional support comes from finding out they are not alone and meeting other parents who are coping. They can also get information by asking questions. Although being able to talk with an understanding and experienced professional can also be helpful at this time, most parents report that personal contact with experienced parents is more important. If such connections are not facilitated in the maternity setting, parents can contact the many outside sources available.

New parents also want straightforward, understandable information about their child's specific disability or diagnosis: what it means; how it may have been caused; and, most important, what they can do to help their baby. They can usually receive such information by contacting the local or national offices of national parent organizations.

Babies with disabilities and their parents can also be assisted by so-called early intervention programs in every state in the United States. These programs provide a range of services, including specific therapies, specialized equipment, and parent education.

When a child is diagnosed as having a disability after parents or professionals have noticed some problem(s) in his development, what happens to the parents and what can they do?

As with parents of newborns with disabilities, these parents are likely to experience a profound sense of disappointment and loss, and begin to mourn for the "ideal" child they had imagined. Again, parents can benefit from support groups of other parents, as well as from the information that is available via local and national organizations.

One important difference is that parents of children diagnosed after birth may also experience a sense of relief upon learning that their own worries were correct. Unfortunately, far too often, when parents become concerned about a baby's behavior and suspect a problem, busy professionals or well-intentioned friends tend to try to reassure them by explaining that individual children develop at different rates and/or that some parents tend to worry too much. It is far more appropriate for professionals to pay attention to and acknowledge parental observations and worries, and to try to determine the source of such concerns, for two reasons. First, research has shown that parents' observations are often accurate; second, when professionals make light of such observations, young children in need may miss out on the opportunities available via early intervention.

If a child is diagnosed before being old enough to go to regular public school, parents need to find out about available early intervention and preschool services. According to federal law, children with disabilities and special health-care needs, and their parents, are eligible to receive a range of intervention services.

When a child has a disability or special need, what kind of discipline should parents employ?

All children benefit from "discipline" that takes into account each individual's strengths and weaknesses, and encourages the child to learn appropriate behaviors and develop self-confidence. As much as possible, parents can "discipline" children with disabilities just as they "discipline" other children in the family. Discipline means far more than rewards or punishments for specific behaviors; it means providing guidance and information about how children are expected to behave as they grow and mature. It is helpful that parents agree on and communicate similar expectations to the developing child, and do so in as consistent a fashion as possible.

Several facts are clear and can be applied to all children—those with disabilities as well as those without disabilities. The most important of these facts is that physical punishment (hitting, spanking, etc.) is not a constructive way to teach appropriate behaviors.

The most effective reward for most children is the approval of their parents. This is one reason why a brief time separated from parents (for example, being sent to the child's room) can be an effective consequence of misbehavior. A parent expressing pride in a child's accomplishments is likely to be far more effective than any actual prize or financial reward. Parents hope that children will learn to feel personally proud of themselves. Sometimes parents may unnecessarily lower their expectations when a child has a disability. Usually this occurs when parents feel that day-to-day life is difficult enough as the child confronts certain limitations caused by a disability. While it is painful to confront one's limitations, parents cannot take away or balance that pain by lowering their expectations.

What can parents do to help the brother or sister of a child with a disability?

Most of all, siblings of children with disabilities need to learn about their brother or sister's disability. Parents can teach about disabilities or illnesses at whatever level a child can understand, and try to answer questions. They can also explain the good and positive characteristics of the child with a disability as well the child's limitations.

It was once believed that a child with a disability in a family had a negative impact on brothers and sisters. Most of the time this is not true. Rather, brothers and sisters of children with disabilities often grow up to be more understanding of and patient with human differences. It seems that a negative impact is more likely when the child's disability is hidden from brothers and sisters and/or is not an acceptable topic of family conversation.

Siblings of children with disabilities or special health-care needs also benefit from opportunities to meet with other boys and girls who are the siblings of children with disabilities. In recent years, more and more programs for children with disabilities and their families have established specific programs for brothers and sisters, too. Such groups have been effective for elementary-school-age children (who may discuss sharing parents' time, teasing by other children, and other topics), and for adolescents, who are likely to discuss future responsibilities and are seeking information about whether their own children are prone to have disabilities.

When a child with a disability reaches school age, is that child better served in an educational program with so-called normal children or in a separate program?

Many children with disabilities are likely to need some special assistance in school on a regular basis. At the same time, many parents and professionals believe that such special needs can be met within a regular school setting without interfering with the academic and social learning that ordinarily takes place in such settings. These parents and professionals are likely to support the "inclusion" of children with disabilities alongside their peers without disabilities. In settings that have sufficient human and financial resources, inclusion programs seem to work well for many children with disabilities.

Most parents and professionals also believe that it is helpful to the personal development of children with disabilities to have opportunities to interact with other children who have similar disabilities. This seems especially important as children approach adolescence.

Sometimes, the needs of some children with disabilities cannot be met within a regular classroom setting. It is also true that the presence of some children with disabilities (or without disabilities) may not be constructive for the educational needs of other children in the same classroom.

Some parents send their children to private schools or religious schools, and some decide to educate their children at home. Parents of children with disabilities do not always have the same choices, because only public schools are required to address the unique educational needs of all children with disabilities.

Which is best? There is no one answer. I believe that parents are the most informed experts about their own children. Some children with disabilities who require highly specialized assistance will need a separate educational setting. When and where it is possible for students with disabilities to be educated with their peers, studies show they tend to do better socially and academically. But each child, family, and educational opportunity must be addressed individually.

Source: Stanley D. Klein, Ph.D., clinical psychologist and educator, co-founder and editor-in-chief, *Exceptional Parent* magazine. Since 1971, *Exceptional Parent,* the only monthly national magazine of its kind, has provided practical information and emotional support for parents and professionals concerned with the day-to-day lives of children and young adults with disabilities and special health-care needs. For information about subscribing or other information, call (800) EPARENT.

Programs for the Gifted

What is *giftedness?*

The U.S. Department of Education defines gifted and talented kids as "...children and youth who

1. give evidence of high performance capability in such areas as intellectual, creative, artistic, or leadership capacity, or in specific academic fields;
2. require services or activities not ordinarily provided by the school in order to develop those capabilities fully."

How are gifted children identified?

School systems may consider a variety of indicators when identifying gifted kids, including achievement tests, which measure scholastic achievement in subjects like math and reading; intelligence tests, which measure general intellectual ability; and creativity tests, which measure the ability to generate original ideas or think in new ways. Schools may also use other kinds of tests to assess talent or glean additional information, especially when a child is from a minority group. In school systems where tests for giftedness are not available, a university education program may be able to point the family toward special programs that do offer such tests.

What can parents do to help their gifted children reach their potential?

Gifted children whose parents take an active role in making sure they are challenged in school, who provide opportunities for learning and growth outside of school, and who help them to nurture friendships with children of both their biological age and their intellectual age are the ones that truly thrive. For a preschool-age child, this might mean a mixed age group (so long as she is not the oldest member). For a middle schooler, it could mean a summer camp designed for the gifted. For a high school student, a class or two at the local community college or a university could fit the bill.

Should gifted children start school early or skip a grade?

Starting school early is a simple way to give gifted kids the additional challenge they crave. When they start early, gifted youngsters have an easier time adjusting to an older peer group. For carefully selected students, skipping a grade is acceptable, provided both the academic profile and the child's social readiness are in sync. Teachers and parents must both support the decision, and monitoring should continue into the academic year.

What kinds of programs are out there?

Some programs offered by states and universities provide advanced study in areas of academic interest, while others let students take a hands-on approach to a professional field, with adult mentors to guide them. Admission criteria vary; being "certified" as gifted by a school system or testing facility may not be necessary. School guidance counselors, public library resource librarians, and university education departments can assist parents in locating appropriate programs.

Are there advantages to choosing a gifted summer program over regular camp?

A chance to spend time with intellectual peers is one of the greatest gifts parents can give their gifted children, whose abilities can set them apart socially from "normal" kids their age. Other advantages of summer programs are an opportunity to focus in depth on a favorite subject; a place to delve into a new area of interest inaccessible during the school year; a chance to explore future career options; and a way to preview college life by staying in a dorm on campus.

How should parents choose a summer gifted program for their children?

After narrowing the choice down to several attainable options, parents should let their children take the lead in selecting a program that really gets them excited about their summer plans. Students who have a say in where and how they will spend their summer get the most out of the experience, as any program counselor knows. And the selection process itself is a growth experience, providing a trial run for college selection a few years down the line.

What should parents and children think about when picking a program?

Aside from cost and location, there are a number of factors to consider:

- *Selection criteria:* How rigorous are the admission requirements? A program that demands writing samples or fluency in a second language attracts a different group than would a program that merely says it admits "gifted middle schoolers."
- *Success and failure:* What provisions are made for those who excel? What kind of support is offered when a child fails at something?
- *Size:* Both program size and staff/student ratio can affect a child's experience. Is there a chance for one-on-one time with teachers?
- *Participant age:* Will the child be among the youngest or oldest there? Is there a chance to interact with undergraduate college students?
- *Staff qualifications:* Expertise makes all the difference—writing programs should feature experienced writers; debate programs, winning coaches and college stars.

Is special financial assistance available for gifted students?

Many summer programs for gifted and talented students offer financial aid based on need, merit, or some combination of the two. Private schools also seek gifted students and may offer financial incentives to attract them. And local chapters of organizations such as the Rotary Club, the League of Women Voters, or the NAACP may offer scholarships for summer programs. Inquire about these options well in advance of the application's due date; the deadline for financial aid requests often occurs much earlier.

Source: Peter Rosenstein, Executive Director, National Association for Gifted Children, Suite 550, 1707 L Street NW, Washington, DC 20036; (202) 785-4268.

Talking to Your Terrible Teen

INTERVIEW WITH DR. CHERYL K. OLSON

Why are the teen years so dreaded?

One of the basic misconceptions people have is that adolescence is going to be hell for the family, and our popular culture promotes this idea—that they are going to be out there stealing cars, taking drugs, having wild sex with strangers, openly rebelling against you and everything you stand for. Research has shown that's just not true, that the values that you've instilled in your kids over the years are pretty much going to be there. And while your kids may have purple hair or more earring holes than you would like, that doesn't mean they aren't seeing the world in much the way you would underneath it all. You don't have to dread it. Dreadful behavior, horrible time is not normal.

What are some ways to get conversation going when my teen is standoffish?

Teenagers do get a little bit more moody, they do want more privacy, but that doesn't mean they don't want to talk or do things with the family sometimes. For example, if your kid comes home looking like he had a bad day, you can say, "You look kind of down, do you want to talk about it?" and he might say, "No," or "Leave me alone." And you can say "Okay" and leave it at that. And he may come back to you later and want to talk. The key is to not make them feel that they *have* to tell you everything, but to let them know that you are available to listen. It can help to start a conversation over a shared activity, such as doing dishes or recycling newspapers. That leaves your teen free to talk without feeling on the spot.

Why is my teenager so argumentative and moody?

The basic task of a teenager is to establish herself as a separate human being. It's not that they are trying to make you look like an idiot, it's that their brains have been maturing at a tremendous rate and they are now able to see shades of gray. They almost can't help getting into discussions, arguments, just because they've got to try out these new ways of looking at the world and to see things from different perspectives. Insist on ground rules. Say, "Look, I want to discuss this with you but I don't want you to call me a 'Butt-head.' I don't mind arguing with you, what I mind is your being rude." Another thing that causes a problem is this feeling that you want your teenager to like you, but they want to know that there are real limits there. If you keep backing up and saying, "Well, maybe I don't feel as strongly about this as I thought," that can be a little scary for them. So it is important that you tell them: Here is what I believe about this and why I believe it. For example, I don't worry so much if someone experiments a little bit with alcohol and has a drink, but I feel very strongly that a teenager should never get into a car with someone who has been drinking and who is planning on driving, because I know that has a very high likelihood of killing them. That's how most teenagers die.

Why do teenagers, who are capable of reasoning and logic, do such stupid, risky, and irresponsible things?

There is this real feeling that "I'm special," that "I'm invulnerable, and nothing bad can really happen to me." That's why we still get kids who think they can't get pregnant the first time. Even if they know intellectually that something can happen, they don't have the perspective that we have as adults; we've seen these things happen. A lot of the information we give them is not put in terms that are relevant to them. If you tell a kid that smoking will give you lung cancer when you are in your 50s or 60s, that's like two centuries from now, they can't picture that. Talk about health risks in a way that they can relate to, like smoking might cut down your performance on the track team, or your breath smells bad when you want to kiss somebody. Or if you drink too much and get drunk, you might throw up and embarrass yourself, or end up in bed with someone you would never want to be with. Also, you can point out other kids their age who have had a problem, or talk about when you were a kid.

What do you say to your teen who wants some of the same freedoms to experiment that we had as teenagers?

I don't think there is anything wrong with saying, "When I was growing up there was this feeling that a really free and independent person would try everything. Here's things that I did that I felt good about and worked, and things I've felt bad about and that didn't work for me." What is important is to not *preach* to the teenager, but to *share* with them. Here is what I hope you would do in these situations, and here is why I hope that. I don't think it is hypocritical to say, "I don't want you to have sex until you are older because I think it will be a harmful experience more than a good experience," or, "I'm afraid it will have a bad consequence, but if you do choose to have sex, I want you to use birth control." Just coming at it with an attitude of honesty, "I'm worried about your making mistakes that will kill you in a car accident, that will cut off options for you as far as future careers." Sex and drugs can affect health and safety, and you owe it to yourself to give as much factual information and to be as straight with them as you can.

Does "just say no" work?

The problem with "just say no" is that it doesn't tell them what to say yes to. If you say, "I don't want you ever to try that," then if they are in a social situation and someone offers them a drink, what do they do to maintain the friendship? You want to make it realistic. They need to have something ready to say, right at hand, to save face in that situation. They might be able to joke about it: They might say they have a driving test tomorrow and can't afford to wake up hungover. And you can practice that with them. But expecting them to "just say no" does a great disservice to teenagers by making it seem that simple-minded.

Are there any benefits to some experimenting?

If your high-schooler tries beer or marijuana, don't panic. Research shows that, for the older teens at least, it is normal to experiment a little bit with drugs and alcohol; in fact, the kids who experiment a little bit seem to be mentally healthier than those who never try anything at all. With younger teens, if they are experimenting, that's more abnormal and that's more of a sign of risk. And all teens should know it's stupid to try drugs such as crack or heroin even once; they pose a real risk of addiction or death. Also, if a child has a family history of drug or alcohol problems, that child should know he or she is at higher risk for bad consequences.

How do I know if my teen has a serious problem?

If you see drastic changes in your child's behavior, where he is suddenly hanging around with a whole new group of friends, where his grades drop, where he stops being interested in things he used to be interested in, or stops taking showers, or he sleeps all the time or he can't sleep, those kinds of drastic changes that persist more than a couple of weeks, that's something to really look into.

It might be a depression or a drug problem. Maybe get some professional advice, because at this age if your kid derails from that track of making friends, passing his courses, it can have lifelong consequences if he has a depression that is not recognized and not treated. About one in ten teenagers will have a serious depression during adolescence, and suicide is one of the top causes of death among teenagers, related heavily to depression. You don't want to ignore drastic, persistent change; that's not the normal teen moodiness.

What are some ways to avoid some of the problems teens generally encounter?

One of the things that seems to get kids into trouble is having nothing productive to do, a feeling that they don't contribute. It's almost like we make it really hard for teenagers to find a useful place in society, especially when they are too young to work legally. It can be really hard for them to find something to do with their creative energy, and sometimes that can turn in destructive ways.

So, you can help your teenagers find something that interests them where they feel needed, where they feel that something they do makes a difference for somebody or some group, such as volunteering at a nursing home or in a community program. Kids need to feel that they matter in the larger society, especially since they are trying to get away from just being part of the family and the feeling that that is their only identity.

I've heard that smoking is on the rise among teenagers. Why?

Almost nobody over 18 or 19 starts smoking; it is typically now junior high kids who are starting to smoke. Part of the problem is that people have always used smoking to rebel, and I think that, in some ways, as adults stigmatize smoking it becomes more attractive as a means of rebellion. And it looks as though this increase in smoking might have something to do with the kid-oriented kind of advertising and the fact that the laws we have that are supposed to prevent kids from getting cigarettes are widely ignored. They look around and think, "Well, if smoking is so bad, how come it's legal, how come they advertise it everywhere?" They think, "This is something I can do to show I'm grown-up." It takes this cycle of smoking occasionally to smoking a little bit more over a few years to become addicted, and they just don't have the reasoning skills to see the damage this can do to them.

How can I help them stop?

Don't ignore it. If you ignore drinking, drug use, or cigarette use, that's like saying that it is really okay that they are doing it. You have to let them know you mind. Say, "I don't want you to smoke because I know that it is really really hard to quit. This is an addictive drug, I don't want you to end up hooked on this, because I love you and don't want you to go through that. I know I cannot control what you do when you are not with me, and I know that you have independence over your own life, and I'm hoping that you will choose not to do that, but I realize that is your choice." To a certain extent that undercuts the need to rebel. You as a parent have to become more aware of both trying to limit access, and having your kid talk to an older teen who is hooked and find out what that's like, trying to quit. Often, that's more credible to them.

What are good tips to adapt to parenting a teen?

The important things are not to crack down like a dictator, but also not to be their friend and say anything goes. You really need to be in between there, letting them know your values but also acknowledging that they are a growing, changing person and deserve more freedom and responsibilities. And that it is important to maintain mutual respect. It is a tough dance because you are trying to let them make mistakes, and learn from those mistakes, without really hurting themselves. But if you are not willing to let them try and fall and learn from those natural consequences of doing this thing, you are really doing them a disservice, because you are not going to be there all the time, and you are not doing your job as a parent.

Source: Cheryl K. Olson, MPH SD, is on the faculty of Harvard Medical School in Psychiatry. She writes frequently about teen issues for *Parents* magazine.

Selecting a College

Selecting a college seems like choosing a fate. Where should I begin?

Start with a look inside yourself—your skills, values, learning style, and career interests—then take a look beyond yourself, to the people around you who can help with this important decision. First, arrange to spend time with someone in your chosen career field and ask his advice on the best preparation, schools, and courses for that profession. Second, have your guidance office direct you to the various directories of educational and career opportunities. Finally, draw on your family contacts to meet other professionals and alumni who can add to your knowledge during this information-gathering stage.

After considering these personal factors, what else should I find out?

List the factors that will affect your selection. Academic programs should come first, of course—they are most important. Then list other factors such as tuition, location, school size, and extracurricular activities, e.g., sports, drama, music, or newspapers and other publications. Finally, consider the difficulty of admission—how selective the school is in admitting applicants.

If a college refuses to send a catalog, how can I find out more about course offerings and degree requirements?

Sometimes colleges will not send catalogs with their first mailing since these are expensive to publish and to mail. But they may have placed the catalog on an electronic database you can access through the Internet on the World Wide

Web; contact the school for the exact address. You could also ask for a viewbook, which is a smaller publication that provides an overview of the college's history, programs, and educational philosophy.

Once I have the catalog, how do I digest this huge volume of information?

First, explore possible majors to determine the number of courses available to you; then see whether special programs of study are available to add marketable skills to your curriculum. For instance, if you are interested in art history as a major, you might wish to find out whether the school offers programs that involve students with local museums.

Should I arrange for an on-campus interview?

If possible, visit the colleges you're considering and schedule an interview with the admissions department. Interviews are seldom required for admission, but they can help you to assess your qualifications and determine whether a school is right for you.

What about an overnight visit?

Many colleges host visitor programs that pair applicants with current students to acquaint them with dorm life and the college environment. Ask the admissions department whether the school offers such a program. If not, consider contacting a high school alum to arrange such a visit.

If I've attended a small high school, should I attend a small college?

There's no set rule as to what environment would serve you best. A student from a rural-based graduating class of 30 students might welcome the breadth of experience a large urban campus provides. A student from the inner city may look forward to the peaceful atmosphere of a small, rural campus. Don't be swayed by stereotypes: Large schools may not be more diverse, nor small schools more intimate. Set aside your preconceptions so that you can more realistically determine the real impact of size as it relates to your own needs and that particular school. Read catalogs, talk to students and professors, and keep your eyes and ears open. You may well find that there are several different types of schools that would suit you well.

Source: Thomas C. Hayden, Vice President of Admissions, Financial Aid and Research, Oberlin College; author of *Peterson's Handbook for College Admissions*, 4th ed., (Princeton, NJ: Peterson's, 1995).

GOVERNMENT AND PUBLIC INSTITUTIONS

————◆————

Amnesty International (AI)

The Electoral College

The Federal Bureau of Investigation (FBI)

The Freedom of Information Act (FOIA)

Guardian Angels • Medicaid

National Aeronautics and Space Administration (NASA)

The National Archives

The National Organization for the Reform of Marijuana Laws (NORML)

The National Organization for Women (NOW)

Paying Federal Taxes

Social Security

U.S. Library of Congress • Voting

Amnesty International (AI)

What is Amnesty International's goal?

A worldwide champion of human rights, Amnesty International campaigns for the rights of "prisoners of conscience"—people detained anywhere for their beliefs or because of their ethnic origin, sex, color, or language—who have not used or advocated violence. AI seeks to:

- free all prisoners of conscience
- ensure fair and prompt trials for political prisoners
- abolish the death penalty, torture, and other cruel treatment of prisoners
- end extrajudicial executions and "disappearances"

Amnesty International also opposes abuses by opposition groups: hostage-taking, torture, and killings of prisoners, and other arbitrary killings.

What is the history of the organization?

Amnesty International was launched in 1961 by a British lawyer, Peter Benenson. His newspaper appeal, "The Forgotten Prisoners," was published worldwide on May 28, 1961, and brought in more than 1,000 offers of support for the idea of an international campaign to protect human rights. Within 12 months the new organization had sent delegations to four countries to make representations on behalf of prisoners, and had taken up 210 cases. AI members had organized national bodies in seven countries.

How many members does Amnesty International have today?

AI has more than 1,100,000 members, subscribers, and regular donors in more than 150 countries and territories, and over 8,000 volunteer groups in more than 70 countries. There are nationally organized sections in 51 countries, 30 of them in Latin America and the Caribbean, Africa, Asia, and the Middle East.

Where is Amnesty International based and how is it organized?

The organization's nerve center is the International Secretariat in London, with more than 290 paid staff and 90 volunteers from more than 50 countries. Amnesty International is governed by a nine-member International Executive Committee.

Are local chapters restricted to involvement with cases in their own regions?

On the contrary. From the beginning, AI emphasized the worldwide commitment to human rights protection. Members were to act on cases worldwide and not become involved in cases in their own countries.

What is Amnesty International's track record?

Since 1961, AI has adopted or investigated more than 43,500 cases. Each case may involve one individual or many; of these cases, 40,753 are now closed. Members around the world work on behalf of prisoners threatened with imprisonment, unfair trials, torture, or execution.

What are some more recent AI accomplishments?

By the end of November 1993, 4,337 volunteer groups were working on behalf of 4,962 named individuals and 6,914 unnamed individuals from 98 countries worldwide. Each "urgent action" can generate hundreds of appeals to the authorities within days of being issued and several thousand within a few weeks.

The new actions covered a variety of concerns: prisoners who might be tortured; those at risk of, or who had been the victim of, extrajudicial execution or "disappearances"; prisoners sentenced to death; and people who had been harassed or had received death threats.

What special assistance can AI members offer prisoners?

Medical groups and networks in more than 30 countries appeal on behalf of seriously ill prisoners without access to medical care; prisoners who have been tortured; those who have died in custody from torture or through lack of medical care; in cases of corporal or capital punishment involving the medical profession; and in cases where medical professionals themselves become the target of abuses because of their professional or human rights activities.

Does Amnesty International have face-to-face dialogue with international powers?

Yes. By the end of November 1993, the organization had sent 73 delegations to 58 countries. Delegates discussed AI's concerns with government authorities, observed political trials, and carried out on-the-spot investigations into human rights abuses. The countries visited ranged from Algeria to Venezuela, from Cambodia to Turkey, from Switzerland to Yemen, and included a number of the new republics in the former USSR. The organization has made over 1,200 visits to different countries since 1961.

Are human rights abuses as widespread today as they were when the organization was founded?

Yes. In fact, prisoners of conscience—jailed solely for the peaceful exercise of their basic human rights—have been held in some 62 countries. At least 300,000 political prisoners have been detained without charge or trial or under administrative detention in more than 60 countries. More than 1,500 political prisoners were imprisoned after unfair trials in at least 30 countries. Detainees were tortured or ill-treated in prisons, police stations, or secret detention centers in at least 110 countries. More than 500 people have died apparently as a result of torture or inhumane prison conditions, or in "suspicious" circumstances in some 48 countries. Suspected government opponents, members of targeted ethnic groups, or people living in opposition strongholds were apparently victims of extrajudicial execution in 45 countries.

In the United States, AI receives news coverage for its anti-execution stance. What are the statistics on executions throughout the world?

During 1992, AI learned of 1,708 prisoners known to have been executed in 35 countries, and 2,697 people who were sentenced to death in 62 countries. The true figures are certainly higher.

Does AI see a trend toward abolishing the death penalty?

Yes. More than 44 percent of countries in the world have abolished the death penalty in law or practice. Some 100 countries and territories retain and use the death penalty for ordinary crimes. China and Iran accounted for 82 percent of all executions recorded by AI in 1992.

Source: Amnesty International; 322 Eighth Avenue, New York, NY 10001; (212) 807-8400.

The Electoral College

What is the *Electoral College* and what does it do?

The Electoral College is a group of people who are elected by popular vote and who in turn are empowered by the U.S. Constitution to elect the president of the United States.

How does the Electoral College work?

Each state is given a number of electors equal to its number of senators (which is always two) and its number of representatives in the U.S. House (which is larger for bigger states). Thus, if your state has ten representatives, it gets to pick 12 electors (ten for the representatives plus two for the senators). In November 1996, if you voted for, say, Bill Clinton, then you would actually be voting for a slate of 12 candidates who were running for elector and who had pledged to vote for Clinton. If the Clinton slate got more votes than any other slate, then the 12 Clinton supporters would be the electors and would cast their twelve votes for Clinton. There are 538 electors. A majority plus one—or 270 electoral votes—is required to be elected president. The way the system works means that a candidate can win the election without actually winning the most popular votes—he just needs to get the majority of the electoral vote.

What if no candidate receives the 270 or more electoral votes required to win the presidency?

In this event, the House of Representatives can elect a president from among the three presidential candidates who received the most electoral votes. The trick is that each of the 50 states casts only one vote, and a majority plus one—or 26 states—is required to win the election. For those states with more than one representative, the representatives will have to vote to decide which candidate receives their one vote. If they deadlock—for instance, 4 votes for one candidate and 4 votes for another—their state will not vote, but the candidate still requires 26 states to win.

What if inauguration day rolls around and no president has been selected by the Electoral College or the House of Representatives?

When the electors voted for president, they also voted for vice president. If no vice-presidential candidate receives a majority of the electoral votes, then the U.S. Senate can elect a vice president choosing between the two candidates who received the most electoral votes for that office. Each senator receives one vote and a majority is required. Choosing between only two candidates, the Senate probably would not deadlock and would pick a vice president. If no president were elected, then the vice president would become acting president on January 20.

Source: Dr. Devin Bent, Department Head, Political Science Department, James Madison University, Mail Stop Code 1101, Maury Hall, Harrisonburg, VA 22807.

The Federal Bureau of Investigation (FBI)

When and how was the FBI established?

The organization known today as the FBI was created in 1908 when Attorney General Charles J. Bonaparte appointed an unnamed force of Special Agents to perform investigations for the U.S. Department of Justice. Prior to this time, the Department of Justice borrowed agents from the U.S. Secret Service to investigate violations of federal criminal laws within its jurisdiction.

How can I tour the FBI?

Tours are open to the public from 8:45 A.M. until 4:45 P.M. weekdays (no weekends). Come to the building on 9th St. and Pennsylvania Ave. NW and wait in line for tickets. During peak season (from the last part of February through Labor Day) it is best to get there before 8:00 A.M.

Who is the most notorious criminal ever captured by the FBI?

Public enemy John Dillinger, a bank robber and murderer, who was killed in an attemped capture on July 22, 1934.

How can one become an FBI agent?

You must be a U.S. citizen between the ages of 23 and 37, with a four-year degree from a college or university. Law and accounting are the best degrees to have, but the FBI also hires people with other degrees, such as languages.

How does someone get on the Ten Most-Wanted list? What are the criteria?

The Most-Wanted Fugitive List was started in 1950. Two different criteria are used. The individual first must have a lengthy record of committing serious crimes and/or be considered a particularly dangerous menace to society due to current criminal charges. Secondly, it must be believed that the nationwide publicity afforded by the program can be of assistance in apprehending the fugitive, who in turn should not already be notorious due to other publicity. The list is *not* ranked.

Does the FBI investigate unidentified flying objects (UFOs)?

The investigation of UFO sightings does not fall within the jurisdiction of the bureau; however, for a limited period of time the FBI did assist the Department of the Air Force in investigating alleged UFO sightings.

For your information, the Department of the Air Force conducted investigations and studies of UFO reports from 1947 to 1969. On December 17, 1969, the secretary of the air force announced the termination of "Project Blue Book," the air force program for the investigation of UFOs. The department has furnished all documents on its investigations to the Modern Military Branch, National Archives and Records Administration, 7th Street and Pennsylvania Avenue NW, Washington, DC 20408, and this data is available for public review and analysis (see *The National Archives,* page 217).

What is the FBI's stance on the rumors about J. Edgar Hoover?

The FBI has no official position or comment on this. However, according to Larry Heim, who worked closely with Hoover's office for 24 years, and is now the media representative for the Society of Former Special Agents, the rumors about Hoover are just that—rumors. Heim points out that J. Edgar Hoover served more than 50 years in the "klieg lights" of Washington, D.C., the home base of the country's ace investigative reporters; not one of them found any evidence regarding the "slanderous rumor" of cross-dressing or homosexuality, and not one alleged victim of blackmailing has ever come forth to substantiate that "vicious rumor." Heim refers to a book by Anthony Summers, which is the source for the rumors of Hoover's involvement with the Mafia and his homosexuality. He states that Summers's work has been refuted by many other journalists who were critics of Hoover themselves, including Sanford Ungar, Les Whitten, and Peter Maas.

Sources: Larry Heim, Society of Former Special Agents of the FBI, and Swanson D. Carter, Special Agent—Unit Chief, Office of Public and Congressional Affairs, Federal Bureau of Investigation.

The Freedom of Information Act (FOIA)

What is the Freedom of Information Act?

Passed in 1966, the Freedom of Information Act makes the records of every government agency available to the public upon request.

Who uses the FOIA and what do they use it for?

Private citizens, advocacy groups, journalists, even public officials have used the act to receive information about their personal records, product safety, workplace hazards, various statistics, government spending, and civil rights issues.

What part of the government is covered by the FOIA?

The FOIA is intended to apply to any federal agency. The act defines "agency" to include the agencies, offices, and departments of the executive branch of the federal government (e.g., the Defense Department or the Office of Management and Budget), as well as independent federal regulatory agencies (e.g., the Federal Trade Commission or the Environmental Protection Agency) and federal government-controlled corporations (e.g., the U.S. Postal Service, the Tennessee Valley Authority, or the Smithsonian Institution). The act does not, however, apply to Congress, the federal courts, or units within the executive office of the president whose sole function is to advise and assist the president (e.g., White House chief of staff).

What kind of information can be obtained?

The act provides access to all "agency records," unless they are specifically exempted. The FOIA does not define this term, but the courts have generally interpreted "agency records" to mean printed documents or other information-bearing materials (e.g., photographs or computer tapes) which (1) were created or obtained by a federal agency, and (2) are, at the time of the request, within both the possession and control of the agency. The act does not require an agency to "create" a record in response to a request if the record does not exist at the time the request is made. Similarly, the act does not require an agency to retrieve a requested record that is not in its possession at the time of the request. The term "control," used to determine whether a record is subject to the FOIA, refers to the power of disposition by the agency over the materials at issue.

Agency records that are accessible under the FOIA may contain information relating to an incredibly diverse range of interests, including public health and consumer product safety, government spending, labor, civil rights, business, taxes, history, foreign policy, national defense, and the economy.

Who can make a request?

The act permits "any person" to request access to agency records. In practice, this includes U.S. citizens, permanent resident aliens, and foreign nationals, as well as corporations, unincorporated associations, universities, and even state and local governments and members of Congress.

How quickly will an agency respond?

In theory, in no more than 30 days. The act requires an agency to respond to an initial request within ten working days and to an administrative appeal within 20 working days—with ten more days allocated to "unusual circumstances" like pulling records from a field facility or processing a large amount of material. In practice, however, most agencies take much longer than ten days to release records. The courts have okayed this, so long as agencies treat each request on a first-come, first-serve basis. What happens most often is that the agency replies within two weeks via a form letter notifying the requester that the request has been placed in line and will be processed as soon as possible—which may mean several months later.

If the records sought are available from a nongovernment source, can an agency defer to that source in denying a request?

No. If the requested records are "agency records" subject to the FOIA, the agency must release them—even if the information is available elsewhere.

On what grounds can an agency deny a request?

The agency can refuse to disclose records only when they fall within one of the nine specific statutory exemptions from the FOIA's disclosure provisions. These include matters that must be suppressed "in the interest of national defense or foreign policy," such as classified records pertaining to foreign intelligence, counterintelligence, or international terrorism investigations; matters that are "related solely to the internal personnel rules and practices of any agency," including law enforcement manuals, which, if released, could risk circumvention of agency regulations or statutes; "trade secrets and commercial or financial information obtained from a person and privileged or confidential," unless the information was generated by the government; material that would not be available to another party unless through litigation with the agency; personnel and medical files; records or information compiled for law enforcement purposes involving a specific suspected violation of law; records pertaining to the regulation or supervision of financial institutions; and geological data concerning oil wells.

Can an agency deny that records exist, even if they really do exist?

Yes, but only if the disclosure of their very existence could reasonably be expected to interfere with a criminal law enforcement proceeding.

It sounds as if agencies have lots of loopholes. Do they withhold information just because they can?

Not necessarily. In fact, these exemptions are discretionary rather than mandatory, which means that an agency can decide to release records to a requester even after it has determined that the records may be withheld pursuant to one or more of the exemptions.

What if only part of a record falls under one of these exemptions? Does that mean a requester can't obtain any of it?

No. The FOIA requires an agency to provide a requester with any "reasonably segregable portion" of a record after deletion of the portions that are exempt from disclosure. This means that an agency may not withhold an entire document on the grounds that some portions of the document are exempt.

Can an agency charge for copies of requested documents?

Yes. Agencies are allowed to charge three types of fees: the costs of searching for documents; the "direct" cost of reviewing documents to decide whether they should be disclosed; and the costs of duplication. In addition, the agency is given discretion to waive fees on a case-by-case basis if the request is "in the public interest because it is likely to contribute significantly to public understanding of the operations or activities of the government and is not in the commercial interest of the requester."

If an individual wants to obtain personal records, it seems the process should be easier. Are there other laws pertaining to this type of search?

Although individuals can use the FOIA to obtain agency records relating to themselves, they can use the Privacy Act for this purpose as well. Requests for personal records should be made under both the FOIA and the Privacy Act. Unlike the FOIA, which merely enables you to obtain access to such records, the Privacy Act establishes your right to correct, amend, or expunge records in which the information about you is not accurate, relevant, timely, or complete. In fact, the Privacy Act permits you to sue the agency for refusal to correct or amend your record, as well as for refusal to give you access.

Why file under both acts? Aren't they about the same?

No—and it is the differences that make it a good idea to file jointly under both acts. Though information obtained under the Privacy Act may cost less, since requesters are charged for copying but not search costs, FOIA favors the requester in several ways:

- FOIA may be used by "any person" to obtain access to any agency records relating to the requester. The Privacy Act may be used only by U.S. citizens or permanent resident aliens, and only to obtain access to specific records that can be retrieved from the system using the individual's name or other identifying code.

- FOIA's exemptions are narrower than the Privacy Act's, particularly for law enforcement records, and some agencies may not routinely consider your request under the law which gives greater access.

- FOIA sets specific time limits for responding and also provides for an administrative appeal. The Privacy Act does not.

- FOIA's statute of limitations for filing a lawsuit is six years; under the Privacy Act, it's only two.

How do I make an FOIA request?

The first order of business in making an FOIA request is to determine which agency should receive it. If you are not sure which agency has the information you want, go to the library and check descriptions of the various agencies in publications like the *United States Government Organization Manual* (U.S. Government Printing Office), or call the local office of your representative in Congress. Then call the FOIA or public affairs office of those agencies for more specific information, including the specific mailing address. Your letter must "reasonably describe" the records being sought.

How do I write a request letter?

Begin by stating that you are making a request under the Freedom of Information Act, 5 U.S.C. Section 552. If your request is for personal files, you will also want to cite the Privacy Act, 5 U.S.C. Section 552a. State that if the agency response is not satisfactory you will make an administrative appeal, and ask for the name of the official to whom such appeals should be addressed. Remind the agency that, although the law allows them to withhold specified categories of exempted information, it requires them to release any "segregable" portions that are left after exempt material is deleted. Some agencies require that Privacy Act requests be notarized; the agency's FOIA office can inform you of its requirements.

Do I have to tell the agency why I am seeking the information?

No. But such an explanation might be necessary if you want the agency to waive its fees or comply more fully with your request. The more precise and accurate the request, the more likely you are to get a prompt and complete response, with lower search fees.

What are some tips for getting a prompt response?

Make the agency's job as easy as possible. Limit your request to what you really want. If you simply ask for "any files relating to" a particular subject (including yourself), you may give the agency an excuse to delay its response and needlessly run up search and copying costs. If you cite specific records or note that the records you seek have already been released, there may be a lower charge.

Source: The American Civil Liberties Union, 132 West 43rd Street, New York, NY 10036-6599; www.aclu.org.

Guardian Angels

What cities do the Guardian Angels work in?

There are Alliance of Guardian Angel chapters all through the United States and Canada, as well as in Australia, England, Germany, Sweden, Denmark, and Puerto Rico. They are starting programs in Russia and Italy. In the United States, there are Guardian Angels in all the major cities—New York, Chicago, Los Angeles, Denver, San Francisco, Miami Beach—and also several smaller ones.

How do you get to be a Guardian Angel? What are the qualifications needed?

You must be 16 or older, have a good attitude, a willingness to help, and no serious criminal record. Men and women of any height and weight are welcome in the program.

Who came up with the outfit?

Curtis Sliwa. It consists of a red jacket with the Guardian Angel design, and Guardian Angels T-shirts. The uniform belongs to the organization, and does not go home with the volunteers. Berets, on the other hand, can be taken home; volunteers can decorate and personalize them.

Where can I get one of those cute red berets?

Any Army-Navy surplus store.

Legally, how far can the Guardian Angels go in defending citizens?

They can exercise the right to make a citizen's arrest. This means that they can restrain someone until the police arrive at the scene. Guardian Angels are always careful to use only equal force, and not to take the law into their own hands.

How closely do the Guardian Angels work with police?

Very closely, in some cities. They can get quite a lot of support from the police. It differs in every city, depending on how long the chapter has been there, but in general the police are supportive.

When did the program start? Who founded it?

Curtis Sliwa, on January 11, 1980.

How many (if any) Guardian Angels have died in the line of duty?

There have been five deaths in the last 18 years.

Do all the Guardian Angels live together?

No. More than 90 percent are part-time volunteers who help out after school or after work. The average time commitment is six to eight hours a week. Volunteers are not paid.

What is the training to be a Guardian Angel?

Some martial arts and self-defense, emergency first aid, CPR, and crisis intervention. Also, teamwork, communications, and scenario role-playing. Depending on the chapter, there different workshops on, among other things, self-esteem, self-confidence, dealing with the mentally ill, and wheelchair safety. The initial training lasts for three months, but then is ongoing as volunteers continue with the program.

What is the primary function of the Guardian Angels?

Providing community safety patrols; being good role models for future generations; promoting volunteer work.

How are they funded?

The alliance is funded solely through public donations. They do their own fund-raising, and are working toward corporate fund-raising.

Source: The Alliance of Guardian Angels, Inc., 982 E. 89th Street, Brooklyn, NY 11236; (718) 649-2607.

Medicaid

What is the relation between Medicaid and Medicare?

Whereas Medicaid is a program for people of all ages, Medicare is generally geared toward those older than 65. In cases where individuals are eligible for both programs, Medicaid is always the "payor of last resort." As each state chooses, services such as eyeglasses, hearing aids, and nursing facility care not covered by Medicare may be provided by the Medicaid program.

What is the Medicaid program?

Medicaid provides health services to certain individuals and families with low incomes and resources.

Does Medicaid provide medical care for all poor people?

No. Even under the broadest provisions of the federal statute (except for emergency services in some cases), the Medicaid program does not provide health-care services, even for very poor people, unless they are in certain designated groups. Low income is only one test for Medicaid eligibility; assets and resources are also tested against established thresholds. People who are eligible for Medicaid may or may not also receive cash assistance from the Aid for Families with Dependent Children (AFDC) program or from the Supplemental Security Income (SSI) program. For example, people who are not poor may become eligible for Medicaid if they incur excessive medical expenses.

Who runs Medicaid—the federal government or the states?

Both. Medicaid is actually a jointly funded cooperative venture between the federal and state governments. But each state administers its own program.

Who is eligible for Medicaid?

Because states are now implementing a welfare reform bill signed into law in August 1996, the requirements are changing. And states do have some discretion in determining which groups their Medicaid programs will cover and the financial criteria for Medicaid eligibility. To be eligible for federal funds, states are required to provide Medicaid coverage for most individuals who receive federally assisted income maintenance payments, as well as for related groups not receiving cash payments. Some examples of the mandatory Medicaid eligibility groups include:

- Infants born to Medicaid-eligible pregnant women. Medicaid eligibility must continue throughout the first year of life so long as the infant remains in the mother's household and she remains eligible, or would be eligible if she were still pregnant.
- Children under age 6 and pregnant women who meet the state's AFDC financial requirements or whose family income is at or below 133 percent of the federal poverty level.
- Recipients of adoption assistance and foster care under Title IV-E of the Social Security Act.
- Special protected groups who lose cash assistance because of the cash programs' rules, but who may keep Medicaid for a period of time.

Who decides who is eligible?

Within broad national guidelines that the federal government provides, each of the states establishes its own eligibility standards; determines the type, amount, duration, and scope of services; and sets the rate of payment for services. So the Medicaid program varies considerably from state to state, and within each state over time. Sometimes, states may use a more liberal standard to decide who qualifies for assistance through Medicaid, especially for aged, blind, and disabled people. But they still have to fall within federal limits for matching funds.

Are the requirements narrowly defined, or do states have some leeway in deciding who can receive Medicaid?

States do have the option to provide Medicaid coverage for other "categorically needy" groups. These optional groups share characteristics of the mandatory groups, but the eligibility criteria are somewhat more liberally defined. States may receive matching federal funds in certain cases in which individuals do not meet mandatory requirements but still need help. For example: infants up to age one and pregnant women not covered under the mandatory rules; certain aged, blind, or disabled adults who have incomes above those requiring mandatory coverage, but below the federal poverty level; children under age 21 who meet income and resources requirements for AFDC but who otherwise are not eligible for AFDC; and institutionalized or homebound individuals with income and resources below specified limits.

What does "medically needy" mean?

States can elect to have a "medically needy" program, which allows them to extend Medicaid eligibility to additional qualified people who may have too much income to qualify. This option allows such people to "spend down" to Medicaid eligibility by incurring medical and/or remedial-care expenses to offset their excess income, thereby reducing it to a level below the maximum allowed by that state's Medicaid plan.

Are there time limits on Medicaid use?

That depends on the state. The amount, duration, and scope of each service must be sufficient to achieve its purpose reasonably. States may place appropriate limits on a Medicaid service based on such criteria as medical necessity or utilization control. For example, states may place a reasonable limit on the number of covered physician visits or may require patients to seek pre-authorization before receiving care.

How do I apply for Medicaid?

Go to your local Medicaid state agency (your local telephone book should list the address and number).

Do states offer other types of medical assistance?

Yes. Most states have additional "state-only" programs to provide medical assistance for specified poor people who do not qualify for the Medicaid program. No federal funds are provided for state-only programs.

What other help is available for those who cannot afford medical care?

As welfare reform continues to restrict government programs, communities throughout the country are increasingly committed to helping out however they can. Free clinics staffed by volunteers can provide free or sliding-scale medical care. And clinics such as Planned Parenthood can provide certain medical services such as pap smears on a sliding-scale basis that costs less for lower-income patients. County health departments usually offer flu shots at cost—generally recommended for the elderly and those with compromised immune systems, but a low-cost investment for anyone hoping to avoid taking a week of sick leave to nurse a bad case of the flu. University communities often have special programs in which medical professionals in training offer free or low-cost care and counseling.

What happens if one family member's expenses jeopardize the finances of the rest of the family?

The Medicare Catastrophic Coverage Act (MCCA) of 1988 accelerated Medicaid eligibility for some nursing home patients by protecting assets for the institutionalized person's spouse at home. Under this law, before an institutionalized person's monthly income is used to pay for the cost of institutional care, a minimum monthly maintenance allowance is deducted from the spouse's income up to a moderate level.

Do I have to shell out money up front and be reimbursed by the state? That sounds like a lot of red tape.

No. Health-care providers bill Medicaid, and Medicaid pays them directly. Known as a "vendor payment program," this program requires providers participating in Medicaid to accept the Medicaid reimbursement level as payment in full. States may impose nominal deductibles, co-insurance, or copayments on some Medicaid recipients for certain routine services.

This sounds like managed care. Can recipients choose their own doctors, or does the state mandate which doctors and hospitals recipients use?

With certain exceptions, a state's Medicaid plan must allow recipients freedom of choice among health-care providers participating in Medicaid. But managed care organizations such as health maintenance organizations (HMOs) are an acceptable alternative. In general, states are required to provide comparable services to all categorically needy eligible people.

What is managed care's role in Medicaid?

As managed care organizations have grown in popularity, so has managed care's enrollment within Medicaid. In 1995, almost a quarter of all Medicaid recipients were enrolled in managed-care plans. One vehicle for the expansion of managed care, and of new eligibility groups, is the 1915(b) waiver process, which allows states to research health-care delivery alternatives to control program costs. And under the Section 1115(b) waiver authority, states are allowed to implement managed-care delivery systems within prescribed parameters.

How has Medicaid changed since its creation in 1965?

Initially, Medicaid was a medical-care extension of federally funded income maintenance programs for the poor, with an emphasis on the aged, the disabled, and dependent children and their mothers. Over time, however, Medicaid has been diverging from a firm tie to eligibility for cash programs. Recent legislation ensures Medicaid coverage to an expanded number of low-income pregnant women, poor children, and some Medicare beneficiaries who are not eligible for any cash assistance program and would not have been eligible for Medicaid under earlier Medicaid rules. Legislative changes focus on enhanced outreach toward specific groups of pregnant women and children, increased access to care, and improved quality of care. The legislation also continued specific benefits beyond the normal run of Medicaid eligibility and placed some restrictions on states' ability to limit certain services.

Source: *1996 HCFA Statistics,* Bureau of Data Management, HCFA Pub. No. 03394, September 1996. For more information on Medicaid statistics, call (410) 786-0165. Press inquiries should be directed to the HCFA Press Office at (202) 690-6145.

National Aeronautics and Space Administration (NASA)
INTERVIEWS WITH JOHN F. PIKE AND ROBERT S. WALKER

Can NASA engineers evaluate my invention, drawing or plans?

No. The agency receives hundreds of such requests each month, and NASA does not have enough engineers to handle this extra work in addition to their regular duties. Since it would be unfair to evaluate some proposals and not others, the agency says, it does not evaluate any. But there is a brochure available about how to submit a formal unsolicited proposal to NASA for funding or joint research and development. The Office of Small and Disadvantaged Business Utilization at NASA Headquarters also has developed a publication about how to do business with NASA.

How does one become an astronaut?

Any adult in excellent physical condition who meets the basic qualifications can be selected for astronaut training. For mission specialists and pilot astronauts, the minimum requirements include a bachelor's degree in engineering, science or mathematics from an accredited institution. Three years of related experience must follow the degree, and an advanced degree is desirable. Pilot astronauts must have at least 1,000 hours of experience in jet aircraft, and they need better vision than mission specialists. Competition is extremely keen, with an average of more than 4,000 applicants for about 20 openings every two years. For more information, write the Astronaut Selection Office, NASA Johnson Space Center, Houston, TX 77058.

How many NASA centers are there in the United States, and where are they?

Ten, including headquarters in Washington, D.C. The others are: Kennedy Space Center at Cape Canaveral Air Force Station in Cocoa Beach, Fla.; Johnson Space Center in Houston; Goddard Space Flight Center in Greenbelt, Md.; Marshall Space Flight Center in Huntsville, Ala.; the Jet Propulsion Lab in Pasadena, Calif.; John C. Stennis Space Center, a rocket-test facility in Hancock County, in southern Mississippi; Langley Air Force Base in Hampton, Va.; Drysden Flight Research Center at Edwards Air Force Base in the Mojave Desert in California; and the Lewis Research Center in Cleveland.

What is NASA's budget-appropriation process?

Walker: We look at NASA as part of the president's overall budget and see if their priorities seem right to us. We usually find much commonality and often argue the details with them. Then there's a hearing's process. We arrive at a policy bill, which we pass through our committee and the House. Meanwhile, the Appropriations Committee arrives at spending commitments. They tend to look at items on an annual basis, and we tend to look at programs on a multiyear basis. The space station, for example, takes place over many years. The Appropriations Committee essentially crunches real-spending numbers using our numbers as guidelines.

Some NASA supporters tout technological spin-offs, such as the first pacemaker, to justify the agency's $13.7 billion budget in light of poverty, homelessness and other social ills prevalent on our own planet. To what extent is it true that NASA has contributed to technological advancements that benefit mankind?

Pike: The identifiable spin-off return on NASA's budget has been about 10 cents on the dollar. I think it's worth a lot of money, but people should not be selling it on the basis of Tang and Velcro. That cheapens it. It's about boldly going where no one has gone before.

How does one go to the bathroom in the weightlessness of space?

Walker: There are vacuum-operated facilities inside the space shuttle and future International Space Station.

How did the Challenger crew die, and what affect has the Challenger shuttle had on the public and press's perceptions of NASA?

Pike: The theory is most of them blacked out after the shuttle fell apart, and they were all killed instantly on impact when it hit water.

Walker: The media has generally given well-balanced accounts of NASA. But in my view there was disproportionate coverage surrounding the Challenger accident. I think some Challenger coverage undermined the NASA mission....With the Challenger, there was a lot of speculation about possible scenarios that did not have validity. In attempting to deal with the issues, the press violated the privacy of families of victims.

Also, the press often has looked at the relation between NASA headquarters [in Washington, D.C.] and its various mission centers across the country as being a difficult relationship," he said. "The press, in getting hold of dialogue between the centers and headquarters, portrays healthy discussion as being dissension.

Pike: The main problem with NASA and the media is that there's not enough coverage of NASA in the sense that it's a very large, very important part of government, and there are only a handful of reporters who attempt to cover this agency full time. The Challenger accident was biggest national tragedy since the Kennedy assassination. There are fewer than a handful of books on Challenger, but entire forests have been slain on the Kennedy assassination.

Is the future in more internationally focused projects?

Walker: Sharing costs have become a major issue. The in-progress International Space Station, which will carry a crew of six and is the size of three football fields, costs the United States $17 billion, with additional costs borne by Russia, Japan, Canada and members of the European Space Agency. NASA expects the project to fly in late 1997. It's also the case that scientists tend to share their work. They're used to working in that kind of atmosphere. Even in the most hostile days of the cold war, American experiments were taken aboard Russian spacecraft and Russian experiments aboard American spacecraft.

What will NASA's future look like?

Pike: NASA will be affected by cuts to federal spending. The government is going to be squeezing a $15 billion agency into a $10 billion budget. NASA's budget peaked in 1990 at $16 billion, and by the end of the century, it will be at $10 billion, because the rest of the government's budget is being reduced. If we continue on a path of budget reduction as we have in the past few years, NASA will shut down within next decade or so.

Walker: Budget restraints will constrict program spending but by no means will signify a total NASA shutdown.

How has NASA's mission changed as a result of budget caps?

Walker: The Apollo mission [which ended with Apollo 17's flight to the moon in 1973] was the most successful project NASA had. We were taking on a mission that no one thought could be done and then extending it to safely land humans on the moon and bringing them back. Never before had a mission achieved that level of technological success, and arguably we have not seen that level of success since. The problem in NASA is that everyone thinks we can run all programs like the Apollo project, but the Apollo project ran on an unlimited budget. Present realities dictate that missions must be designed with cost as a primary consideration.

The Marshall Space Flight Center in Alabama alone trimmed 404 jobs this year. There is no strict policy determining which bases will undergo massive cuts and firings.

We are downsizing as missions change. There is an early out program for NASA personnel to help with the transitions. We have moved away from the nearly unlimited resources of the Apollo program. With the space shuttle program, some centers' missions have changed. There are centers that are devoted to aeronautic work in addition to space-related activities. As there is more and more need for a particular specialty, a center's presence ramps up and others go down.

Sources: John E. Pike has served as director for about 15 years of the Washington, D.C.-based Space Policy Project at Federation of American Scientists, a not-for-profit agency that at times has been a leading NASA critic. Robert S. Walker, a former Republican Pennsylvania congressman for 20 years from Lancaster and Chester counties, served on the House Science Committee and was its chairman for the last two years. That committee authorizes the National Aeronautics and Space Administration's spending and policy framework. Questions 1 and 2 are adapted from NASA Website materials. More NASA FAQs are available at http://www.ksc.nasa.gov/facts/facts.html.

The National Archives

What is the National Archives?

The National Archives and Records Administration (NARA) is the government agency responsible for overseeing the management of the records of the federal government. NARA ensures—for citizens, public servants, Congress, the president, and the courts—ready access to essential evidence that documents the rights of American citizens, the actions of federal officials, and the national experience.

What kinds of documents does the National Archives contain?

Established in 1934, NARA serves as the official repository for all federal records judged to be of enduring value. Its holdings date from the eighteenth century to the present, and include the famous charters of freedom—the original Declaration of Independence, the Constitution, and the Bill of Rights.

Where is the National Archives located?

There are National Archives throughout the United States. But the headquarters is the National Archives Building in Washington, D.C., which houses textual and microfilm records relating to genealogy, Native Americans, pre–World War II military and naval-maritime matters, the New Deal, the District of Columbia, the federal courts, and Congress. Related special media and nontextual records, such as cartographic and architectural records, motion pictures, audio recordings, videocassettes, still pictures, and electronic records, are located at the National Archives at College Park, Md. A fax-on-demand service, for use with the handset on a fax machine, gives information on many topics; call (301) 713-6905.

Who is allowed to do research in the National Archives?

Researchers must be at least 16 years old. Those first visiting the National Archives Building in Washington, D.C., must speak with a consultant archivist, who provides an orientation to the building and records, and conducts the registration procedure.

What restrictions apply to the research rooms?

To protect the valuable documents the Archives contain, researchers are provided with paper and pencils; pens are not allowed. Photocopying is permitted. Researchers may bring approved loose paper research notes, handheld wallets, and coin purses into research rooms, but those items are subject to inspection when researchers enter or leave the research complex.

Researchers may use their own personal computers (laptops, notebooks, etc.), approved scanners, typewriters, tape recorders, cameras, and other equipment, but cases, bags, boxes, and other enclosures are prohibited. Audiocassette tapes and flat-bed scanners without automatic document feed must receive an approval tag before being brought into the research rooms. Personal copiers and auto-feed or handheld scanners are not permitted.

Can people who are not doing research tour the Archives?

Yes. The National Archives is open for tourists who wish to "discover our nation's archival heritage"—not just at its national center but at all locations. The Archives is convenient for visitors to the Mall, located near the National Gallery of Art, the National Museum of Natural History, the National Air and Space Museum, the Old Post Office Pavilion, and the Hirshhorn Museum and Sculpture Garden.

What other special attractions does the Archives offer?

The Museum Shop, located in the Exhibition Hall of the National Archives, has a large selection of books for adults and children relating to the Constitution, the Civil War, foreign relations, genealogy, politics, the presidency, African-American history, and Washingtoniana, as well as biographies. Special merchandise is also purchased and developed for various National Archives and Records Administration exhibitions. More than 250 products have been developed for sale within the National Archives, its presidential libraries, and some regional archives.

Source: The National Archives and Records Administration, 7th Street and Pennsylvania Avenue NW, Washington, DC 20408; (202) 501-5000. For more information on merchandise, call the NARA sales department toll-free at (800) 234-8861.

The National Organization for the Reform of Marijuana Laws (NORML)

Why is marijuana illegal and who advocated that it become so?

Marijuana was made illegal in the United States in 1937 by an act of Congress. The chief proponent for prohibiting marijuana was the head of the Bureau of Narcotics, Harry J. Anslinger. Marijuana was erroneously blamed for causing psychotic and homicidal behavior in individuals. Testifying before a congressional subcommitee, Mr. Anslinger declared that marijuana is "as harmless as a rattlesnake."

When will marijuana be legalized and how much will it cost?

NORML has been trying to re-legalize the marijuana plant and its many uses since 1970. The optimistic answer is that it will not take another 25 years. If the sale of small amounts of marijuana were tolerated in the United States, as is the case in the Netherlands, then marijuana *could* cost $1.00–$3.00 per gram (1 gram = 2 marijuana cigarettes).

Which states have the most tolerant law enforcement on marijuana possession?

Since the mid-1970s, 11 states have passed legislation that has "decriminalized" the possession and use of small amounts of marijuana. These states are: Alaska, California, Colorado, Maine, Minnesota, Mississippi, Nebraska, New York, North Carolina, Ohio, and Oregon.

In what countries of the world is marijuana legal?

Marijuana consumption is legally taxed in the Netherlands, Cambodia, and India. Generally speaking, marijuana use is "decriminalized" throughout most of the world.

Are you guys narcs?

No. NORML's board of directors and its staff are simply a cadre of dedicated individuals who believe that the U.S. government has not demonstrated enough of a compelling interest to arrest, prosecute, and incarcerate the estimated one out of seven Americans who choose to consume marijuana.

Where can an individual, suffering from any number of life- and sense-threatening diseases, get medicinal marijuana?

The only legal source for medicinal marijuana in the United States is from the U.S. government's marijuana farm, located at the University of Mississippi at Oxford. Unfortunately, only *eight* medical patients receive this government-grown marijuana. The patients receive a monthly allotment of medicinal marijuana that averages 350 grams (or roughly 15 joints per day)!

How do you get a job working at NORML?

Get a first-class education, care intensely about the issue, and send a résumé and cover letter expressing your desire to work at NORML.

In a society struggling to cope with the abuse of legal drugs (chiefly alcohol and tobacco), why does NORML want to loosen the laws prohibiting marijuana use?

NORML strongly believes that the social ills and costs associated with marijuana pale compared to those of alcohol and tobacco. (In 1993, an estimated 550,000 Americans died due to alcohol and tobacco abuse—as compared to an estimated 300 "marijuana-related" deaths.) Beyond the obvious health hazards associated with "smoking," NORML believes that the greatest consequence a marijuana consumer faces for choosing to consume marijuna is arrest!

Where does NORML get its operating funds?

NORML has nearly 7,000 members nationwide who pay an annual membership fee of $25. NORML's budget in 1994 was just over $450,000.

Why is cultivating hemp (a nonpsychoactive strain of marijuana) for industrial purposes legal virtually everywhere in the world save for the United States? Wasn't hemp once a major cash crop in the United States?

Prior to its prohibition in 1937, hemp was considered one of America's premier cash crops. In the early 1940s, the U.S. government needed hemp for the war effort and allowed it to be grown once again. But after the war the government upheld marijuana's blanket prohibition. Hemp is grown in nearly every latitude that can support its cultivation. Recently, even Canada has begun cultivating hemp for industrial purposes (fuel, paper, pulp, protein, fodder, building materials, etc.).

Source: Allen St. Pierre, Executive Director of the NORML Foundation, 1001 Connecticut Avenue NW, Suite 1010, Washington, DC 20036; phone: (202) 483-5000; fax: (202) 483-0057.

The National Organization for Women (NOW)

What is the National Organization for Women?

The National Organization for Women, commonly known as NOW, is dedicated to eliminating sexism and ending all oppression by making legal, political, social, and economic change in today's society.

What are NOW's official priorities?

NOW's official priorities are pressing for an amendment to the U.S. Constitution that will guarantee equal rights for women; achieving economic equality for women; championing abortion rights, reproductive freedom, and other women's health issues; supporting civil rights for all and opposing racism; opposing bigotry against lesbians and gays; and ending violence against women.

What are some of NOW's other chief concerns?

NOW also strives to eliminate discrimination and harassment in the workplace, schools, the justice system, and all other sectors of society; to end all forms of violence against women; and to promote equality and justice in our society.

Who decides NOW's policies?

The membership, which holds an annual conference, is the supreme governing body of NOW. The national level of the organization is led by four elected national officers, by the national board of directors, and by national issues committees. These national leaders are responsible for implementing policy as formulated by the annual national conference, for coordinating national actions, and for providing membership services.

How many members does NOW currently have?

NOW is the largest feminist organization in the nation, with more than a quarter of a million members. NOW has more than 550 chapters in all 50 states and the District of Columbia.

Why should I become a member of NOW?

In addition to voicing their support of NOW's goals, policies, and programs, members of this private, nonprofit organization gain access to local NOW chapter activities, receive *National NOW Times* five times a year, as well as any information or national alerts from NOW, and (upon request) messages through the e-mail action alert network.

Does NOW provide legal advice or counseling of any kind?

NOW does not provide individuals with specific legal advice or counseling services, nor does it have a library or research department to assist individuals with projects. As part of its commitment to broad-based change, NOW can refer individuals to other organizations that may be able to help.

What is the relationship of my local NOW chapter to the national organization?

NOW draws its broad-based strength from a nationwide network of local chapters, which are chartered by national NOW and engage in a wide variety of action programs in their communities. State organizations develop chapters, coordinate statewide activities, and provide resources to the chapters. If you become a member of NOW, that membership applies to the local, state, and national organizations.

When and how was NOW founded?

On June 30, 1966, 28 people attending the Third National Conference of the Commission on the Status of Women in Washington, D.C., established the organization. Perhaps its most visible member in these early days was its first president, Betty Friedan, author of *The Feminine Mystique* (New York: Norton Press, 1963). Another founder, the late Reverend Pauli Murray, an African-American woman and Episcopal minister, co-wrote NOW's original Statement of Purpose, which begins: "The purpose of NOW is to take action to bring women into full participation in the mainstream of American society now, exercising all privileges and responsibilities thereof in truly equal partnership with men."

The era of 1970s feminism is long past. Is NOW still walking picket lines?

As long as there is oppression to fight, NOW will remain on the front lines. NOW is still out there, working toward these goals through direct mass actions. That means marching, rallying, picketing, holding counterdemonstrations, and engaging in nonviolent civil disobedience. But it's also doing all it can through the existing channels—intensive lobbying, grassroots political organizing, and litigation, including class-action lawsuits.

Is NOW funded in any way by U.S. tax dollars?

No. NOW is a nonprofit organization that receives all its operating funds from private donations and membership dues.

Is NOW affiliated with any one political party?

No. NOW is a nonpartisan organization. Candidates of all political parties are eligible for endorsement by NOW/PAC (the organization's political action committee) and by state and local NOW political action committees.

What is NOW/PAC?

NOW's political action committee supports candidates for U.S. Congress and the presidency. You must be a member of NOW to contribute to NOW/PAC. NOW/PAC is the only part of the national organization that can endorse federal political candidates. NOW Equality PAC (NEP) supports candidates for state, county, and city offices, from governors to school board members. Many state and local NOW chapters have political action committees that can endorse candidates for governor, the state legislature, and local offices.

Source: National Organization for Women, 1000 16th Street NW, Suite 700, Washington, DC 20036; phone: (202) 331-0066; fax: (202) 785-8576; Web site: http://www.now.org.

Paying Federal Taxes

How long will it take to get my refund and how do I check on its status?

You should receive your refund about four to eight weeks after you mail your return; if you file electronically, it should take about three weeks. The earlier you file, the faster you'll get your refund. To check on the status of your refund, call Tele-Tax at (800) 829-4477.

How can I get forms and publications?

Call (800) TAX-FORM or visit your local IRS office, participating library, bank, or post office.

Do I have to file a return?

This usually depends on your filing status, the amount of your gross income, and whether you can be claimed as a dependent on another person's return for the year before. See your tax forms and instructions booklet for more information.

I just completed my return and I owe the IRS money. What should I do?

Remember to enclose the payment when you file the return. You should file even if you can't pay all of the amount you owe. File by April 15, and pay as much as possible. If you use electronic filing, you can file early but may not have to pay until April 15. By filing on time you avoid the late filing penalty.

How can I get an extension to file my return?

You can get an extension by filing Form 4868, "Application for Automatic Extension of Time to File U.S. Individual Income Tax Return," by April 15. This way you avoid the late filing penalty. However, if you owe tax, you should pay as much as you can with Form 4868.

How can I get my employer to give me my W-2 form?

If you don't get your W-2 form by February 15, call the IRS at (800) 829-1040. They will ask you for certain information, such as your employer's name and address. The IRS will contact your employer requesting that your W-2 form be sent to you.

Which form should I use?

Choose the simplest tax form that fits your tax situation. It may save you time and reduce the possibility of errors if you use one of the shorter forms. Many eligible taxpayers are not taking advantage Form 1040EZ, which could save unnecessary tax preparation costs.

I got married late last year. Do I need to notify the IRS that I changed my name?

If you changed your name because of marriage, divorce, or for other reasons, you should immediately notify the Social Security Administration (SSA). This will help prevent delays in processing your return and issuing your refund, because SSA notifies the IRS of your change in name. Also, by letting the SSA know of the change, you will safeguard your future Social Security benefits. If you get a tax return package with a mailing label, be sure to print your new name on the label.

What is "itemizing"? How can I tell if it will help me?

You itemize deductions by filing Schedule A with Form 1040. On Schedule A, you list amounts you paid during the year for certain items such as medical and dental care, state and local income taxes, real estate taxes, home mortgage interest, and gifts to charity. If your itemized deductions are more than your standard deduction, your federal income tax will be less if you itemize.

Source: IRS Service Center, Holtsville, New York, 00501; (800) 829-1040.

Social Security

What is Social Security?

Under the Social Security system, U.S. workers regularly and automatically pay a percentage of their wages in order to earn benefits that insure against retirement, disability, and death of a wage earner. Employers provide matching contributions. Self-employed workers also contribute. But Social Security provides much more than retirement benefits. It insures workers and their families against the loss of income if they become disabled, and it protects their sur-

vivors if they die during and after their working years. The disability and survivor benefits are particularly important for younger workers.

How many people receive Social Security benefits?

Approximately 44 million Americans receive Social Security benefits each
month.

Who pays for Social Security?

Workers contribute 6.2 percent of their earnings, matched by their employers,
to the Social Security system. Self-employed workers pay an amount equivalent
to the combined employee-employer contribution. Some beneficiaries contribute to the system by paying taxes on Social Security benefits. Individual
beneficiaries with a total income of more than $25,000 and couples with a total
income above $32,000 pay income taxes on up to 85 percent of their benefits.
Most of the revenue from this tax is earmarked for the Social Security program.

What happens to the money I pay into Social Security?

It goes into the Social Security trust funds and is used to pay benefits and accumulate reserves. Most of the payments being made by today's workers and
their employers go to fund today's beneficiaries, but the trust funds are beginning to build substantial reserves.

What will I get if I retire?

The Social Security benefit formula is designed around a formula that calcu-
lates your average earnings for the 35 years of your working life during which
you were paid the most. If your average wages for those 35 years are typical of
American workers and you retire at full retirement age, currently 65, your Social Security benefit will equal about 41 percent of your earnings just before retirement. If your average earnings for that 35-year period reflect the minimum
wage, your benefit will be about 59 percent of your pre-retirement earnings. If
your average earnings for that 35-year period put you in the highest tax
bracket, your benefit will be about 27 percent of your pre-retirement earnings.

I know some retired people with high incomes who get Social Security benefits. Why? They certainly don't need the money.

Social Security benefits are based on people's work records, their wages, and
the contributions they and their employers make throughout their working
lives. We all pay into Social Security, pooling our risks and earning the right to
protection. So it's true that some people who don't need Social Security benefits get them anyway.

Remember that although all workers pay the same percentage of earnings into
the system, the benefit formula is structured so that lower-income workers will receive proportionately higher retirement benefits than higher-income workers—
who, as a rule, have had more opportunities to provide additional protection for

themselves by participating in pension and investment plans and accumulating personal savings. So while higher-income workers do receive Social Security benefits when they retire, those benefits are proportionately lower.

But shouldn't we focus Social Security benefits on those who truly need them?

That's how the benefit formula works. By replacing 59 percent of earnings for those at the bottom of the economic ladder compared to 27 percent for those at the top, the formula assures that those in need will receive proportionately more from their investment in the system.

Why do Social Security beneficiaries get an increase every year?

They don't, really. They get a cost-of-living adjustment (COLA). The COLA adjusts the benefit for the cost of living, which protects the purchasing power of Social Security benefits from being eroded by inflation.

What will my family and I get if I become disabled?

Benefits for a worker who becomes disabled are computed in the same way as old-age benefits. Your dependents—usually spouses or children—receive a benefit equal to half of your benefit, up to a family maximum.

What will my family get if I die?

Children of workers receive a benefit if the worker dies; the widow or widower of a worker also receives a benefit if he or she is caring for surviving children. Each receives three-quarters of what you would have received as a disabled worker, up to a family maximum.

If I had a choice, couldn't I invest my money better?

Maybe, but not everyone could. If the United States abandoned the Social Security system and its citizens set out to provide themselves with equivalent protection, many workers struggling to meet day-to-day needs might not set aside any money for retirement. If employers no longer had to contribute toward the retirement security of their employees, some companies might do so voluntarily, but others would not.

I'm young. Will Social Security be there when I am ready to retire?

Probably. Social Security is one of the most broadly supported of all government programs, vehemently defended by America's growing population of elderly people and by powerful lobbyists representing them. On the other hand, as more people live longer, they put an ever greater demand on the system. It's unclear exactly how the Social Security system will be modified to last for more than another 35 years, but experts are working on the problem.

Concern about the future of Social Security first arose when the nation experienced extraordinary economic problems in the late 1970s and early 1980s. Inflation and unemployment rose rapidly and remained at high levels, while wages lagged. Social Security's benefit payments, which are automatically adjusted to keep pace with inflation, rose steeply, while Social Security's income failed to keep up because of high unemployment and low wages. Congress extended Social Security's functional adequacy with legislation in 1977 and again in 1983.

Today, the Social Security system is set up to work until 2029. Soon, though, Congress is expected to revise the system—possibly by reducing some benefit levels or raising some additional tax revenue to extend this period of financial adequacy.

Source: Tom Margenau, Social Security Administration; (410) 965-8904.

U.S. Library of Congress

Why do they call it the "Library of Congress"?

The Library of Congress serves as the research arm of Congress, answering some 500,000 requests annually. The Congressional Research Service (CRS), the part of the Library that serves Congress, is staffed by specialists on such topics as economics, foreign affairs, and the environment. CRS supplies Congress with unbiased information on a wide variety of subjects. Another department that works closely with Congress is the law library. With collections in foreign, international, and comparative law, it serves as the foreign law research arm of Congress.

Isn't the Library of Congress the National Library of the United States?

Yes. But it's even more than that. The U.S. Library of Congress is the world's largest library. Its collections comprise the world's most comprehensive record of human creativity and knowledge.

Does the Library have a copy of every book published in the United States?

No; but it does have more than 17 million books, in addition to almost 111 million other items, including everything from newspapers to maps to movies, in its other special collections.

That's a lot of books. If you lined the bookshelves end to end, how far would they reach?

Books and other materials are shelved on some 532 miles of shelves in all three buildings—about the distance between Washington, D.C., and Chicago.

With so many books on the shelves, is the Library still acquiring new texts?

Yes—at a rate of 7,000 items per working day! These books and other materials arrive through exchange with libraries in this country and abroad, gifts, transfers from other government agencies, official donations from local, state, and foreign governments, requisition, purchase, and copyright deposits. Selection officers review materials and decide which should be kept and added to the permanent collections. Copyright deposits make up the core of the collections, particularly those in the map, music, motion picture, and prints and photographs divisions.

How is the Library using new technologies?

The expanded Computer Catalog Center adjacent to the Main Reading Room enables patrons to use a simplified automated bibliographic search program to look up titles in the Library's general book collections. Users outside the Library can gain free access to its online catalog of files through the Internet and the National Digital Library.

What is the National Digital Library?

The National Digital Library (NDL) program is the library's initiative to make widely available digitized versions of its unique American collections. Now freely accessible on the Internet are millions of records from the Library, including its entire card catalog; THOMAS, a congressional database; major exhibitions with text and images; and hundreds of thousands of images from the Library's incomparable map, photographic, manuscript, and film collections. The Uniform Resource Locator (URL) for the Library's Home Page is http://www.loc.gov/ or http://lcweb.loc.gov.

Can the general public use this library?

Yes—but not to check books out. In fact, all Library stacks are closed. Instead, patrons must follow a request process and use all books on the premises. But anyone over "high school age" can get a user's card (you'll need a driver's license or passport). Library staffers retrieve requested books or collections items, which patrons then use in the Library's reading rooms.

Is the Library of Congress the best place to start researching my family history?

Probably not. The Library's Local History and Genealogy Section suggests that to make your search easier, you first consult your local public library for guides to genealogical research. That way, you'll know what you're looking for—or at least how to begin. And at your request, the Library of Congress will send you a brochure about its local history and genealogy collection.

If I don't need to do research, is the Library of Congress worth a visit during my next trip to the nation's capital?

History, architecture, and culture buffs would certainly say yes. Opened in 1897, the Library's first permanent building—now called the Thomas Jefferson Building—was intended to be a showplace for the art and culture of the young republic and remains one of the most admired buildings of the period. Throughout the building tourists can view the work of more than 50 American sculptors, painters, and mosaic artists. One tour highlight is the glorious Great Hall, which rises 75 feet from marble floor to stained-glass ceiling. The marble columns, staircases, mosaics, and paintings make this one of the most beautiful public buildings in America. Free guided tours are offered several times a day.

What else can visitors see at the Library of Congress?

The Gutenberg Bible and the Giant Bible of Mainz are on permanent display on the first floor of the Great Hall. Other historic and treasured items from the Library's vast collection are on display on a rotating basis. Changing exhibits are mounted in public areas and reading rooms throughout the Library complex.

How many visitors does the Library serve?

With a staff of approximately 4,100, the Library serves about 1 million readers and visitors annually. Though children cannot request and use Library materials, they are welcome on tours.

What is the Library's Copyright Office?

The U.S. Copyright Office has handled more than 20 million copyright registrations and transfers since 1790, and currently deals with some 600,000 new registrations each year. Its card catalog, with more than 45 million cards, is the largest in the world.

Source: The Library of Congress, 101 Independence Avenue SE, Washington, DC 20540; (202) 707-6200.

Voting

How can I register to vote?

It depends on the state you're living in. The Federal Election Commission (FEC) tells callers the title of the local election official. It could be the county clerk, county auditor, county supervisor of elections, the county board of elections, or the voter registrar. People can look in the phone book under the listings for local government, or under voter information or registration, if the area has it. A January 1995 federal law requires most states to provide voter registration when people apply for or renew their driver's license, when they apply for public assistance, when they apply to an armed forces recruitment office, or when they receive assistance from state-funded disability agencies.

What are the polling hours?

They vary from state to state, but 6 A.M. is the earliest time anywhere. The latest time any state poll is open is 9 P.M. That's a really long time to be open. The pollers get tired and don't get paid very much. In New England states, some jurisdictions stay open shorter hours because of smaller populations.

How do the FEC and the news media get election results?

There are no official results until sometimes as much as three weeks after election. The information available immediately after an election is unofficial, and it's provided by the Voter News Service, a private agency supported by major news services, like the Associated Press and the major TV networks. They're an exit-polling service that identifies bellwether precincts, which indicate the way a state's going. The Voter News Service has people in every county and sometimes at city level who call in unofficial results, and it's all consolidated in a giant database in New York City.

Exit polling and unofficial results are what the news media use to project winners. Sometimes the Voter News Service makes a mistake, as it did with the New Hampshire senate in November 1996. They called it for the Democrats, but when final total came in the Republicans had won.

How many election jurisdictions are there?

There are 10,000 to 13,000 election jurisdictions, because some are run by cities, some by counties. In New England and some midwestern states, elections are run by municipalities. In Virginia, independent cities run elections separate from the counties around them. For most states the election is run at a county level.

How does one get an absentee ballot?

If someone is voting with absentee ballots, he must fill out an application. States have different deadlines. In Arkansas, Connecticut, Delaware, Georgia, and Washington, D.C., you can show up to request an application one day before the election. Rhode Island requires you to apply at least three weeks before the election.

The request for the ballot goes to the local election office to see if the applicant is eligible for absentee voting. In some states, you need to cite a specific reason to vote absentee, such as temporary or permanent disabilities, absence because of college attendance, or business travel or religious reasons. In other states, anyone can vote absentee.

Parties also can appeal to the larger group or approach them as women, owners of small businesses, or labor, etc.

Source: Peggy Sims has been with the Federal Election Commission since 1976 and has served as an election research specialist at the FEC's Office of Election Administration since 1986. The Office of Election Administration collects information about the different laws and procedures that states, counties, and cities use to run federal elections.

THE LAW

—◆—

Adoption

Alternative Dispute Resolution

Automobiles

Copyright

Debt Collection

Disability Law • Discrimination

DNA Testing

Drug Testing • Employment

**Lesbian and Gay
Civil Rights**

Health Law • Finding a Lawyer

Jury Duty

Legal Malpractice • Personal Injury

Products Liability

Search and Seizure • Sentencing

Sexual Harassment

Small Claims Court • Smoking Laws

Traffic Tickets

Victims' Rights • Wills

Workers' Compensation

Adoption

What is *adoption*?

Adoption is the permanent, legal transfer of all parental rights from one person or couple to another person or couple. Adoptive parents have the same rights and responsibilities as parents whose children are born to them. Adoptive parents are real parents.

How many children are adopted in the United States each year?

It is estimated that at least 100,000 adoptions by U.S. citizens occur each year. About half of these adoptions occur between children and persons unrelated to them.

What are the steps in an adoption?

States' laws governing adoption vary widely. In general, the birthparent, or birthparents, sign a consent to the adoption or a relinquishment of parental rights. This consent or relinquishment is not legally binding prior to the birth of the child and can generally be revoked for a limited period of time after birth. The biological father of the child usually must be notified of any adoption plan, but procedures for this notification vary considerably. Separately, the prospective adoptive parents must file a petition to adopt. After a period of court supervision—usually six months to one year, during which the adoptive parents have custody of the child—the adoption is finalized. The adopted child then enjoys the same legal footing in the family as a biological child.

How many Americans want to adopt a child and how many children are in need of adoption?

There are between 1 and 2 million infertile and fertile couples and individuals in the United States who would like to adopt children. It is estimated that no more than 30,000 healthy U.S. infants were legally available for adoption in the most recent year. Given the difference in numbers between babies who need homes and homes waiting to adopt, there's no way that everyone will be able to adopt a healthy baby. There are other alternatives that offer the joy of parenting. Potential adoptive families can adopt a child from another country or a child with special needs. Special needs children are usually older, disabled, or members of sibling groups. There are an estimated 100,000 special needs children waiting to be adopted.

My wife and I have considered adopting a child with a disability, but I don't know how we could afford to pay for the child's special needs.

The federal Adoption Assistance Program (AAP) subsidizes adoptions of special needs children. The AAP provides adoptive parents with monthly payments, the amounts to be determined by the needs of the child and the circumstances of the family. One-time payments of up to $2,000 to cover expenses related to adoption may be paid to adopters of special needs children, whether or not the child qualifies for a continuous monthly subsidy.

Tell me about the role of an adoption agency.

About one-half of all nonrelative adoptions are arranged by private or public adoption agencies. There is a difference between "public" and "private" agencies. A public agency is a state or county agency that places children and is supported by your tax dollars. The private agency is in most cases licensed by the state, but operates using fees from adoptive families and/or charitable contributions. Most private agencies are nonprofit organizations, many with a religious sponsorship. Adoption agencies screen adoptive parents and provide counseling to them. Some provide classes on adoption and teach prospective parents about the various issues involved in understanding adoption, e.g., how and when to tell your child about adoption. Some agencies assist families with questions or issues that arise after the adoption is legally finalized.

How do I choose an adoption agency?

Always begin by calling the department or office in your state that licenses agencies. Find out: if the agency has a current license; when the agency was last visited by a representative of the department; if there are any unresolved complaints about the agency; and if there are any questions about the agency—of a financial or other nature—that appear in the record, or that the person you are speaking with is aware of. Always ask what other departments, organizations, or individuals you might be referred to for additional information. Ask for a copy of the agency's most recent annual report, its most recent outside audited financial statement, and the names of some of the agency's clients.

Your best protection is to do your homework very carefully, reading well-based, sourced books and pamphlets either from your local library, bookstore, or from the National Council For Adoption (NCFA). Beware of much that you will find on the Internet. Proceed cautiously and do not let yourself be pushed or rushed into anything. Avoid any agency that suggests any action that is either illegal or unethical.

Are there alternatives to agency adoptions?

An adoption that is not arranged by an adoption agency is called an "independent adoption." In these cases, families use the services of an adoption attorney or other intermediary. Some people choose independent adoption because they believe that an adoption agency would not accept them. They may be over age 40, not married for very long, or have another situation that they think might cause them to be rejected by an agency. Others seek the services of an attorney because the agencies may have a waiting list of several years. In some states, the attorney or intermediary will identify a pregnant woman considering adoption, just as an agency might, while in other states it is up to the adopting parents to locate the woman. To find a good, ethical adoption attorney or intermediary, ask local parent groups if any of their members have successfully adopted children independently and be sure to use the checklist available from the National Council for Adoption.

How much does adoption cost?

The average fee collected for adopting healthy infants by one group of agencies belonging to the NCFA was $16,100, according to a recent 1996 survey. It is extremely important to obtain fee information in writing from any agency, attorney, intermediary, or consultant before starting the adoption process.

I have just recently been married for the second time. My wife and I would like to start a family by adopting. Will my former divorce and recent marriage hurt our chances?

Generally, divorced parents are accepted as adoptive parents so long as their current marriage is stable and the relationship is good. Many adoption agencies require that couples be married a minimum of three years before adopting.

My husband and I are able to have children but we prefer adoption. Will our fertility be an issue?

Infertile couples usually receive priority for placement of healthy babies; however, this guideline can be waived. For children with special needs, or international adoptions, fertile couples or singles may apply.

Why do some families adopt children from countries other than the United States?

In 1996, Americans adopted over 11,000 children from other countries. Some couples pursue international adoption because they do not wish to wait three or more years to adopt a healthy white infant. Individuals who do not fit the criteria of the average adoption agency (e.g., they are over 40 years of age or single) sometimes look outside the competitive U.S. environment. Couples who are able to have children but believe in providing a home for a needy, already living child are often attracted to international adoptions. Potential parents may seek to adopt a child who shares their own cultural heritage. The International Concerns for Children (ICC) publishes a book of information submitted by various international adoption agencies and a photolisting of children from other countries who are legally available for adoption. The ICC can be contacted at 911 Cypress Drive, Boulder, Colo. 80303; (303) 494-8333.

What records can be found in a sealed birth file?

In most states, once an adoption is final, records such as the original unamended birth certificate, court records, adoption agency case records, and professional working notes and files are sealed; they are then unavailable to the adopted person, adoptive parents, or birthparents without a court order. When courts are asked to open sealed records, the requester must provide good cause, such as a need for critical medical information. Curiosity alone is considered insufficient reason to unseal adoption records. Only three states—Alaska, Hawaii, and Kansas—offer open inspection of original birth records.

In what ways do adopted persons find their birthparents?

Only 1 to 2 percent of adopted adults search for their biological parents. Nearly half of the states have established mutual consent registries that match information on adopted persons and birthparents. When both the birthparent and the adopted child register, identifying information is then shared with each. Twelve states have passed search and consent laws, which enable an adopted adult or birthparent to request that the state social services department or other intermediary initiate a search. If the person being sought is found and consents to having his/her identity released, the agency gives identifying information to the other person.

Some people choose to hire private investigators or to search on their own using information gathered from public records. Others use groups that assist searches. Some of these are: The Adoptees' Liberty Movement Association, P.O. Box 727, Radio City Station, New York, N.Y. 10101-0727; (212) 581-1568; Concerned United Birthparents, Inc., 2000 Walker Street, Des Moines, Iowa 50317; (515) 263-9558; and International Soundex Reunion Registry, P.O. Box 2312, Carson City, Nev. 89702; (702) 882-7755.

Source: William Pierce is president of the National Council For Adoption and author or co-author of several books, including *The Adoption Factbook* and *The Encyclopedia of Adoption*. NCFA is located at 1930 17th Street, NW, Washington, DC 20009-6207; phone: (202) 328-1200; fax: (202) 332-0935; e-mail: www.ncfausa.org; ncfa@juno.com. For more information contact local agencies, state service departments, your local public library, or write for the National Council For Adoption's publication list by sending a self-addressed large envelope with postage for two ounces to: Publications List, NCFA, 1930 17th Street, NW, Washington, DC 20009-6207.

Alternative Dispute Resolution

What is the difference between an *arbitration* and a *mediation*?

In arbitration, both parties agree to present their dispute to one or more impartial persons who will make a final, binding decision regarding their claim. Mediation is a nonbinding, less formal process where the parties submit their dispute to an impartial third person who assists them in reaching their own settlement.

Both processes are separate from the court system and offer disputants an alternative way to resolve conflict. In an attempt to reduce their backlog of cases, all 94 U.S. federal district courts have implemented some type of alternative dispute resolution program, mostly mediation. Some courts not only encourage but mandate that plaintiffs and defendants attempt to resolve their lawsuits by alternate means before entering the courtroom.

What are the advantages of arbitration and mediation?

Disputes are resolved much faster than in court. The average processing time to arbitrate a dispute from filing to award is about four months. Mediation can generally be scheduled in a matter of weeks, and the average meeting time for a mediation is one and a half hours. Hearings are confidential; there is no public record or press coverage. The matter is conducted less formally and strict rules of evidence are not necessary. Legal precedent does not apply in alternative dispute resolution hearings, and therefore solutions are more flexible and can be tailored to the needs of the parties.

What does it cost to arbitrate or mediate a dispute?

Fees vary, though they are often dependent upon the dollar amount at issue in the dispute. The American Arbitration Association charges a nonrefundable filing fee of $500 if the claim is for an amount up to $10,000. Centers for dispute resolution receive an administrative fee (about $150 each day of the hearing), and in most cases claimants pay additional compensation to their arbitrator or mediator. Alternative dispute resolution, however, is generally much less costly than litigation.

Do I need an attorney?

Parties are not required, but are allowed, to be represented by counsel.

A buddy and I started a lawn-care business to pay for our college educations. Now that we've graduated, we are liquidating the business. We disagree about how to divide the equipment and some remaining monies. I don't want to sue my partner but I know what I deserve. How do I initiate an arbitration?

Some business contracts contain a clause that directs future disputes arising out of the contractual relationship to be resolved through arbitration. If you and your partner had such a clause in your partnership agreement, then the process is begun by filing a Demand for Arbitration with the American Arbitration Association. If no such contract clause exists, both parties simply need to agree to arbitrate and complete and sign a written Submission to Arbitration.

How do I prepare my case for arbitration or mediation?

In arbitration, you are trying to convince a decision maker that your claims are right or fair by presenting evidence at a hearing. Although strict rules of evidence do not apply, each arbitration service has rules its arbitrators follow. You will receive a copy of these rules when you agree to arbitration. Rules of the American Arbitration Association allow the presentation of witness testimony, contracts, photographs, diagrams, and other relevant documentation.

Preparation for mediation is different in that you do not prepare evidence in order to convince a third party to award a finding for you. Sharing documents may help disputants gain a better understanding of the other party's position, but time may be better spent considering ways to compromise or inventing creative solutions that both parties can agree on.

I am a medical researcher at a university and a patent dispute recently came up with a pharmaceutical company. I don't have confidence that a judge and jury will understand the complex scientific issues involved. Should I arbitrate?

In alternative dispute resolution, claimants are not stuck with the judge and jury randomly assigned to them. Disputants can use anyone they agree upon as an arbitrator. Arbitration services maintain lists of arbitrators who are experts in all kinds of areas. If the parties do not appoint an arbitrator on their own, the American Arbitration Association will send each party an identical list of arbitrators. Each party strikes three objectionable names from the list and ranks the remaining names in order of preference. From the people approved on both lists, the association invites the acceptance of an arbitrator to serve.

Can I get a refund of the filing fees if the case settles or is withdrawn?

All filing fees are nonrefundable.

What happens after the award is issued?

Most parties voluntarily comply with the arbitrator's award. Judgment on an award can be entered in court so that a prevailing party can take legal steps to collect, such as levying on property or garnishing wages.

What if I don't agree with the arbitrator's decision?

When you agree to arbitrate a claim, your case is decided by a third party who acts like judge and jury. Arbitration awards are final and binding. Appeals are not a matter of course as they are in the court system. You can ask that an arbitrator's decision be reviewed in court, but barring unusual circumstances, the arbitration award will not be overturned.

How many cases are arbitrated each year?

In 1996, a total of 70,516 cases were filed with the American Arbitration Association.

Source: The American Arbitration Association at 140 West 51st Street, New York, NY 10020-1203. For the telephone number of the regional office nearest you, call (800) 778-7879; or visit their Web site at http://www.adr.org. The American Arbitration Association is a not-for-profit, public service organization dedicated to the resolution of disputes through the use of mediation, arbitration, negotiation, elections, and other dispute settlement techniques. With 38 offices nationwide and cooperative agreements with institutions in 52 other nations, the association offers hundreds of education and training programs each year throughout the world.

Automobiles

How can I avoid getting ripped off when buying a used car?

Three critical steps will ensure that you avoid the vast majority of used car ripoffs.

- Insist on buying a one-owner car. If a dealer won't prove to you that the car had only one previous owner, *don't buy the car.* Don't consider buying auction cars, multiple-owner cars, out-of-state cars, former rental or program cars, or demonstrators. This narrows down the field of used cars—and that's the idea. Good cars aren't easily found, but ripoffs are everywhere.

- Before signing anything, making a payment, or handing over a trade-in, talk with the prior owner and ask him about the car. (Was the car purchased new? What problems did the owner have with it? Was it wrecked? Is the odometer correct? Did the owner like the car? Why did the owner trade it in? How much did the dealer give for the trade?) Ask for copies of the service records. Some dealers will insist that they cannot release a previous owner's identity or phone number. Privacy laws generally do not prevent giving this information out; in any case, the dealer could call the previous owner and ask that he/she talk with you. This tack may help to persuade the dealer: either you talk with the previous owner and get satisfactory information or you *don't buy the car.*

- Third, before signing anything or making a payment, have the car examined by a mechanic. Make sure you ask the mechanic to look for signs of wreck damage as well as mechanical problems. Have the mechanic road-test the car.

These three steps should prevent most ripoffs, but there are other things to keep in mind. Rely on *Consumer Reports* buyer's guides, available in any public library, for information on the reliability and quality of various models of cars. Read all documents carefully, especially financing paperwork. Challenge document fees and other items added to the purchase price that you were not told about when you negotiated the price. Don't buy an extended service contract or warranty. If you aren't knowledgeable about cars or skilled at negotiating, bring along someone who is. Check "blue book" wholesale/retail prices on any car that you consider purchasing (blue books are available in bank loan offices).

What should I do if I buy a lemon?

A car is generally considered a lemon under various state lemon laws if the vehicle was bought new and has a certain number of problems or a single problem repeated a number of times. If your new car is malfunctioning, have a well-qualified (preferably ASE-certified), independent mechanic examine the car. If the mechanic determines that the car is not fixable, ask the dealer to buy the car back. Have your mechanic speak to the dealer or write a report to the dealer. If the dealer refuses, get in touch with the manufacturer's zone representative and request a buy-back.

If this effort fails, have the zone representative enter you into the manufacturer's arbitration process, and again, demand a buy-back. Also request reimbursement for your time and inconvenience, lost use of the vehicle, missed work, and disruption of family and personal activities. Payment for these incidentals will help offset monies the arbitrator may deduct for miles driven on the car. If these efforts don't work, your last recourse is to sue.

I bought my neighbor's 15-year-old Plymouth as a second car for my family. I had the car for two weeks and the brakes went out. Can I demand that my neighbor refund my money if I return the car?

Unless the neighbor stated that the brakes were fine when they were not, or otherwise misrepresented or knowingly concealed something material about the car, the neighbor has no obligation to you. In most states, if you establish that the neighbor decided to sell the car only when he found out the brakes needed $500 in repairs, and the neighbor knew that you thought you were buying a car that had no major problems, you would have a valid claim to return the car and receive a refund or to sue for damages.

Are there precautions I should take when selling a car?

Some states require a notarized bill of sale in each sale. Federal law requires that an odometer statement be given in a proper form, although the federal odometer statement is included in the language on your title assignment on most titles issued within the past several years. Some states require that a car be safety-inspected prior to sale. Check with your state motor vehicle office to determine what documents should be prepared and what steps taken in selling your car. Under any circumstances, you should always give a bill of sale that sets out the date and amount of sale, the vehicle ID number, the names and addresses of the buyer and seller, and any substantial, known defects.

Full disclosure of all known defects is the best protection from any claim for misrepresentation. It is also the fair way to do business. Make sure that the buyer signs the bill of sale and any separate federal odometer statement, and that you get a copy of all documents relating to the sale. Avoid selling a car with safety defects unless it is sold to a dealer or mechanic who represents in writing that it will be junked or repaired before use or resale. In completing the financial part of the transaction, insist on cash, cashier's check, or other certified funds before signing over the title or releasing possession of the car. Take your license plates off the vehicle before handing over the keys.

I'm selling my car. Do I have to tell potential buyers about every defect?

State laws vary regarding disclosure requirements, but the safest and fairest practice is to disclose all known defects fully to a buyer. Generally, the law requires disclosure of known defects that are material—that is, defects so significant they may affect the purchaser's willingness to buy or the amount she may pay. It is particularly important that, if asked, the seller answer questions truthfully. If the seller realizes that the purchaser is under an important misconception, (e.g., that the car never was wrecked when it was), the seller must tell the purchaser the truth.

I'm stuck in the second year of a four-year lease and I can't afford the payments anymore. Can I get out of the lease or sell the car?

You will have to live by the terms of the lease, which are harsh when you want to end the lease early. This is one of several reasons why it is generally better to buy a car than to lease it. But the simple answer is, refer to the contract. You can get out of the lease or sell the car; it is just a question of cost.

How can I avoid getting cheated by a mechanic?

As in most consumer affairs, the first issue is knowledge. The more you know about mechanical problems, the less vulnerable you are to fraud. If you don't know much about car repair and either can't or aren't inclined to learn, enlist the help of others. Keep in mind that certain groups of people—such as women, elderly or very young people, minorities, and those who don't speak fluent English—are often targets of scams. For major repairs, get a second opinion, and always shop prices.

Try to hire a mechanic who is ASE-certified. Ask for references. Ask faculty who teach auto-mechanics classes at junior colleges for recommendations. Get estimates in writing, and, if possible, have a written provision stating that the charges will not exceed the estimate. If charges might exceed the estimate, find out exactly how high the cost could go. If the engine is being disassembled for diagnosis, get something in writing about any cost you may have to pay if you choose not to have the repair done. Shops may try to charge a hefty "tear down and reassemble" charge if you decline the repair after diagnosis.

Should I stretch my budget to buy a new car instead of a used car?

As long as you aren't stretching your budget too far, you should spend the extra money to get a new car. Most people are not aware of the enormous amount of fraud in the used car marketing industry. This fraud includes the sale of cars with undisclosed previous wreck damage; false descriptions as "one-owners" when they have had multiple owners and crossed several states; undisclosed histories as "lemons" that have been bought back by the manufacturers; false descriptions as "brass hat" or "executive" cars, when they are mere rental "program" cars; and false descriptions as "in excellent condition" or "having no problems" when there are major known problems.

Even new cars are sometimes sold with fraudulent misrepresentations. In 1987, Chrysler admitted selling some 60,000 cars as new that had been driven with the odometers disconnected and that had in some cases been wrecked and repaired. Chrysler claimed this was standard industry practice. In recent years, 28 states have passed laws permitting cars to be sold as new when they have actually suffered considerable damage (up to 6 percent of their value in damage in some states). This means that a manufacturer or dealer can sell a $25,000 vehicle as new when it has suffered $1,500 in damages, without disclosure.

So, have your new car checked out by a mechanic before buying it, just as you would a used car. The National Highway and Traffic Safety Administration (NHTSA) adopted an exemption that permits car manufacturers to sell cars without disclosing the mileage. If you want to comment on the NHTSA exemption, contact Richard Morse, Chief, Odometer Fraud Section, NHTSA, 400 Seventh St., SW, Room 5321, Washington, D.C. 20590; phone: (202) 366-4761; fax: (202) 366-8065.

Is it better to buy a used car from a dealer or from an individual?

Generally, you are better off buying from an individual. But take all of the precautions described above and ensure that you are dealing with the owner. A number of people pose as individual sellers when in fact they are selling cars for dealers. Insist on having a properly assigned, clear title at the time you pay. It is possible to buy good cars from dealers, too, if you work hard at taking the right precautions. The problem is that a huge number of frauds are perpetrated by dealers who know all the tricks of the trade.

I bought a used car with major problems the dealer did not disclose. What should I do?

Before you contact the dealer, try to find out if the dealer knew that you were being cheated. Especially if safety may be an issue, have the car checked out carefully by a good body shop and/or mechanic, who should look not only for the problems you know about but for other problems like wreck damage or a mileage discrepancy. Ask the mechanic if any problems found would have been obvious to the dealer, and what, if anything, can be done to repair them. Track down the previous owners.

Check for owners' names in records in the glove box or do a title history search with the motor vehicle department. Find out from former owners what problems the dealer was told about. If it becomes clear that the dealer lied to you or concealed problems, you probably have a claim involving actual and punitive damages and attorney's fees. Pay particular attention to any statements the dealer made to you in selling the car, such as, "The car is in excellent condition," or, "This car has never been wrecked." Even if the dealer did not deliberately cheat you, you may have a claim for actual damages or to rescind the contract. After arming yourself with information, you can either contact the dealer to negotiate a resolution of the problem; bring a suit in Small Claims Court; or contact an attorney to pursue legal remedies.

Source: Bernard E. Brown, a private attorney whose practice is primarily devoted to handling cases of fraud in automobile sales. He has won all but one of his numerous jury trials in car fraud cases and his work has set significant precedent in this area of law. Mr. Brown is one of the founders and an original co-chair of the National Association of Consumer Advocates and was the primary draftsman of a bill relating to fraudulent sale of rebuilt wrecked cars offered in the U.S. Congress. In 1993, he appeared in *60 Minutes* in an exposé about the fraudulent resale of wrecked cars. Mr. Brown can be contacted at The Brown Law Firm, Westwood Colonial Building, 4800 Rainbow Boulevard, Westwood, KS 66205-1932; (913) 722-4777.

Copyright

What kinds of works can be *copyrighted*?

Copyright protects art, literature, and information in all types of media: writing, film, music, painting, sculpture, recorded performances, even computer programs and databases. The law states that copyright protects "original works of authorship fixed in any tangible medium of expression, now known or later developed, from which they can be perceived, reproduced, or otherwise communicated, either directly or with the aid of a machine or device." Titles, slogans, and logos can be protected by trademark law, but not by copyright.

What do I have to do to get a copyright?

Nothing. Once your work is put into some tangible form—on paper or in computer disk storage—it is automatically protected. You may want to register it, though.

What can I do with a copyright?

Copyright is just like any other property. The owner of the copyright can sell it, lease it, give it away, or bequeath it in a will. The owner of the copyright has exclusive personal property rights, including the right to prohibit others from copying, disseminating, performing, or displaying the work.

How long does a copyright last?

The basic term of a copyright is the life of the author plus 50 years. In the case of a work created by a company's employees or certain works created under contract, the term is 75 years from first publication. For works published before 1978, the longest possible term is seventy-five years from first publication, but many such works are out of copyright due to noncompliance with requirements of prior law.

I want to quote from a book I found on women's health in a pamphlet I am putting together for my church. Do I need to get permission?

That is probably what is called a "fair use," as long as you give credit to the author and the quotation is kept to a minimum. However, reprinting another church's pamphlet without permission would probably not be a fair use, for that would be "competitive" in the broadest sense.

I got to talking with a man on the bus about his idea for a book. I think it's a terrific book idea. If I write it first, can he sue me?

An idea cannot be copyrighted, only the expression of an idea in a tangible form. At this stage, the book idea is just that—an idea—and open for anyone to use, unless it was disclosed to you with a clear understanding that it was to be kept confidential. You could not, however, take an outline or sample chapters for a book you found and present them as your own.

I teach earth science to high school freshmen. I came across some very interesting data about weather predictions in a newly published book. Can I copy the information and share it with my students?

The data itself is not copyright-protected, but the presentation may be if it has some degree of creativity. In general, teachers may make a single copy of a written work for research purposes or to prepare for teaching a course. For a teacher's purposes, a written work may include a book chapter, a magazine article, a short story, or a graph or cartoon from a newspaper. Whether a teacher can make copies for all of his students depends on several factors, including some rather strict rules about the length of the work to be copied. All classroom copies must include a notice of copyright. A work may not be copied by the same teacher from term to term. If in doubt, you should contact the owner of the copyright for permission or get a copy of the classroom-photocopying guidelines from your local library.

What does it mean when material is in the *public domain*?

When material is in the public domain, it is free for anyone to use without seeking permission. Public domain materials include uncopyrighted works and works in which the copyright has expired.

I've written a "how-to" manual that relates to my job, but I wrote it at home on my own time. Who owns it—me or my company?

If a work is created by an employee within the scope of her job description, it's called "work made for hire." The employer is the "author" and owns the rights; the creator has no rights whatsoever in the work. Some examples of works made for hire are newspapers, movies, dictionaries, greeting cards, and other works created by companies with staffs of writers and authors.

I am writing a mystery story with a cameo appearance by Perry Mason. Am I free to use a character of someone else's invention in my story?

Characters, other than cartoon characters like Mickey Mouse, which are protected as works of art, are usually too amorphous to be protected by copyright. However, a character's distinctive name—such as Perry Mason, James Bond, or even The Cowardly Lion—can be protected as a trademark. And, of course, the actions or dialogue of a character in a story are protected by copyright. So while you could have in your story a lawyer who reveals the murderer by adroit questioning in court, you could not call him Perry Mason or copy the plot or dialogue of a Perry Mason novel.

Should I put a copyright notice on my work?

Copyright notice usually consists of the word "copyright" or the symbol ©, the name of the copyright owner, and in most cases the year of first publication. It is no longer necessary, but still a good idea. Before 1989, it was necessary except on works of foreign authors first published outside the United States.

I recently found some sheet music for a song that did not have a copyright notice. Can I assume that the song is part of the public domain and free to perform?

If the sheet music was first published in the United States before 1978, it is in the public domain. If later than 1977 but before 1989, it is probably in the public domain; even if it is not, you are entitled to rely on the absence of the notice, and your maximum exposure were you sued would be limited to giving up your profits and being enjoined from further use.

Should I register my creative work with the U.S. Copyright Office?

Registration does not create a copyright, but it may be a prerequisite for enforcing one in court. Furthermore, should you bring suit for violation of a copyright, you will not be entitled to attorney's fees and certain statutory damages for infringements that occurred before the registration. Therefore, it is wise to register your work.

How do I register my copyright?

Which registration form you need to complete depends on the type of work being registered. All forms are available from the Information and Publications Section, Copyright Office, Library of Congress, Washington, D.C. 20559; (202) 707-9100. The application form must be accompanied by a $20 fee, and, in most cases, one or two copies of the material to be copyrighted.

Source: William S. Strong, author of *The Copyright Book: A Practical Guide* (4th ed., 1991). Mr. Strong has written extensively on copyright in publications, including the *Journal of the Copyright Society of the USA*. For eight years he was adjunct professor of copyright law at Franklin Pierce Law Center. He received his law degree from Harvard University and is currently a partner in the Boston law firm of Kotin, Crabtree & Strong, One Bowdoin Square, Boston, MA 02114; phone: (617) 227-7031; fax: (617) 367-2988.

Debt Collection

Is there a law that protects consumers with debts?

The federal Fair Debt Collection Practices Act is a consumer law created to eliminate abusive collection practices by debt collectors. The law also ensures that those debt collectors who refrain from using abusive collection practices are not competitively disadvantaged.

I recently bought a fax machine for my small business. I got behind on the payments and the collector is harassing me. Do I have a case under the Fair Debt Collection Practices Act?

No. The act applies only to debts for property or services purchased for personal, family, or household purposes.

My mother-in-law was visiting and answered the phone when a particularly persistent collector called. She gave the collector all kinds of information about where we work and what property we own. Can the collector now use this information to gain payment for the debt?

This collector committed a clear violation of the law. Although he may be able to use the ill-gotten information for collection purposes, he will also be liable under the act. A debt collector may not communicate with any person other than the consumer, his/her attorney, a consumer reporting agency, the creditor, or the creditor's attorney. The law will treat a spouse or parent of a minor buyer like the consumer.

Does a debt collector have to be up front about who they are when contacting you?

In the initial communication, a collector must be honest, telling you that she is attempting to collect a debt, and that any information she obtains from you will be used for that purpose. This disclosure should be clearly given in all communications, including phone calls, personal meetings, corespondence, and other documents. Thereafter, the collector merely needs to inform you that she is a debt collector.

I've gotten in over my head financially and now collection agencies are contacting me all the time. Some of the collectors are quite rude. I know I owe the money, but do I have to put up with their attitude?

Under the act, a debt collector may not engage in any conduct that naturally results in harassment, oppression, or abuse of a debtor. Rudeness is not specifically prohibited, unless it rises to a level of abuse. Obscene or profane language is not allowed.

Can a creditor threaten to bring you up on criminal charges simply because you owe him money?

No. Such a statement would be considered a false or misleading representation. A creditor collecting a debt cannot threaten to take any action that cannot be legally taken, and since you can't be imprisoned for failure to pay a debt, a collector cannot threaten to have you thrown in jail. The act further dictates that a collector can't even state that he is going to take action that is legal but that he has no intention of taking.

One collector kept hounding me about making a payment, but I didn't have the money in my account at the time. He suggested I postdate the check so it would coincide with my payday. I agreed and sent the check. Is this legal?

Debt collectors can encourage payment by accepting postdated checks as long as they notify the debtor in writing not more than ten or less than three business days prior to depositing the check. If you do not receive written notice before your check is deposited, you may file a claim under the Fair Debt Collection Practices Act.

I own an appliance store in a small town, and several customers have not made payments for over six months. I believe I should be able to add interest and collect fees on the amount due. Can I automatically increase their debts for these purposes?

You are not allowed to collect any amount other than what was authorized by the agreement creating the debt. If your sales contract sets out the possibility of a charge for interest and fees in the event of default, then you may pass those costs to the consumer. If your agreement does not specifically mention these charges, you will have to swallow the costs of collection.

A debt collector contacted me recently and claimed that I owed over $1,000. According to my records, I only owe $850. How can I get the amount of debt clarified?

Within five days after the first communication with a consumer, a debt collector must send the consumer a written notice. You have 30 days from receipt of the notice to dispute the amount of the debt. You must make your dispute in writing. The debt collector must then obtain written verification of the debt from the creditor and send a copy to the consumer.

I bought a large-screen TV from Wayne's TV Warehouse. Then I got a notice that I should make payment to some other company. I got so confused I stopped paying at all. Now collectors are calling me. What should I do?

Most likely your debt was sold to a third party. Your debt collector should be able to explain the ownership of the debt to you. At your written request, a collector will provide you with the name and address of the original creditor, if different from the current creditor.

What liability does a collector face who violates the Fair Debt Collection Practices Act?

A debt collector who fails to comply with any provision of the act is liable for actual damages sustained by the consumer. The court may allow additional damages up to $1,000. If you bring action against a debt collector and win, the collector may be liable for court costs and reasonable attorney's fees. If the court finds that a consumer brought a lawsuit in bad faith to harass a debtor, the court may require the consumer to pay attorney's fees and related costs.

Source: The Commercial Law League of America, 150 N. Michigan Avenue, Suite 600, Chicago, IL 60601; phone: (312) 781-2000; fax: (312) 781-2010; e-mail: comlawleag@aol.com. The League, founded over 100 years ago, sets high standards for debt collection procedures among its more than 5,000 members.

Disability Law

What is the Americans with Disabilities Act?

The Americans with Disabilities Act (ADA), passed in 1991, is a federal law that gives civil rights protections to individuals with disabilities similar to those provided to individuals on the basis of race, color, sex, national origin, age, and religion. It guarantees people with disabilities equal opportunity in public accommodations, employment, transportation, state and local government services, and telecommunications.

Who is covered by the act?

To be protected by the ADA, one must have a disability or have a relationship or association with an individual with a disability. An individual with a disability is defined by the ADA as a person who has a physical or mental impairment that substantially limits one or more major life activities; a person who has a history or record of such an impairment; or a person who is perceived by others as having such an impairment.

The ADA applies to persons who have impairments that substantially limit major activities such as seeing, hearing, speaking, walking, breathing, performing manual tasks, learning, caring for oneself, and working. A person with epilepsy, paralysis, HIV infection, AIDS, a substantial hearing or visual impairment, mental retardation, or a specific learning disability is covered; but someone with a minor, nonchronic condition of short duration, such as a sprain, broken limb, or the flu, generally would not be covered. The ADA does not specifically name all of the impairments that are covered.

Does an employer have to give preference to a qualified applicant with a disability over other applicants?

No. An employer is free to select the most qualified applicant available and to make decisions based on reasons unrelated to a disability. Suppose two people apply for a job as a typist, and an essential function of the job is to type 75 words per minute accurately. One applicant, an individual with a disability, who is provided with a reasonable accommodation for a typing test, types 50 words per minute; the other applicant, who has no disability, accurately types 75 words per minute. The employer can hire the applicant with the higher typing speed, if typing is needed for successful performance on the job.

What is "reasonable accommodation"?

Reasonable accommodation is any modification or adjustment to a job or the work environment that will enable a qualified applicant or employee with a disability to participate in the application process or to perform essential job functions. Examples of reasonable accommodation include: making existing facilities used by employees readily accessible to and usable by someone with a disability; restructuring a job; modifying work schedules; acquiring or modifying equipment; providing qualified readers or interpreters; or appropriately modifying examinations, training, or other programs.

Reasonable accommodation also may include reassigning a current employee to a vacant position for which the person is qualified, if that person is unable to do the original job because of a disability even with an accommodation. However, there is no obligation to find a position for an applicant who is not qualified for the position sought. Employers are not required to lower quality or quantity standards as an accommodation; nor are they obligated to provide personal use items such as glasses or hearing aids.

How does an employer know if she must provide a reasonable accommodation?

The decision must be based on the particular facts of each case. An employer should determine whether the accommodation will provide an opportunity for someone with a disability to achieve the same level of performance and to enjoy benefits equal to those of an average, similarly situated person without a disability. However, the accommodation does not have to ensure equal results or provide exactly the same benefits.

In addition, an employer is not required to make an accommodation if it would impose an undue hardship on the operation of the employer's business. "Undue hardship" is defined as an action requiring significant difficulty or expense when considered in light of a number of factors, including the size, resources, nature, and structure of the employer's operation.

Undue hardship is determined on a case-by-case basis. If a particular accommodation would be an undue hardship, the employer must try to identify another accommodation that will not pose such a hardship. Also, if the cost of an accommodation would impose undue hardship on the employer, the individual with a disability should be given the option of paying that portion of the cost that would constitute undue hardship or of providing the entire accommodation themselves. For information on how to accommodate a specific individual with a disability, call the Job Accommodation Network at (800) ADA-WORK (voice/TDD).

Are alcoholics covered by the ADA?

Yes. An alcoholic is a person with a disability, and is protected by the ADA if he is qualified to perform the essential functions of the job. An employer may be required to provide an accommodation to an alcoholic. However, an employer can discipline, discharge, or deny employment to an alcoholic whose use of alcohol adversely affects job performance or conduct. An employer also may prohibit the use of alcohol in the workplace and can require that employees not be under the influence of alcohol while at work.

Under the ADA, are restaurants required to have Braille menus?

No, not if waiters or other employees are made available to read the menu to a blind customer.

Are retail stores required to maintain a sign language interpreter on staff in order to communicate with deaf customers?

No, not if employees communicate by pen and notepad when necessary.

Do businesses need to rearrange furniture and display racks?

Stores may need to reposition displays in order to clear aisles. For example, restaurants could be required to rearrange tables, and department stores could be told to adjust their layout of racks and shelves to permit access to wheelchair users.

Must every feature of a new facility be accessible?

No. Only a specified number of elements, such as parking spaces and drinking fountains, must be accessible in order for a facility to be in compliance with the ADA. Certain nonoccupiable spaces such as elevator pits, elevator penthouses, and piping or equipment catwalks need not be accessible.

Does the ADA cover private apartments and private homes?

The ADA does not cover strictly residential apartments and homes. If, however, a place of public accommodation, such as a doctor's office or day-care center, is located in a private residence, those portions of the residence used for that purpose are subject to the ADA's requirements.

Does the ADA permit someone with a disability to sue a business when that person believes that discrimination is about to occur, or must the individual wait for the discrimination to occur?

The ADA public accommodations provisions permit an individual to allege discrimination based on a reasonable belief that discrimination is about to occur. This provision allows someone who uses a wheelchair to challenge the planned construction of a new place of public accommodation, for example, such as a shopping mall, that would not be accessible to individuals who use wheelchairs. This enables any necessary remedial measures to be incorporated into the planning stage, when such changes are relatively inexpensive.

Source: The U.S. Department of Justice, which enforces the Americans with Disabilities Act as it relates to state and local government activities and public accommodations. For more information, or to file a complaint, contact: Disability Rights Section, Civil Rights Division, U.S. Department of Justice, P.O. Box 66738, Washington, DC 20035-6738; phone: (800) 514-0301; TDD: (800) 514-0383; ADA homepage; http://www.usdoj.gov/crt/ada/adahom1.htm. Charges of disability discrimination in employment may be filed at any U.S. Equal Employment Opportunity Commission field office. For the appropriate field office in your area, call phone: (800) 669-4000; TDD: (800) 669-6820.

Discrimination

What laws exist to protect me from employment discrimination?

In 1964, the federal government passed Title VII of the Civil Rights Act, safeguarding working men and women from discrimination on the basis of race, color, religion, sex, and national origin. The Age Discrimination in Employment Act was passed in 1967 to protect employees from discrimination due to their age. Disability came under the protection of federal law a few years later under the Rehabilitation Act of 1973, and again in 1991 by virtue of the Americans with Disabilities Act. There are also various state and local laws that provide similar protection.

I am the only female Asian manager in a large chain of luggage stores. I have been passed up for promotion three times and am beginning to suspect my company doesn't want a district manager of my race and sex. Have I been discriminated against?

To determine if you have a basis for a claim of employment discrimination, you must first be able to answer four questions in the affirmative:

1. *Are you in a protected class?* In other words, are you a minority, or suffering a disability, or was your sex, religion, or age at issue? In your case, your race and sex put you in a protected class.

2. *Were you qualified for the promotion?* Compare your education, skills, and experience to others who were advanced. How do you stack up? Do you meet the basic qualifications advertised for in the district manager job?

3. *Did you suffer an adverse employment decision?* Yes, you were denied the promotion.

4. *Did the situation occur under circumstances that could be interpreted as a discriminatory action?* For example, was the company's reason for denial of your promotion untrue? Were men of a different race promoted instead of you?

If you answer yes to all four of these questions, you have a basis to seriously consider taking legal action.

How do I file a charge of discrimination against my employer?

The first step is to file a complaint within the time allowed (sometimes 180 days, sometimes 300 days after the discriminatory act) with the Equal Employment Opportunity Commission (EEOC) or with your state's civil rights organization that protects employee rights (your local EEOC and state civil rights agency are listed in the government section of your phone book). After filing your complaint, you have the option of allowing the agency to investigate and seek resolution or proceeding with a lawsuit in federal or state court.

Do I have to file my complaint with the EEOC, and if so, how long will it take the agency to process my complaint?

The EEOC was established to assist in resolving discrimination claims and to prevent the clogging of courts with discrimination cases. Under federal law, employees are required to file with the EEOC or state commission before suing, to give the agency a chance to do its job. However, the EEOC and similar state agencies are so overwhelmed that they can't get to most cases for two, three, or more years. Because of the tremendous backlog, most agencies allow a plaintiff to file a charge (which must then be withdrawn or dismissed) and go directly to court, avoiding the lengthy agency waiting period.

Can I afford to pursue my discrimination case?

The EEOC and state civil rights organization will investigate and render a determination about your case for free. For a lawsuit, attorneys calculate fees in many different ways: some charge an hourly fee, others contract to receive a percentage of any recovery (a *contingency* fee), and still others take a hybrid approach by charging an hourly fee up to a maximum (perhaps $5,000 to $10,000), with the balance as a contingency fee. Court filing fees ($120 to $250), witness fees ($20 to $40 per day for individuals and $2,000 to $4,000 per day for experts), postage, copying, and deposition transcripts ($3 to $6 per page) must also be considered. Who pays these costs, attorney or client, is a matter for negotiation.

It is important to note that as a general proposition, an employee who prevails on any of his discrimination claims at trial is entitled to an award of legal fees from his former employer. The reverse, however, is not true. Even if an employer is successful in defending a discrimination suit, ordinarily it will not be entitled to reimbursement of legal fees from a former employee.

I was recently asked my age in a job interview. When I told the recruiter I was 25 years old, she expressed concern about my ability to handle the position in a mature fashion. Isn't this age discrimination?

You may have been denied employment because of your age, but the federal law only protects persons age 40 and over from age discrimination in employment. Although under federal law an employer can lawfully deny you a job because of your age if you are younger than 40, some state laws protect younger persons.

My boss told me I was fired for excessive tardiness, but I believe my termination was because of my age. What should I write on my unemployment paperwork?

When filing a claim for unemployment benefits, state your reason—not the company's—for termination. This is part of the paper trail in your discrimination suit and it's important that the trail be consistent with your account of discrimination.

Should I try to tape-record my boss making discriminatory statements?

Having your boss on tape admitting that she didn't give you a raise because of your disability or other protected class could be extremely useful in winning your discrimination suit. However, surreptitious taping at work may be grounds for termination.

I'm the last remaining Hispanic on the third shift at the clothing factory. All the other Hispanic employees have transferred or quit because of the harassment waged against us by the supervisor. The nitpicking has become unbearable. But I can't sue if they don't fire me, right?

Many people believe that if they resign from a job, they cannot pursue a discrimination suit or collect unemployment insurance. When a person resigns his position because his employer has created intolerable working conditions, the resignation may qualify as a constructive discharge, which means that it is treated for legal purposes the same as if he had been fired.

I am a secretary in a large financial company. I feel I'm being treated differently from other secretaries because I am a Jehovah's Witness. But if I say anything, I'm afraid things will just get worse. What can I do?

Retaliating in any fashion against a current, or even former, employee for availing herself of her rights under federal antidiscrimination laws is specifically forbidden by Title VII, as well as by a series of major court decisions. If you do nothing more than file a discrimination charge, bring a lawsuit, or voice your belief that you are being discriminated against, any adverse action taken against you by your employer solely because you did so is illegal. If an employer fires you in retaliation, you will have a basis for legal action for unlawful retaliatory discharge. Many employers know this, and so filing a discrimination claim may be like buying an insurance policy against being fired.

This does not mean that your employer may not try for revenge in some other way. So if you have occasion to charge your employer with some form of employment discrimination, be sure to perform your job adequately, be on time for work, don't bad-mouth your boss, or in any other way give the company an excuse to fire you. Even if you take these precautions, you might still have an employer who will make your life on the job unpleasant in the hope that you will quit.

I have filed a discrimination lawsuit against my former employer. I'm worried that my former coworkers will be too fearful of being blackballed to testify honestly on my behalf. I need their truthful account to prevail. Is there any way around this?

Witnesses who testify in discrimination suits are also protected by law from retaliation.

Source: Jeffrey M. Bernbach, an attorney specializing in employment discrimination cases; in 28 years of practice he has successfully represented hundreds of clients (both individuals and large corporations) in job bias lawsuits. Mr. Bernbach has served as chief labor counsel with the Hearst Corporation and legal adviser to the National Labor Relations Board. He is the author of *Job Discrimination: How to Fight, How to Win*. Jeffrey M. Bernbach's office is located at 10 Rockefeller Plaza, New York, NY 10020; (212) 265-3300.

DNA Testing

How does *DNA typing* work?

Each of the cells in our bodies contains two complete copies of our DNA (de-oxyribonucleic acid). DNA is the encyclopedia of information that determines all our inherited characteristics. Most DNA is the same in everyone, but a few of the sentences, known by scientists as *genes,* do vary from person to person. To test these differences, the DNA is first separated from the other sub-stances—proteins, carbohydrates, and fats—that make up our cells. The DNA profiles are then displayed in a bar code–like pattern so the samples being tested can be compared.

How accurate is DNA typing?

The large number of DNA tests available today allow for unique identification. There are two main types of DNA tests that can help solve crimes. First is the RLFP test, which takes several weeks to complete. This test, sometimes called "DNA fingerprinting," is the most commonly applied test in crime laboratories throughout the world. The newer PCR tests work on smaller, more deteriorated samples, and are completed in a few days. In the future, as improvements con-tinue, the PCR will likely completely replace RFLP testing.

What are the predominant uses of DNA typing?

Paternity testing for child support enforcement, forensic testing in criminal cases, and data banking of DNA profiles from convicted violent offenders are the most common uses of DNA testing. Every year almost half a million indi-viduals are DNA-tested as part of the 150,000 paternity cases in which the technology is used. Forensic DNA testing is being applied at the rate of ap-proximately 15,000 cases per year. More than half the states have laws that re-quire convicted violent and sex offenders to have their DNA profiles included in databases. Over 100,000 such profiles are now on record for use by investi-gators in solving crimes.

What is the most common criminal case in which forensic DNA profiling is used?

More than 70 percent of forensic DNA profiling is in sexual assault cases, be-cause semen is such a good source of DNA. Also, other forms of evidence in these cases, such as eyewitnesses, are usually not nearly as reliable as DNA evi-dence. In a typical forensic case, the DNA profile of a semen stain obtained from a rape victim is compared to the DNA profiles obtained by drawing blood from the victim and the suspect. If the profiles of the semen and the suspect match, then it is possible to say with an extremely high degree of certainty that the semen came from the tested individual.

What kinds of samples can be used in a paternity test?

Almost any substance obtained from the human body can be tested. The most common test is blood; but increasingly, swabs taken from the inside of the mouth, called *buccal swabs,* are being used. Another common paternity test is on fetal cells obtained from an expectant mother who is undergoing prenatal testing, or on umbilical cord blood from a newborn baby. Other tested samples include saliva from envelope flaps or cigarette butts, nasal secretions, and tissues from the deceased. Whichever samples are used, it is important to remember that paternity is not a medical test and can be ordered by anyone.

What is the error rate in DNA testing and what would cause an error?

The error rate in DNA testing that would result from a gross human error is too small to measure. Out of the approximately 50,000 forensic DNA cases that have been completed, there has yet to be a case shown to have resulted in a miscarriage of justice. DNA testing represents a great improvement for the justice system because a third of all DNA tests exonerate the accused. More than 30 individuals have been released from prison, some after as long as ten years, as a result of DNA testing.

What causes a sample from a crime scene to be contaminated?

Many evidence samples associated with crimes contain mixtures of DNA from more than one individual. Environmental contaminants such as bacteria may also be present that could accelerate the deterioration of the DNA. Since these occurrences can obscure the results or prevent the laboratory from completing a test, they may result in an inconclusive test, but are not likely to cause a false-positive test. Many safeguards are taken in a well-run laboratory to prevent cross-contamination of samples and to test constantly to detect any contamination that may be present.

How long could blood be at a crime scene and still be good enough for testing?

How long a sample lasts depends on environmental conditions. Direct sunlight or high humidity and temperature will cause degradation of the DNA in a few days or weeks. Where the bloodstain is deposited can also affect the longevity of the DNA. In the O. J. Simpson case, for example, DNA from areas of the sidewalk that were stained by fallen leaves was considerably more degraded than DNA from unstained areas. Despite these factors, blood stains 15 or 20 years old or older have been successfully tested. Bones of the Romanoff family, heirs to the throne of pre-Communist Russia who were murdered in 1918, have been identified using DNA testing.

Are DNA tests always admissible in court?

Of the tens of thousands of DNA cases that have gone to court, there are only a few instances in which the DNA testing has not been admitted. In hundreds of cases the courts have held pretrial evidence hearings—often called *Frye hearings*—

to determine if the technology is "generally accepted by scientists," and therefore admissible as evidence. These hearings have scrutinized DNA testing more thoroughly than any other forensic testing method, including fingerprints and blood alcohol measurements. The question of how well the testing was performed and what the results mean is determined by the "trier of fact," the judge and jury, as part of the trial.

How did DNA testing get started?

DNA testing can trace its roots back to Gregor Mendel, the Franciscan monk who discovered in the 1860s the basic laws of genetics that are still in use today. The forensic use of DNA testing is a spinoff of the biotechnology revolution begun in the 1970s. Other common uses of DNA testing methods include the diagnosis of genetic diseases like cystic fibrosis and Huntington's disease, extinct and endangered animal research, and the identification by the military of war dead, including skeletal remains going back to World War I. Forensic and paternity DNA testing has had a greater impact on people's lives than any other test or medicine to emerge from the biotechnology revolution.

Source: Howard Coleman, president of GeneLex Corporation, a forensic and paternity DNA-testing laboratory. The author of *DNA in the Courtroom: A Trial Watcher's Guide*, Mr. Coleman is an expert in DNA testing who has provided testimony in court cases utilizing DNA typing for over ten years. GeneLex Corporation is located at 2203 Airport Way South, Seattle, WA 98134; phone: (800) 523-6487; fax: (206) 382-6277; Web site: www.genelex.com.

Drug Testing

Can I be required, as a condition of employment, to take a drug-screening test?

Private employers can require a drug test as a condition of employment. However, a small number of states have laws restricting drug testing. In addition, there may be a labor contract that restricts testing. Persons have constitutional protection from drug tests by the government or at the direction of the government; but courts have allowed drug testing of government employees or persons with jobs heavily regulated by the government, such as the transportation and nuclear energy industries, if the employment is safety-sensitive or involves national security.

What are my chances of getting a false-positive, and what causes an erroneous result?

The occurrence of a false-positive depends on what types of testing methods are used and the skill level of the testing operators. Test results can also be affected by how carefully the samples are handled. If the best testing method is used (a sample confirmed by gas chromatography/mass spectrometry) and the procedures are followed accurately and precisely, then testing can be over 99 percent accurate. If shoddy procedures are used, a drug test can be as accurate as a coin toss.

What food products and drugs should I stay away from in order to avoid a false-positive?

Some poppy seed products will cause a false-positive for opiates, so stay away from rolls, bagels, and other foodstuffs containing poppy seeds. Also beware of hemp food products, as they have reportedly caused marijuana positives. In addition, let the people doing the testing know what medications you are on (prescription and over-the-counter). The appropriate testing system has a final step in which a medical review officer examines the test result and considers any substances you have taken that could have caused the positive.

How long are marijuana and other substances retained in the body?

The length of time a substance (or traces of it) is retained in your body depends on a number of factors, including how diluted your urine is. Urine is a poor sample to test because the amount of urine in the body is always changing (unlike blood). When your bladder is full you will generally have a lower level of drug residue in the urine, and when it is empty you will have more. This can determine whether a person tests above or below the cutoff point for a positive test result.

The substance that stays in your system the longest is marijuana residue. A person will test positive for several days to several weeks, depending on how often he consumes marijuana, and other factors such as obesity, since marijuana residue is stored in fatty tissue. The record for a positive marijuana test is 77 days after last use. Other drugs will test positive for shorter periods. Estimates are 48 hours for methamphetamine, two to three days for cocaine, three days for opiates, and eight days for PCP.

Can I test positive if I am around marijuana smokers?

Yes; passive inhalation can cause a showing of marijuana in your system. The question is, will you have a high enough reading to be above the cutoff point for a positive test? Whether your sample produces a positive reading may depend on the conditions of passive inhalation. Were you in a small, smoke-filled room or a large, ventilated area? The amount of urine in your bladder will also make a difference. Larger amounts of fluids decrease the chance of a positive result from passive inhalation.

As an employer, can I single out one employee for drug screening?

If employment is fixed under a labor contract, a drug-testing clause or drug policy statement will determine what the company is contractually allowed to do. Generally, courts frown on picking out one employee for stricter scrutiny unless the employer can document strong evidence of probable cause that the individual is using drugs. Courts prefer to see a clear company policy, evenly applied. The policy should discuss when an employee will be tested and what types of evidence of drug use are needed in order to require a urine sample.

If I am fired for a positive drug screen, but otherwise have an exemplary record, can I sue my employer?

Whether you may take legal action against an employer who terminates you for a positive drug test depends on the type of existing employment relationship. If you have an employment contract, look to that document for what constitutes grounds for discipline or discharge. If you're a private employee without an employment contract, the general rule in the United States is that an employer can hire or fire for any reason or no reason, as long as it is not done discriminatorily. Therefore, in most cases, an employer is justified in firing or refusing to hire a person who tests positive for drugs. If you are a government employee, there is probably an established rule for testing and discipline. Generally, civil servants have certain procedural due process rights such as an appeals hearing before they are fired.

If I am fired for drug use, can I get unemployment benefits?

Some courts find that a positive drug test does not constitute a work-connected discharge because a drug test does not determine whether an employee was impaired at work or when she used drugs. State courts with this bent will usually allow unemployment compensation. Other courts have found that in a company with a clear "no drug policy," the use of drugs is an automatic work-connected violation barring privileges to unemployment monies.

Do student athletes have to take a drug test if the coach requests such as exam?

A school has to put in place a drug-testing policy before the coach can require a urine sample. However, the Supreme Court has greatly broadened the powers of schools to search students, and specifically has upheld the testing of student athletes because of the safety-sensitive nature of sports. The court has expressed concern about requiring testing for other students unless there is probable cause that a specific student is using drugs.

What substances will interfere with a test result and increase the likelihood of a negative result?

People should not attempt to adulterate their urine samples. If someone gets rid of their first urine of the day and drinks a large amount of fluid, they are likely to test negative. There is evidence that bleach, detergent, Drāno, salt, soap, vinegar, Visine, Vanish, and other substances will cause a negative test when added to urine. But urine testing is closely monitored, and the sample may be examined to detect such adulterants.

Source: Kevin B. Zeese, an attorney and the president of Common Sense for Drug Policy. He is the author of many books, including *Drug Testing Legal Manual* and *Drug Law: Strategies and Tactics,* and he serves as editor of *Drug Law Report*. Mr. Zeese has written for newspapers and journals on a range of drug issues and has appeared on every major TV network as a commentator. He served as a consultant to Walter Cronkite for the Discovery Channel special *The Drug Dilemma: War or Peace?* Mr. Zeese's office is located at 3619 Tallwood Terrace, Falls Church, VA 22041; phone: (703) 354-5694; fax: (703) 354-5695; e-mail: kevzeese@laser.net.

Employment

Does my boss have to let me off work for jury duty?

The Jury System Improvement Act of 1978 forbids employers from firing or otherwise disciplining employees who are empaneled to serve on juries in federal cases. Most states have enacted similar laws. Check with your local department of labor to find out if your employer is required to pay your salary while you serve.

Can I be required to take a lie detector test at work?

The Polygraph Protection Act of 1988 makes it illegal for employers to test employees regularly as a matter of policy or in cases of continuing investigation where no suspects have been found. The law forbids employers from using polygraphs to harass or intimidate workers. A supervisor cannot use a lie detector to determine if an employee has used drugs or alcohol, but polygraphs can be used to investigate workplace thefts, embezzlement, sabotage, or money laundering. Even when submission to a test is lawful, however, an employer cannot discharge an employee who refuses to take a test. When a polygraph test is allowed under the law, an employer must explain the nature of the incident under investigation, and must give the worker 48 hours' notice and the opportunity to consult an attorney.

Do I have a right to review my personnel file?

An employee or former employee's access to his/her personnel file depends upon state law. In some states, employees may review their employment files, but they generally will be denied access to documents regarded as confidential, such as letters of reference, information about other employees, or certain investigation reports. Consult an attorney with expertise in your state's employment law to determine your rights regarding review of your personnel records.

I returned from lunch to discover the company security guard rifling through my desk drawer. When I protested, he said he was following company policy. Was his search legal?

In most cases, an employer can search offices and lockers without notice or consent, and can inspect the contents of briefcases upon an employee's leaving work, if the employer has a reasonable basis for suspecting the employee of wrongdoing. Items that are clearly personal cannot be searched. Companies that do routine searches should post notices, disseminate memos, and include information in policy manuals stating search practices. If your company does not publicize its search policy, a court may find you have a reasonable expectation of privacy, and declare the search to be in violation of your constitutional protections.

Recently I've heard a lot about companies spying on their own employees. What are the boundaries for a company doing internal surveillance?

Under federal law it is illegal to tape or eavesdrop on a conversation between employees when the parties expected that their conversation was private (e.g., in an employee bathroom). Since state laws on wiretapping and eavesdropping vary a great deal, you need to check the laws in your state. Employers frequently maintain microphones between counter areas and the boss's office, or instruct the office operator to listen in and monitor suspicious or personal telephone calls by employees. Usually this is illegal, unless the conversation takes place in a public area or one of the parties consents to the taping, or if the employer had genuine suspicion of wrongdoing and monitored only business calls, not personal calls. Courts have found that photographing employees for surveillance purposes does not violate their privacy rights.

Can a company mandate that employees be tested for AIDS?

The law in this area is still uncertain. Some cities require food service workers to be tested for AIDS, venereal disease, and tuberculosis. At least 34 states protect persons with AIDS under disability laws, making it illegal to discriminate against an employee infected with HIV or AIDS. The Americans with Disabilities Act also protects the jobs of persons with AIDS, as long as the employee can perform his/her job duties.

I own a bakery and am famous for my light, fluffy biscuits. My recipe was passed down to me by my great-great-grandmother and I've never told it to anyone but my lead baker, Hank. A friend of Hank's opened a bakery across town and sells biscuits suspiciously like mine. I'm afraid Hank sold me out. What can I do?

Many states have passed laws making it a criminal offense to steal a trade secret. A trade secret is usually something the employer has tried to keep secret and has spent money and effort to develop. A person who sells or receives stolen property worth over $5,000 that has been transported over state lines has committed a federal offense. This stolen property law also applies to trade secrets. You are within your rights to fire Hank, pursue criminal charges, and sue for damages, including profits you've lost to the competing bakery, providing that you have proof of his dishonesty. Still, you may not be able to prevail in court, depending on the facts of the case.

I was recently laid off at work. Am I entitled to severance pay?

As a general rule, there is no legal obligation to give terminated employees severance pay. An employer may have to pay severance if you have a written or oral contract for such reimbursement, if the employee manual states that the company pays severance, or if the employer has created precedent by paying severance to other workers in similar terminations.

When is an employee eligible for unemployment benefits?

You generally cannot collect unemployment benefits if you resign, or if you were fired for misconduct such as fighting on the job, failing to follow company policy, or intoxication on the job. In most states, you can collect if you were fired due to a business reorganization, layoff, job elimination, or other reasons not your fault. You can sometimes even collect if you were fired for poor work performance.

Hearing examiners will seek to determine whether a legitimate company rule was violated and whether or not that rule was justified. At the unemployment hearing you should strive to show either that you did not violate a company policy or that the policy you violated was unreasonable.

I am conducting a job search for a new assistant. Are there interview questions that are forbidden?

Interview questions about an applicant's race, color, age, sex, religion, national origin, need for child care, and marital status are prohibited by Title VII of the Civil Rights Act of 1964 and many state civil rights acts. Employers also may not ask: Do you rent or own a home? What is your maiden name? What is your date of birth? Who will care for your children while you work? Are you married, single, divorced, separated, engaged, or widowed? Are you available to work on the Sabbath? Have you ever been arrested? What is your spouse's nationality? How old are your children? What clubs and societies do you belong to?

Does an employer have to give his employees leaves of absence for emergencies?

Employers are not required by law to allow employees personal leaves of absence, but must apply practices consistently to all employees if they do.

Source: Steven Mitchell Sack, labor attorney, lecturer, and arbitrator of employment disputes. He has appeared on the *Oprah Winfrey Show* and in the *Wall Street Journal* and the *New York Times* as a legal expert. Mr. Sack is the author of *The Employee Rights Handbook* and *Lifetime Legal Guide*. His law firm is located at 135 East 57th Street (12th Floor), New York, NY 10022: contact Steven Sack at phone: (212) 702-9000; fax: (212) 702-9702.

Lesbian and Gay Civil Rights

Is civil marriage for lesbian and gay couples legally recognized?

In no state can same-sex couples lawfully marry. However, a court case headed for the Hawaii Supreme Court may result in a ruling that makes Hawaii the first state to recognize civil marriage for lesbian and gay couples. After that, same-sex couples who live in Hawaii or travel there to get married will expect to have their marriages recognized in their home states and elsewhere, just as others do. Opponents of civil marriage for lesbian and gay couples have already mounted a state-by-state campaign to prohibit these marriages, and by early May 1997, 22 states had passed laws specifically forbidding lesbian and gay couples to marry.

Why do lesbian and gay couples need or want to get married?

For the same reasons that opposite-sex couples do. Most same-sex couples have already taken on many of the same responsibilities as married couples but have none of the legal protections or benefits that accompany civil marriage. Despite taking responsibility for their partner's well-being, both economically and emotionally, same-sex couples legally are treated as nothing more than roommates. For example, one partner is often denied visitation and involvement in medical decision-making when the other is in the hospital. Same-sex couples are often refused "family" health coverage, taxation and inheritance rights, and are denied protection should the relationship end. In addition, lesbian and gay couples are denied the social and emotional security marriage provides for so many people in our society.

Is the sexual orientation of a parent a factor in determining child custody and visitation in divorce cases?

There are an estimated 6 to 10 million lesbian and gay parents in the United States. They are mothers and fathers to an estimated 6 to 14 million children throughout the country. Many lesbians and gay men are the parents of children born to them when they were in a heterosexual relationship. In some instances, when a child's nongay parent discovers that the other parent is gay, he or she may attempt to limit the parenting role of that parent.

In general, the legal standards applied to child custody and visitation cases are vague. They vary considerably from state to state, depending on existing laws and statutes, and usually vest a great deal of discretion in the judge. But although some judges have denied custody and visitation rights solely because of the parent's sexual orientation, this is becoming less common. When confronted with lesbian and gay parenting cases, the vast majority of courts have adopted a "nexus approach," requiring a clear demonstration that the parent's sexual orientation actually causes harm to a child before it is deemed relevant. Under this approach, the child's best interest, not the parent's sexuality, becomes the focus of the case.

How many American households are made up of lesbian and gay couples?

There are no definite statistics. However, the U.S. Bureau of the Census in 1992 found that only 10.2 percent of the nation's 95 million households fit the traditional definition of family—two married parents living with their children. Data revealed that unmarried couples represented 4.5 million households, and one-third of these households consisted of same-sex couples.

Are the children of lesbian and gay parents more likely to become gay?

No; it is a well-established fact that children raised by lesbians and gay men are no more likely to become gay than if they were raised by nongay parents. This is a fact supported by every psychological and sociological study to have examined the issue. But given the many hardships faced by lesbian and gay youth, the real focus should *not* be on whether lesbian and gay parents encourage their children to be gay themselves, but whether lesbian and gay youth are supported by their parents and society.

Are lesbians and gay men allowed to adopt children?

New Hampshire and Florida are the only two jurisdictions with statutory bans on lesbian and gay adoptions, while at least one state (New York) has enacted regulations guaranteeing gay people the same eligibility to become adoptive parents as nongay applicants. Although the majority of states that have considered the issue no longer officially deem lesbians and gay men "unfit" to raise a child, bills barring adoptions by gay people continue to be introduced into state legislatures each year.

The ability of same-sex couples to adopt a child jointly varies considerably from state to state, depending on existing laws and statutes. In some states, couples are able jointly to adopt a child; in others, one partner may adopt a child and later the other parent may also adopt the child through second-parent adoption. Generally, adoption requires that the rights and responsibilities of the legal parent be terminated before an adoption is granted. However, a second-parent adoption maintains the first parent's legal relationship to the child while creating a legally recognized relationship between the second parent and the child. By March 1997, appellate courts in New York, New Jersey, Vermont, Massachusetts, Illinois, Indiana, and the District of Columbia had interpreted their laws to allow second-parent adoption; appeals in Colorado and Wisconsin have been unsuccessful. In the remaining states, second-parent adoptions are permitted or denied depending on the view of the individual trial judges.

Does the law prohibit discrimination in employment on the basis of sexual orientation?

Although no federal law exists which prohibits private employers from discrimination on the basis of sexual orientation, government employees may be protected against such discrimination under the Constitution's equal protection clause and under antidiscrimination policies adopted by many government agencies. In addition, eleven states (California, Connecticut, Hawaii, Maine, Massachusetts, Minnesota, New Hampshire, New Jersey, Rhode Island, Vermont, and Wisconsin) have added sexual orientation to the list of grounds upon which private employers in those states are prohibited from discrimination. Many cities have adopted similar antidiscrimination ordinances, governing employers in those municipalities.

As a result, a majority of all employees in the United States now work in jurisdictions where sexual orientation employment discrimination can give rise to civil liability. Many private employers also have adopted policies prohibiting sexual orientation discrimination in their workplaces, which may be accompanied by internal grievance procedures and may give rise to enforceable claims for breach of contract if such discrimination is not redressed.

Can lesbians and gay men serve in the military with the passage of the "Don't Ask, Don't Tell" law?

The government claims that lesbians and gay men can now serve, although they may not do so openly, and they must comply with onerous rules imposed by the National Defense Authorization Act, often called "Don't Ask, Don't Tell." This law was passed by Congress on November 17, 1993, and signed by President Clinton that same year. The act mandates that a service member will be discharged if one or more of three findings is made:

1. that the member has engaged in, attempted to engage in, or solicited another to engage in a homosexual act or acts;
2. that the member has stated that he or she is a homosexual or bisexual, or words to that effect; or
3. that the member has married or attempted to marry a person known to be of the same biological sex. Under the definition of "homosexual acts," the law prohibits any affectionate or sexual behavior, from hand-holding to intercourse, by homosexuals in the military. This behavior is forbidden to gay people only. Nongay service members are allowed to be sexual as long as they do not violate the military's overall code of conduct. All service members, regardless of sexual orientation, are prohibited from behaviors like sexual harassment, sex in public places, and anal or oral sex.

According to the government, the presence of openly gay or lesbian service members poses an unacceptable risk to the high standards of morale, good order, and discipline essential to military capability. Military leaders assert that homosexual acts interfere with unit cohesion by diminishing other service members' sense of privacy and increasing sexual tension in the barracks. Opponents of the law argue that silencing lesbian and gay service members to make others more comfortable is unconstitutional and intentionally discriminatory, violating rights of free speech, equal protection, and freedom of association. The act is currently being challenged in the courts.

Is it still illegal in some states for lesbians and gay men to engage in consensual sex?

Certain consensual sexual acts are still criminalized in some places for both gay and nongay couples. Private, consensual oral or anal sex between adults is a felony in several states, punishable by fines, imprisonment (as much as life imprisonment in Idaho), or both. As recently as 1961, all 50 states had some sort of "sodomy" laws on their books; today, 14 states have laws making it unlawful for heterosexual or gay couples to engage in oral or anal sex. Six states prohibit oral or anal sex for same-sex partners only. In 1986, the U.S. Supreme Court upheld the constitutionality of sodomy laws, but the laws remain under legal attack and are gradually being struck down by state courts or repealed by state legislatures.

Sources: Lambda Legal Defense and Education Fund, founded in 1973, is the country's oldest and largest national lesbian and gay legal organization committed to achieving full recognition of the civil rights of lesbians, gay men, and people with HIV/AIDS through impact litigation, education, and public policy work. The Lambda Legal Defense and Education Fund is located at 120 Wall Street, Suite 1500, New York, NY 10005-3904; phone: (212) 809-8585; fax: (212) 809-0055.

Health Law

What are *patients' rights?*

A patient has a right to participate in all health-care decisions and to refuse any diagnostic procedure or treatment. Patients may execute an *advance directive* (see page 580) stating their wishes with respect to health-care decisions if the patient becomes incapacitated. A patient may designate another person to make decisions on her behalf in the event of future incapacity: this is called a "durable power-of-attorney for health care." A patient has a right to formulate a *living will* to give direction to physicians and other health-care providers about withholding life-sustaining treatment where the patient suffers from a terminal condition. A patient must not be discriminated against on the basis of race, religion, national origin, sex, or disability in provision of health-care services. A patient has a right of privacy and confidentiality with respect to her medical treatment. Many hospitals establish a patient-rights advocate to assist patients in understanding and enforcing their rights.

Does a patient have an absolute right to refuse treatment?

A competent adult patient has a constitutional right of privacy, which has been held to include free choice and self-determination with regard to medical care. Therefore, a competent adult has a lawful right to refuse treatment even if that refusal would likely result in his death (e.g., by refusing a blood transfusion).

What is *informed consent?*

A physician has a duty to secure a patient's consent to treatment. The patient has a right to be informed of the risks and benefits of any proposed treatment; any unusual or undesirable outcomes; side effects, including any risk of mortality; and alternative treatments. A patient may refuse treatment even against medical advice. If the patient refuses treatment, he must be informed of the medical consequences of such refusal. Also, a patient must give written consent to being subject to any experimental treatment or biomedical research. Should the physician fail to obtain informed consent, the patient may sue for malpractice. Doctors can be liable for exceeding the scope of consent, either with respect to they who treat or what is done.

Does a physician have to disclose to patients that that physician has AIDS?

The risk of HIV (the virus that causes AIDS) transmission in a routine physical exam is very low to nonexistent, but it is much greater when a physician is performing surgery or some other invasive procedure. Therefore, whether a physician must disclose to a patient that he has AIDS may depend on whether the physician is performing an exposure-prone procedure. In some states, an HIV-positive physician performing an invasive procedure has a statutory duty to warn patients and cannot perform invasive procedures unless he obtains the informed consent of the patient and approval from an expert review panel.

Patients have sued physicians for failure to disclose that they are HIV-positive even where the patient has not (yet) tested positive for HIV, seeking recovery from AIDS phobia. Recovery is based on lawsuits for intentional infliction of emotional distress. Symptoms could include headache and worry. Courts have differed on whether recovery exists for AIDS phobia when a person has not actually contracted the virus.

Who has the right to view the medical records of patients?

Traditionally, patients' medical records were viewed as the property of their physicians, and patients were denied access to their own records. Today, at least 27 states grant patients access to their own medical records. Medical records contain personal information on health status, diagnosis, and treatment. A physician has a duty of confidentiality to his patients and therefore cannot provide medical records to third parties without the patient's consent. But this duty is subject to numerous exceptions, such as access by law enforcement officials and public health departments, as long as there is adequate protection of the person's identity.

Insurance companies need a patient's consent to obtain medical records, but the patient typically must agree to release these records as a condition of receiving insurance. To find out more about your state's law, contact the American Medical Association at (202) 789-7400, or the American Health Information Management Association at (312) 787-2672.

When does a physician commit medical *malpractice?*

A physician has a duty to provide care to a patient at the level of "the reasonably competent physician." A physician who does not provide such medical care may have committed medical malpractice if the lack of due care causes injury to the patient. An obvious example would be if a physician amputated the wrong limb. A less obvious example would be if a physician provided care and the condition initially improved, but recurred months (or even years) later, or it emerges that the condition was treated improperly. In both examples, courts would require the testimony of a medical expert to prove that the physician's care failed to meet the professional standard. Patients should question their physician about any medical care they think is out of the ordinary and that may have caused them some injury.

Can an indigent, terminally ill person without health insurance receive medical treatment?

Most states have programs designed to provide health care to people who are indigent, uninsured, and unable to afford medical treatment. In 1965 the federal government created two programs: Medicaid and Medicare. Medicaid is a federally funded health-care program for poor people that is administered by states. Each state has different rules that govern eligibility, and the rules can be quite complicated. Medicare is administered by the federal government and is open to persons 65 and over, persons who are permanently and totally disabled, and persons suffering from end-stage renal (kidney) disease.

What is *physician-assisted suicide,* and is it legal in the United States?

Physician-assisted suicide should be distinguished from euthanasia and the withdrawal of life-sustaining treatment. Euthanasia occurs when a physician accelerates the death of a terminally ill patient through action such as injecting the patient with a lethal drug. Euthanasia is not permitted by any state. Withdrawal of life-sustaining treatment occurs when a physician turns off the life-support machinery, such as a ventilator, of a terminally ill patient. The physician may legally withdraw treatment if the patient was competent when she decided to die, or if the person making treatment decisions for the patient elects to withdraw treatment. This practice has been supported by two U.S. Supreme Court cases as well as by the federal Patient Self-Determination Act.

Physician-assisted suicide occurs when physicians merely give patients the tools to kill themselves, but do not administer the procedure. (Dr. Jack Kevorkian supplies a patient with lethal drugs but does not inject him or her.) In 1997, two cases decided by the U.S. Supreme Court ruled that the legality of physician-assisted suicide is a matter of state law and there is no federal constitutional right to physician-assisted suicide.

Can a patient be denied medical care if he shows up at an emergency room and does not have insurance?

Under the federal Emergency Medical Treatment and Active Labor Act (EMTALA), when an individual enters the hospital in an emergency condition (including active labor), the hospital must either provide medical treatment to stabilize the condition or arrange appropriate transfer to another hospital. The hospital may not transfer an emergency patient unless and until a patient is stabilized, except when:

1. the patient informs the physician in writing that he wishes to be transferred and is aware of the risks; or
2. the physician signs certification that transfer is in the best interest of the patient (e.g., the new hospital has better equipment); or
3. other conditions for an appropriate transfer are met as set out by the law.

EMTALA provides for a federally authorized lawsuit for damages for personal injury and financial loss suffered by a patient where the hospital or physician has refused to treat or appropriately transfer emergency patients who are without insurance. A hospital or physician is subject to a civil penalty of up to $50,000 and possible suspension of their Medicare provider agreement.

Source: The Health Law and Policy Institute at University of Houston Law Center, Houston, TX 77204-6381; phone: (713) 743-2101; fax: (713) 743-2117. The Institute offers the largest health law and policy curriculum in the country, and provides expertise to lawmakers, health-care professionals, and attorneys. *U.S. News & World Report* recently ranked the Institute the leading health law program in the United States. For more information on Medicare, contact the Social Security Administration at (800) 772-1213 or the American Association of Retired Persons at (202) 434-2277. For those having trouble contacting their local health department, the Association of State and Territorial Health Officials at (202) 371-9090 can provide the number.

Finding a Lawyer

What should I look for in a lawyer?

Naturally, you need to keep practical considerations in mind: the lawyer's area of expertise and prior experience, convenience of office location, amount of fees charged, and the length of time a case might take. Your personal preferences as to age, sex, and personality can also be taken into consideration. Be aware that the relationship you will have with any lawyer you hire is very personal. You must feel comfortable enough to tell your lawyer, honestly and completely, personal facts necessary to resolve your problem.

Where do I look?

There are many resources you call use in finding a lawyer, including:

- *Recommendations from others.* Friends, relatives, and acquaintances you trust may be able to suggest someone reliable—but be aware that a lawyer right for someone else may not suit you or your legal problem.
- *Advertisements.* Ads may familiarize you with the names of lawyers, and some ads will also set out a lawyer's area of concentration and quote a fee or price range for a particular case. As with all advertisements, be careful about believing everything you read and hear.
- *Referral services.* Most communities have referral services to assist the public in finding lawyers. Bar associations in most communities can make referrals as well.
- *Legal aid.* Note that most legal aid programs have eligibility requirements often based on where you live, the size of your family, and your income.
- *Prepaid legal services plans.* Recently, employers and labor and credit unions have formed legal insurance plans, which may cover most if not all of the costs of legal consultation.
- *Legal clinics.* Legal clinics are set up primarily to process routine, uncomplicated legal business. These firms generally use standard forms and paralegal assistants. Their main areas of work are wills, personal bankruptcy, divorces, and traffic offenses.

Am I entitled to free legal help under the Constitution?

Yes, but only if you're accused of committing a crime that could result in your being incarcerated six months or more and you can't afford a lawyer. The U.S. Constitution guarantees that you will be represented by a lawyer if you request one in these circumstances.

Does it cost much to get legal advice?

It varies, depending on the case. When you hire a lawyer, you are paying for his/her expertise and time. Sometimes even a seemingly simple, one-page document, or advice given over the phone, might have involved many hours of research.

How can I keep legal costs down?

You can avoid future problems by having a clear understanding of the fees to be charged and, in many cases, by getting that understanding in writing, even before any legal work has started. At your first meeting, the lawyer should estimate how much the total case will cost and clearly set out the method being used to charge for the work. Keep in mind that not all costs can be estimated exactly, because there may be unpredictable changes during the course of your case. You should discuss this with your lawyer. There are a few things you can do as a client to help keep costs down:

- Answer all your lawyer's questions fully and honestly.
- Be organized.
- Be brief.
- Keep your lawyer informed of changes.
- Keep informed about your case.

How do lawyers charge for their services?

Lawyers use several different billing methods. There is nothing improper about asking a lawyer what billing method will be least costly before you agree to hire him/her.

- *Contingent fees.* This type of fee is paid only if your attorney prevails. Such a fee is used only in cases where money is being claimed—most often negligence cases involving personal injury. The lawyer agrees to handle the case for a fixed percentage (often one-third of the amount finally paid to the client). It is especially important to be certain whether the lawyer will take a percentage before or after other costs and expenses have been deducted from the amount won.

- *Fees based on time or an hourly rate.* This is the most common billing method. In general, more experienced lawyers will charge more per hour than those with less experience, but they may also take less time to do the same work. Large firms are often more expensive than small firms, and urban lawyers usually charge more per hour than those in rural areas.

- *Retainer fees.* This is a set amount of money paid regularly to a lawyer to make sure he/she is available for any necessary legal service. This method is generally used by businesses, corporations, or individuals who routinely have a great deal of legal work. Most clients don't see a lawyer regularly and don't need to pay a retainer fee. Be aware that a fee paid in advance of legal work is also known as a "retainer," but this is only a down payment, which will be part of the total amount owed.

- *Fixed fee.* A fixed fee is the total amount that will be charged for routine legal work. Although you might see ads offering "Simple Divorce— $150," don't assume that this is the total amount. Quite often the advertised price won't include court costs and other expenses.

- *Costs and expenses.* Some costs and expenses will be charged regardless of billing method. Your lawyer will usually pay costs such as court filing fees, postage, copying, phone calls, and expert witnesses as they are charged, then bill you at regular intervals or at the close of your case.

• *Referral fees.* If Lawyer A can't help you with your problem but instead refers you to Lawyer B, Lawyer A will sometimes ask to be paid part of the total fee you pay to Lawyer B. If you are referred from one lawyer to another, be sure to ask whether there will be a referral fee paid and, if so, what the agreement is between the lawyers.

What should I do if I'm not satisfied with my lawyer?

First, figure out why you are dissatisfied. You have a right to expect competent representation, but every lawsuit has two sides. You can't always blame your lawyer if your case doesn't turn out the way you thought it would. If, after a realistic look, you still believe you have a worthwhile complaint about your legal representation, there are several things you can do:

• Talk it over with your lawyer.
• Fire your lawyer and hire another.
• File a complaint with the city, county, or state bar association, or with the disciplinary board of your state supreme court.
• Seek available funds. Most states have a client security fund, maintained by fees paid by lawyers, which compensates clients who are defrauded by lawyers.
• Sue your lawyer for malpractice.
• Contact the police. This is a step to be taken only if you suspect that your lawyer has committed a crime, such as stealing your money or property.

Source: The American Bar Association (ABA)'s Division for Public Education, which is dedicated to providing accessible legal information in the form of books, brochures, and videotapes to the public, educators, journalists, lawyers, and judges. The ABA book offerings include *The American Bar Association Family Legal Guide, The American Bar Association Guide to Home Ownership, The American Bar Association Guide to Wills and Estates, The American Bar Association Guide to Family Law, The American Bar Association Guide to Consumer Law,* and *The American Bar Association Guide to Workplace Law.* To order materials by mail, write to ABA Publications Department, P.O. Box 10892, Chicago, IL 60610-0892; phone: (800) 285-2221; fax: (312) 988-5568. Or check the Internet: http://www.abanet.org/store/order.html.

Jury Duty

How was I selected for jury duty?

Names of potential jurors are drawn at random from a variety of sources including voter registration lists, driver's license lists, and state ID lists.

How are members of a particular jury selected?

No one picks anybody to be on a jury; attorneys do not have the ability to select jurors. They remove or "de-select" a limited number of people in the jury pool who they feel would not be fair and impartial in deciding the case. Jury selection is a process of elimination—of removing people who may have difficulty being a suitable juror, until the final jury panel remains. An attorney may choose to remove a potential juror for reasons such as bias or personal acquaintance with the parties involved.

Shouldn't someone who understands the law be sitting here instead of me?

A jury of lay people, ordinary citizens representative of the community, has strong roots in the U.S. legal system. A jury of regular folks serves as protection against abuse of power by government, business, or other powerful entities. Juries guard against the mechanization of justice. If the same fact finder hears similar cases over and over, a real danger exists that he/she will lose the impartiality necessary to decide a particular case on its merits.

In complex technical cases, why don't the experts decide who's liable? If the specialists in the field can't figure it out, how am I supposed to?

The job of an expert witness is to provide an opinion founded on specialized experience and education, which the jury members take into consideration in their deliberation of the case. It is the jury's duty to apply common sense and community values to disputes where scientific or technical experts may disagree. Sure, some issues in lawsuits are technical and difficult to comprehend. It is the lawyer's job, often through expert testimony, to present complex matters in such a way that someone without expertise can understand them.

Do all trials require 12 jury members?

No. The size of the jury varies from state to state. Many jurisdictions have moved from a 12-person jury to an 8- or even 6-person jury.

Why are some juries sequestered?

In criminal cases, at the discretion of the judge, a jury panel may be sequestered either throughout the entire trial or during jury deliberations to avoid exposure to media coverage of the case or influence by the jurors' own families and friends.

Does the jury need to reach a unanimous verdict?

In some jurisdictions a majority verdict instead of a unanimous decision is adequate for a conviction in criminal court or a finding of liability in a civil trial.

What is a *hung jury,* and when this happens, does the entire case have to be retried?

A hung jury occurs when jury members cannot reach agreement on the verdict. The prosecutor or plaintiff may decide to retry the case. In some instances where the jury can agree on everything but one claim or charge, only that claim or charge will be retried.

Can jurors talk to the press or others about their deliberations?

Jurors are free to discuss their verdict with anyone or to remain silent once the case has been decided. The court cannot control what jurors may or may not say after they are done serving on the jury and have left the jurisdiction of the court. Some jurisdictions have rules about whether lawyers or their representatives may contact jurors after the trial is over.

Does the judge have to comply with the jury's decision?

The judge may set aside the jury's verdict if there is enough evidence in the court record to support a contrary decision. The judge may do this at the request of one of the parties or on her own initiative.

What are *compensatory* and *punitive damages* awarded by a jury?

In a civil case, *compensatory damages* refer to money paid to a plaintiff to fairly and adequately compensate him for the injury or harm suffered. Compensatory damages include compensation for medical expenses, lost wages, and pain and suffering. *Punitive damages* refer to money that the defendant must pay as punishment for his wrongdoing, and to discourage the defendant and others from future similar bad acts.

Who gets to keep the money awarded as punitive damages?

Punitive damages go to the plaintiff. Some persons feel that plaintiffs recover their loss fairly with compensatory damages and that large punitive awards are a windfall. Many plaintiffs believe they deserve the often large punitive awards because they suffered a loss as a result of the defendant's wrongdoing and endured the stress and risk of trial.

Source: The National Jury Project, a professional trial-consulting firm, was the first group to apply social science research systematically to litigation. It is dedicated to the continued understanding of the nation's jury system. Each year over 300 law firms, legal departments, and public defenders from across the country seek assistance from the NJP in trial preparation, including pretrial research, change of venue studies, juror interviews, and assistance with jury selection. The National Jury Project has three offices: NJP Midwest, 322 First Avenue North, Suite 500, Minneapolis, MN 55401; (612) 338-2244; NJP East, 285 W. Broadway, Suite 200, New York, NY 10013; (212) 219-8962; NJP West, One Kaiser Place, Suite 1110, Oakland, CA 94612; (510) 832-2583.

Legal Malpractice

What is *legal malpractice?*

Legal malpractice refers to circumstances where a lawyer has failed to meet the professional standard of care for lawyers (usually the care of a reasonable attorney practicing in the same area of the country), either through negligence, mistakes, or intentional behavior, and the client loses rights or is harmed as a result of the lawyer's actions.

What are some examples of legal malpractice?

It's difficult to give examples because finding malpractice always depends on thorough legal analysis of the specific circumstances. Certain situations, such as a lawyer's failure to file a brief on time or loss of evidence through carelessness, might be malpractice. If things don't work out the way you wanted or expected, that does not mean your lawyer has necessarily committed malpractice. There are no guarantees in a lawsuit. Even if with hindsight you see that your lawyer could have done things better, this does not automatically imply malpractice, although it might. Malpractice occurs when a lawyer doesn't live up to the standards of the profession, but those standards don't require perfection.

What should I do if I'm not satisfied with the way my attorney handles my case, or I think there may have been malpractice?

If you're not satisfied with your attorney's work on your behalf, you should first speak to her and ask for an explanation of what was done and why. If the explanation doesn't make sense to you, or doesn't satisfy you, you need to talk to another lawyer or your local bar association and get another legal opinion about what has happened. You always have the right to fire your lawyer if you are dissatisfied, and to seek other counsel, whether or not there has been malpractice.

What would cause a lawyer to be disbarred?

The discipline rules regulating lawyers vary from state to state. Generally, only very serious violations of ethics rules—such as dishonest behavior, behavior causing harm to the public or clients, or behavior indicating an unfitness to practice law—can lead to disbarment. Attorneys are most commonly disbarred for improperly handling, using, or stealing a client's money, or for abandoning clients.

What will happen if I report a lawyer to the local bar association for unethical conduct or malpractice?

Actual procedures will vary by state, but in all cases if there appears to be a problem, it will be investigated. An investigation will likely include someone contacting you to discuss what you have observed and contacting the lawyer to discuss the charges. If the bar investigator believes it's necessary, more formal proceedings may follow, including hearings at which the lawyer has an opportunity to respond to any charges or allegations made. You might be asked to participate in such a hearing. The hearing would result in a public reprimand, suspension, or disbarment, and the lawyer could be ordered to make financial restitution or to pay a fine. Or the finders of fact may decide that the allegations are unsupported by the available evidence and recommend that no action be taken.

If I fire my lawyer for what I believe to be incompetence, do I still have to pay for her services?

In most cases, yes. You are required to pay for services actually rendered by your lawyer before the firing. If you successfully bring a malpractice action, you may recover some or all of what you paid.

Can a lawyer quit in the middle of a case?

Generally, lawyers' ethics rules provide that a lawyer may withdraw from any representation, provided it is done in a way that avoids harming or abandoning the client. When a case is pending before a court or other official body, the lawyer may need permission from the court before being allowed to withdraw. No lawyer may withdraw from a representation without notification and without providing the client a reasonable opportunity to deal with the withdrawal.

My attorney and I disagree about whether I should settle my claim. Must he follow my wishes?

Yes; in most situations your lawyer must follow your wishes about your case, including whether you want to settle. It is your case, and your lawyer works for you, but the lawyer's job includes making recommendations and advising you about what you should do. So you are paying for advice and counsel, and should carefully consider the reasons for your disagreement. Keep in mind that the lawyer will likely have broader experience and expertise, and may also be more objective about your case than you are.

I need legal services and have narrowed my hiring decision down to two lawyers. Is there a way to find out if either attorney has had malpractice complaints filed against him?

There is no practical way to obtain such information, except by asking the attorneys. When selecting a lawyer, you should ask about their previous experience with similar cases and if they've had any disciplinary complaints. You should feel comfortable with the attorney you select. If you don't feel you can communicate honestly and openly, or if you think the attorney is explaining matters to you in a way that you cannot understand, select a different attorney.

My father was in a horrible car accident that made the local newspaper. An attorney called our family about suing. Is this ethical?

No. It is not considered ethical for an attorney to contact you in person or by telephone. Written communications soliciting employment are advertisements and should be labeled as such. The rules regarding solicitation vary from state to state and control both when and how such contact may be made. Your state or local association can tell you what the regulations are in your area.

Source: The American Bar Association Standing Committee on Lawyers' Professional Liability. The American Bar Association is located at 750 North Lake Shore Drive, Chicago, IL 60611; (312) 988-5754; Web site: www.abnet.org.

Personal Injury

What is *personal injury* law?

When a person acting in a negligent fashion injures you or damages your property, that person is responsible for paying for the damage he caused. The civil courts, to be distinguished from the criminal courts, are a means of awarding fair compensation for, among other things, results of accidents that are caused by someone else's negligence.

If I am injured in an accident, do I automatically have a personal injury case?

It is a common misconception that simply because you've been injured in an accident, you are entitled to some kind of compensation. Three criteria must be met for a valid personal injury case to exist:

- The person who caused the accident had to have some type of duty of reasonable care toward the injured person. For instance, anyone driving a car must conform to certain reasonable standards of care, such as driving within the posted speed limits and obeying traffic signs.

- There must be a breach of that duty of reasonable care. In the case of an automobile accident, that breach would occur if someone was driving carelessly or ignoring speed limits and signals.

- The negligent act must have actually caused the accident and the injury. Again, in the example of an auto collision, the negligent act of running a stop sign must have caused the wreck. In some accidents, there is no fault; they just happen, even though everyone involved may have been paying attention and fulfilled any duty of reasonable care.

I was in the produce section of the grocery store and I slipped on some grapes and fell, bruising my knee. Don't I have a clear-cut case against the grocer?

A store owner has a duty to clean any debris that may cause shoppers to fall and injure themselves. If witness testimony shows that the fruit was on the floor for a substantial length of time (say, an hour or more), then it is reasonable to expect an employee to have noticed the mess and removed the danger. However, your injury is minor: a bruised knee that requires no medical attention and does not cause you to miss work. The store owner was negligent, but the damage was so slight that legal action would not be justified. The expense of suing would be higher than any compensation you might receive for such an injury.

How much time do I have to bring a personal injury claim?

Statutes of limitation differ from state to state, but generally, an injured person has from one to three years to file his case. The clock begins to run from the time of the accident and the consequent injury.

If I am driving a friend to the movie and we are in an automobile accident that is determined to be my fault, can my friend sue me for her injuries?

In most states, drivers found guilty of negligence are generally held liable for any injury sustained by passengers in the vehicle. In some states there are exceptions, such as being prohibited from suing a spouse for negligence, or prohibiting a child from suing a parent. In some states a "social" passenger, that is, one who has not paid for the ride, may not sue the driver, even if injuries resulted from that driver's ordinary negligence. However, if the accident was the result of gross negligence, such as extreme speeding or driving under the influence of alcohol, the passenger is permitted to sue.

I recently ran a stoplight, causing an accident. The driver of the other car was not wearing his seat belt and he hit his head on the windshield, badly bruising his face. Will the damages I am required to pay be reduced because he was not wearing his seat belt?

This is certainly a factor a jury can take into consideration when making their decision about liability. You, as defendant, should have experts who will testify that the other driver's injuries could have been prevented, or at least partially mitigated, had he been wearing a seat belt. Many juries have found that drivers who do not wear a seat belt leave themselves open to a charge of comparative negligence, thereby reducing their verdict. Even if the case does not go to trial, the failure to buckle up can be a very strong negotiating point for your insurance carrier.

Do people really get whiplash, or is that just a scam?

Whiplash is an actual soft-tissue injury that occurs frequently in rear-end collisions. Most people don't believe this injury exists until it happens to them. Whiplash does not show up well in X-rays or with other medical tests; as a result, it is difficult to convince a jury that you have suffered the injury. Commonly, whiplash requires four to nine months of medical or physical therapy. The best advice is to see a doctor immediately after an accident and get continued, well-documented treatment.

What should I do if I am in an automobile accident?

If someone is injured in an accident, or if there is damage beyond a small dent or scratch, report the accident to the police. Both parties should remain at the scene of the accident until the police arrive. Exchange the following information with the driver of the other car: name, address, telephone number, license number and license plate number, year and make of the car, and name, address, and telephone number of the insurance company and agent. Get the names, addresses, and license plate numbers of any possible witnesses. Don't talk about the accident and, especially, don't admit any fault, since a statement conceding fault on your part may be used against you later.

If you think the other party did something wrong, tell the police right away. Get the names and badge numbers of police officers who arrive at the scene, as well as the station where their report will be filed and, if available, the report number. Make written or mental notes of the relevant details of the accident, such as road and weather conditions. If possible, have photographs taken of both cars at the scene of the accident from several angles. Look around to see if there are any unusual circumstances, such as nonworking traffic lights or hidden stop signs. Get medical attention, if necessary. Keep a detailed diary of your injuries, including any treatment and expenses incurred. Obtain a written disability slip from your doctor. Contact your attorney even before you contact your insurance agent.

I was collecting donations door-to-door for a charity and was bitten by a dog. Can I sue the pet's owners?

A pet owner has a responsibility to see to it that the public is protected against her pet. In many jurisdictions there is what is called the "first bite doctrine." This doctrine states that pet owners are not held responsible for the first time the animal bites someone; after that, they are liable. But if the owner knew the pet was dangerous and did nothing to prevent it from attacking, the doctrine will not protect a pet owner from liability, even if the pet has never bitten anyone before.

I invited my boss to my home for dinner. As I hung up his coat, he walked into our sunken living room. He did not notice the two steps down, and he tripped, breaking his leg. Am I responsible?

People erroneously believe that they can recover damages simply because they have been injured on someone's property. As with all personal injury cases, in order to collect, someone must have done something wrong; that is, there must have been some negligence or intent to harm. The injured party must prove that there was, in fact, a dangerous condition, the property owner was aware of that dangerous condition, and he did not take reasonable action to deal with the situation.

A property owner has a duty to make that property reasonably free of danger, but does not necessarily have to do everything possible to make the area safe. Having a sunken living room is neither negligent nor evidence of intent to harm, so your boss must bear the cost of his injury himself.

I was visiting a friend on an icy evening. As I left she advised me to take the back door because the steps at the front of the house were slick with ice. I used the front exit anyway and fell, badly injuring my back. Will I prevail if I sue my friend?

No. You knowingly and voluntarily assumed the risk inherent in using the icy stairs.

Source: Gail J. Koff, an attorney and founding partner of Jacoby & Meyers Law Offices, 10 East 40th Street (22nd floor), New York, NY 10016-0201; phone: (212) 726-4400; fax: (212) 726-4444. Jacoby & Meyers has handled tens of thousands of personal injury cases and written several books, including *The Jacoby & Meyers Practical Guide to Personal Injury* and *The Jacoby & Meyers Practical Guide to Everyday Law*.

Products Liability

If a product is on the market, can a consumer assume it is safe?

Manufacturers have a legal duty to make their products reasonably safe, but it is generally up to the company that makes the product to comply with that duty. Some are more conscientious than others. Companies have incentives to keep their products safe because of the potential for bad publicity, because of government regulation, and because of the threat of lawsuits. Still, many product-related injuries do occur, and it is not unusual for consumer groups, government agencies, or juries to find products unsafe.

To sue a manufacturer or supplier for injuries related to their product, must the product be defective?

You can go to court and file a lawsuit for anything. But to win, or even to bring your case to trial, requires more. In order to be successful in a products liability case, you must show that your injuries were caused by a defect inherent in the product—a manufacturing flaw or an inadequate design—or by the manufacturer's or seller's failure to provide adequate warnings or instructions. If you can't show one or more of those problems with the product, the court will dismiss your claim without a trial.

So I could have a claim against a manufacturer if the warnings or instructions were deficient, even if there was nothing wrong with the product itself?

Yes. If you are injured in using a product because the instructions failed to explain everything necessary for its safe use, you would probably have the basis for a successful suit. The manufacturer has a legal duty to warn and instruct as to the safe use of the product, except where the dangers are obvious or widely known to the ordinary consumer.

What about silly warnings we read about in the media, such as warning that a child's Superhero costume won't enable the child to fly? Does the law require that?

Such warnings usually are adopted by manufacturer's caution to the extreme to protect against any possibility of a lawsuit, not because the law specifically requires them. In general, the law does not require warnings about dangers that are obvious or well known to the ordinary consumer. Manufacturers sometimes still give warnings about obvious dangers because they are not sure exactly which dangers will be considered obvious.

If I find something like a mouse or a fingernail in a canned or bottled soft drink, can I sue? How much is such a disgusting discovery worth?

Simply finding something in the drink should get you your money back, but alone would not make for a successful products liability claim. If, however, you were made ill by taking a drink before you discovered the foreign object, you would likely be able to sue and recover any medical expenses, plus some amount for your pain and suffering or emotional distress. A jury would determine the amount, which may vary widely based on the particular circumstances involved. One plaintiff who drank a soft drink containing a tobaccolike substance was awarded $3,168.04, while another made ill by drinking from a soft drink containing batteries was granted $554,000.

My two-year-old daughter was injured when she swallowed a small plastic action figure I purchased for her older brother. The package indicated that the toy was for children five years and older. Is the toy manufacturer at fault for my daughter's injuries?

Probably not. The manufacturer warned against the hazard; so unless you can show there was something else wrong with the product that caused the injury, the manufacturer would not be liable. In view of the warning, the fact that the toy could be dangerous for a two-year-old is not enough.

Why are smokers allowed to sue tobacco companies for health problems resulting from years of smoking, even though the product contains an explicit warning label?

Again, anyone can file a suit about anything. That doesn't mean they will win, or even get a trial. Most smokers who have sued tobacco companies have lost, apparently in part because juries believe that smokers are responsible for the decision to smoke. However, smokers' lawsuits have claimed that the warnings on the packages did not tell everything the companies knew or that consumers need to know. And some smokers have claimed that cigarettes could have been made safer, or that manufacturers deliberately made the product addictive. Those claims could still be successful even with the warning on the package. There have been a number of such lawsuits; as of this writing, tobacco companies have never paid damages to smokers. This may change, however, depending on the outcome of appeals in a 1996 Florida case in which a jury awarded $750,000 to a smoker suffering from lung cancer. Also, recent negotiations among tobacco companies, state attorneys general, and plaintiffs' attorneys have led to a tentative large-scale settlement which, if it becomes final, would involve large payments from the tobacco industry to cover smoking-related health costs.

Does a claim against a manufacturer arise if an advertisement misrepresents the properties of a product?

To have a successful products liability claim, the consumer would have to have been injured because of the misrepresentation. For example, if the advertising indicated that you could use the product in a certain way, and the consumer used it in that way and then was injured, the consumer could probably win. But misleading advertising in itself doesn't create a products liability case.

If a person is injured in the normal use of an inherently dangerous product like a blowtorch, can he sue the manufacturer for damages even if the product was not defective and carried adequate instructions and warnings?

If the person sued just because of the injury, without claiming that there was a defect in the product or lack of adequate warning or instruction, the court would throw out the suit without trial. As the courts often say, the manufacturer is not an insurer of its products, and cannot be held liable just because someone was injured using the product. There must be some defect in manufacture, design, warnings, or instructions that caused the injury.

If I am injured while using a product in a way specifically prohibited in the product's warning, do I have any kind of case against the manufacturer?

You still could have a case if your use of the product was one that the manufacturer should have anticipated and could have protected against, e.g., by changing the design. Manufacturers have a duty to design products to be safe for reasonably foreseeable uses; generally, they can't just tell you not to use it that way. However, in most states your misuse of the product would reduce the amount you could recover from the manufacturer, if you were found partly at fault in causing the injury.

My teenage son's finger was badly cut while he was sticking small tree limbs into the blade of the lawnmower. Clearly, the mower was not meant for this use. Does my son's behavior preclude our family from suing?

It probably would. A teenager is old enough to know better, and would likely be found at fault for what he did. To win the suit you would have to show that the manufacturer could have anticipated this and changed the mower in some way that would have prevented the injury. Even if you succeeded on that point, your compensation would generally be reduced because of your son's conduct.

Is the manufacturer liable if the owner failed to properly maintain and repair a product and it malfunctions and causes injury?

The manufacturer could still be liable if a product defect contributed to the injury, or if the manufacturer could have anticipated the situation and done something to prevent it—such as providing a warning or a design that would have avoided the injury. But if the owner's neglect was part of the cause, the manufacturer's liability would generally be reduced to the extent that the owner's conduct was the cause of the accident.

What about these huge damages awards we read of in the papers? Are companies going broke paying out massive awards in products liability cases?

There have been several very large awards in products liability cases, some in excess of $100 million. Companies complain that these awards are burdensome, and they may well be. However, most such awards are reduced by the courts, and the claims are then settled privately for confidential amounts. The fact that the award was made by a jury does not mean that companies are actually paying out those amounts.

Source: John D. Hodson, Ph.D., J.D., graduated cum laude from Harvard Law School and is a member of the State Bar of New York. He has extensively researched and written about products liability issues as editor or contributing author in several publications, including the *Products Liability Advisory*. He is currently an editor for a publishing firm specializing in legal publications, West Group, 50 Broad Street East, Rochester, NY 14694; (716) 546-1490.

Search and Seizure

If I am stopped for speeding, and the officer asks if he can search my car, can I say no?

Of course you can say no. If the officer has the legal authority to search the car, he will not ask in the first place; he will just search the car. You have a right under the U.S. Constitution to be free from unreasonable searches and seizures. A decision to search the car of a speeder or other traffic offender who is being ticketed, but not arrested, is unreasonable unless objective facts and circumstances cause the officer legitimately to believe he will probably find evidence of a specific crime in the car. A shaved head and earrings are not sufficient to justify such legitimate belief. After all, what crime would the officer be alerted to by a shaved head and earrings—counterfeit jewelry? In this free society, we do not permit officers to conduct searches based on mere hunches.

If I don't have marijuana or other illegal items in my car, what do I have to hide? Why shouldn't I consent?

It's a matter of principle and philosophy. The framers of the Bill of Rights thought of the Fourth Amendment as the great right of Americans to be left alone—to do as we please unless our conduct provides sufficient cause to justify police or government intervention. This right to privacy is vitally important not only for guilty people but for us all, because it draws limits around the power of our government to interfere in our lives.

For what reasons can a police officer enter my home?

The authority of police officers to get past your front door is highly regulated. Essentially, there are three ways for the officer to get into your apartment or house. If you choose to let her in, then the officer is there by your consent. Otherwise, a police officer can enter your home only after she has obtained prior judicial approval to enter (a warrant), or when a near-emergency situation exists that allows her to enter without a warrant.

What does a search warrant allow a police officer to do?

A search warrant is issued by a judge when the police present a sworn statement containing sufficient facts and circumstances to persuade the judge that a crime has been committed and that specific evidence of that crime will be found at the place to be searched. The warrant authorizes police intrusion onto the premises, but it also limits the scope of their search. The warrant must contain a specific description or listing of the items to be searched for, instead of allowing a general exploratory search for any evidence.

Does the requirement that an officer have a warrant to search my home apply to my backyard?

Your backyard is an extension of the living area of your home. Police are restricted from walking into your backyard and nosing around without a warrant, just as they would not be permitted into your home for that purpose.

May a police officer enter my house when he comes to the door because of a neighbor's complaints about a noisy party?

It is unnecessary for the officer to enter your house or apartment just to seek a reduction in noise level, so it is completely up to you whether the officer may come in. Probably the only reason the officer might request entry is to determine whether there are any underage people drinking or whether anyone is using an illegal substance. You are within your rights to refuse the officer's request.

I share an apartment. Can my roommate allow the police to search without my permission?

If a police officer comes to your apartment to search for evidence against you, your roommate may consent to a search. Even if the officer has asked your permission and been refused, your roommate may validly consent to a search of the shared spaces of the apartment, such as the living room and kitchen. However, those parts of the apartment that are yours exclusively may not be searched on the roommate's okay.

When may police search my home without a warrant?

An immediate danger of harm to someone would allow the police to bypass a search warrant and enter a residence. If facts exist which lead police to believe that evidence of a serious crime will be destroyed or immediately removed from a location, police may act without a search warrant rather than risk losing that evidence by taking the time to get a warrant. The evidence may be challenged before it is used in a criminal case, and the police will have to establish the reasonableness of their belief that an emergency justified their search without a warrant.

My roommate and I were having a very noisy, violent fight and someone called the police. An officer came to the door after we quieted down, but he insisted on coming in even though my roommate told him everything was okay. Can he do that legally?

Not only did the circumstances allow for the officer to come in, but if you think about it, you would have approved of his decision to come into your house. A situation like this could lead to a real tragedy if the officer simply accepted the assurance of the person who answers the door, without checking to see whether someone inside is in danger.

In my high school, teachers and principals regularly search lockers. Can they do that?

You have a constitutional right, even in high school, to be free from unreasonable searches and seizures. But one can hardly argue that the presence of weapons, drugs, and alcohol on school premises does not present a hazard to other students and teachers and seriously detract from the learning environment. Therefore, the school may undertake reasonable steps to remove these objects from the school. Students and parents should be notified of the inspection policy, and procedures should be published within the school so that the inspections are not misused.

Source: Lewis R. Katz, John C. Hutchins Professor of Law and Director of Graduate Legal Studies at Case Western Reserve University School of Law in Cleveland, Ohio. As a practicing attorney, Professor Katz participated in two landmark cases before the U.S. Supreme Court. His writing credits include an undergraduate textbook, law review articles, treatises for practicing lawyers, Op-Ed pieces for several major newspapers, and a book focusing on search and seizure issues, *Know Your Rights.* Several of his publications have been cited in opinions of the Supreme Court. Reprinted from Katz, *Know Your Rights,* with permission of the publisher and copyright owner, West Group (Cleveland Office).

Sentencing

How many prisoners are currently incarcerated in the United States?

The number of prisoners has more than doubled in the past decade, and the United States is now second in the world only to Russia in its rate of incarceration. The combined population of our prisons and jails is currently 1.6 million, compared to 800,000 just ten years ago.

How much does it cost to keep one person in prison?

Generally, the cost of incarceration is about $20,000 a year per inmate. New prison cells cost between $50,000 and $80,000, not including long-term financing charges, which are generally twice the initial cost.

How often are convicted felons actually incarcerated?

Four out of five persons convicted of violent offenses are sentenced to incarceration. U.S. Bureau of Justice Statistics data for 1994 (the most recent year for which data are available) show that 62 percent of convicted violent offenders were sentenced to prison. Those who are not incarcerated generally have been convicted of the less serious offenses and/or have less of a previous criminal history.

I read somewhere that only three criminals are actually imprisoned for every 100 serious crimes. Why is the system so soft on serious crime?

The statistic is true, but misleading. Half of all serious crimes are never even reported to the police; only about one in five of those that are reported result in an arrest; and ultimately, fewer than 10 percent of all crimes even result in conviction. Of all the felony offenders actually convicted, about 70 percent are incarcerated in prison or jail. So the problem is not one of "soft" judges, but rather a criminal system that is reactive in nature and can respond only after the fact. This is why many police departments are now moving toward community policing that attempts to solve problems before they escalate into crimes.

How do judges decide what sentences to impose?

Sentencing systems vary significantly by state. Some states permit judges flexibility in deciding a sentence, while others provide guidelines that restrict the judge's choice to a narrow range of sentence lengths. Judges generally try to balance a number of goals at sentencing, including protecting the public, punishing the offender, providing compensation to victims, and addressing the factors that led the offender to commit the crime. Guidelines tend to rely primarily on two factors: the seriousness of the offense and the offender's prior criminal record.

I've heard that some people get long sentences like ten years for possession of marijuana, but a rapist will be sentenced for only seven years. How can this be?

Beginning in the 1980s, most states passed *mandatory sentencing laws* for drug crimes. These laws require harsh, fixed terms that often force judges to treat low-level drug offenders the same as drug kingpins. Many judges oppose these laws, contending that a judge is in a better position to look at the facts and determine a sentence in an individual case than a legislative body passing across-the-board sentencing laws.

How does plea bargaining work?

More than 90 percent of criminal convictions are obtained through a plea bargain rather than a trial. Plea bargains involve an agreement between the prosecutor and defendant to plead guilty to a specified crime, often with an understanding of what the recommended sentence will be.

Why do prosecutors sometimes agree to plea bargains that involve little prison time for serious crimes?

Conducting a criminal trial is very expensive and time-consuming. If all criminal cases went to trial, our already clogged court system would have to shut down. Also, in many cases a prosecutor has only limited evidence: For example, stolen goods may not have been recovered, or there may be few or unreliable witnesses to a crime. So resolving a case through a plea bargain is often the only means of obtaining a conviction, even if it results in a shorter sentence than might be obtained with harder evidence.

Have stricter sentences proven to be a deterrent to crime?

Criminologists have known for many years that it is the *certainty*, not the *severity*, of punishment that produces any deterrent effect. That is, if we can increase the chances that an offender will be apprehended, he may think twice about committing a crime. Merely raising the potential sentence for an offense from five years to ten does little to deter an offender who doesn't believe he will be caught anyway.

How have stricter sentencing laws affected the war on drugs?

From 1980 to 1995, the number of arrests for drug offenses tripled, and the proportion of drug offenders in state prisons rose from about 1 in 16 to almost 1 in 4. There are now about 400,000 offenders in prison or jail either serving time or awaiting trial for a drug offense, compared to about 50,000 in 1983. Despite this enormous increase, drugs remain plentiful in many communities, and teenage drug use has increased in recent years.

The fact is, sentencing some offenders in a community to prison does nothing to alleviate whatever conditions may have existed that contributed to drug usage. Most experts believe that only a broad approach that incorporates emphasis on treatment and prevention will provide long-term benefits.

What do criminologists mean by the "replacement effect"?

One of the reasons why incarceration has only a limited effect on crime is because offenders who are sentenced to prison are often "replaced" on the streets. When a serial rapist is imprisoned, the community is made safer, but when a low-level drug seller is locked up, it only creates an opportunity for another seller to take his place. In the latter case, one more offender is in prison, but the particular drug problem has not been eliminated.

Why do prisoners serve only part of the time for which they are sentenced?

In many states, offenders are sentenced to a minimum and a maximum term in prison. The minimum indicates the lower range of years considered to be sufficient punishment by the judge, assuming that the inmate is well behaved in prison and is planning for release. Prison wardens are generally the first to support "good time" credits, since these provide an incentive for inmates to conform to prison regulations. Thus, to state that a prisoner was released "early" is usually a misnomer; it merely indicates that the inmate met certain conditions established by the sentencing judge and parole board for release after an appropriate period of time.

What are some alternatives to imprisonment?

Incarceration is very expensive for taxpayers, and not every offender convicted of a crime requires such a secure setting. Particularly for persons convicted of nonviolent offenses, programs that incorporate required community service, restitution to victims, substance-abuse treatment, employment, and community supervision have demonstrated that both offenders and victims can benefit from constructive sentencing options.

It seems that defendant rights are now more important than victim rights. Is this true?

It's a mistake to believe a finite number of rights exist that need to be divided between victims and defendants. Victims have needs and rights that should be met, such as compensation for crime costs, counseling, and communication from the court system. Defendant rights, which apply to any citizen accused of a crime, include the right to be presumed innocent, to have access to an attorney, and to have a fair hearing in court. A healthy justice system should be able to meet the needs of all parties without competition.

What is the role of drugs in crime?

Both illegal drugs and alcohol are heavily involved in many crimes. Data from the Bureau of Justice Statistics show that half of all violent offenses were committed by people under the influence of drugs or alcohol. Since much crime is impulsive, these offenders are not necessarily thinking of the consequences of their actions, nor are they deterred by harsh sentencing laws.

Do black people receive harsher sentences than white people?

Research on this issue is mixed. In looking at which offenders receive the death penalty, a number of studies have shown that the race of both the victim and the offender influences the sentence. For other crimes, the research is less conclusive, with the main exception of drug crimes. Most experts believe that African-Americans, particularly in inner cities, are more likely to be arrested when they use drugs and more likely to receive harsher sentences than whites for drug crimes.

Source: The Sentencing Project, 918 F Street, NW, Suite 501, Washington, DC 20004; phone: (202) 628-0871; fax: (202) 628-1091; Web site: www.sproject.com. The Sentencing Project is highly regarded for its reports and analysis highlighting inequities in the criminal justice system; it has helped to establish alternative sentencing programs in more than 20 states.

Sexual Harassment

What laws protect me from *sex discrimination?*

Title VII of the Civil Rights Act (1964) protects you against many forms of discrimination based on sex. It covers decisions made by employers of 15 or more employees regarding hiring, firing, work assignments and conditions, promotions, benefits, training, retirement policy, and wages. The Equal Pay Act (1963) prohibits employers from paying men and women unequal wages for equal work. Persons are protected against sexual harassment by landlords or real estate agents in the sale or rental of a home by the Fair Housing Act. Teachers, students, and other employees in schools receiving federal funding may not commit sex discrimination as mandated by Title IX of the Equal Education Amendments (1972). If any of these laws is violated, you may file suit.

Are there different types of *sexual harassment?*

Courts have recognized two forms of sexual harassment claims: the *quid pro quo claim* and the *hostile environment claim*. A quid pro quo claim (literally, "this for that") involves harassment in which a supervisor demands sexual favors in exchange for job benefits. The classic example of quid pro quo harassment is a male supervisor threatening that if a female employee does not have sex with him, she will be fired. A hostile work environment claim involves unwelcome behavior, either of a sexual nature or based on gender, that is so severe or pervasive that it creates an intimidating, hostile, or abusive work environment or has the effect of unreasonably interfering with an individual's work performance. Such unwelcome behavior could include discriminatory intimidation, ridicule, or insult. Merely offensive conduct would not be enough to establish discrimination.

My coworker, Frank, is constantly propositioning me for sex even though I have plainly told him I am not interested. I don't want to sue my company because I don't feel they are responsible for Frank's actions. Can I take legal action against Frank directly?

Every employer has a duty to stamp out sexual harassment, and you have every right to expect your employer to fulfill that duty. Under Title VII, you cannot sue your coworkers for sexual harassment. However, you can sue your company and high-level supervisors for the harassing and discriminatory actions of your immediate supervisors, or for knowingly allowing your coworkers to continually harass you and make the workplace a hostile environment.

What should I do if I feel I am being sexually harassed?

If an incident of sexual harassment occurs, make it immediately clear to the harasser that you do not welcome his behavior and want it to stop. If you do not feel comfortable confronting the harasser, consider speaking with his or your supervisor. Your legal claims can be hurt if you keep silent. So inform the harasser and/or your employer or supervisor that you do not welcome such behavior. Keep records of all conversations about the harassment, since your employer may later deny that you notified them. Informing your supervisor or employer places the employer on notice so that if you bring a claim later, you can show that the employer knew about the harassment.

Should I be keeping some kind of diary about the harassment I have faced on the job?

You should take notes about all incidents of harassment or other discrimination. Write down the date, time, name of harasser, what happened, what was said, and the names of any witnesses. Be sure to write down when, where, and how superiors may have become aware of the harassment. Note also if you lost any money as a result of the harassment, e.g., by having to take a day off work.

Keep your notes in a safe place at home, separated from personal diaries and records, bearing in mind that these notes may have to be shared with your employer's attorney if the case goes to court. You should always save any notes, cards, or presents that your harasser gives you.

I have a feeling my boss wants to get rid of me because I made a report of sexual harassment about a coworker. I'm worried that my personnel file may be falsified and negative incidents added in an effort to fire me. What can I do to protect my job?

If your employer keeps written records about your job performance and you have a good employment record, immediately mail a sealed copy of those records to yourself and do not open the postmarked envelope. It may provide useful evidence about your job performance before you complained of harassment, and it will be safe from loss or tampering.

My employer has an internal grievance procedure for working through complaints of sexual harassment. Should I use this procedure?

Internal procedures can be beneficial because sorting out a problem without the bother of going to court is preferable. However, you may feel the in-house grievance procedure will only expose you to greater harm. It may require you to complain to your harasser or his friends. Your legal claim should not be hurt if you can show the in-house procedures to be a sham or ineffective. Using an in-house grievance procedure does not mean that you have lost your right to file a lawsuit or complaint with a city, state, or federal agency if your employer fails to resolve your complaint satisfactorily.

If you are a union or a guild member, consider contacting your local representative or shop steward and following the grievance procedures outlined in the contract.

If I file a charge of sexual harassment, will my behavior be scrutinized?

For sexual conduct to constitute sexual harassment, the alleged sexual remarks, advances, or other behavior must be unwelcome. Therefore, the courts may examine the way you respond to the person who is harassing you to determine if the behavior was unwelcome. Most courts have found that responding to sexual harassment with foul language or profanity does not mean that the harassment was not unwelcome. Courts also have found that a woman's life outside the workplace, including posing nude for a magazine, for example, is irrelevant to whether she would find an employer's sexual comments or advances welcome. Some courts have, however, found that plaintiffs who were receptive to, or engaged in, sexually suggestive behavior, did not find it unwelcome. Courts may interpret engaging in sexually suggestive gift giving, exhibiting surgical scars, telling dirty jokes, or making sexually explicit suggestions as indications that alleged harassing behavior was welcome. It is important that you complain of the harassment to a supervisor. Some courts interpret a failure to complain as an indication that you welcomed the harassment.

I am a male flight attendant and I work mostly with women. The whole sexual harassment topic is so sensitive, I'm scared I'm going to say or do the wrong thing and get accused of harassing a fellow employee. Should I be worried?

Courts recognize that people have different levels of sensitivity, so judges and juries must consider whether alleged harassing behavior would result in a work environment that a reasonable person would find hostile or abusive. You will not be responsible for an irrational interpretation of your actions or words. Further, one truly offensive comment will most likely not rise to the level of sexual harassment. Courts look at the severity and pervasiveness of the harassment. One or two sexist comments would probably not be enough to support a hostile environment claim.

I'd like to take action against my employer, but I can't afford an attorney. What other options are available?

The EEOC and similar state and local civil rights agencies provide an alternative forum outside the court system to bring your sexual harassment complaint. In fact, you are required to first file a complaint with the EEOC before bringing a Title VII suit in court. The agency process is designed to avoid lawyers and large expenditures of time and money. There is no filing fee, and the agency does not charge for either investigating or attempting to resolve your complaint.

Be very careful to note the time limits for filing a complaint required by these agencies (sometimes as short as 180 days from the last discriminatory act). If you do not comply with these limits, your complaint may be dismissed. After receiving your complaint, the agency will notify your employer, investigate the charge, and attempt to resolve the problem. Note, however, that because many of these agencies have tremendous backlogs, the agency may instead give you clearance to sue in court. Local telephone numbers for the EEOC and state and local civil rights agencies are listed in the government section of your phone book.

Source: The NOW Legal Defense and Education Fund, 99 Hudson Street, New York, NY 10013-2871; phone: (212) 925-6635; fax: (212) 226-1066. The Fund is the nation's oldest legal advocacy organization for women and girls. For a Legal Resource Kit on sexual discrimination, write to the NOW Legal Defense and Education Fund. (There is a $5 materials charge.)

Small Claims Court

What are the advantages of small claims court?

You get to prepare and present your own case without having to pay a lawyer more than your claim is worth. To file a lawsuit, all you have to do is fill out a few lines on a simple form. And once you're in court, you can talk directly to the judge without using legal jargon. You may present documents or witnesses without the hassles of strict rules of evidence. Perhaps the biggest advantage to small claims court is that it is much quicker than formal court.

How long will I have to wait for a verdict?

Most disputes are heard in court within a month or two from the time the complaint is filed. The hearing itself seldom takes more than 15 minutes. The judge announces his decision in the courtroom on the day of the hearing, or mails it out within a few days.

How much can I sue for?

The maximum amount for which you can sue in small claims court varies from state to state, but it typically ranges from about $2,000 to $5,000. Contact your local small claims court to learn the exact amount.

Can I bring my lawyer?

Lawyers are allowed in most states (though prohibited in some), but the limited financial awards involved usually make it uneconomical for people to hire legal counsel. Besides, the beauty of small claims court is that you don't need a lawyer to pursue your claim.

The city plans to cut down a 50-year-old oak tree near my property. Can I sue the city in small claims court to stop destruction of the tree?

No. With a few exceptions, small claims court does not hear cases unless they are for financial damages. You can't use small claims court to get a divorce, change your name, or do any of the other thousands of things that require some solution other than the payment of money.

In my state, the maximum amount a plaintiff can sue for in small claims court is $2,500, but my damages total at least $3,100. Do I have to file in formal court?

It's legal to reduce a claim for damages so that your case is within the jurisdiction of the small claims court. You can state a claim for just $2,500 of your $3,100 debt, but you forever waive the $600 difference. Still, it is probably advantageous to claim the lesser amount because a lawyer would likely charge considerably more than $600 to represent you in formal court.

I filed a lawsuit in small claims court against my former landlord for failing to return my $500 security deposit. What evidence should I present in court?

A well-prepared tenant will show up in court with the following evidence: photos of the apartment upon moving in, which show any dirt or damage that already existed; photos of the apartment upon moving out, which show clean conditions; receipts for cleaning supplies used in the final clean-up; a copy of the written lease or rental agreement; witnesses who saw the tenant clean up on moving out and who will testify that the apartment was immaculate; and a copy of an inventory of conditions when moving in and out, signed by the landlord and tenant.

Before the court date, the tenant should write a letter to the landlord explaining her position, requesting the full deposit, and stating her intent to sue if the deposit is not returned. This demand letter should also be entered as evidence.

My dry cleaner ruined a leather vest that had been given to me by my father. What are my chances of prevailing in court?

Liability is often easy to prove when clothing is damaged, but the amount of monetary compensation judges award is frequently disappointing to plaintiffs. In theory, that's because a court awards only fair market value of the damaged clothing, not its replacement cost. Used clothing has little actual market value, though it may have been expensive to purchase or may have tremendous sentimental value. In these cases, many judges tend to bend the law a little in favor of the person who has suffered the loss. When you present your case in court, don't forget to bring the damaged vest and, if possible, be ready to prove the purchase price with a canceled check, newspaper ad, or credit card statement.

Can I request a jury in small claims court?

Jury trials are available in small claims courts in less than half the states. But even where it is possible to have a jury, it rarely makes sense to go to the extra time and trouble given the relatively modest amounts of money involved.

How much will it cost to sue?

Fees for filing a case in small claims court are very moderate—no more than $25 to $50 in most states. There is an additional fee for serving papers on the opposing party, but most states allow service by certified or registered mail, so costs are low. If you win, you can get your filing fees and service costs added to the judgment.

The person I want to sue lives in a different county with a separate small claims court. Where do I file?

Chances are you have a choice of courts in which to file. In all states you can sue in the county where the defendant resides or has a place of business. This rule makes sense because if a suit is brought where the defendant is located, he can't complain that it is unduly burdensome to appear. About half the states also allow you to file suit in the county where the injury to the plaintiff or the plaintiff's personal property occurred. In cases involving contracts, many states also permit you to bring your charge in the county where the services under the contract were to be performed.

The judge found my deadbeat neighbor at fault for flooding my yard and destroying my prize-winning rose garden. Now that I've won, how do I collect my award?

The court does not enforce its judgments and collect money for you. Therefore, if you win your case and the defendant does not voluntarily pay the damages awarded by the court, you must act like a collection agency. First, try writing a polite collection letter to the defendant. If you don't see any money within ten days, you can proceed with garnishment of wages. Federal and state laws allow you to collect 25 percent of a person's net wages to satisfy a debt. If you know where a judgment debtor banks, you can order a sheriff, marshall, or constable to levy on a bank account. Most collection costs are recoverable. You can also get interest on the judgment.

Source: Ralph Warner, an attorney, author, and founder of Nolo Press, a publishing company specializing in self-help law books and software. He publishes many books designed to assist people with everyday legal issues, including *Everybody's Guide to Small Claims Court,* now in its sixth edition. Nolo Press is located at 950 Parker Street, Berkeley, CA 94710; phone: (510) 549-1976; fax: (510) 548-5902.

Smoking Laws

Is secondhand smoke harmful?

Environmental tobacco smoke, also known as *secondhand smoke,* is a combination of smoke exhaled by the smoker and sidestream smoke emitted from a burning cigarette. Four thousand seven hundred chemical compounds have been identified in secondhand smoke, including carbon monoxide, nicotine, carcinogenic tars, ammonia, hydrogen cyanide, formaldehyde, benzene, and arsenic. The first comprehensive report on the health effects of environmental tobacco smoke was the Surgeon General's 1986 *Report on the Health Consequences of Involuntary Smoking.* That report concluded that involuntary smoking is a cause of disease, including lung cancer, in healthy nonsmokers.

In 1992, the EPA classified tobacco smoke as a group A carcinogen, a substance known to cause cancer in humans for which there is no safe level of exposure. A University of California, San Francisco, study found that secondhand smoke is the third leading cause of preventable death in the country, killing 53,000 nonsmokers in the United States each year.

I'm confused about smoking laws. My husband can smoke at his place of employment, but where I work employees are only allowed to smoke in designated areas. We often meet for lunch at a restaurant where smoking is not allowed at all. What's going on?

Perhaps you and your husband work in different cities or counties with different smoking laws in force. Or you could be frequenting places that have adopted very different voluntary smoking policies in a local jurisdiction that has not yet passed a clean indoor air ordinance.

Policies limiting smoking, known as clean indoor air or smoke-free policies, fall into two categories: enacted laws and voluntary policies. The most significant enacted laws are municipal ordinances passed by the elected officials in a city or county, or regulations enacted by a local board of health. Smoke-free ordinances restrict smoking in public places and workplaces, often including restaurants, to protect the public and employees from the harmful effects of secondhand smoke.

Voluntary smoking policies are not mandated by law, but are adopted by private employers, business owners, and others for economic, legal, or health reasons. Voluntary policies should not be relied on as an exclusive remedy because only a limited number of workplaces and public places will restrict smoking on their own, and nothing prevents the voluntary policy from being eliminated later on. Workplaces, especially office settings, reflect a strong, voluntary smoke-free trend. Business owners and corporations now know that there is much to be gained by eliminating smoking in the workplace. The legal liability and economic costs associated with workplace smoking do not make good business sense.

What is the status of federal and state laws restricting smoking in public places and workplaces?

The federal government has enacted only a handful of laws protecting nonsmokers from secondhand smoke. Federal laws eliminate smoking on domestic airline flights and in enclosed areas of agencies receiving federal funding that primarily serve youth, such as schools. There are numerous state laws with clean indoor air provisions, but these generally are not very strong. Many state laws restricting smoking are limited to government agencies, or to a few limited places open to the public. Only 21 states have laws restricting smoking in private workplaces. California, Maryland, and Washington attempt to eliminate smoking in all enclosed workplaces. Although 31 states restrict smoking in restaurants, most of these exempt smaller restaurants and require only small nonsmoking sections. Vermont and Utah have enacted laws that completely eliminate smoking in restaurants.

Don't ordinances designed to prohibit smoking discriminate against smokers and violate their civil rights?

Clean indoor air ordinances don't regulate people, they regulate behavior, and therefore are not discriminatory. Smoke-free ordinances do not make smoking illegal; they establish areas where people may not smoke due to the risk to nonsmokers. Smokers can eat in smoke-free restaurants; they just can't light up. In effect, smoke-free ordinances are most similar to drunk driving laws, which do not prohibit drinking but do regulate certain behavior when it presents a danger to others.

How are nonsmoking ordinances enforced?

Studies have found high levels of voluntary compliance with local clean indoor air ordinances. Communities that have passed ordinances have found that posting "no smoking" signs and removing ashtrays represents 99 percent of their enforcement activity. Most ordinances designate violations as civil, not criminal, and offenders may be subject to fines. Ordinances are generally enforced on a complaint-only basis, and citations rarely need to be issued. Most businesses and smokers are law-abiding and will follow the ordinances' requirements as long as they are aware of them.

Is better ventilation a legitimate alternative to smoke-free laws and policies?

Ventilation is an expensive and inefficient means of dealing with secondhand smoke. Both the EPA and the Occupational Safety and Health Administration (OSHA) agree that the only way ventilation can eliminate exposure is if smoking is limited to enclosed areas with a separate ventilation system. Air from a designated smoking area must be funneled directly outside, not recirculated within the building or mixed with the general dilution ventilation. Furthermore, workers should not be required to enter a smoking area to perform work duties. Providing such a ventilation system would be quite costly to businesses, whereas eliminating smoking costs nothing.

Are nonsmoking patrons protected from secondhand smoke when they sit in nonsmoking sections?

No. The Surgeon General states that smoking sections reduce, but do not eliminate, nonsmokers' exposure to secondhand smoke. Air can move freely between smoking and nonsmoking sections, carrying smoke with it. Even if the sections are physically separated, shared ventilation systems still carry smoke from room to room. Let's not overlook the risks to restaurant employees. The most heavily exposed restaurant workers breathe the equivalent of actively smoking 1.5 to 2 packs of cigarettes per day. Researchers have found that wait staff in Massachusetts have a 50 percent greater risk of developing lung cancer compared to other occupations.

Source: Americans for Nonsmokers' Rights, 2530 San Pablo Avenue, Suite J, Berkeley, CA 94702; phone: (510) 841-3032; fax: (510) 841-3071; Web site: www@no-smoke.org. Founded in 1976, Americans for Nonsmokers' Rights is a national public interest organization with over 15,000 members working to protect the rights of nonsmokers to breathe smoke-free air.

Traffic Tickets

If I am pulled over for a traffic violation, how can I convince the officer not to give me a ticket?

Once an officer pulls you over, it is within her discretion whether or not to issue a violation. The best thing you can do to increase your chances of not receiving a ticket is to convey to the officer, through words or actions, a spirit of cooperation and your willingness to comply with the law. Keep your composure. Be friendly and polite without appearing as though you are trying to butter up the officer. Your attitude should convey: I'm not sure if I know exactly what I've done wrong, but I know you had a good reason for stopping me. So I'm at your mercy. Are you willing to discuss the situation for a moment?

What should I do to appear cooperative?

Pull over as soon as possible when you see the officer's blue lights behind you. If you're being signaled to stop while on the freeway, pull onto the shoulder, not into the center divider section. Roll your window down so the officer doesn't have to knock to get your attention. Always keep both hands visible and do not make any sudden movements, or the officer may think you are reaching for a weapon. Turn off your radio. Keep your registration, proof of insurance card, and driver's license where they are easily accessible, in an overhead visor or uncluttered glove compartment. Do not hand the officer your wallet.

Stay in your car unless the officer asks you to step outside. If you seem eager to get out, the officer may suspect you are trying to conceal incriminating evidence like an open container of alcohol or a weapon. Be calm and polite. If the violation is not obvious, politely ask why you were stopped. Don't cry. Don't tell the officer that you will take the matter to the courts, as this could be taken as a challenge.

If I have clearly committed the violation, is there anything I can say to dissuade the officer from issuing the ticket?

Try to get the officer to like and trust you. The following gambits have gotten drivers out of tickets: "I have a perfect driving record. If you just give me a warning this time, I'll do my best to keep it that way"… "Insurance for a person my age is very expensive, so I've been trying to keep my record clean. Could you trust me not to make the same mistake again?"… "My boyfriend/girlfriend just broke up with me and it's hard to concentrate on other things right now. I promise I'll be more careful"… "I'm new to this area. I guess I need to pay closer attention to my driving." Be careful, however, not to admit guilt. If the officer tells you that you were traveling at 70 miles an hour and you respond that you never went over 62, you have admitted to driving well over the speed limit if you're in a 55 mph zone.

Are police required to write a certain amount of tickets each month in order to fulfill a quota?

Police are not required to fill specific quotas. In fact, in many states it is actually illegal for law enforcement agencies to impose a quota on their officers. There is, however, an expectation that a reasonable amount of tickets will be written, based on traffic-flow conditions, accident statistics at a given location, time of day, weather conditions, and the average number of tickets written by other officers patrolling the same or similar roadways. A police officer's performance may be monitored by comparing the number of tickets he has written to other officers working the same beat at the same time of day. After all, a traffic cop who isn't issuing tickets isn't doing his job.

If I sign a ticket, am I admitting that I committed the violation?

No. Your signature on the ticket is only a promise to appear in court. It is not an admission of guilt.

I have a friend who was pulled over and got out of the ticket by telling the officer that she had a medical emergency. Should I try this?

This excuse may get you out of a ticket, but it is risky to lie. Police officers will often take your license number and escort you to the hospital.

What if I am stopped and I don't have my driver's license?

In most states it is illegal to be driving without a driver's license in your possession. If you do not have your driver's license with you, you should provide some other form of official identification (Social Security card, fishing license) with your name on it. You may receive a ticket requiring you to furnish proof of a valid license to the court. This could include a fine. If the officer is not convinced you are who you say you are, she may take you to jail until you are able to prove your identity.

If I drive a sports car, am I more likely to be pulled over by police?

Drivers of unusual vehicles such as sports cars, hot rods, high-performance cars, and motorcycles will attract the attention of the police and are more likely to be pulled over for minor violations than those driving standard cars.

If I am pulled over and I have been drinking, will I automatically be arrested?

Just because you have been drinking doesn't mean you are necessarily going to jail. The officer must determine approximately how much you have had to drink and whether your ability to operate a motor vehicle safely has been affected.

The officer's decision will be based on the following criteria: erratic driving; odor of alcohol on the breath; belligerent attitude; physical appearance such as disheveled clothes or bloodshot eyes; and ability to perform such tests as walking a straight line, reciting the alphabet, or counting backwards. Your driving privilege can be suspended by the Department of Motor Vehicles if you refuse to take a blood alcohol test. If you light a cigarette or pop breath mints, the officer will suspect that you are masking the smell of alcohol. Do not be caught with an open container visible in your car.

Do I have to allow the police to search my car?

The police cannot search your car without probable cause. If an officer asks to do so, say no. Do not give the police an opportunity to find something for which they can arrest you or write a ticket. Simply refusing the request to search does not create probable cause. The following are some examples of instances when the police would have probable cause to search your automobile and therefore would not need your permission to search:

1. an odor of alcohol emanating from within the vehicle, coupled with the observance of spilled liquid or a paper sack about the size of a six-pack;
2. a strong odor of marijuana and a strange-looking cigarette protruding from the ashtray;
3. the neck of a whiskey bottle peeking from under the seat;
4. an empty holster or shell casing on the floorboard.

What happens to my car if I am arrested?

If the car can be parked close by, the officer may choose to lock it up and leave it at the scene. The vehicle could be released to a passenger with a valid driver's license. Most likely, though, a tow truck will be summoned by radio, and the car will be impounded and stored at the owner's expense.

When you are pulled over and the officer takes your driver's license back to the squad car, does he have access to your entire driving record?

Yes. The officer can call the station, and with your driver's license number alone she will be advised as to your entire driving record. Don't tell the officer you have never before received a speeding ticket if you have. She'll find out in a matter of minutes that you are lying and will issue you a ticket this time for sure.

If a cop begins writing a ticket, must she issue that ticket, or can it be torn up?

Once the officer's pen hits the paper, there is no more talking your way out of the ticket. Even if an officer makes a mistake on the citation, she has to get permission from a captain to get the ticket dismissed. All tickets are numbered sequentially, and an officer is accountable for each and every ticket.

Source: David W. Kelley, a California Highway Patrolman for over 26 years who has spent much of his professional life engaged in accident investigations and enforcing traffic laws. Mr. Kelley is the author of *How to Talk Your Way Out of a Traffic Ticket*.

Victims' Rights

What are my chances of becoming a victim of crime?

The U.S. Department of Justice estimates that five out of six people will be victims of violent crime at least once in their lifetime.

Why do victims' advocate groups exist?

In our criminal justice system, a criminal case is brought by the state against the criminal defendant. The victim is not a party in the case. Over time, this has resulted in a criminal justice system that treated the crime victim as little more than a piece of evidence. Among other things, crime victims have an interest in being informed of proceedings in the case, including the trial, and in being allowed to attend those proceedings. They also have interests in being notified if an offender is released or escapes, in having an opportunity to talk with the prosecutor before the case is dismissed or a plea bargain is entered, and in making a statement to the court at sentencing or parole hearings.

Many of the strongest victim advocates are crime victims who were surprised to learn they had no rights in the criminal justice system. They formed advocacy organizations to change the laws and to assist other crime victims, and their actions led to the passage of thousands of victims' rights laws across the country. Today they continue to work to improve and strengthen victims' rights.

What is a "victims' bill of rights"?

A victims' bill of rights is a set of legal protections for crime victims. Some people use the phrase only to describe state constitutional amendments that provide rights for crime victims; other people use it to mean a statute that lists legal rights for victims. The term is probably misleading, because every state has enacted some legal rights for victims, although the rights may not all be contained in one place in the law or in the state's constitutional amendment.

Are most victims notified of the status of the criminal case, an offender's arrest, pretrial hearings, plea bargains, trial date, and disposition of the case?

Most states have laws providing that victims be notified of certain events and proceedings during the criminal justice process. These laws vary quite a bit; for example, most require that the victim be notified of the trial date—far fewer require notice of pretrial hearings. However, these laws are often disregarded, and in most states the victim has no recourse for a violation of rights. Technology is making it easier for states to provide notice consistently, with the use of automated systems that telephone victims about an offender's release or escape, or automatically send postcards with information about court proceedings. Hopefully, automated systems will become more affordable in the next few years and their use expanded.

Do judges listen to the wishes of a victim when determining the sentence to impose on a convicted criminal?

Every state allows victim impact evidence to be considered at sentencing, and most allow a crime victim to make an oral statement to the court at the sentencing hearing. Many of these laws require the court to consider the victim's statement, along with the other evidence received at the hearing, when sentencing the offender. It is important to remember that the court considers numerous factors in sentencing, including statements from the defendant's family or other witnesses who plead for a lenient sentence.

Can alleged rapists be forced to be tested for HIV?

Most states have laws that allow for HIV testing of sex offenders. In many states, the defendant can be tested before conviction if the victim or prosecutor requests HIV testing and the court finds probable cause that the defendant committed the sex offense.

Under what circumstances do criminals have to pay restitution to victims or their families?

In every state, the judge has the authority to order an offender to pay restitution to the victim for the harm caused; in about half of the states, the judge is frequently supposed to order restitution. The victim must ordinarily request restitution and present proof of losses. Restitution generally can include all actual expenses, such as medical expenses, counseling costs, lost wages, and property damage, but does not include damages for pain and suffering or emotional distress.

In most states, the amount of restitution and the payment schedule are at the discretion of the judge, who often considers the offender's ability to pay in making a restitution order. Where the offender is a juvenile, there are usually limits on the amount of restitution. The victim also retains the right to sue the offender for the damages caused. If the criminal court ordered restitution and the victim also wins a civil suit for damages against the offender, the amount of restitution is set off against the civil judgment.

Are newspapers restricted from printing certain information about victims?

No. The Supreme Court has ruled that newspapers can't be prohibited from publishing certain information about victims. However, most newspapers voluntarily refrain from publishing addresses and other personal information about victims, as well as the names of victims of sexual assault or victims who are minors.

Do laws exist that require the community to be informed of the release of sex offenders who might potentially reoffend?

Yes. All states have enacted laws that require sex offenders to register, usually with their local law enforcement agency, although in a few states this requirement may apply only to those sex offenders whose victims were children. Although this information used to be available solely to law enforcement and other criminal justice officials, the passage of federal legislation in 1996 requires that all states release relevant information about sex offenders as is necessary to protect the public. Many states have now expanded their laws to provide notice to community officials, organizations, and members of the public, if that information is needed to ensure the safety of the community. Other states permit public access to sex offender registration information. These laws are often referred to as "Megan's laws," and procedurally vary widely from state to state.

Why do victim advocates want a federal victims' rights constitutional amendment?

Crime victim advocates realize that state laws and state constitutional amendments have not been enough to protect the rights of crime victims. Those laws are often disregarded or not taken seriously, and generally are not enforceable. If victims' rights were enshrined in the U.S. Constitution, they would have to be given the same weight and importance as the rights of criminal defendants. In addition, a victim's rights vary tremendously depending on which state he is in when the crime occurs, and whether the offender is an adult, a juvenile, or a member of the military. In contrast, defendants have the same basic rights no matter where the crime occurred, because their rights are guaranteed in the Constitution.

Is financial help available to victims and their families?

Yes. Every state has a victim compensation program that can help pay the immediate out-of-pocket costs of crime victims, including medical and counseling expenses, burial costs in cases of homicide, and lost wages. There is a cap on the amount of compensation available, which ranges from about $10,000 to about $25,000 per victim or family. To be eligible for compensation, victims must generally report the crime within 72 hours and cooperate fully with authorities in the investigation and prosecution of the crime.

What kinds of groups exist to support victims and their families?

Many organizations exist to assist crime victims. Rape crisis centers, homicide survivor support groups, battered women's shelters, legal aid programs, child advocacy centers, and victim/witness assistants in prosecutor's offices—all of these and more can be found across the country. Yet many victims do not have local assistance. Those in remote areas may have to drive 500 miles to the nearest rape crisis center; domestic violence victims may not have access to a shelter in rural areas; and basic services for crime victims may be located only in the state capital or a few large cities.

Where can I go to get victim assistance in my community?

The National Victim Center's toll-free service (INFOLINK) provides information and referrals to over 8,000 assistance agencies for victims and others concerned about crime. Specialists answer questions about the criminal justice system, local and statewide resources, and legislative updates. Call IN-FOLINK at (800) FYI-CALL.

Source: The National Victim Center at 2111 Wilson Boulevard, Suite 300, Arlington, Virginia 22201; phone: (703) 276-2880; fax: (703) 276-2889; Web site: http://www.nvc.org/. The center was founded in 1985 in honor of Sunny von Bulow by her children. It is dedicated to reducing the consequences of crime on victims and society by promoting victims' rights and victim assistance, and enhancing the dignity and value of human life by eliminating America's acceptance of violence. Call (800) FYI-CALL for information or referrals.

Wills

Do I need a will?

Every state has laws that direct the disposition of property owned by a person who dies without a will. In most states, if you die without a will your property will pass one-half to your surviving spouse and one-half to your children, or all to the children if there is no spouse. This does *not* mean that if such a division is satisfactory to you, you need not bother to make out a will. A will allows you to name the executor of your estate, appoint guardians of minor children, make clear your wishes regarding funeral arrangements, and give specific directions to a guardian.

State law cannot account for the specific circumstances of each diverse family. For instance, laws dealing with dividing a deceased's property do not distinguish between adult and minor children. If you died without a will and you have young children, the court would have to appoint a guardian (even if the children's other parent is still living) who would administer your children's inheritance until they reached adulthood (age 18 in most states). Most people would rather determine for themselves the terms and conditions for providing for their families, depending upon each family's circumstances, and one way to do that is by making a will.

What is *probate?*

Probate is the legal mechanism for dealing with a deceased person's property and estate. Our probate system allows people to make wills and leave their property on their death in almost any manner they choose. If a person dies without a will, then the laws of the state will decide how the decedent's property will be divided. Whether a person has a will or not, the division and transfer of property that is part of the person's probate estate at the time of his death will be done by the probate court. Probate property consists of all assets that are in the deceased's name alone at the time of his death. Probate is the process that determines and governs the distribution of a decedent's estate to the heirs and beneficiaries, the payment of estate debts after death, the resolution of disputes and claims against the estate, and any contests against the will.

My husband and I own a home. If he dies first, will the house have to go through probate?

The house will not be subject to probate on the first death if it is owned in joint tenancy, which is the most common method of home ownership among married couples. Only property that stands in the decedent's name alone at the time of death is considered part of the probate estate. The probate estate would not include jointly held property or assets that are payable to a named beneficiary at death.

What do I need to know about signing my will?

You should read your will before signing it, to be certain it leaves your property as you wish. At the time of signing, you and your witnesses (two or three depending on state law) should be gathered in the same room. You should announce to the witnesses something such as: "This is my will. I have carefully read it and I understand and approve of the contents. Now I would like you to witness my signature." You then initial each page and sign your name in full at the end of the will, in front of the witnesses.

The witnesses then sign, in your presence, and none of the witnesses should leave the room until everyone has signed. The witnesses should also write their addresses beside or below their respective names. If the signature of a witness is not legible, her name should be printed below the signature. Note that witnesses do not need to know the contents of the will. The date of the signing and witnessing should be included.

Whom should I choose to witness the signing of my will?

Witnesses must be competent (legally able to testify that they witnessed the will), but in most states they need not necessarily be adults. The fact that they may later become incompetent, or die before you, has no effect on the validity of your will. A witness should not be a person who is named as a beneficiary under the will, nor should he be the spouse of a beneficiary. If this happens, the beneficiary may not be able to take his inheritance, although for all other purposes the will may still be valid. It is permissible for the named executor or trustee under the will to act as a witness.

Where should I keep my will?

Your original will should be kept in a safe place. Most law firms have vaults to store important documents, so a likely choice is to leave your will in the care of your attorney. For a small fee the probate courts in most states will accept a will for safekeeping. If you store your will with the probate court, it is not released to anyone but you or your personal representative (guardian or conservator) until your death. A third alternative would be to place the will in your safe-deposit box. However, this is less safe, as other people with a personal interest in the will may have access to the box. It is inadvisable to leave your will in a desk drawer or hidden elsewhere in your home, because the document may be difficult to locate at the time of your death, and this type of storage is less secure, leaving the document more susceptible to tampering.

How can I change my will after it is signed?

Changing the terms of a will should be done through the execution of a document called a *codicil*. A codicil is signed and witnessed just like a will. A properly signed codicil also restates the original will and therefore can actually correct a deficiency in the original will. You should never try to amend your will by crossing out pages or paragraphs and substituting new provisions on your own. Initialing or signing your name in the margin beside your change does not make the alteration legal. If you want to make a change that will have the intended effect, do it through a properly executed codicil and avoid the probability of a long and expensive will contest.

Is it possible to disinherit a spouse under a will?

No. When the deceased leaves a will disinheriting a spouse, the surviving spouse can waive the will and take what is called a *forced share*. A forced share is a specific amount, such as one-third of the estate, that is set by state law.

Does divorce automatically revoke a will when the ex-spouse is named as a major beneficiary?

Some states have enacted laws that revoke the specific provisions of a will that favor a divorced spouse, but this is not automatic in all states. If you divorce and no longer wish to leave any property to your former spouse, a codicil should be properly executed, changing the disposition of your estate. You should also be sure to check beneficiary designations of life insurance policies and company benefit plans.

Is it possible to disinherit a child?

Yes. In all states but Louisiana there is no legal obligation on the part of a parent to leave an inheritance to a child, even if the child is a minor. Most states, however, provide that a child born or adopted after the parent made out his or her will is entitled to a share equal to the share the child would receive if the parent died without a will. Some states will not allow an afterborn or adopted child to take a share if it appears that the omission was intentional.

Who can contest a will?

The general rule is that only persons "interested" in the estate have standing and are allowed to contest a will. A person is interested in the estate if she stands to gain something should the will contest be successful. For example, if you die without a will, your estate will pass to your spouse and children. Therefore, your child has standing to contest your will, because if the will is successfully overturned the child will gain a share of the estate. A person who seems to have no connection with the deceased may nevertheless contest a will that excludes her if she was mentioned in a previous will.

On what grounds can you contest a will?

You cannot contest a will simply because you do not like the provisions or because you received less than you felt you deserved. You must have legal grounds, which, if supported by the evidence, would cause the will to be rejected by the probate court. Legal grounds include:

- *Lack of capacity*—the deceased was insane or incompetent at the time the will was signed
- *Improper execution*—there were not enough witnesses, or for some other reason the will was not properly signed
- *Undue influence*—someone took advantage of the deceased's susceptibility and caused him to make out a will different from what he would otherwise have made on his own
- *Fraud or mistake*—the deceased was induced to sign the will as a result of fraud, deceit, or a mistake
- *Revocation*—the will was canceled or revoked by the deceased
- *Bogus will*—the will offered for probate was not the will of the decedent

How can I avoid probate?

There are four ways to transfer property at death, and only one is through probate. The other three are the result of some arrangement or disposition made by the deceased during his/her lifetime but designed to cause a transfer at death. They include:

1. contractual arrangements, such as life insurance, whereby the contract involves a payment or transfer to named beneficiaries on the deceased's death;
2. joint ownership, where on the death of one of the joint owners the jointly held property is supposed to pass to the other; and
3. living trusts.

Even if you believe that you have arranged for the nonprobate transfer of all your property, you still need a will because there is no way of knowing exactly what you will own and how it will be held at the time of your death. If it turns out that in fact you were successful in the nonprobate transfer of all your property, then at the time of your death your will is simply not submitted for probate.

Source: Alexander A. Bove, Jr., a Boston attorney and columnist on legal and financial subjects for the *Boston Globe*. He teaches estate planning at Boston University Law School and is the author of several books, including *The Complete Book of Wills and Estates*. The law offices of Alexander A. Bove, Jr., are located at 10 Tremont Street, Suite 600, Boston, MA 02108; phone: (617) 720-6040; fax: (617) 720-1919.

Workers' Compensation

What is *workers' compensation?*

Workers' compensation laws are designed to protect the relationship between employer and employee by providing quick and automatic compensation to an employee who is injured in a work-related accident. Employees are guaranteed benefits, regardless of who caused the accident, but the trade-off is that the worker gives up the right to sue the employer. This system of coverage is provided by the employer's purchase of workers' compensation insurance.

What benefits are offered under workers' compensation?

Workers' compensation acts as four separate kinds of insurance. First, it is life insurance, as it pays benefits to the family of someone who dies as the result of a work-related accident. Second, it is a medical insurance, paying for the hospital and doctor bills that result from a work-related injury or illness. Third, it makes short-term disability payments to workers who are temporarily disabled. And fourth, it provides compensation for any physical loss (such as the loss of a limb or an eye) that the worker may have suffered.

What does workers' compensation pay for?

Benefits include lost wages and medical expenses. The amount of money an injured employee receives depends upon the seriousness and permanency of the injury and the amount of the worker's salary. Each state has its own schedule of benefits, which determines the percentage of lost wages paid and exactly what medical expenses are covered. Workers' compensation does not compensate for pain and suffering.

I tripped in the company parking lot and sprained my ankle. I hadn't yet punched the time clock since I was on my way in to work. Is my sprain covered by workers' compensation even though my shift had not officially begun?

In most instances, workers are not covered while they are commuting to and from work. Once you reach the parking lot of your place of employment, however, the commute is considered over. Therefore, the injury to your ankle would be covered.

At the request of my boss, I drove to the bank to make a company deposit. On my way back to work, I was rear-ended and as a result was unable to work for two weeks. Do I have a compensation claim?

In general, your medical expenses and absence from work should be reimbursed under workers' compensation and no fault insurance from the person who hit you because you were on a work-related errand at the time of the accident.

How do I make a workers' compensation claim?

A person who has experienced a work-related accident must file notice with the employer and the state industrial accident commission as soon as possible. You will be required to provide information about the time, place, and particulars of the accident, as well as a physician's assessment and medical bills. If your claim is accepted, you will begin receiving benefits.

You may ask for a review by the workers' compensation appeals board if your claim is denied. About 90 percent of cases brought on appeal are settled. If your case is denied in the appeal process, you may file a lawsuit, leaving it up to a court to decide the extent of your disability and the amount of money to which you are entitled.

Can I see my own physician?

Each state has its own rules about whether the employer or the employee chooses the physician. In some states, the worker must visit a doctor chosen by the employer or by the state's Workers' Compensation Agency. Check with your supervisor or company's risk management division for direction about physician restrictions.

I'm a production engineer at a company that manufactures paint. My supervisor keeps insisting I wear safety goggles, but I think they make me look stupid, so I slip them off whenever he's not around. Lately my vision has been blurred. If my eye doctor attributes my loss of vision to paint fumes, can I collect under worker's compensation?

Possibly. Employees who are injured because they willfully disobeyed safety regulations might be disqualified from receiving benefits, but each case must be evaluated on its facts.

Joe, one of my salesmen, somehow fell in the elevator and banged his head, giving him a concussion. At the end of the month I noticed on his expense report that he had a five-martini lunch with a client the day of his accident. I have a suspicion he didn't just fall down—he was falling-down drunk! Can I deny his workers' compensation claim?

Accidents that occur as a result of intoxication are typically not covered by workers' compensation. If Joe was drunk and there was no defect in the elevator to cause a fall, he is not entitled to compensation for his concussion.

I was injured at work and received workers' compensation, but the benefits didn't cover all my expenses and lost wages. What can I do?

An injured worker is always permitted to sue a third party (someone other than the worker's employer) who may also be at fault for the accident. Keep in mind that if you win a third-party lawsuit, many states require that you repay the money you received under workers' compensation. Still, it may be wise to sue a third party if you stand to win substantially more in a lawsuit than from worker's compensation. Be aware that the statute of limitation under which you may sue a third-party defendant varies from state to state and can be as short as 60 days from date of injury.

I do welding at construction sites. While I was standing in an open area, I was hit by a tractor that was backing up. The tractor was not equipped with a backup alarm and was driven not by someone who worked for the construction company I was working for, but by an independent contractor. Who pays for my injuries?

You should immediately apply for and begin receiving workers' compensation benefits. There are also three third-party defendants liable for your accident: the driver of the tractor, who should have taken better care when backing up in a populated area; the owner of the tractor, who should have made sure that his vehicle was equipped with a backup alarm; and the manufacturer of the tractor, for failure to provide a backup alarm.

File a lawsuit against the three third-party defendants. If the court awards you more than your workers' compensation benefits, you will have to reimburse your employer for money you received under worker's compensation, but the rest of the award is yours.

Do I need an attorney for a workers' compensation case?

When you have a work-related accident, it's always a good idea to consult an attorney, if for no other reason than to see if there is a third-party defendant from whom you can recover. But there are further reasons to consult an attorney. In some states, if your employer does not carry workers' compensation insurance, you may collect from a state compensation fund or bring a lawsuit against your employer directly. You may also institute a lawsuit against your employer if your injury came as a result of deliberate misconduct (e.g., you're struck by a hammer thrown by your employer). Although most states give coworkers immunity from lawsuits for accidentally or carelessly injuring another worker, you may be able to sue a coworker who deliberately harms you.

Source: Gail J. Koff is an attorney and founding partner of Jacoby & Meyers Law Offices. She has written several books, including *The Jacoby & Meyers Practical Guide to Personal Injury* and *The Jacoby & Meyers Practical Guide to Everyday Law*. Ms. Koff can be contacted at Jacoby & Meyers Law Offices, 10 East 40th Street (22nd floor), New York, NY 10016-0201; phone: (212) 726-4400; fax: (212) 726-4444.

All answers in this chapter are offered for informational purposes only and are in no way intended as or to be relied upon as legal advice. Legal advice as to a reader's specific circumstances must come from his or her own attorney.

WEDDINGS AND EVENT PLANNING

Buying a Ring

Wedding Etiquette

Planning a Wedding

Wedding Ceremony

The Reception

Invitations

Buying a Ring

How do I get started?

Buying fine jewelry can often be a confusing process. There are so many different gemstones, metals, and jewelers to choose from that the choice can be overwhelming. Get the best information possible before buying any piece of jewelry—do your homework to ensure you ask the right questions and buy the best piece for your money.

What should I look for in a jeweler?

You wouldn't go to a doctor or lawyer who didn't have the proper credentials; don't demand any less from your jeweler. Make sure that he is properly certified and has gemological training. For example, the American Gem Society awards titles to qualified members who study required courses, pass extensive annual exams, and adhere to strict ethical standards.

How do I know I'm buying a quality stone?

This is an important consideration. You should know that the quality of a diamond has nothing to do with size or color alone, but it has everything to do with the four C's: cut, color, clarity, and carat-weight. It's these four characteristics that determine a diamond's quality and value. Purchase the best quality you can afford, as quality is jewelry's most important asset. A smaller stone of higher quality will appreciate more in value over time than a larger stone of lesser quality.

What's the best shape for a diamond engagement ring?

The precision with which your diamond is cut will determine its brilliance, its fire, and its ultimate beauty. However, the shape you select is a matter of personal taste. The round brilliant is the most popular, but there are many other shapes, such as the oval, marquise, pear, emerald, and square. Today, the emphasis is on simple, elegant designs that highlight the beauty of the diamonds themselves.

How do I comparison shop?

Compare like items when comparison shopping, as comparison shopping based on price alone is not enough. For example, a diamond ring selling for $500 may look identical to one costing $1,000, but it may be of a very different quality. Ask the jeweler about the quality and cut of the gemstones and the workmanship of the piece before automatically buying the lower-priced item.

How can I tell if it is real gold or platinum?

Make sure your precious metals are really precious. Gold may be gold, but only karat gold is real gold. Pure gold is 24-karat; gold also comes in 18-karat, 14-karat and 10-karat. Be aware that there are other processes, such as electroplating, that give the illusion of karat-gold jewelry. Only your jeweler can prove the karatage and value of a piece. All gold jewelry should be stamped with a karat mark and trademark.

How much should I spend on an engagement ring?

Get the best quality you can within your budget. Bigger is not necessarily better.

Is buying jewelry on sale a good deal?

Be wary of large discounts. If a sale seems too good to be true, it probably is. An item on sale is often marked up many times its regular price and then marked down to a "sale price." Ask the jeweler when the piece went on sale and how long the sale will last. An ongoing, indefinite sale period may indicate that it's not a real sale.

I've seen some good prices of jewelry in advertisements and catalogs. Can you get good value that way?

Be cautious when buying through the mail or by phone—the photographed piece may bear little resemblance to the actual item. The most important elements in fine jewelry that determine value cannot be seen in a photo: Quality of workmanship, durability, quality of gemstones and metals used, and the service, guarantee, and expertise of the seller are things you will not usually find when buying jewelry through the mail or over the phone.

What policies are important to inquire about when choosing a jeweler?

A reputable jeweler should have policies on returns, repairs, and service. Inquire about the store's policies *before* you buy, instead of discovering the truth later.

Should I consider jewelry to be investment?

Buy jewelry for pleasure, not primarily for investment. Although fine jewelry will appreciate in value over time, don't purchase fine jewelry only for this reason. Instead, buy jewelry as an investment in beauty and pleasure.

Source: American Gem Society, 8881 West Sahara Avenue, Las Vegas, NV 89117. Adapted from *Ten Commandments of Buying Fine Jewelry*. For free consumer information on how to buy jewelry, send a postcard with your name and address to the American Gem Society.

Wedding Etiquette

I'm invited to a wedding ceremony and not to the reception. Do I have to give a gift whether or not I attend?

No obligation to give a gift is attached to a ceremony-only invitation, whether you attend or not. We would feel comfortable giving a gift if we felt close to the bride or groom. However, if a neighbor casually asks you to attend the ceremony, you need not feel obligated.

Help! My fiancé's father refuses to wear formal clothing to the wedding, saying that he isn't participating in the service. Please tell me he's wrong!

He's technically right, and yet sort of wrong. If he has no function other than circulating among the guests, then he can wear the same attire as the guests except that he should wear a boutonniere. However, fathers should consider dressing formally if the bride wants to achieve a uniform look, especially for a very formal wedding.

My stepdaughter is getting married. Both the groom's mother and I would prefer not to wear long dresses, but the bride tells me her mother is wearing a long dress. Why can't we wear what we want?

You can wear whatever length you wish, unless you and the bride's father are the hosts; then you would want to wear a full-length dress. However, the groom's mother is the next to the last to be seated in the church, and she stands in the receiving line at the reception. That's why both mothers should wear the same-length dress.

My daughter has asked two close friends to be matron and maid of honor. Her fiancé invited his closest friend to be best man and his sister's husband, who is also his business associate, to be the usher. I think her future sister-in-law will feel left out.

Your daughter doesn't have to invite more attendants than she wishes. It won't be a balanced grouping if she decides to include his sister, but asking her to be a bridesmaid could cement their relationship. If invited, the bridesmaid and the usher could stand together during the ceremony.

My fiancé's parents are hosting the rehearsal dinner, and intend to invite only those in the wedding party and immediate family members. My parents want us to invite any guests coming to the wedding from out of town, but his parents are reluctant to do so. Who's right?

His parents are right; they don't have to invite out-of-town guests to the rehearsal dinner, but it would be gracious to do so and will create goodwill. Sometimes the bride's parents offer to contribute to the expenses that are incurred in the rehearsal festivities.

I'm in the process of addressing my wedding invitations. I was reminded that I should send one invitation to the pope and one to the president of the United States and his wife. Could you please supply me with the correct titles and addresses?

> The correct title and address for the president is: President William J. Clinton and Mrs. Hillary Rodham Clinton, 1600 Pennsylvania Avenue, Washington, D.C. 20500. The correct title and address for the pope is: His Holiness, Pope John Paul II, 00120, Vatican City, Rome. You may politely direct gifts to be sent to the home address on the bottom of your reception card.

Is it inappropriate to invite single friends without guests?

> This answer isn't as easy as it may sound, but our response is yes. You should, however, take a few things into consideration first. We know of many wedding receptions where single friends were all asked to attend alone because they all knew each other and knew many other people attending. At these receptions, people weren't coupled off, and everyone had a great time together. However, if your single friend does not know many people at the reception, he or she may feel uncomfortable and simply will not enjoy him- or herself. Use your discretion.

This will be my second wedding, but my fiancé's first. He wants to have a rather large wedding (150 people). Should we have attendants and ushers?

> Yes, you should. Having attendants and ushers allows you to have people you care about be part of your very important day. Even though it is your second marriage, we're sure your close friends and family would be honored to stand up for you again. Being an attendant or an usher is an honor, not an obligation. Plus, the role of ushers during the ceremony is to seat your wedding guests. With a large attendance of 150, ushers to escort your guests to their seats are not only appropriate, but necessary.

Is it proper to have the maid of honor as the point of contact for guests to inquire as to wedding gifts? My guests are all from out of the area, and my family members are also scattered. The only problem is that some of my guests don't know my maid of honor. Help!

> This question isn't as uncommon as you may think. When your shower invitations are sent out, ask your maid of honor to place a card within each giving her name, address, and phone number for your guests to contact her for wedding information. It's that simple.

I'm having a bit of a problem over the guest list. My wedding day is in a few months and I'm in the process of working with all the parents to get a final head count. I started a job last year and would like to invite only a couple of immediate coworkers without causing a problem within the group. Any suggestions?

> Unfortunately, our answer may not be what you want to hear. We are under the belief that you should either invite the whole group or none at all. If you invite

only a few people within the group, the others could feel offended and your actual work relationship could drastically change for the worse. If having a few extra people equates to peace on the work front, that may be the best scenario. If you still think you should be able to invite whomever you want (and you shouldn't feel pressured to invite others), by all means invite only your close coworkers. Just prepare yourself for the possibility you may receive a (permanent) cold shoulder from the rest.

We're having an evening wedding and reception. At first my fiancée wanted the ushers and myself to wear morning coats. Then she heard that morning coats are for afternoon weddings. What is traditionally worn at evening weddings?

The type of evening formal wear the groom and ushers wear depends on the degree of formality. At an informal evening wedding, the groom and ushers can wear dark business suits, or in warm weather, white or natural-colored jackets or suits. At a semiformal evening wedding, the attire consists of dinner jackets or dark or light formal suits (depending on the season). Finally, for a formal evening wedding, the attire is a black tuxedo or black tails. Morning coats are usually more appropriate for daytime weddings.

I'm getting married and plan on wearing gloves. My question is, what do I do with them when it's time to exchange vows during the ceremony?

If you are wearing short gloves, simply take them off during the ceremony and hand them to your maid of honor. If you are wearing longer gloves, purchase the kind that have a cut in the ring finger for the ring to slip through easily for the reception. During the ceremony, simply have your groom place the ring on your gloved finger. Afterward, quickly make the switch.

I'm looking for a wedding favor that I have seen recently. It's a fortune cookie, called a Good Fortune Cookie. Where are they available?

You're in luck! There is a company on the Internet that specializes in acrylic glass fortune cookies. There are custom imprints available and they will be happy to match any color. This favor is also available in keychains and refrigerator magnets. If you would like to obtain more information, you may e-mail them at cookiejar@msn.com, or telephone them at (800) MY FORTUNE.

The bride has been married before; the groom has not. The parents of the bride paid for her first wedding. What is the bride's parents' financial responsibility for this second wedding?

The bride's parents don't bear any financial responsibility unless they offer. They do not need to pay this time unless they want to.

My fiancé and I are planning our wedding and reception out of town. We are designing and printing the invitations ourselves. How do we politely ask for gifts to be delivered to our house prior to the wedding?

To be sure that no one is confused or has hurt feelings, you may politely direct that any gifts be sent to the home address you print on the bottom of your reception card.

Source: The Wedding Exchange, Your Single Multimedia Wedding Source, http://www.wedex.com; e-mail: faqs@wedex.com. And *New England Bride Magazine,* 215 Newbury Street, Peabody, MA 01960-2499; phone: (508) 535-4186; fax: (508) 535-3090. To request a free subscription to *New England Bride,* please provide answers to the following questions (via e-mail, mail, or fax) so they can consider your free subscription request: your full name, your address (street/P.O. box, city, state, and ZIP), wedding month and year, and telephone number. If you qualify for a free subscription you will receive your first copy in 4–6 weeks.

Planning a Wedding

How much does a wedding cost?

When someone asks me this question, I tell them it is impossible to give a blanket answer. It is like asking, "How much does a house cost?" or "How much does a car cost?" The answer depends on the kind of wedding (or house, or car) that you want. The national average cost of a wedding in 1994 was $17,001 for a wedding with 150 guests. Keep in mind that the more people you invite, the more your wedding will cost. The biggest pulls on the budget are food and beverages.

If the bride's family pays for the wedding, what does the groom's family pay for?

The groom's family is responsible for the bride's engagement ring and wedding ring, a gift for the bride, the rental of formal wear, the officiant's fee, the marriage license, the bride's bouquet, corsages for the mothers and grandmothers, boutonnieres for the groomsmen and ring bearer, the rehearsal dinner, and the honeymoon expenses.

Who comes to the rehearsal dinner?

Always invite all members of the wedding party, as well as the couple's parents or stepparents. This is also a nice opportunity to invite out-of-town guests, as you will not have much time to spend with them at the wedding.

What percentage of people invited actually show up?

Many different wedding planners will give you an average. The truth, however, is relative to your particular family and friends, as well as their financial ability to travel. The bride and groom should never take a statistic from a book and apply it to their personal circumstances.

What is the difference between an invitation and an announcement?

An announcement allows the person to know you have gotten married. It does not invite the recipient to the event. It is sent on the day of or the day after the wedding. It also does not suggest a gift as strongly as an invitation does.

Source: Maureen Moss' Fairytale Weddings, 3640 North 38th Street, Suite 202, Phoenix, AZ 85018; phone: (602) 224-5514; fax: (602) 954-8194.

Wedding Ceremony

What is the traditional order for the seating and procession?

Here's how it goes at a traditional Christian wedding: The groom's mother is seated first, then the bride's mother. The bride's mother should be the last person to sit down. (Late arrivals should wait at the back for an opportune moment to slip quietly, unescorted, into pews at the back.)

The beginning of the processional music is the cue for the clergyman, groom, and best man to enter the sanctuary and wait at the front of the church. The procession begins with the ushers, two by two if there are a lot of them, in single file if a few. Next come the bridesmaids, also either two by two or singly. After the bridesmaids, the maid of honor walks alone, followed by the flowergirl, then the ringbearer, then the bride on the right arm of her father. After the ceremony, the bride and groom lead the way, followed by the flowergirl and ringbearer, then the best man and maid of honor, then the bridesmaids accompanied by the ushers.

There are no rules that say it has to go this way, however, and no one will mind if you choose a variation; many couples do these days.

How many attendants is common? We are considering seven each right now, but feel that might be excessive. What are the added costs/troubles associated with adding more attendants?

The number of attendants varies according to the region. For instance, very large weddings with upward of 20 attendants are not uncommon in the southern states, whereas it's more common to have two or three bridesmaids and groomsmen in the northern states and Canada. You should choose however many you feel comfortable with. The cost of additional attendants depends on what you've agreed each attendant is going to pay (usually the cost of their clothing) and what you'll be covering (usually transportation to the ceremony and reception on the wedding day, the meal and refreshments, and a thank-you gift for each). It is also considered gracious to cover the cost of accommodation for out-of-town attendants.

If you want to honor some friends or relatives but can't fit them into the wedding party, then ask them to be involved in the ceremony by presenting a special poem, reading, or prayer (check with your officiator first), honor them with a special toast at the reception, or mention them in your speech.

Having my father walk me down the aisle and "give me away" is not an option for me. What can I do instead?

It is your decision whether you want to be escorted down the aisle or not, and if you do, by whom. There are several options:

- Someone other than your father can escort you, someone you are close to who has been influential through your life, such as your mother, your grandfather, an uncle, a brother, etc. Don't let sexism or appearances get in the way of acknowledging and depending upon the right person.
- You can walk alone. This option is a reflection of the times: Brides these days are more mature, more independent, with lives of their own; the idea of being "given away" seems antiquated and perhaps even sexist. By walking down alone, you are symbolizing your personal journey into matrimony.
- You can walk alone halfway and meet your groom, going the rest of the way with him. In this way you symbolize quite literally that you are going forward to make your vows together, unified and giving strength to each other.
- Nowadays, many couples are adopting the Jewish tradition of having both parents walk the bride, and in some cases the groom as well, down the aisle, reflecting their pride in and reliance on family unity.

My stepfather and mother will be paying for my wedding. Does my stepfather have to walk me down the aisle, since he is footing the bill? (I would prefer my father to do it.)

Since your stepfather is paying, he must feel close to you, so do be sensitive to his feelings when making your decision. Also consider your mother's feelings; she may be estranged from your real father and feel very uncomfortable about having him take the spotlight while your stepfather is footing the bill. If you want your natural father to walk you down the aisle, make sure to have a long heart-to-heart with your stepfather and your mother, explaining the reasons for your choice.

I am trying to find a way to have a romantic yet nonreligious wedding. One option is to get married at City Hall, but I don't want it to be that small. Do you have any suggestions?

There are many legal marriage officiators who can perform a nondenominational ceremony that is very romantic, reflecting your personal tastes and sentiments. Look under "Wedding Services" in your local Yellow Pages for a start. Also, check out the Unitarian church, which often appeals to couples who want a meaningful ceremony without specific references to deities, and so on.

Basically, a nonreligious ceremony can be very much like a religious one. Consider your guests when planning your ceremony; an agenda that generally follows the well-known routine of a religious ceremony may be your best bet. You don't want to alienate your guests by creating an event that is completely unfamiliar, perhaps hard to follow, and therefore difficult to glean meaning from. That's really the bottom line—for your friends and family to recognize that you are indeed getting married in a solemn (that doesn't mean sad or exclude joy) and meaningful way.

Source: WEDDINGBELLS.COM. For more information, contact the Web site: www.weddingbells.com.

The Reception

We are considering having a seating arrangement for our reception. Are there any rules about who should sit at which table? How do we direct guests to their places?

Place cards with guests' names printed on them are usually already placed at each place setting. A seating plan should be visible somewhere near the front entrance to the reception. Put a couple of people in charge of greeting guests, to tell them which table they are seated at or to hand them a special small card that indicates the location of their table. Don't have escorts guide guests to their seats, or you'll likely have a traffic jam at the front door (unless you have a very large number of escorts).

There are several ways you can identify the tables. The most common, but not the most romantic, is simply to number them. A more personal touch is to identify each table with a symbol complementing a single theme.

The only rule for seating is that a divorced couple is never seated at the same table. If the wedding officiator is invited to the reception, he/she is seated at the table with the parents of the bride or, if they are divorced, with the mother of the bride. Resist the urge to matchmake when deciding on seating, as this may only cause tension. Also, consider setting up a separate table for children; ask a teenager to help you out by sitting with them. Set the children's table with special favors to keep them occupied.

We are thinking of having a cash bar during our cocktail hour and dinner reception. Is this tacky?

Whether or not to have a cash bar is the hottest question in wedding planning these days. Traditional wedding etiquette has the host(s) providing all beverages, because that is the hospitable thing to do. However, budgets today don't often expand to that degree of hospitality. There are options, though; you can be hospitable to your guests and still stick to a budget. First, you don't have to have a full bar open throughout the reception; ask your caterer about serving a limited selection of beverages: white and red wine, beer, and bottled waters, for instance, with one glass of sparkling wine per guest served for the toasts. A good reception manager will give you an estimate as to how much your guests are likely to drink, based on his/her past experience with large groups of people and what most people in your region prefer to drink.

Our reception is going to be a buffet lunch at a reception hall. What should we do for entertainment? We think it may be too early to hire a DJ. Do you have any other suggestions to help our guests enjoy themselves?

Music and dancing can be a lovely feature to a midday reception. Consider asking a few DJs for suggestions on types of appropriate music before dismissing this idea altogether. You might also want to look into more informal musical entertainment, such as a strolling violinist or a small jazz group. Whatever you decide, do consider that music makes a celebration seem more fun; you don't want guests walking into a dead silent room or listening to the sound of their own voices echoing from the walls. As far as activities go, one sports-loving bride and groom we know had a road rally, with guests on a wild hunt in their cars for various wedding-related souvenirs, as a kickoff to their informal, party-oriented midday reception. You can turn the "clinking glasses for a kiss" tradition into a game that goes on throughout the reception: Give your guests a real challenge, such as singing a verse from a song with the word "love" in it, or reciting a poem or limerick with the words "love," "wedding," and/or "marriage" in it. Think up some activities appropriate to the ages of the guests and the type of environment you'll be in.

We would like to have a proper reception with a sit-down dinner, but our budget is quite small. We both have a lot of relatives who will be coming from out of town and from overseas; I wouldn't want them to come all this way to just see a ceremony and have a drink. Can you recommend some good but fairly inexpensive solutions?

One of the best wedding receptions I've ever been to took place in the public room of a country church. The dinner was a homemade potluck affair provided by various relations of the bride and groom. The food (which was fantastic—obviously cooked with love!) was served buffet-style, and guests sat at simple folding tables on folding chairs, all church property. I know I will always remember that wedding because of the wonderful sentiments, the groaning buffet table filled with family favorites, and the sense of community, all of which had nothing to do with the size of the couple's wedding budget.

My suggestion to you is to get your thinking caps on and see what you can come up with when you set your priorities on having fun and making great memories. For instance, you could have a picnic reception in a park (some public parks have special covered picnic areas ideal for large groups of people in case of rain), serve a cold buffet (consisting in part of trays made up by the local supermarket catering service), and dance the night away under the stars. Remember that your long-distance relatives are coming for a wedding, not a dinner. They want to surround you with their love and support. Give them a good time planned from your heart, and that's what they'll remember.

Do you have any good suggestions for the garter toss besides having all the bridesmaids put their legs up while the groom is blindfolded?

Having all the bridesmaids put their legs up is just one version of this tradition. The garter toss dates back to 14th-century France. Then, it was the bride herself who did the throwing, and what she threw wasn't her garter but her stocking. Unfortunately, male guests often got very enthusiastic in "helping" her when she took it off, which is why this act has been refined to the degree it has. The male guest who catches the garter may be the next to marry.

Many brides today don't care for the sexist connotations of being stripped of their so-called garter by their new husband, and they are choosing to omit this ritual altogether. Why don't you consider not tossing a garter at all? Instead, throw a lacy handkerchief, perhaps embroidered with the wedding date, to all the men gathered around. You can make it easier to throw by weighting it with a small bundle of potpourri or candied almonds around which you gather up and knot the handkerchief.

Source: WEDDINGBELLS.COM. For more information, contact the Web site: www.weddingbells.com.

Invitations

How do I know what kind of invitation to send?

The style of the invitation to social occasions should match the formality (or informality) of the event. While the rules for an informal invitation are much looser than those for a formal invitation, the composition for all invitations contains the same basic information.

What information should be included?

Standard form includes an invitational line, the request line, what the event is, the date, time, location, city, and state, and a reply request line.

What is an example of a formal versus an informal invitation?

A formal invitation might say, "Mr. and Mrs. Stephen Julian Hameroff request the pleasure of your company," whereas an informal one might say, "You are cordially invited for cocktails and dinner," and Janet and Steve would appear on the invitation line. On the reply request line, a formal invitation would say, "The favor of a reply is requested," with no phone number listed, indicating that a formal written reply is necessary; whereas an informal invitation would say something like "Please reply" and have the phone number listed.

How do I prepare a formal dinner invitation?

Formal dinner invitations are properly engraved on ecru or white letter sheets. Black ink should be used. Correspondence cards are sometimes used instead of letter sheets, but they are considered less formal. Black ink is the most formal color, but any conservative ink color engraved on a light-colored card will make a tasteful invitation.

Should my formal invitations be ecru or white?

Your invitations may properly be engraved on either ecru or white paper. Ecru is the more popular of the two in North America, but white is the color of choice in Europe. Either color is acceptable.

How do informal invitations differ?

Informal party invitations reflect the nature of the event: They can be festive, lighthearted, or conservative. More freedom is allowed in designing the invitation, such as using a correspondence card with a bright colored border and a matching lined envelope. The lettering style may be fun and fanciful. This is a chance to be as creative as your imagination allows.

What kind of paper should I use?

This is actually a three-part question, as you need to choose the material from which the paper is made (papers made from cotton are best); the color (formal invitations are ecru or white); and the type of stationery (a sheet that has a fold on the left-hand side is appropriate for a formal wedding).

Why is cotton best?

The finest invitations are made entirely of cotton, creating a soft, rich feel. Cotton's strong, naturally soft fibers intertwine securely, adding texture and durability to your stationery. The result is a luxurious writing surface that will lend an elegant touch to your personal correspondence, and unlike papers made from ordinary wood pulp, cotton fiber papers do not decompose and will last for generations. Cotton papers are environmentally "friendly," in that they are made from fibers that are by-products of the agricultural and textile industries, while trees are cut down to produce wood pulp for ordinary papers and the saplings planted to replace them can take 30 to 50 years to reach maturity.

Should formal invitations be tissued?

Years ago, invitations were engraved with oil-based inks that were slow to dry. Tissues were inserted between the invitations to prevent smudging and were removed before being sent. Many people, however, did not remove the tissues. Over time, tissuing became acceptable, and the inclusion of tissues is now considered elegant and proper. Today, the question of whether or not to remove the tissues is a matter of personal taste, but there is no question that the inclusion of tissues tells your guests that this is a special invitation, offered with great care. Also, modern postal equipment can cause a smudging on some invitations, so it is probably best to leave the tissue in.

Do responses to formal and informal invitations differ?

Yes. Formal invitations should be replied to within two days. Replies are handwritten in black ink on the first page of ecru or white letter sheets. The replies are written in the third person. Acceptances repeat the event, date, and time. Regrets repeat just the event and require a brief reason for the regret. Replies to informal invitations should be as formal or informal as the closeness of your relationship with the host or hostess dictates. A reply sent to a close friend, for example, should be much less formal than one sent to somebody you have just met. If you are sending a regret, you should mention the reason. All replies should be made promptly.

Are fill-in invitations considered appropriate?

Yes. Presidents Reagan and Eisenhower used them regularly. Fill-in or skeleton invitations can be used for more than one occasion. When personalized, they show the host's and/or hostess's name and a request line, followed by spaces to be filled in by hand. They may be purchased over the counter without personalization.

When is a hold-the-date card used?

They are sent to out-of-town guests who might need advance notification of an event so that they have time to make any special arrangements. They are generally sent three to four months before the event, asking the guest to set aside that date. A formal invitation is sent at a later time.

When should reminder cards be sent?

Reminder cards are used when invitations are sent well in advance of the event and when invitations are extended by phone, to confirm any information about the event. They are also sent, as a courtesy, to the guest of honor. They should be mailed so that they arrive one week before the event, and do not require a reply. You may personalize the reminder cards or use fill-ins. A copy of the invitation with the words "To Remind" written on it, and the reply request information crossed out, may also be sent as a reminder card.

What is a *watermark,* and is it important?

A watermark is formed on the paper machine while the paper is still wet. The watermark design is welded to a cylinder made of copper mesh called a *dandy roll,* which rearranges the density of the paper fibers to create lighter or darker areas in the paper. Watermarks can be simple yet elegant, as on social correspondence papers, or as intricate as those found in bank-note papers. For centuries, watermarks have been used to ensure the authenticity of valued documents and to lend additional elegance and prestige to written communications. Using a distinctive watermarked paper for your invitations represents a demonstration of a personal commitment to quality, as well as communicating respect for your guests even within the fibers of the paper.

What is the difference between *engraving* and *thermography?*

The most beautiful invitations are engraved. The wording on your invitation is etched in reverse into a copper plate. The plate is then stamped onto the invitation, creating a beautiful raised impression. The paper is actually raised and ink is applied to that raised surface. Because of this, engraved invitations have a distinctive, elegant look. Thermography is sometimes known as "raised printing," although the printing is not actually raised. Unlike engraving, where the paper is raised, the raise in thermography is created by a resinous powder that is melted over the flat-printed ink. Thermography can give your invitations a look similar to but not quite as nice as engraving.

Sources: Crane and Co., Inc., Paper Makers, Dalton, MA 01226-1799; (800) 5CRANE6. And *Crane's Blue Book of Stationery: The Styles and Etiquette of Letters, Notes, and Invitations* (New York: Doubleday, 1989).

TRAVEL

———◇———

Airline Etiquette

Bureau of Consular Affairs

Business Travelers • Cruising

Cultural Factors for Business Travels

**Customs Restrictions:
Food, Plant, and Animal Products**

Food and Water • Handicapped Travel

**Hepatitis A and Immune
Globulin (IG)**

**HIV/AIDS Prevention
for Travelers**

Medical Care Abroad

**Passports and Citizenship
Documents**

Preventing Typhoid Fever

**United States Customs
Information**

Visas • Yellow Fever

Airline Etiquette

What are the common nuisances people most dread?

The incessant talker, the wrong-seat grabber, the baby in (or out of) diapers, the drunk, the common-cold carrier, the passenger in the window seat with a bladder problem, the carry-on abuser, the snoring sleeper, and the passenger with telephonitis.

Why do people talk too much and why to strangers?

People who are excited tend to talk a lot. People who are frightened tend to do the same thing. Some have personal problems they need to work out. For others, there is the temptation to self-aggrandize.

Incessant talkers might take a tip from the British. That society trains its citizens to refrain from speaking until spoken to; they do not speak to strangers until they are formally introduced. This can be misconstrued as snobbery but, in reality, it allows people to coexist in close quarters without driving each other crazy.

What can I do about it?

Try consciously regulating your level of politeness. Start by not responding to remarks. Smile politely and go back to what you were doing. If they don't take the hint, choose a response like: "I'm sorry, I have something very important to think about (read, work on) and do not wish to talk." There is never any reason to be unpleasant or get angry, of course. Calm, persistent repetition of your desire to be silent is the best strategy.

I have no choice but to travel with my baby. What can I do to minimize the disturbance to others?

Make every effort to have your baby as comfortable as humanly possible. Make sure the baby's plumbing has been attended to and that the bag of baby paraphernalia is as compact as possible. Arrange for an aisle seat and preferably request one at the back of the cabin or close to the galley where as few passengers as possible will be subjected to nursery activities. Make sure the cabin crew is aware of your presence to provide any necessary amenities.

Try to change the baby in the lavatory and place the soiled diaper in an airsick bag; use the trash container to dispose of its contents (although it's best to bring plastic bags along with you in your diaper bag).

Why do people drag all their stuff on board when it would be so much easier to check it with the rest of the baggage?

Some people have had bad experiences with delays at the carousels. For them, "carry-on" is a timesaver worth a few hostile glances. Times have changed, however, and computerized baggage handling has almost eliminated the hassles of retrieving checked bags.

If you wish to carry on some luggage, sizer boxes are available at all boarding gates. Test your carry-on; if it doesn't fit, you should check it. Once on board, don't jam heavy carry-on packages on top of someone's neatly folded overcoat, and don't use other people's bins for extra stowage. Most important, don't ask the person next to you to stow your souvenirs under his seat. He paid for that space and he needs it.

Passengers faced with a carry-on abuser should politely ask the person to remove their belongings from the bin. They can also suggest that the person contact the cabin crew for stowage advice.

I like to have a drink because it relaxes me and I'm a bit frightened of flying. What should I know in advance?

It's important for anyone having a drink to note that altitude exaggerates the effects of alcohol and that one person's euphoria is another's obnoxious invasion of limited personal space. People who don't normally drink can lose their sense of decorum quite swiftly.

If you are drinking out of fear, studies have shown that sugar and alcohol can increase anxiety and panic rather than remove those sensations. If there were an emergency, alcohol would reduce your ability to act swiftly.

What if I'm clearly next to a drunk?

Report the situation to the cabin crew. They are trained to handle it.

What's the best general rule for proper airline etiquette?

The most important tip is for all fliers to do unto others as you would have them do unto you. Courtesy and concern for others will go a long way toward making our skies more friendly whatever airline we choose to fly.

Source: Adapted from "Airline Etiquette: Passengers Struggle to Keep the Skies Friendly," by Larry Benedict, for *Travel ASSIST* magazine; http://www.murrayontravel.com.

Bureau of Consular Affairs

If I become a dual citizen, will it affect my U.S. citizenship?

No. But under limited circumstances the acquisition of a foreign nationality by application and certain other acts may cause loss of U.S. citizenship under Section 349 of the Immigration and Nationality Act. For this to happen, it must be established that the naturalization was obtained by a person 18 years of age or older with the intention of relinquishing U.S. citizenship; this intention may also be shown by the person's statements or conduct.

For the most part, it is assumed that Americans who are naturalized in other countries intend to keep their citizenship. As a result, they have both nationalities.

Is it true that the U.S. government does not endorse dual nationality?

Yes. While the government recognizes the existence of dual nationality, it does not endorse it because claims of other countries upon dual-national U.S. citizens can place them in situations where their obligations to one country are in conflict with the laws of another. Also, their dual nationality may hamper U.S. efforts to provide diplomatic and consular protection to its citizens when they are abroad, especially in the country of their other nationality.

How does one become a U.S. citizen?

By being born in the United States or by being born abroad to a qualifying U.S. citizen parent. Individuals born abroad who do not have a claim to U.S. citizenship and who are currently in the United States can learn how to become eligible for naturalization by checking with the local office of the Immigration and Naturalization Service (INS).

How do I renounce my U.S. citizenship?

You must appear before a U.S. consular officer overseas and file the appropriate documents.

How do I get an international driver's license?

If you intend to drive overseas, check with the embassy or consulate of the country you will visit to learn whether you will need an international driver's license, road permit, and what the auto insurance requirements are. If you need an international driver's license, check with the American Automobile Association or other motor club about obtaining one in the United States before you leave. Some countries may allow you to use your U.S. license.

Are emergency numbers available from the State Department's Bureau of Consular Affairs for, say, robbery and death of an American citizen abroad?

Yes. The Bureau of Consular Affairs has a list of "Important Telephone Numbers" for the following services: The Overseas Citizens Services includes numbers for death abroad, arrest and detention, robbery, missing citizens, crisis, and an after-hours emergency number; the Office of Children's Issues lists telephone numbers for international and child abduction, international adoptions, and recorded information on custody and adoptions; Visa Services offers telephone contacts for visa inquiries and applications, immigrant visa cutoff dates, the Diversity Visa Hotline, and the National Visa Center (for Immigrant visa inquiries). Passport Services offers telephone numbers for inquiries about the passport application process, and the status of an application for an emergency passport.

What are Consular Information Sheets, Travel Warnings, and Public Announcements?

Consular Information Sheets exist for every country in the world. They cover such matters as medical facilities, unusual currency regulations, crime and security conditions, drug penalties, and areas of instability. In addition, there are a number of Travel Warnings that advise Americans to defer travel because of unsafe conditions. These are continuously reviewed by the Department of State, so before leaving, you should check to see if any Travel Warnings have been issued. Public announcements are issued to spread information quickly about terrorist threats and other conditions that affect the security of American travelers.

When I call for information, all I get is a recording. Why can't I talk to a live person?

You can. The recordings provide general information. If you have a question about a specific case or something unique, listen to one message and you will be given an option to speak with an officer.

If I'm traveling to another country, where do I obtain a visa?

From the embassy or consulate of the country you are planning to visit. The booklet *Foreign Entry Requirements* has information on visa/entry requirements, embassy and consulate addresses, and telephone numbers for all foreign missions in the United States.

I need to find the consulate of a particular country in New York. Where do I find the numbers?

Look in the telephone directory. The Office of Protocol publishes a booklet called *Foreign Consular Offices in the United States;* it is available from the U.S. Government Printing Office.

Source: U.S. Department of State, Bureau of Consular Affairs Frequently Asked Questions. To obtain Consular Information Sheets, Travel Warnings, or public announcements, call or write (sending a self-addressed, stamped envelope): Office of Overseas Citizens Services (Room 4800), Department of State, Washington, DC 20520-4818; (202) 647-5225.

Business Travelers

What general rules apply when planning a business itinerary abroad?

Two or three definite appointments, confirmed well in advance and spaced comfortably throughout the day, are more productive and enjoyable than a crowded agenda that forces the businessperson to rush from one meeting to the next before business is really concluded. If possible, schedule an extra day's rest to deal with jet lag before your business appointments begin.

What are some travel tips for business travelers?

- Travel plans should reflect what the company hopes to accomplish.
- The traveler should accomplish as much as possible beforehand by obtaining names of possible contacts, arranging appointments, checking transportation schedules, and so on. Important meetings should be confirmed before the traveler leaves the United States.
- A flexible schedule should allow for unexpected problems (such as transportation delays) as well as unexpected opportunities.
- The traveler should check both the business hours and normal work days for countries to be visited. In many Middle Eastern regions, for example, the work week typically runs from Saturday to Thursday. Foreign holidays also should be taken into account.
- The local Commerce Department district office should be checked to see what travel advisory cables have been issued, if any. They alert travelers to potentially dangerous in-country situations. The U.S. Department of State also has a telephone number for recorded travel advisories.
- An American businessperson should be aware that travel from one country to another may be restricted. For example, a passport containing an Israeli visa may disallow the traveler from entering certain other countries in the Middle East.

At what point before the trip should my travel documents be in hand?

Two to three months before departure, especially if visas are needed. A travel agent can help make arrangements. A valid U.S. passport is required for all travel outside the United States and Canada. Visas, which are required by many countries, are provided for a small fee by the foreign country's embassy or consulate in the United States.

Are visa requirements the same for tourists and business travelers?

No. Some countries that do not require visas for tourist travel do require them for business travel.

What about vaccinations?

The requirements differ from country to country. A travel agent or airline can advise travelers on various requirements. In some cases, vaccinations against typhus, typhoid, and other diseases are advisable even though not required.

What plans should I make for an interpreter?

Find out first whether people you will meet are comfortable speaking English. If not, plans should be made for an interpreter. Business language is generally more technical than the conversational speech with which many travelers are familiar; mistakes can be costly.

Are there any rules on business cards?

In some countries, exchanging business cards at any first meeting is considered a basic part of good business manners. As a matter of courtesy, it is best to carry business cards printed both in English and in the language of the country being visited. Some international airlines arrange this service.

How do I avoid paying import duties when I simply want to carry product samples with me?

In some countries, duties and extensive customs procedures on sample products may be avoided by obtaining an ATA (Admission Temporaire) Carnet. It's a standardized international customs document used to obtain duty-free temporary admission of certain goods into the countries that are signatories to the ATA convention. Applications and inquiries about the ATA should be made to the U.S. Council for International Business.

How can U.S. embassies and consulates help the business traveler?

When planning a trip, business travelers can discuss their needs and the services available at particular embassies with the staff of the local Commerce Department district office. It is also advisable to write directly to the U.S. embassy or consulate in countries to be visited at least two weeks before leaving the United States and to address any communication to the commercial section.

Economic and commercial officers in U.S. embassies and consulates abroad can provide assistance to U.S. exporters, both through in-depth briefings and by arranging introductions to appropriate firms, individuals, or foreign government officials. Because of the value and low cost of these services, the exporter should visit the U.S. embassy soon after arriving in a foreign country.

Is there a travel checklist for business travelers?

Yes, and it also applies to tourists. A travel agent or various travel publications can help you take the following into account: seasonal weather conditions; health care; electric current (transformers and plug adapters); money (exchanging currency, using credit cards and traveler's checks); international dialing codes; using your computer modem abroad; cultural differences; tipping; and U.S. Customs regulations on what can be brought home.

Source: Adapted from *A Guide for Business Travelers,* a publication of the International Trade Administration. For more information on Travel Advisories, call the Department of State at (202) 647-5225.

Cruising

Isn't cruising expensive?

No—a cruise is one of the best travel values. Your fare includes all your meals, your stateroom, daytime activities, nighttime parties and entertainment, plus transportation to some of the most popular ports in the world. For once, you'll know what your vacation will end up costing before you go.

Would our kids enjoy cruising?

If your children enjoy swimming, sports, games, movies, and the adventure of seeing new and exotic places, they'll love cruising. You'll find that kids adapt easily to shipboard life; yet you won't have to wonder where they are and what they're up to every minute because the cruise staff will help keep them busy and entertained. Especially during school holidays, most cruise lines offer a wealth of supervised children's programs. Best of all, children often travel at substantially reduced rates.

Is there a charge for entertainment?

Never. On a cruise vacation, the entertainment is on the house. There's no cover. No minimum. No charge for a ticket. The shows are live. The movies are first-rate. The variety is limitless.

How long are cruises?

As long or short as you want. The more than 35 cruise lines offer itineraries from three days to three months.

How early should I book?

Up to one and a half years ahead of the sailing date. Booking early usually means a reduced total cruise package cost. It also means that you'll have a better chance of getting the exact vacation you want.

Can I book on short notice?

All cruises sometimes have space available because of late cancelations. But to get precisely the ship, cabin, and sailing date you want, you should plan and book early.

Are all ships and cruises the same?

Far from it! You can sail almost anywhere you want to go, with anything from fewer than 100 fellow passengers to nearly 2,500, on ships that range in length from under 200 feet to over 1,000. The atmosphere ranges from casual to formal, classically simple to ultra deluxe. You can even choose between traditional propeller-driven craft and sailing ships.

What's an "air/sea" cruise?

A "fly/cruise" or "air/sea" cruise vacation package includes either free or much-reduced airfare along with your cruise ticket. These money-saving options are available from most major North American cities and include transfers between the airport and ship and baggage handling.

Can I travel alone?

Cruising is ideal for people traveling alone, because it's so easy to meet other people. In fact, most ships have parties just for singles—early on, so you can get involved right away. Most ships also have single cabins as well as single rates for double staterooms. In many cases, a cruise line will even find you a roommate to share a double if you ask them to.

What should I pack?

Pack as you would for any resort. Cruise vacations are casual by day, whether you're on the ship or ashore. In the evening, dress codes vary. For the Captain's Gala, for example, you'll want to wear something more formal, such as a dark suit, or cocktail dress, perhaps even a dinner jacket or gown.

Will I need a tuxedo?

If you have one and like to wear it, bring it along. But don't go out and buy one for the trip. Even on the most formal of ships, a dark suit and tie is just fine. Generally, casual wear (as casual as jeans and a shirt, or shorts and a T-shirt) is fine for daytime activities. A formal night at dinner might require jacket and tie, but other than that you can be as relaxed as you would be on land.

Can I use my hair dryer or shaver?

Certainly. Virtually all ships have 110-volt outlets in the staterooms.

Are there nonsmoking areas?

Today, virtually all ships have smoking and nonsmoking tables and/or sections in the dining rooms and lounges. If you want your dining table in a non-smoking area, just tell your agent when you book. On board, in "open-seating" situations, you can advise your waiter or the maître d'.

Can we stay in touch with the outside?

Quite easily. You can call someone on shore through the ship's radio operator while at sea. And you can make phone calls from most ports of call. Most ships have a daily newsletter with headlines, stock quotes, and sports scores from the outside world, as well as information about on-board activities and special events.

Will I need to carry cash on board?

Only if you intend to visit the on-board casino. Otherwise, your boarding card can be used to make all purchases, including alcohol. You can choose to imprint your boarding card with your credit card information: An itemized list of everything you have purchased during the cruise will be presented to you on the last night, allowing you to track your exact expenses. Or you can choose to keep a tab, which will be presented to you for settling on the last night of the cruise.

What about tipping?

Tipping is, of course, a matter of individual preference, but there are guidelines. A general rule of thumb is to plan for about $2.50 to $3.00 per person per day for your room steward and dining-room waiter, and about half that amount for your busboy. Other personnel can be tipped for special services at your discretion. Generally speaking, many cruise lines simply do not permit tipping during the cruise, and most frown on it. They encourage passengers to wait until the last day to distribute tips. Remember that most drink prices will have a 15 percent gratuity built in—your bill or receipt will tell you for sure. This is to ensure a fair division among the bartending and drink-serving staff, who must take care of alcohol service all over the ship, as opposed to, say, your cabin steward or table waiter, who is with you from the moment you step on board until your cruise is over.

Isn't motion discomfort a problem?

Not really. The most popular cruise areas boast some of the calmest waters in the world. In addition, stabilizers on modern ships, advance accurate weather information, and effective medications have for the most part eliminated the incidence of motion discomfort while at sea.

What about hurricane season?

There is a lot of concern about hurricane season at sea. There is really no such thing. Storms at sea will come up now and then, but most every ship has access to sophisticated meteorological information and can easily avoid trouble spots. Even if your ship does encounter some nasty weather, don't worry. Cruise ships are specifically designed to provide the highest level of safety and comfort—in fact, you would be safer on board ship than you would be on shore if a severe sea storm struck.

Are there medical services on board?

Virtually every cruise ship (except for some smaller vessels in coastal waters) has a fully equipped medical facility and staff to handle almost any emergency.

There's no such thing as a perfect vacation. What are the negatives?

The major complaint we hear over and over again is that cruises end far too soon. Beyond that, it's hard to find any negatives. After all, you don't have to run to make plane connections to get from one port to the next. You don't have the hassles of making dinner or nightclub reservations. You don't have the bother of packing and unpacking again and again as you move from place to place. You don't get unexpected, expensive surprises at restaurants or nightclubs. You have a wealth of options for shopping, adventure, sightseeing, exploring, entertainment, and sports activities. All you have to worry about is relaxing and enjoying your vacation. Most important, every staff member on board is dedicated to making your cruise the best vacation of your life until you top it with your next one!

What should I know before I go?

Insurance: Be sure to inquire about insurance coverage available to cruise ship travelers, including trip cancelation/trip interruption, baggage loss or damage, and accident or illness. Remember that while you are out of the country your own hospitalization insurance may not apply. Check on it now so you can arrange the proper coverage.

Medicare: Take the time to read the small print on your passport. You'll find that Medicare and similar government-sponsored programs do not apply while traveling out of the country. Therefore, don't count on this coverage to protect you while on a foreign-flag ship (and most are) or in a foreign port. This also applies to some supplemental coverage.

Contract of passage: Your cruise ship ticket usually spells out exactly what the limits of liability are for each cruise line. Read this carefully and consider it when arranging baggage insurance or coverage for trip interruption/cancelation. Cruise lines quite regularly charge cancelation penalties, even with a medical excuse. If you must be flown home from a distant port in the case of a medical or family emergency, most cruise lines will assist you only in making arrangements, but will incur no financial liability.

When you book your cruise, your agent should provide you with information about various types of insurance coverage. You should also inquire about some other important areas, such as safety at sea, shore excursions, citizen requirements, and customs.

Source: Vincent Lafek, of Cruise Holidays, the world's oldest and largest network of cruise specialists, adapted from *Frequently Asked Questions About Cruising* (Williams Lake, BC: Image House, Inc., 1995). For more information, answers to questions on any aspect of cruising, and how to book them, contact Cruise Holidays of the North at (800) 667-8864, or on the Web at http://www.imagehouse.com/cruise/faq.html.

Cultural Factors for Business Travelers

How should business executives prepare for their trip?

They should learn about the history, culture, and customs of the countries to be visited.

Do any general principles apply?

Yes. Flexibility and cultural adaptation should be the guiding principles for traveling abroad on business. Business manners and methods, religious customs, dietary practices, humor, and acceptable dress vary widely from country to country.

What are some examples of cultural differences that, without prior knowledge, might offend a host if not taken into account?

There are many. Here are a few examples:

- Never touch the head of a Thai or pass an object over it; the head is considered sacred in Thailand.
- Avoid using triangular shapes in Hong Kong, Korea, and Taiwan; the triangle is considered a negative shape.
- The number 7 is considered bad luck in Kenya and good luck in the Czech Republic, and it has magical connotations in Benin. The number 10 is bad luck in Korea, and 4 means death in Japan.
- Red is a positive color in Denmark, but it represents witchcraft and death in many African countries.
- A nod of the head means no to a Bulgarian, and shaking the head from side to side means yes.
- The "okay" sign commonly used in the United States (thumb and index finger forming a circle and the other fingers raised) means zero in France, is a symbol for money in Japan, and carries a vulgar connotation in Brazil.
- The use of a palm-up hand and moving index finger signals "come here" in the United States and in some other countries, but it is considered vulgar in others.
- In Ethiopia, repeatedly opening and closing the hand palm-down means "come here."

What are the cultural differences most often faced by U.S. firms?

Often they include differences in business styles, attitudes toward development of business relationships, attitudes toward punctuality, negotiating styles, gift-giving customs, greetings, significance of gestures, meanings of colors and numbers, and the use of titles.

What is an example of a business style that differs?

In the Middle East, engaging in small talk before engaging in business is standard practice.

What about punctuality?

Romanians, Japanese, and Germans are very punctual, whereas people in many of the Latin countries have a more relaxed attitude toward time. The Japanese consider it rude to be late for a business meeting, but acceptable, even fashionable, to be late for a social occasion. In Guatemala, on the other hand, one might arrive any time from ten minutes early to 45 minutes late for a luncheon appointment.

What should businessmen and businesswomen be aware of in greetings?

Something as simple as a greeting can be misunderstood. Traditional greetings may be a handshake, a hug, a nose rub, a kiss, or placing hands in the praying position. Lack of awareness of a country's accepted form of greeting can lead to awkward encounters.

What about names and titles?

Proper use of names and titles is often a source of confusion in international business relations. In many countries (including the United Kingdom, France, and Denmark), it is appropriate to use titles until use of first names is suggested. First names are seldom used when doing business in Germany; visiting businesspeople should use the surname preceded by the title. Titles such as "Herr Direktor" are sometimes used to indicate prestige, status, and rank. Thais, on the other hand, address one another by first names and reserve last names for very formal occasions and written communications. In Belgium it is important to address French-speaking business contacts as "Monsieur" or "Madame," while Dutch-speaking contacts should be addressed as "Mr." or "Mrs." To confuse the two is considered a great insult.

I've heard that gift giving is extremely important to understand. Is this true?

Yes. In some cultures gifts are expected and failure to present them is considered an insult, whereas in other countries offering a gift is considered offensive. Business executives also need to know when to present gifts—on the initial visit or afterwards; where to present gifts—in public or private; what type of gift to present; what color it should be; and how many to present.

Gift giving is an important part of doing business in Japan, where gifts are usually exchanged at the first meeting. In sharp contrast, gifts are rarely exchanged in Germany and are usually not appropriate. Gift giving is not a normal custom in Belgium or in the United Kingdom, although in both countries flowers are a suitable gift when invited to someone's home. Check the gift-giving policy of your company as well.

Are there customs concerning the exchange of business cards?

Yes. Although this may seem of minor importance, observing a country's customs on card giving is a key part of business protocol. In Japan, for example, the Western practice of accepting a business card and pocketing it immediately is considered rude. The proper approach is to look carefully at the card after accepting it, observe the title and organization, acknowledge with a nod that the information has been digested, and perhaps make a relevant comment or ask a polite question.

What about rules for negotiating?

Negotiating is complex even between parties of the same nation, and certainly more complicated in international transactions. It is essential to understand the importance of rank in the other country; to know who the decision makers are; to be familiar with the business style of the foreign company; and to master the nature of agreements in the country as well as the significance of gestures and negotiating etiquette.

Source: Adapted from *A Guide for Business Travelers,* an International Trade Administration Publication.

Customs Restrictions: Food, Plant, and Animal Products

Why is the U.S. Department of Agriculture so strict about what can be brought into the country?

Because some prohibited items can harbor foreign animal and plant pests and diseases that could seriously damage America's crops, livestock, pets, and the environment.

What must I declare?

Any meats, fruits, vegetables, plants, animals, and plant and animal products you have with you. Your declaration must cover all items carried in your baggage and hand luggage or in your vehicle.

Do I really have to declare one little piece of fruit or meat?

You should, yes. For example, it's quite likely that a traveler carried in the wormy fruit that brought Mediterranean fruit flies to California in 1979. The three-year fight to eradicate this pest cost more than $100 million. A single link of sausage contaminated with the dreaded virus that causes foot-and-mouth disease could do similar damage to the livestock business.

Are any fruits, vegetables, or plants permitted?

Yes, provided they are declared, inspected, and found free of pests. However, you must get a permit in advance to bring in certain plants and plant parts intended for growing.

What restrictions apply to meat and animal products?

You cannot bring in fresh, dried, or canned meats and meat products from most foreign countries. If any meat is used in preparing a product, it is prohibited. Commercially canned meat is allowed if the inspector can determine that the meat was cooked in the can after it was sealed to make it shelf-stable without refrigeration.

Hunting trophies, game-animal carcasses, and hides are severely restricted. If you intend to bring them in, write to the U.S. Department of Agriculture for information and permit forms.

What's the rule for live animals and birds?

They can enter only subject to certification, permits, inspection, and quarantine rules that vary with the animal and its origin. Dogs that have been in Central and South America pose a special health hazard if they have wounds infested with screwworms. If your dog has even a small wound, be sure to have it treated before you travel to the United States. The U.S. Public Health Service further restricts imports of dogs, cats, monkeys, and turtles.

Pet birds you purchased abroad for your personal use can enter, subject to restrictions by some state departments of agriculture, if quarantined by the USDA for 30 days. Make quarantine arrangements in advance because facilities are limited and available only at certain ports.

I need to bring in some biological materials. What rules apply?

You must have a permit to bring in most organisms, cells and cultures, monoclonal antibodies, vaccines, and related substances—whether of plant or animal origin. This category includes organisms and products used in the biotechnology industry.

What if I have a sentimental need to return with soil from my ancestral homeland?

Unfortunately, you can't. Soilborne organisms threaten both plants and animals. If you visited a farm or ranch overseas, agricultural inspectors may have to disinfect your shoes or clothes. Vehicles must also be cleaned of soil. You may not bring in any soil, earth, or sand, although 1 ounce of decorative beach sand is allowed.

What about rocks, minerals, and shells?

They are all allowed, but all sand and soil must be cleaned off. Products grown in soil (like shamrocks and truffles) must be free of soil.

Source: Adapted from *Traveler's Tips: On Bringing Food, Plant and Animal Products into the United States,* a publication of the USDA Animal and Plant Health Inspection Service. For more information (and a general list of approved products), call your nearest U.S. Department of Agriculture Animal and Plant Health Inspection Service, Plant Protection and Quarantine, or call the central office at (301) 734-8645.

Food and Water

What are the major sources of stomach or intestinal illness when traveling?

Contaminated food and drink. Intestinal problems due to poor sanitation are found in far greater numbers outside the United States and other industrialized nations.

In areas with poor sanitation, what is safe to drink?

Boiled water; hot beverages made with boiled water—such as coffee or tea; canned or bottled carbonated beverages; and beer and wine. Ice may be made from unsafe water and should be avoided. The area of a can or bottle that will touch the mouth should be wiped clean and dry. Where water is contaminated, travelers should not brush their teeth with tap water.

Are there any special instructions for the boiling of water?

Yes. Bring water to a vigorous boil, then allow it to cool; do not add ice. At high altitudes, allow the water to boil vigorously for a few minutes or use chemical disinfectants. Adding a pinch of salt or pouring water from one container to another will improve the taste.

What kinds of chemical disinfectants are used to purify water, and where can I find them?

Iodine or chlorine, with iodine providing greater disinfection for a wider set of circumstances. Both can be found in sporting goods stores and pharmacies. Read and follow the manufacturers' instructions. If the water is cloudy, strain it through a clean cloth, and double the number of disinfectant tablets added. If the water is very cold, either warm it or allow increased time for the disinfectant to work.

What about using portable filters?

The Centers for Disease Control makes no recommendation as to the use of portable filters on the market because test results have not been independently verified.

Which foods cause the greatest concern when traveling?

Salads, uncooked vegetables and fruit, unpasteurized milk and milk products, raw meat, and shellfish are the most worrying. If you peel fruit yourself, it is generally safe. Food that has been cooked and is still hot is generally safe. Any raw food could be contaminated, particularly in areas of poor sanitation.

I've heard that some fish may be unsafe even when cooked. Is this true?

Yes. Some fish have toxins in their flesh. Tropical reef fish, red snapper, amberjack, grouper, and sea bass can occasionally be toxic at unpredictable times if they arc caught on tropical reefs rather than in the open ocean. The barracuda and puffer fish are often toxic, and should generally not be eaten. Highest-risk areas include the islands of the West Indies and the tropical Pacific and Indian Oceans.

What do I do if I'm traveling with an infant?

For infants less than six months of age, breast-feed the child or give him or her powdered commercial formula prepared with boiled water.

What causes traveler's diarrhea and what are its symptoms?

Traveler's diarrhea (TD) is usually acquired through ingestion of fecally contaminated food and water. The typical symptoms are diarrhea, nausea, bloating, urgency, and malaise. It usually lasts three to seven days and is rarely life-threatening.

How should TD be treated?

By oral rehydration, which replaces fluids and salts lost in diarrheal stools. As with all diseases, you should consult a physician rather than attempt self-medication, especially for pregnant women and children.

Source: Adapted from *Food and Water and Traveler's Diarrhea*, a publication of the Centers for Disease Control's Travel Information.

Handicapped Travel

How convenient is air travel if I have a disability?

In 1986 Congress passed a law prohibiting airlines from restricting the right of handicapped persons to travel freely on American aircraft so long as their condition is stable and does not constitute an exceptional safety hazard. Canada has similar laws. If you wish to travel abroad on a non-USA carrier, conditions are regulated by the International Association of Airlines. Since July 1994, rules similar to those in the United States apply for most types of handicaps. All international airlines have special accessible seats.

Will I need to pay extra for my ticket?

No. There are no special fares for handicapped travelers, but there are many discount fares. Check for the one that suits you best and book with the agent who assists you. This is how agents make their living and does not cost you anything. Make sure you tell the agent about any special needs you may have so that he or she can alert the airlines. This must be done at least 48 hours prior to your departure.

What if I require oxygen during the flight?

You may be charged extra, so consult with your agent concerning requirements that must be adhered to and ask him or her to secure a ticket for your destination on a direct flight if possible. Airlines may charge for oxygen for each connecting flight.

Will I encounter any problem traveling with my medication?

You shouldn't if you take a number of precautions. Take copies of your doctor's prescriptions with you in case of accidental loss or to show customs officials if you are going abroad. If you need to keep medication refrigerated, the aircraft crew or the dining car staff on a train will put them in their refrigerator. And finally, take an adequate supply and pack it in your hand baggage in case your checked luggage is lost or delayed.

Do I need to make special arrangements if I have severe arthritis?

Its best to consult with your travel agent on choosing hotels that are accessible even if you are in a wheelchair, so as to avoid unnecessary steps and other obstacles. If you need a wheelchair for transport and are traveling by plane, remember that if you have to change planes en route you will need to arrange for a wheelchair then, as well. Note that since 1990, all handicapped travelers on U.S. carriers are protected by law from discrimination with respect to travel, accommodations, and most other travel arrangements. But it is always practical to make plans well in advance to avoid last-minute problems.

Will I encounter restrictions if I travel with my seeing-eye dog?

You may, so it is best to check and plan in advance. Such information can be obtained from consulates or, in many cases, from the airlines on which one is traveling. Travelers with service animals are advised to carry medical evidence that it is such an animal, as well as veterinary health and rabies vaccination certificates as required by the countries to be visited. Be aware that some island states have strict anti-rabies laws that restrict the entrance of all animals, including service animals. The countries with severe regulations and prolonged quarantines include the state of Hawaii, Australia, New Zealand, Ireland, and the United Kingdom.

What precautions need I take with my deafness?

It is best to tell the flight attendant, train conductor, etc., of your hearing impairment or deafness so that you will be notified of any emergency or other announcements. At check-in time, ask for your boarding gate and time as you will not hear the announcement over the public address system, and request preboarding. Some U.S. airports, however, have already installed assistive listening systems to help remedy this problem, and visual notice boards listing arrivals, departures, and gate number are required for all U.S. depots and terminals.

Will I have a problem finding tours that suit my special needs?

Since the Americans with Disabilities Act became law, it is illegal for tour operators to refuse anyone the right to join any tour. This includes people with sight impairments who cannot move around unaided. However, for people who would prefer to join a tour where they feel more secure, there are tour operators who operate tours for what are known as "slow walkers," as well as those in wheelchairs, namely people who have physical mobility problems or have developmental problems.

Will my diabetes cause any problems while traveling?

It shouldn't if you plan ahead. Check with your physician whether any vaccinations or immunizations required are likely to affect your glucose or insulin balance. Also discuss with you doctor any problems that may arise from changing time zones or your insulin supply, food, and medication. Be sure to inquire as to whether you will be able to use your finger-stick blood glucose tests during your trip, as this is the easiest means of testing available.

How difficult is it to travel cross-country by either train or bus in a wheelchair?

Unfortunately, very few bus companies have lift-equipped long-distance buses, but it is obligatory under the provisions of the Americans with Disabilities Act that they nevertheless transport wheelchairs and provide boarding assistance to passengers with mobility problems. Information on accessible train travel can be obtained from Amtrak. Amtrak trains normally have special facilities both for those with walking impairments and those using wheelchairs.

Information supplied by the Society for the Advancement of Travel for the Handicapped, 347 Fifth Avenue, Suite 610, New York, NY 10016.

Hepatitis A and Immune Globulin (IG)

What is *hepatitis A,* and why is the international traveler at risk?

Hepatitis A is an enterically (intestinally) transmitted viral disease that is highly endemic throughout the developing world but less common in developed countries such as the United States.

How do you get it?

In developing countries, hepatitis A virus (HAV) is usually acquired in childhood, most frequently as mild infection or without visible symptoms.

How is it transmitted?

In several ways: by direct person-to-person contact; from contaminated water, ice, or shellfish harvested from sewage-contaminated water; or from fruits, vegetables, or other foods that are eaten uncooked and that may have become contaminated during handling.

Does anything inactivate the virus?

Yes. Boiling or cooking to 85°C (for one minute); but cooked foods may serve as vehicles for disease if they are contaminated after cooking.

What's the risk of contracting hepatitis A abroad?

The risks vary with living conditions, length of stay, and the incidence of HAV infection in areas visited. In general, travelers to northern and western Europe, Japan, Australia, New Zealand, and North America (except Mexico) are at no greater risk of infection than they would be in the United States.

Areas of the world with intermediate or high rates of hepatitis A do pose an increased risk for travelers. In developing countries, risk of infection increases with duration of travel and is highest for those who live in or visit rural areas, trek in backcountry, or frequently eat or drink in settings of poor sanitation. Recent studies have shown that many cases of travel-related hepatitis A occur in travelers who follow "standard" rules for business itineraries, accommodations, and food and beverage consumption.

How can I avoid getting hepatitis A?

Avoid drinking water (or beverages with ice) of unknown purity and eating uncooked shellfish or uncooked fruits or vegetables that you have not peeled or prepared yourself.

Is there a vaccine?

Yes. Hepatitis A vaccine, or immune globulin (IG), is recommended for all susceptible travelers working in countries with intermediate or high rates of HAV infection. Vaccination of children two years and older, adolescents, and adults with the age-appropriate doses of hepatitis A vaccine is preferred for those who plan to travel repeatedly or reside for long periods in intermediate or high-risk areas. Immune globulin is recommended for children under two years of age.

How safe is the hepatitis A vaccine?

The vaccine has an excellent safety profile for children, adolescents, and adults. The most common side effects are mild problems that usually disappear within one to two days; these may include soreness or swelling at the site of injection, headache, tiredness, and/or loss of appetite. As with any medication, there are very small risks that serious problems such as severe allergic reaction and even death could occur after getting the vaccinc. Most people who have received the vaccine have no problems from it.

How safe is immune globulin?

Intramuscular IG prepared in the United States has an excellent safety profile. IG produced in developing countries may not meet the standards for purity required in most developed countries. Persons needing repeat doses in other countries should use products that meet U.S. license requirements.

Source: Adapted from *Hepatitis A Vaccine and Immune Globulin (IG) Disease and Vaccine Information,* a publication of the Centers for Disease Control's Travel Information. For more information, call the CDC International Travelers Hotline at (404) 332-4559.

HIV/AIDS Prevention for Travelers

To what extent is the international traveler affected by HIV/AIDS?

To the extent that HIV infection and AIDS is a global epidemic, it concerns all travelers. This epidemic has raised several issues about HIV infection and international travel. The first is the need of information for travelers about HIV transmission and how HIV can be prevented.

How can it be prevented?

HIV is transmitted through sexual intercourse, needle or syringe sharing, by medical use of blood or blood components, and perinatally from an infected woman to her baby. HIV is not transmitted through casual contact; air, food, or water routes; contact with inanimate objects; or through mosquitoes or other arthropod vectors.

Can I get HIV/AIDS on an airplane?

No. The use of public conveyances—airplane, automobile, boat, bus, or train—by persons with AIDS or HIV infection does not pose a risk for the crew or other passengers.

How, specifically, are travelers at risk?

Travelers are at risk for AIDS or HIV infection if they: have sexual intercourse (heterosexual or homosexual) with an infected person; use or allow the use of contaminated, unsterilized syringes or needles for any injections or other skin-piercing procedures, including acupuncture, illicit drugs, steroid or vitamin injections, medical/dental procedures, ear or body piercing, or tattooing; use infected blood, blood components, or clotting-factor concentrates. HIV infection by this last route is rare in those countries or cities where donated blood/plasma is screened for antibody to HIV.

With regards to sex, which encounters are particularly risky?

If status of a sexual partner is unknown, travelers should avoid the encounter. This includes avoiding sexual activity with intravenous drug users and persons with multiple sex partners, such as male or female prostitutes. Condoms, when used consistently and correctly, prevent transmission of HIV. Persons who engage in vaginal, anal, or oral-genital intercourse with anyone who is infected with HIV or whose infection status is unknown should always use a condom.

What about the safety of blood and blood products?

In the United States, Australia, New Zealand, Canada, Japan, and western European countries, the risk of infection of transfusion-associated HIV infection has been virtually eliminated through required testing of all donated blood for antibodies to HIV. In the United States, donations of blood and plasma must be screened for antibodies to HIV-1, HIV-2, and HIV-1 p24 antigen.

In less-developed nations there may not be a formal program for testing blood or biological products for antibody to HIV. In these countries, use of unscreened blood clotting-factor concentrates or those of uncertain purity should be avoided (when medically prudent). If transfusion is necessary, the blood should be tested, if at all possible, for HIV antibodies by appropriately trained laboratory technicians using a reliable test.

I'm a diabetic and rely on my injections. What should I do when traveling?

Needles used to draw blood or administer injections should be sterile, preferably of the single-use disposable type, and prepackaged in a sealed container. Insulin-dependent diabetics, hemophiliacs, and other persons who require routine or frequent injections should carry a supply of syringes, needles, and disinfectant swabs (e.g., alcohol wipes) sufficient to last their entire stay abroad.

As an incoming traveler, will I be screened for HIV/AIDS?

Some countries serologically screen incoming travelers (primarily those who plan extended visits for work or study) and deny entry to persons with AIDS and those whose test results indicate infection with HIV. People who are intending to visit a country for a substantial period or to work or study abroad should be informed of the policies and requirements of the particular country. This information is usually available from the consular officials of individual nations.

Source: Adapted from *HIV/AIDS Prevention,* a publication of the Centers for Disease Control's Travel Information.

Medical Care Abroad

Are there any medical steps I should take before leaving?

Yes. Certain diseases may require advance planning and advice from a physician concerning immunization and other preventive measures. If more specific information is needed, travelers should contact their local health department or physician.

What if I take prescription medications?

You should carry an adequate supply, accompanied by a signed and dated statement from a physician. The statement should indicate the major health problems and dosage of such medications in order to provide information for medical authorities in case of emergency. Take along an extra pair of glasses or a lens prescription, and a card, tag, or bracelet that identifies any physical condition that may require emergency care.

Who can provide me with the names of hospitals, physicians, or emergency medical service agencies abroad?

Travel agents or the American Embassy or consulate can usually provide this information. Before leaving, travelers should contact their own insurance companies about their coverage.

Given my concern about acquiring the AIDS virus through blood transfusion, is it possible to have my own blood or blood from my home country available in case of urgent need?

This request raises logistical, technical, and ethical issues that are not easy to resolve. Options include: the use of plasma expanders rather than blood; plasma expanders in addition to an urgent return home; and an attending physician who ensures that blood has been screened for transmissible diseases, including HIV. International travelers should also take active steps to minimize the risk of injury; establish a plan for dealing with medical emergencies; and support the development within countries of safe and adequate blood supplies.

What should I take for motion sickness?

Antimotion sickness pills or antihistamines work well.

What's the best protection against mosquitoes and other mosquito-borne diseases?

Vaccines or chemoprophylactic drugs are available for yellow fever and malaria. For most other mosquito-borne diseases, such as dengue, there are neither vaccines nor drugs.

What other kinds of precautions can I take?

Since ticks and mite-borne infections characteristically are diseases of "place," known areas of disease transmission should be avoided whenever possible. Many infections are transmitted seasonally: simple changes in itinerary may greatly reduce the risk of acquiring infections. Exposure to some bites can be minimized by modifying one's activity or behavior. Some mosquitoes are most active in twilight periods at dawn and dusk or in the evening. Travelers should use repellents and other general protective measures, such as wearing long-sleeved shirts, long pants, shoes, and hats. Shirts should be tucked in. When ticks or mites are a possibility, pants should be tucked into socks and boots should be worn. Travelers should inspect themselves and their clothing for ticks at the end of the day; ticks are detected more easily on light-colored or white clothing.

Are repellents helpful?

Yes. Repellents should be applied to clothing, shoes, tents, mosquito nets, and other gear. Aerosol insecticides and mosquito coils may help to clear rooms of mosquitoes; however, some coils contain DDT and should be used with caution.

Other than being careful with food and water, what causes of medical injuries might I overlook?

Trauma caused by injuries suffered in motor vehicle crashes is the leading cause of death and disability in both developed and developing countries. Inadequate roadway design, hazardous conditions, an inappropriate vehicle or lack of vehicle maintenance, unskilled driving, inattention to pedestrians and cyclists, or driving while under the influence of drugs and alcohol are all preventable or can be abated.

Insist on a vehicle with airbags and antilock brakes; avoid nonessential night driving, alcohol, and riding with persons under the influence of alcohol or drugs. Pedestrian, bicycle, and motorcycle travel can all be dangerous, and the use of a helmet is imperative for bicycle and motorcycle travel.

What about fire?

Fire is a significant cause of injury and death. Check whether hotels have smoke detectors and sprinkler systems, and *do not smoke in bed*. Look for an alternate escape route in rooms in which you are meeting or staying. Also seek out improperly vented heating devices, which may cause carbon monoxide poisoning.

Anything else I should be cautious about?

Yes. Watch for drug reactions from over-the-counter medications you are not familiar with. Also avoid contact with wild animals. In areas with rabies, domestic dogs, cats, or other animals should not be petted. Medical attention should be sought if an insect bite causes redness, swelling, bruising, or persistent pain.

Source: Adapted from *Health Hints for the International Traveler,* a publication of the Centers for Disease Control's Travel Information.

Passports and Citizenship Documents

Where do I get a passport application?

At any regional passport agency or a designated post office or Clerk of Court. You can check your local telephone directory for locations. Look for "Passport Services" under the Department of State listing in the Federal Government Blue Pages of the directory.

I am traveling very soon. How do I get a passport in a hurry?

An expedited passport processing service is available. There is a $30 fee: This includes all passport services—issuance, amendment, extension of validity, and adding visa pages. You are eligible to use expedited processing if you are leaving in less than ten days, or if you are leaving in two to three weeks and require foreign visas. You must document your imminent departure by presenting your plane tickets, an itinerary, or confirmed reservations. Expedited service is also available for passport renewal by mail. Renewals by mail must include all items required to apply for your passport, as well as the $30 expediting fee and proof of imminent departure. Clearly mark the envelope "Expedite." Expedited passports are processed within three working days of receipt by the passport agency. If you would like overnight or express delivery, payment for this service should be included with the other items.

How do I renew my passport?

You must meet certain criteria to be able to renew your passport by mail:

1. You can submit your most recent passport.
2. You were at least 18 years old when your most recent passport was issued.
3. Your most recent passport was issued less than 12 years ago.
4. You have the same name as on your most recent passport, or you have had your name changed by marriage or court order and you can submit proper documentation to reflect your name change.

If you do not meet all of these criteria, or if your previous passport was lost or stolen, you must apply in person using Form DSP-11. Send your most recent passport, with $55 payment, two photos, and a completed Form DSP-82 to the National Passport Center. The address is on the back of the Form DSP-82, along with detailed instructions.

I'm renewing my passport. Do I get the old one back?

Yes, the old, canceled passport is returned to you. It is a good idea to keep it in a safe place as it is considered proof of your U.S. citizenship.

I was recently married/divorced. How do I change my name on my passport?

You will need to complete Form DSP-19, Passport Amendment/Validation Application, and send it along with certified documentation of your name change and your current, valid passport to the nearest passport agency. The agencies are listed on the back of the form. Your documentation will be returned to you with your amended passport. There is no fee for this service unless you require expedited service.

I was born abroad. How do I get a birth certificate?

If you were born in a foreign country to a U.S. citizen parent or parents, your parent registered your birth at a U.S. embassy or consulate in the form of a Consular Report of Birth (Form FS-240), and you would like evidence of your birth and U.S. citizenship, you should submit a written request that includes the following five items:

1. The subject's full name at birth, and date and country of birth.
2. Parents' full names, including mother's maiden name, and their dates and places of birth and nationality.
3. A daytime telephone number.
4. Signature of the subject or parents. A legal guardian's signature is acceptable only when accompanied by a certified copy of the guardianship papers or court order of adoption.
5. A $10 fee per document. The check or money order should be made payable to the U.S. Department of State. All requests should be mailed to: Passport Services Correspondence Branch, Suite 510, 1111 19th Street NW, Washington, D.C. 20522-1705.

What should I do if my baby is born abroad?

The birth of a child abroad to a U.S. citizen parent or parents should be reported as soon as possible to the nearest U.S. embassy or consulate to establish an official record of the child's claim to U.S. citizenship at birth. The official record is called a Consular Report of Birth of a Citizen of the United States of America, or Form FS-240. This document, known as the Consular Report of Birth Abroad, is a basic citizenship document. An original FS-240 is furnished to the parents at the time the registration is approved. Additional copies must be ordered for $10 each from Passport Services. A Consular Report of Birth can be prepared only at a U.S. embassy or consulate; it cannot be prepared if the child has been brought back into the United States or if the person is 18 years of age or older at the time the application is made.

What do I do if there is no birth record on file for me?

If you were born in a foreign country to a U.S. citizen parent or parents and your parent did not register your birth in the form of a Consular Report of Birth FS-240, it is suggested that you apply to a U.S. passport agency for a U.S. passport, or, alternatively, to the INS for a Certificate of Citizenship to document your U.S. citizenship. If you submit satisfactory proof that you acquired citizenship at birth, a Certificate of Citizenship will be issued in your name. For more information, contact your local office of the INS. Consult your local phone book for the telephone number listed under the U.S. Department of Justice. A U.S. passport is also proof of U.S. citizenship.

I have run out of pages in my passport. How do I get more pages added?

You will need to complete Form DSP-19, Passport Amendment/Validation Application, and send it along with your current, valid passport to the nearest passport agency. The agencies are listed on the back of the form. Write in the "Other Action Requested" space: "Add visa pages" or "Add extra pages." Your passport will be returned to you with the extra pages inserted. There is no fee for this service unless you require expedited service. If you plan to travel extensively, you may request a 48-page passport at no extra cost.

How do I get a U.S. passport if: I have never had a U.S. passport; my passport was lost or stolen; my child who is under 18 needs a passport.

You will need to appear in person before an agent authorized to accept passport applications at either a post office, courthouse, or passport agency. You need to bring the following four items with you:

1. *Proof of U.S. citizenship (one of these):* Previous U.S. passport, certified birth certificate, Consular Report of Birth Abroad, Naturalization Certificate, Certificate of Citizenship. If none of these is available, you will need:

a) A "Letter of No Record" issued by the state, stating the name, date of birth, years searched for a record, and that there is no birth certificate on file for the person, plus other documentation of birth in the United States such as:

- baptismal certificate
- hospital birth certificate
- census record
- certificate of circumcision
- early school record
- family Bible record
- doctor's record of postnatal care

Any of this documentation must be a public record, showing the date and place of birth, and created within the first five years of life.

b) An affidavit or Form DSP-10A from an older blood relative familiar with the circumstances of the birth, such as a parent, aunt, uncle, sibling. This must be notarized or have the seal and signature of the acceptance agent.

c) A Delayed Birth Certificate filed more than one year after the birth, listing the documentation used to create it. This must be signed by the attending physician or midwife, or list an affidavit by the parents, or show early public records. (No voter registration cards. No army discharge papers.)

2. *Proof of identity (one of these):* Previous U.S. passport; Naturalization Certificate; Certificate of Citizenship; current, valid driver's license; government ID: city, state, or federal ID; military ID (military and dependents' ID); work ID (must be currently employed by the company); student ID (must be currently enrolled); Merchant Marines card (also known as a "Seamen's" or "Z" card); pilot or flight attendant ID. Social Security cards are not considered acceptable as identification. If none of these is available, you will need to find a person who can vouch for the applicant. This person must have known the applicant for at least two years, be a U.S. citizen or permanent resident, and have valid ID. They will need to fill out a Form DSP-71 in front of the passport agent, and the passport applicant must have some form of signature ID, such as a Social Security card, credit card, bank card, or library card.

If applying for a child under the age of 13, the child need not appear in person. A parent or legal guardian can apply for the child. The parent or guardian must show current, valid ID. If the parent is not a citizen, they must show an alien registration card ("green card"), a valid foreign passport, or other ID such as a driver's license. If the parent does not have acceptable ID, someone with current, valid ID must vouch for the parent as described above.

If applying for a child age 13 to 18, the child must appear in person with the parent.

3. *Two passport photographs,* which must be 2 x 2 inches in size. The image size from the bottom of the chin to the top of the head should be between 1 and 1⅜ inches. Photos may be in color or black and white. They must be full-face, front view, with a plain white or off-white background. Photographs should be taken in normal street attire, without a hat or headgear that obscures the hair or hairline. Uniforms should not be worn in photographs with the exception of religious attire that is worn daily. If prescription glasses, a hearing device, wig, or similar articles are normally and consistently worn, they should be worn when the picture is taken. Dark glasses or nonprescription glasses with tinted lenses are not acceptable unless required for medical reasons. A medical certificate may be required to support the wearing of such glasses in photographs.

4. *The applicable fee:*

- $65 for those 18 years and older (includes $10 execution fee for DSP-11), plus the $30 expedited fee if you need your passport in a hurry.
- $40 for those under age 18 (includes $10 execution fee for DSP-11), plus the $30 expedited fee if you need your passport in a hurry.

In addition, if your passport was lost or stolen, you will need to complete and submit a DSP-64 Lost or Stolen Passport Form.

My child is too young to sign her own passport. How do I sign my child's passport?

In the space provided for the signature, the mother or father must print the child's name and sign their own name. Then, in parentheses by the parent's name, write the word "mother" or "father" so the Department of State knows who signed for the child.

Source: U.S. Department of State, Bureau of Consular Affairs. For inquiries about the passport application process, the status of an application, or an emergency passport, contact the National Passport Information Center at (900) 225-5674 (there is a fee for the call). Passport applications as well as additional information on international travel can be obtained from the Web site: http://travel.state.gov.

Preventing Typhoid Fever

What is *typhoid fever?*

Typhoid fever is a life-threatening illness caused by the bacterium *Salmonella typhi*. In the United States, about 400 cases occur each year, and 70 percent of these are acquired while traveling internationally. Typhoid fever is still common in the developing world, where it affects about 12.5 million people each year.

How is it spread?

Salmonella typhi lives only in humans. Persons with typhoid fever carry the bacteria in their bloodstream and intestinal tract. In addition, a small number of people, called "carriers," recover from typhoid fever but continue to carry the bacteria. Both people who are ill and carriers shed *Salmonella typhi* in their stool.

You can get typhoid fever if you eat food or drink beverages that have been handled by a person who is shedding *Salmonella typhi*, or if sewage contaminated with *Salmonella typhi* bacteria gets into the water you use for drinking or washing food. Once *Salmonella typhi* bacteria are eaten or drunk, they multiply and spread into the bloodstream. The body reacts with fever and other symptoms.

Where in the world do you catch it?

Typhoid fever is common in most parts of the world, except industrialized regions such as the United States, Canada, western Europe, Australia, and Japan. Over the past ten years, travelers from the United States to Asia, Africa, and Latin America have been especially at risk.

How do I know if I have typhoid fever?

The symptoms are: a fever as high as 103° or 104°F; plus weakness, stomach pains, headache, or loss of appetite. In some cases, patients have a rash of flat, rose-colored spots. The only way to know for sure, however, is to have samples of stool or blood tested for the presence of *Salmonella typhi*.

What do I do if I suspect I have it while traveling?

See a doctor immediately. If you are traveling in a foreign country, you can usually call the U.S. consulate for a list of recommended doctors.

How is typhoid fever treated?

With antibiotics.

When the symptoms go away, is the danger over?

No. You may still be carrying *Salmonella typhi*. If so, the illness could return, or you could pass it to other people. That's why, if you are being treated for typhoid fever, it is important to do the following: Keep taking the prescribed antibiotics for as long as the doctor has asked you to take them; wash your hands carefully with soap and water after using the bathroom, and do not prepare or serve food to other people; and have your doctor perform a series of stool cultures to ensure that no *Salmonella typhi* bacteria remain in your body.

How can I avoid typhoid fever?

By staying away from risky foods and drinks and by getting vaccinated against typhoid fever.

Are vaccines completely effective?

No. That's why it's just as important to watch what you eat and drink when you travel. Avoiding risky foods will also help protect you from other illnesses, including traveler's diarrhea, cholera, dysentery, and hepatitis A.

Source: Adapted from *Preventing Typhoid Fever: A Guide for Travelers,* a Centers for Disease Control Travel Information publication. For more information, call the CDC International Travelers Hotline at (404) 332-4559, or contact: The Division of Bacterial and Mycotic Diseases, National Center for Infectious Diseases, Centers for Disease Control and Prevention, 1600 Clifton Road NE, MS C-09, Atlanta, GA 30333.

United States Customs Information

When I return from my trip, what must I declare?

For the most part, items include: any articles that you purchase; articles presented to you while abroad—such as wedding and birthday presents or inherited items; articles purchased in duty-free shops or on board a carrier; repairs or alterations made to any articles taken abroad and returned, whether or not repairs or alterations were free of charge; items you have been requested to bring home for another person; and all articles you intend to sell or use in your business (promotional items and samples for customs purposes are only those items that are valued at $1 or less).

Do I have to list a price?

Yes. For each article, the price in U.S. currency must be stated on your declaration or its equivalent in the country of acquisition. The state price must include any "value added tax" (VAT) if it was not refunded prior to arrival.

What if the article was not purchased?

Then you should obtain an estimate of its fair retail value in the country in which it was acquired.

What are the consequences of not declaring?

The article will be subject to seizure and/or retention, but you will be liable for personal penalty in an amount equal to the value of the article in the United States. In addition, you may also be liable for criminal prosecution.

What if I'm wearing a dress or piece of jewelry acquired abroad?

What you wear is not exempt from duty. It must be declared at the price you paid for it.

Where do I get the U.S. Customs declaration forms?

They are distributed on vessels and planes and should be prepared in advance of arrival for presentation to immigration and customs inspectors.

What's required for an oral declaration?

You may declare orally to the customs inspector the articles you acquired abroad if the articles are accompanying you and have not exceeded the duty-free exemption allowed.

When is a written declaration called for?

A written declaration is necessary when the total retail value of articles acquired abroad exceeds your personal exemption; when more than 1 liter (33.8 fluid ounces) of alcoholic beverages, 200 cigarettes (one carton), and 100 cigars are included; if some of the items are not intended for your personal household use, such as commercial samples, items for sale or use in your business, or articles you are bringing home for another person; if articles acquired in the U.S. Virgin Islands, American Samoa, Guam, or a Caribbean Basin Economic Recovery Act country are being sent to the United States; if a customs duty or Internal Revenue Tax is collectible on any article in your possession; or if you have used your exemption in the last 30 days.

What is a "family declaration"?

The head of a family may make a joint declaration for all members residing in the same household and returning together to the United States. Family members making a joint declaration may combine their personal exemptions. For example, Mrs. Smith purchased an item for $600, but Mr. Smith purchased only $200 worth of merchandise. Mr. and Mrs. Smith may combine their $400 exemptions and will not have to pay duty on the items they acquired.

What is a "returning U.S. resident" and how does this affect my exemption status?

Generally speaking, if you leave the United States for purposes of traveling, working or studying abroad, and return to resume residency in the United States, you are considered a returning resident by U.S. Customs.

As a returning resident, you are allowed certain exemptions from the payment of duty on items obtained while abroad. Sometimes this means that articles acquired abroad with a total value of up to $400 will be admitted duty-free (though there are some limitations on liquors, cigarettes, and cigars). For instance, suppose a traveler buys a $300 gold bracelet, a $40 hat, and a $60 purse. Duty would not be charged on these items because they qualify for the $400 exemption. In addition, this same traveler buys a $200 unframed painting. Because fine art is not subject to duty, the traveler will be able to bring in $600 worth of goods without paying any duty (be aware that if the painting were to be framed, duty could be charged on the value of the frame).

What if I bring my camera, watch, or tape recorder with me? Will customs inspectors make me pay a customs duty when I return?

You should register them at the U.S. Customs office nearest you before leaving, by using a readily identified serial number or permanently affixed marking. This Certificate of Registration allows you to expedite free entry for these items when you return. You can keep the certificate for future trips.

How do I know which articles are dutiable and not covered by my exemption?

Since all regulations of U.S. Customs and other agencies cannot be covered in full, customs offices will be glad to advise you of current regulations.

Which items are restricted or prohibited altogether?

Articles considered injurious or detrimental to the general welfare of the United States are prohibited entry by law. Among these are: lottery tickets, narcotics and dangerous drugs, obscene articles and publications, seditious and treasonable materials, and hazardous articles (fireworks, dangerous toys, and toxic or poisonous substances).

Also included: alcohol and tobacco; food/plant products; objects coming from countries with whom the U.S. has restricted trade (Persian carpets, etc.); fish and wildlife products; medicines and narcotics; biological materials; firearms, and ammunition; and trademark or copyright items (handbags, watches, software, compact discs, videotapes, etc.).

Source: Adapted from *Know Before You Go*, a publication of the U.S. Customs Service. For more information, consult your local telephone directory under "U.S. Government, Department of Treasury, U.S. Customs Service," for the telephone number of your nearest Customs Office.

Visas

What is a *visa*?

There are many types of visas, but essentially, for U.S. citizens traveling to foreign countries, a visa is an endorsement or stamp placed by officials of a foreign country on a U.S. passport that allows the bearer to visit that country. This applies to citizens traveling on tourism/business; it does not apply to persons planning to emigrate to foreign countries.

I'm an American citizen traveling to another country. Where do I get my visa?

From the embassy or consulate of the country you are planning to visit. The booklet *Foreign Entry Requirements* has information on visa/entry requirements, embassy and consulate addresses, and telephone numbers for all foreign missions in the United States, although this listing is prepared from information obtained from foreign embassies and is subject to change. It is best to check entry requirements with the consular officials of the countries to be visited directly. You can also obtain the addresses of foreign consular offices in the United States by consulting the *Congressional Directory* in your local library.

How do I find out whether I need a visa?

It is the responsibility of the traveler to find out if visas are necessary and to obtain visas, when required, from the appropriate embassy or nearest consulate of the country that you are planning to visit.

When should I get my visa?

Visas should be obtained before proceeding abroad. Allow sufficient time for processing your visa application, especially if you are applying by mail.

Does getting a visa from one country have any impact on my travels to other countries?

Sometimes; for instance, some Arab or African countries will not issue visas or allow entry if your passport indicates travel to Israel. Consult the nearest U.S. passport agency for guidance if this applies to you.

What does an applicant need for a visitor visa to this country?

An applicant must have a passport, valid for six months beyond duration of the proposed visit; one passport-size photograph; and proof of social, family, economic, professional, or other compelling ties to a residence outside the United States to which he will be expected to return after the visit. It is helpful for an applicant to have a letter of invitation and support, if he is visiting someone in the United States.

What must be done to invite someone for a visit to the United States?

A guest of a United States host can be helped by sending him a letter of invitation. The letter should include the invitee's name, reason for visit, period of stay in the U.S., and method of payment of expenses. If the guest is paying his own expenses, he must be prepared to show the consular officer that sufficient funds are available for the trip. If the American host is paying the expenses, an affidavit of support may be included.

How can I help my employee, friend, or relative get a visitor visa to the United States?

Unfortunately, there is little a U.S. sponsor can do to help an applicant qualify. The amount of money the U.S. sponsor has is not relevant; there is no way the United States sponsor can guarantee that the applicant will leave the U.S. at the end of his stay. It is up to the applicant to show that he meets the requirements.

What is the difference between an *immigrant* and a *nonimmigrant* visa?

An immigrant visa is the visa issued to persons wishing to live permanently in the United States. A nonimmigrant visa is the visa issued to persons with permanent residence outside the United States but who wish to be in the United States on a temporary basis—e.g., for tourism, medical treatment, business, temporary work, or study.

Who can I call for information on visa cases and what can they do about specific visa cases?

You can call the Visa Services Telephone Inquiries Branch; the number is (202) 663-1225. This contains recorded information for visa applicants. After listening to one message, there is an option to speak to an officer between 8:30 A.M. and 5:00 P.M. They can usually explain what aspects of immigration law and regulation are applicable in certain cases. They can also check if a case has been returned to the State Department for an advisory opinion, which is an opinion rendered by Visa Services when a post has a question about the interpretation of immigration law and needs the State Department to make a determination on a point of that law.

Source: U.S. Department of State, Bureau of Consular Affairs. For more information and inquiries about visa cases and the application process, call Visa Services at (202) 663-1225. General information can also be obtained from the Web site at http://travel.state.gov. The booklet *Foreign Entry Requirements* for visa information for U.S. citizens traveling abroad can be obtained from the Web site directly or obtained for 50 cents from the Consumer Information Center, Pueblo, CO 81009.

Yellow Fever

What is *yellow fever?*

Yellow fever is a viral disease transmitted between humans by a mosquito. It's a very rare cause of illness in travelers, but most countries have regulations for yellow fever vaccinations that must be met prior to entering the country.

Where does it occur?

Only in Africa and South America. In South America, sporadic infections appear almost exclusively in forestry and agricultural workers who are exposed occupationally in or near forests. In Africa, the virus is transmitted in three geographic regions: the moist savanna zones of west and central Africa during the rainy season; occasionally, in urban locations and villages in Africa; and to a lesser extent in jungle regions.

What general precautions should be taken?

Avoid insect bites by using insect repellent, protective clothing, and mosquito netting.

How does the vaccine work and where can I get it?

Yellow fever is a live virus vaccine. A single dose confers long-lived immunity lasting ten years or more. Administration of immune globulin does not interfere with the antibody response to yellow fever vaccine. The vaccine has been used for several decades and has a very low rate of adverse reactions.

One dose of yellow fever vaccine may be administered to adults and children over nine months of age. This vaccine is only administered at designated yellow fever centers, usually your local health department. Consult your local health department for vaccination sites near you. If you are at continued risk of yellow fever infection, a booster dose is needed every ten years.

Who should not receive the yellow fever vaccine?

Unless the risk of yellow fever infection outweighs the risk of vaccine, the following groups of people should not receive the vaccine: infants under six months of age, due to a risk of developing viral encephalitis; pregnant women, because of a theoretical risk that the developing fetus may become infected from the vaccine; people who are hypersensitive to eggs, because the vaccine is prepared in embryonated eggs; persons with an immuno-suppressed condition associated with AIDS or HIV infection, or those whose immune system has been altered either by diseases such as leukemia and lymphoma or through drugs and radiation.

Are there any side effects from the vaccine?

Fewer than 5 percent of those vaccinated develop mild headache, muscle pain, or other minor symptoms five to ten days after vaccination.

What kind of paperwork do I need to travel with if I am not a candidate for vaccination?

If you have a medical reason for not receiving the yellow fever vaccination, then the Centers for Disease Control recommends that you obtain a written waiver from consular or embassy officials before departure. Typically, a physician's letter stating the reason for withholding the vaccination, written on letterhead stationery, is required by the embassy or consulate. The letter should bear the stamp used by a health department or official immunization center to validate the International Certificate of Vaccination.

Most countries will accept a medical waiver for persons who have a medical reason for not receiving the vaccination.

If I have received the yellow fever vaccination, what kind of paperwork do I need to bring with me?

After immunization, an International Certificate of Vaccination is issued. It is valid ten days after vaccination to meet entry and exit requirements for all countries. The certificate is good for ten years. You must take the certificate with you.

Source: Adapted from *Yellow Fever: Disease and Vaccine Information,* a Centers for Disease Control Travel Information publication.

BUSINESS
AND FINANCE

—◇—

Bankruptcy • Buying a Home

Buying a New Car • Buying a Used Car

Car Repair and Maintenance

Choosing a Bank • Cover Letters

Credit Report

Finding an Accountant

Futures/Options

Choosing Home Insurance

Home Shopping/Mail Order

Investment Clubs

Job Interviews • Life Insurance

Living Within a Budget • Mortgages

Mutual Funds • Paying for College

Personal Investment • Résumés

Selecting Stocks • Starting a Business

The Stock Market • The Fed

Unemployment Insurance

Working at Home

Bankruptcy

What is *bankruptcy*?

Bankruptcy is a federal court proceeding that provides a business or individual with protection against creditors. It allows the debtor to put aside much of his/her debt for the moment, and gives the debtor time to regain control of his/her finances without harassment. Bankruptcy also provides relief to creditors, in that it arranges a system of payment by which the creditor can receive at least a partial payment of the outstanding debt.

Is it common for an individual to file for bankruptcy?

Every year over 800,000 Americans file for personal bankruptcy protection. While some have abused their credit and managed their money irresponsibly, many others are individuals and families who have been unexpectedly displaced from a job or stricken with sudden debt.

What is *Chapter 11* bankruptcy?

Chapter 11 is a form of bankruptcy that is normally used by businesses that cannot meet their payments to creditors. It allows the business to continue operating while its finances are reorganized by the court.

The two types of bankruptcy that are most commonly used by individuals are *Chapter 13* and *Chapter 7*. In Chapter 13 bankruptcy, debtors who still have a regular income are given a plan to pay their debt over a period of time. Chapter 7 provides for many of the debtor's possessions and assets to be sold at auction; the money raised is used to make partial payments to the creditors. Some assets can be exempted from sale under certain state and federal laws; a debtor filing Chapter 7 may be allowed to keep such things as clothing, cars, or tools of the trade.

Does bankruptcy affect all of a debtor's outstanding loans and debts?

No; some types of debt are considered "nondischargeable," or exempt from protection. These include legal fines and penalties, most taxes, direct student loans, and alimony or child support.

How do I know whether I should file for bankruptcy?

Before considering bankruptcy, consult a credit counselor. Most state governments offer such credit advice free of charge. An attorney may be able to help you reach an out-of-court settlement with some or all of your creditors, and to avoid filing. Keep in mind that bankruptcy is a last resort and never desirable; also remember that once you start a bankruptcy proceeding, it may be difficult to stop.

What documents will I need?

You will need to pull together all of your important financial information, including: tax documents from the past two years; any loan contracts, including home mortgages, car loans, and student or personal loans; all legal papers relating to current debts or past bankruptcies; deeds to your properties and assets; current bills relating to all kinds of outstanding debt; and records of all current bank accounts.

Do I need an attorney?

If you can afford to hire an attorney, it is most helpful. Attorneys generally charge anywhere from $500 to $1,000 and up for bankruptcy proceedings, so be sure to settle the fee up front. If your case is a very simple one, involving one large creditor only, for example, you may want to muddle through on your own.

How long do the proceedings take?

If your case is straightforward, it should take about four to six months from beginning to end. If there are points of contention between you and your creditors, or if your filing is otherwise complicated, the proceedings can be dragged out considerably.

Can an individual file for bankruptcy more than once?

You can file for Chapter 7 bankruptcy only once every six years. There is no such limit on Chapter 13 filings, though they tend to be dragged out over a long period of time in any event.

How does filing for bankruptcy affect my credit?

Very badly. Not many things look worse on a credit report than a bankruptcy filing, which is one reason that bankruptcy is a last resort. A record of the filing stays on your credit report for seven to ten years. That does not mean, however, that you can never have good credit again. Every on-time payment made thereafter is a step toward refurbishing your credit rating.

What is a "secured" credit card?

A secured credit card is one of the ways you can begin to repair your credit after a bankruptcy filing. It is not a true credit card, because it only allows you to charge such amounts as you have in a bank account that acts as collateral against your debt. A secured card offers the same payment structure and convenience as a regular card, though, and is an excellent first step back into the world of credit.

Where can I get the forms and information I need to make a bankruptcy filing?

You can obtain all of the necessary forms from the Clerk of Courts in the local bankruptcy court. Be prepared to pay a hefty filing fee; naturally, if you can't pay it all, an installment plan can be worked out.

Source: Bankruptcy Overview, The American Bankruptcy Institute, 44 Canal Center Plaza, Suite 404, Alexandria, VA 22314-1592; (707) 739-0800.

Buying a Home

Can I afford to buy a home?

One way to find out would be to try to "pre-qualify" for a mortgage. Most lending banks offer this service free of charge. You file an application that provides the bank with detailed information about your income, your assets, and your credit history. The bank then processes your application and tells you what type of mortgage you can afford, if any. You may even find that you can finance a home for the same monthly payment (or less) than your current rent.

What is a real estate broker?

A real estate broker, or Realtor, is a middleman or agent who sells property on a commission basis. The Realtor does not have title to the property, but represents the owner in the sale. Most home sales in the United States are accomplished through Realtors, due to the complicated paperwork involved in selling a home. A good Realtor will be able to show you a wide variety of properties in your price range.

How can I find a good Realtor?

Look for a Realtor who is well-established in the area you want to buy. An agent who works for a large company will have a bigger base of homes to choose from; on the other hand, independent Realtors often have a more thorough knowledge of the small area they serve. Ask a potential Realtor the questions that are important to you, especially about issues other than property. A good one will be able to furnish information about local tax rates, school districts, neighborhoods, and the character of the community. The Realtor's commission comes from the seller, not the buyer; any service she provides you should be free.

What should I know before I start house-hunting?

All homes have different features and characteristics, and all buyers have different needs. For this reason, it is helpful to make up two lists before you start looking: one of the things you *need* in a home, and one of the things you would *like*. If you don't drive, you need a home that has access to public transportation; to look at one that doesn't would be a waste of time. On the other hand, if you do drive but occasionally use the bus, you might be willing to take a look. Discuss the things that you must have and the things that you might be prepared to sacrifice. Let your Realtor know; this will help him in deciding what to show you. Your lists may change from the beginning of your search to the end, but they are an excellent starting point.

What determines a house's value?

A combination of factors contributes to the value of a home. The size of a home, the number of bathrooms and bedrooms, and the size of the property as a whole will partially determine the asking price. Also to be considered are age, structural condition, and state of repair. Does the roof leak? Does it need a paint job? Location, too, is vitally important; a house worth $45,000 in rural Maine might fetch ten times that much in suburban Connecticut.

Local tax rates, school systems, proximity to shopping and work, and many other small details combine to make one town, street, or neighborhood more marketable than the next. Of course there are also intangible factors, such as "character" or "charm." If you have doubts about a home's value, ask for the result of the most recent appraisal; most homes are independently appraised for tax purposes every five to ten years.

What should I look for when inspecting a home?

Look for the characteristics on your "must have" and "like to have" lists, and note things that you like and dislike about each house. It is extremely helpful to write things down in detail since you may be looking at five or more houses in a day. It may be difficult to remember which house had what feature, or how big that third bedroom was. Keep your eye out for obvious trouble signs, like water leakage or structural cracking or settling. Finally, if you like a home, take the time to have a second look around. Get as much information as you can, so that you can make an informed decision about which properties merit a return visit with family or friends.

What is a *condominium*?

A condominium is an individually owned dwelling, or apartment, within a larger building or development, where individual owners have an interest in the common areas and facilities that serve the entire building or development. If you purchase a condominium, you own your own unit outright; normally, however, you must pay a monthly fee to maintain common areas and services.

What is a *cooperative*?

A cooperative is an apartment house or a group of dwellings owned by a corporation, the stockholders of which are the residents of the dwellings. It is operated by an elected board of directors, which has the right to approve new resident-stockholders. If you buy into a cooperative, you do not own your unit; however, you are entitled to live in the unit for as long as you own the stock. Again, monthly fees apply.

I've found the home I want. What do I do now?

You will want to make a written offer to the seller, through the broker. It is probably not wise to offer the full asking price; the seller may be willing to bargain. Make an offer that you feel is reasonable; the seller may accept your price, or make a compromise offer. A written offer is not always binding, depending on the circumstances. Read any documents that you sign carefully, and seek the advice of an attorney.

My mortgage lender requires a home inspection and appraisal. Do I need to worry about this?

No, it is common practice. The lender wants to be sure that the house is worth the purchase price, since the house is being used as collateral to secure the loan. In fact, you should welcome a home inspection; if there are any major structural problems with the house, you will want to know before you buy it, not afterward.

My offer was accepted, and my mortgage was approved. What closing costs will I be expected to pay?

This should be spelled out clearly in the purchase and sale agreement, which is the written contract between buyer and seller. Typically, the buyer is expected to pay for documentary stamps on notes, recording fees, escrow fees, an attorney's fee, title insurance, and the cost of the inspection and appraisal. These costs must be paid at the closing, where all contracts are signed and the formalities of the sale are carried out.

Source: *The Mortgage Almanac,* Summer 1996, including "Top Ten Tips for First Time Buyers," by Robin Cileno. All material © 1996 by The Mortgage Almanac, Inc., Fairfield, CT; (800) 409-9640. Used by permission.

Buying a New Car

What do I need to know before I go to the car dealership?

It's a good idea to get your financing in order before you go to buy a car. This will help to avoid a situation where you end up paying high interest rates because the dealer makes you feel trapped. For example, if you spend a few hours inspecting the car and negotiating the price, the last thing you want is for the deal to fall through over financing. The dealer knows this, and will use it to his advantage in negotiating loan terms. Avoid the entire problem by securing financing from a bank or credit union beforehand; if the dealer then wants to make a better offer, he can.

Also, know what kind of a car you want to buy. There are hundreds of publications available at the library that will tell you everything you need to know about the current crop of new cars, including performance, durability, gas mileage, and price. Research the cars on your own, so that you don't have to depend on the dealer's information; the more you know about what you want, the better.

What should I do with my old car?

You may be able to make a better deal by selling it yourself, through the newspaper, than by trading it in. This approach, though, comes with its own headaches. It can take weeks to sell a car on your own, whereas a trade-in can easily be made on the same day as your purchase. Whether you choose to sell or trade your car in, you should determine a fair price beforehand. Consult pricing publications, or try fishing for offers from a used car dealer; this will give you a reasonable idea of your car's value. Keep in mind that the dealer will rarely give you the full wholesale value of the car for a trade-in; a good goal would be a little bit less than the book price.

I find car dealers very intimidating. What can I do to avoid being taken advantage of?

Car dealers are intimidating; it is their job to negotiate aggressively, and they have the advantage of knowing the business a lot better than you. In order to avoid being cheated, you must take advantage of your position as the buyer. You are the one with the money to spend, and you can choose the time and place where you spend it. Remember that you have the right to walk out of a dealership at any time. If you feel that the dealer is putting too much pressure on you, or that he is deliberately misleading you in some way, you should feel free to exercise that right. The dealer very much wants to sell you a car; let him know that you are willing to go elsewhere if you're not satisfied.

How do I get the dealer to take me seriously as a buyer?

You must convince the dealership that you are serious about buying a car if you expect them to put time and effort into selling you one. It helps to tell them specifics; you want to buy this car, here, today. Show them that you are prepared, and that your finances are in order. Act in a businesslike manner and you will be treated similarly. Let it be known that you expect to be treated like a real buyer, or you will take your business elsewhere. All of this will put you in a stronger position when it comes time to negotiate a price.

Should I take a test drive?

Yes. Even if you think you know exactly what kind of car you want, be sure to test-drive it before making a final decision. Of course, you may want to test-drive several models to comparison shop. If you know what kind of car you want, and you are seeking to trade your old car in, ask that the trade-in price be evaluated during your test drive. This should set the negotiation process in motion.

When should I set the price for my trade-in?

Before you start haggling over the price of the new car, tell the dealer you would like to settle the price of the trade-in. Dealers love to compensate for the "deal" they give you on the new car price by bilking you on the trade-in price. As with the financing, come prepared with a previous offer—or at least a firm idea of the car's worth. Remember to consider the deal you get on the trade-in as one aspect of the whole deal. Taking care of the trade-in first will help you accomplish this.

How do I negotiate a good deal?

Again, research. Know the dealer's costs when you come in; published price guides will tell you roughly how much the car costs him. If you can negotiate a price that is between 2 and 5 percent over the cost, you are doing very well. The "sticker price," which should be used as a starting point, will be marked up between about 8 and 10 percent (or perhaps more). Depending on how anxious the dealer is to sell the car, you should be able to negotiate a figure that is substantially below the sticker price.

If you get stuck on a higher price than you think is appropriate, perhaps you could try a bit of comparison shopping at another dealership. Who knows? Maybe the salesman will come running after you with a better offer.

I'm a marshmallow when it comes to bartering. Any tips?

Toughness helps, but it may not be in your nature. Your most important tools are preparation and stubbornness. If you know what you want, and you know what the approximate market value of the car is, you simply have to wait for the dealer to meet you halfway. Certainly, this can be an unpleasant chore; not as unpleasant as those monthly payments, though, when you know they should have been lower. If you have the patience and the perseverance not to cave in, you needn't be aggressive; a good dealer will eventually give you a fair price.

Should I bring my father with me? I know that seems pathetic, but he's a much better negotiator than I am.

By all means, bring Dad. Or bring a friend, or a spouse, or anyone who can support you when you're at your weakest. Remember, a dealer is more experienced than you; he fights this battle every day. You need all the support you can get.

What should I bring to the dealership with me (along with my checkbook)?

Bring the research notes you have done on financing, value of your trade-in, dealer costs on the car you want to buy, etc. Don't feel timid about this; you want to present yourself as a well-prepared buyer. Also, bring a calculator and a notepad. You always want to check the dealer's figures, and take notes on any verbal promises or claims made during the bartering process. These notes will serve as a checklist of things to look for in the written warranty or service contract.

What dealer tricks and techniques should I look out for?

There are hundreds of them, and many are older than the automobile itself. "Bait and Switch," "Good Cop/Bad Cop," and "Take It or Leave It" are just a few of the games salesmen play with their customers. The only way to beat them at their own game is to know what you want and stick to your guns. Be aware of the gimmicks, and respond to them like a broken record. Eventually, the salesman will realize that you will accept only a straightforward negotiation. Otherwise, say good-bye.

Source: *The Insider's Guide to Buying a New or Used Car,* Burke Leon and Stephanie Leon. Used by permission of Betterway Books, a division of F&W Publications, Inc., Cincinnati, OH; (800) 289-0963.

Buying a Used Car

Is buying a used car a good deal in the long run?

That depends on the car. Remember that the true cost of a car is not limited to the purchase price. Other important factors include loan terms (if you finance the car), maintenance costs, gas mileage, and insurance costs. A used car can easily become just as expensive as a new car if these considerations are ignored.

How can I find out which cars are most reliable?

A number of publications available at libraries publish frequency-of-repair records, consumer satisfaction ratings, safety test results, and gasoline mileage ratings. These are an excellent source for comparison shopping. Also, the Department of Transportation offers an Auto Safety Hotline at (800) 424-9393 that will inform you whether or not a particular model has ever been subject to recall for any reason.

Should I buy from a dealer?

Used car dealers have a terrible reputation for dishonesty, but they may be your best option. Dealers are subject to certain laws and regulations that private sellers are not, including the FTC's Used Car Rule. Each car on a dealer's lot must have a *"Buyers Guide"* sticker on the window, which provides important information about the warranties and protections the car comes with. The guide also offers warnings and suggestions about what potential buyers should look out for.

Is it safe to buy a car privately, through the classified ads in the newspaper?

Buying a car from a private party, or an individual who sells less than six cars a year, is somewhat different than buying from a dealer. Private sellers are not required to use the *Buyers Guide,* and private sales are generally not covered by the "implied warranties" protections that dealer sales are. This means that unless you sign a specific written contract with the seller, the sale is on an as is basis. This is an especially good reason to have your own mechanic inspect the car before you buy it.

You may want to obtain a copy of the *Buyers Guide* from the FTC, to use as a reference during the sale. Be aware that warranties and service contracts may not transfer from one owner to the next. Be sure to inspect all warranty-related documents closely before considering them as part of the value of the car.

What is an "implied" warranty?

Certain limited protections for used car buyers exist under state laws, whether or not a written warranty exists. These protections are known as implied warranties, and they vary from state to state. The most common implied warranty requires the seller to guarantee simply that the car runs for a reasonable length of time.

What legal paperwork do I have to complete when purchasing a car from a private party?

You should receive a signed bill of sale, stating the date, model of the car, serial number, and purchase price. This is simply proof of your ownership of the car. You should also receive the original title deed, which should be in the possession of the current owner.

Should I expect to be allowed to test-drive the car before I buy it?

Absolutely. Try the car at different speeds and under different conditions; on hills, highways, sharp turns, and in stop-and-go traffic.

Should I try to negotiate for a lower price?

Most dealers and private sellers leave room in the asking price for a bit of bartering, so it would be foolish not to make an attempt, at least.

Should I purchase a service contract?

Consider the value of the car, the price of the service contract, and the likelihood that the car will need repairs. Does the contract cover all repairs, including both parts and labor? Is a deductible required? Does the contract duplicate coverage that you get from the warranty? How long are you likely to own the car? Service contracts vary a great deal in what they cover, and they are not necessarily a good deal. If a third party (such as a service center or garage) is required to carry out the terms of the contract, be sure to investigate that company's reputation.

I just bought my used car, and I'm already having problems. What should I do?

First, try to resolve the problem with the dealer. He or she may be eager to resolve any problems quickly in order to protect the dealership's reputation. If the car is under a manufacturer's warranty and you have a dispute about service with the dealer, contact the "zone representative" of the manufacturer, who might intervene on your behalf.

I don't have a written warranty. If I get stuck with a lemon, does the dealer have any legal responsibility to compensate me?

Yes, unless the dealer tells you in writing that implied warranties do not apply. Most states have the "must run" implied warranty, along with other limited protections. For example, if a dealer suggests to you that a car is suitable for a particular purpose, such as hauling a trailer, the implied warranty guarantees that the car must perform that duty. In some states, the dealer can negate the implied warranties by modifying the contract, usually using the phrases "as is" or "with all faults." Nearly half of all cars sold by dealers come as is, which means that all repairs are the responsibility of the buyer. A number of states do not permit such as is sales by dealers.

When I bought my car, the dealer promised that he would cover any repairs during the first year. Now he refuses. I didn't put the promise in writing. Do I have any recourse?

Oral contracts are nearly impossible to enforce; for this reason, you should insist that all promises be put in writing. Otherwise, if the dealer and his superiors are uncooperative, your only legal protection would be any implied warranties that apply.

Who can help me to enforce a written warranty or service contract if I cannot resolve my service problem with the dealer?

Contact the Better Business Bureau, the state attorney general, or any local consumer protection office, and ask if they can intervene on your behalf. Some states have offices that mediate disputes of this nature. Another possibility would be to ask a dispute resolution organization, such as the Automotive Consumer Action Program, to arbitrate your disagreement.

What if I am unable to get satisfaction from the dealer or any of the agencies I call?

A last resort would be Small Claims Court (for disputes involving small amounts) or a full-fledged lawsuit. There are substantial consumer protections in place that allow you to collect attorney fees and damages if you can prove breach of warranty, whether express or implied. Seek a lawyer's advice if you think you have a case.

Source: *Buying a Used Car,* Consumer Information from the Federal Trade Commission, 6th Street and Pennsylvania Avenue NW, Washington, DC 20580; (202) 326-2502.

Car Repair and Maintenance

I know next to nothing about cars. Is there anything I should be doing to check up on my car between tune-ups?

Some simple routine maintenance can save you a great deal of money and aggravation down the road, if you're willing to put in the time now. Start by monitoring the various lubricating and cooling fluids that keep your engine running smoothly, the most important of which is engine oil.

How often do I need to check the oil level?

Have your oil checked at every other fill-up. If you pump your own gas, it is quite easy to check it on your own. Locate the reservoir, and remove the dipstick; wipe it with a rag, replace it, and remove it a second time to get an accurate reading. If the level is in the "low" area, add oil. Be careful not to overfill the car with oil, and to use the correct oil for your car.

How often does the oil need to be changed?

For the best performance and long-term maintenance, it should be changed completely every three months or 3,000 miles, whichever comes first. If you change the oil yourself, be sure that it is disposed of in accordance with local regulations. The oil filter should be changed along with the oil.

What about the other fluids in the car? Do they need to be checked?

Yes. The antifreeze/coolant level should be checked weekly. This must be done when the car is off and the engine is cool. Remove the pressure cap from the radiator and fill the reservoir to the "level" marking with a solution of half antifreeze and half water. The brake, transmission, and power-steering fluid should be checked monthly. Use the Owner's Manual to locate the reservoirs for these fluids; when filling, be sure to use the correct fluids, and be very careful not to overfill. Poor brake or steering performance or hesitation in shifting gears can be signs of low fluid levels.

What else should I be checking on?

Keep an eye on the ground under your car for signs of fluid leakage. Inspect the hoses and belts in the engine about once a month; check them for any signs of leaks, breaks, brittleness, slackness, or general wear and tear. Check the air filter periodically, and have it changed when it gets dirty. Watch the terminals on top of the battery for signs of decay or corrosion. Keep your windshield wipers in good condition; change the blades every year, or whenever they start to smear or stick. In general, keep an eye out for any changes in your car's performance; alert your mechanic to any problems or questions at the next tune-up.

What can I do to keep my tires in good shape?

Keep them inflated to the recommended pressure. Most gas stations will have a gauge available with the air hose that you use to fill the tires. Check for excessive or uneven wear on the treads; uneven wear might indicate a poor alignment. Look for cuts or bulges on the sides of the tires. Rotate the tires every 7,500 miles; this will help keep them evenly balanced.

My car bounces like a trampoline. What's wrong?

Excessive bouncing or bumpiness indicates worn or leaking shock absorbers, which should be replaced immediately. Keeping the suspension system in good working order is essential, not only for comfort but for safety.

What spare parts and supplies should I keep in the car?

A spare tire, jack, and lug wrench, along with spare engine coolant, are absolutely essential. It is also a good idea to keep a spare can of oil and other lubricating fluids on hand for long trips, in case of unexpected leakage. A canister of dry gas is a good security measure, as are safety flares, a good flashlight, replacement lamps for headlights and flashers, and jumper cables.

I live near the ocean, and rust is a problem. What should I look out for?

Check the underside of your car for signs of rot and rust, or even holes, particularly in the muffler and exhaust pipe. Also, be sure the support clamps that hold up the exhaust system are sturdy and free of corrosion. Excessive noise indicates problems with the muffler. Have the exhaust system checked yearly, both for safety and to assure that it complies with emissions standards.

How often does my car need a tune-up?

A rule of thumb is to have your car tuned up yearly, or every 10,000 miles, whichever comes first. At the tune-up, the oil should be changed; the fluids and replaceable parts should be checked and adjusted; all of the major systems should be checked; and any complaints or questions you have should be evaluated. Regular tune-ups are an excellent way of prolonging the life of your car, and avoiding larger expenses later on.

How can I find a good mechanic?

Word of mouth is the most reliable way to find an honest, competent mechanic or garage. If you find a good one, stay loyal; you are much less likely to get cheated by a mechanic who knows that you're a repeat customer. Most people have at least one story about being burned by a mechanic who performed unnecessary work. If you don't know much about cars, good mechanics are like gold; you might want to put extra effort into developing a good, long-term relationship with yours.

If you are unable to find a mechanic through referrals from friends, one of the auto clubs, like AAA (the American Automobile Association) might be able to help. These clubs can be useful to belong to, because they provide road service in case of a breakdown far from home. This helps to avoid the night-mare scenario of rolling into the first available garage in a strange town, completely at the mercy of the mechanic on duty. There are also online databases that provide unofficial referrals, such as the one at www.cartalk.com, the Web site of the National Public Radio car repair talk show.

Source: "How to Find Your Way Under the Hood and Around the Car," Maintenance Awareness Program, 4600 East West Highway, Bethesda, MD 20814.

Choosing a Bank

How do I choose a bank, and what difference does it make what bank I choose?

Any bank will take your money, but not every bank meets your needs. If you choose the wrong bank, you may have to pay unnecessary fees, miss out on deals you would have been able to take advantage of at another bank, or have to hike across town to do business at an inconvenient branch.

The best way to find a good bank may be to ask around. Talk to your coworkers and people who live near you; ask where they bank and whether they're happy with their banks. You also can look in the newspaper for banks running promotions that fit your needs, or stop by a bank branch that's near your home or place of work. Make sure the bank you choose fits the details of your life—if you need to be able to deposit your paycheck on Saturday after-noon, then you should look for a bank that enables you to do so.

What kinds of charges can my bank collect from me?

Banks can collect several different fees from you, even if you have only a sim-ple checking account. When inquiring about a bank's checking accounts, ask these questions:

- Is there a minimum balance? Minimum balances can be as low as $0 or as high as $5,000 or more, depending on the benefits you get by main-taining that balance.
- What happens if my balance falls below the minimum? Depending on the particular bank or account, fees could run as high as $10 or more if your average balance for a month falls below the minimum.
- Is there a per check charge? Often, banks will give you an allowance of free checks each month—usually 10 or 15. For every check you write above the allowance, you're charged a dime or a quarter.
- Will the money in my account collect interest? If so, at what rate? Not all checking accounts accumulate interest. Those that do may have higher minimum balances. Savings accounts do gather interest—2 to 4 percent is typical.

- Are there ATM usage fees? Frequently, banks let you use their own ATMs without charge but charge you $1–$2 for each transaction you make with other banks' ATMs.
- Are there any special features, such as discounts on loans? How do those features work?

This bank in my town is advertising "budget" checking. What does that mean?

You should look carefully at the offer. This generally means the price is extra low, but there may be trade-offs like a limit on the number of checks you can write; beyond that number you'll be charged a fee. Some banks have free checking, with no minimum balance, no per check fees, and no monthly service charges. You have to shop around.

I can't lose all my money in a bank failure, can I? I mean, the government protects us from that, right?

As long as your bank is insured by the Federal Deposit Insurance Corporation (FDIC)—most banks are, but you should ask to be sure—your deposits, up to $100,000, are insured. If the bank fails and cannot give you back the money you deposited, the FDIC will give you up to $100,000 to cover your losses.

What does that mean? If you're really rich, it means you should ask a bank officer how to protect your money, including interest. If you're not really rich, it means that in the unlikely event that your bank goes under, you will get your money back, even if it takes the FDIC a while to get it to you. Keep in mind that the insurance applies to each *depositor*, not each *account*.

Should I shun a local bank with only a few branches? Don't the huge regional banks offer inexpensive service?

Though it's true that large banks often can save money by automating the banking of millions of people, they lack the personal touch of small, local banks. If you have a problem with your account at a big bank, you may end up dealing with an anonymous customer service representative. If you have a problem with a local bank, you're more likely to be able to get someone you know on the phone—and you'll probably know the bank president, in case things get really hairy. But you shouldn't judge a bank based only on size. Fees will vary at each bank. Is convenience more important than personal service? You have to decide what you want.

What about savings and loan institutions?

As a practical matter, savings and loan institutions, often called S&Ls, can be thought of in the same way as banks. S&Ls offer checking and savings accounts that work exactly like those banks offer. You should shop for an account at an S&L in the same way you should investigate banks.

S&Ls got a black eye in the early 1990s when it was discovered that many S&L operators had invested in very risky real estate. When the real estate lost its value, the S&L operators didn't have enough money to cover their customers' withdrawals and the federal government had to spend a great deal of money to straighten everything out (and send many of the dastardly S&L owners to prison). That is the past. Now, S&Ls are much more tightly regulated than they were before the crisis, and they're safe places to keep your money.

Is it okay to deal with one bank for my checking account, another bank for my car loan, an S&L for my mortgage, and buy shares in mutual funds through a totally separate company?

Sure. Most people operate this way. But be on the lookout for banks that offer deals on loans for people who maintain checking and savings accounts—usually with a minimum balance—with them. You may save enough money on your loan by moving your accounts to a new bank to justify the trouble. Many banks offer access to mutual funds and other uninsured investments too.

What about online banking?

Some banks offer you the ability to do your banking via your home computer. They let you do things like check your balance, see what checks have cleared, and transfer money from one account to another electronically. Many people, especially those who are handicapped or otherwise find it hard (or a waste of time) to go to the bank, consider online banking the best financial development since the demise of shiny beads.

Personal finance software packages, including Quicken from Intuit and Microsoft Money, contain online banking features. They can contact your bank and reconcile the bank's records with the records you've been keeping on your computer. To use the online banking features of these software packages, you'll need a computer equipped with a modem and a connection to a telephone line. Some banks charge a monthly fee for online banking services.

Source: Virginia McGuire, American Bankers' Association; (202) 663-5000.

Cover Letters

What is a *cover letter?*

A cover letter is a letter of inquiry to a potential employer. A formal cover letter should be included with any résumé or application that you send out.

How should I address a formal cover letter?

Try to find out exactly who will be receiving the letter, and address it accordingly: "Dear Ms. Henshaw:" If possible, address the letter to the person who has the power to hire you, which probably means your potential supervisor.

Call the company to verify this information; they should be happy to provide it to you. Be particularly careful to spell the name correctly. If you are unable to address the letter personally, avoid using "Dear Sirs," because the person receiving the letter is equally likely to be a woman. Be as specific as possible: "Dear Hiring Manager" is better than "To Whom It May Concern."

Should I always sign my letters "Sincerely"?

"Sincerely" is a perfectly acceptable standard closing, though it certainly won't set your letter on fire. If you want more punch to your closing, try matching it to the tone of the letter; "With great enthusiasm" or "With much anticipation" are sharper and more to the point.

How can I capture the reader's attention?

In your opening sentences, refer to what you already know about the company. Research your potential employer, and let them know why you want to work for them. Mention favorable things you have heard or read about the company in the business press. This accomplishes two things: It captures the reader's attention, and it lets the reader know that you are serious about working for this company in particular.

What specifics should the letter address?

Clearly state the title of the job that you are applying for, and how you discovered the job opening. If you are answering a classified ad, say so; if you were referred to the company by a friend or colleague, mention that person by name. Briefly summarize your related experience and qualifications, and why you think they are appropriate for this particular job. Refer to your résumé, highlighting whatever you think is most important or impressive.

Should I request an interview?

Yes. Suggest a convenient time for an interview, and state that you will call to follow up on the letter with the hope of confirming an appointment.

Should I repeat the information about my qualifications that appears on my résumé?

Briefly summarize your qualifications, rather than repeating them. Your cover letter should be an introduction to your résumé, where a more detailed description of your experience can be found.

What sort of paper should I use?

Use plain white or off-white paper of a quality stock. Keep the entire format simple, crisp, and uncluttered.

Does it help to use elaborate fonts for my letters?

No. Cover letters should look conservative and businesslike. Using different sizes of print or unusual typefaces tends to distract from the message you are trying to convey.

How many lines should I leave between the closing and my typed name?

Three or four spaces should allow you to sign your name legibly between the complimentary closing ("sincerely," etc.) and your typed name. Don't forget to sign; it personalizes the letter.

Where should I put my phone number?

Your phone number should appear clearly at the top of your résumé, so if the résumé is attached you need not put the number in the cover letter. If you do want the number to appear in the cover letter, the best place is probably directly below your name. The reader will be able to find it quickly, rather than having to scan the text for it.

What are some common mistakes to avoid?

Cover letters must be typed perfectly; grammatical or typographical errors must be avoided at all costs. Proofread each letter carefully before it goes in the mail. If you don't have word processing equipment that will produce a sufficiently clear and neat letter, consider renting equipment, or paying a résumé service to type your letters for you.

Source: *Occupational Outlook Quarterly,* Bureau of Labor Statistics, Publications Sales Center, P.O. Box 2145, Chicago, IL 60690; Neale Baxter, Managing Editor.

Credit Report

What is a *credit report*?

A credit report is a record of your relationships with people who have loaned you money. Credit reports tell whether you lived up to your side of lending agreements—that is, whether you paid your debts in full and on time. Other potential creditors use your credit report in deciding whether to lend you more money. Potential employers and landlords also review credit records.

How can I see my credit report?

Credit bureaus—agencies that collect information on the creditworthiness of individuals—keep credit records. Credit bureaus distribute information via three automated reporting systems: Equifax Credit Information Services, Experian (formerly TRW Information Services), and Trans Union Corporation.

Regardless of whether you've had any debt problems, you need to keep track of your credit history. You can get copies of your credit report from each of the three major reporting services. If you've been denied credit in the past 60 days, you're entitled to a free copy of your record from the credit bureau that supplied your report to the organization that denied you credit. Fees vary. All three require written requests that include detailed personal information, so call first to get instructions.

Equifax Credit Information Services
P.O. Box 105873
Atlanta, GA 30348
(800) 685-1111

Experian
National Consumer Assistance Center
P.O. Box 949
Allen, TX 75013
(800) 682-7654

Trans Union Corporation
National Disclosure Center
P.O. Box 390
Springfield, PA 19064
(800) 916-8800

How do I establish a good credit history?

You establish a good credit history by borrowing money and paying it back according to the terms of your credit agreement, such as:

- Getting a credit card at a local store and promptly paying back charges
- Getting and paying back a small loan from a credit union
- Applying for a loan or credit card with a co-signer who guarantees your creditworthiness
- Starting and maintaining a savings or checking account at a financial institution that offers credit cards
- Renting a home or apartment and making payments on time
- Getting a secured credit card from a bank. A secured credit card is one for which you put up money—say $500—that the bank holds as security against your not paying your credit card debts

How do I get a copy of my credit report?

If you write to a credit reporting agency and include the proper identification, the bureau is legally required to show you everything in your file and its origin as often as once every year. You might want to request your credit report every one or two years.

What do I do if there's a mistake on my credit report?

Write the credit bureau, which will try to verify the information with the creditor. If the bureau cannot confirm the information it has in your file, it must delete or change it.

How long will negative information stay on my record?

Accurate negative information can stay on your credit report for seven years (except in the case of bankruptcy, which stays on up to ten years).

I run a balance on my credit card—I don't pay it off in full each month. Will that have a negative effect on my credit report?

No, as long as you're sending in at least the minimum payment each month, your acount is considered current.

How do I get negative information taken off my credit report?

Unless it is wrong or obsolete, you can't get it removed until seven years have passed. But negative information weighs less with the passage of time, so problems you had five years ago might not be a big deal today if other indicators demonstrate that you are worthy of credit.

I haven't been able to pay my bills. How do I improve my credit rating?

By paying bills and loans promptly over time. Call a member of the National Foundation for Consumer Credit (a nonprofit organization) at (800) 388-2227 and ask for help in setting up a plan for paying off your debts. After you get everything paid off, any factually correct information about your troubles will remain on your credit report for seven years.

I'm withholding payment on a credit card purchase because of unsatisfactory service. How do I make sure this doesn't end up on my credit report?

Make sure you communicate in writing with your creditor, explaining why you're withholding payment. Keep copies of all correspondence and records of all telephone calls to the creditor, including the date, time, and name of the person with whom you spoke.

Can I be denied credit for no reason at all?

No. By law, you have a right to know why you have been denied credit.

Source: National Foundation for Consumer Credit; call (301) 589-5600 for more information.

Finding an Accountant

I'm not particularly rich. What use do I have for an accountant?

An accountant can help you in all areas of your personal financial planning, from tax preparation to saving for your children's college tuition to building retirement plans. They are a good source for information and advice, particularly if you don't have a firm grasp on financial matters. You certainly don't have to be rich to use the services of an accountant. In this age of high education costs, declining pensions, and uncertainty about the future of Social Security, most working families will need some type of financial advice to plan for the future.

What is a CPA?

In order to be classified as a CPA, or Certified Public Accountant, an accountant must pass a uniform nationwide licensing examination. In addition, CPAs must fulfill all licensing requirements for the state in which they practice. Many of these guidelines are quite strict, requiring postgraduate study or further testing. CPAs are frequently required to take continuing education courses to maintain their certification.

Where do CPAs work?

Like lawyers, CPAs work in a variety of settings. Some operate private practices, concentrating on serving the financial needs of individuals and families. Many businesses and organizations employ CPAs, either on staff or as consultants; they provide auditing services, advice on developing and maintaining effective accounting systems, and tax assistance. In recent years, CPAs have often become involved in designing and installing computerized accounting systems for businesses. The government also uses CPAs frequently, especially as auditors and examiners.

Is there a legal difference between CPAs and other accountants?

Yes. CPA licensing is necessary for an accountant to perform certain tasks, particularly regarding tax and legal documents. It also indicates that the accountant has a broad knowledge of finance.

How can I find a good accountant?

One of the best ways to locate a reliable accountant, as with a doctor or a lawyer, is through referrals from friends, colleagues, or business contacts. If you need an accountant for a specific purpose, such as setting up a small business, contact established businesses in related fields for a referral. There are also state CPA societies and government agencies that operate CPA referral services.

What qualifications should I look for?

Your accountant should be willing to provide proof of license to practice in your state. You may want to ask for references from professional organizations or past clients. Most important, see to it that your accountant's manner and areas of expertise are compatible with your needs.

What should a CPA charge?

There are no standard rate schedules, though CPAs normally charge by the hour. The rate will depend on several factors, including experience, expertise, and the prevailing rate in your area. The best way to find a fair price is to comparison shop; talk to several accountants, and consider how their fees relate to the services they offer.

I usually pay a service to have my taxes done. What extra services does an accountant offer?

Most accountants are able to go beyond simple tax return preparation. The more complicated your taxes, the more useful an accountant can be to you. If you have income from investments, rental property, or sources other than work, an accountant may be able to help you develop a tax strategy to protect your money more effectively. Accountants are also best qualified to represent you before the tax authorities, in the case of an audit, for example.

I'm setting up a very small business, which I plan to run on my own. Should I consult an accountant?

You may have to. Depending on the laws of your state, and on what classification of business (sole proprietorship, limited partnership, corporation, etc.) you are starting, it may be necessary for a lawyer or CPA to complete some of the paperwork. Your city hall or chamber of commerce will be able to advise you of local requirements.

Even if not required by law, it is probably advisable to talk with an accountant. Any business, no matter how small, needs to set up an effective accounting system in order to operate smoothly. An accountant with expertise in your area of business can be a vital resource for information on financing, budgeting, taxes, financial statements, and data processing systems.

Do accountants give advice on investments?

Some do. Finding an accountant who will help you develop a complete financial plan for your family is probably the best value for your money. Again, try to find one with a broad knowledge who can advise you on all investment strategies, loans, taxes, insurance needs, even estate planning. Developing an overall strategy will allow your accountant to get to know your family and its needs, making it easier to give you sound advice.

I want to become a CPA. What do I have to do?

Before you start your quest, make sure you know the exact certification requirements for CPAs in your state. Contact the state board of certification or the agency that deals with CPA licensing. They will be able to provide you with a complete list of requirements and qualifications, including information on the national certification exam.

The first step, if you don't have one, will likely be to earn a bachelor's degree, either in accounting or in a related field. Colleges and universities offer programs of study in a wide variety of majors related to business and finance; some programs and courses are specifically designed to prepare you for the certification exam. Perhaps the best way to wade through your options is to talk to qualified CPAs. Ask them about programs in the area, and seek their advice on what the best path is for you.

Source: *How to Choose and Use a CPA*, The American Institute of Certified Public Accountants, 1211 Avenue of the Americas, New York, NY 10036-8775; contact Dave Disgupta, AICPA, (212) 596-6200.

Futures/Options

What are *futures markets?*

Futures markets, simply put, are markets where futures contracts are bought and sold. Futures contracts establish a price now for items to be delivered later. They exist largely to ensure both buyers and sellers of commodities against rapid changes in price. The list of commodities that are traded in futures markets has expanded significantly over the past 25 years, and now includes agricultural products, metals, petroleum, financial instruments, foreign currencies, and stock indexes.

Who participates in futures markets?

The active participants in futures markets—that is, the people actually on the floor yelling and signaling prices to each other—represent three major categories. *Hedgers* are individuals or firms that are dealing in the market in order to establish a known price level for some commodity that they intend to buy or sell later on for cash; they are hedging their bets, so to speak.

The person or concern on the other side of the transaction would be a *speculator;* a speculator has an opinion about what will happen to the actual price of the commodity, and seeks to profit from it by purchasing contracts (if they expect a price increase) or by selling contracts (if they expect prices to fall). When selling contracts, the speculator hopes to buy back offsetting contracts at a lower price, thus realizing a profit. This is known as "going short."

The third type of participant is the *floor trader,* who hopes to make quick, same-day profits by buying and selling contracts when a hedger cannot immediately find a speculator (or vice versa).

That's pretty confusing. How exactly do the markets work?

Take, for example, a manufacturer of grape juice. To make a profit, she counts on the price of grapes remaining at $1 per pound; however, she suspects that the price is going up. In order to hedge against this price increase, she buys a futures contract for a certain amount of grapes at $1 per pound. A speculator, who thinks the price of grapes is going down, sells her the contract; he hopes to realize a profit by buying a contract—to offset the one he has sold to the juice maker—at a lower price.

Time passes, and the price of grapes goes down to 90 cents. The juice maker sells her contract for a lower price than she paid, and realizes a loss. That loss, however, is offset by the fact that she only has to pay 90 cents for grapes. She has, in essence, locked the price in at $1. The speculator, on the other hand, makes a profit; to fulfill his contract that he sold, he simply needs to buy one at the new, lower price.

Suppose the price had gone up to $1.10. The juice maker sells her contract at a profit; this makes up for her losses due to the higher price of grapes. The speculator, in this case, takes a loss.

Instead of selling the contract, why doesn't the juice maker just take delivery on the grapes?

In theory, she could. But the markets rarely work this way in practice; delivery of the goods is the exception rather than the rule. As a manufacturer, the juice maker doubtless has an efficient supply system in place; she uses the futures market simply to stabilize her costs.

How does the floor trader fit in?

The floor trader keeps the market "liquid." Perhaps when the juice maker wanted to buy her contract at 90 cents, there was no speculator ready to sell. The floor trader might agree to sell her a contract at 91 cents. An hour later, when the speculator wants to sell at 90 cents but can't find a buyer, the floor trader buys at 89 cents. He has made a quick, modest profit at the expense of both the juice maker and the speculator; in turn he has smoothed the transaction between them. Many transactions of this sort create the chaotic selling floors that we see on television.

How do "regular" investors participate in the futures markets?

Some of those traders classified as speculators represent individual investors, either directly (as brokers) or indirectly (as part of investment firms managing their money). It is possible to call up a brokerage house and purchase a futures contract, but it is not advisable unless you know exactly what you're doing.

What is an *option* on a futures contract?

Investing in "put" and "call" options is a less risky way to play the futures markets. The investor pays a premium for the right (but not the obligation) to buy (call) or sell (put) a futures contract at a particular price. The transaction amounts to a straight gamble on the direction of the price of that commodity. If the price changes in the right direction, a profit can be made; either the option rights can be sold for more than they cost, or the right to buy or sell at the set price can be exercised. The most an investor can lose in such a transaction is the amount of the premium; if the price goes in the wrong direction, there is no obligation to buy or sell.

Are futures contracts a high-risk investment?

Yes. Because of volatile prices, and because of the fact that futures markets are highly leveraged (much is bought on margin), futures markets are quite high risk. Substantial profits and substantial losses can happen extremely quickly. Futures trading is for investors who have enough money to risk a portion of it for the chance at a big gain; it is not for the casual investor. The markets are quite complicated, and even experienced investors should seek advice before taking the plunge.

Source: *Understanding Opportunities and Risks in Futures Trading,* National Futures Association, 200 West Madison Street, Suite 1600, Chicago, IL 60606-3447; (800) 621-3570.

Choosing Home Insurance

Is home insurance required for everyone who owns a home?

No, but most mortgage lenders require that an adequate home insurance policy be purchased before the loan contracts are signed. Therefore, unless you pay cash for your home, you will probably have to buy a policy. How much coverage you buy beyond the minimums specified by your mortgage is up to you.

What does home insurance cover?

Coverage varies from policy to policy. A standard policy will cover your home against most losses and damage occurring as a result of fire, theft, vandalism, weather, and unexpected accidents or mechanical failure.

What factors can effect the price of my insurance?

The company you buy your policy from, the amount of coverage you get, and the type of policy you buy can affect the total cost of your home insurance by hundreds of dollars. There are some important factors over which you have very little control, though, including: the age of your home; the condition of its electrical, plumbing, and heating systems; the soundness of its structure; the materials that it is constructed of; and the physical properties of the area in which it is located. All of these elements contribute to the overall likelihood that your home will be damaged in some way, whether by fire, flood, wind, theft, or other means. The more apparent dangers that face your house, the higher your premium will tend to be.

What is a *deductible*?

A deductible is a set amount that you must pay toward the repair of damage or loss before your insurance coverage kicks in; that is, before the insurance company begins paying its share of the bill as set out by your policy. For example, if you have a policy that covers fire damage at 100 percent with a $200 deductible, that means that in the case of a fire, you will pay the first $200 in repairs and replacement costs; after that payment is satisfied, the insurance company will pay all other costs within the scope of the policy.

Is there an advantage in having a high deductible?

There can be, in that it helps to keep premiums down. If you have a new home with new systems located in a low-risk area, a policy with a high deductible might make sense; essentially, you would be paying less in premiums in the hope that you will never need to use the policy, and thus that your deductible will never be met.

What other ways can I keep the price of my home insurance down?

As with other types of insurance, careful comparison shopping is the most effective way to get a good price. If you already have a trusted agent you have used to find business or auto insurance, she may be able to provide the same service for your home insurance, possibly even at a discount. If not, you should be able to locate a reliable agent through referrals from friends or relatives.

If you prefer not to use an agent, information is available from state insurance agencies, consumer organizations, and guidebooks. When you feel confident that you know what you want from your policy, start making calls to insurance companies. Note the quality and range of service they offer, and ask what they can do to lower your costs. When you have found three or four companies you are comfortable with, ask for and compare price quotes.

In choosing between specific policies, there are several ways you can save money. Make sure that you are insuring the value of your home only, and not the land that it sits on. The land is not at risk of damage from fire or theft, so it need not be covered; however, many homeowners forget that the value of the land was included in the purchase price of their house. If you have a number of insurance policies with the same company, you may qualify for a discount.

Some companies offer group discounts to members of large organizations such as unions and alumni or business associations. Retired people qualify for certain discounts based on the fact that they have more time to maintain their homes, and that they are more likely to be at home at the time of a given emergency. Alarm systems and other security measures also may qualify you for a break on theft coverage. Ask your agent or provider to thoroughly review your cost-cutting options; these discounts can save a significant amount of money on your premiums.

I'm buying a house near the waterfront, and I understand the area has had problems with flooding. Will flood damage be covered by my regular policy?

No. You will likely be required by your mortgage lender to buy a separate flood insurance policy. Homeowners' insurance does not cover flood damage.

Will my policy cover other possessions that I keep inside my home against theft or damage?

Most policies allow you to buy additional coverage for major purchases to protect them against theft or damage. One way to save money on your policy is to compare the value of your property to the extent of your coverage on a regular basis; if the value of your possessions has decreased, you may find that you have more coverage than you need.

Source: *Twelve Ways to Lower Your Homeowners Insurance Costs,* Insurance Information Institute, Consumer Information Center, P.O. Box 100, Pueblo, CO 81002.

Home Shopping/Mail Order

I hear so much about mail-order fraud. Is shopping through the mail ever a good idea?

Many mail-order businesses are legitimate, and want to please their customers in order to generate repeat business. Buying by mail can be a convenient and economical way to shop. The fact remains, however, that the mail-order business has been, and continues to be, a breeding ground for fraud, theft, and shady business practices. The government and the Better Business Bureau receive thousands of complaints every year from consumers who have been cheated or misled by fraudulent companies operating mail-order businesses through direct-mail soliciting, television or radio advertising, telemarketing, and classified advertising.

How can I tell the good companies from the bad?

Unless you (or someone you know) has done business with a company in the past, it is difficult to be sure that it is legitimate. The best defense against fraudulent offers is a healthy dose of vigilance. Be skeptical of exaggerated claims and unrealistically low prices for merchandise. The old cliché, "if it sounds too good to be true, it probably is," is a reliable yardstick.

If you are ordering from an unfamiliar company, be sure to check with your local Better Business Bureau first; they can provide information on outstanding complaints and warnings against suspect companies. Carefully read all the fine print of catalogues and print advertisements; always keep a copy of the ad you are ordering from. Pay by check or money order; never send cash through the mail. Keep clear records of all aspects of the transaction: Make copies of all order forms, delivery receipts, packing lists, and canceled checks.

Is it safe to pay by credit card through the mail or over the telephone?

Yes and no. Credit card fraud is widespread, and giving your number out to an unknown company is one way to expose yourself to it. In our increasingly cashless society, however, it is becoming more and more difficult to keep our credit card information completely secure. If a company charges your credit card for goods or services that you did not receive, you have the right to dispute the charge with your merchant bank.

If a company has your signature on an order form, and some sort of record that the goods were delivered to you, they are likely to recover the charge. If they have no signature, and only a name and number, they will be required to prove that you ordered the merchandise. Be aware that giving your address, telephone number, or any personal information to a shady mail-order business could provide them with such ammunition. Most important, be sure to investigate the company thoroughly before any credit card transaction.

How soon should I expect delivery on items that I order?

The Federal Trade Commission's Mail Order Rule provides strict time guidelines for mail-order delivery. The rule does not apply to telephone orders that are paid by credit card. The company must state in advance the exact time period in which the items will be delivered; if they don't, you have the right to expect them within 30 days. If there is a delay in shipping, the company must notify you by mail or telephone, and must give you the opportunity and the means (such as a stamped reply card) to cancel your order. If you agree to the delay, and the company is still unable to ship after 30 days, they must again give you the option to cancel. If you then choose to cancel, the company must refund any payment you have made in full.

What can I do if I have a problem with my mail-order purchase?

If you have paid for goods that were never delivered, or feel that you were otherwise defrauded, and you have not been able to resolve the problem directly with the company, contact your local branch of the Better Business Bureau. Disputes are slow, time-consuming, and difficult to resolve; checking up beforehand is by far the wisest course.

I often get junk mail telling me that I've won a vacation in Bermuda, or some other fabulous prize. What are these people up to?

The "free vacation" offer is one of the most widespread scams in the direct-mail and telemarketing businesses. You receive a phone call or a letter notifying you that you have won a "free" cruise or beach vacation. Upon further investigation, you find that you have to pay an outrageous membership fee to join a travel club; or perhaps it turns out to be a "two for one" discount; or you need to attend a sales promotion at a timeshare resort; or the package is loaded with entry fees and shipping and processing charges.

All variations on this scheme boil down to the fact that people love to go on vacation; images of sun, sand, and sea are an excellent way to divert their attention while their pockets are being picked. A rule of thumb: When you hear or see the words "free" and "vacation" in the same sentence, alarm bells should be pealing inside your head.

Can I do anything to stop those irritating telemarketing calls?

Some steps can be taken to reduce the volume of calls, at least. Long-distance companies tend to top people's lists of bothersome beggars of the dinner hour; the major ones all have customer relations departments to which you can return the favor. Call them up, and ask that they please remove your name from their marketing lists; show the same persistence that they do, and you are likely to have success. Getting an unlisted telephone number can cut down on (but not necessarily eliminate) the number of lists your household appears on.

The most effective tactic, however, is to be stingy with your personal information. Wherever you shop—be it the supermarket, the telephone, or the Internet—don't give out your address or telephone number unless you absolutely must. Marketing lists are developed by cross-referencing information about your finances and buying habits; if you want to stay off the lists, keep those things a secret where possible.

What about "home shopping" television channels? Are they safe?

Television channels devoted entirely to mail order have lately joined program-length "infomercials" among the most effective of direct marketing media. Infomercials generally use a "hard-sell" technique; wildly enthusiastic hosts rave about the products as viewers are assaulted with a barrage of information.

Home shopping channel spokesmen rely on a number of techniques, from the venerable "time is running out and there are a limited number in stock" routine to a more New Age "I feel your pain, come join the club" approach. The same caveats apply here as with all mail-order business: Check out all unfamiliar companies in advance, and ask about fine print issues such as return policies.

I see ads in the "Help Wanted" section that advertise "work from home" offers that sound like great deals. Are any of them legitimate?

Rarely. Work-at-home schemes that require money up front (even just $2) are likely fraudulent. For the money you put up, you may be sent nothing more than a set of instructions on how to dupe other job seekers. Beware of any employer who refuses to make a written offer of a fixed salary, or who seems to exaggerate income potential. Above all, avoid pyramid schemes, which promise huge earnings from a small investment. Most work-at-home ads are designed to take advantage of people who are naive and inexperienced in the workforce.

Source: *Shopping by Mail; Homework Offers; Avoid Telemarketing Fraud;* and *Buying by Mail,* © 1996, Council of Better Business Bureaus (www.bbb.org).

Investment Clubs

Exactly what is an *investment club*?

An investment club is a group of people who follow a common investment strategy, pool their money and knowledge, and invest in stocks regularly. Investments clubs date back to the late 1800s in the United States. The National Association of Investors Corporation (NAIC) has helped over four million investment clubs and individuals since 1951.

What are the advantages of forming an investment club?

An investment club pools not just the financial resources of its members but their experience and expertise as well. While many clubs take their membership from just one profession, many successful clubs seek to build a diverse membership. Having members well versed in different industries and professions adds to the club's overall savvy.

An obvious advantage is in the dollar amount available to be invested. Since investment clubs seek to build wealth by reinvesting dividends and compounding their gains, the more money in the pool, the better the results.

How many members does a club usually have?

Anywhere from 12 to 20 people. The NAIC average is 16 members per club.

How should members be chosen?

The first qualification is that members should enjoy one another's company. After all, this is a long-term program, and members will be seeing a lot of each other. Next, they have to agree on a fundamental investment philosophy they're going to follow—this prevents fundamental disagreement at a later date. Then a club partnership agreement must be signed and the club can begin.

Aren't investment clubs really just a form of social activity?

An investment club does offer a pleasant social opportunity, but anyone who regards the activity as a "night out" has the wrong idea. An investment club is a lifetime program of investing and financial study, and each member must be willing to participate fully in the club's activities—from investigating and analyzing securities to making periodic reports to the rest of the membership.

Once a club has enough members, how does it get started?

The club's founders hold a meeting for all potential members, at which the philosophy, operation, and goals of the club are explained. If enough people are interested, the club proceeds with the following steps:

- adopting an operation agreement
- setting operation policies

- electing officers
- determining the responsibility of each member
- setting regular meetings
- deciding the amount of monthly deposit
- selecting a broker
- attaining a tax identification number with the IRS
- naming the club
- joining the National Association of Investment Clubs

How often does an investment club meet?

Once a month, as a rule.

How soon can a club expect to become fabulously wealthy?

An investment club isn't a get-rich-quick scheme. If anything, it is a build-wealth-slowly plan. Most investment clubs have the goal of long-term, consistent investing.

Okay, how do you build wealth slowly?

By following four conservative, time-proven principles:

1. Invest a set sum once a month in common stocks, regardless of general conditions.
2. Reinvest dividends and capital gains immediately. This is compound income at work.
3. Buy growth stocks—companies that should be stronger five years from now.
4. Diversify your investments. This spreads both risk and opportunity.

Can members contribute different amounts of money?

Yes. In fact, in most clubs the members' contributions vary. But it's a good idea for beginning clubs to have their members invest the same amount each month for the first two years, in order to understand the accounting system.

What happens if I want to leave my club?

Every member's share in the club is valued in units (usually $10), and a valuation is done each month before the club meeting. Any member withdrawing is paid in cash, or in stock based on his/her valuation at time of withdrawal.

Source: National Association of Investors Corporation; contact Jonathan Strong, Manager, Member Services; phone: (248) 583-6242; fax: (248) 583-4880. For more information on how to start a profitable investment club, write the NAIC, P.O. Box 220, Royal Oak, MI 48068.

Job Interviews

How should I dress for a job interview?

If you are interviewing for a professional, administrative, or secretarial position, an attractive, conservative suit is always best. Impeccable grooming and a pleasant, nonthreatening appearance will keep the interviewer's attention focused on your skills, where you presumably want it. Even companies with a reputation for casual work environments and lax dress codes will most likely expect you to meet this standard, particularly for a first interview.

For nonoffice jobs the rules may vary, but the goal remains the same; while it might be considered bizarre to show up in a Gucci suit to interview for a position as a cocktail server, looking neat and orderly is important in all cases. If you have doubts, it is probably better to risk overdressing a bit.

What are the most commonly asked questions in job interviews?

Interviewing techniques and tactics vary widely, but you should certainly be prepared to answer a few general questions about why you want the job and why the employer should give it to you. The best way to prepare for such questions is to come armed with information. Find out all you can about the job in advance, so that you can say what it is in your background that qualifies you for it. Know something about the company or institution as well: what it does, where and how it does it, and how you might be able to help.

You will almost certainly be asked questions about your job history; answer them honestly, but with an strong emphasis on the positive. Avoid disparaging remarks about your former employers or bosses, no matter how true they are; interviewers tend to find such things alarming. Concentrate on what you have accomplished, and on what you enjoyed, at previous jobs; if these things don't come easily to mind, you might want to prepare a short list.

Another common type of question is the personal. You may be asked about your goals, your strengths, your fears, or your expectations of the future. These questions can be quite vague and open-ended, and thus difficult to answer; they are designed to show how well you can "think on your feet." There is no way to prepare an answer for every potential question; the best plan is to decide what you want to highlight about yourself, so that you can guide your answers in positive directions.

How can I overcome my nervousness at job interviews?

Try to treat the interview as a conversation (though admittedly a rather constrained one) rather than as a test. It is an opportunity for you to meet with a possible employer to discuss a possible job, and nothing more. If you think of the interviewer as an interrogator, trying to pry information from you, you will likely appear defensive and ill at ease. If you tend to be nervous meeting new people, try turning the tables by concentrating on putting the interviewer at ease. Once the ice is broken and a friendly tone is set, you should begin to feel more comfortable.

How can I make a good impression on an interviewer?

Arrive 15 minutes early, and bring extra résumés. Show the interviewer that you are able to listen; engage yourself in the conversation. Take an interest in the company, its history, and its plans for the future. In your answers to questions, keep the focus on the job and on your skills and abilities.

If you are asked about a negative aspect of your past experience, such as having been fired from a job, don't be evasive; stress what you learned from the episode, and how it might have helped you to become a more effective worker. Be courteous; listen attentively, answer what is asked to the best of your ability, and allow the interviewer to lead you through the process.

Interviewers always seem to ask me to comment on my "greatest weakness" or "a past regret." Is there a right way to answer those types of questions?

Yes. Mention a weakness that is actually a strength, or something that you regret that shows you in a good light as an employee. You certainly don't want to discuss your untidiness, or the fact that you can't get out of bed in the morning. Yes, it may make you squirm or feel evasive to manipulate the question; don't let that affect your answer. If an interviewer has the nerve to ask you why she shouldn't hire you, then you should feel free to turn the tables. "I find that I sometimes care too much about my work," or some variation thereof, should do the trick.

Should I be prepared to ask questions at a first interview, or should I take a more passive approach?

The interview is for your benefit as well as your potential employer's, and you should feel free to ask questions. After all, if the job isn't right for you, neither one of you will want to waste any more of your time than necessary. Stay away from specifics like salary and hours; those issues can be settled when and if the job is offered to you. Stick to general questions that indicate your interest in learning and growing in the position, and in challenging yourself. When listening to the interviewer's answers to your questions, try, if possible, to link them to some aspect of your experience or abilities.

I always seem to do well until the very end. How can I end an interview without awkwardness?

Be sure to thank the interviewer for his time, and, if appropriate, emphasize your interest in the job. Politely inquire what the next step in the process will be; find out if there will be another round of interviews, if you should contact the interviewer again, or if you can provide him with further information. Be sure to keep your composure right to the end, in order to leave the interviewer with a pleasant final impression; don't rush out as if from a burning building.

How can I effectively follow up on an interview?

Send a letter, rather than telephoning. State your interest in the job again, and try to provide some new information that relates to what was discussed in the interview. Keep it brief and polite, and don't apply any pressure. As with all correspondence in your job search, be sure that the letter is perfectly typed and organized. If the company does not contact you within a reasonable amount of time, call and ask if the position has been filled. Remember that companies are often choosing from a large pool of applicants; try not to take rejections personally.

Source: *Occupational Outlook Quarterly,* Bureau of Labor Statistics, Publications Sales Center, P.O. Box 2145, Chicago, IL 60690; Neale Baxter, Managing Editor.

Life Insurance

What is the purpose of life insurance?

Most people buy life insurance to protect their dependents from debt and loss of support in the event of their death. A policy is bought during the lifetime of an individual, and is paid off to the named beneficiary after the death of that individual.

How much life insurance do I need?

The factors that should be examined when deciding how much life insurance to buy include: the costs related to your death, including medical bills; funeral and burial expenses; the need for funds during the period of your family's adjustment after your death; and the financial need that will be caused in your family by the loss of your income. Life insurance works best when it is part of a larger financial plan that is carefully worked out with the help of knowledgeable advisers.

What is the difference between *term* and *permanent* insurance?

Term insurance covers only a specific time period (anywhere from one to 20 years) and pays off only if you die during that period. It is designed to correspond to your need for insurance at a given time of life. For example, a man aged 45 with several children might feel that it would be particularly disastrous for his family if he died whithin the next ten years; they would be losing his entire income, and yet would still have the burden of all of the costs associated with feeding, clothing, sheltering, and educating the children. In this case, he might buy a term policy covering those years extensively. At age 55, when the policy expires, perhaps most of the children are grown; he and his wife are ready to sell their home, and are planning for retirement. In this case he might feel that the situation is more secure, and less coverage is needed; he would buy a policy with lower premiums and less coverage.

Permanent insurance is designed to last your entire lifetime; as long as the premiums are kept up, the death benefit will be paid. The benefit remains roughly the same, whether the premiums are paid for 40 months or 40 years.

What are the differences between the various types of permanent insurance?

The array of permanent insurance classifications includes so-called whole life or ordinary life, universal or adjustable life, and variable life. *Whole life* is a common, straightforward arrangement in which premiums remain the same and are paid at regular intervals over the course of the buyer's life. The *universal life* variation allows the buyer to pay premiums when she wants and in the amounts she wants within certain parameters; according to this payment schedule, the amount of the potential death benefit fluctuates. This allows the policyholder to adjust the amount of coverage according to the family's needs at any given time. *Variable life* is both insurance and a type of investment; the amount of the benefit depends on the performance of a portfolio of stocks and securities the policy is attached to.

What should my life insurance agent do for me?

Your agent should be able to explain the various options available to you, and to help you evaluate how much and what variety of insurance your family needs. Some agents represent a particular company; others are independent, and sell policies from a variety of providers. There are strict licensing procedures for life insurance agents in all states, and your agent should be willing to provide you with all the necessary proof of her credentials.

I have an appointment with my agent. What will she be asking me?

You should be prepared to discuss all aspects of your family's finances. Your agent will help you to determine your net worth, and will ask questions designed to help her understand the way in which your family's finances are structured. Finally, she will discuss your various policy options with you.

Will she ask questions about my health?

Yes. In fact, during the initial appointment you will have to go into great detail about your health. Be prepared to answer questions about personal and family medical history, illnesses, and personal habits such as smoking, drinking, diet, and exercise. Answer these questions carefully; evasive answers might cause problems later on, when your beneficiaries try to collect.

Medical questions can sometimes seem overly personal, even invasive. Keep in mind that the agent's job, morbid as it may sound, is to assess how long you are likely to live. This assessment will affect your premiums, the benefit rate, and what type of policy is recommended.

Will I have to take a medical exam?

In most cases, yes. Insurance companies usually require a physical exam to confirm the medical information you have given. Some high-premium, low-benefit policies aimed at the elderly offer a "no exam" clause as a selling point.

My agent has made a recommendation about what sort of insurance she thinks I should purchase. What should I watch for when looking over the proposal?

The agent will often provide you with a written description of her recommendations, called a "policy illustration." Study this illustration point by point to be sure that it meets your needs; make sure that the agent clearly explains anything that is unclear to you. Try to anticipate potential problems, like the missing of a payment or the need to cancel suddenly, and find out what flexibility the policy allows. If you have reservations, ask your agent for other possible options; don't feel that you need to accept the recommendation completely. The agent wants you as a client, and should be glad to show you other available choices.

Source: *What You Should Know About Buying Life Insurance,* American Council of Life Insurance, 1001 Pennsylvania Avenue, NW, Washington, DC 20004.

Living Within a Budget

Where does all of my money go?

If you don't have a clear idea where your money is being spent, it would probably be a good idea to make the effort to find out. Working out a personal budget can help you find those areas where your hard-earned cash is evaporating, and can give you a model to follow for more responsible spending. You may find that a large portion of your paycheck is going for essentially nothing; "phantom" expenses such as interest on loans, banking fees and errors, late charges, and excessive retail markups can account for a large share of costs, for which you receive nothing in return.

What is the most effective way of making my money last?

Comparison shopping is vitally important in a consumer economy. Buy the same product in ten different stores and you may pay as many as ten different prices for it. By shopping at low-price grocery stores, for example, you can save hundreds of dollars a year; the high markups of convenience stores wreak havoc on your budget. For any purchase, from airline tickets to insurance, from a new car to a can of tuna fish, comparison shopping is the key to keeping costs down.

How can I avoid unnecessary banking fees and charges?

When selecting a checking account, try to find one with a minimum balance requirement that you can easily maintain. This will help you to avoid fees for check writing and ATM transactions. Many bank accounts waive checking fees if your paycheck is direct-deposited electronically; ask your employer if they provide this service. Keeping accurate records of your bank accounts will help both in detecting errors made by the bank and in avoiding charges for bounced checks.

My credit card bills are killing me. What can I do?

The most obvious plan is to pay the entire balance of your credit cards each month; of course, this requires some restraint in spending. If you are able to avoid carrying over balances, you can save yourself hundreds of dollars over the course of a year.

If you do find yourself with revolving debt, there are several strategies to follow to limit the damage. Begin by consolidating the debt on one or two cards with a low annual percentage rate (APR) of interest. If all of your cards have high APRs, it would be worthwhile to apply for a card with a lower rate. Many cards offer low promotional APRs that last from two to twelve months. Make the largest payments on cards with the highest APRs, regardless of balance. Keeping only one or two cards will also help to cut down on fees. Avoid late payments, which result in additional fees and damage your credit rating.

Is it less expensive to lease a new car than to buy one?

That depends on the terms of the lease. Your monthly payments may well be lower for a lease than for a loan to buy, but there are other factors to consider. Remember that at the end of the lease, the car will not belong to you, and thus will have no trade-in value. (Some lease contracts will provide you the opportunity to buy the car at this stage.)

Lease contacts often require that you return the car in a certain condition, or below a certain mileage. Beware of hidden costs, and find out what penalties you will incur if you decide you don't want to complete the lease. Leasing a car is a complicated matter, and all aspects of a lease should be closely examined in order to determine if there will be a real savings over buying.

My car takes up such a large portion of my budget. How can I reduce these expenses?

Keeping your car well tuned and your tires properly inflated can save you hundreds of dollars each year in gasoline. Pumping gas yourself at self-service stations, and using the least expensive gas that your Owner's Manual recommends, can further reduce these costs. Finding a competent and fair mechanic is a huge step forward in saving money on your car over the long run. Careful comparison shopping when buying a car, selecting an insurance policy, or finding financing will also help keep your transportation budget under control.

How can I keep my insurance premiums down?

When purchasing any insurance policy, buy from a licensed agent who has demonstrated the willingness to get you the best price possible. You may be able to reduce your premiums by purchasing all of your policies from the same company. With auto insurance, consider raising deductibles on collision and comprehensive coverage; if you have an old car, you might want to consider dropping these coverages altogether. With homeowner insurance, be certain that you have just enough coverage to replace the house and its contents; too much coverage can be as costly as too little. With life insurance, be sure that you understand the difference between term and whole life policies, and select the coverage that is appropriate for your needs to avoid unnecessary expense (see *Choosing Home Insurance,* page 381, and *Life Insurance,* page 390).

What is the best way to invest my money safely but still get a good return?

Certificates of Deposit (CDs) and Treasury Notes are two forms of investment that offer a better return on your savings than standard savings accounts with little or no risk. Be sure to compare rates on all investment products before buying; rates will vary widely from bank to bank (see *Selecting Stocks,* page 409, and *Mutual Funds,* page 398).

What types of loans are best for my overall financial health?

When financing a home, make careful computations to determine which mortgages will save you money in the long run. Consider not just the interest rate, but the points, closing costs, duration of the loan, and all other variables. A small difference in the interest rate can cost you thousands of dollars over the course of repayment. Taking a 15-year loan over a 30-year loan, where possible, will greatly reduce the amount of total interest while increasing the monthly payments. A large down payment will reduce both monthly payments and interest charges.

Be wary of taking out home equity loans, because they reduce the amount of equity you have in your home. Remember that if you are unable to make the payments on a home equity loan, you are in danger of losing your home. For loans other than home mortgages, consider all available sources, including credit unions, finance companies, and banks.

Should I refinance my mortgage?

If you can qualify for a mortgage that has an interest rate that is at least one full point lower than your current one, you may want to consider refinancing. In order to determine whether refinancing is worthwhile, however, you must consider all costs, charges, and fees that are associated with the new loan. Ask an accountant to help you calculate the costs and benefits of refinancing.

Source: *66 Ways to Save Money,* Consumer Literacy Consortium, Consumer Federation of America, 1424 16th Street NW, Suite 604, Washington, DC 20036.

Mortgages

What is a *mortgage*?

A mortgage is an agreement under which a lender, such as a mortgage company or bank, holds the title to a piece of property until the borrower fulfills certain obligations, such as making a series of payments, even though the borrower uses the piece of property during the time he is fulfilling the terms of the agreement.

Typically, mortgages are ways for consumers to finance homes and for businesses to finance buildings and massively expensive equipment. This text assumes you're a consumer looking to finance a house with a mortgage.

How do I know how much house I can afford?

As a general guide, you can purchase a home with a value of two or three times your annual household income, depending upon your savings and debts. However, you may be able to take advantage of special loan programs (especially those for first-time buyers) to purchase a home with a higher value.

When should I talk to a mortgage lender?

You should approach a lender when you start thinking about buying a home. True, you can't actually apply for a mortgage until you've chosen your home and signed a contract to buy it, but you shouldn't wait until then to start talking with a lender. Any reputable mortgage lender will be happy to help you look for a home—determining what you can afford, helping steer you to special mortgages for first-time home buyers, and perhaps making suggestions to help get the best mortgage for you. When it comes time to actually apply for a mortgage, you'll already have a good relationship with a lender.

How do I choose a mortgage lender?

When most people think about choosing a mortgage lender, they think only about finding the lowest rate. Financial considerations are important to every home buyer, and you certainly should consider the different rates lenders in your area offer on comparable loans. But you also want a lender you can trust, and someone you can work with effectively. So don't let rates be your only criterion. Here are some suggestions:

- *Build a list of lenders.* Talk to people you know who have bought or refinanced a home recently. Check the newspaper's real estate or business section, or look in the Yellow Pages under "Mortgages."

- *Talk to loan officers.* Call or visit the lenders on your list. Get a feel for what it will be like to work with them, and how they approach your needs. If you're still uncertain, ask for references—recent home buyers like yourself—and talk to them.

• *Compare rates, fees, and other costs for loans—not just rates.* Use the mortgage calculators that come with personal finance software to compare mortgages fairly.

What is a *mortgage broker?* Should I use one?

A mortgage broker is a person who represents multiple lenders—a good analogy is to a travel agent, who represents more than one airline. A bank's mortgage officer will tell you only about the mortgages offered by his/her bank, for better or for worse. A mortgage broker tells you what deals multiple lenders will offer you, but collects a fee for his/her service. It's usually worth your time to hire a mortgage broker if the shopping time they'll save you is worth the fee they charge.

What kinds of mortgages are there?

There are two basic kinds of mortgages: *fixed-* and *adjustable-rate.*

• *Fixed-rate mortgages:* With this type of mortgage, your monthly payments for interest and principal never change. Property taxes and homeowner's insurance premiums may increase, but generally your monthly payments will be stable. Fixed-rate mortgages are available for 30, 20, 15, and 10 years.

• *Adjustable-rate mortgages (ARMs):* These loans generally begin with an interest rate that is 2 to 3 percent below a comparable fixed-rate mortgage, and could allow you to buy a more expensive home. However, the interest rate changes at specified intervals (say, every year) depending upon changing market conditions; if interest rates go up, your monthly mortgage payment will go up too. If rates go down, your mortgage payment will drop.

There are also mortgages that combine aspects of fixed- and adjustable-rate mortgages—starting at a low fixed-rate for seven to ten years, for example, then adjusting to market conditions. "Bi-weekly" mortgages shorten the loan period by calling for half the monthly payment every two weeks. (Since there are 52 weeks in a year, you make 26 payments, or 13 "months" worth every year.) Ask your mortgage lender about these and other special kinds of mortgages that fit your needs.

How do I know which type of mortgage is best for me?

The right type of mortgage for you depends on many factors, including:

• your financial picture
• how you expect your finances to change
• how long you intend to keep your house
• how comfortable you are with your mortgage payment changing from time to time

For example, a 15-year fixed-rate mortgage can save you thousands of dollars in interest in comparison to a 30-year mortgage, but your monthly payments will be much higher. An adjustable-rate mortgage may get you started with a lower monthly payment than a fixed-rate mortgage, but your payments could get higher when the interest rate changes.

The best way to find the "right" answer is to discuss your finances, your plans and financial prospects, and your preferences frankly with a mortgage lender.

What are *points* and *closing costs?*

Points, sometimes called *discount points,* are paid at the closing of the mortgage deal. For each point you pay (a point is equal to 1 percent of the mortgage amount), your interest rate is reduced incrementally. Generally, you don't want to pay more than half a point.

Closing costs are fees paid to a third party that arranges the mortgage closing. These fees can't be avoided—even so-called zero closing cost mortgages. In such deals, the closing costs are hidden in higher interest rates. Just pay the closing costs in cash at closing and be done with them.

Do they really need to know everything about me for the mortgage application?

It may seem that way, but actually all your mortgage lender needs to know about you is the nature of your employment and your financial condition, in addition to information about the home you want to buy. Lenders need many details about these issues, though, so be prepared with tax documents, paycheck stubs, and other financial information.

How much will my credit history affect my ability to get a mortgage?

Less than you think, probably. Still, it's a good idea to get a copy of your credit report to review before you apply for your mortgage. That way, if there are any errors, you can take steps to correct them before you make your application.

If you have had credit problems, be prepared to discuss them honestly with your mortgage lender, and come to your application meeting with a written explanation. Responsible mortgage lenders know there can be legitimate reasons for credit problems, such as unemployment and illness. If you had a problem that's been corrected, and your payments have been on time for a year or more, your credit will probably be considered satisfactory for the mortgage.

What happens after I've applied for a mortgage, and how long will it take?

Your lender will begin the work of verifying all the information you've provided. This process can take anywhere from one to six weeks, depending on the type of mortgage you choose, whether you're buying a home outside your local community, and other factors.

Within three business days after your application, the lender must give you an estimate of your closing costs. (The closing is the actual settlement of your loan.) You'll also get a statement that shows your estimated monthly payment, the cost of your finance charges, and other facts about your mortgage.

Some home buyers find the closing process to be one of the most intimidating aspects of buying a home because it's so unfamiliar. Ask your mortgage lender what to expect at your closing.

How much will I need for the down payment?

It varies. Generally, your down payment can be anywhere from 3 to 20 percent of the home's value. Down payments can be lower for first-time buyers. Some military veterans and those in active military service can obtain loans with no down payment at all. The larger your down payment, the less interest you'll be charged over the life of the mortgage. Save up to make the largest possible down payment.

What does my mortgage payment include?

For most homeowners, the monthly mortgage payments include three separate parts: a payment on the principal of the loan (that is, the amount borrowed); a payment on the interest; and payments into a special account (called an *escrow* account) that your lender maintains to pay for things like hazard insurance and property taxes. You can remember the components of your payment with the mnemonic "PITI," which stands for Principal, Interest, Taxes, and Insurance.

If I can, should I make larger payments than I have to?

Under most mortgage agreements, yes. Usually, any money you pay to your mortgage lender in addition to the required payment goes toward reducing the principal of your loan, thereby reducing the amount of interest you pay on it. Check your particular mortgage to be sure.

Source: Mike Schlerf, Mortgage Bankers Association of America; Mike Schlerf@mbaa.org.

Mutual Funds

What is a *mutual fund*?

Mutual funds enable small-time investors—that is, most of us—to invest our money more wisely than we could by buying individual stocks, bonds, or other investments. Here's how they work.

Ideally, the investments of a person or organization are diversified—that is, they're spread around among various stocks, various bonds, and cash to protect against volatility in each kind of investment. An investor might own shares of several big companies, some small companies, a few tax-protected municipal bonds, a handful of corporate bonds, and some U.S. dollars.

This method is dandy if you have lots of money to invest. Considering that you usually have to buy stocks in lots of 100 and bonds in lots of 10, the cost of amassing a diversified investment portfolio can be enormous. Owning just

100 shares of each of ten stocks that cost $20 per share comes to $20,000—and that's before you take brokers' commissions into account.

Mutual funds come to the rescue of people who want to invest, but who don't have that kind of money. They enable you to buy into a diversified portfolio of investments with relatively small amounts of money. Think of mutual funds as baskets containing many different securities. A single mutual fund might own shares in hundreds of companies in several different countries, as well as some bonds and some cash. Instead of buying into each security individually, you can just buy a share of the basket and enjoy the benefits of owning all the investments the basket contains. Further, you don't have to worry about picking the fund's investments yourself, since funds employ teams of expert managers who work full time managing your money.

What kinds of mutual funds exist?

There are funds for everyone. You can buy funds that invest only in particular kinds of companies, only in bonds, only in real estate securities, or only in commodities, like gold. You can buy aggressive funds with high risk and high potential reward, and you can buy more sedate funds that don't try for huge returns, but minimize risk. Some funds enable you to invest in foreign companies, while others try to provide their investors with a stream of income.

What kind of fund is right for me?

As with everything, it depends on your situation. If you're young and plan to leave your money in the fund for many years, your best bet is probably an aggressive fund, since any short-term declines in the value of stocks almost certainly will be overshadowed by a long-term upward trend. If you're retired and need income from your investments, then a bond fund more likely is right for you.

Your personality should play a big role in selecting a fund. If you have no stomach for volatility, do not choose an aggressive fund—you'd look in the paper the morning after some bad news in the biotech industry and faint! On the other hand, if you're willing to take some risks in exchange for the promise of larger returns (and that is the one ironclad rule of investing), don't put your money in a conservative bond fund. Something in between might be for you.

Ideally, you should diversify your mutual fund investments. Find two or more funds—preferably ones with different investment bases, such as one international fund and one U.S. stock fund—that you like, and divide your money among them.

How do I ascertain the value of a mutual fund?

The value of a fund is the total value of the assets—stocks, bonds, currencies or whatever—that it owns. Since people buy pieces (also called "shares") of funds, the total value of the fund's holdings is divided by the number of shares held by investors. The result of this division is called the net asset value (NAV) of the fund. Sometimes, the NAV is called the share price. A fund's NAV is calculated at the end of each business day and appears in newspapers and other information sources the next morning. You can think of the NAV as the equivalent of a stock price—when you sell at a higher NAV than you bought, you make money; when you sell at a lower NAV than you bought, you lose money.

The NAV is the figure to watch when you own or are researching a fund. Let's say you invest $500 in a fund whose NAV is $15.73. You own 31.786 shares of the fund (unlike stocks, it's okay to own a fraction of a share of a mutual fund). Then, over time, the assets of the mutual fund increase in value until the NAV is $18.50. You can sell your 31.786 shares at $18.50 each—a total of $588.04. How do I spot a good fund? "Good" means different things to different people. The first question to ask when you're shopping for a mutual fund is one we covered earlier—Which kind of fund is right for me? Once you've decided what kind of fund you want, based on your investment goals and time constraints, you can hunt for the best fund in that category. A good way to start is by getting a comprehensive mutual fund report from an independent source. The *Wall Street Journal* publishes a special funds roundup section every quarter, and personal finance magazines like *Kiplinger's* and *Worth* regularly publish such reports, too. A company called Morningstar publishes a directory of mutual funds that rates each fund like a movie—with one to five stars. Look in your public library for recent issues of these publications.

Mutual fund reports typically give investment return figures for each of several time periods, usually one year, two years, five years, and the entire life of the fund. Compare how various funds have performed over time. Has one fund consistently outperformed other, similar funds in the long haul? If so, that may be your fund.

Once you've narrowed the field to three or four funds, contact them—their phone numbers should be in the report—and ask for investor's kits. These will contain more information, including information about fees. Call back and ask specific questions if you're unclear about anything.

What are the risks of investing in mutual funds?

The risk is the possibility that you will lose some of the money you invest. It's hard to lose *all* the money you invest in a fund, the way you can if you invest in the stock of a company that goes bankrupt—it's never happened before.

The likelihood that you will lose the money you invest in a particular fund is a function of several factors, including the kinds of securities the fund invests in and the skill of the people managing the fund. Generally, funds that invest in the stocks of large, established companies are less likely to lose significant percentages of their value than those that hold the stocks of small companies, and high-quality bond funds are safer investments than stock funds of any kind.

What is an acceptable risk? That's a matter of personal taste, but a good rule to follow is never to invest more money than you can afford to lose. Always be prepared for the worst—securities values are quite volatile.

How do I invest in a mutual fund?

You can buy funds through stockbrokers, but frequently you'll have to pay them a commission for their services. You can save brokers' commissions by investing directly in funds, without a middleman. Once you've decided which funds you think will best meet your needs, use the forms and envelopes that came with the investor's kit to send checks to each of the funds you want to invest in. The fund companies will set up accounts for you and send you a statement confirming that you've purchased shares. If you later decide you want to cash out of a fund, call the fund company and explain what you want to do. You'll get a check from the fund company in a few days.

What are "load" and "no-load" mutual funds?

Some mutual funds, mainly those sold through stockbrokers, take a percentage of the money you invest and give it to the selling broker as payment. This percentage is called a "load." Funds that collect loads—and they're in the minority—are called load mutual funds. Logically, funds that collect no loads are called "no-load" mutual funds.

Different load funds collect their loads at different times. Some take their percentages when you invest money—these are front-end load funds. Others collect when you cash out of a fund—these are back-end load funds.

What do loads mean? In general, they mean you should think twice before investing in the funds that charge them. There are so many good no-load funds out there that you should be able to find a fund that meets your investment needs without taking away part of your money.

Can I make a mutual fund part of my individual retirement account (IRA)?

Certainly. Many people designate money invested in mutual funds as all or part of their IRAs. To designate the money you've invested in a fund as part of your IRA, tell your fund company what you want. They'll send you appropriate paperwork.

Many funds charge IRA account holders a small amount—typically $10—each year to cover the costs of administrating your account and mailing statements to you. These custodial fees aren't large, and you should pay them without complaint. Many fund companies waive their custodial fees when you have a certain amount of money, say $10,000 or more, in your IRA.

Source: Wasatch Advisors, manager of the Wasatch Funds family, provided expert consultation for this FAQ. Contact Jeff Cardon at (801) 533-0777.

Paying for College

I don't think I can afford the college I want to attend. Should I apply to a cheaper school?

Yes, but don't let that keep you from applying to your first preference, too. There are literally hundreds of sources of financial aid for college students. With federal grants and guaranteed student loans, academic and athletic scholarships, grants from community or professional organizations, and the resources of the colleges themselves, there is no reason you cannot attend the college of your choice.

Who gives out financial aid for college?

The federal government administers a large percentage of the aid given to students, through a number of programs. Colleges and universities operate financial aid offices that give advice and often distribute their own funds to students who demonstrate need. State governments offer aid programs to supplement the federal programs; private sources, such as labor unions, companies, foundations, religious organizations, civic groups, and even individual donors, provide additional support for students.

What type of aid does the federal government give?

The U.S. Department of Education distributes Federal Pell Grants, Work Study Grants, Supplemental Educational Opportunity Grants (FSEOG), and a variety of low-interest loan programs. Pell Grants and FSEOGs are direct aid that you will not have to pay back. Work Study programs provide part-time jobs to help pay for your expenses. Loans, naturally, have to be paid back; however, they are deferred until you complete your studies.

Which type should I apply for?

Fortunately, you can apply for all of these programs by filling out one application. The Free Application for Federal Student Aid is available at nearly all colleges and universities, or can be obtained by calling (800) 4-FED-AID. You must complete the application and return it between January 1st of the school year you are beginning to study, and June 30 of the following year. For example, to apply for federal aid for the 1998–99 school year, you must send the application between January 1, 1998, and June 30, 1999.

For obvious reasons, it is highly recommended that you apply as early as possible; sources tend to get used up over time, and it certainly makes sense to have your finances in order before the school year starts. Also, most individual schools set earlier deadlines for certain types of aid. Keep in mind that the application is somewhat complicated and requires some documentation; allow yourself a reasonable amount of time to work on it. If you are dependent on your parents, they will need to provide a substantial amount of information about their finances.

What happens after I apply?

About a month after your application is received, you will be sent a Student Aid Report that will tell you your "Expected Family Contribution." This figure will be used in determining your eligibility for aid. It will also tell you what types of federal aid you are eligible for, if any.

What do I do next?

You need to forward a copy of your Student Aid Report to the financial aid office of the school you want to attend. The school will use the report to determine how much you are capable of paying; they will then offer you a financial aid package, taking all of your resources and expenses into account. You should go through this process for all schools to which you have been accepted; you may find that one school is willing to give you a better deal by supplementing your federal or private aid with its own scholarship funds.

How is my need determined?

Your "financial need" is the difference between your entire cost of attendance (including room and board, tuition, fees, and expenses) and your expected family contribution, which is determined by a standard formula. The formula weighs many factors, including your income (or the income of your parents, if you are a dependent); the number of children in your family who are attending college; and your family's assets, including savings and investments. The school's Financial Aid Administrator determines the cost of attendance, and has the ability to adjust your financial need assessment based on the information you provide.

If I get a private scholarship or grant, does that affect my need?

Yes. Any additional source of aid you are expected to receive is considered when determining the cost of attendance.

What is a Stafford Loan?

A Stafford Loan is the major form of guaranteed student loan offered through the federal government. Subsidized Stafford Loans are awarded on the basis of need; the interest is subsidized by the government until repayment begins, which keeps payments lower. Unsubsidized loans are available to all students regardless of need; interest begins to accumulate from the time the loan is made. Many colleges participate in a direct loan program, which means that loan funds come to you directly from the government; other loan sources include banks and credit unions. Fees and interest rates on Stafford Loans are generally lower than the market rate.

What other types of loan can I get?

PLUS loans are federally subsidized loans available to some parents of college-age children. There are also loans that allow you to consolidate several loans under one interest rate and repayment schedule. Banks and credit unions offer private loans, of course; interest rates and fees tend to be higher, and these loans generally have to be secured with collateral.

When do I pay back my loans?

After you graduate, quit school, or drop below half-time enrollment, you will have a six-month grace period before you begin repayment. Repayment schedules and options vary, depending on the loan type.

What if I can't make the payments?

Under certain circumstances of financial hardship, you may be able to defer repayment of your loans, or at least reduce the payments. Some possible reasons for deferment, or "forbearance," include poor health or family emergencies; serving in a medical internship or residency; unanticipated personal problems; or having federal loan payments that are greater than 20 percent of your income. These deferments are not automatic and must be applied for through the lender or agency that holds your loan.

What other sources should I check out?

Contact the financial aid office at the school you want to attend, for information about scholarships or additional resources. The state higher education agency in your home state can provide you with information about state aid. Your employer or labor union (or your parents) may offer aid programs or one-time scholarships. If you have a particular field of interest, check with organizations connected with that field. Finally, high school guidance departments are expert sources of information on scholarships from local institutions and benefactors.

Source: *The Student Guide,* a guide to student financial aid from the U.S. Department of Education, Federal Student Aid Information Center, P.O. Box 84, Washington, DC 20011-0084.

Personal Investment

What is a financial planner?

The title "financial planner" is not a legally defined term. It is used by individuals in a variety of professions, including accountants, bankers, stockbrokers, insurance agents, and others. Generally, a financial planner is meant to be someone who provides comprehensive financial advice, coordinating all aspects of your finances with your personal needs. A financial planner would typically be expected to advise you on investments, employee benefits, savings for college or retirement, insurance, and tax matters.

Do I need one?

Not everyone needs a financial planner, but whether you have one or not, it is highly advisable to educate yourself and keep up to date about financial matters. By reading advisory publications or taking classes you can certainly gather enough information to take care of your own financial planning. If you lack confidence in this area, or prefer not to spend too much time researching, a financial planner could be helpful to you. Keep in mind, though, that you must be aware of the general state of your finances in order to make good use of the planner's recommendations.

You should consider hiring a financial planner only if you have some discretionary, or extra, income that you want to invest. Before spending in this manner, you should first take care of your basic needs, such as housing, pension plans, and insurance. If these needs are not being met, you should concentrate on making a basic long-term financial plan rather than on hiring a planner.

Take stock of everything you own and everything you owe; consider what your income is now, and what it will be later on; and think hard about what is important to you financially. This will help you to get a better idea of the current state of your finances, and of the task ahead if you want to realize your goals. Working out a basic strategy is something a good financial planner would have you do on your own as a first step, so it makes sense to do it before thinking about hiring one.

How can I find a good financial planner?

Since the profession is not regulated, almost anyone can call themselves a financial planner; this does not necessarily mean they have the training to give you the comprehensive advice you are seeking. Check credentials carefully, and ask for references from other clients. Look for someone who has a wide variety of experiences and training rather than a narrow focus on one aspect of finance. Though most planners are trustworthy and legitimate, people associated with fraudulent investment schemes have at times passed themselves off as financial planners. Remember, financial planners are likely to earn all or part of their income from commissions on the products that they sell. This should indicate caution on your part; know your finances well, so that you can weigh any investment decisions carefully before acting. Most financial planners are quite responsible, but they still may be in the position of having to sell you a product in order to make their profit. In the end, only you can decide what is best for your interests. As always, be very wary of anyone who promises an easy profit or a get-rich-quick scheme. Careful financial planning in the long term is the only way to provide yourself with security.

Are there any professional certifications that I should look for in a financial planner?

The National Association of Certified Financial Planners and the Institute of Certified Financial Planners are among the organizations that represent those financial planners who have taken courses and passed a certification test. Bear in mind that certification from these or any organizations does not guarantee that someone is a wise financial planner; it simply means that she has demonstrated a certain depth of knowledge and training.

What is a "Registered Investment Adviser"?

These are individuals who advise investors for a fee, and who are registered as such with the Securities and Exchange Commission (SEC). The title does not imply any particular knowledge or training, but it does mean that the SEC has information on the person's background on file. A financial planner may or may not have this classification.

What will a good financial planner do for me?

She will help you to review all aspects of your finances, including tax returns, income statements, investments and assets held, and retirement or savings plans already in place. She will review your financial goals, while also taking into account the level of risk that you are prepared to accept, both financially and psychologically. The planner will then help you to create a timetable for accomplishing your goals in the most efficient way possible, including specific recommendations for investments and savings plans.

A good planner should be able to identify potential problem areas in your finances, such as high debt levels or insufficient funds for retirement. She should be willing to sign the written financial plan that you both develop, and to give you any help you need in putting it into action. Finally, she should agree to periodic reviews of the plan to assess the need for changes or adjustments.

What is an appropriate fee for a financial planner?

Financial planners may operate on a fee-only basis, or on commission, or a combination of the two. Fees vary, and commissions are not always disclosed, so it is sometimes difficult to determine how much you are paying your planner. Careful comparison shopping is the only reliable way to ensure that you are paying a fair price; this means considering not only the fees a planner charges but the services she offers, and the price of the products she sells.

I'm not sure that I'm comfortable with what my financial planner is telling me. Should I trust her as the expert?

No. Until you develop a trusting relationship with any adviser, you ought to proceed with caution. Beware of high-pressure sales techniques, and don't go ahead with any investment that you don't fully understand or feel comfortable with. You, after all, have the highest stake in what happens to your money.

Source: *Facts About Financial Planners,* American Association of Retired Persons, Consumer Affairs, Program Department, 1909 K Street, NW, Washington, DC 20049; (202) 728-4355.

Résumés

Do I need a résumé?

That depends on the job you are applying for. Typically, a résumé is necessary for those jobs that require substantial training and experience; this would include most professional, administrative, and technical positions. It is also a standard requirement for most clerical and secretarial work. Some employers may request a résumé for skilled jobs, such as building or culinary trades, and semiskilled jobs, such as security or assembly positions. Unskilled, quick turnover jobs, particularly those in the retail and food service industries, generally do not require résumés.

What are employers looking for in a résumé?

A résumé is meant to be scanned quickly, to give the employer a general idea of your qualifications and experience. It should "sell" the reader on your skills in the top half of the first page, because that may be all that is read. Your strongest skills and credentials should be listed either at the top of the résumé in a "Summary of Qualifications" or in the first job description. Company names and titles should be easy to pick out. It should look spare, clean, and professional, with plenty of space between sections. If possible, it should be kept to one page.

But I have so much experience that I want the employer to know about. How can I fit it all on one neat and legible page?

Remember that a résumé is a summary of your experience, meant to highlight your accomplishments; it is not an exhaustive autobiography. If you develop a great résumé, you will most likely have the chance to go into detail about yourself during the interview process.

What information should appear on my résumé?

It should contain a clear and succinct work history, detailing the last three to five positions, or the last ten years of employment. Devote the most space to your last position, and summarize earlier ones (unless you want to highlight something particularly relevant).

Is there a standard format that works best?

Research has shown that employers prefer the reverse chronological format, where your most recent job is listed first. Opening sections entitled "Summary of Qualifications," "Highlights," or "Executive Summary" are effective eye-catchers.

What about education?

If you have completed a college degree (or a training course specifically for the work desired) within the past five years, you may want to put that information first, particularly if your work experience is somewhat sparse. Otherwise, it follows your work history. There is no fixed rule of organization; emphasize your best and most relevant credentials.

What typeface and layout should I use?

Use simple, legible fonts, and arrange the information in a way that is pleasing to the eye. Center or justify all headings, and be consistent about the use of italics and boldface. Remember that your résumé may be the hundredth in the pile; you don't want to jangle the reader's nerves with loud, irritating typefaces. Understated professionalism usually wins out.

Should I use one standard résumé for all employers I contact?

Take the time to tailor your résumé for each potential employer. Do your best to match your qualifications with what the employer is seeking. Don't lie; emphasize. Your efforts will save you time in the long run.

I got fired from one of my previous jobs, and the circumstances were fairly bad. Should I put it on my résumé?

If the job constitutes only a small portion of your experience, leave it off. Calling attention to a poor relationship with a past employer is the last thing you want to do, regardless of who was at fault. If cutting it out means a huge gap, however, it may be time for some damage control. Contact the old employer; find out if they are giving a usable reference or a damaging one. If necessary, consider using a functional résumé.

What is a "functional résumé"?

A functional résumé emphasizes quality and variety of experience rather than chronology. It is useful for people just entering the workforce, and for those who have taken unusual career paths. If you have changed careers, are returning to work after a long period, or don't feel that your recent work experiences represent you at your best, a functional résumé may be the wisest choice. They are not the preferred form among employers, but can be effective if they contain specific, appropriate, and verifiable references. A good résumé guide will give several examples of creative functional résumés; choose one that works well for you.

I'm just out of college, like thousands of other job hunters. How can I create a résumé that stands out?

Include any work history or internships, no matter how humble they may seem. Employers recognize that a recent college graduate is going to be short on experience; don't try to fill out your résumé with irrelevant information. Highlight a few interesting activities, and keep it succinct.

How often do employers really check references?

Almost always. Resist the temptation to fabricate your credentials. Work with what you've got.

Source: *Tips for Finding the Right Job*, U.S. Department of Labor—Employment and Training Administration.

Selecting Stocks

I have some money I want to invest. Where should I begin?

The first step before investing in securities is to find a brokerage firm, or broker/dealer. Within the brokerage firm, you will likely be dealing with an individual stockbroker, who will help you manage your account. Before you make a decision about which broker to use, think about your financial objectives. Ask yourself why you want to invest and how much you are willing to risk. When you feel that you have a firm grasp on these questions, call around to several firms; ask the salespeople you talk to about their backgrounds, what sort of clientele they serve, and what they can do to help you accomplish your goals.

Keep in mind that not all brokerage firms are the same, and some may prey on inexperienced investors. Shop around, and ask for referrals from trusted friends or colleagues. If you have a question about the integrity of a particular firm, or if you simply want to check up on your firm before opening an account, the National Association of Securities Dealers operates a toll-free hotline at (800) 289-9999. This service can provide you with information about any past disciplinary actions that may have been taken against a firm.

What is the difference between a full service broker and a discount broker?

A discount brokerage firm provides only "execution" services; that is, it buys securities for you on the exchange, according to your instructions. A full service broker, in addition to the execution of your transactions, provides you with advice, research, and recommendations about what securities to invest in. Of course, a full service broker's commission rates and/or fees will tend to be higher.

What is a "new account agreement"?

Most brokerage firms will ask you, as an investor, to sign a contract that sets out the terms by which your investments will be carried out; this contract is known as a new account agreement. Typically, your broker will sit down with you to review your goals and objectives and your financial situation, in order to determine which type of account will best suit your needs. Be sure to carefully review this agreement before signing it, because the terms of it will affect your rights as an investor.

What initial decisions will I have to make about my account?

First, you will need to decide whether you or your broker will be making the final investment decisions for your account. Unless the contract specifically gives the broker "discretionary authority" to make such decisions, the final say rests with you. If you do decide to grant this authority to your broker, bear in mind that he is then authorized to invest as much of your account, at whatever price, in whatever security he sees fit; he need not even consult you. While this may be acceptable to some investors who prefer to stay out of the decision-making process, you should take the time to investigate the firm and the broker carefully before entering such an arrangement.

What is the difference between a *cash* account and a *margin* account?

A cash account, the type most commonly held by investors, requires cash payment up front for any security you purchase. A margin account allows you to buy on credit that is extended to you by the brokerage firm. Margin accounts come with certain caveats; for example, if the value of the securities in your portfolio should suddenly decline, the firm has the right to sell any of your stocks in order to make up the difference. If the total value of your portfolio dips below the total amount of credit that has been extended, you are immediately liable for the difference, which must be paid in cash. Buying securities on margin is a way of increasing risk, and it can bring about substantial gains and losses very quickly.

How do I choose a "risk level"?

Your new account agreement will specify the amount of risk that you are prepared to accept. Be sure you understand all the terms in this part of the agreement, and that the amount of risk you agree to is in line with your overall financial goals.

How can I investigate the recommendations my broker makes before making the decision to invest?

There are various information sources you can consult. Ask your broker to provide you with all available literature on the security he is recommending, including the prospectus and the most recent annual report of the company. Read this material carefully, and look for independent information from the vast array of periodicals devoted to business and investing. If you don't feel that you completely understand the security you are investing in, seek advice from an independent source, such as another firm or an experienced investor.

What risks should I be aware of?

All investments involve some element of risk; that is the nature of the game. Remember that investments that offer the potential of quick and substantial gains, such as futures, also contain an inherently higher risk. Some types of investments, such as government bonds, may penalize you for selling before the maturity date; be aware of all such penalties, and don't put yourself in a position where you have to sell these investments quickly.

Above all, remember that the securities markets are tremendously complicated. Your investments are not insured against loss, the way that your bank accounts are; don't risk more than you can afford to lose, and seek the advice of experienced investors and brokers.

What warning signs should I be on the alert for while investing?

Be very wary of any high-pressure, hard-sell tactics that you encounter from salespersons. Keep careful records of where your checks are sent to, and have confirmation documents mailed directly to you. Keep these documents in a safe place, as with all records pertaining to your investments; good bookkeeping is your best defense against fraud.

Indications that something might be wrong with an investment include: any advice based on so-called insider information; an inordinately high number of transactions in your account, resulting in excessive commissions; any investment that is presented as low in risk and high in potential gain; and guarantees that you will not lose money on a particular investment. The market does not work this way; as always, anything that sounds too good to be true almost certainly is.

Source: *Invest Wisely: Advice from Your Securities Industry Regulators,* U.S. Securities and Exchange Commission, Office of Consumer Affairs, 450 5th Street, NW, Washington, DC 20549; (202) 942-7040.

Starting a Business

Do I have what it takes to run my own small business?

Small businesses require a great deal of time, money, and skill. Before deciding to start a business of your own, you should ask yourself some important questions. How much time are you willing to invest? How much capital do you have available for start-up costs? What technical skills and experience do you bring to the table? Does your desire for financial independence and creative freedom outweigh your need for job security? Starting a new business also requires considerable research and planning; it can take months or years of effort before a profit is made, and there are no guarantees. You must decide whether the sacrifice is worthwhile.

What is the best business for me to choose?

When deciding what product or service to sell, consider both what you can do and what you enjoy doing. When you have settled on a product, identify the niche that your business will occupy. Is there a need for your product? How much competition will there be? What advantages will you have over your competition? What obstacles will you face?

What is a *business plan,* and why do I need one?

A business plan is a thorough written description of the business you plan to start and its goals. It should discuss the product or service your business will be offering, your marketing strategy, your sources of capital, and how the business will be operated on a daily basis. The plan should include a monthly operating budget for the first year, a discussion of how your accounting records will be maintained, and a projection of the return on your investment over the first two years. It should be as detailed as possible, including all of your research and anticipating potential problems. You need a business plan to focus your efforts and minimize mistakes in the crucial start-up period. And, a good business plan is essential if you need to attract investment or obtain financing.

What legal aspects do I have to consider?

First, you need to determine that you have a legal right to produce and market your product; that you are not, for example, impinging on someone else's copyright. Then you must establish your business legally; this you can do with the help of the local government of the city or county in which the business will be located. If you are establishing a sole proprietorship, or a business owned and operated exclusively by one person, the process will be relatively simple.

How much money do I need to get started?

The amount of cash you have on hand, and the amount of money you are able to borrow or raise, should be a determining factor in what business you choose. Your business plan should include a section that describes the financial management of your company: How much monthly expenditure will be needed, how much income can be expected, and what the initial investment will be. Start-up costs to consider include the rental of space, investment in market and product research, licensing fees, and purchase or rental of equipment.

How can I raise money to start my business?

One option is to raise capital through selling equity (a financial stake) in the company, either to a personal acquaintance (friends, family members, previous business contacts) or to a professional investor (a venture capitalist or a small business investment company). Another is to take out a personal loan from a bank, credit union, or savings and loan association. You will have to secure this type of loan by putting up real estate or other assets for collateral. Unless you have run a successful business before, it is unlikely that you will be able to obtain an unsecured business loan. The Small Business Administration, banks, and commercial finance companies all offer business loans with various terms and requirements. If you do not have sufficient personal assets to secure a loan, you could consider leasing necessary space and equipment in the short term.

What do I need to know about accounting?

Strict accounting records must be kept in all businesses, even the smallest. The IRS will provide you with guidelines on tax documentation and information on tax collection and payment rules. Good accounting is not only legally necessary but is essential in running the business smoothly and effectively. If you are not familiar with accounting procedures, consider hiring or contracting with someone who is.

What do I need to know about advertising?

That depends on the business you're in. Some businesses run largely on reputation or word of mouth, some on location and quality of service, and some depend heavily on advertising. If advertising is a large part of your marketing plan, contact an advertising consultant or agency to help you determine costs and strategies.

How do I set price levels?

The costs of research and development, raw materials, labor, and overhead (such as leasing the site of your business) constitute only the production costs: that is, the total expense of making the product. In order to turn a profit, you will need to calculate the costs of marketing and distributing the product, and price accordingly. These costs include advertising budgets, paying any sales or marketing staff, and transportation costs. You will not be able to calculate the exact total cost of your product or service, but you must be as accurate as possible in order to maintain enough profit to keep your business going.

Another consideration is that your prices must keep pace with your competition. You must offer your customer either superior quality or a lower price in order to gain an advantage. Balancing the need for competitive prices against the need for a sufficient profit margin is the key to successful pricing.

What legal responsibilities do I have toward my employees?

There is a huge amount of legislation regarding the rights of employees, and you are responsible for complying with all laws and regulations. Employment law varies from state to state, but some standards are set by the federal government. These include a minimum wage, workplace safety standards, limits on child labor, unemployment compensation taxes, overtime regulations, and antidiscrimination measures. If you plan to hire employees, you should request a complete set of guidelines from your local, state, and federal governments to ensure your compliance with all regulations; failure to do so could lead to disaster.

Where can I go for help?

The Small Business Administration offers free counseling and resources in offices around the United States. Their answer desk can be reached at (800) 827-5722. Most states have economic development agencies that are excellent sources for information on markets, business opportunities, and local assistance programs. Other useful resources include schools, libraries, business periodicals, local chambers of commerce, and banks.

Source: *How to Start a Small Business,* U.S. Small Business Administration, Office of Business Development, 409 3rd Street NW, Washington, DC 20416. Thirty-one most asked questions provided by the help desk of the Small Business Administration; (800) 827-5722.

The Stock Market

What is the difference between a *stock* and a *bond*?

A stock, or "share," is an ownership interest in a company; in other words, a small piece of the company. A bond is a certificate attesting to a debt that is owed to the holder by a firm or institution, which is to be paid back with interest over a specific time period. The term "stock market" is broadly used to describe the securities markets, in which a wide range of investment instruments are traded; these include stocks, bonds, mutual funds, and options. The best-known securities market in the United States is the New York Stock Exchange; however, there is a network of similar exchanges located in cities around the country.

What is Wall Street?

Wall Street is the main street of New York City's financial district in lower Manhattan. A large portion of the country's important financial institutions are located on or near the street.

What is an "over-the-counter" stock?

Over-the-counter stocks are not traded on an exchange; instead, they are traded over the telephone through a network of dealers and brokers. The National Association of Securities Dealers operates an "automated quotation system" known as NASDAQ, which functions as an online system for organizing and tracking over-the-counter transactions.

Who are those people on the floor of the stock exchange, and why are they yelling?

They are *floor traders,* and their actions determine stock prices. Some of the traders represent investment companies or other financial institutions; others are buying and selling on behalf of brokerage firms, who in turn represent individual investors. To maintain the smooth operation of the market, certain traders are employed as specialists; when it is practical, they are expected to step in as short-term buyers and sellers if the number of buyers and sellers do not balance. The rest of the exchange is populated by various functionaries, regulators, observers, and clerks.

What appears to be chaos and yelling on the trading floor is simply the settling of prices by a system that operates somewhat like an auction. Investors communicate their needs to traders on the floor, who hash out prices through a bidding system. Quotations, or "quotes," which are the going prices for particular stocks at a given time, are communicated to various reporting companies, who transmit with great speed to businesses and media outlets all over the country. During high-volume trading, the signaling and bidding can become quite frenzied.

Is the government involved in the stock exchange?

Yes. All types of securities trading are overseen by the SEC, which is a federal regulatory agency. The SEC monitors trading practices, sets rules and standards, and mediates disputes.

What are the stock figures that are listed every day in the newspaper?

Newspapers generally print stock quotations as they stood at the close of trading on the previous day. They are meant to be an estimate of the value of a particular stock, and of its performance on the market that day.

What is the Dow Jones?

The Dow Jones Industrial Average is a stock index that is meant to be a rough indicator of how the market is performing. An index is a survey of the performance of certain securities that are reliable "key indicators" of the general direction of the market. The Dow Jones is the most widely reported index.

What does a stockbroker do?

A stockbroker, or a brokerage firm, acts as an intermediary between the individual investor and the floor trader. For a fee or commission, a broker will instruct a trader to complete any transactions requested by his/her client. In addition, brokers often give investment advice to their clients or help them manage their accounts.

Do I need one to invest in the market?

Yes, for all practical purposes. That's the way the system works; you won't be allowed to stroll out onto the floor of the exchange and start trading. If you want to play the market on your own, there are so-called discount brokerage firms that offer no-frills service at a reduced commission; be sure, though, that you understand the basic principles of investment before taking the plunge.

What is the difference between a *money market* fund and a *mutual* fund?

A mutual fund is an array of stocks that is purchased by a group of investors and managed by an investment company. A money market fund is a type of mutual fund that typically invests in low-risk "short-term debt instruments," such as government bonds and bank certificates of deposit.

What is a *dividend*?

A dividend is a payment from a company to its shareholders, usually representing a share of the profits. Dividends are paid on a quarterly or yearly basis. Not all stocks pay dividends.

Why is it that when the stock market figures are reported on television, there is always the sound of a bell in the background?

That sound represents the closing bell on the New York Stock Exchange, which rings at the end of each day's trading.

Source: *What Every Investor Should Know,* a handbook from the U.S. Securities and Exchange Commission, Office of Public Affairs, 450 5th Street NW, Washington, DC 20549; (202) 942-7040.

The Fed

What is "the Fed"?

The Federal Reserve, or "the Fed," as it is often called, is the central bank of the United States. The Federal Reserve System is composed of twelve regional Reserve Banks, the Board of Governors in Washington, the Federal Open Market Committee, the Federal Advisory Council, and the Consumer Advisory Council. The current system was begun in 1913.

What is the main purpose of the Federal Reserve System?

The Federal Reserve regulates the money supply of the nation. It puts currency into circulation, formulates the government's monetary policy, supervises and regulates the banking industry, and provides banking services to the federal government and to commercial banks. The twelve regional banks oversee banks in their districts, issue currency, and process government financial instruments such as bonds, food stamps, and Treasury Notes. They examine member banks on a regular basis to ensure their financial soundness.

I hear a lot about the chairman of the Federal Reserve. What is his job?

The chairman is the head of the Board of Governors of the Federal Reserve, which is located in Washington. The Board of Governors supervises the regional Reserve banks and is responsible for setting the country's monetary policy. The board has seven members, who are appointed by the U.S. president with the consent of the Senate. Each member receives a 14-year term; every four years, one of the members is elected chairman.

The chairman is a rather high-profile figure in Washington, because he is influential in policy matters and because he often speaks for the board. Federal Reserve policy has a significant effect on the national economy. In recent years, much attention has been paid to the Fed's use of interest rates to balance the need for economic growth against the fear of inflation. Adjustments in interest rates directly affect the securities markets; for this reason, public statements by the chairman of the Fed often receive extensive media coverage.

Does the president have control over the Fed?

Not directly. One of the important features of the Fed is that it operates independently of the other branches of the government. Though the President and the Senate have control over the nomination process for the Board of Governors, they have little power over sitting members. However, the board often seeks the counsel of the president, and is expected to explain its actions to the Congress.

What does the Fed have to do with interest rates?

One of the tasks of the Federal Reserve System is to provide liquidity in the banking system; a major method of accomplishing this is to provide member banks with credit at a discounted rate, so that they may in turn lend the money to their clients. Naturally, the discount rate at which the Fed lends to its member banks directly affects the interest rates the banks charge. Raising or lowering this rate influences not only interest rates but the supply of money in the economy.

What do interest rates have to do with controlling inflation?

To simplify a rather complex set of circumstances: Low interest rates encourage businesses to expand by taking out loans; they encourage consumers to buy expensive things (like houses or cars) that require loans; the result is the stimulation and growth of the economy. The flip side: Low interest rates mean that the Fed has increased the money supply; according to the laws of supply and demand, this means that the value of a dollar is lower because it is easier to come by; as the value of a dollar decreases, prices must increase to compensate. This is what is meant by inflation.

The Fed can also regulate the money supply and implement its policies by buying and selling government bonds and other securities in the open market. When it wishes to encourage the expansion of credit in the economy, it buys securities. Federal Reserve checks are paid to securities dealers, who deposit them with member banks; in turn, the member banks redeposit the checks with the Fed, which expands their line of credit. When the Fed wishes to encourage the contraction of credit, it sells securities; this causes checks to be drawn on member banks by dealers, depleting their available lending funds. These transactions are carried out by the Federal Reserve Bank of New York, under the supervision of the Federal Open Market Committee.

Are all banks members of the Federal Reserve System?

All national banks—those banks that are chartered by the federal government—must be members by law. Banks chartered by state governments may also become members if they meet certain standards.

Does the Fed insure all money that is deposited in banks against bank failure?

The Federal Deposit Insurance Corporation, which was formed in response to the bank failures of the twenties and thirties, insures all funds deposited into eligible banks by individuals up to $100,000. All member banks of the Federal Reserve are covered by the FDIC, as are most state-chartered nonmember banks. Banks often display the FDIC seal prominently in their public spaces as a symbol of stability and reliability.

I've heard that all paper currency issued by the U.S. government must be "backed up" by gold or silver. Where do they keep all of it?

U.S. currency is no longer tied to a gold or silver standard; this is one reason that the Fed is so important. The paper currency has no intrinsic value; its value comes from the secure knowledge that the Fed will release only a certain amount of it into circulation. That is not to say, however, that the government does not hold reserves of precious metals. In fact, the gold reserves of the central banks and financial institutions of many countries are held in the gold vault of the New York Fed, 80 feet deep in the bedrock below the streets of Manhattan.

Source: *The New York Fed: Who We Are and What We Do*, Federal Reserve Bank of New York, 33 Liberty Street, New York, NY 10045.

Unemployment Insurance

What is *unemployment insurance?*

Unemployment insurance, or unemployment compensation, is temporary income that is distributed by state governments to eligible workers who have become unemployed through no fault of their own. It is designed as a temporary safety net to hold displaced workers over while they search for new jobs. The revenue for unemployment benefits comes from a payroll tax on employers; most states do not take deductions from workers' paychecks for this purpose.

Am I covered?

Since the programs are operated by state governments, the eligibility requirements vary from state to state. In general, most workers are covered. However, many states have rules that exclude certain categories of employment from coverage. Some common examples include: employees of religious organizations; real estate brokers (and others working on commission only); people working as consultants or independent contractors; and workers employed in publicly administered training programs. Contact the employment department of your state government for rules.

How do I know if I am eligible to collect unemployment compensation?

Generally, you are eligible if you have become unemployed through no fault of your own (through a layoff, for example), and if you are actively seeking full-time employment. The amount of money you have earned during a specific "base" period is also considered, both in determining eligibility and in calculating benefits.

If I quit my job, does that mean I cannot collect benefits?

You are not likely to qualify if you left your job voluntarily without good cause. "Good cause," though, can mean different things in different states. If you feel as though you were forced to resign your job, or that your work environment was intolerable, or that you left your job due to circumstances beyond your control, it might be worthwhile to file a claim.

I was fired from my job. Am I eligible to collect benefits?

That probably depends on why you were fired. Most states have rules which disqualify you from receiving benefits if you were fired for "deliberate misconduct" or violation of company rules or standards. The best way to find out is to contact a help desk or information line run by your local unemployment office; describe the circumstances of your dismissal, and they will advise you if it is worthwhile to file a claim.

What if my claim is denied?

Most states provide you (as well as your employer) the opportunity to appeal a decision on a claim. Before putting time and effort into an appeal, however, it would be wise to find out exactly why the claim was denied. If you feel that you are qualified by law to collect benefits and that they have been unfairly denied, ask your case worker how you can file an appeal.

I have qualified for benefits. What do I have to do to remain eligible?

All states require that you document your job search. This could involve filling out forms describing what employers you contacted over a period of time, or meeting with an employment counselor, or making use of other job search services. Also, you must not decline any suitable offer of work; here again, rules vary on what constitutes a suitable job offer.

Can I collect benefits while working?

When you return to work full time, you must stop collecting benefits. If you find part-time or temporary employment, it may be possible to continue collecting partial benefits while working, depending on how much you earn. All income must be reported while you are collecting benefits; not to do so would constitute fraud.

What if I want to move to a different state to look for a new job?

You may be allowed to continue collecting benefits from your old home state, as long as you continue to meet its eligibility requirements. Contact your local agency to ask about interstate claims. Benefit checks will not be forwarded to you by the Postal Service, even to a new address within the same state; be sure to notify your agency of any changes in address.

How are my benefits calculated?

Most states use formulas that are based on your earnings from the first four of the last five completed calendar quarters. This one-year period constitutes a "base" from which the amount of your benefits and the maximum number of weeks that you can collect is figured. In general, you can collect a weekly check for about half of your average weekly wages before deductions during the base period. However, state law will normally set a "maximum benefit amount" based on the average weekly wage in your state, which your benefits will not be allowed to exceed.

Is there a time limit on how long I can collect?

Yes. Normally you can collect "regular benefits" for 26 weeks, as long as you continue to meet your state's eligibility requirements. Some states provide for longer benefit periods. In some instances, the federal government will help to pay for an extended period of benefits in states where a threshold of prolonged high unemployment rates has been reached; however, this situation has been relatively rare since the 1980s.

Do I need to pay taxes on the money I have collected?

Yes. All unemployment compensation is considered taxable income, both at the state and the federal level. Be aware that taxes are often not deducted from your benefit checks the way they are from your wages; this could cause you to owe tax payments at the end of the year.

What about incumbent politicians who lose an election (and their jobs)? Are they allowed to collect benefits?

No. Most states have laws that prevent elected officials, and those who advise them in policy matters, from receiving unemployment benefits.

Source: Eldred Hill, National Foundation for Unemployment Compensation and Workers Compensation, 1201 New York Avenue NW, Suite 700, Washington, DC 20005; (202) 682-1517.

Working at Home

Has working at home become a more common practice with all of the recent advances in technology?

Yes. In 1995, more than 8 million Americans were estimated to have had their primary workplace at home. In addition, many more workers now utilize alternatives to the traditional commute to the centralized office; satellite offices, regional work centers, shared office space, and many other arrangements are part of a distinct trend away from long commutes.

What are the benefits of working at home?

Some companies that have participated in work-at-home programs have found that such arrangements seem to increase employee morale and productivity. Employees who work at home tend to have an easier time balancing family and personal needs with work pressures; they have more time, more scheduling flexibility, and fewer logistical problems to consider. The consequent reduction in stress can lead to better productivity and more job satisfaction. Nontraditional work arrangements have also helped employers keep valuable employees they might otherwise have lost because of changes in their personal lives, such as parenthood or relocation. Furthermore, companies and entrepreneurs can benefit by cutting down on overhead costs associated with maintaining large centralized offices.

There are also obvious advantages to the society at large when the number of long-distance commuters is reduced. Traffic congestion and air pollution—two major environmental problems associated with the widespread use of cars for commuting purposes—can be decreased as more workers are allowed to work from home. Public and private expenditures on such things as transportation, infrastructure, and child care can be curtailed, which benefits both the finances of families and the economy as a whole.

Are employers open to the idea of their employees working at home rather than in a controlled office setting?

More and more companies are becoming aware of the benefits of work-at-home programs. Studies indicate that many of those companies that have already participated in such programs are planning to expand them, and that more are planning to start programs in the near future. As competition increases and technology improves, businesses are increasingly willing to look at unconventional ways of increasing productivity; home offices are an important part of this trend.

There are still some negative perceptions about telecommuting in the corporate world. One of the most common concerns voiced by employers and managers has been the loss of direct supervision and control over the work environment. Because the work-at-home arrangement goes against many traditional assumptions about work and management, those seeking to implement such plans can expect a measure of resistance along the way.

What is meant by the term *telecommuting*?

Telecommuting is an umbrella term used to describe a wide range of alternative office strategies that seek to substitute communications technology for the geographical commute from home to office; in other words, to use the telephone, the Internet, the fax machine, and other devices to bring a team of workers in different areas together, rather than asking them all to travel to the same workplace every day. Telecommuters may perform their jobs from home offices, or from regional telecommuting centers nearby.

What is a *telecommuting center*?

A telecommuting center offers all the equipment and resources that a worker needs to perform a particular job, in a location that is more convenient than the central office of the employer. Space and equipment at these centers are shared by many employees. In some cases, an employee might work from home for most of the week, then spend a day or two at a telecommuting center when additional resources are needed; in others, a worker might work her entire schedule in a center only five minutes from her home.

What type of work lends itself to being done in a home office situation?

Jobs that are project-oriented, with clearly defined objectives, are well suited to the home office, because they tend to require less direct supervision. Naturally, careful consideration must be given to the resources that are necessary to perform certain tasks. How many of these resources are available only at the office? How much face-to-face contact is required, and how much can be accomplished through telephone, written, or electronic correspondence? These questions can help determine how much of your job could be performed from a home office.

Do I have the right personality to work at home successfully?

Those who are successful in home-based jobs tend to be very self-motivated, well-organized people who have the ability to manage their time well. Flexibility, excellent communications skills, and a strong knowledge of the job are also important. If you are contemplating the idea of working at home, you also might want to consider whether your home environment is conducive to getting work done. Perhaps the distractions you would face at home would offset any potential benefit.

What sort of equipment will I need to work from home?

The requirements vary with the job, of course, but a typical setup might include a computer, necessary software, a modem, a fax machine, a printer, and enough telephone capacity to run this equipment effectively. In some instances, an employer will provide all or some of this equipment for you; in others, you may have to buy it yourself. Hundreds of publications now devote themselves to office technology of all kinds, and some of these are specifically aimed at telecommuters and their needs. They can advise you on how to organize a home office, help you assess your equipment needs, and keep you abreast of new trends in technology.

I would like to work from home, but my job requires certain things that need to be done at the office. Can I work it out?

Consider a compromise. A large portion of telecommuters spend at least part of their work week in the office, attending to those aspects of their jobs that can only be accomplished in person. Try to work out a schedule that allows you to do as much of your work as possible from home, and you may find that you can cut your commuting down to one or two days a week.

Source: *Telecommute America: Discover a New Workplace,* Telecommute America, P.O. Box 9539, Scottsdale, AZ 85252-9536. Telecommute America is a joint national public awareness initiative founded with the participation of the U.S. Department of Commerce, the U.S. Department of Transportation, the U.S. Environmental Protection Agency, and the U.S. General Services Administration.

FAMILY HEALTH

—◇—

Birth Control • Blood Donation
Choosing a Doctor
Choosing a Hospital
Circumcision
Dental Hygiene • Eyeglasses
Hysterectomy
Infertility • Lamaze
Menopause
Pregnancy • Safer Sex
Vasectomy • Water Birth

Birth Control

What factors should I consider when choosing a birth control method?

Your contraceptive needs may change throughout your life. To decide which method to use now, consider how well each one will work for you. Questions to ask include: How well will it fit into my lifestyle? How effective, safe, affordable, and reversible will it be? Will it help prevent sexually transmitted diseases (STDs)? A wide range of contraceptive choices is available today: continuous abstinence, outercourse, sterilization, vasectomy, Norplant®, Depo-Provera®, IUD (intrauterine device), the Pill, the condom, diaphragm, cervical cap, withdrawal, over-the-counter methods for women, periodic abstinence, and fertility awareness.

I've known what abstinence is, but I've never heard the term "outercourse." What's the difference?

Continuous abstinence involves no sex play. Outercourse involves sex play without vaginal intercourse. Both methods will keep sperm from joining the egg. Continuous abstinence is 100 percent effective, and prevents sexually transmitted infections (STIs). The advantages are that there are no medical or hormonal side effects, and some religions endorse abstinence for unmarried people. Possible problems include the difficulty for many people to abstain from sex play for long periods, and that people often forget to protect themselves against pregnancy or STIs when they stop abstaining.

Outercourse is nearly 100 percent effective, but pregnancy is possible if semen or pre-ejaculate is spilled on the vulva. Outercourse is effective against HIV and other serious STIs, unless body fluids are exchanged through oral or anal intercourse. The advantages are that there are no medical or hormonal side effects, it can be used as safer sex if no body fluids are exchanged, and it may prolong sex play and enhance orgasm. But it may be difficult for many people to abstain from vaginal intercourse for long periods.

How do periodic abstinence or fertility awareness methods (FAMs) work?

A professional will teach you how to chart your menstrual cycle and to detect certain physical signs to help predict "unsafe" days. Abstain from intercourse (periodic abstinence) or use barrier contraceptives during the nine or more "unsafe" days. This includes: checking temperature daily, checking cervical mucus daily, and recording menstrual cycles on a calendar. These methods range from 80 to 99 percent in effectiveness. Periodic abstinence is not effective against STIs. There are no medical or hormonal side effects; calendars, thermometers, and charts are easy to get; and most religions accept periodic abstinence.

Possible problems for these methods are uncooperative partners, taking risks during "unsafe" days, and poor record keeping; illness and lack of sleep may also affect body temperature, vaginal infections and douches change mucus, and you cannot use these methods if you have irregular periods or temperature patterns.

Is withdrawal an effective means of birth control?

Withdrawal, when the man pulls his penis out of the vagina before he "comes" to keep the sperm from joining the egg, is effective 81 to 96 percent of the time. Pre-ejaculate can contain enough sperm to cause pregnancy, which is also possible if the semen or pre-ejaculate is spilled on the vulva. This method is not effective against STIs, but has the advantage that it can be used to prevent pregnancy when no other method is available. However, it requires great self-control, experience, and trust. It is not appropriate for men who are likely to have "premature" ejaculation, or who can't tell when they have to pull out. It is not recommended for sexually inexperienced men or for teens.

How effective is the condom?

The condom offers 88 to 98 percent effectiveness for birth control, and latex condoms are good and effective choices for protection against STIs, including HIV, the virus that can cause AIDS. This method involves covering the penis with a sheath before intercourse to keep sperm from joining the egg. The sheath may be made of thin latex, plastic, or animal tissue. There are things you can do to increase your birth control protection, such as lubricating condoms with spermicide to immobilize sperm.

Do not use oil-based lubricants like Vaseline on latex condoms. Use the condom correctly by putting a drop or two of a water-based lubricant, like K-Y jelly, in the tip of the condom. Place the rolled condom on the tip of the hard penis. Leave a ½ inch space at tip. Pull back the foreskin and roll the condom down over the penis. Smooth out any air bubbles. Lubricate generously to prevent breakage. Hold the condom against the penis to withdraw.

Condoms are easy to buy in drugstores, supermarkets, etc.; they can help relieve premature ejaculation, can be put on as part of sex play, and can be used with other methods to prevent STIs. Possible problems include allergies, loss of sensation, and breakage.

What products are available over the counter for women?

Currently, women can buy the vaginal pouch (female condom) or spermicides, which come in the form of contraceptive foam, cream, jelly, film, or suppository. Instructions for each of these methods are given in the packaging information. These methods are inserted deep into the vagina shortly before intercourse to keep sperm from joining the egg. Spermicides immobilize sperm. Follow the package instructions to remove a pouch; other methods dissolve in the vagina. The pouch is 79 to 95 percent effective, and contraceptive foams, creams, jellies, films, and suppositories range from 72 percent to 97 percent effective. The pouch provides some protection against STIs, including HIV. Use a condom with all other methods for STI protection.

Advantages for these methods: They are easy to buy in drugstores, supermarkets, etc.; insertion may be part of sex play; and an erection is unnecessary to keep the pouch in place. Possible problems are that they can be messy, people may be allergic, they may irritate the vagina or penis, the pouch may be difficult to insert, and the outer ring of the pouch may slip into the vagina during intercourse.

What's the difference between a diaphragm and a cervical cap?

The *diaphragm* is a shallow latex cup and the *cervical cap* a thimble-shaped latex cap. In both cases, your clinician with fit you and show you how to coat them with spermicide and put them in your vagina to keep the sperm from joining the egg. The diaphragm is 82 to 94 percent effective, and the cervical cap is 82 to 91 percent effective for women who have not had a child, and 64 to 74 percent effective for women who have. Neither is effective against STIs.

There are no major health concerns for either one, and these methods can last several years. Possible problems are that they can be messy; allergies may exist to latex or spermicide; and they cannot be used during vaginal bleeding or infection. With the diaphragm, there is increased risk of bladder infection. The cervical cap is difficult for some women to use, as it is sometimes hard to fit and only comes in four sizes.

How does an IUD work?

Your clinician will put a small plastic device in the uterus. The IUD (intrauterine device) contains copper or hormones that keep sperm from joining the egg and prevent a fertilized egg from implanting in the uterus. This method is 97.4 to 99.2 percent effective, but it is not effective against STIs. Advantages are, there is nothing to put in place before intercourse; copper IUDs may be left in place for up to 10 years; there is no daily pill; no effect on hormone levels in the body; and IUDs with hormones may reduce menstrual cramps and can be left in place for one year.

Problems may include an increase in cramps, spotting between periods, heavier and longer periods, and an increased chance of tubal infection (which may lead to sterility) for women with new partners, women with more than one sex partner, or women whose partners have other partners. Also, though rarely, the wall of the uterus may be punctured.

If I decide on the Pill, how do I know which kind of pill to choose and how do they differ?

Your clinician will prescribe the right Pill for you. Take one pill once a day. Complete one pill pack every month. Combination pills contain estrogen and progestin; mini-pills contain only progestin. Pills contain hormones that work in different ways. The combination pills prevent release of an egg. Both types thicken cervical mucus to keep sperm from joining the egg, and both types also may prevent a fertilized egg from implanting in the uterus. The Pill is 97 to 99.9 percent effective, but not effective against STIs.

What are the advantages and disadvantages with the Pill?

There is nothing to put in place before intercourse, periods are more regular, and there is less menstrual cramping, acne, iron deficiency anemia, and premenstrual tension. The Pill protects against ovarian and endometrial cancers, pelvic inflammatory disease, noncancerous breast tumors, and ovarian cysts, and there are fewer tubal pregnancies. Disadvantages are that it must be taken daily, and there are rare but serious health risks, including blood clots, heart attack, and stroke—women over 35 who smoke and those who are greatly over-weight are at greater risk. Side effects include temporary irregular bleeding, de-pression, nausea, and other discomforts.

I've heard a lot about two other long-term methods—Depo-Provera® and Norplant®. How do they differ?

For Norplant, your clinician will put six small capsules under the skin of your upper arm. Capsules constantly release small amounts of hormone that prevent release of the egg and thicken cervical mucus to keep sperm from joining the egg. Removal can be done at any time, though it must be done by a clinician.

Depo-Provera involves a hormone shot by your clinician in your arm or buttock every 12 weeks to prevent release of an egg, to thicken cervical mucus to keep sperm from joining the egg, and to prevent a fertilized egg from im-planting in the uterus. Norplant is 99.96 percent effective, and protects against pregnancy for five years. Depo-Provera is 99.7 percent effective, protecting against pregnancy for 12 weeks. Neither is effective against STIs.

What are the advantages and disadvantages of each?

The advantages for both are: no daily pill, nothing to put in place before inter-course, can be used while breastfeeding (six weeks after delivery), and can be used by some women who cannot take the Pill. Additionally, Depo-Provera pro-tects against cancer of the lining of the uterus, and iron deficiency anemia. Pos-sible problems for Norplant include side effects such as irregular bleeding, and other discomforts such as headaches, nausea, depression, nervousness, dizziness, and weight gain. Also, a medical procedure is needed for insertion and removal, which can cause possible scarring and (rarely) infection at the insertion site.

Depo-Provera's side effects include irregular bleeding and other discom-forts, such as weight gain, headaches, depression, and abdominal pain. These side effects cannot be reversed until the medication wears off, which is up to 12 weeks. Additionally, Depo-Provera may cause a delay in getting pregnant after shots are stopped.

What permanent methods of birth control are available?

Tubal sterilization, intended to permanently block a woman's tubes where sperm joins egg; and vasectomy, intended to permanently block a man's tubes that carry sperm. Each method involves an operation. Effectiveness ranges from 99.6 percent to 99.8 percent, but neither method is effective against STIs. The advantages of tubal sterilization are permanent protection against pregnancy, no lasting side effects, no effect on sexual pleasure, and protection to women whose health would be seriously threatened by pregnancy. Possible problems include mild bleeding or infection right after the operation, reaction to the sur-gical anesthesia, and the fact that some people later regret not being able to have children. Reversibility cannot be guaranteed, although occasionally tubes re-open, allowing pregnancy to occur. Pregnancies that do occur, however, are more likely to be in the tubes (ectopic). Tubal sterilization may involve bruising where the incision is made, and, very rarely, injury to blood vessels or bowel. Vasectomy can involve infection or blood clotting in or near the testicles, and temporary bruising, swelling, or tenderness of the scrotum; sperm leakage may form temporary small lumps near testicles.

What is "emergency contraception"?

Emergency contraception is designed to prevent pregnancy *after* unprotected vaginal intercourse, such as if the man's condom broke or slipped off and he ejaculated inside your vagina, or if you forgot to take your birth control pill. It is also called postcoital or "morning after" contraception. It is provided in two ways: emergency hormonal contraception (doses of birth control pills) within 72 hours of intercourse, or insertion of an IUD within five days of intercourse. It is for use if a woman is sure she is not already pregnant, as it prevents pregnancy by preventing fertilization or implantation. It will not cause an abortion. All of Planned Parenthood's 900 clinics nationwide can provide emergency contraception, or can make a referral.

Source: Planned Parenthood® Federation of America, Inc., the world's oldest and largest voluntary family planning organization. Adapted with permission from *Your Contraceptive Choices*, and other materials, © 1996 Planned Parenthood Federation of America, Inc. All rights reserved. To order the complete booklet, call (800) 669-0156. Check out the free materials at your nearest Planned Parenthood health center. To make an appointment at the Planned Parenthood health center nearest you, call (800) 230-PLAN.

Blood Donation

How long does blood donation take?

The procedure is done by a skilled, specially trained technician (called a *phlebotomist*) and takes seven to ten minutes. You will rest after donation, and be served refreshments. Plan to spend about an hour at the blood drive.

Does the needle hurt the entire time?

There is a little sting when the needle is inserted, but there is no pain during the donation.

How long will it take to replenish the pint?

Blood volume or plasma is replaced within 24 hours. Red cells need about four to eight weeks for complete replacement.

How will I feel after the donation?

Donors who know what to expect and have eaten regular meals before donating are usually fine. After donating, drink extra fluids for the next 24 hours.

Can a woman donate during her menstrual period?

Yes. If you're feeling well, there is no problem.

How soon after donating can I practice sports?

Just avoid heavy muscular or strenuous activity such as lifting, pushing, or picking up heavy objects for at least four or five hours after giving blood.

What happens to my blood after donating?

After donation, your blood will be tested for blood type, hepatitis, HIV (AIDS antibody), HALVE-1, and syphilis. Then it can be used either as whole blood for one patient or, after separation into components, to help several patients.

How often can I give blood?

You can give blood every 56 days (eight weeks) up to five times a year.

Is it true I can get AIDS if I give blood?

No. You cannot get AIDS or any other disease by giving blood. The materials, including the needle used for your donation, are new, sterile, disposable, and used only once, for your blood donation.

Are there any qualifications for an individual donating blood?

Anyone in good health between the ages of 17 and 75 may donate blood. Healthy individuals over 75 must have written permission from their physician dated within two weeks of their donation. Donors must weigh 110 pounds or more. There are some medical conditions that can temporarily or even permanently keep you from giving blood, such as low iron in the blood. People who may have been exposed to hepatitis or the AIDS virus are asked not to donate blood.

Source: New Jersey Blood Services, 167 New Street, New Brunswick, NJ 08901; (800) 403-7879.

Choosing a Doctor

What is the best way to find a new doctor?

Some of the easiest and best ways to find a new doctor include getting a recommendation from a previous doctor if you are moving to a new area, recommendations from friends, or hospital referral lines.

Do I need a primary-care physician rather than just a specialist?

Yes. A primary-care physician will be able to notice and diagnose a disease or illness that could develop gradually. There are other good reasons, including the fact that a primary-care physician will be better able to treat you as a "whole," can deal with preventive medicine, and can better steer you to a specialist—helping you to keep your costs down.

What should I consider in getting a primary-care doctor?

The doctor's professional preparation, including education, residency training, board certification, and fellowships; professional reputation; office and practice arrangement; professional (or "bedside") manner; and confidentiality are all points to consider.

Is it rude to interview a new doctor?

No. Some doctors may engage in brief interviews for a lower-than-standard or no fee; some prefer the telephone. Ask the staff what the doctor's credentials are, and about office hours and billing practices so you don't waste the doctor's time.

What are some questions I should ask?

You'll obviously have your own questions, but some routine ones might be: What is your experience in treating any particular illness or condition? Are you open to treatment and therapies that do not rely heavily on medication? What preventive program do you suggest for someone of my age, sex, and health status?

What is the best way to select a specialist?

Ask your primary-care doctor to find out about a specialist's training and experience. You might also want to ask if the specialist is someone your primary-care doctor would go to.

When should I get a second opinion?

Second opinions are best sought before major surgery, when the diagnosis is serious or life-threatening; if a rare disease is diagnosed; if you are uncomfortable with a prescribed diagnosis and treatment; if a course of treatment is not working; or if your insurance company requires it.

Is there any way to check if a doctor is *not* qualified?

There are two ways: You can call the appropriate state agency, or check the names in a book called *10,289 Questionable Doctors,* published by the Public Citizen's Health Research Group.

What do I do if my doctor has done something wrong?

Contact the appropriate local medical society in the county, or the state medical society. The state health department can be helpful on disciplinary actions.

Is it appropriate to discuss a living will with my doctor?

Yes, but go over it with an attorney as well.

Source: Adapted from *How to Find the Best Doctors, Hospitals, and HMOs for You and Your Family*, Castle Connolly Medical Ltd., 150 E. 58th Street (37th Floor), New York, NY 10126.

Choosing a Hospital

What is the difference between a community hospital and an academic or teaching hospital?

Community hospitals tend to be smaller, with between 50 and 300 beds, offering a full range of basic and advanced services as well as certain specialties. Community hospitals also tend to take care of the poor, more often than not. Academic hospitals are typically larger and always affiliated with a medical school; usually they have over 300 beds and more services, offering more sophisticated programs.

Do proprietary or for-profit hospitals provide worse care?

Most of these hospitals are owned by corporations, so they seek to generate a profit. Some people claim they cut corners, while these hospitals defend themselves by saying they serve patients more effectively. But quite often they do not provide programs deemed to be too expensive.

What are the advantages of a teaching hospital?

Teaching hospitals tend to have students and recently graduated students involved in patient care under the supervision of highly skilled teachers. They also tend to offer the most sophisticated services, have the latest equipment, and attract the top specialists. You should be warned that you may be prodded or probed by medical students.

What are "resident-run services"?

Attending doctors allow residents-in-training to supervise patient care without appropriate supervision. This is not recommended, since a doctor may not be providing proper attention to you but leaving it to the residents.

What happens if my doctor isn't allowed admitting privileges at the hospital I've chosen?

That is a choice you will have to make. If you choose a certain hospital, you will not be likely to have your own doctor if she is not affiliated with that institution.

What does "accreditation" mean?

Accreditation in more than 5,000 of the approximately 6,500 hospitals in the United States is done by the Joint Commission on Accreditation of Healthcare Organizations, a team of professionals that includes nurses and health-care administrators as well as doctors.

What are some of the things to look for in a hospital staff?

Call the hospital's community relations department for information and look for a 70 to 80 percent range of board-certified physicians; 75 percent or higher of nurses who are registered nurses (RNs); and the size of the residency department, showing the hospital's commitment to its teaching programs.

What are the advantages of outpatient care in choosing a hospital that may offer it?

Convenience, cost savings, and safety (from infections) are some of the advantages. More than two-thirds of U.S. hospitals offer outpatient surgery.

Is it possible to see a list of the medical staff at a hospital?

It is usually possible. This helps if you discover a large number of doctors from foreign universities, indicating perhaps a less selective board.

Is it possible to tour the hospital before you choose?

Yes, but ask the hospital public information office for permission. Notice whether the building is clean and in good repair, staff members are busy, the staff is helpful, and equipment is stored properly, not lying unprotected in hallways.

Source: Adapted from *How to Find the Best Doctors, Hospitals, and HMOs for You and Your Family,* Castle Connolly Medical Ltd., 150 E. 58th Street (37th Floor), New York, NY 10126.

Circumcision

What is *circumcision*?

Circumcision is the surgical removal (cutting off) of the fold of skin that normally covers and protects the *glans* (head) of the penis. This part of the penis, the prepuce, is more commonly known as the foreskin.

What is the purpose of the foreskin?

The foreskin has three known functions: protective, sensory, and sexual. During infancy, the foreskin is attached to the glans and protects it from urine, feces, and diaper abrasion. Throughout life, the foreskin keeps the glans soft and moist and protects it from trauma and injury. Without this protection, the glans becomes dry, callused, and desensitized from exposure and chafing. In adulthood, specialized nerve endings in the foreskin enhance sexual pleasure.

When and why did doctors start circumcising babies?

Circumcision began in the English-speaking countries during the mid-1800s supposedly to prevent masturbation, which was believed to cause many diseases. According to the American Academy of Pediatrics, circumcision prevents *phimosis* (inability to retract a fully differentiated foreskin), *paraphimosis* (edema of the prepuce and glans), *balanoposthitis* (inflammation of the glans and prepuce), and has been shown to decrease the incidence of cancer of the penis among American men. It may also result in a decreased incidence of urinary tract infection. However, the National Organization of Circumcision Information Resource Centers (NOCIRC) holds the position that circumcision is unnecessary because none of the reasons doctors give for circumcision has been proven.

Is circumcision painful?

According to NOCIRC, circumcision is extremely painful—and traumatic—for a baby. The doctors and nurses at NOCIRC argue that babies are as sensitive to pain as anyone else and scream frantically when their foreskins are cut off. The babies that don't cry are prevented from doing so because they are in a state of shock. They believe it is additionally inhumane because no pain medication is given after the surgery or during the week to ten days it takes the wound to heal. The Academy of American Pediatrics mentions anesthesia as a way to reduce the pain and stress of newborn circumcision, but cautions that experience with local anesthesia in newborn circumcision is limited, and the procedure is not without risk.

What are the risks of circumcision?

The Academy of American Pediatrics recommends circumcision as an elective procedure, to be performed only in healthy and stable infants. The exact incidence of postoperative complications is unknown, but studies indicate that the rate is low, approximately 0.2 to 0.6 percent. As with any surgery, circumcision has inherent risks, including hemorrhage, infection, surgical mishap, and although rare, even death. (The AAP's review of the literature for the past 25 years documented two deaths.) NOCIRC reports postsurgical problems such as extensive scars, skin bridges, missing hunks and slices, curvatures, tight and painful erections, bleeding at the scar site, and retarded orgasms due to lost sensitivity and impotence.

It is NOCIRC's position that all circumcised males lose some or most of the sensitivity in their glans and all of the sensitivity in their foreskin.

Does the foreskin need special hygiene?

The intact penis of an infant or child needs no special care. During the first years of life, the foreskin and glans are connected by a common membrane called the *synechia*. This connective tissue dissolves naturally sometime during the first 18 years of life in a process that should never be hurried. The first person to retract a child's foreskin should be the child himself. Once he makes this discovery, he can easily learn to care for himself. A simple explanation of "how to" may be helpful:

1. Gently slip the foreskin back.
2. Rinse the head of the penis and the inside fold of the foreskin with warm water.
3. Pull the foreskin forward, back in place over the glans.

If my son isn't circumcised, won't he be teased?

Parents may believe their child should be circumcised to look like Dad or older brothers, yet children can easily accept individual differences. As parents, we can help our children to feel good about their own bodies and to respect differences in one another. The circumcision rate in the United States is steadily decreasing, so parents will no longer need to worry that their sons might be teased for not being circumcised. In 1994, more than 40 percent of newborn boys left the hospital intact. Worldwide, 85 percent of males are intact.

Can the foreskin be restored?

According to NOCIRC, the rich supply of nerve endings and blood vessels that are amputated with the foreskin can never be restored. Nevertheless, surgical and nonsurgical techniques are being used successfully by thousands of men to re-cover the glans. Reports indicate that sensitivity of the glans returns when it is protected from abrasive clothing.

Sources: American Academy of Pediatrics (AAP). Marilyn Fayre Milos, R.N., Executive Director, National Organization of Circumcision Information Resource Centers (NOCIRC), P.O. Box 2512, San Anselmo, CA 94979-2512; phone: (415) 488-9883; fax: (415) 488-9660.

Dental Hygiene

How often should I brush my teeth?

Ideally, three times a day, after every meal. If you can't do that, it's most important to brush right before bedtime and in the morning.

Should I brush up-and-down or side-to-side?

Here are instructions from the American Dental Hygienists' Association for proper brushing: Place the brush bristles at a 45° angle to your teeth, the bristles pointing toward the gums. With small circular motions starting at the gumline, brush the front, back, and chewing surfaces. Brush the tongue, too, from back to front to remove odor-producing bacteria. Always use a fluoride toothpaste and replace your toothbrush every two to three months or when the bristles become worn.

How often should I floss my teeth and what is the proper way to floss?

Once a day, before or after brushing, wrap an 18-inch piece of floss around the third finger of each hand. Hold about 1 inch of floss tightly between the thumb and forefinger of each hand. Keeping the floss taut, work it in between the teeth. Then wrap the floss around each tooth and gently rub up and down. Use a clean section of floss as it becomes soiled or frayed.

Are the new plaque-removing rinses effective (the ones you use before brushing)?

The literature shows that these rinses reduce plaque accumulation to a small degree. They are not a substitute for proper brushing and flossing. There is no evidence that they are effective in treating periodontal disease.

What is periodontal disease?

Periodontal disease is a disease of the bone and other structures that support teeth. Symptoms include puffy or red gums, bleeding gums, persistent bad breath, widening spaces between the teeth, loose teeth, and receding gums.

Should I use a soft or hard toothbrush?

Soft. The hard brushes damage the gums and can abrade the root surface of the tooth. The soft brushes are also able to reach more areas of the tooth structure.

My gums bleed when I brush my teeth. Is there something wrong?

Yes. If this is occurring on a daily basis, you should go see a dentist. Bleeding gums often signal the beginning stages of periodontal disease.

What about brushing with baking soda? Or using the new baking soda toothpastes?

Baking soda alone does not contain fluoride. The new baking soda toothpastes which contain fluoride may be of benefit since baking soda may increase the pH level in the mouth and thus may reduce cavity formation.

And what about the whitening toothpastes? Are they really effective?

While some whitening toothpastes effectively keep the teeth cleaner and, therefore, looking whiter, some are more abrasive than others. The stronger toothpastes rely on abrasion to remove external stains as opposed to actually changing the color of the teeth.

I brush twice a day every day, but my teeth are just naturally yellowish. Is there anything I can do?

Yes. You can bleach them at the dentist's office or you can restore the teeth with porcelain veneers or bonding to cover them in any shade you want. Bleaching costs anywhere from $300 to $500, for a home treatment at night for two weeks. Porcelain veneers cost from $700 to $1,200 a tooth. They are shell-like facings that can be bonded onto stained teeth. Bonding is similar to porcelain veneers, but a little less expensive (between $300 and $700 per tooth).

Source: American Dental Hygienists' Association Oral Health Hotline, 444 North Michigan Ave, Chicago, IL 60611; (800) 847-6718.

Eyeglasses

What is the difference between *shatterproof* and *impact-resistant* lenses?

There's no such thing as truly shatterproof lenses. Today's eyeglass lenses must meet federal impact-resistant standards, but they can break, depending on the size and the speed of the object striking them. For eye-hazardous jobs or sports, nonprescription safety eyewear that meets American National Standards Institute (ANSI Z87.1 standard) can be purchased from optometrists or hardware and sporting goods stores. Optometrists can also provide prescription safety eyewear that meets the ANSI standard.

What is the difference between an *optometrist*, an *ophthalmologist*, and an *optician*, and which of these people give prescriptions and which fill them?

An optometrist examines the eyes to evaluate eye health and visual abilities, diagnoses eye diseases and conditions of the eye and visual system, and provides necessary treatment and, in most states, drugs to treat eye disease. An ophthalmologist is a physician who concentrates on treating eye disease with drugs or surgery, but may also prescribe glasses or contact lenses. An optician is a technician who dispenses eyeglasses according to prescriptions written by optometrists and ophthalmologists.

Is one pair of glasses enough?

This depends upon your condition and needs. Many people feel that one type of eyewear doesn't fulfill all their needs. A librarian or retail clerk may need trifocals on the job but bifocals for driving. Some contact lens wearers prefer to wear reading glasses over their contacts rather than switch to bifocal contact lenses. In order to determine what sort and how many different kinds of eyewear you need, examine the different uses to which you consistently put your eyes. Prescription sunglasses are felt to be a "must" for many eyeglass wearers. Final decisions should be made in consultation with an optometrist or ophthalmologist.

What exactly are those lens coatings optometrists often recommend, and do I really need them?

Various lens coatings can be applied to the surface of the lens. Your need for them depends upon when you wear your glasses and your lifestyle. The most popular types are scratch-resistant, which is important for the protection of plastic lenses; antireflection, which eliminates reflections in the lens, is often beneficial for dusk or night driving, and also combats indoor glare; and ultraviolet, often found on sunglasses, which is used to block hazardous ultraviolet radiation.

When picking frames, how important is it that the shape of the frame "match" the shape of my face?

Frame styles can highlight good facial features and play down those that are less attractive. Stylists advise never selecting a frame shape that matches your face shape—round, square, oval, rectangular, or heart-shaped. For example, a square-faced person should not wear square lenses and frames. People with heart-shaped faces should wear frames that draw attention away from their chins, while those with rectangular faces can shorten their face with dropped temple pieces on their frames. People with oval faces have it best: They can wear practically anything.

What are the general guidelines for picking the color for frames, barring fashion trends?

Frame and lens color together make a great impact on the face and should not be chosen lightly. The easiest and most widely used color system is seasonal: winter, spring, summer, and autumn. People in the winter and summer color categories (pale skin and blond hair or dark skin and hair) look best in cool colors such as blue and gray. People in the spring and autumn categories (pale or peach skin and strawberry blond or brown hair) look best in warm colors such as brown and peach.

Lens tints, if desired, should match the color of the frames. Pale fashion lens tints usually will not affect color perception and generally can be worn for most day and evening activities. Deeper tints, however, can affect color perception somewhat, and reduce nighttime visibility. These are not recommended for full-time wear.

Which are better, glass or plastic lenses?

In general, plastic lenses are often a better choice as they are lighter and safer. Plastic lenses, however, are a very broad category, with many subsets. The two largest categories are regular hard resin lenses and polycarbonate lenses that are thinner. Both glass and plastic lenses can be ground into bifocals or trifocals as well as made polarizing (glare-resistant) and photochromatic (automatically shading), so the desire for these features need not sway your decision. Plastic lenses tend to be slightly cheaper; that, plus their lighter weight on the nose, make them a more popular choice.

Source: The American Optometric Association, 243 North Lindbergh Boulevard, St. Louis, MO 63141; phone: (314) 991-4100; fax: (314) 991-4101. Contact Charlotte A. Rancilio.

Hysterectomy

What is a hysterectomy?

A hysterectomy is the surgical removal of the uterus. After a hysterectomy, a woman no longer menstruates, but removing the uterus does not cause menopause. If the ovaries are left intact, they continue to produce eggs and release hormones until menopause.

How common are hysterectomies?

Each year approximately 600,000 American women have hysterectomies. That means one out of every three women in the United States will have had a hysterectomy by age 60. The United States leads Western countries in this surgical procedure. Within this country, hysterectomy rates are highest in the South and Midwest, and the rates are higher for African-American women.

Are all hysterectomies the same?

No. There are three types of hysterectomy surgery: A *total* or complete hysterectomy removes the uterus, including the cervix. A *radical* hysterectomy is performed for certain cancers of the reproductive organs: It removes the uterus, cervix, supporting ligaments and tissues, the upper portion of the vagina, and the pelvic lymph nodes. A *subtotal* or partial hysterectomy removes the uterus only and not the cervix. This type of hysterectomy is rare, however. It is mostly performed only in extreme situations, such as when a patient is unstable and the surgery needs to be completed quickly, or when there is difficulty visualizing the lower uterine segment during surgery.

How often are the ovaries removed during a hysterectomy?

According to the National Center for Health Statistics, approximately 45 percent of hysterectomies are performed with both ovaries removed. When the fallopian tubes and the ovaries are removed with the uterus, the procedure is referred to "as a total hysterectomy with bi-lateral salpingo-oophorectomy" (meaning both ovaries are removed). In some cases, as when one ovary is diseased, for instance, only one ovary may be removed. Older women are more likely than younger women to have oopherectomies.

Does menopause begin when the ovaries are removed?

Yes. This is known as "surgical menopause"—symptoms such as hot flashes, vaginal dryness, dizziness, and night sweats can be sudden and severe. However, the immediate initiation of hormone replacement therapy after oophorectomy can help to lessen or alleviate these symptoms.

How is a hysterectomy performed?

The uterus may be removed either through an incision in the abdomen or through an incision in the vagina. Seventy to 80 percent of hysterectomies are abdominal surgeries, which require a longer hospitalization and recovery. Abdominal hysterectomies are usually performed when more extensive disease is present.

How is the type of surgery decided on?

The choice of how a hysterectomy will be performed is usually influenced by the condition for which it is recommended, the woman's anatomy, and the physician's training. Vaginal hysterectomies are often performed when the uterus is small, or when close inspection of other reproductive organs is not warranted.

How long does it take to recover from surgery?

Hospitalization following hysterectomy averages three to five days. Although normal activities may be resumed gradually, a woman should not expect to feel fully recovered before four to six weeks after surgery. For some women the effects of surgery may continue after this time. Fatigue is a commonly reported symptom after the six-week recovery period.

What are the risks for hysterectomy?

Recent figures cited in the *New England Journal of Medicine* report the risk of death from hysterectomy ranging from 6 to 11 per 10,000 cases for indications not involving pregnancy or cancer; from 29 to 38 per 10,000 when complications with pregnancy are involved; and between 70 to 200 per 10,000 when cancer is involved.

What kinds of problems may result from surgery?

According to the Center for Health Statistics, 25 to 50 percent of hysterectomy patients may experience one or more complications from surgery. Most of these problems are minor and reversible. They can include:

- fever and infection following surgery
- urinary tract infections or discomfort
- sudden hormonal decreases, which may produce menopausal symptoms such as hot flashes, night sweats, dizziness (these symptoms may be temporary when the ovaries are not removed during surgery and regain some level of functioning; physicians may also offset hormonal decreases by

administering hormone replacement/supplement prior to or immediately following surgery)
- constipation
- fatigue and/or decreased energy
- depression
- pain or discomfort during intercourse
- loss of sexual pleasure and/or interest
- ovarian failure

Are there any serious complications resulting from hysterectomy?

Yes. They can include:

- hemorrhage requiring transfusion
- injury to the bowel or bladder during surgery, requiring repair
- life-threatening cardiopulmonary incidents

What are the medical reasons for a hysterectomy?

In the rare situation when a woman's life is threatened by severe uterine bleeding—following childbirth, for example, or when severe infection exists, such as when a tubal abscess ruptures—a hysterectomy may be the only procedure to offer immediate and complete treatment. Hysterectomy is also recommended for treating cancer of the uterus and fallopian tube, and may be recommended for managing colon, rectum, or bladder cancers. Invasive cervical cancer is also an indication for hysterectomy.

Has the need or indications of hysterectomy changed from the past?

Yes. For example, removing the uterus and cervix was once standard practice for a common precancerous form of dysplasia (abnormal cell development) known as cervical intraepithelial neoplasia (CIN). More than 55,000 women develop CIN yearly. Today, effective treatments, including cutting, burning, or freezing the diseased portion of the cervix, are generally recommended for CIN instead of hysterectomy, depending on the severity and location of the disorder, age, clinical status, and a woman's interest in preserving her childbearing ability.

When is a hysterectomy generally recommended?

Hysterectomy is often recommended to relieve chronic pain and/or heavy bleeding that can be caused by fibroids, endometriosis, dysfunctional uterine bleeding, and other disorders. Genital proclapse, which can be accompanied by difficulty with bladder and bowel control, may also be an indication for hysterectomy. Women should explore all of their treatment options and possible alternatives to surgery as part of their decision-making process about this important women's health issue.

How does a hysterectomy affect a woman emotionally?

The decision to have a hysterectomy is a highly personal one, and each woman's condition is unique. For some women, the recommendation of removing the uterus is a distressing proposition, bringing up many feelings associated with the loss and function of body parts, a diminished sense of femininity and attractiveness, and anxiety about issues surrounding sexuality. For others, a hysterectomy may be welcomed as a relief from painful and/or unacceptable symptoms, such as heavy bleeding. In many cases, alternatives to hysterectomy are available, also with risks and benefits to consider. Some women's health centers and hospitals offer hysterectomy support groups or have social workers who can help people discuss their feelings prior to or following surgery. Women interested in finding a support group should begin by asking their physicians for more information.

Source: Adapted from *National Women's Health Report*, (March–April 1994), vol. 16, no.3, published by the National Women's Health Resource Center, Washington, DC. More information about hysterectomy and other women's health topics is available from the National Women's Health Resource Center (NWHRC), an independent organization that serves as a clearinghouse for women's health information. Consumers may write or call to request information about publications and services. National Women's Health Resource Center (NWHRC), 5255 Loughboro Road NW, Washington, DC 20016; (202) 537-4015; www.healthywomen.org.

Infertility

What is *infertility?*

Infertility is a disease of the reproductive system that impairs one of the body's most basic functions: the conception of children. Conception is a complicated process that depends upon many factors: the production of healthy sperm by the man and healthy eggs by the woman; unblocked fallopian tubes that allow the sperm to reach the egg; the sperm's ability to fertilize the egg when they meet; the ability of the fertilized egg (embryo) to become implanted in the woman's uterus; and sufficient embryo quality. Finally, for the pregnancy to continue to full term, the embryo must be healthy and the woman's hormonal environment adequate for its development. When just one of these factors is impaired, infertility can result.

How common is it?

Infertility is a disease that strikes men and women with almost equal frequency, affecting about 5.3 million women and their partners in the United States, or about 10 percent of the reproductive-age population. In fact, one out of seven couples will have trouble conceiving sometime during their reproductive years.

What causes infertility?

Nobody can be blamed for infertility, any more than someone is to blame for diabetes or leukemia. In rough terms, about one-third of infertility cases can be attributed to male factors and about one-third to factors that affect women. For the remaining one-third of infertile couples, infertility is caused by a combination of problems in both partners or, in about 20 percent of cases, is unexplained.

The most common male infertility factors include azoospermia (no sperm cells are produced) and oligospermia (few sperm cells are produced). Sometimes, sperm cells are malformed, or they die before they can reach the egg. In rare cases, infertility in men is caused by a genetic disease such as cystic fibrosis or a chromosomal abnormality.

The most common female infertility factor is an ovulation disorder. Other causes include blocked fallopian tubes, which can occur when a woman has had pelvic inflammatory disease, or endometriosis (a condition causing adhesions and cysts that is sometimes painful). Congenital anomalies (birth defects) involving the structure of the uterus and uterine fibroids are associated with repeated miscarriages. Pelvic inflammatory disease (PID) is the most common preventable cause of infertility in the United States. PID is often the result of an untreated sexually transmitted disease (STD) in a woman. About one in four couples are unable to conceive due to STDs, which are the number one preventable cause of infertility.

How is infertility diagnosed?

Couples are generally advised to seek medical help if they are unable to achieve pregnancy after a year of unprotected intercourse. The doctor will conduct a physical examination of both partners to determine their general health and to evaluate physical disorders that may be causing infertility. Usually, both partners are interviewed about their sexual habits in order to determine whether intercourse is taking place properly for conception.

If no cause can be determined at this point, more specific tests may be recommended. For women, these include an analysis of body temperature and ovulation, X-ray of the fallopian tubes and uterus, and laparoscopy. For men, initial tests focus on semen analysis. In approximately 40 percent of infertile couples, the male partner is either the sole or a contributing cause of infertility.

Where does a woman go for the first-time visit?

You may choose to be initially evaluated by a general obstetrician/gynecologist (ob/gyn), or you can go directly to an infertility specialist. Some infertility specialists are general gynecologists with a special interest in the treatment of infertility; others are reproductive endocrinologists. You and your partner should attend the first meeting together.

What specific questions will the doctor ask us?

In a typical interview, the physician asks the woman if she has irregular periods, severe menstrual cramps, pelvic pain, abnormal vaginal bleeding or discharge, a history of genital infection, or any medical illness. Also, expect questions concerning prior conceptions, prior miscarriages, pregnancies, operations, and methods of contraception. The man will be asked questions about possible genital injury, operations, infection, drug and/or medication usage, history of prior paternity, and any medical illnesses. Your physician will ask both of you how long you've been trying to conceive, how often you have sexual intercourse, if you use lubricants during intercourse, and if anyone in your family has birth defects. Since 25 percent of infertile couples have more than one factor causing infertility, it is very important to evaluate everything that may affect both male and female partners.

How is infertility treated?

Most infertility cases—85 to 90 percent—are treated with conventional therapies such as drug treatment or surgery.

How many couples who have fertility problems will achieve a pregnancy?

In most cases today, experts can identify the male and female factors that reduce fertility, so there is renewed hope to infertile couples for a successful pregnancy, now possible for more than half of the couples pursuing treatment. This is due to recent advancements in medication, microsurgery, and *in vitro* fertilization (IVF) techniques.

What is *in vitro* fertilization?

In infertile couples where women have blocked or absent fallopian tubes, or where men have low sperm counts, *in vitro* fertilization offers a chance at parenthood to couples who until recently would have had no hope of conceiving a "biologically related" child. In IVF, eggs are surgically removed from the ovary and mixed with sperm outside the body in a petri dish (*in vitro* is Latin for "in glass"). After about 40 hours, the eggs are examined to see if they have become fertilized by the sperm and are dividing into cells. These fertilized eggs (embryos) are then placed in the woman's uterus, thus bypassing the fallopian tubes. IVF has received a great deal of media attention since it was first introduced in 1978, but it actually accounts for less than 5 percent of all infertility treatment in the United States.

Is *in vitro* fertilization expensive?

In 1993, the average cost of an IVF cycle was $6,233 in the United States, but can it be as high as $10,000. Like other extremely delicate medical procedures, IVF involves highly trained professionals with sophisticated laboratories and equipment, and the cycle may need to be repeated to be successful. Though IVF and other assisted reproductive technologies are not inexpensive, they account for less than 1 percent of total U.S. health-care costs.

Does *in vitro* fertilization work?

Yes. Since 1981, when IVF was introduced in the United States, more than 33,000 American babies have been born from IVF and over 55,000 from all assisted reproductive technologies. The average live delivery rate for IVF according to the latest statistics is 21.1 percent, comparable to the 20 percent chance in any given month that a reproductively healthy couple has of achieving pregnancy and carrying a baby to term.

Do insurance plans cover infertility treatment?

The degree of services covered depends on where you live and the type of insurance plan you have. Twelve states currently have laws that require insurers to either cover or offer to cover some form of infertility diagnosis and treatment. Those states are Arkansas, California, Connecticut, Hawaii, Illinois, Maryland, Massachusetts, Montana, New York, Ohio, Rhode Island, and Texas. However, the laws vary greatly in their scope of what is and is not required to be covered. (For more information about the specific laws for each of those states, contact the American Society for Reproductive Medicine or refer to the State Infertility Insurance Laws page of the ASRM Web site.) Whether or not you live in a state with an infertility insurance law, you may want to consult with your employer's director of human resources to determine the exact coverage your plan provides. If that isn't an option, an excellent resource for determining coverage is a booklet entitled *Infertility Insurance Advisor—An Insurance Counseling Program for Infertile Couples,* available for a small fee from RESOLVE, an infertility patient advocacy and information organization.

What are some of the psychological implications?

Infertility is a medical condition that has many emotional overtones for couples. Couples may experience feelings such as frustration, anger, sadness, jealousy, guilt, and anxiety. These feelings can affect your self-esteem and your self-image. You may find it difficult to share such feelings with family and friends, which can lead to isolation. It is important to know that they are normal and that you are not alone in what you are experiencing. While it is your physician's responsibility to discuss realistically what your chances of pregnancy may be, only you and your partner can decide how far you want to go in your attempts to conceive. Evaluation and therapy are frequently stressful in many ways. Coming to a joint decision about goals and acceptable therapies is important. In many cases, setting endpoints for therapy is also advisable. Support groups can help with these issues, and your physician can refer you to a local counselor who can work with you on an ongoing basis.

Source: The American Society for Reproductive Medicine (formerly The American Fertility Society) is a private, nonprofit medical organization devoted to advancing knowledge and expertise in all phases of reproductive medicine and health care. For more information, contact: American Society for Reproductive Medicine, Patient Information Department, 1209 Montgomery Highway, Birmingham, AL 35216-2809; phone: (205) 978-5000 ext. 300; fax: (205) 978-5005. E-mail: asrm@asrm.com; Web site: http://www.asrm.com. RESOLVE, Inc., a national support group for infertile couples, can provide resources on local support groups, reading materials, and infertility counselors: 1310 Broadway, Somerville, MA 02144-1731; (617) 623-0744.

Lamaze

What is *Lamaze?*

Lamaze refers to a method of childbirth preparation based on the ASPO/Lamaze philosophy of birth. In addition to early pregnancy classes focusing on pregnancy and the growth and development of the baby taught by some Lamaze teachers, all Lamaze educators teach a series of classes for women and their partners during the last trimester of pregnancy that prepares them for labor and birth. These classes focus on the normal process of labor and birth and strategies that women and their partners can use to enhance the progress of labor and to reduce pain and fear. Information about complications and medical options is also included so that parents can make informed decisions should they need to do so.

What is the philosophy behind a Lamaze birth?

ASPO/Lamaze believes that birth is normal, natural, and healthy. The experience of birth profoundly affects women and their families. Women's inner wisdom guides them through birth. Their confidence and ability to give birth is either enhanced or diminished by the care provider and place of birth. Women have a right to give birth free from routine medical interventions; birth can safely take place in birth centers and homes. Childbirth education empowers women to make informed choices in health care, to assume responsibility for their health, and to trust their inner wisdom.

How long have women been using Lamaze, and how did it get started?

In 1951, Dr. Ferdinand Lamaze introduced a method of childbirth in France by incorporating techniques he observed in Russia. The method, consisting of childbirth education classes, relaxation and breathing techniques, and continuous emotional support by the husband and a specially trained nurse, became known as the "Lamaze method." Word of mouth spread in the United States during the late 1950s, after Marjorie Karmel wrote of her childbirth experience in a book titled *Thank You, Dr. Lamaze*. The book inspired many women to approach childbirth as a shared event for both mother and father. In 1960, Marjorie Karmel and physical therapist Elizabeth Bing formed ASPO/Lamaze, a nonprofit organization to spread the word about Lamaze and to set the standards for Lamaze childbirth education.

Why should I attend Lamaze childbirth classes?

Women have always prepared for the birth of their babies. Until recent times, they learned about childbirth from their own mothers and sisters. Birth took place at home and family rituals and traditions ensured that women were confident in their ability to give birth, surrounded by family and wise women who provided comfort and encouragement through labor and in the days and weeks after birth. Such confidence and wisdom is often difficult to achieve in the high-tech world of modern obstetrics. Lamaze childbirth classes provide the knowledge, skills, and support that will help you give birth with confidence and joy as women have done for centuries.

What is covered in Lamaze classes?

True Lamaze classes today focus on much more than just the "breathing." Most Lamaze teachers concentrate class time on normal labor, birth, and on the many choices that expectant parents have today. Pregnant women and their partners practice various positions that will facilitate the normal progress of labor and birth. Partners and other support persons learn massage techniques to ease the pain of labor and to enhance relaxation. Comfort measures such as hydrotherapy, the use of heat and cold, and pressure are discussed and, when possible, practiced.

Much time is spent on relaxation skills, including breathing strategies— skills that can be used throughout life in times of stress. Communication skills are also practiced—both for the pregnant woman and her partner or other support person, and for the pregnant woman and other members of the health-care team. Class members discuss what they would like for their childbirth experience and what they can do to help make that experience happen.

Are common problems that arise during a delivery discussed?

Yes. Some time is spent on problems that could occur during labor and birth and what the pregnant woman and her partner might need to know. Information is provided about anesthesia and medical procedures so that women can make informed choices about what is appropriate for their particular experience. Fear is reduced by learning what happens during labor and birth, and confidence is increased by learning skills that help the pregnant woman to manage the pain and stress of labor and birth. New innovations in maternity care, such as the benefits of a *doula,* or professional labor support person, are discussed. Most classes also spend time on getting breastfeeding off to a good start, other aspects of the postpartum period, and making the most of short-ened stays in the hospital or other birth place.

Why do people actually need to attend classes to learn Lamaze techniques?

It's natural to wonder why classes are important, rather than reading a book or watching videotapes to prepare for childbirth. Information gained this way can be helpful and is certainly better than no preparation for birth. However, attending Lamaze classes provides actual demonstration of techniques, as well as the opportunity to share your concerns and discuss your plans with other expectant parents and with your childbirth educator. Classes also give you more motivation to practice Lamaze techniques, the benefit of feedback from your instructor on how well you are learning them, and the chance to develop new skills each week. We would strongly recommend that you take the full series of Lamaze classes. After all, birth is a physical and emotional rather than an intellectual activity!

What if it is a second or subsequent pregnancy—do I still need to take classes?

If you have taken a good-quality, full series course of Lamaze classes in the recent past, consider a refresher course.

Has the use of the Lamaze technique changed American birth practices?

Yes. Over the past 37 years, Lamaze techniques have changed childbirth for millions of families, and have firmly established the childbirth educator as a recognized professional in the health-care field. The visible impact of advocacy and increased consumer awareness over the years includes the proliferation of homelike birthing rooms in hospitals, fathers in the delivery room, sibling visits, and family involvement. Childbirth education has become such a normal part of prenatal care that there is rarely a hospital that does not offer classes to pregnant women and their partners.

What is important to look for in childbirth preparation classes?

The qualifications of childbirth educators and the focus of childbirth classes vary widely. The following guidelines can help you determine which class is best for you:

- *The qualifications of the childbirth educator.* Where was she formally prepared to teach childbirth classes? Is the instructor certified as a childbirth educator by a nationally recognized organization? For instance, childbirth educators who complete the certification program conducted by ASPO/Lamaze, one of the most comprehensive programs available, receive the credential ACCE, which stands for ASPO-certified childbirth educator.

- *Class size.* The most appropriate size is 8 to 12 couples. This allows individual attention, time for discussion, and adequate floor space for practice.

- *Focus of the class.* In addition to providing the basic information of pregnancy and childbirth, the instructor should discuss birthing options, develop an individualized birth plan, and provide guidelines on how to make informed personal choices.

- *Length of class series.* A Lamaze course for first-time parents should include at least 12 hours of instruction, with plenty of time to practice skills and comfort measures, and plenty of time for class discussions.

How many women use Lamaze a year?

An exact number is not available, but we do know that today the majority of expectant parents attend Lamaze classes to prepare for childbirth. ASPO/Lamaze-certified childbirth educators teach over 150,000 classes every year, which are attended by more than 2 million parents, representing approximately one-quarter of all American women who give birth.

How can a woman find out more about Lamaze classes in her area?

ASPO/Lamaze has a list of ASPO/Lamaze-certified educators throughout the United States and in some foreign countries. They operate a toll-free telephone service to provide consumers with information on prepared childbirth and how to locate childbirth educators in your area. Many childbirth educators offer private as well as group classes.

Source: The American Society for Psychoprophylaxis in Obstetrics is an international, not-for-profit organization that promotes normal, natural, healthy, and fulfilling childbearing experiences for women and families through, education, advocacy, and reform. For more information, contact: ASPO/Lamaze (American Society for Psychoprophylaxis in Obstetrics, Inc.), 1200 19th Street NW, Suite 300, Washington, DC 20036. Call (800) 368-4404 or (202) 857-1128 in Washington, DC. E-mail: ASPO@sba.com. http://www.lamaze-childbirth.com.

Menopause

What is *menopause*?

Menopause is the point in a woman's life when menstruation stops permanently, signifying the end of her ability to have children. Known as "the change of life," menopause is the last stage of a gradual biological process in which the ovaries reduce their production of female sex hormones—a process that begins about three to five years before the final menstrual period.

How do you know when menopause is actually over?

Menopause is considered complete when a woman has been without periods for one year. On average, this occurs at about age 50. But like the beginning of menstruation in adolescence, timing varies from person to person. Cigarette smokers tend to reach menopause earlier than nonsmokers. With a life expectancy of about 81 years, a 50-year-old woman can expect to live more than one-third of her life after menopause.

How does it happen?

The ovaries contain structures called *follicles* that hold the egg cells. A woman is born with about 500,000 egg cells, and by puberty there are about 75,000 left. Only about 400 to 500 ever mature fully to be released during the menstrual cycle; the rest degenerate over the years. During the reproductive years, a gland in the brain generates hormones that cause a new egg to be released from its follicle each month. The follicle then produces the sex hormones estrogen and progesterone, which thicken the lining of the uterus. This enriched lining is prepared to receive and nourish a fertilized egg, which could develop into a baby. If fertilization does not occur, estrogen and progesterone levels drop, the lining of the uterus breaks down, and menstruation occurs.

For unknown reasons, the ovaries begin to decline in hormone production during a woman's mid-30s. In the late 40s the process accelerates and hormones fluctuate more, causing irregular menstrual cycles and unpredictable episodes of heavy bleeding. By the early to mid-50s, periods finally end altogether. However, estrogen production does not completely stop. The ovaries decrease their output significantly, but still may produce a small amount. Also, some estrogen is produced in fat cells with help from the adrenal glands (near the kidney).

Progesterone, the other female hormone, works during the second half of the menstrual cycle to create a lining in the uterus as a viable home for an egg, and to shed the lining if the egg is not fertilized. If you skip a period, your body may not be making enough progesterone to break down the uterine lining. However, your estrogen levels may remain high even though you are not menstruating.

At menopause, hormone levels don't always decline uniformly; they alternately rise and fall again. Changing ovarian hormone levels affect the other glands in the body, which together make up the endocrine system. The endocrine system controls growth, metabolism, and reproduction. This system must constantly readjust itself to work effectively. Ovarian hormones also affect all other tissues, including the breasts, vagina, bones, blood vessels, gastrointestinal tract, urinary tract, and skin.

What should I expect at menopause?

Menopause is an individualized experience. Some women notice little difference in their bodies or moods, while others find the change extremely bothersome and disruptive. Estrogen and progesterone affect virtually all tissues in the body, but everyone is influenced by them differently.

I've heard so much about "hot flashes." What are they?

Hot flashes, or flushes, are the most common symptom of menopause, affecting more than 60 percent of menopausal women in the United States. A hot flash is a sudden sensation of intense heat in the upper part or all of the body. The face and neck may become flushed, with red blotches appearing on the chest, back, and arms. This is often followed by profuse sweating and then cold shivering as the body temperature readjusts.

How long do hot flashes usually last and how often do they occur?

A hot flash can last a few moments or 30 minutes or longer. Hot flashes occur sporadically and often start several years before other signs of menopause. They gradually decline in frequency and intensity as you age. Eighty percent of all women with hot flashes have them for two years or less, while a small percentage have them for more than five years. Hot flashes can happen at any time. They can be as mild as a light blush or severe enough to wake you from a deep sleep. Some women even develop insomnia; others have found that caffeine, alcohol, hot drinks, spicy foods, and stressful or frightening events can sometimes trigger a hot flash. However, avoiding these triggers will not necessarily prevent all episodes.

What causes hot flashes?

Hot flashes appear to be a direct result of decreasing estrogen levels. If there is no estrogen, your glands release other hormones that dilate blood vessels and destabilize body temperature. Hormone therapy relieves the discomfort of hot flashes in most cases. Some women claim that vitamin E offers minor relief, although there has never been a study to confirm it. Aside from hormone therapy, which is not for everyone, here are some suggestions for coping with hot flashes:

- Dress in layers, so you can remove a layer at the first sign of a flash
- Drink a glass of cold water or juice at the onset of a flash
- At night keep a thermos of ice water or an icepack by your bed
- Use cotton sheets, lingerie, and clothing to let your skin "breathe"

What about sex? Is there any effect on the vagina?

With advancing age, the walls of the vagina become thinner, dryer, less elastic, and more vulnerable to infection. These changes can make sexual intercourse uncomfortable or painful. For some women, but by no means all, menopause brings a decrease in sexual activity. Reduced hormone levels cause subtle changes in the genital tissues and are thought to be linked also to a decline in sexual interest.

Estrogen creams and oral estrogen can restore secretions and tissue elasticity. Water-soluble lubricants can also help. Water-soluble lubricants are preferable, as they help reduce the chance of infection. Try to avoid petroleum jelly; many women are allergic, and it damages condoms. Be sure to see your gynecologist if problems persist.

Is it true that menopause causes incontinence and urinary tract infections?

Tissues in the urinary tract also change with age, sometimes leaving women more susceptible to involuntary loss of urine (incontinence), particularly if certain chronic illnesses or urinary infections are also present. Exercise, coughing, laughing, lifting heavy objects, or similar movements that put pressure on the bladder may cause small amounts of urine to leak. Lack of regular physical exercise may contribute to this condition.

It's important to know that incontinence is not a normal part of aging, to be masked by using adult diapers. Rather, it is usually a treatable condition that warrants medical evaluation. Recent research has shown that bladder training is a simple and effective treatment for most cases of incontinence and is less expensive and safer than medication or surgery.

Within four or five years after the final menstrual period, there is an increased chance of vaginal and urinary tract infections. If symptoms such as painful or overly frequent urination occur, consult your doctor. Infections are easily treated with antibiotics, but often tend to reoccur. To help prevent these infections, urinate before and after intercourse, be sure your bladder is not full for long periods, drink plenty of fluids, and keep your genital area clean. Douching is not thought to be effective in preventing infection.

What effect does menopause generally have on a person's mental health?

A popular myth pictures the menopausal woman shifting from raging, angry moods into depressive, doleful slumps with no apparent reason or warning. However, a study by psychologists at the University of Pittsburgh suggests that menopause does not cause unpredictable mood swings, depression, or even stress in most women; in fact, it may even improve mental health for some. This gives further support to the idea that menopause is not necessarily a negative experience. The Pittsburgh findings are supported by a New England Research Institute study, which found that menopausal women were no more depressed than the general population: about 10 percent are occasionally depressed and 5 percent are persistently depressed. The exception is women who undergo surgical menopause. Their depression rate is reportedly double that of women who have a natural menopause. Studies have also indicated that many cases of depression relate more to life stresses or "midlife crisis" than to menopause.

Are the symptoms any different when a woman has surgery before menopause would naturally occur?

Premenopausal women who have both their ovaries removed surgically experience an abrupt menopause. They may be hit harder by menopausal symptoms than are those who experience it naturally. Their hot flashes may be more severe, more frequent, and last longer. They may have a greater risk of heart disease and osteoporosis, and may be more likely to become depressed. The reasons for this are unknown. When only one ovary is removed, menopause usually occurs naturally. When the uterus is removed (hysterectomy) and the ovaries remain, menstrual periods stop but other menopausal symptoms (if any) usually occur at the same age that they would naturally. However, some women who have a hysterectomy may experience menopausal symptoms at a younger age, possibly due to a decreased blood supply to the ovaries as a result of surgery.

What are some of the long-term effects of estrogen deficiency?

One of the most important health issues for middle-aged women is the threat of osteoporosis—the condition in which bones become thin, fragile, and highly prone to fracture. Numerous studies over the past ten years have linked estrogen insufficiency to this gradual yet debilitating disease. In fact, osteoporosis is more closely related to menopause than to a woman's chronological age. The other main area affected is cardiovascular diseases (CVD), which are disorders of the heart and circulatory system. After menopause, the incidence of CVD increases, with each passing year posing a greater risk.

Are there any tips to avoid some of these problems?

Hereditary factors are important in determining peak bone mass, as well as ensuring that you have an adequate intake of dietary calcium and vitamin D, exposure to sunlight, and enough physical exercise. These elements also help slow the rate of bone loss. CVD can be prevented or at least reduced by early recognition, lifestyle changes, and, many physicians believe, hormone replacement therapy. Good nutrition and regular physical exercise are thought to improve overall health. Some doctors feel these factors can also affect menopause.

What is *hormone replacement therapy?*

To combat the symptoms associated with falling estrogen levels, doctors have turned to hormone replacement therapy (HRT), which is the administration of the female hormones estrogen and progesterone. Estrogen replacement therapy (ERT) refers to administration of estrogen alone. The hormones are usually given in pill form, though sometimes skin patches and vaginal creams (just estrogen) are used. ERT is thought to help prevent the devastating effects of heart disease and osteoporosis—conditions that are often difficult and expensive to treat once they appear. The cardiovascular effects of progesterone, however, are yet unknown.

Is it safe?

Hormone treatment for menopause is still quite controversial. Its long-term safety and efficacy remain matters of great concern. There is not enough existing data for physicians to suggest that HRT is the right choice for all women. Several large studies are currently attempting to resolve the questions, though it will take several more years to reach any definitive answers.

Source: Adapted from *Menopause*, prepared by the National Institute on Aging, National Institutes of Health, a division of the U.S. Department of Health and Human Services, Public Health Service. For the complete booklet on menopause, and other related information on aging, contact: National Institute on Aging (NIA), 9000 Rockville Pike, Bethesda, MD 20892. Call the Information Center at (800) 222-2225.

Pregnancy

Is it important to plan your pregnancy?

Yes. Pregnancy is a major event. If you plan for it, you can make wise decisions that will benefit both your own health and that of your baby. Good health before pregnancy can help you cope with the stress of pregnancy, labor, and delivery. It can also help ensure that neither you nor your baby is exposed to factors that could be harmful during pregnancy. Getting good health care before you become pregnant—sometimes called "preconception care"—will help you throughout your pregnancy. It also provides a chance to find any risks and treat any medical problems you may have.

Why can't you wait till after you know you're pregnant to seek care?

Many women do not know they are pregnant until several weeks after they have conceived. These early weeks are some of the most crucial ones for the fetus (the baby growing inside you during pregnancy). It is during this time that the organs are formed. Certain substances such as cigarettes, alcohol, and some medications can interfere with normal growth, whereas healthy habits can help promote it.

What goes on during a preconception visit?

As part of your visit, you will be asked questions about your family and medical history, medications you take, your diet and lifestyle, and any past pregnancies. Your answers should be honest and open because they will help show whether you could need special care during pregnancy. This is also a time for you to ask questions, so don't hesitate to seek advice or discuss any concerns you might have. There are many questions to consider, such as: Do I or a member of my family have a disorder that could be inherited? Could any medications I'm taking cause problems during my pregnancy? Can I continue my present exercise program? Does my work expose me to things that could be harmful during pregnancy?

How do I know if I'm pregnant?

There are some early signs of pregnancy to watch for. The first sign that most women relate to being pregnant is a missed menstrual period. Not all women have regular periods, though. Menstrual periods can be affected by stress or illness, so it is best to watch for a number of other signs and symptoms:

- Light menstrual period or spotting
- Tender breasts
- Feeling very tired
- Upset stomach or nausea
- Feeling bloated
- Needing to urinate often

If you have one or more of these symptoms along with a missed period, you could be pregnant, even if you have been using birth control.

How can I know for sure?

Pregnancy can be confirmed by the time you've missed a period. During early pregnancy, the hormone called *human chorionic gonadotropin (hCG),* which is made by the developing placenta, is in the mother's urine and blood. You can be tested by your doctor or at a clinic, or you can test yourself with a home pregnancy test kit.

How do you use home pregnancy kits?

You can buy most kits without a prescription. If your body has made enough hCG, a chemical in the test kit will react with the hCG in your urine. The test shows the presence of the hCG in different ways. In some, a ring forms in a liquid or a bead changes color. They can easily give a wrong result if the directions are not followed. Therefore, it is very important to follow all the directions on the kit carefully. If a home test shows that you are pregnant, you should make plans to begin prenatal care.

Are these tests accurate?

Home pregnancy tests can be very accurate, but no test is 100 percent foolproof. False-negative results (results showing that you are not pregnant when you really are) can occur in a small number of cases. If you think there is even a small chance that you could be pregnant despite getting negative results from a home pregnancy test, see your doctor as soon as possible. He may choose to confirm the results with more accurate tests.

Once I know I'm pregnant, then what happens?

Pregnant women have many choices to make. You need to decide where you want the baby to be delivered, who will deliver it, and how best to prepare for childbirth. You'll want to explore choices regarding breastfeeding, circumcision, and other aspects of your own and your baby's care. These important decisions will affect how comfortable you will be with your care and how confident you will feel as you approach the birth. It's important to think over your options early and discuss them with your partner and your health-care provider so you can make the best decisions possible.

How do you choose a health-care provider and what are the options available?

Choosing who will care for you and your baby during your pregnancy and delivery may be one of your first decisions. Many women ask friends or relatives who have had children to recommend a health-care provider. Some women decide on a hospital where they would like to deliver their baby and ask the staff there for a referral. Keep in mind that your health insurance policy may have restrictions that affect your choices. Babies can be delivered by three types of health-care providers: certified nurse-midwives; doctors in family practice; or obstetrician-gynecologists. Sometimes a doctor and a nurse-midwife work as a team.

Are most pregnancies normal?

Yes, most pregnancies proceed normally, but there are some risks. Assessing these risks is a key part of prenatal care. At each visit, you will be examined and the course of your pregnancy charted. Tests or studies of the fetus may be done to help point out problems that could arise. Even if you had a problem-free pregnancy in the past, you should receive prenatal care as early as possible in pregnancy. No two pregnancies are alike, and problems can come up without warning.

What kinds of tests are available for the developing baby?

Many techniques are used to check the well-being of your fetus, such as ultrasound, fetal kick counts, fetal heart rate monitoring, and others. Most of the time these tests offer reassurance that all is going well. They may be done to confirm other test results or to provide further information. When problems arise, the tests can help pinpoint them early. These tests cannot cure a problem, nor can they guarantee a healthy baby. What they can do is draw attention to the need for special care. When they show no signs of trouble, such techniques help you feel more secure about your baby's health.

Depending on the results of routine tests or risk factors, other tests may be needed to diagnose a problem. These tests may include *amniocentesis* or *chorionic villus sampling*. In amniocentesis, a sample of amniotic fluid (the liquid around the fetus inside the uterus) is drawn through a thin needle that is inserted through the abdomen into the uterus. In chorionic villus sampling, a sample of the chorionic villi is taken from the placenta through the abdomen and uterus, or through a thin tube passed through the vagina and cervix.

What should I know about genetic disorders and birth defects?

Most children in the United States are born healthy. Of each 100 babies, about two or three are born with some type of major birth defect. Some birth defects may be inherited from the parents; others may result from exposure to something harmful during the pregnancy, such as an infection or a drug or medication. Often the reason for the defect is unknown. Most babies with birth defects are born to couples with no special risk factors. Each pregnancy is different and each baby has its own genetic makeup. A birth defect can occur even if you've had normal children and have no history of genetic problems.

However, the risk of birth defects—including genetic disorders—is higher when certain risk factors are present. In some couples, these factors can be identified in advance through tests done before or during pregnancy. These tests, combined with counseling, give information about the risk of having a baby with certain birth defects. The decision to have these tests is a personal one. Prospective parents should know what the tests can and cannot do, and what the results mean, when making decisions.

If there are no apparent risks, why is prenatal care important?

Prenatal care is an important part of making sure you and your growing baby are as healthy as possible. Regular prenatal visits give you a chance to ask questions, be informed about your pregnancy, and make the decisions that are best for you. They also allow your progress, and that of your fetus, to be checked throughout pregnancy. If you are getting regular prenatal care, your doctor may be able to detect signs of problems early. Advances in medicine have helped both to decrease the risks of childbirth and to improve the health of babies at birth.

By planning your pregnancy, starting prenatal care early, making well-thought-out decisions, and having a healthy lifestyle, you can take an active role in your pregnancy and be assured that you're doing all you can to have a healthy baby.

Source: The American College of Obstetricians and Gynecologists (ACOG). Adapted from *Planning for Pregnancy, Birth, and Beyond,* 2nd ed. To obtain the complete book, (1) ask your physician for a copy (if he has one); (2) check a local bookstore; or (3) call (800) 762-2264 ext. 197 to order it ($12.95 plus shipping). For a free pamphlet on pregnancy, send a business-size stamped addressed envelope to: ACOG Resource Center, APO56, P.O. Box 96920, Washington, DC 20090-6920.

Safer Sex

What is "safer sex"?

Safer sex is anything we do to lower our risks of getting an STI (sexually transmitted infection). It's about getting more pleasure with less risk.

Do most people take risks?

Yes. Most of us have taken risks to have sex. We take so many risks that one out of four of us becomes infected sometime in our lives.

Why is safe sex important?

The risks we take can be dangerous. Many sexually transmitted infections last a lifetime, put stress on relationships, cause sterility, cause birth defects, and even lead to major illness and death. We know that safer sex reduces our risks, but many of us don't make the effort because we think safer sex will be less satisfying. It does not have to be. Some of us think safer sex is only about condoms. It's not. We may think it's only about AIDS. It's not. Safer sex is about a lot more. It's also about sexual pleasure. Exploring safer sex can make sex more satisfying. It can improve partner communication, increase intimacy and trust, prolong sex play, enhance orgasm, add variety to sexual pleasure, relieve anxiety, and strengthen relationships.

What basic guidelines should people follow?

Sex partners should have one another's consent, be honest with one another, treat one another as equals, be attentive to one another's pleasure, and protect one another against physical and emotional harm, unintended pregnancy, and sexually transmitted infection. They should accept responsibility for their actions, and have access to safe and effective means to prevent unintended pregnancy and sexually transmitted infection.

How can you practice safe sex?

Here are three steps to safer sex:

1. Become honest with ourselves about the risks we take.
2. Decide which risks we are willing to take—and which ones we aren't willing to take.
3. Find ways to make our safer sex play as satisfying as possible. The most important way to reduce your risk is to keep your partner's body fluids out of your body. The body fluids to be most careful about are blood, semen, preejaculate fluid, vaginal fluids, and the discharges from sores caused by STIs.

How do you keep body fluids out?

There are only two basic rules: Keep your partner's body fluids out of your vagina, anus, and mouth, and don't touch sores that are caused by STIs. Safer sex also means protecting your partner, so return the favor. Don't allow your body fluids to get into your partner's body. Don't have sex if you have sores or other STI symptoms. Get checked for STIs every year, and get the correct treatment if you become infected.

What kind of sex is highest risk?

Unprotected vaginal and anal intercourse have the highest risks for the most dangerous STIs. Lower-risk sex play includes masturbation, mutual masturbation, mutual pleasuring, outercourse, erotic massage, body rubbing, kissing, deep kissing, oral sex, vaginal intercourse with a condom or vaginal pouch (female condom), and anal intercourse with a condom or vaginal pouch.

Are all STIs transmitted the same way?

No! You need to know a little bit about how you might get an STI. Here are the basics about your risks:

If you have unprotected vaginal or anal intercourse, you are at high risk for: trichomoniasis, bacterial vaginosis, gonorrhea, chlamydia, syphilis, chancroid, human papilloma viruses (HPVs) that can cause genital warts, herpes simplex virus (HSV) that can cause genital herpes, pelvic inflammatory disease (PID) that can cause sterility, hepatitis B virus (HBV), cytomegalovirus (CMV), pubic lice, scabies, and human immunodeficiency virus (HIV) that can cause AIDS.

If you have unprotected oral sex, you are at high risk for: gonorrhea, syphilis, chancroid, HSV, HPV, and CMV.

If you have sex play without sexual intercourse you are at risk for: HSV, CMV, HPV, pubic lice, scabies. Lots of other diseases, from the flu to mononucleosis, can also be transmitted sexually.

Are women at greater risk of getting STIs than men?

Yes. A woman's vagina and rectum are more easily infected than a man's penis. A woman's chance of being infected by a man with HIV is twice as great as a man's chance of being infected by a woman with HIV. Women generally have fewer symptoms than men; they are less likely to know if they are infected. Lots of damage can be done, even if there are no symptoms. Many women develop pelvic inflammatory disease because they don't know they have an STI. PID increases the risk of sterility and ectopic pregnancy.

Is it safe to have sex with only one partner?

Maybe. The ideal for many people is to have sex with only one partner. Women and men don't need to worry about getting STIs if neither partner ever had sex with anyone else, if neither partner ever shared needles, and if neither partner was ever infected. Most of us have more than one sex partner during our lives. We may not plan it that way, but it happens. We may also get an infection from one partner and carry it to another. The partners who gave it to us may not have known they were infected, may have hoped they wouldn't infect us, or may not have been totally honest about their sexual history. Some of us have only one partner, but our partner may "cheat." Most women who got HIV from having sex thought they were their sex partners' only sex partners.

You and your sex partner may want to give up safer sex because you've decided to have sex with no one else. Before you do, be sure that neither of you is infected. Some infections, like HIV, may take years to develop symptoms. You may not even know they are there. See your local Planned Parenthood or health-care provider and get yourselves checked out for STIs.

Whom can we trust?

Many of us know how it feels to discover that a sex partner has been dishonest with us. More than one out of three people will lie about their feelings to have sex with someone else. A similar number will lie about their sexual history. The same number will lie about whether or not they have HIV! When it comes to safer sex, rely on yourself. You're the only one you know you can trust. Believing you are your sex partner's only sex partner will not make it true.

Here are some questions to think over: Do I know how my partner spends time away from me? Is my partner always open about everything with me? Does my partner get upset if I want to have a "serious" talk about our relationship? Does my partner keep secrets from me? Does my partner ever say, "I'm just going out," or, "It's none of your business"? Is my partner always respectful to me?

We all want partners we can trust. The key is to make sure our partners earn our trust. We should never just give it away.

Can sex be very satisfying without intercourse?

Yes! Great sex is about a lot more than penetration with a penis. It's about exploring the many ways you can turn your partner on. It's exploring the many ways that you can be turned on. It's about finding new turn-ons and rediscovering old ones. You don't have to be shy about your sexual pleasure. Partners who explore safer sex with one another may discover new sexual excitements. They can be clear about how and where they like to be caressed, and help one another enjoy sex even more.

Sex play without penetration is called "mutual pleasuring" or "outercourse." A lot of people have vaginal intercourse because they think they're supposed to. For a long time, women and men were taught that "good sex" only meant having an orgasm during vaginal intercourse. Nothing could be less true. Most women don't have orgasms from vaginal stimulation. Most of them get orgasms when the clitoris is stimulated—whether or not they are being penetrated by a penis. Men also enjoy outercourse—even if they're shy about letting their partners know. Outercourse with many partners can be safer than intercourse with only one.

What kind of birth control is best for safer sex?

Condoms are the best protection for avoiding STIs while enjoying sexual intercourse. Condoms help make sex last longer. Condoms help prevent premature ejaculation. Latex condoms offer good protection against vaginitis caused by infections like trichomoniasis, as well as PID, gonorrhea, chlamydia, syphilis, chancroid, and HIV/AIDS. Latex condoms offer some protection against genital warts, herpes, and hepatitis B virus.

What else should I know about STIs and birth control?

Most forms of birth control do not protect against STIs. If there is a risk of STI infection, use a condom or vaginal pouch every time you have vaginal intercourse—even if you use the Pill, Norplant, Depo-Provera, IUD, diaphragm, cervical cap, fertility awareness methods, withdrawal, foam, cream, jelly, film, or suppository—in fact, even if you are sterilized. Spermicide offers some protection against chlamydia, gonorrhea, and trichomoniasis; do not rely on it to protect against viruses like HIV, HSV, and HPV. Vaginal pouches also protect against STIs. The pouch is a polyurethane sheath, with a flexible ring at each end, which is inserted deep into the vagina like a diaphragm. It stays in place even if a guy loses his erection. Condoms can be used for protection during oral sex on men. Cut-open condoms, dental dams, and plastic wrap provide protection during oral sex on women.

Why do people take risks when they know it may be dangerous?

Many people have mixed feelings about sex. As much as we like sex, it embarrasses a lot of us. Sometimes we can't admit we enjoy it. Some of us use alcohol or other drugs to feel less self-conscious about enjoying ourselves. But drugs also encourage us to take risks we wouldn't take if we weren't high. The more we use drugs when we have sex, the more likely we are to take risks. We also have a lot of feelings that encourage taking risks with sex—among them passion, desire to be swept away, fear of losing a partner, low self-esteem, need to be wanted, embarrassment, insecurity, anger, and shyness.

Women and men who are comfortable with their sexuality are more likely to enjoy safer sex. If drug use, shame, or other feelings block your safer sex plans, make an appointment to talk with a sexual health counselor. A counselor can help you work through the feelings that keep you from having safer sex.

Source: Planned Parenthood® Federation of America, Inc. Adapted with permission from *Sex—Safer and Satisfying: A Guide for the Sexually Active*, © 1996 Planned Parenthood Federation of America, Inc. All rights reserved. To order the complete booklet, call (800) 669-0156. For more information about STIs, check out the free materials at your nearest Planned Parenthood health center. They can tell you all you need to know about effects, symptoms, diagnosis, treatment, and prevention. To make an appointment at the Planned Parenthood health center nearest you, call (800) 230-PLAN.

Vasectomy

Why choose vasectomy?

Vasectomy is the most reliable of all birth control methods, is a convenient office procedure, acts as permanent birth control for the man, and, over time, is the least expensive method of birth control.

What family planning issues ought to be considered?

Several choices are available for contraception, and each couple must choose the method that best suits their needs. Permanent methods include sterilization by tubal ligation in the woman or by vasectomy in the man. These procedures are generally considered irreversible, so sterilization should be chosen only by those who have decided that they will not wish to have more children. There are a number of temporary and reversible methods of birth control available as well.

While no one can predict the future, you must take into consideration the possibility of unforeseen changes in your life or in the lives of your spouse and children. Can you imagine a situation in which you would regret having chosen sterilization? Would you consider the alternative of adoption? You should also consider the risks and consequences of having an unintended pregnancy while using a reversible method of contraception instead of sterilization.

Is vasectomy a "sure thing"?

Vasectomy is the most effective of all the methods of birth control; it also ranks among the safest and most effective of surgeries. But nothing is perfect, and no surgery is 100 percent safe or effective. The failure rate for this method of vasectomy has been reported as 0.4 percent. That is to say, four out of 1,000 men would remain fertile, even several months after the vasectomy. If you are still fertile, the clinic that performed your vasectomy may offer to repeat the procedure at no cost. Some doctors may refer the patient for repeat vasectomy, which would usually mean another fee. Patients should ask about this policy in advance.

How much pain or discomfort will I experience during the procedure?

This varies with the individual, but most men say the discomfort is quite mild, and that there is no pain after the anesthetic is given. You might think of it as similar to making a donation at your local blood bank. After an initial sting, you rest fairly comfortably through the ten-minute procedure, then get up and go home.

Will my sex life be affected?

Sex drive, erection, orgasm, and ejaculation are not interfered with by the operation. Vasectomy only blocks the sperm from coming out. The male sex hormones in the blood do not change. If a man or his partner had negative feelings about vasectomy, like other feelings it could affect sexual performance. However, many men and women have said that the relief from worry about pregnancy has improved their sex lives after vasectomy.

Why is vasectomy not effective immediately?

During vasectomy, the vas deferens from each side is cut high in the scrotum. The sperm stored "downstream" in the seminal vesicles can still be ejaculated and cause pregnancy until the system is emptied, which is usually complete after 15 ejaculations and six weeks' time.

What is the risk of complications?

As with any surgical procedure, complications do occasionally occur. With vasectomy, the risk is about 5 percent, or one in 20 men, who will have a complication. The majority of these are minor and temporary, easily treated with rest and medication. More serious complications occur in less than 1 percent of vasectomies.

What is the "no-scalpel technique"?

The basic technique of vasectomy, using *electrocautery*, has become popular worldwide and has proven to have a high success rate. Recent refinements in technique, based on work done by Dr. Li in China, allow the entire procedure to be done without cutting with a scalpel. There are other effective techniques that may be preferred by different surgeons. You should ask about the technique your doctor uses.

The doctor locates each vas deferens and injects a local anesthetic to numb the skin and both vasa. The left vas deferens is then held just under the skin of the scrotum while a small puncture opening less than $\frac{1}{8}$ inch long is made in the skin to expose the vas. The vas is separated from the sheath of surrounding tissues and brought out through the opening. It is then cut and one or both ends are sealed using an electric cautery needle.

The sealing effect of cautery is temporary, but it stimulates formation of a strong scar which blocks the vas. The two ends of the vas are then separated by using an absorbable suture to pull the sheath tissue between the cut ends. This step helps to ensure that when healing is taking place, the ends of the vas will not heal back together, allowing sperm to cross the cut. The left vas is put back in place, and the right vas is located and held where it can be reached through the same opening. The right vas is cut, sealed, and sutured, just like the left, then put back into place. The small skin opening closes itself without stitches.

Can I have the vasectomy reversed?

With microscopic surgery by a skilled and experience surgeon, it can be reconnected. But even after making this attempt, as many as half of all patients will not succeed in having children. Vasectomy should be considered a permanent operation.

Are there men who should not have vasectomy?

Yes. If a man does not want vasectomy and is having it because he is told he should, he may feel resentment. If he is having problems with impotence or sexual fears or an unhappy marriage, it is not likely that vasectomy will help any of these problems.

How do I find a reliable doctor to perform the vasectomy?

My advice to patients is to ask their family doctor about vasectomy. All family doctors will perform this procedure themselves or know where to refer their patients.

Source: Charles L. Wilson, M.D., founded The Vasectomy Clinic in 1987. He is a Clinical Associate Professor of Family Medicine at the University of Washington School of Medicine, is a Fellow of the American Academy of Family Physicians, and on the faculty of the AAFP Clinical Procedures Workshops on no-scalpel vasectomy. The Vasectomy Clinic, 3216 NE 45th Street, Suite 220, Seattle, WA 98105; (206) 525-4090 (a message is available 24 hours a day).

Water Birth

Why do women choose to have their babies in water?

Water birth is more a philosophy of nonintervention than a method of giving birth—it profoundly demonstrates that a women is empowered by "giving birth," not "being delivered." Having labor and giving birth in water is a natural, gentle alternative—warm water is used to control pain, aid relaxation, and provide an environment for more control and freedom of movement. Water birth provides a gentle transition for both mother and baby, and among many health-care practitioners around the world it is considered the best non-narcotic pain relief for laboring women.

Is it new?

It is just beginning to become well-known and offered as an option in the United States, but this method is currently quite popular in many European countries. The use of water at birth has been an accepted practice around the world for thousands of years in many indigenous cultures.

Is it safe?

To date, there are estimates that more than 40,000 water births have taken place worldwide, with no reports of life-threatening complications for either the mother or the baby.

How does the baby breathe?

Understanding how a newborn takes its first breath helps to dispel any fears about the safety of water birth. There is a complex physiological mechanism which inhibits the baby from taking a breath when it is born in water. It is commonly believed that the stimulus to breathe is caused by the baby's face coming into direct contact with air. During those first seconds after birth, when the newborn is under the water up until the time it is lifted out, the baby receives oxygen from its mother via the placenta and the umbilical cord, just as it has for the prior nine months in the womb. The newborn baby also has an innate reflex—the dive reflex—which allows it to be in the water without inhaling. That is why infants swim so easily in water and don't have problems with breathing.

When do you take the baby out of the water?

We do not advocate leaving the baby in the water for any reason after the full body is birthed. As long as the umbilical cord is intact and the placenta is functioning, the baby will remain in the same steady state it was before and during birth. However, if the placenta were to detach from the uterine wall, it would interrupt the baby's flow of oxygenated blood. That is why it is essential for the newborn to be brought out of the water immediately after birth. Without hurrying, someone reaches down—it can be the mother, father, midwife, or doctor—and gently lifts the baby up, and hands it to the mother. Everything stops at that point as the new arrival and the mother luxuriate in the warmth of the water and the quiet that surrounds them.

Will the mother get an infection from the water?

In the 1950s, women were told that it was unsafe to take a bath in the latter stages of pregnancy because the cervix was opening and the uterus could be infected by germs in the water. This edict against bathing is still printed in some childbirth books read by women today. If a woman's bag of water has ruptured before labor begins, most doctors will advise her to stay out of the bath until labor is initiated and progressing. Otherwise, bathing, especially during labor, is encouraged without worry of infection. The only precaution is to make sure that the water for bathing is clean.

Some couples go to the extreme of using purified water for the tub in which they intend to give birth. Regular tap water is usually sufficient. During labor, everything is moving down and out. The baby is descending into the birth canal. It does not make sense that bacteria from the water would go up into the uterus. In fact, the concentration of bacteria in and around the vagina is actually diluted by the water, lessening the possibility of infection.

What are the tubs like?

The standard home bathtub and even the hospital Jacuzzi are just too small to be comfortable for the mother, and midwives find it difficult to assist with a birth. Many women use the bathtub for labor, but get out to give birth. Molded fiberglass hot tubs are used by some couples, especially if they live in warm climates. These hot tubs are actually too deep. The best tubs we have found are either inflatable or collapsible portable ones. These portable tubs frequently have features that make them ideal for hospital installation; they are available for sale, or rental, and are generally kept by a couple for a minimum four-week period. Many couples have taken their own tubs into hospitals or birth centers. Fathers often report that they enjoy being in charge of setting up and filling the labor pools for their partners. It gives them something practical to do for the birth in addition to being there for emotional support.

How hot should the water be?

Water should be maintained at a temperature that is comfortable for the mother, usually 95–100°F. If the water is too hot, dehydration becomes a problem, as well as overheating, which can cause the baby's heart rate to go up.

At what stage of labor do you get in the water?

A woman should be encouraged to use the labor pool whenever she wants. In early labor, the contractions will sometimes space out or stop altogether, so the woman needs to get out of the pool and walk to keep labor established. Labor often progresses quickly when a woman waits until her cervix is at least 5 cm dilated before getting into water. Most women don't get out again once they get in!

Do all hospitals offer water birth as an option?

No. Not in this country, where water birth is just beginning to take hold, although the number of hospitals that have accepted water birth has grown exponentially in the past year. Currently, about 10 percent of the hospitals that have maternity units have bathtubs or Jacuzzis for water birth. Hospitals are more cooperative today as more doctors and midwives see the benefits of allowing women to make their own choices. Between 1995 and the beginning of 1997, over 40 new hospitals began offering water birth. Water birth is much more common in Europe and other parts of the world. In fact, the National Health Service in England has encouraged the use of water by installing baths in 219 British hospitals.

How are emergencies handled in the water?

The physicians and midwives who include water birth in their practices carefully monitor the progress of the birth and the baby's status throughout labor, just as in any birth. If an emergency is encountered, the situation is assessed and the proper course of action taken. The mother may be required to get out of the tub or simply change positions. Practitioners use their own judgment and level of experience during labor and birth to guide them.

Are most women pleased with the experience?

Yes! The Global Maternal/Child Health Association (GMCHA) has been sending out surveys to parents who have experienced a water birth since 1989.

The stories that come back are nothing short of incredible. One of the questions that we ask is: "Would you consider giving birth in water again?" Out of approximately 1,200 returned surveys, only one woman wrote that she would not give birth in water again, but attached was a little note that said, "This is number seven. I'm *done!*" So 100 percent of the women we surveyed who had one water birth would do it again, given the right circumstances.

Source: Barbara Harper is President of Global Maternal/Child Health Association, a nonprofit organization that directs the Waterbirth International Resource and Referral Service, which provides information and resources on waterbirth. Ms. Harper is the author of *Gentle Birth Choices* (Rochester, VT: Inner Traditions, 1994) and the forthcoming *Waterbirth: Dispelling the Myth—Embracing the Magic.* For more information, contact: Global Maternal/Child Health Association (GMCHA), P.O. Box 1400, Wilsonville, OR 97070; phone: (503) 682-3600; fax: (503) 682-3434; e-mail: waterbirth@aol.com; Web site: www.geocities.com/hotsprings/2840.

ILLNESSES AND DISEASES

———◆———

AIDS • Alcoholism

Allergies and Asthma

Arthritis • Cancer • Brain Tumors

Breast Cancer • Lymphoma

Prostate Cancer

Cerebral Palsy • Chicken Pox

Chronic Fatigue
Syndrome

Cystic Fibrosis • Diabetes

Heart Attack • Hepatitis

High Blood Pressure • Insomnia

Kidney Disease and
Kidney Stones

Lupus • Lyme Disease

Multiple Sclerosis • Osteoporosis

Stroke • Venereal Diseases

AIDS

What causes AIDS?

AIDS (acquired immune deficiency syndrome) is caused by the human immunodeficiency virus (HIV). HIV destroys the body's ability to fight infections by killing or impairing cells of the immune system. This leaves the immune system open to microbes that cause illness which would easily be dealt with in healthy human beings.

Do only homosexuals get AIDS?

No, although they run a greater risk of getting the disease if not careful. HIV is most commonly spread by sexual contact, but also may be passed through blood, sharing contaminated needles, and even from mother to child during pregnancy.

When was the first case of AIDS in the United States reported?

AIDS was first reported in the United States in 1981.

What are the early symptoms of this disease?

Although not everyone develops symptoms when they first become infected with HIV, some people contract flulike symptoms within a month or two after exposure to the virus, as well as fever, headaches, malaise, and enlarged lymph nodes. These symptoms may be mistaken for other illnesses, and more persistent or severe symptoms may not surface for a decade or more after infection in an adult.

Is it possible to become infected with HIV and not contract AIDS?

A small number of people initially infected with HIV have not developed symptoms of AIDS in over a decade of their infection.

How can you be diagnosed if you are infected with HIV?

Because early HIV infection often causes no symptoms, it is primarily detected by testing a person's blood for the presence of *antibodies* (disease-fighting proteins) to HIV. HIV antibodies generally do not reach detectable levels until one to three months following infection, and may take as long as six months to be generated in quantities large enough to show up in standard blood tests.

Do children of HIV-infected mothers always get AIDS?

Not necessarily. Infants born of infected mothers may or may not be infected by the virus, but all carry their mother's antibodies to HIV for several months.

They can be tested after about 15 months to see whether they have produced their own antibodies if infected.

Is there any treatment for people suffering with AIDS?

When AIDS first surfaced in the United States, no drugs were available to combat the underlying immune deficiency and few treatments existed for the diseases that developed. In the past ten years, the FDA has approved eight drugs for treatment, including AZT, which, along with other drugs, may slow the spread of HIV in the body.

Is there any way to prevent getting AIDS?

Since no vaccine for HIV is available, the only way to prevent infection by the virus is to avoid behaviors that put a person at risk of infection, such as having unprotected sex and sharing needles.

How many people have AIDS?

More than 500,000 cases of AIDS have been reported in the United States since 1981, and as many as 900,000 Americans are believed to be infected with HIV.

Source: National Institute of Allergy and Infectious Disease, Department of Health & Human Services, Bethesda, MD 20892; (301) 496-5717.

Alcoholism

What is *alcoholism*?

Alcoholism, which is also known as *alcohol dependence syndrome*, is a disease characterized by the following elements: craving (a strong need or compulsion to drink); loss of control (the frequent inability to stop drinking once a person has begun); physical dependence (the occurrence of withdrawal symptoms such as nausea, sweating, shakiness, and anxiety); and tolerance (the need for increasing amounts of alcohol in order to get "high").

Why can't most alcoholics drink just a little alcohol?

Because alcoholics are in the grip of a powerful craving for alcohol, a need that can feel as strong as the need for food or water. Alcoholism has little to do with what kind of alcohol one drinks, how long one has been drinking, or even exactly how much alcohol one consumes. It has a great deal to do with a person's uncontrollable need for alcohol.

How can I tell if I or someone close to me has a drinking problem?

By answering the following questions: Have you ever felt you should cut down on your drinking? Have people annoyed you by criticizing your drinking? Have you ever felt bad or guilty about your drinking? Have you ever had a drink first thing in the morning to steady your nerves or to get rid of a hangover?

One "yes" response suggests a possible alcohol problem. If you responded "yes" to more than one question, it is highly likely that a problem exists. Even if you answered no to all the above questions, if you are encountering drinking-related problems with your job, relationships, health, or with the law, you should still seek professional help.

What are the consequences of alcohol misuse?

Heavy drinking can increase the risk for certain cancers, especially those of the liver, esophagus, throat, and larynx (voice box). It can also cause liver cirrhosis, immune system problems, brain damage, and harm to the fetus during pregnancy. In addition, drinking increases the risk of death from automobile crashes, recreational accidents, and on-the-job accidents. And it increases the likelihood of homicide and suicide.

Why can some individuals use alcohol without problems, while others are unable to control their drinking?

Recent research supported by the National Institute on Alcohol Abuse and Alcoholism has demonstrated that for many people, a vulnerability to alcoholism is inherited. Yet it is important to recognize that aspects of a person's environment—such as peer influences and the availability of alcohol—are also significant. Both inherited and environmental influences are called "risk factors." But risk is not destiny. Just because alcoholism tends to run in families doesn't mean that a child of an alcoholic parent will automatically develop alcoholism.

What's the treatment for alcoholism?

It depends on the severity of the individual's alcoholism and the resources available in his/her community. Treatment may include *detoxification* (the process of safely getting alcohol out of one's system); taking doctor-prescribed medications to help prevent a return to drinking once drinking has stopped; and individual and/or group counseling.

What role does Alcoholics Anonymous play in treatment?

Virtually all alcoholism treatment programs also include meetings of Alcoholics Anonymous (AA), which describes itself as a "worldwide fellowship of men and women who help each other to stay sober." While AA is generally recognized as an effective mutual help program for recovering alcoholics, not everyone responds to AA's style and message, and other approaches are available. Even those who are helped usually find that AA works best in combination with other elements of treatment, including counseling and medical care.

Can alcoholism be cured?

Alcoholism is a treatable disease, but a cure is not yet available. That means that even if an alcoholic has been sober for a long while and has regained health, he remains susceptible to relapse and must continue to avoid all alcoholic beverages.

What if an alcoholic has a relapse?

Relapses are very common. They do *not* mean that a person has failed or cannot eventually recover from alcoholism.

Source: *Alcoholism*, a publication of the National Institute on Alcohol Abuse and Alcoholism. For more information, call or write: Alcoholics Anonymous (AA) World Services, 475 Riverside Drive (11th floor), New York, NY 10115; (212) 870-3400.

Allergies and Asthma

What is an *allergy*?

An allergy is an inherited trait, a genetic susceptibility toward the production of an allergy antibody called IgE. These allergy antibodies act like fuses on the outside of the allergy mast cells. Once the fuse, IgE, comes into contact with foreign materials such as pollen or cat dander that originally triggered the allergy, then the mast cell explodes. This allergic explosion releases histamine and other chemicals into the surrounding area, and may produces the immediate symptoms of sneezing, wheezing, hives, and itching so characteristic of allergic reactions.

What's the connection between allergies and asthma?

Not everybody with allergies has asthma, and vice versa. But there is a connection. Ninety percent or more of children with asthma have allergies, while 50 percent of adult asthmatics are affected.

Is it possible for a person to outgrow allergies and asthma?

A recent study conducted in the Netherlands by Dutch and American researchers adds to the evidence that most children do not outgrow asthma. This study found that breathing difficulties in about 75 percent of children with moderate to severe asthma persisted or recurred by the time they reached their mid-20s. For some with very mild asthma, symptoms do subside, but those with moderate or severe asthma usually continue to experience symptoms into their adult lives. As children mature, their airways grow, sometimes easing the symptoms.

An allergic reaction is an abnormal response a person has to a substance that is ordinarily harmless. This response depends on a person's individual genetic makeup and is not outgrown.

473

Are asthma and allergies inherited?

The tendency to develop asthma or allergies is most often inherited, although the chances of developing asthma are influenced by a variety of factors, including allergies, infections, irritants, and the environment. Cigarette smoking by parents; exposure to dust mites, cockroaches, and cats; humidifier use; high concentrations of nitrogen dioxide (mainly from gas stoves); and electric heating in the home are all factors that may increase the risk of a child developing asthma. Currently, 20 percent of the population suffers from allergies. If one parent is allergic, a child has a 40 percent chance of having allergies; if both parents are allergy sufferers, their child has an 80 percent chance.

Do people die from asthma?

Yes. Approximately 15 people die from asthma-related deaths each day. Nearly all of these deaths are preventable.

What are the worst areas of the United States for people allergic to pollen?

Every area has pollen, but ragweed, which is a major culprit, grows most heavily in the middle of the country, causing problems from August through the first frost. People on the West Coast aren't exposed to ragweed. The East Coast has ragweed growth which is significant but less than the Midwest. Moving to a different climate isn't necessarily going to give relief of symptoms, though. While the argument for making an asthma-related move is to avoid triggers such as cold air or high humidity and moldiness, many people find that they just trade old allergies for new ones after a move.

Why do my allergies seem to get worse every year?

Your level of tolerance may be declining, but a likely reason for your worsening allergies is that once you have an allergic reaction in the eyes, nose, or throat, these areas are more reactive to other substances. That is, they become increasingly more irritable. If your perfume makes you sneeze during your allergy season but not during the rest of the year, this is most likely the case.

If you are treating yourself with over-the-counter antihistamines, it's also possible that you are becoming less and less responsive to these medications.

What is an *allergen?*

An allergen is a very small protein substance capable of inducing an allergic or other immune system response. Physicians use allergens to skin-test patients in order to diagnose exactly which allergens cause the symptoms of allergy or asthma.

Is it safe to take antihistamines for long periods of time?

Yes, although they may become slightly less effective over time.

What's the scoop on these new, prescription-only nose sprays everyone's talking about?

They are called *intranasal corticosteroids*. Corticosteroids work to prevent the allergic reaction (by preventing your body's release of histamine) as well as to prevent and reverse inflammation that goes along with it. Other nasal sprays, like Nasalcrom, block the allergic reaction but do not reverse inflammation. The latter must be taken before the reaction begins to work.

Physicians warn to keep off antihistamines for at least three days before taking a skin test for allergies, as they will block the reaction.

Why do antihistimines make you sleepy?

This is a direct effect on the brain induced by conventional antihistamines when they cross from the bloodstream into the brain. The newer prescription-only antihistamines do not cross into the brain and therefore do not cause sleepiness.

Are there nondrowsy antihistamines that work?

First of all, most over-the-counter allergy relief medicines that say "nondrowsy" on the packaging are not antihistamines. The antihistamine is what makes you drowsy, but it is also the most effective over-the-counter agent in combating allergies because it works to stop the symptoms caused by release of histamine from your mast cells.

Some effective, nondrowsy antihistamines, available by prescription only, are Claritin, Zyrtec, and Allegra.

Are cortisone injections a viable option for people who don't want to take allergy pills?

No. It's probably used in some places, but cortisone can do structural damage to the nose and causes many other negative side affects, such as cataracts, calcium leaching from bones, puffiness of the skin, and muscle weakness. Cortisone injections should not be used as a substitute for allergy medicine.

Do allergy shots help?

Immunotherapy is a program consisting of injections of the particular allergens to which a person is allergic. Treatments begin with low doses every week, usually lasting from 4 to 12 months. They then continue every other week for approximately six months; then every three weeks for another 15 to 18 months. The average course of treatment is three to five years. Allergy injections are most effective for those who are allergic to seasonal pollens, animal dander, and dust. Although not a cure, they can help to reduce symptoms and the need for medication. About 85 percent of patients receiving immunotherapy have a dramatic reduction in asthma and allergy symptoms within one year.

What's the difference between a cold and an allergy?

A cold will most likely have been caught from another person who was sick; it will be gone in a week to ten days. An allergy induces similar symptoms but is more itchy than a cold and lasts for a longer time. Allergies usually occur during the same seasons year after year.

What are *hives,* and how are they related to allergies?

Hives are a swelling of the skin, often caused by an allergic reaction. The rash is composed of *wheals,* the pale or raised areas, and *flares,* the red areas around the raised areas. Hives look like bug bites and can appear anywhere on the body. They usually occur because an individual is experiencing an allergic reaction to a particular substance. Hives are a warning sign that your body can't handle something. Food and drugs are the most common causes of hives.

Should I worry if I have hives?

If you are experiencing head-to-toe itching, play it safe and get medical help. If the hives only cover a small area on the body, and they have been present for less than three days, try easing the itch by taking an antihistamine, applying hydrocortisone cream, or taking a lukewarm bath in Aveeno or another natural-based, soothing product. Don't overbathe, however, as this will dry out the skin and could worsen the rash.

If I get hives once, will I get them again?

Possibly, and the next time you could have a worse reaction to whatever caused the problem.

Try to find the culprit by using common sense: Look for a change in detergent or soap. If you have just eaten something unusual or taken an antibiotic, see a physician.

How serious is it if I'm stung by a bee?

The site of the sting may swell and itch, and hives may follow. But if you are: hit with an asthma attack, lightheaded or flushed, faint, have diarrhea, hives, or other signs of a real allergic reaction, you should be treated accordingly, then tested. If you are allergic to bee stings, you can be desensitized with a series of shots that lower the chances of an allergic reaction from 60 percent down to about one percent.

Source: Institute for Asthma and Allergy, Washington Hospital Center, 106 Irving Street NW, Suite 108, Washington, DC 20010; (202) 877-8777; (800) ASTHMA-5.

Arthritis

What are some common forms of arthritis?

Osteoarthritis (OA), at one time called *degenerative joint disease,* is the most common type of arthritis in older people. Symptoms can range from stiffness and mild pain that comes and goes to severe joint pain and even disability.

Rheumatoid arthritis (RA) can be one of the more disabling forms of arthritis. Signs of RA often include morning stiffness, swelling in three or more joints, swelling of the same joints on both sides of the body (both hands, for example), and bumps (or nodules) under the skin most commonly found near the elbow. RA can occur at any age; it affects women about three times more often than men.

Gout occurs most often in older men. It affects the toes, ankles, elbows, wrists, and hands.

What are OA's symptoms and causes?

OA usually affects the hands and the large, weight-bearing joints of the body: the knees and hips. Early in the disease, pain occurs after activity and rest brings relief; later on, pain occurs with every little movement, even during rest.

Scientists think that several factors may cause OA in joints. OA in the hands or hips may run in families. OA in the knees is linked to being overweight. Injuries or overuse may cause OA in joints such as knees, hips, or hands.

What are RA's symptoms and causes?

Scientists think RA has something to do with a breakdown in the immune system, the body's defense against disease. It is also likely that people who get RA have certain inherited traits (genes) that cause a disturbance in the immune system.

What about gout's symptoms?

An acute attack of gout is very painful. Swelling may cause the skin to pull tightly around the joint (usually toes, ankles, elbows, wrists, and hands) and make the area red or purple and extremely tender.

What are the common warning signs for arthritis?

Warning signs include: swelling in one or more joint(s); morning stiffness lasting 30 minutes or longer; joint pain or tenderness that is constant or that comes and goes; not being able to move a joint in the normal way; redness or warmth in a joint; weight loss, fever, or weakness and joint pain that can't be explained. If any one of these symptoms lasts longer than two weeks, see your regular doctor or a doctor who specializes in arthritis (a rheumatologist).

What treatments are available for arthritis?

Treatments for arthritis work to reduce pain and swelling, keep joints moving safely, and avoid further damage to the joints. Treatments include medicines, special exercise, use of heat or cold, weight control, and surgery.

What kind of medicine is used?

Acetaminophen (ACT) should be the first drug used to control pain in patients with osteoarthritis. Patients who don't respond to acetaminophen and patients with rheumatoid arthritis and gout are most commonly treated with nonsteroidal anti-inflammatory drugs such as ibuprofen. People taking medicine for any form of arthritis should limit the amount of alcohol they drink.

What type of exercise is recommended?

A daily walk or swim keep joints moving, reduces pain, and strengthens muscles around the joints. Rest is also important for the joints affected by arthritis. Physical therapists can develop personal programs that balance exercise and rest.

Does anything help reduce the pain?

Other than medicine and exercise, some people find that soaking in a warm bath, swimming in a heated pool, or applying heat or cold to the area around the joint helps reduce the pain. Controlling or losing weight can reduce the stress on joints and help avoid further damage.

When is surgery recommended?

If damage to the joints becomes disabling or when other treatments fail to reduce pain, your doctor may suggest surgery. Surgeons can repair or replace damaged joints with artificial ones. The most common operations are hip and knee replacements.

Do copper bracelets really help?

No, they're useless. And snake venom, another quack cure, is harmful. In general, watch for the following kinds of claims: those that say they work for all types of arthritis and other diseases as well (often with lotions or creams); those whose scientific support comes only from one research study; those whose labels have no directions for use or warnings about side effects.

Source: *Arthritis Advice,* a brochure published by the National Institute on Aging. For more information, call or write: National Institute of Arthritis and Musculoskeletal and Skin Diseases, Building 31, Room 4C05, Bethesda, MD 20892; (301) 496-8188.

Cancer

What is *cancer*?

Cancer is a large group of diseases characterized by uncontrolled growth and spread of abnormal cells.

How do cancer cells behave differently from normal cells?

Normal cells reproduce in an orderly manner and grow for a purpose, such as to replace worn-out tissues or repair injuries. Cancer cells grow for no reason. They multiply uncontrollably, destroying normal cells, and can spread to other parts of the body.

Does a lump always mean I have cancer?

No. A lump which is diagnosed as a benign tumor is made up of cells that are not cancerous. Benign tumors do not spread to other parts of the body. They are usually harmless.

What is a *precancerous lesion*?

A precancerous lesion is made up of atypical cells that have the potential of becoming cancer.

How does cancer spread?

Cancer cells invade neighboring tissues, and spread to distant parts of the body by way of the bloodstream or lymph vessels. The spread of cancer is called *metastasis*.

How fast does cancer grow?

The rate of cancer growth varies. Some cancers grow rapidly; others may grow slowly over a period of years.

How many different kinds of cancer are there?

More than 100 forms of cancer occur in any tissue or organ of the body, including the blood (*leukemia*) and lymphatic system (*lymphomas*).

Can anyone get cancer?

Yes, cancer can develop in people of all races, ethnic backgrounds, and at any age.

What are the most common cancers?

In men, the most common cancers are skin, prostate, lung, and colon-rectum; in women, they are cancers of the skin, breast, colon-rectum, lung, and uterus. For both sexes combined, the most common cancers are skin, breast, lung, and colon-rectum.

Certain types of cancer occur more frequently in different parts of the world. The incidence of colon cancer is high in the United States, for example, and extremely low in Africa. Breast cancer, the second leading cause of cancer death in American women, is much less common in Japan. On the other hand, stomach cancer is much more common in Europe and Asia than in this country. Scientists are exploring the reasons for these variations.

How many people will develop cancer and is the incidence rate of cancer higher among black people?

About 76 million Americans now living will eventually develop cancer—roughly 30 percent according to present rates. Statistics from an ongoing National Cancer Institute program show that cancer is more common in black men than white men. Black and white women have about the same rates. Of the leading sites of cancer, blacks have a higher incidence of cancers of the lung, prostate, and uterine cervix than do whites. These differences are probably related to economic, environmental, and social factors, rather than to biological characteristics.

Are more people surviving cancer today?

Yes. In the 1930s, less than one in five cancer patients was alive five years after treatment; in the 1940s, one in four survived five years. Today, almost four out of ten patients, or 40 percent, are alive five years after diagnosis of cancer. The relative survival rate is 54 percent.

How many people die of cancer?

One out of every five deaths from all causes each year in the United States is due to cancer.

Why does cancer start?

The exact mechanism is still unclear, but several factors have been identified as *carcinogenic,* or cancer-producing. These include the use of tobacco products, exposure to occupational substances like fluorocarbons and asbestos, certain chemicals, radiation, and excessive exposure to sunlight.

Does cigarette smoking really cause cancer?

Smoking is responsible for 87 percent of all lung cancers. Smokers are also more likely to develop cancer of the mouth, pharynx, larynx, esophagus, pancreas, bladder, cervix, and kidney. In fact, smoking accounts for 30 percent of all cancer deaths. It is also a major source of heart disease, stroke, chronic bronchitis, and emphysema.

Can air and water pollution cause cancer?

Pollutants in air and water do include chemical and radioactive materials that have carcinogenic potential. The concentrations, when present, are usually very low, and human population studies have not clearly shown any increased cancer risks. Where risks have been suggested, they are far smaller than those associated with cigarette smoking. Lung cancer risks from indoor radon air pollution are much greater for smokers than for nonsmokers.

Do certain occupations carry a higher risk for cancer?

Yes. Workers exposed to asbestos, benzene, coal-tar pitch, and uranium are more likely to develop lung cancer. These risks greatly increase if the occupational exposure is combined with cigarette smoking. Workers exposed to arsenic have a higher incidence of lung and skin cancers. Vinyl chloride workers have experienced a higher incidence of liver cancer. Workers in rubber and aniline plants are at greater risk for bladder cancer.

Can diet cause or prevent cancer?

Although no direct cause-effect relationship has been observed in humans, many scientific studies suggest that a high-fat diet may be associated with colon and rectum cancer, as well as prostate, uterus, and breast cancer. Fruits and vegetables might be protective against several types of cancer.

Is heavy alcohol consumption related to the development of cancer?

Heavy use of alcohol, especially when accompanied by cigarette smoking, increases the risk of cancers of the mouth, esophagus, liver, larynx, and stomach.

Is cancer inherited?

Some familial tendencies have been noted in cancers of the breast, colon, stomach, prostate, lung, ovary, and in leukemia. Relatives of patients with these cancers may need more frequent cancer-related checkups.

Do viruses cause cancer?

Viral agents have long been known to cause cancer in animals, but their role in human cancers is not yet clear. A few viruses can, however, be linked: HTLV-I virus with certain leukemias; hepatitis B virus with liver cancer; papilloma and herpes virus with cervical cancer; Epstein-Barr virus with certain lymphomas and nasopharynx cancer.

Can radiation cause cancer?

Yes. High-energy (ionizing) radiation is a known cause of leukemia, breast cancer, and lung cancer. Ultraviolet radiation from excessive sun exposures causes skin cancer. Lower-dose radiation (such as medical and dental X-rays), where exposures are much less than normally present on earth, has negligible effects. Lower-energy radiation (microwave and electromagnetic fields) does not appear to have any clear carcinogenic potential.

Can cancer be prevented?

Some, not all. Most lung cancers can be prevented by not smoking cigarettes; most skin cancers can be prevented by avoiding excessive sunlight and using protective sunscreens. Certain cancers caused by occupational or environmental factors can also be prevented by eliminating or reducing contact with known carcinogens. Also, needless deaths can be prevented by early detection.

What are the seven warning signals used by the American Cancer Society?

They are symptoms or changes that could be a sign of cancer:

1. a change in bowel or bladder habits
2. a sore throat that does not heal
3. unusual bleeding or discharge
4. thickening or a lump in the breast or elsewhere
5. indigestion or difficulty in swallowing
6. an obvious change in a wart or mole
7. nagging cough or hoarseness

Source: *Answering Your Questions About Cancer,* a publication of the American Cancer Society. For more information, call the American Cancer Society toll-free at (800) ACS-2345.

Brain Tumors

What is a *brain tumor?*

Tumors are a collection of abnormal, unnecessary cells in the brain. Since the adult body reproduces cells only to replace old or damaged ones, a tumor may develop when unneeded cells are produced, or if something occurs that disturbs this development function.

Can anyone get a brain tumor?

Primary brain tumors (tumors that start in the brain) can occur in people of any age, but statistically, children below 15 and older adults are more likely to get them. Malignant tumors (those that are life-threatening) make up about 1.3 percent of all cancers diagnosed in the United States.

What is the difference between a *benign* and a *malignant* brain tumor?

Benign tumor cells are usually slow-growing, distinct to one area, and can be removed by surgery rather easily. Malignant tumors are life-threatening and must be treated with one or more of the following procedures: surgery, radiation therapy, or chemotherapy.

What causes brain tumors?

The primary cause of brain tumors is as yet unknown.

What are the symptoms?

There are no specific symptoms that are common to all brain tumors; in fact, tumors may mimic the symptoms of other diseases, making them difficult to diagnose. Some general symptoms include frequent headaches due to pressure in the brain, nausea, dizziness, seizures; and frequent mental changes, including problems with speech, memory, and concentration.

What are the chances of mortality if a person is afflicted with a malignant brain tumor?

Primary malignant brain tumors represent 2.4 percent of deaths due to cancer in the United States. They are the second most common cause of cancer death in people ages 15 to 34.

What is the treatment for brain tumors?

The most common treatments are surgery, chemotherapy, radiation therapy, or a combination of the above. Surgery is most often used for accessible areas of the brain that have been found to have tumorous growth.

What are the chances of a child suffering from a brain tumor?

This disease is fairly rare among children, affecting only about 2,000 children a year; it is more likely in boys than girls.

What is *chemotherapy*?

Chemotherapy uses certain drugs to destroy tumor cells. The drugs may be taken orally, through the bloodstream, or placed into the cerebrospinal fluid.

Is the rate of brain tumors increasing or decreasing?

The rate could possibly be increasing, due to the fact that cancer patients today are living longer, which increases the opportunity for stray cancer cells to make their way into the brain.

Source: American Brain Tumor Association. For more information, call or write: American Brain Tumor Association, 2720 River Road, Suite 146, Des Plaines, IL 60018-4117; (800) 886-2282.

Breast Cancer

Are there some factors that increase the risk of breast cancer?

Risk is higher in women who have a family history of the disease, those who started menstruation at a young age, had menopause later than 50, never bore children, or used long-term estrogen replacement therapy. Risk increases with age.

How prevalent is breast cancer?

The American Cancer Society estimates that 184,300 new cases of breast cancer were diagnosed among women in the United States in 1996.

Is breast cancer becoming more prevalent?

The incidence rates for women have increased about 4 percent a year between 1982 and 1987, but appear to be leveling off at a rate of about one in eight. Between 1987 and 1992, incidence of developing breast cancer appeared to stabilize at approximately 109.6 cases per 100,000 women. One of the reasons for the leveling off is that more women are undergoing *mammography,* which is able to detect cancer at earlier stages. A second reason is improvement in breast cancer treatment.

How many people die a year from breast cancer?

The American Cancer Society estimates that 43,900 women and 290 men will die of breast cancer in 1997. Breast cancer is the second major cause of cancer death in women (lung cancer is the first).

What can be done to prevent breast cancer?

Since little is known about what causes breast cancer, there are no established rules for prevention.

How can I detect breast cancer?

A self-exam performed by women over 20 years of age every month is recommended, and a clinical breast examination by a physician every three years for women between the ages of 20 and 40, as well as a mammogram before they reach 40. Those between 40 and 50 should get a mammogram every one to two years, and those over 50 should get one every year.

What is a *biopsy?*

In a biopsy, a portion of breast tissue is removed and examined under a microscope to determine whether it is cancerous or not. This can be done on an outpatient basis.

What is the treatment for breast cancer?

Various types of treatments and combinations may be utilized by your physicians. Some common surgical ones include: *lumpectomy,* in which the cancerous lump is removed; *modified* or *simple mastectomy,* in which only the breast tissue is removed; *Halsted radical mastectomy,* in which the breast tissue and and the muscle underlying the breast are removed. Other treatments include radiation and chemotherapy.

Are there side effects of chemotherapy?

Side effects depend upon which drugs are utilized by your physician, as well as the dosage amount. Nausea and vomiting are common, as are a loss of appetite, hair loss, mouth or vaginal sores, fatigue, changes in the menstrual cycle, and increased chance of infections.

Are there side effects from surgery?

Yes. *Lymphedema* may occur if the lymph glands beneath the arm have been removed or treated with radiation therapy. Lymphedema is a swelling of the hand or arm due to collection of fluid. If left untreated, this can interfere with wound healing.

Source: American Cancer Society, New York City Division, Inc., 19 West 56th Street, New York, NY 10019-3984. For more information, call the American Cancer Society toll-free at (800) ACS-2345.

Lymphoma

What is *lymphoma?*

Lymphoma, simply put, is a cancer of the lymph system, part of the body's immune system. Because lymph tissue is in many parts of the body, the disease can start almost any place. Lymphoma is categorized in two separate ways; *Hodgkin's disease* and *non-Hodgkin's lymphoma.*

What are the types of lymphomas?

The three major types of non-Hodgkin's lymphomas are *low grade* (indolent types), *intermediate grade* (aggressive types), and *high grade* (very aggressive types).

What are the symptoms of lymphoma?

There are a number of different symptoms, including persistent fatigue, fever and chills, painless swelling of lymph nodes in the armpit, neck, or groin, night sweats, severe itching, and weight loss.

How prevalent is lymphoma?

According to the American Cancer Society, 61,100 new cases will be diagnosed in 1997. About 53,600 of these patients will have non-Hodgkins lymphoma.

How is lymphoma treated?

The most common treatment is chemotherapy plus low doses of radiation therapy, but treatment may differ depending on the stage and type of disease. Some patients are treated with radiation, bone, or cell transplants or newer biological therapics.

What are the stages that characterize lymphoma?

In stage one, cancer is found in only one lymph node area or in only one area or organ outside the lymph nodes. In stage two, cancer is found in two or more lymph node areas on the same side of the diaphragm (the thin muscle under the lungs that helps you breathe). In stage three, cancer is found in lymph node areas on both sides of the diaphragm. In stage four, cancer has spread to an organ or organs outside the lymph system.

How does a physician diagnose this disease?

Initially, the physician will ask about previous medical conditions, conduct an examination, take X-rays, and obtain a test of blood. But the most important will be a lymph node biopsy. If traces of lymphoma are found, a bone marrow biopsy or other similar tests may be necessary.

How serious is non-Hodgkin's lymphoma?

Low-grade non-Hodgkin's lymphoma is not curable at this time but is very responsive to initial therapy. There are many new treatments in clinical trials. The intermediate- and high-grade lymphomas progress more rapidly, but many patients achieve remission and may be cured.

How serious is Hodgkin's lymphoma?

If detected in early stages, there is a 90 percent survival rate. Fifty to 80 percent of those with advanced cases are disease-free after ten years of chemotherapy.

Where can people learn to get help?

Clinical trials are occurring around the country for most stages of lymphoma. If you want more information, contact the Cancer Information Service listed below.

Source: Cure for Lymphoma Foundation, 215 Lexington Avenue, New York, NY 10016; (212) 213-9595. For more information, call the Cancer Information Service toll-free at (800) 4-CANCER.

Prostate Cancer

What is the *prostate*?

The prostate is a gland—about an inch and a half in diameter or the size of a walnut—in men that is located just below the bladder and in front of the rectum. It wraps around a tube called the *urethra,* and produces a fluid that is part of semen.

Who is most likely to get prostate cancer?

It occurs most frequently in men over 50 years of age, and is most common in men over 65. Those with close family members who have had the cancer and African-American men are also more prone to prostate cancer, which is the most common type of cancer found in American men.

How can you diagnose prostate cancer?

A biopsy is the only positive way to diagnose the condition. After doing a digital rectal exam the physician routinely removes a small piece of the prostate through a thin needle and examines it for cancerous growth. For early detection, the American Cancer Society recommends that men age 50 and over have an annual prostate-specific antigen blood test.

How will I know the extent or stage of the cancer?

The doctor will order a variety of tests to insure proper diagnoses. These may include a prostate-specific antigen blood test, a bone scan, a CAT scan, magnetic resonance imaging, ultrasound, conventional X-rays, or a combination of such tests.

How does the doctor know if the cells are cancerous?

Cancer cells taken during the biopsy are graded by how closely they resemble normal cells. Aggressive cancer cells lack specific characteristics and distinguishing marks of normal cells.

Is surgery the only type of treatment for prostate cancer?

No. Along with surgery (called *radical prostatectomy*), radiation therapy, hormone therapy, and even "watchful waiting" are all common treatments for prostate cancer.

Are there side effects to prostate cancer treatment?

Unfortunately, yes. Incontinence and impotence are the most common side effects accompanying surgery. Fatigue, diarrhea, and irritated intestines may occur with radiation therapy. With hormone therapy, the attempt is to lower the level of testosterone, occasionally causing hot flashes and loss of sexual desire.

Is there any way to prevent prostate cancer?

Since the medical community is still unsure what causes prostate cancer, it does not know how to prevent it. Although doctors suggest a diet low in fat, the link between prostate cancer and saturated fat has still not been conclusively proven.

Are there any symptoms of prostate cancer that one can recognize?

There is little a layperson can do to detect prostate cancer, since in its earliest stages it usually causes no pain or other symptoms. Warning signs include pain in urination or weak or interrupted urine flow, but these could also result from a simple urinary infection which should still be evaluated by a physician. Other warning signs are continuing pain in the lower back, pelvis, or upper thighs.

What are the rates of survival?

Almost 87 percent of American men with prostate cancer can expect to live at least five years after the cancer has been diagnosed. For men with prostate cancer that has not spread farther than the prostate gland, the percentage rises to 99 percent.

Source: American Cancer Society, New York Division, Inc., 19 West 56th Street, New York, NY 10019-3984; (800) 227-2345.

Cerebral Palsy

What is *cerebral palsy*?

Cerebral palsy is a term used to describe a group of conditions that affect both muscle coordination and body movement. "Cerebral" refers to the brain, and "palsy" refers to weakness or poor control of muscle movement.

What causes cerebral palsy?

There are a number of factors that may injure the developing brain: low birth weight or premature delivery; lack of oxygen to the baby during or after birth; brain infection; a head injury; or viral diseases in pregnancy.

Is the condition of cerebral palsy inherited?

No.

What are its effects?

Cerebral palsy's effects include an inability to control motor function—in particular, muscle control and coordination. Very relaxed or very stiff muscles, difficulty moving arms and legs, difficulty in speech and hearing, loss of bladder and bowel control, and sight problems are some of the effects. Cerebral palsy can affect different parts of the body, such as one or both legs, or the whole body.

Is there more than one type of cerebral palsy?

There are three generally accepted types of this condition: *spastic*, which is characterized by stiff and difficult movement; *ataxic*, which causes a disturbed sense of balance and depth perception; and *athetoid*, which is characterized by involuntary movement in groups of muscles.

Can cerebral palsy be prevented?

Yes. A variety of tests and preventive approaches can be undertaken by physicians, such as the test for the Rh factor and subsequent immunization if necessary. The emphasis, though, lies in quality prenatal care, and in protecting infants from head injury and brain infections.

If I have a child with cerebral palsy, will the next child have it as well?

This is unlikely, but it is best to check with your physician to determine what caused cerebral palsy in your child in the first place to see if it can be prevented with subsequent children.

Does cerebral palsy become progressively worse?

No. The brain damage does not get worse; however, the disabilities associated with it may become worse, stay the same, or improve.

Is cerebral palsy curable?

No, not in the medical sense. But therapy and training can improve functions, helping to improve the quality of life.

How many people in the United States have cerebral palsy?

It is estimated that about 500,000 people in the United States manifest one or more symptoms of cerebral palsy.

Source: United Cerebral Palsy Association, 1660 L Street NW, Suite 700, Washington, DC 20036-5602; (202) 776-0406.

Chicken Pox

What is chicken pox?

Chicken pox is one of the most common childhood viral diseases, affecting most children in the United States before their tenth birthday. It is usually mild and not life-threatening to children who are otherwise healthy. The most noticeable sign of chicken pox is a skin rash that develops on the child's scalp and body, then spreads to the face, arms, and legs over a period of three to four days. The rash forms between 250 and 500 itchy blisters that dry up into scabs two to four days later. School-age children often get a mild fever for one or two days before the rash appears. Other symptoms of chicken pox are chills, fussiness, loss of appetite, and headaches.

Is chicken pox contagious?

Yes, chicken pox is highly contagious. It is spread in one of the following ways:

- by direct contact with an infected person, usually through fluid from broken blisters
- through the air when an infected person coughs or sneezes
- through direct contact through lesions (sores) from a person with shingles

When is a person contagious?

A person who has chicken pox is contagious from one to two days before the rash starts and for six days after you first see the rash. A child will have to stay home from day care or school until she is no longer contagious. An adult or child who has never has chicken pox is at risk for getting it and may not show symptoms for 10 to 21 days after being exposed to the virus. Within households, 80 to 90 percent of at-risk persons will develop chicken pox if they are exposed to a family member who has it.

Who gets chicken pox?

There are about 3.9 million cases of chicken pox in the United States each year, with more than 95 percent of all people developing the disease in their lifetime. Cases occur most frequently in children aged six to ten.

When are people most likely to get chicken pox?

Chicken pox can occur at any time throughout the year, but it peaks in the winter and early spring, especially in moderate climates.

What is the treatment for?

You may remember from when you were a child how itchy chicken pox can be. If your child scratches the blisters before they are able to heal, they can get infected, turn into small sores, and possibly leave scars. Discourage scratching, but keep her fingernails trimmed short just in case.

Oatmeal baths can help relieve the itching, and acetaminophen may help reduce a child's fever. Do not give your child aspirin or salicylate (a compound found in aspirin) as they have been associated with Reye's syndrome, a disease that affects the liver and the brain. If the child's fever lasts longer than four days or rises above 102°F, call or see your pediatrician. Also let your pediatrician know if areas of the rash get very red, warm, or tender; this may mean the child has a bacterial infection and needs other treatment.

Acyclovir, an oral drug, is used for certain patients who are at risk of developing severe chicken pox, including adolescents and children with skin or lung disease. To be effective, acyclovir must be given within the first 24 hours of the onset of the rash. You may want to discuss this with your pediatrician.

Can chicken pox cause complications?

Most children who are otherwise healthy won't have any complications from the disease. However, each year in the United States about 9,000 people are hospitalized for chicken pox and 90 people die from the disease. The most common complication is bacterial infection of the skin; the next most common problems are viral or bacterial pneumonia and encephalitis. The following groups of people are at higher risk of developing these problems:

- people who have weak immune systems
- infants under one year of age
- adolescents and adults
- newborns whose mothers had chicken pox around the time of delivery
- premature infants whose mothers have not had chicken pox
- children with eczema and other skin conditions
- children receiving salicylate therapy

What happens when adults get chicken pox?

In adults, the disease usually lasts longer and is more severe, often developing into pneumonia. Adults are almost 10 times more likely than children under 14 to need hospitalization from chicken pox and more than 20 times more likely to die from the disease. If a pregnant woman develops chicken pox, her unborn baby may have complications.

What is *shingles?*

Once you have had chicken pox, the virus that caused it stays forever in your nerve roots. Later in life, the virus in these nerve roots can reappear and cause shingles. Shingles can occur at any age, but usually appears after a person is 50 years old. About 10 to 20 percent of all people who have had chicken pox develop shingles. Symptoms typically include numbness and itching or severe pain in the skin areas where the affected nerve roots are. Within three to four days, clusters of blisterlike lesions develop that last for two to three weeks.

Is there a new vaccine?

Yes. Until recently, chicken pox could not easily be prevented with a vaccine, only treated. Now, parents can have their children immunized with a new vaccine, which is beneficial in protecting against chicken pox and preventing the discomfort and possible serious complications it can cause.

When should my child get the vaccine?

The American Academy of Pediatrics recommends the chicken pox vaccine for all children between 12 and 18 months who do not have a history of chicken pox. Older children should be immunized at the earliest opportunity, also with a single dose. Healthy children who are older than 13, have no history of the disease, and have never been immunized should get two doses of the vaccine four to eight weeks apart.

Regular medical care includes vaccinations, which are an important part of a child's total health care. Your child can get the chicken pox vaccine at the same time she gets the measles-mumps-rubella (MMR) vaccine. If the pediatrician doesn't administer the chicken pox and MMR vaccines at the same time, you should wait at least one month between getting each vaccine. Otherwise, your child can get the vaccine for chicken pox at the same time or any time before or after vaccines for diphtheria, tetanus, pertussis (DTP), polio, hepatitis B, and "Haemophilus influenzae" type b.

What are the benefits of vaccinating my child against chicken pox?

Although chicken pox is usually mild, routinely vaccinating all children at age one can prevent medical problems and reduce the costs related to the disease. Chicken pox is expensive and inconvenient. Parents may have to miss work while their children are home from school or child care. In the average household, a child with chicken pox misses eight or nine days of school, and adult caretakers lose up to two days of work.

The vaccine is 70 to 90 percent effective in preventing chicken pox. If vaccinated children do get the disease, they generally have a much milder form of the disease—fewer skin lesions (15 to 32), a lower fever, and a quicker recovery. In fact, the attack may be so mild that the skin lesions look like insect bites. But remember, vaccinated children with a mild case of chicken pox can still infect others at risk. Currently, a booster for the vaccine is not recommended. Studies are under way to determine how long protection from the vaccine lasts and whether a booster will be needed in the future.

Is the new vaccine safe?

In the early 1970s a vaccine for chicken pox was developed in Japan. More than 2 million doses of that vaccine have been given in Japan and Korea. Since the early 1980s a similar vaccine has been tested in the United States in over 9,400 healthy children and over 1,600 adults. These tests have shown this vaccine to be safe and effective.

Are there ever adverse reactions?

Adverse reactions from the chicken pox vaccine generally are mild. They include redness, stiffness, soreness, and swelling where the shot was given; tiredness; fussiness; fever; and nausea. Also, a rash of several small bumps or pimples may develop at the spot where the shot was given or on other parts of the body. This can occur up to a month after immunization and can last for several days.

Are there some people who shouldn't get the vaccine?

Although the chicken pox vaccine is approved for use in otherwise healthy children, certain groups of people, such as children with a weakened immune system or pregnant women, should not receive it. Talk to your pediatrician about whether your child falls into any of the high-risk categories and should not be vaccinated.

Source: Reprinted with permission from American Academy of Pediatrics, from *Chickenpox and the New Vaccine-Guidelines for Parents*, © 1995, rev. February 1996. Note that the above information should not be used as a substitute for the medical care and advice of your pediatrician. There may be variations in treatment that your pediatrician may recommend, based on individual facts and circumstances.

Chronic Fatigue Syndrome

What is *chronic fatigue syndrome?*

Chronic fatigue syndrome (CFS) is characterized by six months or more of profound persistent or relapsing fatigue that is unrelieved by rest. This fatigue occurs together with other symptoms—most often recurrent sore throats, muscle pain, multijoint pain, tender lymph nodes, new types or patterns of headaches, and neuropsychological complaints such as impaired memory or concentration.

How do people get chronic fatigue syndrome?

For a number of people, CFS follows an acute infection such as hepatitis, bronchitis, or even the common cold; others may feel this extreme fatigue after a bout of mononucleosis. Some develop it more gradually, slowly losing their energy over an extended period of time with no known triggering event. Still others notice it after going through a period of high stress.

Who is more likely to get chronic fatigue syndrome?

CFS is diagnosed two to four times more often in females than in males. This may be attributed to psychological reasons in that women could be more likely to report symptoms to a doctor; or it may have a biological explanation, similar in nature to multiple sclerosis and lupus, which both exhibit a strong gender preference toward women.

Why is chronic fatigue syndrome called the "yuppie flu"?

Research done in the 1980s centered on the complaints of mainly well-educated, affluent women in their 30s and 40s, giving rise to CFS's modern stereotype. As research continues, a more diverse patient population will likely emerge when CFS is recognized by the greater medical community as a legitimate disorder.

How would I know if I had CFS?

Diagnosis for CFS is tricky because it shares symptoms with so many other diseases. When evaluating patients, physicians need to rule out diseases that seem similar, such as lupus and multiple sclerosis. After this weeding-out process, if a person still exhibits the debilitating signs of severe tiredness, CFS may be considered as a culprit.

How many people have chronic fatigue syndrome?

Based on the first three years of an ongoing study in four U.S. cities, the Centers for Disease Control and Prevention estimates the minimum prevalence rate of CFS in the United States is 4 to 10 cases per 100,000 adults 18 years of age or older.

When was chronic fatigue syndrome first diagnosed?

As early as the 1860s Dr. George Beard called the syndrome *neurasthenia,* thinking it to be a neurosis caused by weakness and fatigue. Since then, doctors have repeatedly tried to explain this malaise in various fashions; iron-poor blood, low blood sugar, environmental allergies, brucellosis, or a bodywide yeast infection. In the mid-1980s, the illness gained the moniker "chronic EBV" after laboratory tests led scientists to speculate that the collection of symptoms may be caused by the Epstein-Barr virus (EBV). Recent evidence has caused researchers to doubt the notion that the Epstein-Barr virus is the sole factor causing CFS.

What is the *Epstein-Barr virus?*

EBV is one of the many microbes found in normal healthy people. It is common for people to become infected with EBV through saliva contact when very young, usually without subsequent signs of illness. Antibodies in the immune system keep the infection under control if the virus remains in the body for life. EBV can be a significant cause of mononucleosis in young adults who were not exposed to the virus as children.

How many people have the Epstein-Barr virus?

Researchers have estimated that over 80 percent of the population have been infected by the virus by the time they reach 40 years of age.

Is there any treatment for chronic fatigue syndrome?

No specific treatment has yet proven effective against this illness. Some doctors have had success with certain drugs, but no procedure has yet met with universal acceptance.

Source: National Institute of Allergy and Infectious Disease, Department of Health and Human Services, Bethesda, MD 20892; (301) 496-5717.

Cystic Fibrosis

What is *cystic fibrosis*?

Cystic fibrosis causes the body to produce an abnormally thick, sticky mucus. This abnormal mucus clogs the lungs and leads to fatal infections. The thick CF mucus also obstructs the pancreas, preventing enzymes from reaching the intestines to digest food.

How common is cystic fibrosis?

Cystic fibrosis is the most common fatal genetic disease in the United States. It affects approximately 30,000 children and young adults, and occurs in about one of every 3,300 live births.

How long is a person expected to live with cystic fibrosis?

The median survival age of a person with cystic fibrosis is about 30 years.

What are the symptoms of cystic fibrosis?

The most common symptoms are: persistent coughing, wheezing, or pneumonia; extremely salty-tasting skin; excessive appetite but little weight gain; and bulky, foul-smelling stools.

Why are cystic fibrosis cells different from others?

The main defect of the cystic fibrosis cell is that it does not transport sodium and chloride (salt) within the epithelial cells (which line organs such as the pancreas and lungs) to their outer surfaces.

Is there a treatment for cystic fibrosis?

Treatment often depends upon the stage of the disease and which organs have been affected. Chest physical therapy involves active percussion, using cupped hands on the patient's chest and back to dislodge mucus from the lungs. Intravenous antibiotics and medicated vapors are also used. Unfortunately, these treatments tackle the symptoms of the disease but not the underlying cause. The best bet for a cure to date is research utilizing gene therapy.

What is *gene therapy*?

Gene therapy involves manufacturing normal cells in the laboratory using biotechnology and then introducing them into the body.

Is there a test to diagnose for cystic fibrosis?

The standard test is known as the "sweat test." This painless test measures the amount of salt in the sweat. An excessive level of salt indicates that the person has cystic fibrosis.

Is it possible to be a carrier for the disease and not know it?

Yes. More than 10 million Americans are unknowing, symptomless carriers of the defective gene.

What are the chances of a parent giving cystic fibrosis to his or her child?

The child must first inherit a copy of the defective gene from each of their parents to have the disease. Whenever two carriers conceive, there is a 25 percent chance that the child will develop cystic fibrosis, a 50 percent chance that the child will be a carrier, and a 25 percent chance that the child will not develop CF and will not be a carrier.

Source: Cystic Fibrosis Foundation, 6931 Arlington Road, Bethesda, MD 20814-5200; (800) 344-4823 (FIGHT CF); www.cff.org.

Diabetes

What is *diabetes*?

Diabetes is a disorder of metabolism—the way our bodies use digested food for growth and energy. Most of the food we eat is broken down by the digestive juices into a simple sugar called *glucose,* which is the main source of fuel for the body. For this glucose to pass into the bloodstream, where it becomes available for body cells to use for growth and energy, insulin must be present. Insulin is a hormone produced by the pancreas, a large gland behind the stomach.

In people with diabetes, the pancreas either produces little or no insulin, or the body does not respond to the insulin that is produced. As a result, glucose builds up in the blood, overflows into the urine, and passes out of the body. Thus the body loses its main source of fuel, even though the blood contains large amounts of glucose.

Are there different types of diabetes?

Yes. Three kinds: *insulin-dependent diabetes mellitus* (IDDM) or type I diabetes; *noninsulin-dependent diabetes mellitus* (NIDDM) or type II diabetes; and *gestational diabetes.*

Insulin-dependent diabetes is considered an autoimmune disease; that means that the body's system for fighting infection (the immune system) turns against parts of the body. In diabetes, the immune system attacks the insulin-producing beta cells in the pancreas and destroys them. The pancreas then makes little or no insulin. Someone with IDDM needs daily injections of insulin to live.

What are the symptoms of IDDM?

Increased thirst and urination, constant hunger, weight loss, blurred vision, and extreme tiredness. If not diagnosed and treated with insulin, a person can lapse into a life-threatening coma. IDDM develops most often in children and young adults, though it can appear at any age.

What causes IDDM?

Scientists believe that both genetic factors and viruses are involved.

What is the most common type of diabetes?

The second type, noninsulin-dependent diabetes (NIDDM), accounts for 90 to 95 percent of people with diabetes. In NIDDM, the pancreas usually produces insulin, but the body is unable to use it. The end result is the same as for IDDM—an unhealthy buildup of glucose in the blood and a body that can't use the glucose.

Are the symptoms for NIDDM the same as for IDDM?

Yes, but they also include frequent infections and the slow healing of sores. Also, the symptoms of NIDDM develop more gradually and are not as noticeable as in IDDM.

What about the third type, gestational diabetes?

It develops or is discovered during pregnancy, and usually disappears when the pregnancy is over. But women who have had gestational diabetes have a greater risk of developing NIDDM later in their lives.

How widespread is diabetes?

Diabetes is widely recognized as one of the leading causes of death and disability in the United States. Long-term complications from the disease contribute to blindness, heart disease, strokes, kidney failure, amputations, and nerve damage. Uncontrolled diabetes can complicate pregnancy, and birth defects are more common to women with diabetes.

Who gets diabetes?

Certain risk factors can increase one's chance of getting diabetes. People who have family members with diabetes (especially NIDDM), who are overweight, or who are African-American, Hispanic, or Native American, are all at greater risk of developing diabetes.

IDDM occurs equally among males and females, but it is more common in whites than in nonwhites. Data from the World Health Organization's Multinational Project for Childhood Diabetes indicate that IDDM is rare in most Asian, African, and Native American populations. On the other hand, some northern European countries, including Finland and Sweden, have high rates of IDDM.

NIDDM is more common in older people, especially older women who are overweight, and occurs most often among African-Americans, Hispanics, and Native Americans. Compared with non-Hispanic whites, diabetes rates are about 60 percent higher in African-Americans and 110 to 120 percent higher in Mexican-Americans and Puerto Ricans. Native Americans have the highest rate of diabetes in the world.

How is diabetes treated?

Daily injections of insulin are the basic therapy for IDDM. Insulin injections must be balanced with meals and daily activities, and glucose levels must be closely monitored through frequent blood sugar testing. Diet, exercise, and blood testing for glucose are also the basis for management of NIDDM. In addition, some people with NIDDM take oral drugs or insulin to lower their blood glucose levels.

People with diabetes should be treated by a doctor who monitors their diabetes control and checks for complications. Doctors who specialize in diabetes are called *endocrinologists* or *diabetologists*. In addition, people with diabetes often see ophthalmologists for eye examinations, podiatrists for routine foot care, dietitians for help in planning meals, and diabetes educators for instruction in day-to-day care.

Recent studies prove that keeping blood sugar levels as close to normal as possible reduces the risk of developing major complications of diabetes.

Source: *Diabetes Overview*, a publication of the National Institute of Diabetes and Digestive Kidney Diseases. For more information, call or write: National Diabetes Information Clearinghouse, One Information Way, Bethesda, MD 20892-3560; (301) 654-3327.

Heart Attack

What are the warning signs of heart attack?

- Uncomfortable pressure, fullness, squeezing, or pain in the center of the chest lasting more than a few minutes
- Pain may spread to the shoulders, neck, or arms
- Chest discomfort with lightheadedness, fainting, sweating, nausea, or shortness of breath

Not all these signs occur in every attack. Sometimes they subside and then return. If some of them occur, get help by calling the emergency rescue service or, if it's faster, by having someone drive you to the hospital. Prompt action can reduce the risk of a fatal heart attack.

What causes a heart attack?

Coronary atherosclerosis causes heart attack. It's a slow process that can go on for years without causing any symptoms. Fatty deposits build up along the inner walls of the arteries to the heart. Much like lime deposits forming in a water pipe, atherosclerosis coats the inside of the artery channels and gradually narrows them. The fatty buildup reduces the flow of blood from the artery to an area of the heart muscle. When the blood flow stops due to a blockage—usually from a blood clot—heart attack results.

How can I reduce my risk of heart attack?

By slowing down the risk factors that cause atherosclerosis. These coronary risk factors include: high blood pressure; high blood cholesterol levels; cigarette smoke; and lack of physical exercise. Obesity and diabetes can also increase your risk.

Risk factors that neither you nor your doctor can change include heredity and race, increasing age, and male gender. Some families have a tendency toward heart attack. African-Americans, for example, have a greater risk of heart attack because they're more prone to high blood pressure. The incidence of heart attack also increases with age. And men are likely to suffer heart attacks earlier in life than women.

I've heard that the pain for a heart attack resembles indigestion. Is this true?

Sometimes, yes. But the pain of heart attack isn't exactly the same for everyone. It might be an intense pain for one person and a milder pain for another—often mistaken for indigestion.

Why is prompt action so crucial?

Because cardiac arrest is usually reversible if it's treated within a few minutes with a defibrillator.

Also, the amount of heart muscle that dies from lack of blood flow can be reduced when flow is restored very early (usually by clot-dissolving medicines called *thrombolytics*).

Is it possible for the heart to heal?

Yes. If blood flow is good, the healing process starts promptly. The portions of the heart muscle that are permanently damaged are replaced by scar tissue. At the same time, new scar tissue develops to build up the damaged area.

Can people who've had a heart attack return to work?

Yes. They can and should return to work, though some people may have to change occupations or alter their lifestyles.

Source: *Heart Attack*, a brochure published by the American Heart Association. For more information, contact your nearest American Heart Association, or call (800) AHA-USA1 [(800) 242-8721].

Hepatitis

What is *hepatitis*?

Hepatitis is an inflammation of the liver caused by certain viruses and other factors, such as alcohol abuse, some medications, and trauma. Although many cases of hepatitis are not a serious threat to health, the disease can become chronic (long-lasting) and can sometimes lead to liver failure and death.

What are the major types of viral hepatitis?

Hepatitis A, caused by infection with the hepatitis A virus, usually a mild disease that does not become chronic. The virus is sometimes passed on through sexual practices involving oral-anal contact. It is most commonly spread by food and water contamination.

Hepatitis B, caused by infection with the hepatitis B virus (HBV), may be mild or severe, acute or chronic. HBV is most commonly passed on to a sexual partner during intercourse, especially during anal sex. It can also be transmitted by sharing drug needles; from a mother to newborn; and in a health-care setting. It is not spread through casual contact, such as shaking hands or sharing a workspace.

Non-A, non-B hepatitis is primarily caused by the hepatitis C virus (HCV). It is generally a mild condition, but is more likely than hepatitis B to lead to chronic liver disease. HCV appears to be spread through sexual contact, as well as sharing drug needles. Sexual spread, however, is less common than it is for HBV. Since new tests have been developed to screen blood donors, only a very small percentage of persons with HCV become infected through blood transfusions.

Hepatitis E is another type of non-A, non-B hepatitis. It is principally spread through contaminated water in areas with poor sanitation. This form of hepatitis does not occur in the United States and is not known to be passed on through sexual contact.

Delta hepatitis occurs only in people infected with HBV. A potentially severe disease, it is caused by a virus (HDV) that can produce disease only when HBV is also present. Most cases occur among people who are exposed to blood and blood products, such as people with hemophilia. Small-scale epidemics have occurred among injection drug users who share contaminated needles.

What are the symptoms of *viral hepatitis?*

Most people infected with viral hepatitis have no symptoms. For example, one-third of the people infected with HBV have a completely "silent" disease. The most common early symptoms are mild fever, headache, muscle aches, fatigue, loss of appetite, nausea, vomiting, or diarrhea. Later, symptoms may include dark and foamy urine and pale feces; abdominal pain; and yellowing of the skin and whites of the eyes (jaundice).

Fifteen to 20 percent of patients with severe HBV develop short-term arthritis-like symptoms; another third of those with HBV develop only mild flulike symptoms without jaundice. Very severe (fulminant) HBV is rare, but life-threatening: its signs are personality changes and agitated behavior. It requires immediate medical attention.

At least half of all HCV carriers will develop chronic liver disease, regardless of whether of not they have symptoms.

How is viral hepatitis diagnosed?

For HBV, several types of blood tests are used, even before symptoms develop. These tests measure liver function and identify HBV *antigens* (proteins of the virus) or *antibodies* (proteins produced by the body in response to the virus) in the blood.

Delta hepatitis, until recently, could be diagnosed only by liver biopsy, in which a tiny piece of the liver is removed and examined. Scientists supported by the National Institute of Allergy and Infectious Diseases have developed a procedure to detect part of the genetic material in a patient's blood, allowing for a faster diagnosis. A blood test is also now available.

A test is available, too, for hepatitis C. It identifies antibody to HCV, which is present in more than 50 percent of persons with acute hepatitis C and in almost all with chronic hepatitis.

How is viral hepatitis treated?

There are no specific treatments for the acute symptoms of viral hepatitis. Doctors recommend bed rest, a healthy diet, and avoidance of alcoholic beverages. Most patients with mild to severe acute hepatitis begin to feel better in two to three weeks and recover completely within four to eight weeks.

Many chronic carriers remain symptom-free or develop only a mild condition, *chronic persistent hepatitis*. A small percentage go on to develop the most serious complications of viral hepatitis: cirrhosis of the liver, liver cancer, and immune system disorders.

How can I protect myself against viral hepatitis?

By avoiding the blood, saliva, semen, or vaginal secretions of infected individuals. People with acute or chronic viral hepatitis should avoid sharing items that could infect others, such as razors or toothbrushes. They should also protect sex partners from exposure to their semen, vaginal fluids, or blood. Properly used condoms may be effective in preventing sexual transmission.

Several vaccines are available to prevent hepatitis B. People at high risk of infection should consider vaccination. In an effort to eliminate chronic carriers, the Centers for Disease Control and Prevention recommends that all newborn babies be vaccinated.

No vaccines yet exist for HCV or HDV; however, HBV vaccine will prevent delta hepatitis as well.

Source: *Hepatitis,* a publication of the National Institute of Allergy and Infectious Diseases. For more information, call or write: American Liver Foundation, 998 Pompton Avenue, Cedar Grove, NJ 07009; (800) 223-0179.

High Blood Pressure

What is *high blood pressure?*

High blood pressure (HBP), or hypertension, is a serious condition that can lead to stroke, heart disease, kidney failure, and other health problems. As blood flows from the heart out to the blood vessels, it creates pressure against the blood vessel walls. Your blood pressure reading is a measure of this pressure. When the reading goes above a certain point, it is called *high blood pressure* or *hypertension*.

How is it tested?

A doctor or a nurse places a cuff around your arm above the elbow, pumps air into the cuff, then releases the measurements as the air is let out. Because HBP is so common, everyone should have his blood pressure tested once a year. Blood pressure readings are given in two numbers. The average reading for adults is 120/80; a slightly higher or lower reading (for either number) may not be a problem. If blood pressure goes above 140/90, however, some form of treatment—diet or drugs—may be needed. Lower blood pressure readings (e.g., 110/70) are thought to be safe for most people.

What if just the first number is high?

Often in older adults the first number (the upper or *systolic* number) is high while the second (the lower or *diastolic*) number is normal. This condition is called *isolated systolic hypertension,* and it also should be treated. Studies prove that lowering the systolic number cuts down on strokes and heart attacks in people age 60 and over.

What causes high blood pressure?

Some cases of HBP are caused by other illnesses. This kind of HBP is called *secondary hypertension,* and it is often cured once the original medical problem is cured. Most HBP, however, is *essential* or *primary hypertension.* This kind cannot be cured but can be kept under control by regular, ongoing treatment. Doctors think that many things combine to cause HBP. Being overweight, drinking too much alcohol, and eating too much salt are risk factors because they raise your risk of having HBP. They do not cause it directly.

Blood pressure goes up in all people during periods of stress or exercise. But avoiding stress will not prevent high blood pressure. You can have HBP even though you are usually a calm, relaxed person.

How is high blood pressure treated?

If you have mild HBP, your doctor may suggest that you lose weight and keep it off, eat less salt, cut down on alcohol, and get more exercise. That may bring it down. If medicine is needed, these daily habits may help it work better.

Once my high blood pressure is under control, do I still need treatment?

Yes. If your doctor has prescribed medication, you may need to take it for the rest of your life. Later on, though, you may be able to take less.

Can high blood pressure be prevented?

For some people, yes. The keys to prevention are: keeping your weight moderate; cutting down on salt; exercising regularly; and, if you drink, having no more than two drinks a day.

Source: *High Blood Pressure: A Common But Controllable Disorder,* a publication of the National Institute on Aging. For more information, call or write: National Heart, Lung, and Blood Information Center, P.O. Box 30105, Bethesda, MD 20824-0105; (301) 251-1222.

Insomnia

What is *insomnia*?

Insomnia is the perception or complaint of inadequate or poor-quality sleep because of one or more of the following factors: difficulty falling asleep; waking up frequently during the night with difficulty returning to sleep; waking up too early in the morning; unrefreshing sleep.

Does the number of hours someone sleeps help determine whether the condition is insomnia?

No, because people vary in their need for sleep.

Are there different kinds of insomnia?

Yes. Insomnia lasting from a single night to a few weeks is referred to as "transient." If episodes of insomnia occur from time to time, the insomnia is said to be "intermittent." Insomnia is said to be "chronic" if it occurs on most nights and lasts a month or more.

What causes insomnia?

Certain conditions seem to make individuals more likely to experience insomnia. They include: advanced age (insomnia occurs more frequently in those over 60); female gender; a history of depression. If other conditions (stress, anxiety, a medical problem, or the use of certain medications) occur along with these conditions, insomnia is more likely.

Transient and intermittent insomnia generally occur in people who are temporarily experiencing one or more of the following: stress; environmental noise; extreme temperatures; change in the surrounding environment; sleep/wake schedule problems such as those due to jet lag; side effects from medication.

Chronic insomnia is more complex and usually results from a combination of factors, including underlying physical and mental disorders. One of the most common causes is depression. Other underlying causes include: arthritis, kidney disease, heart failure, asthma, sleep apnea, narcolepsy, restless legs syndrome, Parkinson's disease, and hyperthyroidism. Chronic insomnia may also be due to behavioral factors, including the misuse of caffeine and alcohol; disrupted sleep/wake cycles, as may occur with shift work or other nighttime schedules; and chronic stress.

Who gets insomnia?

Men and women of all age groups, although it seems to be more common in females (especially after menopause) and in the elderly. The ability to sleep, rather than the need for sleep, appears to decrease with advancing age.

How is insomnia diagnosed?

Patients are evaluated with the help of a medical history and a sleep history. The sleep history may be obtained from a "sleep diary" filled out by the patient or by an interview with the patient's bed partner on the quality and quantity of the patient's sleep. Specialized sleep studies may be recommended, but only if there is a suspicion that the patient may have a primary sleep disorder such as *sleep apnea* or *narcolepsy*.

Are over-the-counter sleep medicines helpful?

They are usually not recommended for the treatment of insomnia.

What's the appropriate treatment?

First, diagnosing and treating underlying medical or psychological problems. Second, identifying behaviors that may worsen insomnia and preventing them. Third, the possible use of sleeping pills—at the lowest dose, for the shortest duration, and with medical supervision. Finally, the use of behavioral techniques, such as relaxation therapy and reconditioning.

What is *relaxation therapy*?

It's a technique that helps the body eliminate anxiety and tension. As a result, the person's mind is able to stop "racing," the muscles can relax, and restful sleep can occur.

What about *reconditioning*?

This treatment helps people associate their bed and bedtime with sleep. For most people, this means not using their beds for any activities other than sleep and sex. The person is advised to go to bed only when sleepy and, if unable to fall asleep, to get up, stay up until sleepy, and then return to bed. During this treatment, napping should be avoided and the person should go to bed at the same time each day.

Source: *Insomnia,* a fact sheet published by the National Heart, Lung and Blood Institute Information Center. For more information, call or write: National Center on Sleep Disorders Research, Two Rockledge Centre, Suite 7024, 6701 Rockledge Drive, MSC 7920, Bethesda, MD 20892-7920; phone: (301) 435-0199; fax: (301) 480-3451.

Kidney Disease and Kidney Stones

What happens when the kidneys fail?

If the kidneys are seriously impaired by disease (usually effecting both kidneys), excess fluid may be retained in the body, causing severe swelling and symptoms of kidney failure.

Are there different types of kidney disease?

Yes. Some of the most common types are diabetes (not a kidney disease, but may affect the kidneys), glomerulonephritis (inflammation of the kidney's filtering units), congenital diseases, and polycystic kidney disease (formation of cysts in the kidneys that can grow over time and cause kidney damage and failure).

What are some of the warning signs of kidney disease?

An increase in the frequency of urination, a burning sensation when urinating, passing blood in the urine, high blood pressure, and pain in the back just below the ribs.

Is kidney disease treatable?

Some kidney disease can be treated easily and conveniently. Doctor-supervised control of such factors as high blood pressure and diabetes can retard or even prevent kidney disease. Some diseases may progress to a point where kidney failure can occur, requiring dialysis or transplantation.

When is treatment necessary?

Usually when the patient has lost up to 85 to 90 percent of total kidney function. Obviously, you should consult a doctor long before this so that permanent kidney failure may not occur.

How do kidney stones form?

When certain chemicals that are produced from dissolving food do not pass through the urine, they tend to build up. The chemicals can form crystals, which in turn may produce kidney stones that stay in the kidneys or lodge in the urinary tract.

Are all kidney stones the same size?

No. They can be as small as grains of sand, which pass easily through the urinary tract, or as large as eggs, which require a procedure to remove them.

What are some ways to prevent kidney stones?

The most recommended prevention is to drink plenty of water every day. Maintain your sugar levels if you have diabetes, eat well, exercise, avoid tobacco, and maintain a healthy weight.

Can kidney stones return if I have already had them?

Most likely. If you have experienced a kidney stone in the past, there is a greater chance that you may develop others. Some people have a recurrence of kidney stones every couple of years (or more often, in some cases).

How many people are afflicted with kidney disease?

There are believed to be over 20 million Americans suffering from one type of kidney disease or another. Of this number, over 260,000 patients need to be treated by dialysis or transplantation.

For more information, contact: National Kidney Foundation, Inc.; 30 East 33rd Street, New York, NY 10016; (800) 622-9010.

Lupus

What is *lupus?*

Lupus is a chronic inflammatory disease that can affect various parts of the body—especially the skin, joints, blood, and kidneys. In an *autoimmune disorder* such as lupus, the immune system loses its ability to tell the difference between foreign substances (antigens) and its own cells and tissues.

How widespread an illness is it?

Lupus Foundation of America market research data show that between 1,400,000 and 2,000,000 Americans reported to have been diagnosed with lupus. Ninety percent of them are women. Lupus affects one out of every 185 Americans. The disease is more prevalent in African-Americans, Latinos, Native Americans, and Asians.

What causes lupus?

The causes of lupus are unknown, but environmental and genetic factors are involved. While scientists believe there is a genetic predisposition, it is known that environmental factors also play a critical role in triggering the disease. Some of these factors are: infections, antibiotics (especially those in the sulfa and penicillin groups), ultraviolet light, extreme stress, and certain drugs.

Is lupus inheritable?

Only 10 percent of lupus patients will have a close relative (parent or sibling) who already has or may develop lupus. Statistics show that only about 5 percent of the children born to individuals with lupus will develop the illness.

Why is lupus sometimes called a "woman's disease"?

Lupus can occur at any age, and in either sex, although it occurs 10 to 15 times more frequently among adult females than among adult males. Hormonal factors may explain why lupus occurs more frequently in females. The increase of disease symptoms before menstrual periods and/or during pregnancy supports the belief that hormones, particularly estrogen, may be involved.

Should a woman with lupus risk pregnancy?

The current general view is that there is no absolute reason why a lupus patient should not get pregnant, unless she has moderate to severe organ involvement (i.e., central nervous system, kidney, or heart and lungs) which would place the mother at risk. However, there is some increased risk of disease activity during or immediately (three to four weeks) after pregnancy. If a patient is monitored carefully, the danger can be minimized.

What are some of the symptoms?

Achy joints, fever over 100°F, and arthritis occur in over 90 percent of patients. Some other noticeable symptoms are prolonged or extreme fatigue, skin rashes, anemia, kidney involvement, light-sensitivity, and butterfly-shaped rashes across the cheeks and nose.

What triggers an attack of lupus in a susceptible person?

Scientists have noted common features in many lupus patients. In some, exposure to the sun causes sudden development of a rash and then possibly other symptoms. In others, an infection—perhaps a cold or a more serious infection—does not get better, and then complications arise.

Is there a treatment for lupus?

For the vast majority of patients, effective treatment can minimize the symptoms, reduce the inflammation, and maintain normal bodily functions. Some commonly prescribed medications include: nonsteroidal anti-inflammatory drugs, acetaminophen (e.g., Tylenol), corticosteroids, anti-malarials, and cytotoxic drugs.

Is lupus always fatal?

This is one of the greatest misconceptions of the disease. It is true that medical science has not yet developed a method for curing lupus, and some people do die from the disease, but 80 to 90 percent of patients may live normal lives if they follow the advice of their physicians and take their medications as prescribed.

Source: Lupus Foundation of America, Inc., 1300 Piccard Drive, Suite 200, Rockville, MD 20850-4303; (800) 558-0121; http://www.lupus.org/lupus.

Lyme Disease

What is Lyme disease?

Lyme disease is an infection carried by deer ticks. It is caused by a type of bacteria called a *spirochete*. A tick with Lyme disease may pass it on to any human or animal it bites.

How can I get Lyme disease?

First, you cannot get Lyme disease directly from other people, pets, or insects. You can only get it through being bitten by a tick carrying the disease.

Where do the ticks live that pass on Lyme disease?

The ticks that pass on Lyme disease are deer ticks which live primarily in the eastern United States, as well as the upper Midwest. Western black-legged ticks, also carriers, live in the Pacific coastal states. Ticks prefer moist woody areas, but can also be found in well-manicured lawns. They are present mostly where deer and other animals roam frequently.

Will I know immediately if I have been bitten by a deer tick?

No, and chances are you will not be able to see it either. Deer ticks in their "nymphal stage" are little larger than a poppy seed.

How can I remove a tick?

Do not attempt to remove a tick with your fingers, or by covering it with nail polish or petroleum jelly, because the tick may inject you with the Lyme disease bacteria as a defense mechanism. Instead, get a pair of tweezers: Grab the tick as close to the skin as possible and pull outward.

What are the symptoms of the disease if I am infected?

Nearly 60 to 80 percent of those infected with the Lyme disease bacteria develop a reddish bull's-eye rash somewhere on the skin. This is known as *Erythema migrans*. Other symptoms include severe headaches, joint pain, and fatigue.

Is Lyme disease curable?

If diagnosed early, Lyme disease is almost always curable. In rare cases, if left undiagnosed, it may cause permanent damage.

How is the disease treated?

In mild cases, three to four weeks of antibiotics are usually prescribed by a physician. In severe cases, intravenous antibiotics may be recommended.

Is there any way to reduce the risk of getting the disease?

The obvious is to stay away from areas known to be breeding grounds for ticks. If you live in an area where ticks are known to be present, use insect repellents and tuck your pant legs into your shoes. Give yourself and your children thorough daily examinations to discover if any ticks are present on the skin.

Where are ticks apt to bite?

They appear to prefer the areas of the groin, the back of the neck, the armpits, and the backs of the knees.

Source: American Lyme Disease Foundation, Inc., Mill Pond Offices, 293 Route 100, Somers, NY 10589; (800) 876-LYME.

Multiple Sclerosis

What is *multiple sclerosis*?

Multiple sclerosis (MS) is a disease of the central nervous system. It is a chronic, often progressive, illness that hampers the brain's ability to send and receive messages. "Multiple" indicates that the disease may strike in more than just one area of the brain and spinal cord, and "sclerosis" merely means hardened, describing what happens to tissue.

How many people are affected by MS?

About a third of a million people are known to have MS in the United States.

What are the symptoms?

The symptoms of people suffering from MS can vary, including: muscle spasms or stiffness; loss of balance; loss of bladder or bowel control; weakness or excessive tiredness; eye problems; speech and memory problems; and complete or partial paralysis of any part of the body. These symptoms can also vary in severity from patient to patient.

Why do these symptoms occur?

When *scarring* (sclerosis) occurs in the nerve fibers in the central nervous system, the fatty substance surrounding them becomes damaged, distorting and even blocking nerve messages. It is similar to an electrical wire losing its insulating material, interfering with the signals being transmitted.

Is MS contagious, and is it fatal?

There has been no evidence to prove that MS can be passed on through casual or even sexual contact. The majority of people suffering from MS have a normal life expectancy.

What causes MS?

Though the cause is as yet unknown, it is believed that in people with MS the body's defense system begins to attack its own healthy cells instead of destroying foreign viruses and bacteria.

Is there a test that will confirm whether or not a person has MS?

As yet no single test is used to confirm or rule out MS, but various procedures do help in a diagnosis, including CAT scans, which use X-rays to produce pictures of the spinal column and brain; spinal taps, which allow the physician to check the spinal fluid for the disease; and MRI scans, which give highly detailed views of the spinal cord and brain.

Will I be able to have children if I suffer from MS?

It is best to consult with your physician but, barring a severe disability, this should pose no problem.

Is MS a hereditary disease?

In the way we commonly describe hereditary disease, no. But for as yet undetermined reasons, some families are more susceptible to MS than are others.

Are certain people more likely to develop MS?

Yes. People of northern European ancestry, women, people living farther away from the equator, and people between the ages of 20 and 40 appear more likely to get MS.

Source: National Multiple Sclerosis Society, 733 Third Avenue (6th floor), New York, NY 10017-3288; (800) 344-4867.

Osteoporosis

What is *osteoporosis?*

Osteoporosis is a disease that thins and weakens bones to the point where they break easily—especially bones in the hip, spine, and wrist. It's called "the silent disease" because you may not notice any symptoms. People can lose bone over many years, but not know they have osteoporosis until a bone breaks. About 25 million Americans have osteoporosis; 80 percent are women.

What is it caused by?

Experts don't understand all the causes. They do know that when women go through menopause, levels of the female hormone estrogen drop. Lower hormone levels can lead to bone loss and osteoporosis. Other causes of bone loss and osteoporosis include a diet too low in calcium and not getting enough exercise.

Who gets osteoporosis?

One out of two women and one in eight men over age 50 will have an osteoporosis-related fracture. White and Asian women are most likely to get osteoporosis. Women who have a family history of osteoporosis, an early menopause, or who have small body frames are at greatest risk. Men have less risk because they do not experience the same kinds of hormone losses as women. Osteoporosis can strike at any age, but the risk increases as you get older.

How is the disease diagnosed?

Losing height or breaking a bone may be the first sign of osteoporosis. Doctors use several tests. The dual-energy X-ray absorptiometry (DEXA) is the most exact way to measure bone density in the wrist, hip, and lower spine. Other tests doctors may use include single-photon absorptiometry, dual-energy absorptiometry, and quantitative computed tomography. Ask your doctor about these tests if you think you are at risk.

Is osteoporosis preventable?

Yes. A diet that is rich in calcium and vitamin D, and a lifestyle that includes regular weight-bearing exercise, are the best ways to prevent osteoporosis.

How much calcium should I take?

Calcium is what builds strong bones. Men and women age 25 to 65 should have 1,000 milligrams of calcium every day; women near or past menopause should have 1,500 milligrams of calcium. Make foods that are high in calcium part of your diet. They include low-fat dairy products such as cheese, yogurt, and milk; canned fish with bones you can eat such as salmon and sardines; dark green leafy vegetables such as kale, collard, and broccoli; and breads made with calcium-fortified flour.

If you don't get enough calcium from your food, you might think about taking a calcium supplement. Always check with your doctor before taking any dietary supplement.

Why do I need vitamin D?

Your body uses vitamin D to absorb calcium. Being out in the sun for even a short period of time every day gives most people enough vitamin D. You can also get this vitamin from supplements, as well as from cereal and milk fortified with vitamin D.

What are some common weight-bearing exercises?

Walking, jogging, and playing tennis.

How is osteoporosis treated?

Treatment is aimed at stopping bone loss and preventing falls, since osteoporosis is the cause of 1.5 million fractures each year, including more than 300,000 hip fractures. Doctors sometimes prescribe estrogen to replace the hormones lost during menopause and to slow the rate of bone loss. This treatment is called *hormone replacement therapy* (HRT). HRT also prevents against heart disease and stroke. However, experts do not know all the risks of long-term use of HRT.

Women should discuss the benefits, risks, and possible side effects of HRT with their doctors. *Calcitonin* is a naturally occurring hormone that increases bone density in the spine and can reduce the pain of fractures. It comes in two forms—injections or nasal sprays. You can also ask your doctor about the drug *alendronate*. This drug increases bone mass in women past menopause.

Source: *Osteoporosis: The Silent Bone Thinner,* a brochure published by the National Institute on Aging. For more information, call or write: National Osteoporosis Foundation, 1150 17th Street NW, Suite 602, Washington, DC 20036-2226; (800) 223-9994.

Stroke

What is a *stroke*?

A stroke or "brain attack" occurs when blood circulation to the brain fails. Brain cells can die from decreased blood flow and the resulting lack of oxygen.

Are there different kinds of strokes?

Yes. There are two broad categories of stroke: those caused by blockage of blood flow, and those caused by bleeding. The strokes caused by blockage— often of a blood vessel in the brain or neck—while usually not fatal, are responsible for about 80 percent of strokes. The second type is caused by bleeding to the brain, or the spaces surrounding the brain; it's called a *hemorrhagic stroke*.

In the case of the more common stroke, which blockages cause the stroke?

A *thrombosis* involves the formation of a clot within a blood vessel of the brain or neck. An *embolism* is the movement of one clot to another part of the body, such as the heart, the neck, or the brain. A *stenosis* is the severe narrowing of an artery in or leading to the brain.

What are the warning signs?

Any one of the following signs provides a clue that your brain is not receiving enough oxygen:

- sudden weakness or numbness of the face, arm, or leg on one side of the body
- sudden dimness or loss of vision, particularly in one eye
- sudden difficulty speaking or trouble understanding speech
- sudden severe headache with no known cause
- unexplained dizziness or sudden falls, especially with any of the other signs

If you observe one or more of these signs of stroke, don't wait: call a doctor or 911 right away.

What if the signs only last a few moments, then disappear?

Other signs may include double vision, drowsiness, and nausea or vomiting. They may be brief episodes, known as *transient ischemic attacks,* or "mini-strokes." Although brief, they identify an underlying serious condition that isn't going away without medical help. Since they clear up, many people ignore them. Don't. Heeding them can save your life.

What's a "risk factor"?

A risk factor is a condition or behavior that occurs more frequently in those who have, or are at a greater risk of getting, a disease than in those who don't. Having a risk factor doesn't mean that you'll have a stroke; on the other hand, not having a risk factor doesn't mean you'll avoid one. The risk of stroke grows as the number and severity of risk factors increase.

Are some groups at greater risk than others?

Yes. While stroke occurs in all age groups, in both sexes, and in all races in every country, scientists have found more severe risk factors in some minority groups. In African-Americans, the death rate from stroke is almost twice that of the white population.

What are the risks that I can do something about?

Control your blood pressure. High blood pressure, also called *hypertension,* is the most potent risk factor, and it is treatable. Other than medicines your doctor may prescribe, some ways to lower blood pressure include: maintaining your proper weight; avoiding drugs known to raise blood pressure; cutting down on salt; eating food, particularly vegetables to increase the potassium in your diet; and exercise.

Quit smoking. Cigarette smoking has been linked to the buildup of fatty substances in the carotid artery, which is the main neck artery supplying blood to the brain. Blockage of this artery is the leading cause of stroke in Americans. Also, nicotine raises blood pressure; carbon monoxide reduces the amount of oxygen your blood can carry to the brain; and cigarette smoke makes your blood thicker and more likely to clot.

Treat heart disease. Heart disease—which includes common heart disorders such as coronary heart disease, valve defects, irregular heartbeat, and enlargement of one of the heart's chambers—can result in blood clots that may break loose and block vessels in or leading to the brain. The most common blood vessel disease, caused by the buildup of fatty deposits in or leading to the brain, is *atherosclerosis.* Your doctor will treat your heart disease and may prescribe medication, such as aspirin, to help prevent the formation of clots; or surgery, to clean out a clogged neck artery.

Control diabetes. Diabetes, which affects the body's ability to use sugar, also causes destructive changes in blood vessels throughout the body, including the brain. If blood glucose levels are high at the time of a stroke, then brain damage is usually more severe and extensive. Treating diabetes can delay the onset of complications that increase the risk of stroke.

Report warning signs. Transient ischemic attacks, the brief episodes of stroke's warning signs, should be treated immediately. If you've had a stroke in the past, this is especially important, since a second stroke can be twice as bad.

Has the controlling of risk factors proven successful?

Yes. Americans have shown that stroke is preventable and treatable. A better understanding of the causes of stroke has helped people make lifestyle changes that have cut the stroke death rate in the United States nearly in half compared to the last two decades.

Source: *Brain Basics: Preventing Stroke,* a publication of the National Institute of Neurological Disorders and Stroke. For more information, call or write: National Institute of Neurological Disorders and Stroke, Information Office, P.O. Box 5801, Bethesda, MD 20824; (800) 352-9424.

Venereal Diseases

Does a condom protect you from venereal disease (VD)?

The latex (rubber) condom is an important risk-reducing factor in the prevention of AIDS and other sexually transmitted diseases (STDs), acting as a physical barrier for the areas involved during sex activities, and protecting each partner from the spread of germs that may be present in the bodily fluids of the other.

What is the best way to avoid STDs?

A sexual relationship with one person is preferable. Having multiple sex partners places one in a high-risk group with increased exposure to STD.

Is it possible to contract more than one type of STD in a single encounter?

Yes. More than one STD may be transmitted on the occasion of one sex contact.

Is an STD similar to chicken pox; once I get it, will I be immune from it thereafter?

No. Having had an STD does not provide immunity; reinfection is possible upon exposure to that disease. AIDS (HIV) infection, however, is permanent.

Do spermicidal jellies and foams protect the participant from STDs during intercourse?

Laboratory experiments indicated particularly that those products containing nonoxynol-9 have germicidal properties which are active against the infectious agents of certain sexually transmitted diseases. These spermicides are recommended for use along with the condom and the diaphragm.

Do intrauterine devices (IUDs) provide any protection against disease?

Neither the birth control pill nor the IUD prevents STDs; both serve only as contraceptives.

Is it possible to contract STDs through casual contact?

It is unlikely. Germs such as syphilis and gonorrhea require warmth and moisture for survival and die quickly upon drying outside the human body. Therefore, it would seem unlikely for these diseases to be acquired, as rumored, from toilet seats, towels, or drinking cups.

How is syphilis contracted?

Through infected blood, bodily fluids, or sexual contact with a person who has a syphilitic lesion. The germ enters the body through a mucus membrane or break in the skin and invades the bloodstream. Unsterilized acupuncture, tattoo, or hypodermic needles contaminated by blood during previous use on an infected person may transmit syphilis.

What are the symptoms of herpes?

When the virus is active, it appears with small, painful, fluid-filled bumps or blisters. The first outbreak, which is always more severe than those following, may be accompanied by flulike symptoms such as fever, aches, and malaise; the blisters may last for three weeks, or much longer if they become infected. It is estimated that as many as 70 percent of cases of genital herpes are transmitted without an outbreak and in the absence of symptoms.

What happens if STDs are left untreated?

Frequent STD exams for the sexually active are essential. For example, untreated *Chlamydia trachomatis* infection and gonorrhea in women can lead to serious consequences such as infertility and ectopic (outside the uterus) pregnancy, which can cause death if not promptly treated.

Source: American Foundation for the Prevention of Venereal Disease, Inc., 799 Broadway, Suite 638, New York, NY 10003; (212) 759-2069.

MENTAL HEALTH

◆

Alzheimer's Disease

Manic Depression

Depression

**Eating Disorders:
Anorexia, Bulimia, and Binge Eating**

Obsessive-Compulsive Disorder

Panic Attacks

Schizophrenia

Alzheimer's Disease

What is *Alzheimer's?*

Alzheimer's is a brain disease that leads to the loss of mental and physical functions. Most people with Alzheimer's are over 65. The disease is neither curable nor reversible.

What causes it?

The cause is unknown.

What are the signs of someone with Alzheimer's?

The onset of Alzheimer's disease is usually very slow and gradual, seldom occurring before the age of 65. Over time, however, it follows a progressively more serious course.

Problems of memory, particularly recent or short-term memory, are common. For example, a person might, on repeated occasions, forget to turn off the iron or not recall which of their morning medicines they had taken. Mild personality changes, such as apathy and withdrawal, may occur early in the illness. As the disease progresses, a person might have trouble with figures when working on bills or with understanding what is being read. Agitation, irritability, and diminishing ability to dress appropriately may also occur at this point.

Later, the affected person may become confused or disoriented about what month or year it is and be unable to accurately describe where he or she lives. Eventually, patients may wander and be unable to engage in conversation. They may seem inattentive, uncooperative, and become incapable of caring for themselves in the final stages.

Is the rate of decline the same for all Alzheimer's sufferers?

No; it can vary considerably. In fact, most people with Alzheimer's can function at a reasonable level and remain at home far into the course of the disorder. Throughout much of their illness, individuals maintain the ability to give and receive love, and to participate in activities with their family and friends. The chessboard might be put away, but tennis or gardening are possibilities; math might be difficult, but reading a magazine might be possible; playing the piano might be too stressful, but singing along might be a good option.

Is the disease easy to diagnose?

No. Alzheimer's is currently the most overdiagnosed and misdiagnosed disorder of mental functioning in older adults. There's no specific clinical test or finding that is unique to Alzheimer's disease. That's why diagnostic workups can be so frustrating, both for patients and their families. They are not told that Alzheimer's disease has been specifically diagnosed; rather, they are told that other possible diagnoses have been dismissed—leaving Alzheimer's as the likely diagnosis by the process of elimination.

Can Alzheimer's be treated?

For some patients, depression and delusion can aggravate Alzheimer's disease. By treating the depression alone, which can mimic dementia, clinical improvement can result—even though the underlying disease process is advancing. The patient's symptoms can be reduced, the suffering lowered, the capacity to cope buttressed, with the family's burden eased as a result.

The patient's immediate environment can also add to the level of impairment. Modifying the surroundings can reduce stress imposed by environmental factors. Protecting a person from wandering toward a stairway and perhaps falling will lower his frustration level. At some point, the most protective but least restrictive setting for care may involve a move away from home to a nursing home or other facility equipped to deal with those who have Alzheimer's disease.

Though Alzheimer's disease cannot at present be cured, reversed, or stopped in its progression, much can be done to help both patient and family live through the course of the illness with greater dignity and less discomfort. Toward this goal, appropriate clinical interventions and community services should be vigorously sought.

Source: *Alzheimer's Disease*, a brochure published by the National Institute for Mental Health (a division of the U.S. Department of Health and Human Services), the federal government's primary agency for biomedical and behavioral research. For more information, call or write your state agency on aging, or: Alzheimer's Association, Inc., 919 North Michigan Avenue, Suite 1000, Chicago, IL 60611; (312) 335-8700; (800) 272-3900 (Illinois); (800) 621-0379 (national).

Manic Depression

What is *manic depression*?

Manic depression, or *bipolar disorder*, is a mental illness involving episodes of serious mania and depression. The person's mood usually swings from an overly "high" and irritable one to a sad and hopeless one, then back again, with periods of normal mood in between.

What are the symptoms?

For mania, the symptoms include discrete periods of racing thoughts; rapid talking; increased energy, activity, and restlessness; excessive "high" or euphoric feelings; extreme irritability and distractibility; decreased need for sleep; unrealistic beliefs in one's abilities and powers; uncharacteristically poor judgment; increased sex drive; abuse of drugs, particularly cocaine, alcohol, and sleeping medications; provocative, intrusive, or aggressive behavior; and denial that anything is wrong.

For depression, the symptoms include discrete periods of persistent, sad, anxious, or empty moods; feelings of hopelessness or pessimism; feelings of guilt or worthlessness; loss of interest or pleasure in ordinary activities, including sex; decreased energy; a feeling of fatigue or of being "slowed down"; difficulty concentrating, remembering, and making decisions; restlessness or irritability; sleep disturbances; loss of appetite and weight, or weight gain; chronic pain or other persistent bodily symptoms that are not caused by physical disease; thoughts of death or suicide; suicide attempts.

Is manic depression easy to detect?

No. Manic-depressive illness is often not recognized by the patient, relatives, friends, or even physicians. Descriptions provided by the patients themselves offer valuable insights into the continuous range of moods associated with bipolar disorder. At one end is severe depression, which shades into moderate depression; then come mild and brief mood disturbances that many call "the blues"; then a normal mood again, then *hypomania* (a mild form of mania), and then mania. Some examples follow.

Depression: "I doubt my ability to do anything well. It seems as though my mind has slowed down and burned out to the point of being virtually useless. I'm haunted by the total, desperate hopelessness of it all. If I can't feel, move, think, or care, then what on earth is the point?"

Hypomania: "At first when I'm high, it's tremendous. Ideas come fast, like shooting stars you follow until brighter ones appear. All shyness disappears, the right words and gestures are suddenly there. Uninteresting people, things, become intensely interesting. Sensuality is pervasive, the desire to seduce and be seduced irresistible. Your marrow is infused with unbelievable feelings of ease, power, well-being, omnipotence, euphoria. You can do anything, but, somewhere, this changes."

Mania: "The fast ideas become too fast and there are far too many of them. Overwhelming confusion replaces clarity. I stop keeping up with it. Memory goes. Infectious humor ceases to amuse. My friends become frightened. Everything is now against the grain. I'm irritable, angry, frightened, uncontrollable—and feel trapped."

Why is manic depression so hard to recognize?

For several reasons. First, because an early sign of the illness is hypomania, the state which often feels good to the person experiencing it. So much so that she may deny that anything is wrong. Second, in its early stages, bipolar disorder may masquerade as a problem other than mental illness. For example, it could first appear in the form of alcohol or drug abuse, poor work or school performance, or wild spending sprees.

What causes it?

Bipolar disorder tends to run in families and is believed to be inherited in many cases.

How serious can some of the episodes get?

The person in the midst of a severe episode may have to be committed to a hospital, for his own protection. Untreated, some of the more devastating manic-depressive episodes can lead to suicide.

How can manic depression be treated?

One medication, lithium, is usually very effective in controlling mania and preventing the recurrence of both manic and depressive episodes. Mood-stabilizing anticonvulsants have also been found useful. Often these medications are combined with lithium for maximum effect.

Electroconvulsive therapy (ECT) is often helpful in the treatment of severe depression and/or mixed mania that does not respond to medications. Psychotherapy can work in concert with medication to provide support, education, and guidance to the patient and his family. Anyone with bipolar disorder should be under the care of a psychiatrist skilled in the diagnosis and treatment of the disease.

Almost everyone with bipolar disorder—even in its most severe forms—can obtain substantial stabilization for their mood swings.

Does manic depression ever go away completely?

No. It is important for patients to understand that bipolar disorder will not go away. Ongoing encouragement and support are necessary because it may take a while to discover what therapeutic regimen is needed to keep the disease under control.

Source: *Bipolar Disorder,* a pamphlet published by the National Institute of Mental Health Office of Scientific Information. For more information, call or write: National Depressive and Manic Depressive Association, 730 Franklin Street, Suite 501, Chicago, IL 60610; phone: (312) 642-0049 or (800) 826-3632; fax: (312) 642-7243.

Depression

What is *depression?*

Depressive illnesses are more than temporary "blue" moods or periods of grief after loss. Symptoms of depression affect thoughts, feelings, body, and behaviors. Without treatment, the symptoms can last for months, years, or a lifetime.

Are there different kinds of depression?

Yes. Some depressive episodes occur suddenly, for no apparent reason; some are triggered by a stressful experience. Some people have one episode in a lifetime; others recurrent episodes. Some people's symptoms are so severe they are unable to function; others have ongoing, chronic symptoms that do not interfere with functioning, but keep them from feeling really well. Some people have *bipolar disorder* (see *Manic Depression,* page 521). They experience cycles of terrible "lows" and inappropriate "highs."

What are the symptoms?

Symptoms of depression can include: persistent sad or "empty" moods; loss of interest or pleasure in ordinary activities, including sex; decreased energy, fatigue, feeling "slowed down"; sleep disturbances (insomnia, early-morning waking, or oversleeping); eating disturbances (loss of appetite or weight, or weight gain); difficulty concentrating, remembering, or making decisions; feelings of guilt, worthlessness, and helplessness; irritability; excessive crying; chronic aches and pains that don't respond to treatment, such as headaches and digestive disorders; thoughts of death or suicide; and suicide attempts.

Symptoms of mania can include: abnormally elevated moods; irritability; severe insomnia; grandiose notions; increased talking; racing thoughts; increased activity, including sex; markedly increased energy; poor judgment that leads to risk-taking behavior; and inappropriate social behavior. If five or more symptoms last for two weeks or longer, or are severe enough to interfere with normal functioning, an evaluation for clinical depression by a qualified health or mental health professional is recommended.

Is depression easy to spot?

No. Nearly two-thirds of depressed people do not get appropriate treatment because their symptoms are either not recognized, are blamed on personal weakness, are so disabling that the person cannot reach out for help, or are misdiagnosed and wrongly treated.

How many people does it affect?

Approximately 17.6 million Americans each year are afflicted by depression.

Is there a connection between depression and alcohol or mood-altering drugs?

Yes, but only insofar as some people mistakenly try to "reduce" their depressive symptoms by using alcohol and drugs. While such drugs may provide temporary relief, they will eventually complicate the depressive disorder and its treatment, and can lead to dependence and the life problems that come with it. It's estimated that as many as half of all people with alcohol and drug problems suffer from mood disorder, especially bipolar disorder.

Are some people more at risk for depression than others?

There are no differences in rates of depression among ethnic/racial groups, but the rate of clinical depression for women is about double that of men; in bipolar disorder, the rates are about the same.

The highest overall age of onset is between 25 and 44. Depression may be associated with life events such as loss (of spouses, children, jobs) or major financial reverses. Personality factors such as undue dependency and low self-esteem may also be associated with a vulnerability to depression. There's a risk for developing depression when there is a family history of these illnesses, with a somewhat higher rate for those with bipolar disorder.

Can depression be masked by other symptoms?

Yes. When depression occurs with medical, psychiatric, and substance-abuse disorders, its presence frequently goes unrecognized. For example, physical illnesses (stroke, heart disease, cancer, and diabetes) are risk factors for depression. A higher than average occurrence with other psychiatric disorders such as anxiety and eating disorders has been documented. Recent studies show that one out of three depressed people (32 percent) also suffer from some form of substance abuse or dependence.

Can depression be treated?

Yes. Drugs and psychological treatments are available; often, they are used in combination. In severe depression, medication is generally required. Other treatments include light therapy and electroconvulsive therapy (ECT). With treatment, up to 80 percent of those suffering from depression can improve and return to daily activities, usually in a matter of weeks.

Source: D/ART (Depression Awareness, Recognition, and Treatment) brochures on depression. D/ART, 5600 Fishers Lane, Rockville, MD 20857. For more information, call or write: National Alliance for the Mentally Ill, 200 North Glebe Road, Suite 1015, Arlington, VA 22203-3754; (703) 524-7600; (800) 950-NAMI (6264); fax: (703) 524-9094. For free brochures on depression and its treatment, call D/ART at (800) 421-4211.

Eating Disorders: Anorexia, Bulimia, and Binge Eating

What are the major eating disorders?

Anorexia nervosa, which affects approximately 1 percent of adolescent girls, is a dangerous condition in which sufferers can literally starve themselves to death. Another 2 to 3 percent of young women develop *bulimia nervosa*, a destructive pattern of overeating followed by vomiting and other "purging" behaviors to control their weight. *Binge eating*, like bulimia, also involves uncontrolled eating, but it differs from bulimia because its sufferers do not purge their bodies of excess food.

Do eating disorders affect women in particular? And if so, why?

Ninety percent of those afflicted are adolescent and young women. One reason is that women in this age group are particularly likely to go on strict diets to achieve an "ideal" figure. Researchers have found that stringent dieting can play a role in triggering eating disorders.

What is *anorexia nervosa?*

People who intentionally starve themselves suffer from anorexia nervosa. The disorder usually begins around the time of puberty and involves extreme weight loss—at least 15 percent below the individual's normal body weight. Many people with the disorder look emaciated but are convinced they are overweight. Sometimes they have to be hospitalized to prevent starvation. Eventually, half of those with anorexia will develop bulimia.

What is *bulimia nervosa?*

People with bulimia nervosa consume large amounts of food and then rid their bodies of the excess calories by vomiting, abusing laxatives or diuretics, taking enemas, or exercising obsessively. Because many individuals with bulimia "binge and purge" in secret and maintain normal or above-average body weight, they can often successfully hide their problem from others for years.

What is *binge-eating disorder?*

Individuals with this disorder feel that they lose control of themselves when eating. They eat large quantities of food and do not stop until they are uncomfortably full. Most of these people are obese and have a history of weight fluctuations.

Are eating disorders dangerous?

Yes. For patients with anorexia, starvation can damage vital organs such as the heart and brain. They can also lose calcium from their bones or experience irregular heart rhythms and heart failure. For patients with bulimia nervosa—even those of normal weight—purging may result in heart failure due to loss of vital minerals such as potassium.

People with binge-eating disorder are usually overweight, so they are prone to the serious medical problems associated with obesity, such as high cholesterol, high blood pressure, and diabetes. Obese individuals also have a higher risk for gall-bladder disease, heart disease, and some types of cancer; and they have high rates of psychiatric illness—especially depression—occurring in concert with their disorder.

What causes eating disorders?

Scientists have studied the personalities, genetic history, environments, and biochemistry of people with these illnesses. The more that is learned, the more complex the roots of eating disorders appear. However, most people with eating disorders share certain personality traits: low self-esteem, feelings of helplessness, and fear of becoming fat. In anorexia, bulimia, and binge-eating disorder, eating behaviors seem to develop as a way of handling stress and anxieties.

Eating disorders appear to run in families. One recent study found that mothers who are overly concerned about their daughters' weight and physical attractiveness may put the girls at increased risk of developing an eating disorder. In addition, girls with eating disorders often have a father and brothers who are overly critical of their weight. There also appears to be a connection between depression and eating disorders, as well as one between people with eating disorders and *obsessive-compulsive disorder* (see this page). Key chemical messengers in the central nervous system, such as neurotransmitters like *serotonin,* are known to occur at abnormal levels in people with these disorders.

Are some people more at risk than others?

People pursuing professional activities that emphasize thinness—such as modeling, dancing, gymnastics, wrestling, and long-distance running—are more susceptible to the problem. In contrast to other eating disorders, one-third to one-fourth of all patients with binge-eating disorders are men. Preliminary studies also show that the condition occurs equally among African-Americans and Caucasians. Although most victims of anorexia and bulimia are adolescent and young women, these illnesses also affect men and older women.

How can eating disorders be treated?

When it comes to treatment, the sooner the better. But this is difficult to do: People with anorexia may not receive medical or psychological attention until they are dangerously thin and malnourished; people with bulimia often have a normal weight and can hide their illness for years; and eating disorders in males may be overlooked because they are relatively rare.

The complex interaction of emotional and physiological problems in eating disorders calls for a comprehensive treatment plan. Ideally, the team should include an internist, a nutritionist, a psychotherapist, and a psychopharmacologist—someone who knows which medications are useful in treating these disorders.

Source: *Eating Disorders,* a pamphlet published by the Office of Scientific Information at the National Institute of Mental Health (NIMH). For more information, call or write: National Association of Anorexia Nervosa and Associated Disorders (ANAD), P.O. Box 7, Highland Park, IL 60035; (708) 831-3438.

Obsessive-Compulsive Disorder

What is *obsessive-compulsive disorder?*

Obsessive-compulsive disorder (OCD), one of the anxiety disorders, is a potentially disabling condition that can persist throughout a person's life. The individual becomes trapped in a pattern of repetitive thoughts and behaviors that are senseless and distressing, but extremely difficult to overcome. OCD occurs in a spectrum from mild to severe, but if severe and left untreated, it can destroy a person's capacity to function at work, school, or in the home.

What are *obsessions?*

Obsessions are unwanted ideas or impulses that repeatedly well up in the mind of a person with OCD: persistent fears that harm may come to oneself or a loved one, an unreasonable belief that one has a terrible illness, or an excessive need to do things correctly or perfectly are common. "My hands may be contaminated; I must wash them"..."I may have left the gas on"..."I am going to injure my child" are typical thoughts that are intrusive, unpleasant, and produce a high degree of anxiety. Often the obsessions are of a violent or sexual nature, or concern illness.

What's the compulsive aspect of OCD?

Compulsions are the receptive behaviors that people with OCD resort to in response to the obsessions. The most common ones are washing and checking. Others include counting (often while performing another compulsive action such as hand washing); repeating; hoarding; and endlessly rearranging objects in an effort to keep them in precise alignment with each other. Performing these rituals may give the person with OCD some relief from anxiety—they are intended to ward off harm to the person with OCD or others—but any such relief is temporary.

But aren't a lot of people compulsive?

Yes. People who hold themselves to a high standard of performance, who are perfectionistic and very organized, are sometimes called "compulsive." But this type of compulsiveness often serves a valuable purpose, contributing to a person's self-esteem and success on the job. It differs from the life-wrecking obsessions and rituals of the person with OCD.

What signs can I look for?

Other than obsession and compulsion, key features of OCD include: insight (self-knowledge about the problem, but an inability to stop obsessing or carrying out rituals); resistance (keeping OCD impulses under control during "working hours"); shame and secrecy (hiding the disorder, sometimes successfully); and long-lasting symptoms (despite the attempts to conceal the illness, the symptoms, for most people, are chronic).

Can you give a few examples of how people with OCD behave?

The following case histories are typical:

Isobel is intelligent, but is failing her first-period class in biology because she is either late to class or absent. She gets up at five o'clock, hoping to get to school on time. The next three hours are spent taking a long shower, followed by changing clothes repeatedly until it "feels right." She packs and repacks her books until they are just right, opens the front door, and prepares to walk down the front steps. She pauses on each step for a particular length of time. She recognizes her thoughts and behaviors are senseless, but she feels compelled to complete these rituals. Once completed, she makes a mad dash for school and arrives when the first period is over...

Meredith and her husband proudly brought a perfect, beautiful baby boy home from the hospital. She fed, bathed, and comforted the baby, and became a competent young mother. Then the obessional thoughts began; she feared that she might harm her child and, over and over again, she imagined herself stabbing the baby. She became terrified to use kitchen knives or her sewing scissors. She knew she did not want to harm her child, but she wondered why she has such distressing, alien thoughts...

During his last year at college, John became aware that he was spending more and more time preparing for classes, yet he graduated in the top 10 percent of his class with a major in accounting. He accepted a job in a prestigious accounting firm in his hometown and began working with high hopes for the future. Within weeks, the firm was having second thoughts about John. Work that should have taken two or three hours was delayed by his constant review of the figures, checking and rechecking—spending more than a week on a task. He knew it was taking too long to get each job done, but he felt compelled to continue checking. When his probation period was over, the company let him go.

How common is OCD?

According to a survey conducted by the National Institute of Mental Health (NIMH), OCD affects more than 2 percent of the population, making it more common than schizophrenia, bipolar disorder, or panic disorder.

When does OCD typically begin?

During the teenage years or early adulthood, though recent studies indicate that some children develop the illness at earlier stages. One-third of adults with OCD showed signs of the disorder in childhood.

What causes OCD?

The old belief that OCD was the result of life experiences the patient learned in early childhood—an inordinate emphasis on cleanliness, or a belief that certain thoughts are dangerous or unacceptable—has given way to growing evidence that biological factors are a primary cause.

Brain-imaging studies show abnormal neurochemical activity in regions known to play a role in neurological disorders. There is an increased rate of OCD in people with Tourette's syndrome, an illness characterized by involuntary movements or vocalizations. Another illness that may be linked to OCD is *trichotillomania* (the repeated urge to pull out scalp hair, eyelashes, or eyebrows). Genetic studies of OCD and other related conditions may help scientists pinpoint the molecular basis of these disorders.

How is OCD treated?

A combination of drugs and behavior therapy is often effective, though some people respond best to one over the other. Drug therapy (pharmacotherapy) is based on clinical trials that show how drugs affecting the neurotransmitter serotonin can significantly decrease the symptoms of OCD. The FDA has approved two serotonin reuptake inhibitors (SRIs), clomipramine (Anafranil) and fluoxetine (Prozac). Other SRIs, which have been studied in controlled, clinical trials, have also proved effective.

If medication is discontinued, relapse will follow. Most patients benefit from a combination of medication and behavioral therapy. Traditional psychotherapy, aimed at helping the patient develop insight into his problem, is generally not helpful for people with OCD. A specific "exposure and response prevention" therapy, in which the patient is deliberately and voluntarily exposed to the feared object (or idea), then denied the usual compulsive response, can produce long-lasting benefits. For example, a compulsive hand washer may be urged to touch an object believed to be contaminated, then denied the opportunity to wash for several hours. For therapy to succeed, it's important to be sure that the therapist is well trained in the specific method developed, that the patient is highly motivated, and that the patient's family is cooperative.

Source: *Obsessive-Compulsive Disorder,* a pamphlet published by the National Institute of Mental Health's Office of Scientific Information. For more information, write or call: Anxiety Disorders Association of America, 6000 Executive Boulevard, Suite 513, Rockville, MD 20852; (310) 231-9350.

Panic Attacks

How do I know if I'm having a *panic attack?*

The symptoms appear suddenly, without any apparent cause. They include: racing or pounding heartbeat; chest pains; dizziness, lightheadedness, nausea; difficulty breathing; tingling or numbness in the hands; flushes or chills; dreamlike sensations or perceptual distortions; fear of losing control and doing something embarrassing; fear of dying; and terror—a sense that something horrible is about to occur and you are powerless to prevent it.

How long does an attack last and will it happen again?

The typical panic attack lasts for several minutes. Most people who have one attack will have others. When someone has repeated attacks, or feels severe anxiety about having another attack, she is said to have *panic disorder.*

What is panic disorder?

Panic disorder is a serious health problem that affects at least 3 million adult Americans at some time in their lives. The disorder is strikingly different from other types of anxiety because panic attacks are sudden, appear to be unprovoked, and are often disabling.

When someone has a panic attack while driving, shopping in a crowded store, or riding in an elevator, she may develop irrational fears, called *phobias*, about these situations and begin to avoid them. This type of panic disorder, when someone fears driving or stepping out of the house, is compounded by *agoraphobia* (fear of spaces). Panic disorder can have a serious impact on a person's daily life—unless they receive effective treatment.

Does anything in particular trigger it?

The first attacks are usually triggered by physical illness, a major life stress, or certain medications.

What causes panic attacks?

One theory is that the body's normal "alarm system" is triggered unnecessarily. Scientists don't know why this happens. Panic disorder has been found to run in families, and this may mean that inheritance (genes) plays a strong role in determining who will get it. However, many people who have no family history of the disorder also develop it.

Is panic disorder sometimes mistaken for other illnesses?

Yes—for heart disease or other life-threatening medical illnesses. People frequently go to hospital emergency rooms, where extensive medical tests may be performed to rule out these illnesses.

Is panic disorder serious?

Yes. Expressions such as "nothing serious," "all in your head," and "nothing to worry about" give the incorrect impression that there is no real problem and that treatment is not possible or necessary.

What is the treatment for panic disorder?

A variety of treatments are available, including several effective medications and specific forms of psychotherapy. Often, a combination of psychotherapy and medications produces good results—sometime, in a short period of time, about six to eight weeks. Proper treatment can, at the very least, reduce the severity and frequency of panic attacks, bringing relief for 70 to 90 percent of people with the disorder.

What happens if panic disorder is not treated?

It tends to continue for months or years. Typically, it begins in young adulthood, but the symptoms may arise earlier or later in life. If left untreated, the disorder may worsen to the point where the person's life is seriously affected by panic attacks and by attempts to avoid or conceal them. In fact, many people have had problems with friends and family or lost jobs while struggling to cope with this disorder.

Source: *Panic Disorder,* a Panic Disorder Education Program pamphlet published by NIMH. For more information, write or call: National Institute of Mental Health Panic Disorder Education Program, 5600 Fisher Lane, Room 7-99, Rockville, MD 20857-8030; (301) 443-4536; (301) 443-0008; or call (800) 64-PANIC.

Schizophrenia

What is *schizophrenia?*

Schizophrenia is the most chronic and disabling of the major mental illnesses, as well as the most puzzling. Few generalizations hold true for all people diagnosed with schizophrenia because it's a complex illness that may be one disorder or many disorders with different causes.

When does it strike?

The first psychotic symptoms—when the sufferer is out of touch with reality or unable to separate real from unreal experiences—are often seen in the teens or 20s in men and in the 20s or early 30s in women. Less obvious symptoms, such as social isolation, withdrawal, and unusual speech, thinking, or behavior may precede and/or follow the psychotic symptoms.

What are its symptoms?

The schizophrenic's sense of reality can appear distorted, changeable, and lacking in reliable landmarks we all use to anchor ourselves to reality. As a result, the person may feel anxious, confused, and seem distant, detached, or preoccupied. He may even sit rigidly as stone, not moving for hours and not uttering a sound. It's also possible for a person with schizophrenia to move about constantly, always occupied, wide awake, vigilant, and alert. Different kinds of behavior may be exhibited at different times.

Hallucinations are part of a schizophrenic's world. The person may sense things that in reality do not exist. Hearing voices that tell them what to do, seeing people or objects that are not really there, or feeling invisible fingers touching their bodies—these are all possible hallucinations that can be quite frightening for the schizophrenic. Delusions are also a common symptom. These are false and irrational beliefs that can include themes of persecution or grandeur. They are often quite bizarre—for instance, believing that a neighbor is controlling the schizophrenic's behavior with magnetic waves or that people on TV are directing special messages to the sufferer. Delusions of persecution, which are common in paranoid schizophrenics, lead the individual to feel he is being cheated, harassed, poisoned, or conspired against.

Disordered thinking, another symptom, involves thoughts that come and go so rapidly that it is not possible for the schizophrenic to "catch them." He may not be able to connect thoughts into logical sequences, and may jump from topic to topic in a way that is totally confusing to others.

Finally, people with schizophrenia sometimes exhibit "inappropriate affect." This means that they show emotion that is inconsistent with their speech or thoughts. For example, a schizophrenic may say that he is being persecuted by demons, and then laugh.

Can a schizophrenic ever appear normal?

Yes. Unless in the midst of an extremely disorganized state, many schizophrenic people often think, feel, and act in a normal fashion. They will share the common sense of reality (knowing that most people eat three times a day and sleep at night, for example) but sometimes will have an experience—such as hearing a voice of warning—which is clearly a distortion of reality.

Is schizophrenia the same as "split personality"?

No. In fact, this Dr. Jekyll–Mr. Hyde switch in character, or *split personality* is an entirely different disorder that, along with *multiple personality,* is quite rare.

Can children be schizophrenic?

Children over the age of five can develop schizophrenia, but it is very rare for them to have it before adolescence.

Are all schizophrenics violent?

No, most are not violent. More typically, they prefer to withdraw and be left alone. Some acutely disturbed patients become physically violent, but such outbursts have become relatively infrequent, especially following the use of antipsychotic medications. There is general agreement that most violent crimes are not committed by schizophrenic persons and that most schizophrenic persons do not commit violent crimes.

What about suicide?

People with schizophrenia appear to have a higher rate of suicide than the general population.

Is schizophrenia inherited?

It has long been known that schizophrenia runs in families. Most scientists agree that what may be inherited is a vulnerability or predisposition to the disorder. This inherited potential, given a certain set of factors, can lead to schizophrenia.

How is schizophrenia treated?

Since schizophrenia may not be a single condition and its causes are not yet known, current treatment methods are chosen on the basis of their ability to reduce symptoms and lessen the chance that they will return. Antipsychotic drugs are the best treatment now available, but they do not "cure" schizophrenia or assure sufferers that psychotic episodes will not recur. These medications may diminish the hallucinations, agitation, confusion, distortions, and delusions, allowing the schizophrenic to make decisions more rationally. Not all patients, however, respond to such medications.

Psychosocial approaches to treatment, involving various forms of therapy, have limited value for acutely psychotic patients (who are out of touch with reality or have prominent hallucinations or delusions), but may be useful for those with less severe symptoms or for those whose psychotic symptoms are under control.

Source: *Schizophrenia: Questions and Answers,* a brochure published by the National Institute of Mental Health. For more information, call or write: The National Alliance for the Mentally Ill, 200 North Glebe Road, Suite 1015, Arlington, VA 22203-3754, (703) 524-7600 or (800) NAMI (6264).

ALTERNATIVE MEDICINE

Acupuncture
Aromatherapy
Chiropractic
Homeopathy
Yoga

Acupuncture

What is *acupuncture*?

Acupuncture is the gentle insertion of hair-fine needles into specific points on the body to stimulate the flow of one's *Qi* (pronounced "chee") or natural healing energy. Sometimes, rather than just inserting a needle into an acupoint, an acupuncturist may choose to apply heat to the point, or stimulate it with very low voltage electricity (no more than is generated by a transistor radio battery). These techniques are known as "Moxibustion" and "electro-stimulation." They are additional tools that your practitioner may use to further stimulate the natural healing powers of your body.

Does acupuncture hurt?

Most people are surprised to learn that acupuncture needles are very thin and flexible, about the diameter of a human hair. Several acupuncture needles can fit into one conventional hypodermic needle. Acupuncture bears no resemblance to the feeling of receiving an injection, since the main source of pain from injections is the larger-diameter, hollow needle and the medication being forced into the tissue by pressure. Acupuncturists can attain a high level of skill in placing these tiny needles into the skin with a minimum of discomfort. Depending on the type of needle manipulation that is used, you may experience a sense of heaviness or electricity in the area of insertion. However, most patients find the treatments very relaxing and many fall asleep. In some cases, it is not necessary to use needles at all.

How do I know the needles are sterile?

Acupuncture needles used today in the United States are all sterile and generally disposable. In the past, before AIDS was an issue, acupuncturists used a special machine called an *autoclave* to treat used medical equipment with heat to sterilize it. This technique is still allowed, but depending on the state laws, e.g. in California, most licensed acupunturists choose to use the new disposable type of needles. They come in sterile containers, are used once, and then disposed of. Some practitioners use reusable needles and keep an individual set for each patient. You should discuss the type of needles to be used if you have a preference.

Is acupuncture safe?

In the hands of a comprehensively trained acupuncturist, your safety is assured. Acupuncture and herbal treatments are drug-free, so you avoid side effects or dependency. However, you should always inform any health practitioner about preexisting conditions, the names of all medications you are taking, whether you are or could be pregnant, and if you have a cardiac pacemaker or cosmetic implants. Your acupuncturist will evaluate your specific situation with this information to ensure the best results.

What is Oriental medicine?

Traditional Oriental medicine is a comprehensive system of health care with a continuous clinical tradition of over 3,000 years. It includes acupuncture and herbal treatment, as well as Oriental bodywork such as tuina and shiatsu, dietary therapy, meditation, and exercise. These therapies work with the natural vital energy inherent within all living things to promote the body's ability to heal itself. This system of health care is used extensively by one-quarter of the world's population in the East and is rapidly growing in popularity in the West.

How does it work?

Oriental medicine is based on an energetic model rather than the biochemical model of Western medicine. The ancient Chinese recognized the vital energy behind all life forms and life processes. They called this energy *Qi*. In developing an understanding of the prevention and cure of disease, the ancient practitioners discovered a system of cyclic energy flowing in the human body along specific pathways termed *meridians*. Each pathway is associated with a particular physiological system and internal organ.

Disease is considered to arise because of a deficiency or imbalance of vital energy in the meridians and their associated physiological systems. The meridians communicate with the surface of the body at specific locations called *acupuncture points*. Each point has a predictable effect upon the vital energy passing through it. Modern science has been able to measure the electrical charge at these points, thus corroborating the locations of the meridians mapped by the ancients.

Traditional Oriental medicine has also developed methods of determining the flow in the meridian system, using an intricate combination of pulse and tongue diagnosis, palpation of acupuncture points, medical history, and other signs and symptoms to create a composite diagnosis. A treatment plan is then formulated to induce the body to a balanced state of health.

If I use acupuncture, does it mean I can't use traditional Western treatments?

Not at all. Acupuncture treatment may be used along with other medical care to great advantage. It has been used for pain control with other medical or dental procedures, for improving healing, and to lessen the side effects of some drugs, including those used in chemotherapy.

What can it treat?

Traditional Oriental medicine is used for any medical need—hormonal, neurological, psychological, metabolic, immune system, and to alleviate pain. There are treatments for everything. The World Health Organization recognizes acupuncture and Oriental medicine's ability to treat over 43 commonly encountered clinical disorders.

What can I expect if treated?

Many conditions may be alleviated very rapidly when treated by acupuncture, herbs, and/or Oriental bodywork. However, some conditions that have arisen over the course of years will be relieved only with slow, steady progress. As in any form of healing, the patient's attitude, diet, determination, and lifestyle will affect the outcome.

Although there are techniques in traditional Oriental medicine for healing most conditions, certain medical circumstances can be dealt with more effectively by Western medicine. In such cases, your practitioner will recommend that you contact a Western medical doctor. As is the case in China, acupuncture and Oriental medicine should be seen as complementary to Western medicine.

How do I find a qualified practitioner?

You should look for a practitioner who has been comprehensively trained in the area of Oriental medicine that you are seeking. The national standards for the practice of acupuncture, established by the national certification agency for practitioners and the national accreditation agency for colleges, require a minimum of three years of training to practice acupuncture and four years training in acupuncture and Chinese herbology for those who practice both. As a consumer, there are two methods for choosing a qualified practitioner who has been comprehensively trained. One is through state licensure; the other is through national board certification.

The laws in different states vary. For example, some jurisdictions include the practice of Chinese herbology within the scope of acupuncture, others do not. In some states, acupuncturists are regulated by a state board of acupuncture, in others they are under the department of health, licensing, or education, or the board of medical examiners. Practitioners may be called Licensed Acupuncturist (L.Ac. or Lic.Ac.), Registered Acupuncturist (R.Ac.), Certified Acupuncturist (C.A.), Acupuncturist, Doctor of Oriental Medicine (New Mexico and Nevada), or Doctor of Acupuncture (Rhode Island). However, in each case, state licensure means an individual has met eligibility requirements established by the state to practice acupuncture and/or Oriental medicine. If you live in a regulated jurisdiction, seek a comprehensively trained acupuncturist.

The second mechanism for selecting a fully trained practitioner of acupuncture or Oriental medicine is through national board certification by the National Certification Commission for Acupuncture and Oriental Medicine (NCCA). If you live in an unregulated state, in order to ensure the highest-quality health care, you should seek a practitioner certified by the NCCA.

Sources: National Acupuncture and Oriental Medicine Alliance, the national professional membership association for acupuncture and Oriental medicine in the United States. The National Alliance is an excellent source of information on the profession, legislation, Oriental medicine schools, referrals to qualified practitioners, upcoming workshops, etc. Al Stone is the creator of "Acupuncture.com," a Web site that offers a wealth of general information on acupuncture and related disciplines. Mr. Stone maintains an acupuncture practice in Santa Monica, California. For more information, contact: National Acupuncture and Oriental Medicine Alliance, 14637 Starr Road, S.E., Olalla, WA 98359; phone: (253) 851-6896; fax: (253) 851-6883; Web site: http://www.Acupuncture.com.

Aromatherapy

What is *aromatherapy*?

Aromatherapy is the use of natural plant essential oils to promote personal health, well-being, or simply to add to the sensual experiences of life.

What are "essential oils"?

Essential oils are the volatile fragrant essence that a plant produces in specialized cells. Essential oils and hydrosols, the tools of aromatherapy, are obtained from plants by a process called *distillation*. Plant materials are heated with water in a pot known as a still, so that their aromatic oils are released from the plant, vaporize, and rise with the steam of the heated water. The steam and vapor move through a tube to a condensing coil, where they are cooled and return to a liquid state. The essential oil, which is an easily evaporated (volatile) liquid having the characteristic odor of the plant, floats on top of the water. The resulting water, containing water-soluble parts of the plant and micro-molecules of essential oil, is called the *hydrosol*. Both of these products of distillation are considered valuable therapeutic substances, and are used by application and inhalation to achieve physical, emotional, mental, and spiritual balance and harmony.

Is using anything with a scent considered aromatherapy?

No. Aromatherapy is not simply the use of products containing fragrance. To practice true aromatherapy, pure essential oils from plants, which have not been adulterated with synthetic substances, must appear in quantities considered to therapeutic. By the same token, hydrosols must be fresh, as must be the water collected from the condenser after the process of distillation. Other products, such as essential oils added to distilled water, are sometimes mistaken for hydrosols. It is always wise to read the ingredients when choosing products labeled as "aromatherapy."

How does aromatherapy work?

The inhalation of essential oils and hydrosols affects our bodies in several ways. The aroma of essential oil is inhaled from a handkerchief, or is "diffused" throughout the room. Hydrosols are spritzed in the air or on the face and body and inhaled with a deep, relaxing breath. When inhaled, micro-molecules of essential oils travel through the nasal passages to the limbic system of the brain, which is the seat of memory and emotion. The inhalation of essential oils triggers memories and emotions within the limbic system, which in turn stimulates a response within the entire system.

What's an example of this?

If the aroma of cinnamon is reminiscent of hot apple pie baking in the oven, an emotional response such as comfort, warmth, and security may accompany the inhalation of cinnamon essential oil. This emotional response, triggered by a mental association, creates a relaxed and comforted response from the body. Yet many essential oils produce a relaxed, stimulated, or soothed state even if we have no memory associated with them. This is because of the chemical composition of the essential oil. The chemical composition of essential oils can also affect the user physically. Eucalyptus essential oil, when inhaled through the mouth and nose, clears sinus passages and can aid in the treatment of chest colds and flus. If you use essential oils in a bath, or while having a massage, the oils are absorbed through the skin and carried to the main body systems, such as the nervous and muscular systems.

What else can you do with these oils?

Your imagination is the limit. You can use these oils in a relaxing bath, for a massage, in body-care products, for aromatherapy perfumes, candles, humidifiers; or spritzed around the house, car, and office to spread pure, pleasurable aromas. Essential oils can be added to potpourris; room sprays are also great ways to incorporate the benefits of aromatherapy. Try adding a few drops of essential oil to your laundry during the final rinse, or a few drops at night on your pillowcase. They can be added to cleaning agents to decrease harmful bacteria.

Hydrosols are equally versatile, and are used for body care, symptoms of menopause, stress relief, and in culinary preparations. They can also be used in medicinal and first-aid preparations. Many practitioners believe that essential oils have the ability to permeate the skin and are carried via the bloodstream throughout the body to strengthen and heal internal systems. In other preparations, essential oils are used for their astringent, antibacterial, antibiotic, or anti-inflammatory properties. In perfumes, they are used for aesthetic, aphrodisiac, warming, and other emotional effects. Essential oils can even be inhaled to reduce one's appetite and help achieve weight loss.

How can aromatherapy help weight loss?

What good would an inhalation of essential oil do to your ravenous appetite, you may ask? Our sense of smell is responsible for 90 percent of our experience of taste. By overloading our sense of smell regularly throughout the day, particularly by inhaling culinary oils such as dill weed, ginger, cumin seed, lemon, vanilla, and spearmint, we can suppress our desire to taste, and thereby, to eat. Try it yourself. Whenever you feel hungry but prefer not to indulge, choose one of the oils and put it to your nose for 3 to 5 minutes. Feel your taste buds actually being filled and your desire for food being satiated. The instinctive message from the brain saying you are hungry simply gets turned off.

This should be done as many times during the day as you need, but change scents daily so as to not get overloaded on one. And make sure to smell the oil for at least 3 to 5 minutes. If only whiffed briefly, culinary oils can have the reverse effect of stimulating the appetite (as they are intended to do in cooking).

How does a "diffusor" work?

Diffusors are devices used to fill a room with essential oils to maximize the therapeutic benefits of inhalation. Some diffusors use heat as a means of evaporating the essential oils, spreading tiny molecules of essential oils throughout the room. Candle diffusors and ceramic rings placed on lightbulbs are common forms. Other diffusors are electric and consist of an electronically powered air pump and a glass vessel that holds the essential oil. Air is blasted through a tube connected to the vessel holding the volatile oil, which separates into tiny droplets small enough to be carried on currents of air and spread throughout a room.

I've heard a lot about aromatherapy lately... is it new?

Not at all. Essential oils and their effects on the body have been known about and used since the year 1500, but aromatic substances have been in use for thousands of years. In fact, aromatherapy is often referred to as an ancient healing art, dating back to Egyptian and Greek times. Hippocrates, considered the father of Western medicine, is said to have believed that "the way to health is to have an aromatic bath and scented massage every day." A variety of aromatic substances are mentioned throughout the Bible as well. These substances from aromatic plants have been used throughout history in a variety of ways to increase spiritual awareness and to aid meditation practice.

What are some of them?

Everyone knows frankincense, which is a much-favored incense for churches and other places of spiritual ritual. This essential oil has a calming effect, and also awakens higher consciousness. It is also useful in coping with grief to soothe the mind and emotions, is good for respiratory conditions, and is used for aging skin.

Myrrh, another familiar one, has been around since before the time of Christ, when this luxury oil was used for cosmetics and perfumery. It calms fears about the future, and is antiseptic to the lungs and good for problems of the throat. Spikenard, known for its deep, powerful aroma, is good for regulating the heartbeat, reducing fevers, and for incurable skin conditions, with its balancing, soothing, harmonizing effect.

Can aromatherapy ever be dangerous, or are there times when certain oils shouldn't be used?

The main thing to remember is that these oils are concentrated and need to be diluted before you put them on your skin, otherwise they can be damaging. Anything can be dangerous if used immoderately. Drops are always used—unless you are using a ready-to-use blend. Various vegetable oils, such as almond oil, are mixed with the essential oil for massage, and in a bath there are large amounts of water to dilute the oil. Be mindful when pregnant or nursing to use only the gentlest of essential oils.

Do I need an aromatherapist, or can I do it myself?

Many of the uses of aromatherapy, such as massaging your feet with lavender to help relaxation and stress reduction, and many of the ones listed above are quite simple and can be easily used at home. Many people consider aromatherapy among the simple home remedies, but it is in fact both a specific science and a deeply complex art. Essential oils are not like prescriptions, in which a particular pill is considered best for a particular malady; rather, the skilled aromatherapist works with the client to develop a blend of oils that will suit his total profile. The essential oils chosen work well together aesthetically, as well as for the client's particular complaint.

For instance, when addressing muscle pain, an aromatherapist may create a blend of essential oils that will relieve the tension of the muscle, yet will also act upon the client mentally and emotionally to address the underlying cause of the muscle tension. This blend of oils, in which the whole is greater than its parts, is known as "synergy." The knowledge, awareness, and listening skills required to create synergies are quite complex.

How do I find an aromatherapist?

There are no legal standards for aromatherapy training or certification in the United States, but many schools and individuals offer aromatherapy training. Those practitioners calling themselves aromatherapists are most often trained in some other form of therapy, such as massage or chiropractic, and have incorporated the use of essential oils into their practice. When seeking aromatherapy training, it is important for students to know the background and experience of the teacher. The National Association for Holistic Aromatherapy (NAHA) has devised a set of standards for aromatherapy certification in an effort to provide guidelines for students and teachers.

Source: Jeanne Rose, president emeritus of NAHA. She has written extensively on aromatherapy, has been a practicing aromatherapist and educator on the subject for many years, and provides a home-study course that follows NAHA's guidelines. Call (415) 564-6785 for information. Jeanne Rose can be reached at 219 Carl Street, San Francisco, CA 94117.

Chiropractic

What is *chiropractic?*

Chiropractic is a branch of the healing arts that is concerned with human health and disease processes. Doctors of chiropractic are physicians who consider man as an integrated being and pay special attention to the physiological and biochemical aspects of the body, including structural, spinal, musculoskeletal, neurological, vascular, nutritional, emotional, and environmental relationships.

The practice and procedures employed by doctors of chiropractic are based on an academic and clinical training received through accredited chiropractic colleges. They include, but are not limited to, the use of current diagnostic and therapeutic procedures. Such procedures specifically include the adjustment and manipulation of the articulations and adjacent tissues of the human body, particularly the spinal column, and the treatment of intersegmental aberrations to alleviate related functional disorders.

Chiropractic is a drug-free, nonsurgical science, and as such does not include pharmaceuticals or incisive surgery. State laws, as well as the nation's antitrust laws, may allow doctors of chiropractic to utilize ancillary health-care procedures commonly referred to as being in the common domain.

What is a chiropractor?

Chiropractors are first-contact physicians who possess the diagnostic skills to differentiate health conditions that are amenable to their management from those conditions that require referral or co-management. Chiropractors provide conservative management of neuromusculoskeletal disorders and related functional clinical conditions, including, but not limited to, back pain, neck pain, and headaches.

Chiropractors are expert providers of spinal and other therapeutic manipulation/adjustments. They also employ a variety of manual, mechanical, and electrical therapies. Chiropractors can provide patient evaluations and instructions on disease prevention and the promotion of well-being through proper nutrition, exercise, and lifestyle modification.

What are the current educational requirements to become a doctor of chiropractic?

Chiropractic colleges require a minimum of four academic years of professional resident study, including clinical experience under strict supervision, preceded by a minimum of two years of college work with a curriculum concentrated in the biological and basic sciences, and clinical disciplines. The remaining two years emphasize practical or clinical studies dealing with the diagnosis and treatment of disease, with approximately half the time spent in college clinics.

How do you go about choosing a chiropractor?

It would be a rare community that did not list several doctors of chiropractic in the local telephone directory's Yellow Pages. In choosing a particular practitioner, one of the best guidelines is the doctor's reputation within his community. Because stringent educational and professional standards are required for state licensing, the public is assured of academic competence and clinical experience—even with recent graduates. A patient should select a doctor based on confidence in that person's ability. However, as in all professions, the personal rapport between doctor and patient is also important.

How do you know when to use a doctor of chiropractic?

Doctors of chiropractic (DCs) are primary-care physicians, so defined in federal and state regulations, who serve as portals of entry into the health-care system. Under chiropractic care, a patient receives a comprehensive differential diagnosis, arrived at by utilizing an orthopedic and neurologic examination, an X-ray examination, laboratory procedures, or whatever other procedure is deemed necessary. By consultation and examination, the doctor of chiropractic will arrive at a chiropractic prognosis, or else refer the patient to appropriate care.

Is chiropractic treatment dangerous?

With rare exceptions, the answer is no. Any form of health treatment contains a degree of inherent risk, but there is little danger in chiropractic care administered by a licensed practitioner. To assure competency and make certain the discipline is conducted in a scientific and professional manner, all states require that DCs, as well as MDs and DOs, be board-qualified, licensed, and regulated according to stringent criteria. Statistics show that patient risk is substantially lower in chiropractic as opposed to medical care, where the iatrogenic threat of prescription drugs and surgery pose greater risk. These two hazards, which are avoided in chiropractic care, represent the overwhelming concerns in health science today.

Recognizing that, with rare exceptions, the community relationship between medical and chiropractic physicians is cordial and cooperative, how does the American Chiropractic Association interpret criticisms from organized medicine at the national level, especially the AMA?

The American Chiropractic Association encourages its members to cooperate within the healing arts whenever such cooperation will enhance the health of an individual or public health objectives. No profession offers a panacea to public health needs; thus, more interprofessional dialogue and cooperation are still needed.

Are chiropractors well-educated in the use of diagnostic X-rays, and are full-spine exposures exceptionally dangerous?

Chiropractic education provides more hours of education in diagnostic X-ray than allopathic and osteopathic predoctoral education does. About 90 percent of chiropractors utilize diagnostic X-rays; full spine X-rays constitute less than 17 percent of all X-ray procedures. Chiropractic doctors are trained to administer a full-spine X-ray of good diagnostic quality, with a smaller dose of X-ray to vital body areas and reproductive organs, than would be received if separate films of each spinal area were taken to see the entire spinal column. Properly taken, the full-spine study may be superior to the use of films of each spinal region by allowing the relationships between several spinal areas to be better understood.

Are chiropractors allowed to practice in many hospitals or use their outpatient facilities?

Chiropractors are being recognized to admit and treat patients in hospitals, and to use outpatient clinical facilities (labs, X-rays, etc.) for their nonhospitalized patients. Hospital privileges were first granted in 1983.

Source: The American Chiropractic Association, a national, nonprofit professional organization representing the majority of licensed practicing doctors of chiropractic in the United States. For more information, write to them: American Chiropractic Association, 1701 Clarendon Boulevard, Arlington, VA 22209. Or call toll-free, (800) 986-4636. You can also visit their Web site, Chiropractic OnLine, at http://www.amerchiro.org for information.

Homeopathy

What is *homeopathy*?

Homeopathy is a system of medicine that uses small doses of natural substances to stimulate the body's defense mechanism. It was developed in Germany in the early 1800s by the physician Christian Frederich Samuel Hahnemann (1755–1843). The word "homeopathy" means "similar suffering"—a homeopathic medicine is given based upon its ability to mimic the disease state. Homeopathy was very popular in the United States in the late 1800s and early 1900s, but declined during the first half of the 20th century. Today it is enjoying a resurgence of interest and continues to be widely used in Europe, Asia, and Latin America. Homeopathy is used not only to treat illness but also to prevent illness and maintain overall health.

How does it work?

Homeopathy is based on the principle of similars, which means that a substance that can cause certain symptoms in a healthy person can cure a sick person with similar symptoms. For example, if a person has a cold or hay fever and is experiencing watery eyes and a burning nasal discharge, he might be treated with a homeopathic preparation of onion—a substance known to make the eyes water and the nose run. If a person can't sleep because she is too agitated or her mind too active, she might be treated with a homeopathic preparation of coffee. In other words, "like cures like." This principle is incorporated by conventional medicine in its use of vaccinations and allergy treatments.

How does the concept of homeopathy differ from that of conventional medicine?

Instead of looking at symptoms as something wrong that must be set right, homeopathy regards symptoms as the body's attempt to restore itself to health. Homeopathy looks at individuals, not diseases. For instance, each of us suffers a cold in his or her unique way. While conventional medicine assumes that all colds are alike and uses drugs to control the symptoms, a homeopath will use a remedy that matches the unique symptoms of the individual and encourages their self-healing mechanism to respond more efficiently. In conventional medical therapy, the aim is often to control the illness through regular use of medicines; if the medicine is withdrawn, the person returns to illness. A person who takes a pill every day for high blood pressure is not undergoing a cure but managing symptoms. Homeopathy's aim is the cure.

What ailments is homeopathy best used for?

Homeopathy is effective in a wide range of conditions, from simple first aid and self-limiting conditions to more serious complaints. Some common ailments that can be effectively treated by homeopathy are

- Sports and exercise injuries
- Sore throats, cough, and flu

- Earaches, teething, colic, and other childhood conditions
- Allergies, asthma, bronchitis, and hay fever
- Headaches and migraine headaches
- PMS, menopause, and morning sickness
- Arthritis
- Digestive disorders
- Eczema and dermatitis
- Chronic fatigue syndrome
- Depression and anxiety

What are the medicines?

There are approximately 1,300 medicines catalogued in the *Homeopathic Pharmacopoeia* of the United States, the official manufacturing manual. Most are made from plants, such as daisy and chamomile; some are made from minerals, such as calcium and table salt; the rest are from animal sources, such as cuttlefish ink and bee venom. Some are even made from synthetic drugs such as penicillin.

These substances are prepared by a process of serial dilution and succussion, or vigorous shaking, until little of the original remains. Because of the small doses used in homeopathy, the medicines are nontoxic. The manufacture and sale of homeopathic medicines is regulated by the U.S. Food and Drug Administration.

Where do you get the medicines?

The majority of homeopathic medicines are available over the counter in the United States and can be purchased from health-food stores, many corner drugstores, or by mail directly from the manufacturers. There are seven major homeopathic manufacturing companies in the United States.

Are the medicines expensive?

Homeopathic medicines are much less expensive than conventional medicines, costing on average $4 to $7 per bottle. Often only a single dose of a medicine is needed to effect a return to health.

If I can get most medicines over the counter, why do I need to go to a professional?

Self-care is not appropriate for all conditions. Consumers can learn simple first aid and how to treat acute conditions effectively with the aid of a homeopathic self-care book or by attending homeopathic classes, but serious conditions should always be treated by an experienced homeopathic practitioner.

Who practices homeopathy?

Homeopathy is practiced by a wide variety of health-care providers, including medical doctors, osteopaths, naturopathic physicians, nurse practitioners, physician assistants, dentists, veterinarians, chiropractors, licensed acupuncturists, certified nurse-midwives, and podiatrists. Homeopathy is considered the practice of medicine by most states; licensing requirements vary by state and profession. Professional education in homeopathy is offered by independent postgraduate training programs. There are approximately 3,000 homeopathic practitioners in the United States at present.

How do I find a homeopath?

Word of mouth is generally the best way to find any kind of practitioner. Seek the advice of friends or coworkers who have visited a homeopath. Obtain the National Center for Homeopathy (NCH)'s *Directory of Homeopathic Practitioners,* a listing of licensed health-care providers who dedicate 25 to 100 percent of their practice to homeopathy. Then research the practitioners in your area. The NCH directory also lists study groups, which are valuable sources of information about local practitioners.

What kind of questions should I ask to help identify a good practitioner?

The questions will vary with each case, but a few pertinent ones might be: Does the practitioner specialize in homeopathy? Does the practitioner use classical homeopathy? Where was the practitioner trained? How long has she been using homeopathy? Has the practitioner had experience with the diagnostic category in which your condition fits? Is the practitioner board-certified in homeopathy? Some other important issues might be how far the practitioner is from your home, and whether or not your insurance will cover the visit. You may wish to seek the care of a practitioner who has more extensive general medical training if your condition is chronic or serious.

What happens during a homeopathic consultation, and what does it cost?

The first visit to a homeopath usually lasts 60 to 90 minutes. During the visit the homeopath will review the patient's medical history, elicit a full picture of the symptoms—mental, emotional, and physical—and find a homeopathic medicine to match that symptom picture. Follow-up visits are scheduled four to six weeks later, depending on the case, and last about 30 minutes. A 1992 survey of members of the American Institute of Homeopathy (AIH), an organization of homeopathic medical doctors and osteopaths, found that the average first visit to a homeopathic physician cost $137 and the average follow-up $55. Prices have likely increased since that survey.

Will my health insurance cover it?

Health insurance covers visits to most homeopathic practitioners by virtue of their health-care license. As a general rule, if your homeopath has the type of license that is covered by your insurance (MD, DO, ND, DC), then the visit will be covered. In addition, many insurers are investigating homeopathy for its cost-saving potential. In January 1996, Blue Cross of Washington and Alaska initiated a health plan covering the services of homeopathic and naturopathic physicians and acupuncturists. (In France, where homeopathy is widely practiced, total costs for homeopathic physicians are 42 percent lower per year than for conventional physicians, and pharmacy prescriptions are 48 percent less.)

Is there research to support homeopathy?

Yes. Several good-quality studies have shown homeopathy to be effective in various conditions. Most homeopathic research has been conducted in Europe, but more is under way in the United States, some of it sponsored by the National Institutes of Health Office of Alternative Medicine. The exact mechanism by which homeopathy works is still unknown, but 200 years of use worldwide have shown it to be a safe and effective form of treatment.

Source: The National Center for Homeopathy, a nonprofit membership organization which provides information and education about homeopathy to the public. It publishes a monthly magazine, *Homeopathy Today,* as well as the national *Directory of Homeopathic Practitioners;* and it conducts study groups and training programs. For more information, contact: National Center for Homeopathy, 801 North Fairfax Street, Suite 306, Alexandria, VA 22314; phone: (703) 548-7790; fax: (703) 548-7792; e-mail: nchinfo@igc.org; Web site: http://www.homeopathic.org.

Yoga

What is *yoga?*

Many people confuse yoga with physical contortion, or think it is a religion. Yoga is none of these things. It is a system of physical, mental, and spiritual training handed down through teacher to student. Yoga is basically a way of life that enables one to conserve energy and coodinate the power of body-mind consciousness, which keeps the body healthy and the mind relaxed.

What does the word "yoga" mean?

It comes from the Sanskrit language, and means "union."

What is the philosophy behind it?

Yoga is based on the principle of correct breathing. Yoga exercises are built on the ancient disciplines designed to maintain a healthy body so that the mind may also become healthy. The aim of yoga is self-discipline. It contributes to greater concentration, which in turn helps to improve your involvement, no matter what you are doing. It is a scientific system of physical and mental excercises, designed for every part of the body, that keeps the student in top condition. Yoga postures, based on stretching of the entire muscular system and slow movements, make the body more supple, agile, and relaxed.

How do you do it?

In yoga, methods of relaxation and special breathing techniques are part of the training. Yoga students learn the breathing techniques and the many postures that keep the body flexible; they are also introduced to proper eating habits. Relaxation exercises rid one of the buildup of stress from today's hectic pace.

Is it good for you?

Yes! Yoga gives you better health. The correct and regular participation in yoga can result in substantial health benefits. Yoga exercise stretches and tones the muscles. It increases endurance and improves flexibility; controls weight; relieves anxiety and tension; and helps manage stress. Yoga's body movements strengthen your back, firm your stomach, and redistribute weight properly. Yoga exercise postures can relieve problems such as headaches, nervousness, menstrual cramps, back pain, and many others. The combination of breathing and movement, practiced on a regular basis, can improve the circulation, regulate blood pressure, and be instrumental in disease prevention. Yoga, as it renews the spirit and body, provides well-being through physical and mental harmony.

Why is the breathing so important?

Deep rhythmic breathing provides deep tension release and a noticeable rise in energy level. We learn how to relieve stress, which these days concerns us all. A study at Harvard University Medical School, conducted by doctors, stated that "A simple breathing technique can lower blood pressure and decrease anxiety. The results of proper breathing applied on heart patients have proven extremely helpful."

How does yoga help you relax?

Correct rhythmic breathing, concentration, and the practicing of the various positions and exercises can lead to deep, profound mind and body relaxation. Systematic relaxation of the muscles and mind through Hatha Yoga relaxation exercises once or twice a day, on awakening and retiring, pays dividends in well-being and a sense of peace. These methods, inspired by natural habits, are fundamentally based on concentration and relaxation, rhythm of breath and rhythm of body. The relaxation method assures that the body grows stronger and the mind calmer as a person acquires the know-how to remain happy and healthy in the feverish excitement of a busy life.

The practice of relaxing every muscle brings rest to the body and mind. Eventually the tension is relieved and you will not waste any energy. Those who know how to relax can close their eyes for a few minutes and do the mental relaxation any time; without any preparation, they simply "let go." During that short period the entire system is recharged, like a new battery, energy and vigor flowing into every organ, muscle, and nerve.

How many different kinds of yoga are there?

There are many variations, or schools, of yoga, but the most popular form in this country is called Hatha Yoga, which is a system of physical fitness that can lead the way to good health, and involves mastering the exercise positions, called *asanas,* such as a spinal twist or back bend, to gain physical control of your body, which in turn gives control over your mind.

Can children do yoga?

Absolutely. Yoga can prove a positive experience for anyone—adults, families, children. There is no age limit—you can be as young as five or as old as 80 or 90. Kids love yoga because they can pretend. Most of the yoga postures have animal names, inspired by the movements of the animals they are named after—"the crow," "the cobra," "the tortoise"—and as kids do these positions they are carried into the world of make-believe. Yoga improves children's coordination and their ability to concentrate. It's lots of fun to do, and beneficial for their health as well.

Is there anyone who shouldn't do yoga?

People of all ages, with a range of physical abilities, can do yoga. You'll often hear of middle-aged or older people beginning yoga. But, as with any type of regular exercise, you should start slowly, gradually increasing the number of the various positions. And it is important to consult with your physician first, before you start, to check for high blood pressure, heart condition, or any other ailments.

How long has yoga been around?

It isn't known for certain, but yoga has been around for a very long time. Some sources claim it is about 5,000 years old, while others believe it is even older. Yoga has its origins in India.

Source: Renee Taylor has taught yoga for over 40 years, written books, produced award-winning videos, and has lectured and conducted workshops internationally. Well over 90, Renee was awarded the title Woman of the Year, 1991, by the Biographical Institute of America. For more information, contact her at P.O. Box 696, Redondo Beach, CA 90277-0696; (800) 288-0733; Web site: www.homevideos.com/yoga. Or write the *Yoga Journal,* P.O. Box 12008-3008, Berkeley, CA 94712-3008; (800) I-DO-YOGA (436-9642); Web site: www.yogajournal.com.

RETIREMENT

◆

AARP

Gray Panthers

Easing into Retirement

Money for Retirement

AARP

What is the AARP?

AARP stands for the American Association of Retired Persons, a nonprofit, nonpartisan organization dedicated to helping older Americans achieve lives of independence, dignity, and purpose. Founded in 1958 by retired educator Dr. Ethel Percy Andrus, AARP is today the nation's oldest and largest organization of older Americans, with a membership of more than 30 million.

What are the goals of the organization?

AARP's long-term goals are to reduce poverty and promote economic security for individuals as they age; to lead in achieving universal access to comprehensive and affordable health care, including long-term care; to enhance dignity and quality in the workplace through positive attitudes, practices, and policies toward work and retirement; to provide quality service to members, communities, volunteers, and staff; to employ tools, methods, applications, processes, and systems that enable AARP to maximize the effectiveness of its volunteers, staff, and technological and fiscal resources; and to conduct and support research to understand and help meet the needs of an aging population.

How does AARP attempt to accomplish these goals?

There are a variety of ways, one of the most important being community service. More than 160,000 AARP volunteers are involved nationwide in community service programs that reinforce self-worth and self-reliance among older people while improving the lives of others. Through these programs, older Americans are given the opportunity to share their wisdom, experience, and abilities with those of all ages who are in need. AARP's motto, "To Serve, Not to Be Served," and its vision statement, "AARP Excels as a Dynamic Presence in Every Community, Shaping and Enriching the Experience of Aging for Each Member and for Society," reflect the importance of community service, and are supported by the activities of members who are involved in community, state, and national affairs.

What are some of these community service programs?

There are many of them, for just about any issue concerning seniors you can think of. They run the gamut, from such traditional areas as employment, legal council for the elderly, consumer affairs, housing, health, and helping older Americans prepare their tax forms each year, to innovative programs such as the "Grandparent Information Center," which provides grandparents who are raising their grandchildren with a wide variety of educational materials and referrals to local support groups. The "55 Alive/ Mature Driving" program is the nation's first driver-retraining program specifically designed for motorists age 50 and older.

Does the AARP get involved nationally?

Yes. AARP is quite active in legislative advocacy on the national level, representing a population that includes workers and retirees; women reentering the workforce and older women living alone; people with comfortable standards of living and those who struggle daily. Developing legislative policy recommendations to serve such a diverse group of older Americans is a formidable task, but advocacy for their needs and interests is a major reason why millions of people join AARP.

How are AARP members made aware of these policies?

One of the ways these national issues are brought home is through the AARP/VOTE volunteer advocacy program, which is designed to educate and involve voters on issues of concern to older Americans at large. The program neither endorses candidates nor contributes money to campaigns. It is strictly nonpartisan, and focuses on issues, not on candidates or their political affiliations.

Who can join AARP?

Membership is open to anyone age 50 or older, whether working or retired.

You don't have to be retired to join?

No. In fact, over one-third of the association's membership is in the work force.

Where is AARP located?

National headquarters are in Washington, D.C., but there are more than 4,000 local chapters throughout the United States. AARP also maintains a network of regional and state offices.

What are some of the member services?

There are many different programs providing a variety of services, such as insurance coverage (health, homeowners, life, automobile, and even mobile home insurance), and investment and consumer assistance. The "Pharmacy Service" provides prescription medicine and other health-care items to members by mail or direct purchase. Members can use a toll-free number.

"On-Line Computer Services" offers AARP On-Line, featured on Prodigy, America Online, CompuServe, and AARP's own page, providing AARP members and the general public with an incredible wreath of information on issues such as Social Security, Medicare, health care, financial planning, and consumer protection. This service also provides a wide array of bulletin boards, interactive forums, publications, and information databases.

AARP members receive the bimonthly *Modern Maturity* magazine, and the AARP/NRTA (National Retired Teachers Association Division) *Bulletin* 11 times per year. The association distributes a wide range of more than 400 specialized publications, many of which are available free of charge in limited quantities upon request. These authoritative materials are researched by experts in the many fields, including health, consumer affairs, crime prevention, retirement planning, and lifetime learning.

Source: American Association of Retired Persons (AARP), 601 E Street NW, Washington, DC 20049. For further information, call toll-free at (800) 434-3410.

Gray Panthers

Who are the *Gray Panthers*?

The Gray Panthers is a national organization of activists dedicated to social change. Its motto, "Age and Youth in Action," reflects its vision of a better world—that people of all ages can work together toward common ground and solutions to today's problems. The Gray Panthers takes on our society's toughest problems—peace, housing, jobs, antidiscrimination, family security, rights for the disabled—and speaks out on many other issues that affect each of us.

The Gray Panthers fights to change laws and attitudes to achieve social justice for all. It believes that all Americans should benefit from our country's abundance, and that dignity comes with having an adequate job, decent housing, health care, a healthy environment, and a peaceful world.

Who can be a Gray Panther?

Anyone who believes in the Gray Panthers' mission. Gray Panthers brings together groups of people of all ages—young, old, women, men, persons of all ethnic, racial, and economic backgrounds. It is not just an organization for older people; in fact, it encourages all of its members to think intergenerationally.

I thought the "Gray" in the name referred to aging, and this group was just for older people?

Not at all. Gray Panthers has always been for people of all ages. In fact, the organization was originally called "Consultation of Older and Younger Adults for Social Change," and was renamed in 1972. Many people have the same understanding of the title "Gray," which actually refers to "gray" issues, the spectrum of issues, not just the black and the white, that are of concern. Though the Gray Panthers has had a powerful impact on the image and issues of aging, its purpose and policies have always been more encompassing. For 25 years, Gray Panthers has been effective in creating change, working to make America a better place to live for the young, the old, and everyone in between.

How did the Gray Panthers get started?

The Gray Panthers was founded in 1970 by social activist Maggie Kuhn, who at age 65, upon completing her career as a Presbyterian social education and action leader, faced a dual challenge: how to resist enforced retirement at 65, and how to participate actively with young people in the struggle against the Vietnam War. The confluence of those two concerns propelled her into leadership of the Gray Panthers, a movement that has focused national attention on patterns of "ageism" and alternative social policy responses.

What are some notable changes the Gray Panthers has been responsible for?

Over the years, Gray Panthers has been instrumental in numerous national reforms, among them: stopping forced retirement at age 65; nursing home reform and exposing nursing home abuse and legislative measures to achieve health-care access; new organizations to overcome race and age-segregated housing; hearing aid fraud; and removing barriers to senior volunteer service (through an amendment to the Older Americans Act).

How do Gray Panthers' members get involved?

Gray Panthers are free to choose their own level of participation. If there is a local network in your area, you might attend meetings, serve on a committee, or help with a local event. National members bring about social change by serving on task forces, contributing to Gray Panthers publications, and through financial support.

What are the task forces?

Gray Panthers Task Forces are groups that work to identify areas of needed change. They offer a vision of hope and methods to achieve the Gray Panthers' goals through research and analysis.

What are some of the ways the Gray Panthers work toward their goals?

Gray Panthers work to achieve change through two groups. The first is membership of local chapters, referred to as "networks." These members tackle issues that affect their local communities, and are organized in cities and towns around the country. These individuals are also part of a second group—the national membership. Both groups promote change through the national office in Washington, D.C.

How many Gray Panthers are there?

Currently, there are over 50 local networks and 50,000 members nationwide.

Source: Gray Panthers, P.O. Box 21477, Washington, DC 20009. Call their toll-free number, (800) 280-5362 for more information.

Easing into Retirement

How can I be assured I will have enough money to live comfortably after I retire?

Consult with a financial planner who charges by the hour. You should choose a planner who has no vested interest in *how* you ultimately decide to invest your money. First, you must consider your projected retirement budget. Then add up the income from your pension, IRA, 401(k), Keogh, Social Security, fixed assets, investments, and savings. The planner will help you assess your financial needs and your potential income. Do as much research as you can, and then be prepared to ask questions. Do not make any decisions until you completely understand your financial position.

What is the best way to provide for worry-free health care?

Be familiar with the provisions of Medicare. Then decide whether you need and can afford Medigap coverage. Medigap is coverage that pays for what Medicare doesn't pay for. Do not overlook the option of an HMO. Explore buying a long-term insurance policy, for nursing home and/or home health care.

Should I relocate to a warmer climate?

This is a personal decision—do not make the move on a permanent basis until you have rented or spent a year in any area you are considering. Popular areas for retired people are often university towns, which rank high because they offer many cultural activities at low costs. Some popular states are North Carolina, Kentucky, Florida, and Oregon.

What is the best living situation for retirees?

This, too, is a personal decision. Retirement communities appeal to many retirees. As the population ages, many communities are offering homes with golf, tennis, and other facilities. There are also apartment facilities, called Lifecare housing, that provide meals and activities, an option for retirees with health problems. Some retirees opt to travel the country in an RV until they find a place to settle down. Others never change their lifestyle at all.

What am I going to do with my time when I retire?

This requires some self-assessment. What are your needs for social contact? Do you like group activities or can you pursue your interests on your own? Do you have an interest in physical activities? If you need structure in your life, you may want to consider some educational activities or some volunteer work. Think about trying something you've never done before, like learning computers or joining a theater group. This personal decision may change as your retirement needs change.

How can I make friends if I relocate?

Join whatever organizations interest you. Church groups, community groups, professional organizations, and special interest groups are all available and welcoming. You are more likely to find that you are interested in people who have joined the organizations that interest you. Be sure to volunteer for committees and special assignments within these groups. Take a course at a local high school or college. Be prepared to extend invitations to people you met. Relationships grow slowly and they need your help.

I have enjoyed my retirement, but I want to do something more with my time.

It's not unusual for retirees to take a part-time job after several years of leisure. Employers often welcome these older workers because of their maturity and sense of responsibility. Volunteering is a way of being useful and giving back to the community. Hospitals, libraries, schools, even the courts have programs for people to volunteer their time and skills.

I have recently become almost a full-time caretaker to my spouse and I am starting to feel overwhelmed.

It is important for you to have time away. Find a support group for caregivers in your community. You can do this by calling your local hospital or organization for a chronic illness, even if it is not the specific one you are caregiving. Caregivers all experience the same difficulties. Make arrangements for a friend, a family member, or a paid worker to give you a few hours several times a week so you can have some time for yourself.

Is it okay for me to be dating at the age of 70? I am alone and many of my friends have joined a singles club.

It is very much okay. People are living longer and in better health than ever before, and it is not unusual for them to begin a new life and find a new love after their mourning period is over.

Where can I find more information on retirement?

Check your State Unit on Aging. Join the AARP. Look in your library and local bookstore for books that address your specific concerns. There are several magazines which target the retiree. *Successful Retirement* is a bimonthly publication with many articles of interest.

Source: Compiled by Diana Cort Van Arsdale and Phyllis Newman, authors of *Transitions: A Woman's Guide to Successful Retirement*, and columnists for *Successful Retirement* magazine.

Money for Retirement

How long, on average, do people spend in retirement?

The average American will live approximately 18 years after retirement from full-time work. That amounts to nearly half the time that most will have spent in the workforce, and more than most will have spent in school.

How much will Social Security pay me when I retire?

On average, Social Security pays retirees about 40 percent of what they made in real dollars when they were in the labor force.

Will I be able to maintain my standard of living on that income?

Absolutely not. In order to maintain the standard of living to which you have been accustomed, you will need to have a total retirement income of approximately 70 to 90 percent of what you made preretirement. With the decline of that reliable old institution, the pension plan, this could mean scrambling to cobble together a collection of savings and investments that will be sufficient to cover the difference. It is estimated that more than half of all Americans who are established in the labor market have yet to put aside so much as a dime for their retirement; if you've been putting it off, you are in good company.

My employer does not offer a pension plan. What other ways can I effectively save for my retirement?

In recent years, the most popular options for retirement savings have been Individual Retirement Accounts (IRAs) and 401(k) plans. IRAs allow you to invest $2,000 every year and not pay taxes on your investment earnings until you reach retirement age. This allows your money to grow unshackled over the years, which makes a surprisingly large difference in how much you end up with. 401(k) plans are tax-sheltered savings plans; again, taxes are deferred until retirement, which allows for more growth. Many employers have replaced their pension plans with 401(k) plans, and will kick in a percentage every time you contribute; they may even match your contribution. Automatic deductions from your paycheck make your 401(k) convenient to use.

When should I start thinking about saving for retirement?

Assuming you have a regular job, now. It is absolutely never too early to start saving. Even small contributions to a pension or 401(k) plan early in your working years can turn into substantial amounts later on; remember, early money grows for a long period of time.

I'm carrying a lot of revolving debt, and I'd like to get that taken care of first. Does that make sense?

Yes. Credit card debt will kill you, there is no question about it. However, consider putting even the tiniest amount toward retirement now; it's a good habit to get into, and the earlier you start, the better.

But I'm in my 50s! Did I miss the boat?

No, certainly not. Just as it's never too early to start planning and saving, it's also never too late. In fact, the decade before retirement can be the crucial one in deciding how you spend your golden years. For one thing, you are probably at your peak earning power, and may even have less household expenses than you did in your 30s and 40s. For another, you are probably developing a clearer picture of how you want to spend your retirement. Whether you envision yourself in a penthouse on the Florida coast or cruising the interstate system in a secondhand camper, now is the time to decide what you want and how you intend to get it. Money matters must be discussed openly.

All right, we need to talk about it. So what do we talk about?

Talk about reducing your debts; pay off your mortgage, or sell the big house and buy a nice bungalow. Talk about the expenses you might face in retirement; will you still have children or parents to support? What will you do in case of illness? Is it really realistic to retire at 65? Get a running dialogue going (assuming there are two of you).

It seems that my retirement savings are a bit behind schedule. I don't want to postpone my retirement, though; what options do I have?

You could think about working part time for a stretch; some retirees find part-time work a welcome bit of routine in their suddenly unstructured lives. Perhaps you could consider selling off any assets that you have to help meet expenses. Could you live in a smaller home? Is buying the Land Rover that you've always wanted worth two extra years of work? Scaling down your expectations a bit can help make early retirement a more realistic possibility.

My wife has always handled all of our money; all loans and credit cards are in her name. If I survive her, does her good credit transfer to my name?

No. It is important for both spouses to develop individual lines of credit to avoid credit problems in the event of the other's death. Credit histories do not transfer between spouses.

Is Medicare sufficient coverage for our retirement, or do we have to worry about that, too?

Medicare does not cover all health-care costs, and many retirees are unduly burdened by the costs of a long-term or serious illness. Determine whether or not your health-care plan is sufficient for your retirement years; if not, you will want to seek supplemental insurance. So-called Medigap plans, which are meant to cover those areas that Medicare does not, should be carefully investigated; you don't want to duplicate coverage you already have, nor do you want to leave any important gap uncovered.

Source: *Staying Independent: Planning for Financial Independence in Later Life,* American Express Company, Consumer Affairs Office, World Financial Center, New York, NY 10285-4700.

DEATH
AND DYING

◆

What to Do When Someone Dies
Funerals • Grieving
Cremation • Hospice Care
The "Right-to-Die" Dilemma
When a Pet Dies

What to Do When Someone Dies

What do I need to do when someone dies?

After a death, the family's first responsibility is to make phone calls. By calling a few professionals, close relatives, and friends, you can get all the help, support, and comfort you need during this difficult time. In some states, a doctor must be present to declare a person dead and state the cause of death. If the doctor isn't sure of the cause of death, or if the death may have been caused by suicide, homicide, or an accident, the county medical examiner or coroner may be called.

Call your funeral director and clergy person right away, even if death occurs during the night or holidays, or while the deceased was away from home. Their immediate assistance and guidance will be extremely valuable to you, and will help you prepare for the details that need attention, especially if you are faced with the added difficulty of making initial arrangements from a distance.

Who do I call first?

After the professional calls are made, the family must make sure friends and relatives are told of the death, although they needn't make all the calls themselves. Immediate family members should be called first, personally—parents, grandparents, children, and siblings of the deceased. Again, do not worry about waking others. Grief researchers say those close to the deceased feel left out if they aren't told about death immediately.

It's not necessary or practical for you to call every nonimmediate family member and friend. News of a death travels quickly. Rely on others to make sure everyone is notified. Although it may be difficult to do, telling others of a death is therapeutic. By saying aloud that a loved one has died, the death is confirmed in your mind, an important step in the grief process.

Do I need to have a funeral director?

In most states, a licensed and registered funeral director must arrange for and supervise the transport of the deceased person's body from the place of death to the funeral home, and handle the care, preparation, and final disposition of the body.

What is the funeral director's role?

Your funeral director will help coordinate all of the details during this important and difficult transition in your life. Most important, your funeral director will assist you in planning a personal ceremony to help you begin the healing process. Experts estimate 200 to 300 separate activities are conducted and coordinated by funeral directors, in just two or three days, in preparation for and during a funeral. Among these many services are care and preparation of the deceased; conferences with your family; and securing information for and filing the death certificate, which you will need for various estate settlement purposes.

Funeral directors also help you select funeral merchandise, such as a casket, outer burial container, urn, memorial stone, marker, or other items. They make arrangements with the cemetery, or crematory, or other place of disposition; help with paperwork, including obituary notices and a variety of government benefit claim forms such as Social Security and Veterans benefits; and help you notify the deceased person's employer, attorney, insurance companies, and banks. Many funeral homes offer free after-care services or can make referrals to support groups or bereavement counselors in the community to help you work through your grief, if necessary.

What should I consider when selecting a funeral home?

Give thought to this decision as you would when selecting any professional to handle something important for you. Choose a funeral home that has a good reputation in the community. If you are unfamiliar with the homes in your area, ask a relative, friend, clergy person, doctor, or hospice worker for a recommendation, or call the National Funeral Directors Association for a listing of funeral directors in your community. Consider meeting with a few different directors in advance to determine whether you are comfortable and to check out the range of services offered at a cost that meets your needs.

What options exist for the final care of my loved one?

Perhaps no other moment in the funeral process is as powerful as the final disposition, the final care of a loved one's body. For survivors, this is a strong symbolic moment, a confirmation that they must let go of the person who died and look ahead to a changed life. For this reason, it is important that families choose the kind of final disposition most significant to them and most appropriate for the deceased. Several options are available:

- *Earth burial* is the most common in this country. Americans seem to prefer the idea of a final resting place and a gravesite where they can go to remember the person who died.
- *Entombment,* like burial, offers a fixed, final resting place. When a body is entombed, the casket is placed in a mausoleum, an above-ground structure normally made of marble or stone. Mausoleums, usually found on cemetery grounds, vary greatly in size and design. Some are large enough for entire families, with a separate room for each person's casket.
- *Cremation* is a process that exposes the body to intense heat (flames) and evaporation, reducing it primarily to fine bone fragments.
- *Anatomical gifts* offers two different options: body donation for medical research, and organ donations for transplants. Usually a body is donated for one of these sources, not both.

A meaningful ceremony can accompany any method of disposition chosen.

Is a viewing possible with cremation or anatomical gifts?

Yes. Sometimes families will refuse to donate their loved one's organs because they are afraid the body won't be available for an open-casket viewing. This simply isn't true. Whether the entire body or just the organs are donated, medical personnel can usually make arrangements for the body to be present at the funeral. When organs are removed, the funeral director can use his restorative arts to return the body to a natural-looking state for the viewing and funeral.

What should I know about embalming?

Embalming is the use of chemicals to disinfect, retard decomposition, and temporarily preserve the body for a public viewing by restoring it to an acceptable physical appearance. The foremost reason for embalming is the protection of public health. Contrary to the old belief that "the germ dies with the host," human remains begin to decompose almost immediately, therefore offering an ideal environment for microbial growth. Untreated remains pose serious public health concerns. Further, in America's highly mobile society, embalming permits friends and family the time to travel from great distances to attend the funeral ceremony, and allows the body to be buried at some place other than where death occurred.

Do most people have their loved one's body embalmed?

Yes. The practice of embalming has existed since early recorded history throughout many lands and cultures. In the United States, the vast majority of bodies are embalmed.

Do I have to have the body embalmed?

No. Embalming is not routinely required by law in all states, and the Federal Trade Commission requires that funeral homes explain in writing the reason embalming may be necessary. Situations require embalming:

- if the death is due to certain diseases
- if final disposition is not made within a prescribed period of time, or if refrigeration is not available
- if a body has to be transported between states or internationally in a common carrier such as an airline
- some states require embalming for transportation within the state, beyond the place where death occurred
- funeral directors may require embalming if the funeral ceremony selected by a family includes viewing and they are required to ask permission of the deceased's next-of-kin verbally or in writing.

Who should I contact to resolve any issues I felt weren't handled properly by my funeral director?

Most consumer concerns are resolved when expressed to the funeral director or management of the funeral home. If, however, you remain unsatisfied, contact the Funeral Service Consumer Assistance Program at (800) 662-7666 to help resolve your complaint. Most states have regulatory boards that enforce the laws pertaining to the practice and business of funeral directing, and that investigate complaints.

Source: National Funeral Directors Association (NFDA), 11121 West Oklahoma Avenue, Milwaukee, WI 53227-4096. For more information, contact the NFDA's Learning Resource Center for educational materials and free consumer brochures on dying, death, bereavement, and funeral customs at phone: (800) 228-6332; fax: (414) 541-1909; e-mail: nfda@nfda.org; Web site: www.nfda.org.

Funerals

Is it important to have a ceremony?

You might wonder why funerals are so important that virtually every culture has them in one form or another. There are several reasons. Just as we have rituals for other passages of life, such as graduations and weddings, we need a ritual for death—one of the most significant of all passages. Funerals don't just recognize that a life has ended; they recognize that a person has lived. They offer survivors a chance to gather and recall what mattered to them about the deceased's life: his/her accomplishments, friendship, guidance, or love. Experts say ceremonies provide closure for the bereaved, and help the survivors to heal emotionally by focusing their emotions and bringing meaning to the experience of death. A funeral gives "permission" to express feelings of sadness and loss.

Have funerals always been a part of our culture?

As far back as anthropologists can trace civilization, human beings have recognized death with a ritual or ceremony. In some cultures, funerals were large gatherings with uninhibited public displays of grief; mourners tore their clothes or even injured themselves to demonstrate their emotional pain. In others, the dead were buried with their favorite belongings to comfort them in the next world. Today, of course, people all over the world still commemorate their loved ones with ceremonies that reflect their religious or cultural attitudes toward death.

Why are viewings held?

A viewing of the deceased's body helps confirm the reality of a death to the person's loved ones—an important step in the healing process we call grieving.

What is a memorial service?

A memorial service is held without the presence of a body and offers a grief-healing alternative and/or addition to a funeral. For example, planting a memorial tree can be beneficial in helping to release feelings of grief at a painful time and for years to come.

What is a "traditional" funeral?

Traditional funerals are becoming more difficult to define. Most ceremonies are personalized. Today's funeral directors offer a variety of options to those choosing a funeral ceremony, which may include ethnic or nonreligious ceremonies.

What religious ceremonies are most common in this country, and how do they differ?

Religious ceremonies often change over time, and have many differences within particular denominations, but this is how the most common ones have traditionally been practiced:

- *Protestant funerals* are generally preceded by a visitation period. The casket will be open or closed, depending on the family's wishes, but it is usually closed during the actual funeral service. Those attending a Protestant service often send flowers or gifts as an expression of their concern and feelings. Protestant ceremonies usually include scripture lessons that relate to death and the Christian concept of resurrection. The service may also include prayers, a sermon, and a group reading or singing of hymns.

- *The Roman Catholic funeral* follows relatively formal guidelines. On the evening before a Roman Catholic funeral, a wake is held at the funeral home. Friends and family may send flowers or gifts, although it is not uncommon for the family to request a donation to charity in lieu of flowers. Friends from other parishes can also ask that a mass be said for the repose of the deceased person's soul, then send a mass card to the family. The funeral ceremony often begins at the funeral home, proceeds to the church for mass, then proceeds to the graveside, where additional liturgy is performed. The casket is closed at a Roman Catholic funeral service, but usually open at the wake.

- *Jewish funeral* services vary somewhat among the Orthodox, Conservative, and Reform branches, but in general the funeral itself is the beginning of ceremonies instead of the end. Traditional Jewish families remain at home for seven days after the funeral. During this time, friends and relatives visit to offer their support. The emphasis is on people getting together to share feelings and memories, not on religious teachings. A deceased Jewish person's memorial stone or tablet is often unveiled one year after the funeral, which gives family and friends another opportunity to gather in remembrance. The deceased person's name is also read aloud during synagogue service every year on the anniversary of his/her death.

What do people who aren't religious do for a funeral ceremony?

Although religious ceremonies serve their important role, some Americans are not formally religious. These people often request a religious funeral from a church they had a relationship with in the past; or they choose to create a humanistic or nonreligious service. Because relating death to religious teachings is only one purpose of a funeral, many nonreligious people these days elect to hold humanistic ceremonies. During humanistic ceremonies, as in religious ceremonies, families and friends gather to acknowledge the death, offer support to each other, and express their grief.

A friend or family member may preside over the ceremony, or the family may ask a pastor to conduct a ceremony that avoids religious imagery. Families who choose a humanistic ceremony should ask their funeral director for assistance. Humanistic ceremonies commonly feature music, group singing, and readings of poetry or literature that held meaning for the deceased.

How much does a funeral cost?

Funeral costs will vary greatly depending on the services and merchandise selections made. Under FTC regulation, funeral directors must provide a general price list of itemized costs of all options offered by their funeral home at the time arrangements are first discussed, or over the telephone if a consumer inquires about the cost of a funeral. All costs should be clearly explained and understood, and you should only be charged for those services used. Like any consumer transaction, it is important to understand exactly what kind of merchandise and type of service you will receive for the price you pay. You decide what the cost will be, based on your selections.

What type of financial assistance is available to help with funeral costs?

Your funeral director can help determine whether or not you're qualified for financial assistance. Potential resources include Social Security, Veterans benefits, union or employer pension funds, life and accident insurance policies, worker's compensation, and fraternal order or professional group benefits. Your funeral director will help secure certified death certificates to aid you in claiming these benefits.

What does preplanning a funeral mean?

Preplanning can be as simple as recording your wishes and letting a loved one know about them, or meeting with a funeral director to prearrange the details of final wishes.

What are the benefits to preplanning?

Preplanning removes some of the emotional burden from survivors and ensures the consumer and his/her family that final wishes will be met. Those preplanning also have the peace of mind that a spouse or child will not be left making important decisions at a difficult time.

Families take comfort at the time of death knowing their loved one's funeral reflects his/her wishes. It also allows consumers the advantage of being able to think about what they really want before purchasing merchandise and choosing a funeral director. A prefunding arrangement is a good option for some and should be discussed with your funeral director because there may be Medicaid (see page 210) guidelines or state requirements to consider. Seniors can set aside funds to cover the cost of a funeral, all or part of which may not be counted as resources when determining eligibility for Supplemental Security Income (SSI), Medicaid, or other public benefits.

How do you prepay for a funeral?

There are three basic ways to prefund a funeral:

- A regulated trust can be established by a licensed funeral director.
- A life insurance policy can be purchased equal to the value of a funeral.
- Individuals can establish a savings or certificate of deposit account, earmarked for their funeral expense. The account can be designated as "payable on death" to the funeral home.

Source: National Funeral Directors Association (NFDA), 11121 West Oklahoma Avenue, Milwaukee, WI 53227-4096. For more information, contact the NFDA's Learning Resource Center for educational materials and free consumer brochures on dying, death, bereavement and funeral customs at phone: (800) 228-6332; fax: (414) 541-1909; e-mail: nfda@nfda.org; Web site: www.nfda.org.

Grieving

Why do people mourn or grieve, and are these the same thing?

Mourning is the open, shared expression of your thoughts and feelings regarding the death and the person who has died, while grief is the internalized thought and feeling of loss and pain. Mourning is a difficult but important process people should allow themselves. Our society grieves well, but doesn't mourn well, which gets us into trouble. Both are essential parts of healing, and the beginning of a journey that is often frightening, painful, overwhelming, and sometimes lonely.

Why is it important to grieve *and* mourn?

The capacity to love requires the necessity to grieve and mourn when someone you loved dies. You can't heal unless you openly express your grief. Denying your grief will only make it become more confusing and overwhelming. Embrace your grief and heal. Reconciling your grief will not happen quickly.

Remember, grief is a process, not an event. Be patient and tolerant with yourself. Never forget that the death of someone loved changes your life forever. It's not that you won't be happy again. It's simply that you will never be exactly the same as you were before the death. The experience of grief is powerful. So, too, is your ability to help yourself heal. In doing the work of grieving, you are moving toward a renewed sense of meaning and purpose in your life.

Do most people grieve in the same way?

No. You should realize your grief is unique. No one will grieve in exactly the same way. Your experience will be influenced by a variety of factors: the relationship you had with the person who died; the circumstances surrounding the death; your emotional support system; and your cultural and religious background. As a result of these factors, you will grieve in your own special way. Don't try to compare your experience with that of other people or to adopt assumptions about just how long your grief should last. Consider taking a "one-day-at-a-time" approach that allows you to grieve at your own pace.

How much of what I am feeling should I share?

It is important to talk about your grief, to express your grief openly, or mourn. By sharing your grief outside yourself, healing occurs. Ignoring your grief won't make it go away; talking about it often makes you feel better. Allow yourself to speak from your heart, not just your head. Doing so doesn't mean you are losing control, or "going crazy." It is a normal part of your grief journey.

Find caring friends and relatives who will listen without judging. Seek out those persons who will "walk with," not "in front of" or "behind" you in your journey through grief. Avoid people who are critical or who try to steal your grief from you. They may tell you, "Keep your chin up," or "Carry on," or, "Be happy." These comments may be well intended, but you do not have to accept them. You have the right to express your grief; no one has the right to take it away from you.

What kinds of feelings will I experience?

Expect to feel a multitude of emotions. Experiencing a loss affects your head, heart, and spirit. So, you may experience a variety of feelings as part of your grief work. Confusion, disorganization, fear, guilt, relief, or explosive emotions are just a few of the emotions you may undergo. Sometimes these emotions will follow each other within a short period of time. Or they may occur simultaneously.

Are all these different emotions okay to have?

As strange as some of these emotions may seem, they are normal and healthy. Allow yourself to learn from these feelings. And don't be surprised if out of nowhere you experience "grief bursts"—sudden, powerful surges of grief, even at the most unexpected times. These attacks can be frightening and leave you feeling overwhelmed. They are, however, a natural response to the death of someone loved. Find someone who understands your feelings and will allow you to talk about them.

Is feeling a little detached also normal?

You should allow for numbness. Feeling dazed or numb when someone loved dies is often part of your early grief experience. This numbness serves a valuable purpose: It gives your emotions time to catch up with what your mind has told you. The feeling helps create insulation from the reality of the death until you are more able to tolerate what you don't want to believe.

How does grief affect a person physically?

Your feelings of loss and sadness will probably leave you fatigued, so be tolerant of your physical and emotional limits. Your ability to think clearly and make decisions may be impaired. And your low energy level may naturally slow you down.

Respect what your body and mind are telling you. Nurture yourself. Get daily rest. Eat balanced meals. Lighten your schedule as much as possible. Caring for yourself doesn't mean feeling sorry for yourself; it means you are using survival skills.

How much should I rely on family and friends?

Reaching out to others and accepting support is often difficult, particularly when you hurt so much. But the most compassionate thing you can do for yourself at this difficult time is to find a support system of caring friends and relatives who will provide the understanding you need. Develop that support system. Find those people who encourage you to be yourself and acknowledge your feelings—both happy and sad.

I've heard people say that it's important to have a funeral. Why?

The funeral ritual does more than acknowledge the death of someone loved. It helps provide you with the support of caring people. Most important, the funeral is a way for you to mourn. If you eliminate this ritual, you often set yourself up to repress your feelings, and you cheat everyone who cares for a chance to pay tribute to someone who was, and always will be, loved.

How important is religion in the grieving process?

You should embrace your spirituality. If faith is part of your life, express it in ways that seem appropriate to you. Allow yourself to be around people who understand and support your religious beliefs. If you are angry at God because of the death of someone you loved, realize this feeling as a normal part of your grief work. Find someone to talk with who won't be critical of whatever thoughts and feelings you need to explore. You may hear someone say, "With faith, you don't need to grieve." Don't believe it. Having your personal faith does not insulate you from needing to talk out and explore your thoughts and feelings. To deny our grief is to invite problems that build up inside. Express your faith, but express your grief as well.

How important are memories in the grieving process?

Treasure your memories; they are one of the best legacies that exist after someone loved dies. Share them with your family and friends. Recognize that your memories may make you laugh or cry. In either case, they are a lasting part of the relationship you had with a very special person in your life.

Source: Dr. Alan Wolfelt, a noted author, educator, and practicing clinical thanatologist, adapted from *Helping Yourself Heal When Someone Dies* (Batesville, IN: Batesville Management Services, 1991). Dr.

Wolfelt serves as director of the Center for Loss and Life Transition and is on the faculty at the University of Colorado Medical School in the Department of Family Medicine. As a leading authority in the field of thanatology, he is known internationally for his outstanding work in the areas of adult and childhood grief. Among Dr. Wolfelt's numerous publications and books is *Understanding Grief: Helping Yourself Heal* (Bristol, PA: Taylor & Francis Publishers, 1992). In addition, he is the editor of the "Children and Grief" department of *Bereavement* magazine and is a regular contributor to the journal *Thanatos*. For more information and publications about grief, contact: Center for Loss and Life Transition, 3735 Broken Bow Road, Fort Collins, CO 80526; phone: (970) 226-6050; fax: (800) 922-6051, e-mail: wolfelt@centerforloss.com.

Cremation

What is cremation?

Cremation is another method of disposition of human remains at the time of death. In cremation, the person's body is reduced to small pieces of bone fragments by a process of intense heat. The end result is referred to as "cremated remains," "ashes," or, sometimes, "cremains." After cremation is completed, the bone fragments and residue are encased in a small metal or plastic container and returned to the family or a designated person, such as the funeral director.

What is the history of cremation?

Cremation is a very old process, dating back as far as the Stone Age. For much of human history, cremation was very common in both the East and the West. In the early Christian era the practice declined in the West, since early Christians preferred earth burial. Current interest in cremation was revived in the Western world in the late 1800s.

Is cremation now common in the United States?

Cremation is the second most preferred form of final disposition in the United States. The most common is earth burial. Cremation currently accounts for over one-eighth of all final dispositions. Some predict that this figure will rise to 25 percent by the year 2000. Cremation tends to be most popular on the East and West coasts.

Are there religious objections to cremation?

Most Christian churches do not object to cremation, considering it an alternate choice for their members. Traditional Jewish and Islamic laws prohibit cremation; however, Hinduism and Buddhism do permit cremation. If you have any questions about your religious denomination's views on cremation, you may wish to discuss this with a member of your clergy, or with your funeral director.

What happens to the cremated remains?

Family members have a variety of choices. They may elect to have the remains buried in a family plot or placed within a mausoleum. The family may place the remains in an urn. This urn then can be placed in a *columbarium*, which is a building especially designed to store urns. The urns are assigned recessed compartments, called "niches," which are encased in glass or ornamental stone. The urn may also be put in a special urn garden in a cemetery.

Some families may select to keep the cremated remains at home, perhaps burying them in their garden, or scattering them. If this is the case, it is important to check any local laws and ordinances. Your funeral director will be able to advise you on this. However, you may want to think very carefully before scattering cremated remains, as this is very final and irreversible. In addition, some people find that the actual scattering is a traumatic experience. Many crematories have gardens especially designed for scattering cremated remains, where families have the option of choosing a personal memorial to the deceased within the garden and are reassured that the site will not be developed or used for other purposes in the future.

Does cremation affect the process of grief?

With any method of funeral or final disposition, three aspects are important. The first is that survivors be comfortable with the choices made. Second, people often find it therapeutic to observe a death with some form of ceremony or memorial service. Third, over a period of time, the bereaved find it reassuring to have some type of memorial to the person they've loved which they can visit later.

As long as these three considerations are dealt with, the form of final disposition should not affect the grieving process. Sometimes with cremation there is a tendency to shorten the time for grief. The grief process requires a period of time for recovery, for which each individual's need is different. It should be noted that even though the Jewish faith has a funeral and burial shortly after death, it calls for a grieving period of seven days following the service in which mourners do not work or do household duties. Psychologically, people need to deal with their grief at the time of loss. This therapy enhances one's capacity to cope with the adjustment period that follows.

If I choose cremation, can I also have a funeral or memorial service?

Yes, you can. Many people who choose cremation elect to have some form of religious service and/or secular remembrance. Some have a funeral service with the casket present, while others will have a memorial service, either prior to or following the cremation. Most psychologists and grief counselors find these services to be very therapeutic for the bereaved family and friends.

Can I have a viewing?

Yes. Cremation may follow a traditional funeral service that includes visitation, viewing, and a service with an open or closed casket.

Is embalming necessary?

The purpose of embalming is to disinfect and preserve a body for a limited period of time. If there is to be viewing with visitation, and/or funeral services with the body present, embalming is essential. There may also be health, legal, or religious reasons that make embalming desirable or necessary.

Do I have to purchase a casket?

Some form of rigid container or casket will be needed to transport the body to the crematory and place it in the cremation chamber. Generally, this is made of a combustible material, such as wood. If viewing with visitation and services is desired, a casket will be needed. In some states funeral homes may rent caskets for a funeral, and make available for purchase another container for the cremation.

Is an urn necessary?

Many people prefer to have the cremated remains placed in an urn. In some cases, these urns have very special meanings. People may elect to purchase urns that they consider appropriate to or symbolic of the deceased, or they may even make an urn to hold the cremated remains. In one case, a woman's cremated remains were placed in a vase that had been very special to her; in another, a noted ceramic artist made an urn for her late husband's cremated remains. If you are planning to use a columbarium, urn garden, mausoleum, or cemetery, you will need to review any requirements they may have.

What is the cost of cremation?

In general, the cost of a cremation is less than that of a burial. However, because families have so many options with a cremation, these costs can vary widely. The concept that cremation is selected because of perceived lower funeral costs or lack of land for earth burial is totally inaccurate. Only in rare instances is land a concern, and funeral costs are based on fixed expenses and a family's selection of merchandise and services. You may wish to discuss this with your funeral director to obtain an estimate for the selections you prefer.

Is there a waiting period before cremation?

In some instances a person can be cremated immediately, although many states have a 48-hour waiting period from the time of death until the time a person can be cremated. This situation does necessitate embalming and/or refrigeration services when available. In all cases there is a time frame for obtaining necessary information and filling required permits and authorizations.

Can I make arrangements for cremation in advance?

Yes, you can. In fact, it is wise to make any funeral arrangements prior to the time of a death, for survivors are often in shock, confused, and grieving at that time. As with other prearrangements for a funeral, it is recommended that you discuss your plans in detail with members of your family.

Source: Kenneth J. Doka, Ph.D., is Professor of Gerontology at the College of New Rochelle in New York; he is also an ordained Lutheran minister. Dr. Doka has been active in the field of death education and counseling for over 20 years. He has published many articles, and is the author of *Disenfranchised Grief* (Lexington, MA: Lexington Books, 1989). Excerpted from *Cremation—Guidelines*, from the Guideline Publications Company, publishers of educational and counseling material on death and dying. For more information, call Guideline Publications toll-free at (800) 552-1076. Or contact: Guideline Publications Co., P.O. Box 1141, Madison, AL 35758.

Hospice Care

What is hospice care?

Hospice care is a comprehensive, medically directed, team-oriented program of care that seeks to treat and comfort terminally ill patients and their families at home or in a homelike setting.

Is hospice a place that you go to?

No. In fact, that is one of the biggest misconceptions. Hospice is a philosophy of care rather than a specific place. While most hospice care takes place in a patient's home, some patients live in nursing homes or centers where hospice care is delivered. On average, each year 90 percent of hospice-care hours take place in a patient's home, and about 77 percent of hospice patients die in their own personal residence.

Do most people want to die at their homes?

Yes. A recent Gallup poll revealed that, given six months to live, nine out of ten of those surveyed would choose to be cared for and die in their own or a family member's home.

What are the goals of hospice care?

Hospice care's clinical goals are pain management and symptom control, and the understanding that psychological and spiritual pain are as significant as physical pain. Hospice has a philosophy of care that accepts death as a natural part of life, seeking neither to hasten nor prolong the dying process. It provides caring that strives to help patients truly "live until they die"—without fear of dying in pain, dying alone, or losing control.

Do a lot of people receive hospice care?

Yes. Over the past five years, growth in the number of hospice patients nationwide has risen steadily. In 1996, hospices cared for more than 450,000 patients and families, and approximately one out of every seven deaths in America from all causes were tended to by a hospice program. Hospices care for about one out of every three cancer and AIDS-related deaths in this country. Currently, there are approximately 2,800 hospice programs in all 50 states and Puerto Rico, with new programs added each year.

How long do people generally stay in hospice programs?

The average length of stay for patients admitted to hospice is about 64 days.

Is hospice care just for the elderly?

No, not at all. While the majority of patients who receive hospice care are over 65, the services are available to terminally ill people of any age, including children.

Who administers hospice care?

Hospice services are available as necessary 24 hours a day, every day, guided by a plan of care developed by an interdisciplinary team that includes a physician, a nurse, a spiritual caregiver, a therapist, a social worker, volunteers, and aides. Hospices employ more than 25,000 paid professionals, aided by 96,000 volunteers, who in a recent year contributed more than 5 million hours of service.

What additional services may hospice care offer?

In addition to standard hospice care, many hospices offer further services to their patients, families, and communities that vary program to program. Some of these include memorial services, individual and family counseling, emergency-room support, and specific children's programs. Programs involve family, and include support for family members and friends while their loved one is dying, as well as bereavement care after the person has died. Many are not just for those served directly by hospice, but for the community at large.

Do hospices have to be accredited or licensed?

There is no current mandatory nationwide accreditation or "seal of approval" for hospices, although many programs are certified voluntarily by Medicare, the Joint Commission on Accreditation of Healthcare Organizations (JCAHO), or by the Community Health Accreditation Program (CHAP). Additionally, 38 states have hospice licensure laws, 36 of which require licensure. The remaining 12 states do not have laws governing licensure, although currently six have laws pending. These statistics are representative of all 50 states, Puerto Rico, and the District of Columbia.

How much does hospice care cost and is it cheaper than standard medical care?

There is no nationwide standard on what the cost of caring for a hospice patient is. The closest determination is Medicare per diem rates, which are currently around $92.32 per day for home care and $410.72 per day for general in-patient care. More than 90 percent of hospice-care hours are provided in patients' homes, thus substituting for more expensive multiple hospitalizations. A recent study showed savings of $3,192 in the last month of life for hospice patients over those in standard hospitalizations.

Who pays for it?

Hospice care is part of the covered benefits of Medicare, which accounts for about 68 percent of the cases. Most private insurance plans cover hospice care as well, as does Medicaid in 40 states and the District of Columbia.

Recently, there has been increased public attention and focus on the issue of voluntary euthanasia and assisted suicide. What stand do hospices take on this issue?

The National Hospice Organization (NHO), considered the voice of the nation's hospice community, is often requested to provide comment to Congress, government agencies, the courts, other national organizations, the media, and the general public. The NHO supports a patient's right to chose palliative care and refuse unwanted medical intervention, including the provision of artificially supplied hydration and nutrition, but does not support the legalization of voluntary euthanasia and assisted suicide; it believes hospice care is a better choice.

The proponents of change in the legal status of these practices often paint a stark picture in which a patient's choice is between painful existence devoid of value on the one hand and voluntary euthanasia or assisted suicide on the other. The NHO is committed to the value of the end of life, and to the philosophy that hospice care neither hastens nor postpones death. It supports improved access to hospice care for terminally ill patients and their families, including those who have expressed a desire for assistance with suicide.

Source: National Hospice Organization, 1901 N. Moore Street, Suite 901, Arlington, VA 22209; (703) 243-5900; Web site: http://www.nho.org. For more information, call the NHO's toll-free Hospice Helpline at (800) 658-8898 to find out about hospices in your local community.

The "Right-to-Die" Dilemma

What is the "right to die"?

Although the concept of how to achieve a "good" death has interested philosophers since the time of the Greeks, it was not until recently that the issue became a pertinent and widespread social concern. By the 1950s, advances in medical technology had allowed terminally ill and permanently unconscious patients—individuals who once died quickly from complications or from an inability to eat and drink—to be kept alive dramatically longer than ever before. This newfound capacity of medical science brought difficult end-of-life decision-making issues into the lives of many dying patients and their loved ones. Whereas the course of nature once seemed unalterable, now doctors, patients, and families suddenly needed to make decisions about when life should end. *Advance directives* (see page 580), the general term for a living will and a medical power of attorney, are important ways for individuals to plan about end-of-life decisions. The range of issues related to such decision making is sometimes referred to as "right-to-die" issues.

What is *euthanasia*?

Euthanasia, translated literally, simply means a "good death." The term has traditionally been used to refer to the hastening of a suffering person's death, or "mercy killing." *Involuntary euthanasia* is one of the least accepted social policies. It refers to an intervention that ends a patient's life without obtaining the informed consent of that patient. *Voluntary active euthanasia* involves an intervention requested by a competent individual that is administered to that individual to cause death. Although no law currently authorizes the practice, polls show that a growing number of Americans support honoring a patient's request for active euthanasia.

What is *assisted suicide*?

Assisted suicide refers to the act of providing the means to commit suicide knowing that the recipient plans to use them to end her life. *Physician-assisted suicide* specifically refers to a physician providing medications or other interventions with the understanding that a patient plans to use them to commit suicide. An example of physician-assisted suicide can be found in the activities of Dr. Jack Kevorkian of Michigan.

Where does society stand on this issue?

This is a rapidly evolving area of social, ethical, and legal controversy. On one side, individual patients want control over the final days and moments of their lives. On the other, society has a broader interest in protecting life and the ability of medicine to cure and care for the ill. Controversy over right-to-die issues often involves a tension between these two competing claims.

A number of court cases have helped define social policy on these issues. Our society has shown itself to be more comfortable with policies that authorize a passive role with respect to an individual's right to die, such as honoring a terminally ill patient's request to withhold or withdraw certain aggressive medical interventions, rather than an active role in hastening death, as in assisted suicide.

There's been a lot in the press recently on physician-assisted suicide. What is the legal status?

Currently, 35 states explicitly criminalize assisted suicide; nine states and the District of Columbia have jurisdictions that criminalize assisted suicide through common law; and five states have laws that are unclear concerning the legality of assisted suicide. In 1994, an Oregon voter ballot measure created a law permitting doctors to prescribe medications for terminally ill patients to commit suicide. This law was immediately challenged in the courts, but the lawsuit was dismissed before it could reach the U.S. Supreme Court.

Why is there so much debate over assisted suicide?

Supporters of assisted-suicide measures see the request for assistance in dying as an extension of an individual's legal right to accept or refuse end-of-life medical treatment, including life support. Others argue that if assisted suicide is legalized, a "right to die" will become a "duty to die." They fear that the elderly and the dependent—those who may not be considered as making a substantial contribution to society—will be made to feel guilty for not dying soon enough, and thereby coerced into suicide.

What is *life support*?

Life-sustaining treatments, often called *life support*, are medical procedures that replace or support a failing bodily function. When patients have curable or treatable conditions, life support is used temporarily until the illness or disease can be stabilized and the body can resume normal functioning. At times, the body never regains the ability to function without life support. An individual has a constitutional right to request the withdrawal or withholding of medical treatment, even if this procedure will result in the person's death. Honoring a person's right to refuse medical treatment at the end of life is the most widely practiced and widely accepted right-to-die policy in our society. In addition, there is broad consensus that no ethical or legal distinction exists between an individual's request to have life-sustaining treatment removed and a request to withhold this treatment.

How do you decide what to do?

When making decisions about specific forms of life support, gather the facts you need to make informed decisions. In particular, understand the benefit as well as the burden the treatment will offer you or your loved one. A treatment may be beneficial if it relieves suffering, restores functioning, or enhances the quality of life. The same treatment can be considered burdensome if it causes pain, prolongs the dying process without offering a benefit, or adds to the perception of a diminished quality of life.

What are some of the main life-support measures?

The most commonly used medical treatments that could sustain or prolong life include feeding tubes, ventilators, antibiotics, and treatments to provide cardiopulmonary resuscitation (CPR).

What should I know about "tube feeding"?

Artificial nutrition and hydration (or *tube feeding*) supplements or replaces ordinary eating and drinking by giving a chemically balanced mix of nutrients and fluids through a tube placed directly into the stomach, the upper intestine, or a vein. Artificial nutrition and hydration can save lives when used until the body heals. Long-term artificial nutrition and hydration may be given to people with serious intestinal disorders that impair their ability to digest food, thereby helping them to enjoy a quality of life that is important to them.

But long-term use of tube feeding is also frequently given to people with irreversible end-stage conditions. Often the treatment will not reverse the cause of the disease itself or improve the quality of life; in fact, it can increase a dying person's discomfort. Some health-care facilities and physicians may not agree with stopping or withdrawing tube feeding. Therefore, explore the issue with your loved ones and physician, and state your wishes about artificial nutrition and hydration clearly in your advance directive.

When should a person use CPR?

The decision whether to resuscitate someone who has a cardiac or respiratory arrest is one of the most common end-of-life medical decisions that individuals and their families must face. Cardiopulmonary resuscitation (CPR) is a group of treatments used when someone's heart and/or breathing stops. CPR is used in an attempt to restart the heart and breathing. It may consist only of mouth-to-mouth breathing, or it may include pressing on the chest to mimic the heart's function and to cause the blood to circulate. Electric shock and drugs also are used frequently to stimulate the heart. When used quickly in response to a sudden event like a heart attack or drowning, CPR can be life-saving. But the success rate is extremely low for people who are at the end of a terminal disease. Critically ill patients who receive CPR have small chance of recovering and leaving the hospital.

If you do not wish to receive CPR under certain circumstances, and you are in the hospital, your doctor must write a separate *do-not-resuscitate* (DNR) order on the chart. If you are at home, some states allow for a *nonhospital* DNR order. This order is written by a physician and directs emergency workers not to start CPR.

What do ventilators do?

Mechanical ventilation is used to support or replace the function of the lungs. A machine called a *ventilator* (or *respirator*) forces air into the lungs.

The ventilator is attached to a tube inserted in the nose or mouth and down into the windpipe (or trachea). Mechanical ventilation is often used to assist a person through a short-term problem or for prolonged periods if irreversible respiratory failure exists due to injuries to the upper spinal cord or a progressive neurological disease. Some people on long-term mechanical ventilation are able to enjoy themselves and live a quality of life that is important to them. For the dying patient, however, mechanical ventilation often merely prolongs the dying process until some other body system fails. It may supply oxygen, but it cannot improve the underlying condition.

When discussing end-of-life wishes, make clear to loved ones and your physician whether you would want mechanical ventilation if you would never regain the ability to breathe on your own or return to a quality of life acceptable to you.

What are advance directives?

Advance directive is a general term that refers to your oral and written instructions about your future medical care, in the event you become unable to speak for yourself. There are two different types of advance directives:

- A *living will* allows individuals to put into writing their wishes about medical treatments they wish to accept or refuse at the end of life.
- A *medical power of attorney* allows you to appoint someone you trust to make decisions about your medical care if you cannot speak for yourself. This type of advance directive may also be known as a "health-care proxy" or "appointment of a health-care agent." The person you appoint may be called your health-care agent, surrogate, attorney-in-fact, or proxy. In many states, the person you appoint through a medical power of attorney is authorized to speak for you any time you are unable to make your own medical decisions, not solely at the end of life.

Why do I need an advance directive?

Advance directives give you a voice in decisions about your medical care, even when you are unconscious or too ill to communicate. As long as you are able to express your own decisions, your advance directives will not be used, and you can accept or refuse any medical treatment. But if you become seriously ill, you may lose the ability to participate in decisions about your own treatment.

What laws govern the use of advance directives?

Both federal and state laws govern the use of advance directives. The Patient Self-Determination Act requires health-care facilities that receive Medicaid and Medicare funds to inform patients of their rights to execute advance directives. All 50 states and the District of Columbia also have laws recognizing the use of advance directives, and each state regulates their use differently.

Once a medical treatment is started, can it ever be stopped?

Yes. There is no legal or ethical difference between withholding and withdrawing a medical treatment in accordance with the patient's wishes. If a distinction existed, people might not even try a potentially helpful treatment for fear that once started, it could not be removed. However, state laws may affect how that decision is made for patients who can no longer make their own decisions.

How can I plan for end-of-life health care?

You can prepare for a potential medical crisis by taking steps today that ensure your participation in future health-care decisions:

1. Gather the information you need to make the right choices for you.
2. Talk about end-of-life decisions with your family, friends, doctor, clergy, and any others close to you to help determine what quality of life and which decisions are important to you.

3. Prepare and sign advance directives that accurately reflect your decisions and comply with your state's law.

4. Inform your loved ones and doctor about your preferences, and give them copies of your advance directive.

From the numerous calls Choice In Dying (CID) receives each month from patients and providers, the majority of problems arise when an individual has not issued or discussed clear instructions about his/her medical treatment wishes, leaving family, loved ones, and health-care providers uncertain about how to proceed.

What if I change my mind?

Any advance directive you make may be changed or canceled by you at any time, either verbally or in writing. It is a good idea to review your advance directive from time to time to make sure it is still in agreement with your wishes. If you make a change, you must redo and re-execute the forms. When updating your advance directive forms, be sure to give new copies to everyone who is involved with your health care—your proxy, your physician, your clergy person, and so forth.

Source: Choice In Dying, creators of the living will form over 25 years ago, 200 Varick Street, New York, NY 10014-4810; Web site: http://www.choices.org. For more information, contact the CID national hotline at (800) 989-WILL (9455) for counseling and assistance on end-of-life crises; information on obtaining advance directives tailored to your state; advice about state and federal laws regarding end-of-life medical decisions; educational materials; and referrals to other resources. A CID staff member is available 24 hours a day in case of emergency.

When a Pet Dies

It was "just an animal." Why do I feel so sad that my pet died?

You have suffered a loss, and your grief is a natural, human feeling. Rather than "just an animal," your pet was a friend and companion who meant a lot to you. Don't be ashamed of feeling depressed or lonely, or even of crying. Others who have felt such a loss will understand.

Talk with your family and friends. Tell them how you feel. If you are sad, it's all right to show it—as times passes, the sadness will decrease. However, it's important not to pretend to be sad if you are not.

When will I feel happy again?

Like sorrow over any important loss, there are several stages of grieving people usually go through, some more quickly than others. At first there may be disbelief and denial, particularly if the loss was unexpected. This may be followed by anxiety or a sense of having been abandoned by your pet. As this anxiety lessens, you may feel anger, even self-blame. After these stages you will feel sad—maybe even depressed— but eventually you should be able to remember your pet without sorrow, and concentrate on the positive memories. Only be concerned if your grief persists too long without easing, or if it results in severe depression, personality changes, difficulties in school or at work, or changes in your daily routine of sleeping or eating.

Can the loss of a pet cause extended emotional problems?

Usually, a person will work through the grieving process in a few weeks. In rare cases, perhaps because of feelings of self-blame or extreme emotional attachment to the pet, recovery is very difficult. This is sometimes called abnormal grief. Society teaches us to conceal our emotions. We are told, "Keep a stiff upper lip," "Be tough," "Don't be a baby." We want to cry, but don't. In some persons this causes an unusual condition known as fear of grieving. They bottle up their feelings inside and lose their ability to complete the grieving process. This can cause extended or severe emotional problems, and professional help may be needed.

Is it possible to feel worse about the loss of a pet than the death of a relative?

To most people, particularly those not involved in the relationship, the relative would be more important than the pet. However, we are not measuring value here, but rather the sense of loss felt by the pet's master. The anxiety and sorrow over the separation from a well-loved pet may be very great. On the other hand, the emotional attachment to the relative who died may not have been very strong at all. Thus, the distress over the loss of a pet may indeed be worse, and the pet owner need not feel guilty about it.

Our pet is terminally ill. How should we prepare?

"Terminally ill" means that the pet will die soon from its illness. Knowing this will happen often begins the grieving process in the family. Denial, anger, guilt, and depression may occur. Deal openly and truthfully with children involved in the relationship with the pet. If ending the pet's life (called *euthanasia*) must be considered, include the children in the decision-making process. Everyone's feelings of grief, whether strong or mild, should be anticipated and considered normal. If the adults involved let their own feelings of sorrow show, the children probably will follow their example.

Why should euthanasia be considered?

Sometimes a pet is in pain or distress and there is no hope that it can recover and lead a happy, pain-free life. Then it may be an act of kindness to end the life of the animal. This is not an easy choice to make. Both the veterinarian and the pet owner would like the pet to recover. But when that's not possible, the animal deserves a humane, dignified, pain-free end to life. The veterinarian and the pet's family, including children, should understand and decide together to do what is most merciful for the animal and the family.

Should I be present during euthanasia?

The presence of the pet's master can be very comforting to the pet. Also, seeing the dead body may provide the pet owner with a sense of finality—or closure—most helpful in grief recovery. Whether children should be present or not depends on their age, emotional state, and sense of understanding. Perhaps viewing the pet after death, or merely being told that the pet is dead, will provide the closure they need, too.

Are animals buried when they die?

Several choices are available for disposing of the body of a deceased pet—burial being one of them. The place of burial can vary from a backyard to a pet cemetery, depending on the size of the pet and the laws or ordinances of your community. It is wise to check these first. Some communities have pet funeral directors or pet cemeteries who will handle all the necessary details. Your veterinarian may have more information about this. If home burial is chosen, the grave should be several feet deep and the body should be in a container—a cloth or box, or a special holder obtained from a pet store, veterinarian, funeral director, or pet cemetery. This is necessary so that other animals do not dig it up, and to abide by any local regulations or ordinances.

Can my pet's body be cremated?

Yes. Most veterinarians can help arrange for cremation, which is the use of extreme heat to reduce the dead body of the animal to ashes. The ashes then can be disposed of by the veterinarian or returned to the owner to be buried or scattered in some place that was special to the pet or its master. They also may be kept in a special container—called an urn—at the pet owner's residence or at a pet cemetery.

Can I have a service for my dead pet?

Yes, you can hold a funeral service in connection with the disposal of a pet's ashes or the burial of the body. Or you can have a memorial service later. Such a service can be simply a gathering of the family, sharing memories of the pet. An extensive service by a pet funeral director, with casket, flowers, memorable quotes, and more, also is possible. Whatever you choose, remember the service really is for the benefit of the people to whom that pet was important. It will comfort and help them accept the finality of their loss—a necessary step in the recovery from grief.

What can I do to memorialize my pet?

"Memorializing" means doing something to keep alive the memory of your pet. If you buried your pet, place a temporary memorial of flowers on the grave, or use a more permanent marker of wood, bronze, or stone. Plant a shrub or tree in the name of your pet. Make a contribution of time or money to your local humane society or animal shelter. Make a donation in your pet's name to one of the many fine organizations trying to save the world's animals and sea mammals, and so increase the benefits of people and animals together. Just a talk, story, or poem honoring your pet or a visit to its resting place is a memorial, too. Letters of thanks to your veterinarian and others who helped would be appreciated by them. Whatever you decide is a way to help you keep the memory of your loving friend in your heart.

Can a new pet ever take the place of a lost one?

In a family, new members join by birth, adoption, or marriage. They leave by marriage, death, or for other reasons. Pets also join and leave the family, but a new pet does not replace the previous one. Instead, it is a fresh, different, family member, who will develop its own relationship within the family. The previous pet had its own habits and personality, and the memories of it will live on with each family member. It usually takes a while to sort out the feelings about having another pet, so a new pet should not be brought in too quickly or without a lot of thoughtful consideration. Nevertheless, a new pet may be a wonderful addition to the family and may help ease the grief you feel.

Source: Excerpted from the illustrated booklet *Death of a Pet: Answers to Questions for Children and Animal Lovers of All Ages*, compiled by Shirley and Jim Potter and George J. Koss, and published by the Guideline Publications Company, publishers of educational, counseling, and public relations materials on death and dying. For more information, call Guideline Publications toll-free at (800) 552-1076. Or contact: Guidelines Publications Co., P.O. Box 1141, Madison, AL 35758.

PERSONAL CARE

—◇—

Beauty Alert

Which skin-care products cause the irritations dermatologists see most often?

Bath soaps, detergents, antiperspirants, eye cosmetics, moisturizers, permanent hair-waving solutions, and shampoos cause what we call *allergic contact dermatitis* in susceptible people, but the average person has no problem with most products.

What are the most common allergic reactions?

Someone is allergic when they react to a specific ingredient. Fragrances cause more allergic contact dermatitis than any other ingredient (see *Decoding Cosmetic Labels,* page 588). More than 5,000 fragrances are used in skin-care products—and they appear in everything from perfume to toilet paper.

Preservatives are the second most common cause of skin reactions. They're necessary to prevent bacterial and fungal growth and to protect products from oxygen and light damage. All cosmetics that contain water must include a preservative. The good news is that someone who is allergic to one preservative won't necessarily react to them all.

Finally, lanolin, which is used as a skin conditioner, also can cause allergic reactions.

Is acne caused by dirt or bad hygiene?

Neither. In fact, it's important not to wash too often because it could make your acne worse. Acne is linked to rising hormone levels—most often during puberty, but not always. It's not caused by the foods you eat, nor does sunlight cure it.

What's the rule on shelf life?

Eye cosmetics should never be shared and should be replaced every three to four months. There's no hard-and-fast rule for other cosmetics, which are designed to last from one to three years, but if they've been exposed to too much light or heat, all bets are off; improper storage will cause a radically reduced shelf life.

How many times a year is it safe to dye my hair?

First of all, you should always test both semipermanent (they wash out after four to six shampoos) and permanent hair dyes on a small patch of skin—either behind your ear or inside your elbow. Do this 24 hours before you color your whole head, because ammonium persulfate can cause both irritant and allergic contact dermatitis, as well as hives and wheezing.

What about perms?

Make sure you've got an experienced hairdresser. Permanent waving breaks the chemical bonds in straight hair to make it curl. The process can damage the hair, which is why perms shouldn't be done more than every three months. If the perming solution is left on too long or is applied to hair that's already damaged, your hair might break up and scalp irritation may occur.

Are any precautions necessary for nail cosmetics?

Yes. Don't cut, poke, or remove nail cuticles. They prevent infection and protect nail-forming cells. If you use artificial nails, beware of glues with methacrylate, a known allergen. Even glues that are methacrylate-free may cause the underlying nail to peel and crack. Sculptured nails, custom-made to fit permanently over natural nails, are the worst offenders. They can promote infection of the skin around the nail and might cause you to lose your nail. The rule is to remove artificial nails every three months to allow your natural nails to rest.

Source: Adapted from the American Academy of Dermatology's *Cosmetics and Skin Care Products*. For more information, contact: The American Academy of Dermatology, 930 North Meacham Road, Schaumburg, IL 60173-4965; phone: (847) 330-0230; fax: (847) 330-0050.

Cosmetic Dentistry

My teeth are discolored. How can I make them "white" again?

The process of teeth whitening, or bleaching, can be done by the dentist in-office or through dentist-supervised, at-home systems. After several office sessions, teeth will be whitened to the desired shade. At-home systems should be individually fitted and monitored by a cosmetic dentist.

There's a big gap between my two front teeth. Can that be changed?

Chipped or fractured teeth, gaps between teeth, and/or discolored teeth can be redesigned through *bonding* and *veneering* to help create the "perfect" smile many people desire. Bonding generally requires one office visit, while veneering takes two. In addition to aiding good oral hygiene and a healthy lifestyle, both are inexpensive ways to enhance a smile. A cosmetic dentist can explain the various techniques and the best ones for tailored needs.

My back teeth have too much silver and gold. Is there a less obvious way to fill cavities?

Years ago gold and silver fillings were the only options for fillings. Today, new advances in tooth-colored porcelain and composite materials not only allow fillings to go unnoticed but are stronger and more wear-resistant.

Most of my teeth are bunched toward the front of my mouth. Is there a way to get rid of that "crowded" look?

Through *movable orthodontics, cosmetic contouring,* and/or bonding and veneering, teeth can be reshaped and polished, resulting in a straighter, less crowded-looking, and generally more attractive dental appearance. The results of these procedures are long-lasting.

I know my smile needs some work, but I don't know if cosmetic dentistry is right for me. Just how much does it cost for these procedures?

Some cosmetic dental options are covered by insurance, and the cost varies with how much work you want done. Like any cosmetic process, the amount of money spent will increase with the amount of product or service you desire. Your actual cost will depend on factors such as the extent and complexity of the treatment and the types of changes you and your cosmetic dentist decide on.

My semiprofessional boxing career left me missing one tooth. Is there anything that can be done for this problem?

Crown or bridge work is best for correcting a major functional or structural problem with individual teeth, missing teeth, or general bite dysfunction. New porcelain and ceramic technology is available to replace missing and/or severely broken teeth so that no one can tell that replacements are not real. Furthermore, implants are currently being used successfully to replace teeth in people of all ages.

Source: American Academy of Cosmetic Dentistry, 270 Corporate Drive, Madison, WI 53714; phone: (608) 241-5857; fax: (608) 241-7709.

Decoding Cosmetic Labels

Are cosmetic ingredients listed in any particular order?

Yes. Federal regulations require that the main ingredients be listed first; the others follow in descending order by quantity. That's why water is usually at the top of the list. This FDA regulation applies only to product labels on retail cosmetics intended for home use. Free cosmetic samples and products marked "For Professional Use Only" are not required to declare ingredients.

I read labels religiously, but why do some of the ingredients still mystify me?

Because they're written in the language of chemistry, which is why, for instance, a common preservative in shampoo is listed as methyl paraben and vitamin E as tocopherol.

Where do I go to get more information about any one ingredient?

The *International Cosmetic Ingredient Dictionary,* published by the Cosmetic, Toiletries and Fragrance Association, lists the most widely known cosmetic ingredients, along with their definitions and trade names.

Do vitamins contribute to a healthier cosmetic?

No. The health claims are not recognized by the FDA (see *Skin Care,* page 604), and, in cosmetics, vitamins C and E are used as preservatives. Topical vitamin E can sometimes cause rashes (contact dermatitis) or hives.

I have sensitive skin and am moderately allergic, so I try to be careful, but I'm most confused by the terms that sound as if they're protecting me. What does it really mean for a cosmetic to be "hypoallergenic"?

Whatever the manufacturer wants it to mean. Hypoallergenic cosmetics are products the manufacturers claim produce fewer allergic reactions (*hypo* means "less than"), but there are no federal standards or definitions to govern the use of the term. Dermatologists say it has very little meaning since many products labeled "hypoallergenic" contain the skin conditioner lanolin, which for some people produces swelling, itching, and redness of the eyelids. For the most part, the basic ingredients in so-called hypoallergenic cosmetics are the same as those used in other cosmetics.

Am I safer choosing a "natural" product?

Not necessarily. "Natural" ingredients are extracted directly from plants or animal products, rather than synthetically. This doesn't guarantee purer and cleaner products, since plants—including those used in cosmetics—can be contaminated with bacteria, pesticides, or chemical fertilizers. Also, lanolin is a natural extract of sheep wool. Finally, certain naturally occurring vitamins are, for some, a potent allergen.

What does "alcohol-free" mean?

"Alcohol-free" means that cosmetics don't contain ethyl ("grain") alcohol. But they very well might contain fatty alcohols, such as cetyl, stearyl, cetearyl, or lanolin, which don't tend to have the same drying effect on skin.

Is there any difference between a "fragrance-free" cosmetic and an "unscented" one?

Neither one guarantees that a fragrance has not been used. Since many of the raw materials used to make cosmetics just plain stink, manufacturers add ingredients to cover up odors. In the case of "fragrance-free" or "unscented" cosmetics, companies are adding enough fragrance to cover an unpleasant odor, but less than they'd use to produce a noticeable scent. By reading the ingredients list you'll be able to see the word "fragrance" if one has been added.

Why do some cosmetics list an "active ingredient" as a first entry on the product label?

Because they're not just cosmetics. As defined in the Federal Food, Drug, and Cosmetic Act (1938), cosmetics are "articles (other than soap) intended to be applied to the human body for cleansing, beautifying, promoting attractiveness, or altering the appearance without affecting the body's structure or functions." Drugs, on the other hand, are articles intended to treat, prevent disease, or to alter the structure or function of the body. Dandruff shampoo and fluoride toothpaste are both cosmetics and drugs. The "active ingredient" is the one that behaves like a drug.

What does "noncomedogenic" mean?

It means that common pore-clogging ingredients that can lead to acne are not used by the cosmetic manufacturer.

Sources: Adapted from the following U.S. Food and Drug Administration publications: *Cosmetic Safety: More Complex Than at First Blush; Thigh Creams; Cosmetic Labeling; Hypoallergenic Cosmetics; Alcohol Free; On the Teen Scene: Cosmetics and Reality;* and *Fragrance Free and Unscented.* For more information, call the FDA Hotline at (800) 270-8869. Or write: U.S. Food and Drug Administration, Director of the Cosmetics and Color Section, 200 C Street SW, Washington, DC 20204.

Finding a Facial Plastic Surgeon

Who is qualified to perform facial plastic surgery?

A facial plastic surgeon is typically board-certified in *otolaryngology,* the specialty that addresses surgery of the head and neck. The training includes one year of postgraduate training in general surgery and a minimum of four additional years in both head and neck surgery and facial plastic surgery.

For what reasons do people seek facial plastic surgery?

To remove birthmarks and to repair cleft palates or congenital deformities. Other clients are burn and accident victims. Many simply choose to change the way they look—to reshape a facial feature or to alter some of the signs of premature aging.

What kinds of surgery do facial plastic surgeons perform?

The most common surgeries are: nose jobs, or *rhinoplasty;* eyelid surgery, or *blepharoplasty;* face-lifts, or *rhytidectomy;* forehead-lifts; double chin removal, or *submental lipectomy;* chin augmentation and reduction, or *mentoplasty;* ear surgery (shaped and "pinned back"), or *otoplasty;* smoothing skin with laser skin resurfacing; facial reconstruction for cancer and facial trauma victims (also for birth defects); collagen implants (injections) to raise skin tissue and smooth out wrinkles; chemical peels to remove the outer layer of skin; and dermabrasion to smooth wrinkled skin.

What are the recovery times for the most common cosmetic operations and how long do the results last?

Nose jobs require a week's recovery; results are permanent. Eye surgery needs about a week to heal; lower lid changes are permanent, whereas upper lids last ten years.

For a face-lift, the recovery period is two weeks. Depending on the patient, results can last ten years. The surgery for eliminating the fat beneath the chin is usually permanent.

What's the best way to go about finding a facial plastic surgeon?

Word of mouth is often best. And ask if your contact would return to the same surgeon for another procedure.

The American Academy of Facial Plastic and Reconstructive Surgery has instituted a toll-free number, (800) 332-FACE, that can provide you with names, addresses, and telephone numbers of surgeons in your area.

Once I find a surgeon, what are the key questions I should ask?

During your first consultation, be sure to ask the following questions:

- Am I a good candidate for this procedure?
- How long will the operation take?
- What is the recovery time?
- What are the risks involved?
- Is postoperative medication necessary?
- How much do you charge?

What does the plastic surgeon need to know about me?

Your medical history: medications, allergies, habits, and even your expectations should be shared with your surgeon. Computer imaging might give you a picture of what to expect, and the appropriate anesthesia should be discussed.

Source: Adapted from *Understanding Facial Plastic Surgery: What Is a Facial Plastic Surgeon?*, a publication of the American Academy of Facial Plastic and Reconstructive Surgery. For more information write or call: American Academy of Facial Plastic and Reconstructive Surgery, Inc., 1110 Vermont Avenue NW, Suite 220, Washington, DC 20005-3522; (800) 332-FACE; (202) 842-4500.

Hair Care

What type of brush is best to use on different types of hair?

The best brush is no brush all, but if you need to use one, buy the cheapest brush with the long white bendable plastic bristles. Get a gentle one that bends a lot, so it won't damage and pull out your hair. There is no point to buying very expensive brushes, particularly the pure bristle sort, because these are often barbed and can snag into the hair.

In general, although gentle brushing for styling is fine, brushing isn't very good for your hair because it wears your hair out. When you do brush, be careful not to tug at the hair too much because this traction on the hair can pull it out.

How often can I get a perm without damaging my hair?

Perming always damages hair no matter how often you do it. The average woman perms her hair every four to five months, and when you consider that hair only grows 2 inches in that time, you realize that the remainder of the hair is getting re-permed repeatedly. For this reason, one should be very careful about perming too often, particularly if the hair seems damaged or dry.

If hair is permed often, protect the ends by putting heavy cream on them to keep the perm solution away from them. Have the perm done professionally, if possible. Also, use conditioner more often—permed hair needs extra care because it is much more vulnerable to breakage.

Is it true that your hair grows faster if you cut it often?

Absolutely not. This is a total myth. Your hair is not a lawn, and cutting has no effect on the rate of growth.

What can I do to avoid split ends?

Three words: Condition, condition, and condition. Use a leave-in conditioner just on the ends (a nongreasy one that won't weigh hair down). Try not to over-perm, over-color, or over-bleach. Brushing too much or too hard can also lead to split ends. Once you have split ends, the only way to get rid of them is to cut them off, so it is best to prevent this from happening at all.

What can I do to combat damage from heat-styling methods (curling irons, hot rollers, blow-dryers)?

The blow-dryer is not the problem, but the way you use it. If you stop immediately when your hair is dry, you won't damage your hair. It's using it on dry hair that causes damage. When you use hot rollers, wrap the ends of hair in a tissue to protect them from splitting. The rule about conditioning applies here as well—if your hair is in good condition, it won't damage as easily.

Is it safe to wash my hair every day or will I damage it/dry it out? How about twice a day if I'm exercising frequently?

Yes, just as it is safe to wash your face every day. Twice a day is fine too. You won't dry it out if you're using the right products, chosen according to your hair texture and shape (fine hair will require a different product from coarse, thick hair). Make sure to use a conditioner, which will also keep the hair from drying out.

I'm a swimmer—how can I protect my hair from chlorine without wearing a cap?

There is a product called swim cap cream, which you put on your hair and it behaves like a cap to protect it. The cream is water-, sun-, and chlorine-resistant, and washes off completely after use.

I've heard that you're not supposed to brush your hair when it's wet because this causes breakage. Is this true?

Wet hair is stretched hair, and brushing adds traction, leading to greater chances for breakage. You should therefore never *brush* tangles out of wet hair, but comb them out with a wide-toothed comb. The comb you use should be saw-cut (created out of one piece) and not molded, because the joint lines of a molded comb cut into the hair shaft and damage the hair.

What about hair products with alcohol in them? Are they damaging to the hair?

This pervasive hair myth is total balderdash. The alcohols used in hair products are fatty or oily alcohol—cetyl alcohol, for example, is very waxy and oily and is also used in moisturizing face creams. *Rubbing* alcohol may be drying, but no one in their right mind would use it in a hair-care product. "Alcohol free" on a hair product thus means nothing; the product could actually be more drying than a product that contains an oily alcohol.

Does dandruff signify a dry scalp?

No, it usually signals an oily scalp. Use a dandruff shampoo for either condition, but don't use it all the time, because it is bad for the hair.

Source: Philip Kingsley, trichologist (hair scientist), with practices in London and New York City. He is the author of *Hair: An Owner's Handbook* (London, UK: Aurum Press, 1995).

Hair Coloring

How do I know which hair coloring product is right for me?

Consider three factors:

- *How long* do you want your color to last? You can choose semipermanent, long-lasting, or permanent hair color.
- *What shade* do you want? If you're coloring your own hair, stay within your own shade range. The closer you stay to nature, the safer your choice will be. Going lighter is usually best. Lighter hair softens the face. A dark color might be too drastic; you can always go darker later. Think of hair color in relation to your whole self—skin, eyes, length of hair, the clothes you wear.
- *What kind of results* do you want to achieve? To cover gray or enhance your natural color, use a semipermanent or long-lasting semipermanent hair color. To lighten, go redder, make a dramatic color change, or cover gray, choose a permanent hair color.

I intend to color my hair and get a perm. Which should I do first? How long do I need to wait between procedures?

Have the perm first, and then wait at least one week before coloring your hair. Shampoo your hair at least once (to remove excess traces of the perm solution) before you color your hair.

Can I mix a semipermanent with a permanent hair color if they are both from the same manufacturer? I'm a very creative person, and I like to mix hair color shades to achieve the color I want.

No. The chemical formulation of each hair color product line is different, and not necessarily compatible. It is perfectly all right to mix shades within the same product line, however. For example, permanent and permanent.

I use hair color and mix two shades together. Can I save the unused portion for my next retouch?

Only if they have not been mixed with the developer. Save your half-used bottles of color in a cool, dark place. Keep them tightly capped and they'll remain fresh for up to six weeks. But once the color has been mixed with the developer, use it up or toss it out, because the chemical process is already taking place.

I have about 25 percent gray in my hair, and it's really making me feel older and feel lousy. What can I do to feel and look better without making a drastic change?

There is no getting around it—gray hair makes people look older. It might not be fair, but it's certainly true. Think about turning your grays into highlights or just gently covering your gray hair with a semipermanent, no-peroxide, no-ammonia product in a shade lighter than your natural hair. If you have light brown hair, a golden blond shade will turn your gray strands into golden highlights. Be sure to strand-test first to preview the color results.

Should people who want to cover gray hair use different products from those who don't need gray coverage?

It depends on the percent of gray hair you have. There are two ways to color gray hair. If you have a small percentage of gray (35% or less), you would want to use a semipermanent product (levels 1 or 2), which would highlight gray hair while enhancing your natural color. If, on the other hand, you have a lot of gray (50% or more) and want to cover it completely, you would use a permanent product (level 3). Women who don't have gray hair but who want to enhance their color can use levels 1, 2, or 3.

I've used shampoo-in permanent hair color for years with excellent results. Now it doesn't cover my gray hair.

Permanent hair colorings are formulated to cover 50 percent gray or more. You might have more gray now than you did when you first started to use hair coloring. Besides, gray hair tends to get resistant and is often the most difficult to color. You might want to try keeping the formula on for an extra five minutes or changing your color to a deeper tone in your shade category. An added tip: If you notice that certain areas of gray hair tend to be resistant to color, apply your hair coloring to those areas first.

Is it safe for those with sensitive skin and scalp conditions to color their hair?

With any product there is a possibility of allergy to some of the ingredients, so a patch test should always be done before using any hair color. Permanent hair-coloring products are mixed with hydrogen peroxide (developer) before they are applied to the hair. Usually they contain ammonia, which might cause irritation to some people with sensitive skin and scalp conditions. Semipermanent products are more gentle because they have no ammonia or peroxide. If you have sensitive skin or a scalp condition, it is best to consult a doctor if there are any doubts.

Should individuals from different ethnic backgrounds use different color products?

We recommend that a strand test be done before you apply any level of hair color to the whole head. Asian hair is harder to color and generally requires longer application times. Hair that has been chemically treated with relaxers, perms, or even old hair color is more porous and tends to take the color more quickly.

If I use a shampoo-in hair coloring, will it shampoo out just as easily if I don't like the results?

No. The shampoo-in designation refers to the formula. Although these are products that are easy to apply, unlike a regular shampoo, they won't wash out immediately. For example, a semipermanent product will rinse out after 6 to 12 shampoos. A permanent hair color will not wash out and needs to be reapplied every 4 to 6 weeks.

When I was younger, my hair was nearly black. Now it's salt and pepper. I want to cover the gray, but I'm afraid if I use a black hair coloring it will be too dark for my mature face. What do you think?

Black hair tends to look harsh. Most women find that a hair color a shade *lighter* than their own is a better choice. The new color looks softer and more flattering—remember that just as your hair color changes, so does your skin tone. Try a natural deep brown or a chestnut brown color to warm up your face. It will look dark enough to you (you've been looking gray, after all), but will be more flattering now than the black your hair once was.

Can you color your hair too often?

It depends on the type of hair color product. Permanent hair color products need to be reapplied when your regrowth begins to show, usually from four to six weeks. Follow the directions in the insert for touch-ups. Semipermanent hair color products last from six to eight shampoos and need to be used more often than permanent hair color. Semipermanent hair color does not change your hair color; it just deposits color, covers grey, and enhances your own natural hair color.

Source: Clairol, 345 Park Avenue, New York, NY 10154. For more information, call (800) 223-5800 or visit the Clairol Web site at www.clairol.com.

Hair Loss

What's the most common form of permanent hair loss and what causes it?

The most common form of hair loss is *androgenetic alopecia* (genetic hair loss or pattern balding). To date, approximately 38 million men, 27 million women, and 8 million children in the United States are affected. Contrary to the popular belief that the gene is passed on by the mother, baldness is a trait that can be determined by either the mother or the father.

What is it about hair loss that makes people feel particularly vulnerable?

It's chiefly that people feel like outsiders in a setting that shows us images of tall, thin, good-looking men and women with hair. We live in an extremely visual society, and few people have the time to get to know the person behind the image.

What everyday factors can cause temporary hair loss?

In women, hormonal changes can cause hair loss, as can pregnancy.

For men and women, anesthesia, anemia, chemotherapy, skin disorders, stress, rapid weight loss, and megadosing of certain vitamins, particularly A and E, can also cause hair loss. The hair grows back when the body corrects itself, but in the case of radiation therapy, the hair loss (to the treated area) is permanent.

What beauty-related techniques can cause hair loss?

If a licensed beauty professional takes all the proper steps, there's no need to worry. Any hair thinning is always temporary. In rare cases, hair dye can cause a severe allergic reaction, which could result in hair loss. All chemical treatments should be preceded by a skin test.

What about wearing a wig or a hat?

This is one of the many myths about what causes hair loss. Others include: washing your hair too frequently; having dandruff; getting a crew cut; or even being an intellectual. There are also myths about keeping hair, such as that standing on your head or brushing your hair 100 times a day will produce a healthier head of hair.

What is Rogaine? Does it work? For whom? And for what kind of baldness?

Rogaine is the brand name developed by Upjohn Laboratories for monoxidol, a medication developed for the treatment of high blood pressure. One of its side effects was an increase in the growth of body hair. After several years of study, a topical solution of monoxidol was developed.

While there is no absolute cure for baldness, monoxidol may significantly slow down hair loss. The ideal candidates are younger people who are at the beginning stages of hair loss (mainly in the crown).

What are monoxidol's side effects?

The most common side effects from Rogaine include itchy scalp, headaches, increased heart rate, weight gain, and the shakes.

How much does monoxidol cost?

The average cost of monoxidol is between $20 and $30 a month. It used to cost a lot more—$80 to $100 a month, not including physician visits.

What clearly *won't* work for hair loss?

Shaving your head to grow healthier, thicker hair; stimulating the scalp; removing the dirt from the follicles. Again, these are all myths. There is no absolute cure for androgenetic hair loss to date.

How can I figure out if my children will experience hair loss?

Look at your family's ancestry. If there is baldness on either side of the family, there's a good chance that the child will experience some form of hair loss. If there's hair loss on both sides, there's a much greater chance. It's possible for hair loss to skip a generation, and sometimes the amount of hair loss can vary among family members.

If I'm experiencing hair loss, will I eventually lose all my hair?

Probably not. Men tend to lose their hair in a defined pattern—typically confined to the top of the head, from the forehead to the crown. Women don't usually experience total hair loss in any specific area, unless they are suffering from some form of alopecia or chemical exposure.

What are my options for treatment?

- Professional counseling to accept hair loss.
- Cosmetic enhancements, such as perms, color, or temporary fillers.
- Pharmaceuticals such as monoxidol (Rogaine—the only FDA-approved medication available to date).
- Hair additions. Technological advancements in the materials and the construction of hair additions, as well as their methods of attachment and technical skills, are making this option better than ever.
- Hair replacement surgery.

What's currently being tested?

One drug, finasteride (Proscar), currently used for the treatment of enlarged prostate glands, diminishes testosterone in the body. It theoretically reduces dyhydratestosterone on the scalp, encouraging hair to grow back. The drug is currently being tested, and FDA approval may be one to three years away if it is shown to be an acceptable solution with minimal adverse effects.

Source: Anthony Santangelo, president of the American Hair Loss Council; he is also president of AMS Designs, Inc., and vice-president of Taylormade Corp., hair replacement salons and hair product manufacturers. For more information: The AHLC (American Hair Loss Council) keeps a list of both surgical and nonsurgical hair replacement professionals in your area. Call (312) 321-5128. Or write: The American Hair Loss Council, 401 North Michigan Avenue, Chicago, IL 60631.

Hair Removal

How do I get rid of unwanted hair?

For do-it-yourselfers, a variety of home-use hair removal products are available over the counter. They include shaving creams, foams, and gels; waxes; chemical depilatories; and electrolysis devices. Professionals at beauty and skin-care salons and in dermatologists' offices provide waxing, electrolysis, and, most recently, laser treatments to remove hair. In April 1995 the FDA cleared the first laser for this use.

Does shaving make my hair grow faster?

No. Contrary to what many believe, shaving does not change the texture, color, or rate of hair growth.

How does a depilatory work and what precautions should I take?

Depilatories act like a chemical razor blade. You'll find them in gel, cream, lotion, aerosol, and roll-on forms. They all contain a highly alkaline chemical—usually calcium thioglycolate—that dissolves the protein structure of the hair, causing it to separate easily from the skin surface.

Make sure you do a skin test first. If you're allergic or have a sensitivity to the chemical, the depilatory could cause a serious skin irritation or even a chemical burn.

Contact with the skin should be kept to between four and 15 minutes, depending on how fine or coarse the hair is. Above all, don't use a depilatory near your eyes; neither should you apply it on inflamed or broken skin.

How do I choose between using a depilatory and tweezing or waxing?

Unlike depilatories, which remove hair at the skin's surface, "epilatories," such as tweezers and waxes, pluck hairs from below the surface of the skin. They're a bit more painful, but the results last longer, and new growth isn't visible for some weeks. Tweezing is impractical for large areas, so it's used most often for shaping eyebrows and removing facial hair.

Waxing, too, is mostly done to shape the eyebrows and remove hair on the chin and upper lip. Many women also have their legs, underarms, and bikini line waxed.

Where do men commonly want their hair removed?

They usually come for treatment on their chest or back. Bodybuilders often want their skin to look smooth for competitions. Other men are uncomfortable with unwanted back hair.

What's the difference between a hot and a cold wax?

All waxes use a combination of substances—usually paraffin and beeswax, oils or fats, and a resin that makes the wax adhere to the skin. With hot waxing, a thin layer of heated wax is applied to the skin in the direction of the hair growth; the hair becomes embedded as the wax cools and hardens. The wax is then pulled off in the opposite direction, taking the uprooted hair with it.

Cold waxes work pretty much the same way. Strips precoated with wax are pressed on the skin in the direction of hair growth and pulled off in the opposite direction. The strips come in different sizes, for use on the eyebrows, upper lip, chin, and bikini area.

Who shouldn't use wax?

People with diabetes and circulatory problems are particularly susceptible to infection. Waxes should not be used over varicose veins, moles, or warts, nor should they come into contact with eyelashes, ears, nipples, genital areas, or the inside of the nose. Finally, wax should never be applied to chapped, irritated, or sunburned skin. A small area should be tested for sensitivity or allergic reaction before treating the entire area. And though epilatory waxes are available for home use, some hair removal experts recommend professional waxing for best results.

How does electrolysis work?

Needle electrolysis introduces a fine wire close to the hair shaft. The electric current travels down the wire and destroys the hair root at the bottom of the follicle. The loosened hair is then removed with tweezers. Every hair is treated individually.

Which areas are most commonly selected for electrolysis?

Men are treated for areas between their eyebrows, around the outside of the ears, and their shoulders.

Women usually come in for facial hair—lip, chin, eyebrows, and neck. Body work includes bikini line, abdomen, breast, forearms, and underarms.

Is electrolysis a one-shot deal?

No. It involves a series of treatments over a period of time. A forearm, for example, requires appointments once a week for about a year. Successful electrolysis requires considerable time and money, but when done properly, hair removal is permanent.

What are the risks?

Electrical shock, if the needle is not properly insulated; infection from an unsterile needle; and scarring from improper technique.

How do I find a licensed and certified electrologist?

A list of licensed and certified electrologists is available from the International Guild of Professional Electrologists: (800) 830-3247.

How does a laser remove hair?

A topical black-colored solution is applied to the treatment area before a laser scans across it. The solution penetrates the hair follicles, and the black material in it absorbs the laser wavelength, which heats and destroys the follicles.

Are there any side effects?

Yes. Redness, caused by heating the tissue, and possibly darkening of fair skin or lightening of dark skin. There's also a risk of scarring, and sunlight should be avoided during healing to avoid a change in pigment.

Source: Marian Segal. Adapted from her article, "Hair Today, Gone Tomorrow," *FDA Consumer* magazine (September 1996). For more information, call the FDA Consumer Hotline at (800) FDA-4010.

Makeup Application Tips from a Pro INTERVIEW WITH MARET ASARO

What are a few beauty tips that apply both to the plain-looking makeup user and to the professional model?

Beautiful faces come in all shapes and sizes, but one thing that separates the beautiful from the homely is perfectly shaped eyebrows. Every makeup artist, supermodel, and female impersonator knows the importance of a tweezer.

Skin care comes next. Women spend too much time covering up their problem skin with makeup rather than fixing the problem itself. Your skin should be cleansed at least once a day. A cleansing lotion should be followed by a toner, then by a good moisturizer. Another trick of the trade is to drink plenty of water. Water will hydrate your skin and get rid of toxins from the inside.

To sum up: Arch those eyebrows, clean that skin (don't just cover it), and drink lots of water.

What is the best makeup on the market?

If there were one perfect brand, we wouldn't need thousands of manufacturers. The point is for you to find a foundation that is appropriate for your skin type and tone—and stick with it.

When should I throw my makeup away?

When it smells like crayons, it has bacteria in it. Also, for aesthetic reasons, don't use an eye pencil or mascara that melts on your face. Makeup shouldn't run after it's applied.

Which brand is best for people who are allergic to makeup?

The first instinct is to buy makeup that boasts it's "hypoallergenic" (see *Decoding Cosmetic Labels,* page 588). This generally means the product does not contain perfumes that might irritate the skin. But it might still cause a reaction. Most of the time, someone with sensitive skin is allergic to lanolin, mineral oil, preservatives, or one of the pigments. A dermatologist will test you to find out the ingredients you should avoid.

What are the most common makeup mistakes or misapplications?

• *Penciled-in eyebrows.* If your eyebrows are shaped, but have bald spots, use eyeshadow to fill them in. Women with dark to light brown eyebrows should invest in taupe-colored eyeshadow. To apply it, use a small, angled brush. If you don't have eyebrows, use a pencil, but apply a softer color powder on the top of the penciled line for a softer, less shiny and waxy, natural look.

• *Don't be a painted lady.* The woman behind the cosmetic counter wants your money. She's going to insist that you need all the products she has to sell. Let her do your makeup, then walk outside and see how what she's done holds up under natural light. With a clean tissue, wipe off the colors you hate and bring back those tissues. Tell her you'll take everything except the items on the tissues. You'll probably walk out with a lipstick, one of the three blushes she applied, and an eyeshadow or two (not five!). Remember: Sometimes less is more.

• *Match your foundation to your skin.* Don't pick a base color that's two to four shades darker because you like a tan look. Start with a foundation that matches, then apply a slightly darker bronzing powder with a dome duster brush. Dust the powder all over your face and throat (being careful not to put any where it will rub off onto your collar); it will look more natural.

I have fair skin and blue eyes. What can I do to draw attention to my eyes?

The only color liner to use with blue eyes is charcoal brown. Don't use black. Dark brown, greens, or blues will only draw attention away from your eyes rather than get them noticed.

What are the best eyeshadows for African-American women?

Honey mustard on the eyelid, with a raisin red in the creases. A darker nutmeg color should be added to the outer corner off the crease, finished with a pale shimmering gold on the brow bone. It's very natural and very beautiful.

How do I get my cheeks to look fuller if my skin tone is darker than many contour colors on the market?

Just because a product says it's eyeshadow doesn't mean you can't use it on your cheeks. Take a very shimmery bronze color and, using a powder brush, smile a big smile and apply to the apple of the cheeks. This will make your cheeks pick up the light in the room.

How do I get my makeup to look like it was done by an artist?

Artists are nothing without their tools. Invest in sable or squirrel hair brushes. Buy good tweezers, powder puffs, and latex sponges—which, in addition to helping you apply foundation, are great for blending out hard lines of eyeshadow and blush. Always keep your makeup well blended.

Is there a way to play down my ruddy complexion?

Yes. Green neutralizes red. Find a concealer with a green undertone. Then apply your foundation over the concealer.

Is it possible to conceal those dark circles under my eyes?

Yes. The circles under your eyes are blue. Yellow neutralizes blue. Use a flesh-tone concealer that is two to three shades lighter than your skin tone and make sure it has yellow undertones.

How do I know if I'm applying my makeup properly?

The idea is to bring out your best features and exaggerate the contour of your face. Take a light to your mirror and observe how the shadows reflect the highlights and lowlights on your face. The features closest to the light (bridge of your nose; apple of your cheek; chin, eyelid, brow bone, and center of your lower lip) will be pale in color, whereas the features set into your face (sides of nose; crease of eyes; outer corner of eyelids; beneath jawline and cheekbones) are darker. The point of the makeup is to subtly pop out the highlights and draw back the lowlights.

You should use three to four colors of eyeshadow, two colors on your cheeks, and three colors on your lips. Line the lips and fill in the outer corners with the lipliner pencil. Using your fingers, blend the lines and then fill in the lips with a lighter lipstick color. Finish up with a dot of pale gold lipstick to the bottom center of your lower lip. Rubbing the lips together will blend the colors properly. Remember to keep all your colors neutral and well blended for a natural, classic, and beautiful look.

What distinguishes professional makeup from drugstore or department store makeup?

Professional makeup, such as the products Alcone sells, offer customers the highest quality makeup at very low prices. That's because customers aren't paying for advertising, fancy packaging, perfumes, or unnecessary cosmetic additives. Instead, they're buying highly pigmented makeup, handcrafted from simple ingredients by makeup artists for makeup artists.

Source: Interview with Maret Asaro, in-house Makeup Artist at Alcone, where, according to *Mirabella*, "top makeup artists stock up"—235 West 19th Street, New York, NY 10011. For more information, call Alcone at (800) 466-7446; (212) 633-0551. Or write: Alcone Company, Inc., 5-49 49th Avenue, Long Island City, NY 11101.

Skin Care INTERVIEW WITH DR. NELSON NOVICK

Can you recommend a basic skin-care regimen that cuts through the maze of expensive skin-care products?

Yes. Basic skin care has three parts. First and foremost comes adequate sun protection. The effects of ultraviolet rays are the single most aging factor to the skin, bar none. Wearing paba-free sunscreen, a 4-inch brimmed hat, and avoiding the sun between 10 A.M. and 2 P.M.—especially during the high sun season of mid-April through mid-October—are essential steps to basic skin care. There are a whole variety of sophisticated sunless tanning preparations that contain dihydroxyaceton (DHA); they can produce natural-looking skin coloration and cause no damage whatsoever.

Second comes cleansing. I advocate doing a sensitive skin cleaning. Americans are the most overwashed and overbathed people in the world, to their skin's own detriment. The truth is that the skin's natural process sheds dead cells at the surface. Our surface layer of skin, the *stratum corneum,* is a dead layer of cells that migrated up from a living layer. So, without scraping or rubbing, dead skin cells come off naturally.

When it comes to cleansing, you want to use the mildest product because anything harsher will abrade the living layers. For that, I suggest any bar or cleanser that's labeled "sensitive skin." I like Formula 405's Facial and Body Cleanser because it's soapless and nondrying. Also, wash with your fingertips, not a polyester scrub, and lightly pat dry with a towel.

Proper moisturizing is the last step. For most people, a cheap, over-the-counter moisturizer is just fine. It shouldn't contain a host of ridiculous, exotic ingredients such as collagen, pro-collagen, elastin, vitamin E, vitamin A, tocopherol, egg's milk, honey oil, bee jelly, DNA, and liposome. The molecules of these ingredients are too large to be absorbed by the skin; it's akin to driving a railroad train through the opening of an anthill.

In the moisturizer, first look for an *occlusive* ingredient (one that locks in moisture) like petrolatum, simethicone, or a light mineral oil that doesn't block pores. The second ingredient to look for is a *humectant,* which draws moisture from the deeper layers of the skin. Glycerin is a common humectant. I usually recommend Formula 405's Facial Day Cream to patients because it contains a paba-free sunscreen and 6 percent lactic acid, which is an alpha-hydroxy acid *and* humectant.

For people who have tough, dry skin, I recommend an over-the-counter product like Carmol 10 lotion or Carmol 20 cream; they contain very high concentrations of urea, a wonderful humectant.

Can moisturizers prevent wrinkles?

No. Sun damage, genetics, and the tug of gravity cause wrinkly skin. Moisturizers combat dryness and improve the appearance of the skin.

What about Retin-A? Does it work against wrinkles?

It appears to. Retin-A seems to increase new blood vessel formation, collagen synthesis, and possibly even elastic fiber synthesis. It also seems to speed up the turnover of cells—the cycle from living to dying—that generates fresh skin. But some people are allergic to Retin-A, and even 90 percent of those who are not allergic can anticipate an initial reaction. Retin-A tends to be drying. That's why they brought out Renova, which is for more mature skin. All Retin-A products can be obtained only by prescription.

But I thought you said that vitamins couldn't be absorbed by the skin? Isn't Retin-A a vitamin?

Retin-A is different. It's retinoic acid. Certain chemicals can be absorbed by the skin; if that weren't the case, then patches for seasickness, estrogen, or topical treatments for hypertension would be useless. But the molecules have been modified. For example, certain vitamin C preparations, like Cellex-C, tested at Duke University, are believed to be absorbed by the skin and to work as an antioxidant. An antioxidant attacks free radicals, which are highly reactive molecules looking to combine with your skin's molecules to break them up (and "rust" them the way a cut apple oxidizes) and destroy skin cells.

Research suggests that the *orally* administered antioxidants, like vitamin C, vitamin E, and beta-carotene, are shunted to the body's priority organs—the heart, the liver, the kidneys. So the skin is treated like a lower-priority organ, which is probably why taking these vitamins orally doesn't affect the skin that much. If we apply the *modified* vitamins topically with any success, then we're administering them directly to the skin. But the products you're seeing that boast vitamins in their ingredients don't contain the modified vitamins I'm talking about.

You mentioned alpha-hydroxy acids. What do they do?

They're derived from fruits and used by dermatologists in high concentrations to remove age spots and to resurface wrinkled, damaged skin. You'll also see them used in skin products. They not only serve to resurface the skin and exfoliate dead skin cells, but are believed to increase collagen synthesis and plump up the gelatinous matrix in the dermis, which supports collagen and elastin fibers.

Are facials good for your skin?

If you have perfectly normal skin and want to listen to music and be pampered by somebody with a white coat in a dimly lit room, they're fine. But don't do it too often; and get a facial *only* if you have nothing wrong with your skin. If you do have something wrong, it's likely to get worse. I get patients who run in and say, "I just went in for a facial and now I'm all broken out!" That's because there's too much manipulation of the skin—caking, masking, vibrators, hot towels, and creams. Even when they remove a blackhead, the overstimulation of the skin often provokes the surrounding clogged pores (whiteheads) underneath the surface to rupture, causing inflamed skin.

Isn't it good to remove blackheads?

Yes. But it requires scalpels or special extractors and sterile equipment, and this is best left to medical hands. When a dermatologist removes blackheads and whiteheads, it's called *acne surgery*. There's less manipulation of the skin, and afterwards we inject an anti-inflammatory.

What do the phrases "dermatologist tested" and "clinically tested" mean?

There is no medical or legal definition for those terms. They really provide you with little substantive help.

Source: Nelson Lee Novick, M.D., Associate Clinical Professor of Dermatology at Mt. Sinai School of Medicine, New York City, and the author of *You Can Look Younger at Any Age: A Leading Dermatologist's Guide* (New York: Henry Holt & Company, 1996). For more information, call the American Academy of Dermatology at (847) 330-0230; (847) 330-0050 (for fax inquiries). Or write: The American Academy of Dermatology, 930 North Meacham Road, Schaumburg, IL 60173-4965.

Sun Safety

Is tanning safe?

No, because it presents risks. By exposing your skin to ultraviolet rays, you increase your chances of skin cancer and premature wrinkling.

But I don't burn. I get a dark, even tan.

Any tan indicates skin damage. A tan will shield you somewhat from burning, but it won't fully protect you against wrinkling or skin cancer. Fair-skinned individuals who burn easily should be especially careful; but for those who tan well, the deeper the color of the tan, the more extensive the skin damage.

I look better with a tan. If I'm determined to get one, what precautions should I take?

Limit sun exposure between 10 A.M. and 3 P.M. Use a sunscreen with an SPF (sun protection factor) of at least 15. Because some skin ingredients may cause irritation, you may want to first test a product by applying a small amount to a limited area of your skin.

I don't understand what the SPF numbers mean.

If you would normally burn in 10 minutes without a sunscreen, an SPF of 15 gives you 150 minutes in the sun before you burn. Note that swimming and perspiration might reduce the SPF factor, which is why a sunscreen must be reapplied.

Does SPF offer full sun protection?

No. Sunlight exposes you to two kinds of ultraviolet light: UVA and UVB. Both can cause skin damage, including wrinkling and skin cancer. SPF sunscreen numbers apply *only* to UVB rays. That means that SPF will reduce your risk of skin damage and cancer, but not entirely eliminate it. Look for products that provide "broad spectrum" or "UVA protection."

If I'm determined to tan year-round, what precautions should I take for indoor tanning?

Find out the exposure limits for your skin type (the salon staff or manufacturer of the tanning device should know). Make sure there's a timer you can set that either signals when your exposure time is up or one that automatically shuts off.

Since artificial ultraviolet light is more intense, it can cause skin damage and cancer. You also risk doing harm to your corneas, so make sure to use UV-blocking goggles. The salon should sterilize all goggles after each use to prevent eye infection.

Since artificial ultraviolet light is more intense, are there any other safety measures I should take?

Yes—consider your medical history. If you are undergoing treatment for lupus or diabetes or are susceptible to cold sores, your condition can be severely aggravated by UV light from tanning devices, sunlamps, or natural sunlight.

What about medications and ultraviolet light?

Run all medications (both oral and topical) by your doctor. Antihistamines, tranquilizers, and birth control pills, to name a few, increase your likelihood of rashes, sunburns, and other allergic-type reactions. Advil, Nuprin, Motrin (ibuprofen), and Bactrim (trimethoprim) are a few of the common photosensitizers (so called because light "photo" increases your sensitivity to them). Other products applied to the skin can cause photoallergic reactions; among them are cosmetics with musk ambrette, sandalwood oil, and bergamot oil.

Source: Adapted from *Sunscreens: Fast Facts*; *Indoor Tanning: Fast Facts;* publications of the Federal Trade Commission. See also *Chemical Photosensitivity: Another Reason to Be Careful in the Sun,* (FDA publication). For more information, write: Federal Trade Commission, Public Reference Branch, Washington, DC 20580; (202) 326-2222. Or sign onto the Web site: http://www.FTC.gov.

DIETS AND FOOD RISKS

———◇———

Deli Meat • Eggs

Food Product Dating

The Food Pyramid

Freezing • Healthy Heart Diet

Kitchen Safety

Poultry and Game

Preparing a Turkey

Red Meat

Safe Defrosting • Vegetarian Diets

Deli Meat

I don't know how long I've had some deli cold cuts in my refrigerator. If they smell good, are they safe to eat?

You can't see, smell or taste the bacteria that cause foodborne illness. If the cold cuts have been opened and refrigerated more than a week, discard them.

CAUTION: If meat is slimy or sticky, has an off-odor, or is discolored, food spoilage and possibly foodborne bacteria could be present. Do not use it.

Generally you can freeze cold cuts that won't be used soon after purchase.

The store clerk was handling some raw meat and didn't wash his hands before picking up my deli meat to slice it. Is it safe?

Whether you're a clerk or a home cook, you should always wash your hands before and after touching raw meat. Bacteria from raw juices can cross-contaminate cooked foods. Since cold cuts are usually eaten without further cooking, any bacteria would not be destroyed. Eating a sandwich made at this deli could be risky.

The potato salad I just purchased at the deli tastes spoiled. Where should I complain?

Potato salad is not a product under USDA jurisdiction. Foods purchased at food service establishments and supermarkets are regulated by your state and local health departments. Contact these officials, listed in your phone book.

Processed deli meats like cold cuts or a sealed carton of chicken salad are inspected by the USDA. If you have a concern about this type of product, call the hotline at (800) 535-4555.

The sliced ham and roast beef I bought from the deli shimmers with green iridescent colors. Does this mean it is spoiled?

Not necessarily. Meat contains fat, iron, and many other compounds. When light hits a slice of meat, it splits into colors like a rainbow. There are also various pigments in meat compounds that can give it an iridescent or greenish cast when exposed to heat and processing. Spoiled meat would probably also be slimy or sticky and have an off-odor.

Is it safe to buy uncooked, prestuffed meats from the deli?

The USDA recommends against purchasing previously stuffed whole poultry products because these items are highly dense and perishable. Cold storage may not stop bacteria from growing in the stuffing inside the bird's cavity. But smaller products like stuffed pork chops or chicken breasts are safe to buy.

What are BHA and BHT and why are they used in some processed meats?

BHA and BHT are antioxidants. They are used to inhibit the development of off-flavors caused by rancidity.

What meats are commonly used in sausages?

Fresh meat trimmings (similar to what is used in ground beef and ground pork) are the primary ingredients. The amount and type vary with the sausage products. If variety meats are included in a cooked sausage product, such as frankfurters, the words "contains variety meat" are prominently identified on the label. Examples of variety meats include heart, tongue, liver, and kidney.

Why is meat cured and/or smoked?

Curing and/or smoking develop the characteristic flavor and color of sausage and smoked meats, extend shelf life, and ensure safe, wholesome, nutritious, and varied meat products.

What's the nutrition profile of a frankfurter?

America's most popular sausage is a source of high-quality protein, B vitamins, iron, and zinc. The traditional frank has 10 to 13 grams of fat; however, many new products contain as little as 1 to 2 grams per serving.

Sources: Deli/Prepared Meats Committee of the National Live Stock and Meat Board/USDA Meat and Poultry Hotline at (800) 535-4555.

Eggs

Do eggs have to be refrigerated?

If eggs are not cared for properly, they can slip in grading. Continual refrigeration keeps them fresher. There are only two situations where eggs should be at room temperature. If you've creamed together butter and sugar and you add cold eggs, you will harden that mixture and your batter runs the risk of curdling. If you are whipping egg whites, they will reach their fullest volume when beaten at room temperature. Let eggs stand for a period of up to 30 minutes after they are taken from the refrigerator.

What does it mean if there is a red dot on the yolk of my egg?

This is a blood spot, and it is not harmful. It is the equivalent of a bruise, obtained when the egg is being formed and the hen's blood vessel has ruptured. Less than 1 percent of eggs produced have blood spots, and through candling most of these eggs are removed. If you do find an egg with a blood spot it is totally safe to eat, but if you don't like the way it looks, use the tip of a knife to remove it.

How can I tell if an egg is fresh?

The best way is to look at the Julian date on the carton (the name is taken from the emperor Julius Caesar). Starting with January 1 as 1 and ending with December 31 as 365, these numbers printed on the carton represent the consecutive days of the year when the eggs were packed. From this packing date you can keep eggs in the refrigerator for at least four to five weeks with no significant freshness loss. The date is the best and most consistent way to measure freshness, because as long as the eggs are sold within 30 days of their pack date, there are no federal regulations on dating—it can vary from state to state or even by supermarket.

Store eggs in the carton on an inside shelf of the fridge, not on the door shelf, because they are exposed to frequent temperature changes there. The carton also protects them from food odors, which eggs very easily pick up. In the new frost-free refrigerators, eggs will dry out faster if they are not protected.

If you don't keep the eggs in the carton, and forget when you've bought them, there is no way to tell how fresh they are without breaking them open. Once cracked, the more the egg spreads out, the older it is.

Is it okay to eat raw cookie dough?

There have been no recorded food-poisoning outbreaks from eating raw cookie dough.

Can I get salmonella from eggs?

Many years ago, there was a form of salmonella found on eggshells. The egg industry worked with the government to get new laws passed to require washing and santizing eggshells, and the bacteria were eradicated. Unfortunately, the bacteria mutated: this new form can be found in the egg itself, not just the shell. The U.S. government, scientists, and the egg industry are all working to eliminate it, but in the meantime they recommend always cooking eggs that are used for consumption.

In the food industry, salmonella usually results from time and temperature abuse of eggs—they haven't been cooked long enough or kept at a high enough temperature when serving. Consumers have problems related to ice cream, so it is recommended that dishes like ice cream and eggnog be prepared with a cooked egg custard base. For most other egg dishes, cook the egg until the white is completely set and the yolk is beginning to thicken.

What are those icky white things in my egg? Are they safe to eat?

These are the *chalazae*, and they are entirely edible. They are caused by the motion of the egg yolk in the white as it is formed in the hen's body. The more prominent the chalazae, the fresher the egg. These natural parts of the egg albumen do not interfere with the cooking or beating of the white and need not be removed, although some cooks like to strain them from stirred custard.

What is the best way to separate an egg?

Use an inexpensive egg separator, rather than passing the egg yolk back and forth from shell half to shell half. Minute bacteria can be present in the pores of the shell, and can posssibly contaminate your egg if you use the shell method. Eggs are easiest to separate when cold.

What's the difference between brown and white eggs?

Only the shell. Different-colored eggshells are produced by different breeds of hens, but there is no difference in the actual eggs. The majority of egg-laying hens in America are White Leghorn types, which lay white eggs. In New England, people prefer brown shells laid by Rhode Island Red, New Hampshire, or Plymouth Rock hens. The brown egg-layers are larger birds and require more food, so brown eggs are slightly more expensive than white.

What are free-range eggs?

The strict definition of "free-range" refers to eggs produced by hens that are raised outdoors or have daily access to the outdoors. Based on seasonal conditions, however, very few hens are actually raised outdoors. Instead, some egg farms are actually indoor floor operations that often are erroneously called free-range. Contrary to rumor, free-range eggs do not have less cholesterol than supermarket eggs.

I've seen green eggs before. How do those come about?

There all kinds of different varieties of birds that lay all different colors of eggs. The Aracauna hen lays green eggs, but these are the same thing as a regular egg, only with a different-colored shell. Rumors that green eggs have less cholesterol are also not true.

Do larger eggs come from larger chickens?

When a hen first begins laying, as a general rule, she lays smaller eggs. As she matures, the eggs become larger. Her maturity, not her size, is thus the factor in the size of eggs that she produces. Interestingly enough, one hen will always produce roughly the same amount of shell material, regardless of the size of the egg. This means that a larger egg will have a slightly thinner shell. To have a strong shell, the hen must also be getting enough calcium in her diet, as the shell is mostly composed of calcium carbonate.

The official size of an egg is determined by the weight per dozen. Large eggs must weigh a minimum of 24 ounces in the carton; Jumbo eggs will weigh 30 ounces; Extra Large, 27; Medium, 21; Small, 18; and Peewee, 15 ounces per dozen.

Explain the grading process. Most eggs in the supermarket are grade A. Is there such a thing as grade B or C?

Grading is separate from sizing, and is based on outside and inside quality. Graders judge how attractive the shell is on the outside; they check the inside to make sure that the yolk is nicely centered, and that there are no flaws in the egg.

Grading the inside is done through a process called *candling*. In the old days, graders would hold the egg up to a candle to see the outline of the yolk in the egg and judge the size of the aircell (the empty space between the white and shell at the large end of the egg). Nowadays, eggs pass through a very bright light on a conveyor belt. The person monitoring the process touches the flawed eggs with an electronic wand so they can be automatically pulled from the belt.

The possible grades are "AA," "A," and "B." "B" eggs rarely reach the retail market. Most are broken and are used by egg product manufacturers for such items as egg substitutes, cake mixes, and frozen waffles. An "AA" egg will stand up tall, its yolk will be firm, and the area covered by the white small. It will have a large proportion of thick white to thin white. In an "A" egg, the white covers a relatively small area. The yolk will be round and upstanding. The thick white is large in proportion to thin and will stand fairly well around the yolk. "B" eggs spread out more and their yolks are flattened. They have the same amount or more thin white than thick white.

Source: The American Egg Board, 1460 Renaissance Drive, Park Ridge, IL 60068; www.aeb.org.

Food Product Dating

What is dating?

"Open dating" (using a calendar date instead of a code) on a food product is stamped on the package to help the store determine how long to display the product for sale. It also helps the consumer determine the time limit to purchase or use the product at its best quality. *It is not a safety date.*

What kinds of foods are dated?

Open dating is used mostly for perishable foods such as meat, poultry, eggs, and dairy products. "Closed" or "coded" dates often appear on shelf-stable products such as cans and boxes of food.

Is dating required by federal law?

Only for infant formula and some baby food. But if a calendar date is used, it must express both the month and day of the month (and the year in the case of shelf-stable and frozen products). A phrase explaining the meaning of that date must also be displayed immediately adjacent to the date ("Sell by" or "Use by," for example).

There are so many different phrases. What do they mean?

• "Sell by" tells the store how long to display the product for sale. You should buy this product before the date expires.

- "Best if used by" (or "Before") is a date recommended for best flavor or quality. It is not a purchase by or safety date.
- "Use by" is a date determined by the manufacturer. It is the last date recommended for use of the product while at "peak quality."
- "Closed" or "coded" dates are packing numbers for use by the manufacturer.

After these dates expire, are the products still safe to consume?

Generally, yes. That is: If a date expires during home storage, the product should be safe, wholesome, and of good quality *if handled properly and if kept at 40°F or below*. Only the "Use by" date refers to home storage and use after purchase.

If the food develops an off-odor, flavor, or appearance due to spoilage bacteria, don't use it. Also, don't use food that's been left out too long (even if the date *hasn't* expired); this applies, for example, to hot dogs left out several hours at a picnic.

I heard that it's sometimes legal for a retailer to change the expiration date. Is this true?

Yes and no. Yes, for example, if wholesome, fresh meat has been cut up and wrapped in the meat department of the supermarket. But it is not legal to modify a label on a product packaged under federal inspection. In this case, the meat, if still wholesome, can be sold, but the date cannot be altered, changed, or covered up by a new date.

I've noticed the codes on cans. Are they meant for consumers?

No. There's no book on how to translate the codes into dates. Here's a good general rule for canned goods: High-acid canned foods such as tomatoes, grapefruit, and pineapple can be stored on the shelf for 12 to 18 months. Low-acid canned foods such as meat, poultry, fish, and most vegetables will keep for two to five years—if the can remains in good condition and has been stored in a cool, clean, dry place.

What about dates on egg cartons?

As long as you purchase the eggs before the expiration date, you should be able to use all the eggs safely in three to five weeks after the date you *purchase* them.

I have several cans of food that accidentally froze. Are they still safe to use?

Frozen canned goods, whether left in a car, basement, or cabin, can present health problems. Seams on cans may be compromised when cans freeze and the contents swell. The cans should be moved immediately to a refrigerator and allowed to thaw. After thawing, cook and use the food or cook and refreeze.

If cans were not thawed in the refrigerator, or if you suspect that the foods may have frozen and thawed more than once, discard them.

My neighbor stores leftover food right in the can. I thought this was dangerous because lead can leach into food.

It is best to transfer leftover food to a storage container intended for refrigerator use. Food left in the can may develop an off-taste as the food reacts with metals used in the can. However, this is a quality issue, not a safety issue. Fortunately, lead has been virtually eliminated as a metal used in the U.S. canning industry. According to the National Food Processors Association, the percentage of food packed in lead-soldered containers dropped from 90.3 percent in 1979 to 3.07 percent in the first quarter of 1990.

I've started buying the new shelf-stable entrees to take to work and heat in the microwave. How long can I expect to safely keep these products on my kitchen shelf?

Many new types of packaging use plastic or paper containers instead of metal cans or glass jars. Think of these new plastic and paper type containers as "flexible cans." Like cans, the contents have been heat-treated (sterilized) to make them shelf-stable. Assuming there are no breaks or tears in the package, these products should maintain top quality for over a year if stored in a cool, dry place.

I still don't have a sense of how long products are good after I get them home. What are good general rules for some of the most commonly purchased food products—opened and unopened?

Purchase products before their expiration date. If perishable, take the food home immediately and refrigerate it promptly. If you freeze the product fresh, the matter of the expiration date is insignificant because foods kept frozen are safe indefinitely. Follow all handling recommendations.

If a product has a "Use by" date, follow it. If it has a "Sell by" date, then cook or freeze it according to the following guidelines after purchase (assume a refrigerator kept at 40°F or below):

• Uncooked poultry	1 or 2 days
• Cooked poultry (unopened)	3 to 4 days
• Cooked poultry (opened)	3 to 4 days
• Uncooked beef, veal, pork, and lamb	3 to 5 days
• Raw eggs	3 to 5 weeks
• Hot dogs (unopened)	2 weeks (but no longer than 1 week after the "Sell by" date)
• Hot dogs (opened)	7 days

Meat and poultry products come in so many different kinds of packages these days. How can I tell if a package requires refrigeration?

Read the label carefully. If refrigeration is necessary for safety, the label must say "Keep refrigerated." If the package was purchased off the shelf, chances are the product will not require refrigeration until opened.

Source: Bessie Berry, Manager, USDA Meat and Poultry Hotline. Adapted from *Focus On: Food Product Dating*, U.S. Department of Agriculture, Food Safety Inspection Service publication. For more information, call the USDA Meat and Poultry Hotline at (800) 535-4555. Or write: Information and Legislative Affairs, Food Safety and Inspection Service, Room 1175—South Building, Washington, DC 20250; (202) 720-7943; fax: (202) 720-1843.

The Food Pyramid

What is the food pyramid?

The pyramid is an outline of what to eat each day. It's not a prescription, but a general guide that lets you choose a healthful diet that's right for you. It calls for eating a variety of foods—including bread, pasta, fruits, vegetables, meats, and milk—to get the nutrients you need and, at the same time, the right amount of calories to maintain a healthy weight. The pyramid also focuses on fat because most American diets are too high in fat, especially saturated fat.

How are the pieces of the pyramid divided?

The pyramid is divided into five food groups. At the base are breads, cereals, rice, and pasta—all foods from grains. You need the most of these foods each day. The next level up includes foods that come from plants—vegetables and fruits. Most people need to eat more of these foods for the vitamins, minerals, and fiber they supply. On the next level up are two groups of foods that come mostly from animals: milk, yogurt, and cheese; and meat, poultry, fish, dry beans, eggs, and nuts. These foods are important for protein, calcium, iron, and zinc. Finally, at the small tip of the pyramid are fats, oils, and sweets. These include items such as salad dressings and oils, cream, butter, margarine, sugars, soft drinks, candies, and sweet desserts that provide calories and little else nutritionally. Most people should use them sparingly.

Is any one food group more important than another?

No. For good health, you need all five food groups.

How many calories are right for me?

That depends on your age, sex, and size, and how active you are: 1,600 calories is about right for many sedentary women and some older adults; 2,200 calories is about right for most children, teenage girls, active women, and many sedentary men. Women who are pregnant or breastfeeding may need somewhat more. For teenage boys, many active men, and some very active women, 2,800 calories is about right.

For younger children, it's hard to know. If you're unsure, check with your doctor. Preschool children require the same variety of foods as older family members do, but may need less than 1,600 calories. For fewer calories, they can eat smaller servings. However, it is very important that they have the equivalent of 2 cups of milk a day.

How many servings are right for me?

That depends on the number of calories you need, but almost everyone should have at least the lowest number of servings in the ranges provided: 6 to 11 servings from the bread group; 2 to 4 from the fruit group; 3 to 5 from the vegetable group; 2 to 3 from the meat group; and 2 to 3 from the milk group.

How much fat can I have?

The USDA Dietary Guidelines recommend that Americans limit fat in their diets to 30 percent of calories. You will get up to half this fat even if you pick the lowest fat choices from each food group and add no fat to your foods in preparation or at the table. These guidelines translate to: 53 grams of fat in a 1,600 calorie diet; 73 grams of fat in a 2,200 calorie diet; and 93 grams of fat in a 2,800 calorie diet.

Saturated fat—from meat and dairy products and in some vegetable fats such as coconut, palm, and palm kernel oils—should be limited to less than 10 percent of calories (or one-third of total fat intake). Eating too much saturated fat raises blood cholesterol levels in many people, increasing their risk for heart disease.

Are fats and cholesterol the same thing?

No. Cholesterol is a fatlike substance present in all animal foods—meat, poultry, fish, milk and milk products, and egg yolks.

Do I have to give up salt?

No. But most people eat more than they need. Some health authorities say that sodium intake should not be more than 2,400 to 3,000 milligrams a day (1 teaspoon of salt provides about 2,000 mg of sodium).

What about sugars?

Sugars include white sugar, brown sugar, raw sugar, corn syrup, honey, and molasses; they supply calories and little else nutritionally. Try to limit your added sugars to 6 teaspoons a day if you eat about 1,600 calories, 12 teaspoons a day at 2,200 calories, or 18 teaspoons at 2,800 calories.

Added sugars are in products like candy and soft drinks, as well as jams, jellies, and sugars you add at the table.

Why are breads, cereals, rice, and pasta important?

Because they provide complex carbohydrates (starches), which are an important source of energy, especially in low-fat diets. They also provide vitamins, minerals, and fiber.

What do vegetables provide?

Vegetables provide vitamins, such as vitamins A and C, folic acid, and minerals, such as iron and magnesium. They are naturally low in fat and also provide fiber.

Why are fruits important?

Fruits and fruit juices provide important amounts of vitamins A and C and potassium. They are low in fat and sodium.

What do meat, poultry, fish, and other foods in the same group add to the diet?

Protein, B vitamins, iron, and zinc. For low-fat choices: Choose lean meat, poultry without skin, fish, dry beans, and peas; prepare meats by trimming the fat you can see, or by broiling or roasting (instead of frying). Go easy on egg yolks—they are high in cholesterol; and eat nuts and seeds in moderation (they're high in fat).

Why are milk products important?

Milk provides protein, vitamins, and minerals. Milk, yogurt, and cheese are the best sources of calcium. For low-fat selections: Choose skim milk and nonfat yogurt often; choose "part skim" or low-fat cheeses when available and lower-fat milk desserts, like ice milk or frozen yogurt. Go easy on high-fat cheese and ice cream.

Source: *The Food Guide Pyramid,* a brochure prepared by the Human Nutrition Information Service, USDA, Home and Garden Bulletin Number 252. For more information, write: U.S. Department of Agriculture, Human Nutrition Information Service, 6505 Belcrest Road, Hyattsville, MD 20782.

Freezing

Can any food be frozen?

Just about any food. Cans of food or eggs in shells cannot, but once the food—ham, for example—is out of the can, you may freeze it.

Remember, though, that just because food can be frozen doesn't mean it will taste good; that's the case with mayonnaise, cream sauce, and lettuce. Also, raw meat and poultry maintain their quality longer than do their cooked counterparts because moisture is lost during cooking.

Is frozen food safe?

Yes. Food stored constantly at 0°F will always be safe. Only the quality suffers with lengthy freezer storage.

How does freezing work to keep food safe?

Freezing food slows down the movement of its molecules. That means that microbes enter a dormant phase, which prevents the growth of micro-organisms. (It is these microorganisms that cause both food spoilage and foodborne illness.)

Does freezing destroy bacteria and parasites?

No. At 0°F, it just inactivates the bacteria, yeast, and molds present in food. This means that food, once thawed, has active microbes that can multiply and lead to foodborne illness, which is why it's important to handle thawed items as you would fresh food. While some parasites can be destroyed by subzero freezing (under strictly supervised government conditions), home freezing usually cannot be counted on to do so. Only thorough cooking destroys bacteria and parasites.

Does freezing destroy nutrients?

No. In meat and poultry products, there's little change.

What about enzymes?

Enzyme activity can lead to the deterioration of food quality. Most vegetables that freeze well are low in acid and require a brief, partial cooking to prevent deterioration. This process is called *blanching*. Such partial cooking before freezing can be done in boiling water or in a microwave oven. After blanching, the vegetables should be chilled quickly, then frozen.

Enzyme activity does not affect frozen meats or fish. Nor does it harm frozen fruits, whose acids neutralize the enzymes.

What does freezer burn look like? Is it unsafe?

Freezer burn appears as grayish-brown, leathery spots and is caused by air reaching the surface of the food. It's not unsafe; it just makes food dry in spots. Cut freezer-burned portions away, either before or after cooking the food. Heavily freezer-burned foods have to be discarded for quality reasons.

What's the proper way to package food I intend to freeze?

It's safe to freeze meat or poultry directly in its supermarket wrapping, but this type of wrap is permeable to air. Unless you plan to use the food in a month or two, overwrap the package—using airtight heavy-duty foil, plastic wrap, freezer paper, or by placing the package inside a plastic bag.

Use these same materials to repackage family packs into smaller portions for freezing or to freeze foods from opened packages. Note that you don't have to rinse meat and poultry before freezing and that you can freeze unopened vacuum packages as is. If a package has accidentally torn or has opened during freezing, overwrap or rewrap it; it's still safe to use.

What kinds of color changes can I expect?

The bright red color of meat as purchased usually turns to dark or pale brown depending on its variety. This may be due to lack of oxygen, freezer burn, or abnormally long storage. Freezing doesn't usually cause color change in poultry, but the bones and the meat near those bones can become dark. Bone darkening is the result of pigment seeping through the porous bones of young poultry into the surrounding tissues when poultry meat is frozen and thawed.

The dulling of color in frozen vegetables and cooked foods is usually the result of excessive drying due to improper packaging or over-lengthy storage.

What's the best and safest way to go about freezing?

Freeze food as quickly as possible to maintain its quality. Rapid freezing prevents undesirably large ice crystals from forming throughout the product. Slow freezing creates large, disruptive ice crystals. During thawing, these crystals damage cells and dissolve emulsions. This causes meat to "drip" and lose its juiciness. Emulsions such as mayonnaise or cream will separate and appear curdled.

Ideally, a food 2 inches thick should freeze completely in about two hours. If your home freezer has a "quick-freeze" shelf, use it. Never stack packages to be frozen. Instead, spread them out in one layer on various shelves, stacking them only after they've been frozen solid.

If your freezing compartment can't maintain zero degrees, or if the door is opened frequently, use it for short-term food storage. Eat those foods as soon as possible for best quality. For long-term storage, use a free-standing freezer set at 0°F or below. Keep a thermometer in your freezing compartment or freezer to check the temperature.

For how long can I freeze food?

Freezing keeps food safe almost indefinitely, so recommended storage times are for quality only. With this in mind, the following storage times apply: ham, hot dogs, lunch meats—1 to 2 months; soups and stews—2 to 3 months; whole poultry (uncooked)—12 months; poultry parts (uncooked)—9 months; ground meat (uncooked)—3 to 4 months; steak or chops (uncooked)—4 to 6 months; casseroles, bacon, and sausage—1 to 2 months.

Can I cook frozen food directly without thawing?

Yes, but it will take longer—about one and a half times longer than the usual cooking time. Discard any wrapping or absorbent paper from meat or poultry. Make sure to read the label of the USDA-inspected frozen meat and poultry products. Some foods, such as prestuffed whole birds, *must* be cooked from the frozen state to ensure a safely cooked product. When cooking whole poultry, remove the giblet pack from the cavity as soon as you can loosen it (giblets must be cooked separately).

After a power outage, how long does frozen food stay safe?

If the door of a fully packed freezer is kept shut, about two days; for a half-packed freezer, about one day. The freezing compartment in a refrigerator may not keep foods frozen as long. If the freezer is not full, quickly group packages together so they will retain the cold more effectively. Separate meat and poultry items from other foods in case they begin to thaw; their juices won't drip onto other foods.

For short-term power outages—less than six hours—leave the door closed unless the power returns. If the outage lasts longer, you may want to put dry ice, block ice, or bags of ice in the freezer, or transfer your food to a friend's freezer until power is restored. Use an appliance thermometer to monitor the temperature.

If it's freezing outside, don't be tempted to use the great outdoors as your freezer. Food stored outdoors is exposed to the sun, environmental contamination, and roaming animals and birds—so keep it indoors.

When the power goes back on, how do I know if my food is safe?

Check each item's condition and temperature. If food is partially frozen, or has ice crystals, or is as cold as it would be in your refrigerator (40°F), it's safe to refreeze or use. *Discard foods that have been warmer than 40°F for more than 2 hours. Also throw out any foods that have been contaminated by raw meat juices.* Dispose of soft or melted ice cream for quality's sake.

I left canned goods in my car and they froze. How do I determine their safety?

Accidentally frozen cans, such as those left in a car or basement in subzero temperatures, can present health problems. If the cans are merely frozen—and you are sure the swelling is caused by freezing—they may still be usable. Let the can thaw in the refrigerator before opening. If the product doesn't look or smell normal, throw it out. *Do not taste it!* If it looks and smells normal (and if the seams haven't rusted or burst), immediately cook the contents by boiling for 10 to 20 minutes.

Source: *Focus On: Freezing* (December 1994), U.S. Department of Agriculture, Food Safety Inspection Service consumer publication. For more information, call the USDA Meat and Poultry Hotline at (800) 535-4555, 10 A.M. to 4:00 P.M. (EST). Food safety recordings run 24 hours a day using touch-tone phone. Or write: Information and Legislative Affairs, Food Safety and Inspection Service, Room 1175—South Building, Washington, DC 20250; phone: (202) 720-7943; fax: (202) 720-1843.

Healthy Heart Diet

Are there risk factors for heart disease that I can do something about?

Yes. High blood pressure, high blood cholesterol, smoking, obesity, diabetes, and physical inactivity are all risk factors for heart disease. The three most important ones are high blood pressure, smoking, and high blood cholesterol; each one, on the average, doubles your chance of developing heart disease. Regular exercise and good nutrition are essential to reducing your high blood pressure, high blood cholesterol, and excess weight.

Is the most effective dietary way to lower my blood cholesterol to eat foods low in cholesterol?

No. Reducing the amount of blood cholesterol in your diet is important; however, eating foods low in saturated fat is the most effective dietary way to lower blood cholesterol levels—along with eating less total fat and cholesterol.

Which foods are low in saturated fat?

Grains, fruits, and vegetables; low-fat or skim milk and 1 percent milk; lean cuts of meat; fish; and poultry.

Which foods are high in saturated fat?

Animal products such as butter, cheese, whole milk, ice cream, cream, and fatty meats. Saturated fats are also found in some vegetable oils—coconut, palm, and palm kernel oils.

Is there a way to prepare meat that cuts down on fat?

Yes. Trim fat from meat before cooking. Bake or broil meat, rather than frying it; use less fat and oil; and take the skin off chicken and turkey.

What's the best way to lose weight?

The best way to lose weight is to increase your physical activity and to cut back on calories. You burn off calories by exercising. Cutting down on calories—especially calories from fat—is key to losing weight. Combining this with a regular physical activity, like walking, cycling, jogging, or swimming, can both help you lose weight and maintain weight loss.

Losing weight, if you are overweight, may also reduce your blood pressure, lower your LDL-cholesterol ("bad" cholesterol), and raise your HDL-cholesterol.

To lower my blood cholesterol level, do I have to give up meat?

No. Although some red meat is high in saturated fat and cholesterol, which can raise your blood cholesterol, you do not need to stop eating it or any other single food. Red meat is an important source of protein, iron, and other vitamins and minerals. You should choose lean cuts of meat with the fat trimmed and watch your portion sizes (no more than 6 ounces of meat a day—the size of two decks of playing cards).

Is it true that fish oil supplements reduce blood cholesterol levels?

No. Fish oils are a source of omega-3 fatty acids, which are a type of polyunsaturated fat. Fish oil supplements generally do not reduce blood cholesterol levels. Further, the effect of long-term use of fish oil supplements is unknown. However, fish is a good choice because it is low in saturated fat.

What kinds of changes can I expect if I eat less fat?

Generally, your blood cholesterol level should begin to drop a few weeks after you start. How much your level drops depends on the amounts of saturated fat and cholesterol you used to eat, how high your blood cholesterol is, how much weight you lose if you are overweight, and how your body responds to the changes you make. Over time, you may reduce your blood cholesterol level by 10 to 50 mg/dL or even more.

I heard that all vegetable oils help lower blood cholesterol. Is this true?

No. Most vegetable oils—canola, corn, olive, safflower, soybean, and sunflower oils—contain chiefly monounsaturated and polyunsaturated fats, which can help lower blood cholesterol when used in place of saturated fats. However, a few vegetable oils—coconut, palm, and palm kernel oils—contain more saturated than unsaturated fat.

What kind of fat does margarine contain?

A special kind of fat called *trans fat* is formed when vegetable oil is hardened to become margarine or shortening, through a process known as hydrogenation. The harder the margarine or shortening, the more likely it is to contain more trans fat.

What kind of margarine should I pick?

Choose margarine containing liquid vegetable oil as the first ingredient. Just be sure to limit the total amount of any fats or oils, since even those that are unsaturated are rich sources of calories.

If I get my fat intake under control and lower my blood cholesterol, what else can I do if I also need to lower my blood pressure?

According to the National High Blood Pressure Education Program, the following preventive measures show promise: controlling weight, increasing physical activity; and, in addition to other dietary factors, reducing sodium intake and avoiding excessive alcohol consumption.

How much salt is too much?

More than 6 grams of sodium chloride (table salt) daily.

How much alcohol is too much?

More than two drinks a day.

Sources: The National High Blood Pressure Education Program and the National Cholesterol Education Program, both divisions of the National Heart, Lung and Blood Institute (NHLBI), U.S. Department of Health and Human Services. For more information, contact: NHLBI Information Center, P.O. Box 30105, Bethesda, MD 20824-0105; phone: (301) 251-1222; fax: (301) 251-1223. Or: American Heart Association; (800) AHA-USA [(800) 242-8721].

Kitchen Safety

How cold should I keep my refrigerator?

At 41°F (or 5°C) or less. To make sure, test the temperature with a thermometer and, if needed, adjust the control dial. The idea is to slow the growth of most bacteria. The temperature won't kill all the bacteria, but it can keep them from multiplying. The fewer there are, the less likely you are to get sick.

How often should I clean my kitchen sink drain and how do I go about it?

The kitchen sink drain, disposal, and connecting pipe are often overlooked, but they should be sanitized periodically by pouring down the following solution: 1 teaspoon chlorine bleach in 1 quart of water. You can also use a commercial kitchen cleaning agent according to product directions. Proper sanitizing will prevent food particles from getting trapped in an ideal environment for bacterial growth.

What's the proper way to safely use my cutting board?

The first rule is: Never allow raw meat, poultry, and fish to come into contact with other foods. Second, the cutting board should be washed with soap and hot water, then sanitized with a mild bleach solution. Improper washing with a damp cloth, for example, will not remove bacteria.

What about my kitchen counters?

Bleach and commercial kitchen cleaning agents are the best sanitizers, but only if they're diluted according to the product's directions. Hot water and soap does a good job, but it may not kill all strains of bacteria. Water alone can get rid of visible dirt but not bacteria.

Be sure to keep dishcloths and sponges clean too, because when wet they harbor bacteria.

I was taught never to leave dishes in the sink. Why?

Because dishes that sit in water, combined with food particles, create a kind of "soup" in which bacteria multiply. When washing dishes by hand, try to do so within two hours. It's also best to air-dry them so you don't handle them while they're wet.

What's the proper way to defrost?

Thaw foods in the refrigerator, or, if on the counter, make sure to thaw food in watertight plastic bags submerged in cold water (water should be changed every 30 minutes). The cold water slows bacterial growth.

When microwaving, follow package instructions. Leave about 2 inches between the food and the inside surface of the microwave to allow heat to circulate. Smaller items will defrost more evenly than larger pieces of food. Foods defrosted in the microwave should be cooked immediately after thawing.

How long can I leave hot foods out after cooking?

Hot food should be refrigerated within two hours after cooking. Otherwise, throw it away. Don't taste-test it, because even a small amount of contaminated food can cause illness.

How long can I keep leftovers?

The general rule is that you can refrigerate and use them for three to five days. If in doubt, though, throw it out. It's a good idea to date leftovers so you can use them within a safe period.

What's the safest way to eat hamburgers?

Cook them until they are no longer red in the middle and until the juices run clear. That's not going to be the case with rare or even medium hamburgers.

The internal temperature should be at least 160°F in order to prevent food-borne illness. It's usually the well-done meats that reach that temperature.

To be on the safe side, check the internal temperature of your meat, fish, and poultry with a thermometer. To do so with microwaved food, make sure to follow directions, including the standing time (either in or out of the microwave). Microwave cooking creates pockets of heat in the food that will spread out more evenly if the food is allowed to stand.

What's the safest way to test products I'm baking with eggs?

Consider substituting pasteurized eggs for raw eggs. They are usually sold in the grocer's refrigerated dairy case and carry no salmonella risk. That way, you can safely sample homemade dough or batter. Commercial cookie dough is not a food hazard because all commercial products are made with pasteurized eggs.

How often should I wash my hands?

Before and after handling food, especially raw meat poultry and fish. If you have an infection or cut on your hands, wear rubber or plastic gloves. Make sure to wash gloved hands as often as bare hands because the gloves can pick up bacteria.

Sources: Pamela Kurtzweil, Public Affairs Specialist, FDA. *FDA Consumer* magazine, "Can Your Kitchen Pass the Food Safety Test?" (October 1995). For more information, call the FDA Consumer Information Line at (800) 532-4440, 10 A.M. to 4 P.M. EST (Mon. thru Fri.). Or contact: Food and Drug Administration, 5600 Fisher's Lane HFI-40, Rockville, MD 20857; phone: (301) 443-5094; fax: (301) 443-9057.

Poultry and Game

Do bacteria from poultry contaminate the counter and everything they contact? Can bacteria pass from object to object or into cuts on my hands?

Poultry, like all raw foods of animal origin, carries salmonella and other bacteria. It should be handled carefully to prevent cross-contamination. Never let raw poultry or its juices contact cooked foods or foods that will be eaten raw, such as salad ingredients. Salmonella bacteria must be eaten to cause illness. They cannot enter the body through a cut on your hand. Refrigeration slows the growth of salmonella, and thorough cooking destroys it.

After I left the grocery, I did more shopping. The turkey roast was in my van for three hours on a 90° day. Is it safe?

Absolutely not. Don't leave poultry in a hot car for more than 30 minutes. The supermarket should be your last stop before heading home, and perishable foods like turkey should be the last you choose before checkout. Unload perishables from your car first and refrigerate them immediately.

Sometimes when I buy chicken, it looks frozen. But by the time I get it home, it is defrosted. Is it safe to freeze?

Yes. What you have observed is only frozen surface tissues. The entire chicken is not frozen. Processors quickly chill and store fresh chicken at 28° to 32°F to prevent the rapid growth of bacteria and to increase its shelf life.

I've had a thawed turkey breast in the refrigerator eight days. Is it safe to cook? I'm 90 and I don't want to get sick.

Senior citizens, pregnant women, very young children, and people who suffer from chronic illnesses are especially vulnerable to foodborne bacteria. But for persons of any age, eight days is too long to refrigerate raw or cooked poultry. The safe time limit for refrigerating raw poultry is one to two days; three to four days if it's cooked. Your turkey may have begun to spoil. Even without spoilage indicators like an off-odor or sticky surface, harmful bacteria may be present. Discard it.

I'm concerned about the dark color of meat around the bones of chicken. How do you prevent it?

First, it's perfectly safe to eat chicken meat that turns dark during cooking. The darkening around bones occurs primarily in young broiler-fryers seven to nine weeks old. Since their bones have not calcified completely, pigment from the bone marrow can seep through the porous bones. When the chicken is cooked, the pigment turns dark. Try buying a more mature baking hen that weighs 5 to 7 pounds, or debone the chicken before cooking.

How long is it safe to keep a turkey or whole game bird in the freezer?

It's safe to keep food in the freezer indefinitely as long as it stays frozen. But for quality, cook a whole turkey within one year; it's safe after this but not as flavorful. Cured meats don't tend to freeze well from a quality standpoint. It's best to use them within a few months.

Source: Deli/Prepared Meats Committee of the National Live Stock and Meat Board/USDA Meat and Poultry Hotline—(800) 535-4555.

Preparing a Turkey

What's the best way to thaw a turkey?

Refrigerator thawing is recommended. However, if short on time, you can submerge the turkey in cold water. Thawing turkey at room temperature allows bacterial growth and is *not recommended*.

Refrigerator thawing: Thaw breast side up in its unopened wrapper on a tray in the refrigerator. Allow at least one day of thawing for every 4 pounds of turkey.

Cold-water thawing: Place breast down in its unopened wrapper in cold water to cover. Change the water every 30 minutes to keep surface cold. Estimate thawing time to be 30 minutes per pound for whole turkey.

What's the best way to roast a turkey?

1. Place thawed or fresh turkey, breast up, on a flat rack in a shallow pan, 2–2½ inches deep.
2. Insert oven-safe meat thermometer into the thickest part of the thigh.
3. Brush or rub skin with oil to prevent drying of the skin and to enhance the golden color.
4. Place in a preheated 325°F oven.
5. When the skin is a golden color and the turkey is about two-thirds done, shield the breast loosely with a tent of lightweight foil to prevent its over-cooking.

Use the following roasting schedule as a guideline (start checking for doneness one half hour before recommended end times):

Net Weight (pounds)	Unstuffed (hours)	Stuffed (hours)
10–18	3–3½	3¾–4½
18–22	3½–4	4½–5
22–24	4–4½	4½–5
24–30	4½–5	5½–6¼

How do you recommend handling a turkey so it's safe to eat?

Follow these food safety guidelines (refer to specific categories for additional directions):

- Thaw frozen turkey in the refrigerator or cold water.
- Keep thawed or fresh turkey in refrigerator.
- Prevent juices from dripping onto other foods in the refrigerator by placing wrapped turkey on a tray.
- Thawed turkey may be kept in a refrigerator up to four days before cooking.
- Roast fresh turkey as soon as possible, but no later than the "Use by" date on the packaging.
- Place raw poultry on nonporous surfaces; these are easy to clean. Avoid wooden cutting boards.
- Use paper towels, not cloth, to dry off turkey and wipe up juices.
- Stuff turkey just before roasting, *not* the night before.
- Wash your hands, surfaces, and the utensils touched by raw poultry and its juices with hot, soapy water.
- Use cooking methods that allow the turkey to reach an internal temperature of 140°F in less than four hours. Avoid low roasting temperatures or partial cooking methods.
- Use a meat thermometer to determine turkey's doneness.
- Store turkey, stuffing, gravy, broth, and other cooked foods properly within two hours after cooking.

How can leftover turkey be stored safely?

Within two hours after roasting, remove stuffing from turkey and carve the meat off the bones, then place in refrigerator or freezer.

Refrigerator storage: Wrap turkey slices and stuffing separately and use within three days.

Frozen storage: Wrap in heavy foil, freezer wrap, or place in freezer container; for optimum taste, use stuffing within one month and turkey within two months.

Where does the meat thermometer go?

The tip of any oven-safe meat thermometer should be placed in the thigh muscle just above and beyond the lower part of the thigh bone, but not touching the bone, and pointing toward the body. Turn the thermometer so it can be read while the turkey is in the oven.

How do you know when the turkey is done?

Turkey is done when the meat thermometer reaches the following temperatures:

180° to 185°F deep in the thigh; also, juices should be clear, not pink, when thigh muscle is pierced deeply

170° to 175°F in the thickest part of the breast, just above the rib bones

160° to 165°F in the center of the stuffing, if turkey is stuffed

What do you need to do to a turkey just before roasting it?

1. Remove original plastic wrapper from thawed or fresh turkey.
2. Remove the neck and giblets from the body and neck cavities.
3. Drain juices and blot turkey dry with paper towels.
4. Stuff the turkey (optional) just before roasting. Ingredients may be prepared earlier, but keep moist and dry ingredients separate and combine just before stuffing.
5. Return legs to tucked position, if untucked.
6. Insert oven-safe meat thermometer into the deepest part of the thigh.
7. Brush with oil to prevent drying of the skin.
8. Follow roasting directions on packet.

What's the proper way to stuff a turkey?

Generations of Americans have been enjoying turkeys—stuffed and unstuffed. Whether you choose to stuff your turkey or cook stuffing in a casserole dish is a matter of personal preference. As with any preparation involving raw food ingredients, it's imperative to follow proper food safety and handling procedures carefully to ensure a safe and picture-perfect turkey every time. For consumers who choose to stuff their turkey, we recommend the following four guidelines.

- Prepare the stuffing *just before* placing in turkey. Use only cooked ingredients in stuffing—sauté vegetables, use only cooked meats and seafood (oysters), and use pasteurized egg products instead of raw eggs. Place prepared stuffing in turkey *just before* roasting. Do not stuff the turkey the night before roasting.

- Stuff both neck and body cavities of *completely thawed* turkey, allowing ½ to ¾ cup of stuffing per pound of turkey. Do not pack stuffing tightly in turkey.

- Always use a meat thermometer. The turkey is done when the thigh temperature reaches 180°F on a meat thermometer inserted into the thickest part of the thigh next to body, not touching bone. Move the thermometer to the center of stuffing; temperature should be 160° to 165°F. When the stuffed turkey is done, remove from the oven and let stand 15 to 20 minutes. This stand time provides an added measure of safety for stuffing temperature to reach 165°F.

- When the turkey is cooked on an outdoor grill, water smoker, or by fast cooking methods where the bird typically gets done faster than the stuffing, it is recommended that the turkey be cooked unstuffed.

Should I buy a fresh or frozen turkey?

Selecting a fresh or frozen turkey is your choice. Fresh turkeys need no thawing and are ready to cook. Frozen turkeys can be purchased months in advance, but plan enough thawing time before roasting.

Is it necessary to baste a turkey?

No. Basting throughout the roasting process is unnecessary. Pouring juices over a turkey's surface while it roasts will not make the meat any juicier. The liquid penetrates only about ⅛ to ¼ of an inch beneath the skin, and most of the juice will run off into the pan. Opening the oven door periodically to baste a turkey can cool the oven and possibly lengthen the roasting time. Before roasting, lightly coat the turkey's skin with oil, shortening, or vegetable cooking spray to prevent the skin from drying.

Source: Butterball Turkey Talk-Line. The preceding questions were the ten most popular during the 1995 holiday season. A total of more than 200,000 inquiries were made. The Talk-Line provides specially trained home economists to answer questions. It can be accessed during November and December by dialing (800) 323-4848. The service is provided to Butterball Turkey by Edelman Public Relations, 200 E. Randolph, (63rd floor), Chicago, IL 60601; (312) 240-3000.

Red Meat

Is it safe to eat rare hamburgers and rare steak?

Ground meat by its nature can present risks because it has much more surface area to be exposed and handled. In addition, during the grinding process these surface bacteria can be transferred to the interior of the meat. It therefore needs to be cooked more than you would a steak.

All forms of ground beef, including patties, loaves, meatballs, and crumbles, should be cooked to medium—160°F—doneness. To be safe, a steak should be brought to a temperature of at least 145°, medium or medium well done. A roast needs to be cooked to at least 145°, but 160° is really better.

How do I know the ground beef I am purchasing is fresh?

A bright, cherry red color indicates fresh ground beef. However, fresh ground beef does go through a number of color changes during its shelf life.

- A darker, purplish red color is typical of vacuum-packaged ground beef or the interior of packaged ground beef that has not been exposed to oxygen.
- Once exposed to oxygen, ground beef will turn from darker red to bright red.
- With extended exposure to oxygen, beef will take on a brown color. These color changes are normal. Ground beef remains wholesome and safe to eat if purchased by the "Sell by" date on the package label.

How long is it safe to keep a smoked ham in the refrigerator? Will a vacuum-packaged ham keep longer?

Both plastic-wrapped and vacuum-packaged hams must be refrigerated. A plastic-wrapped ham will keep about one week. The smoking process adds flavor but does not preserve the ham. A vacuum-packed ham should be consumed by the "Use by" date, or within one week after the "Sell by" date listed on the package.

How long is it safe to keep fresh meat in the refrigerator? I was always told to use it within several days, yet supermarkets seem to keep meat for a week or so. Why the difference?

Ground beef and poultry should be used within one to two days. Red meats can be stored in the home refrigerator for three to five days. Commercial refrigerators can safely store meat for longer periods because they are significantly colder than home refrigerators. Meats are held in commercial refrigerators or lockers in the back of the store until rotated out to display cases for purchase.

Sometimes when I make a meat loaf or other ground beef dish, it still appears pink even though it has cooked the specified length of time. Why is it still pink and how do I tell if a ground beef dish is cooked?

Due to the natural nitrate content of certain ingredients like onions, celery, and bell peppers, ground beef dishes such as meat loaf may remain pink in the center even if a 160°F internal temperature is reached. Always check the temperature with a meat thermometer to make sure it reaches 160°F.

Sources: National Live Stock and Meat Board/USDA Meat and Poultry Hotline;(800) 535-4555.

Safe Defrosting

What's the safest way to thaw frozen food?

There are actually three safe ways to defrost food: in the refrigerator; in cold water; and in the microwave (cooking must follow immediately).

What's unsafe?

Thawing on your kitchen counter for more than two hours or overnight is unsafe. The center of the package may still be frozen, but the food's outer layer will be in the "danger zone"—between 40°F and 140°. This is the zone in which bacteria multiply rapidly.

What should I consider when thawing food in the refrigerator?

Plan ahead. Small amounts of frozen food—one pound of ground meat or boneless chicken breasts—require a full day to thaw.

Should I take into account my refrigerator's temperature?

Yes. Food takes longer to thaw in a refrigerator set at 35°F than one set at 40°. Also, glass shelves retard the thawing process longer than wire shelves. Finally, food placed in the coldest part of the refrigerator will take longer.

After ground meat or poultry is thawed in my refrigerator, for how long is it safe?

For another day or two. Red meat should last for three to five days.

Can I refreeze meat or poultry that's been defrosted in the refrigerator?

Yes. If you haven't cooked it and want to refreeze it, do so within the safe period (mentioned above). There might be some loss of quality, however.

I've heard that cold-water thawing is faster than refrigerator thawing. Is this true?

Yes. But it requires more attention. For cold-water thawing, make sure the food is in a leakproof package or plastic bag. If the bag leaks, bacteria from the surrounding environment could be introduced into the food.

Proper thawing requires you to immerse the bag in cold tap water and to check the water frequently to make sure it stays cold. Change the water every 30 minutes until the food is thawed. After thawing, refrigerate until you're ready to use it.

Can I refreeze food that's been thawed by the cold-water method?

No. Not unless you cook it first.

What about microwave thawing?

You must plan to cook the food immediately after thawing with a microwave, because some areas of the food might become warm and begin to cook during microwave thawing. Partially cooked food contains bacteria that haven't been destroyed.

Source: *The Big Thaw—Safe Defrosting Methods*, U.S. Department of Agriculture, Food Safety and Inspection Service publication. For more information, call the USDA Meat and Poultry Hotline at (800) 535-4555. Or contact: Information and Legislative Affairs, Food Safety and Inspection Service, Room 1175—South Building, Washington, DC 20250; phone: (202) 720-7943; fax: (202) 720-1843.

Vegetarian Diets

What kinds of vegetarians are there?

Vegans, who eat no animal foods; ovo-vegetarians, who eat eggs but no dairy food or animal flesh; semivegetarians, who eat dairy foods, eggs, chicken, and fish, but no other animal flesh; pesco-vegetarians, who eat dairy foods, eggs, and fish, but no other animal flesh; lacto-ovo-vegetarians, who eat dairy foods and eggs, but not animal flesh; and lacto-vegetarians, who eat dairy foods, but no animal flesh or eggs.

Can veggies prevent cancer?

Vegetables from the cabbage family may reduce cancer risk. Diets low in fat and high in fiber-rich foods may reduce the risk of cancers of the colon and rectum, and diets rich in foods containing vitamin A, vitamin C, and beta-carotene, such as fruits and vegetables, may reduce the risk of certain cancers.

Can veggies prevent heart disease?

Plant foods low in fat content may give protection against coronary heart disease.

Are vegetarians healthier?

Some data point to the finding that vegetarians are at lesser risk for obesity, atonic (reduced muscle tone) constipation, lung cancer, and alcoholism. Evidence is good that the risks for hypertension, coronary artery disease, type II diabetes, and gallstones are lower.

Are there any risks to a vegetarian diet?

Vegetarians who abstain from all dairy products or animal flesh face the greatest nutritional risks because some nutrients naturally occur mainly or almost exclusively in animal foods. For this reason, careful planning is necessary to include enough calcium, riboflavin, iron, and vitamin D.

For vegetarians who eat no meat, fish, poultry, or dairy foods, what are the nonanimal sources for those nutrients found to be lacking?

Fortified soy milk and cereals for vitamin B_{12}: fortified margarine and exposure to sunshine.

For vitamin D: tofu, broccoli, seeds, nuts, kale, bok choy, peas, beans, greens, calcium-enriched grain products, and lime-processed tortillas for calcium.

For iron: peas and beans, tofu, green leafy vegetables, dried fruit, whole grains, and iron-fortified cereals and breads, especially whole wheat (absorption is improved by vitamin C, found in citrus fruits and juices, tomatoes, strawberries, broccoli, peppers, dark green leafy vegetables, and potatoes with skins).

For zinc: whole grains (especially the germ and the bran), whole-wheat bread, legumes, nuts, and tofu.

What about protein?

Nearly every animal food, including egg whites and milk, provides all eight of the essential amino acids in the balance needed by humans and therefore constitutes "complete" protein.

Plant foods contain fewer of these amino acids than animal foods, but all plant foods, including fruit, contain some protein. By eating a variety of fruits, vegetables, and grains, even vegans who don't eat dairy products or animal flesh can get enough of this nutrient.

To make sure you're getting enough protein and to improve the quality of that protein, combine legumes such as black-eyed peas, chickpeas, peas, peanuts, lentils, sprouts, and black, broad, kidney, lima, mung, navy, and soy beans with grains such as rice, wheat, corn, rye, bulgur, oats, millet, barley, and buckwheat.

There are also foods made to look like meats (protein analogs) such as hot dogs, sausage, and bacon. These are usually made from soybeans and many are fortified with vitamin B_{12}.

Source: "Vegetarian Diets: The Pluses and the Pitfalls," by Dixie Farley in an article from *FDA Consumer* (May 1992). For more information, call or write: The American Dietetic Association, 216 West Jackson Blvd., Suite 800, Chicago, IL 60606; (800) 366-1655; (312) 899-0040.

INDULGENCES

——◇——

**Beer • Chocolate
Cigars • Coffee
Coca-Cola
Pipe Smoking • Wine**

Beer

What country consumes the most beer per capita? And where does the United States fall in this ranking?

Germany is first. In 1991 (the last time this ranking was done) the United States was 13th, with 87.4 liters per capita. A recent poll done by the Gallup Organization showed that Denmark is the country where the most households drank beer—in 1996 a whopping 85 percent consumed the beverage. The United States was actually lowest, with 44 percent. Germany was at 72 percent, the third highest, after Japan at 74 percent.

What's the difference between malt liquor and the new ice beers? I've heard that they're actually the same thing.

Ice beer is high-alcohol liquor, so technically it is malt liquor, because the United States government stipulates that any beverage with over 4 percent alcohol is no longer beer, but malt liquor, ale, or stout. However, ice beer and malt liquor (such as Mickey's) are brewed using different processes. Malt liquor is high-gravity beer, brewed at 8 percent, then watered back to 5 percent. It is not made with an ice process.

What is the most popular beer in the United States?

Budweiser is the most popular. Bud Light is second, and Miller Lite third. Budweiser is also the most popular beer in the world.

What is the best seasonal beer available in the United States?

Sierra Nevada Celebration. It is available in 38 states during the fall.

What is the worst beer?

Any cheap beer that's not a major brand. They often contain food coloring, chemicals, and other bad by-products. Your best bet is to stick with the major brands, which are brewed to very high standards. Miller Genuine Draft, Coors, and Bud are all excellent value for the money, and well crafted for the mainstream marketplace.

How big is the beer industry in the United States?

It is a $40 billion industry composed of 85 million beer drinkers. Approximately 5.9 billion gallons are sold each year. Per capita, wine consumption is 2.5 gallons, hard liquor is 2.5 gallons, and beer is an amazing 24 gallons!

What is a brewpub?

A brewpub brews and sells fresh, unpasteurized beer on the premises. There are currently 525 of them in America, and in a decade there will easily be 2,000, since the industry is growing at a rate of three a week. Brewpubs right now are a billion-dollar industry—1 percent of the total beer market. This percentage should grow to 12 to 18 percent in the next two decades.

What is a *fruit* beer?

Beer brewed with essence of raspberry, apricot, or other various fruits. Buffalo Bill's Brewpub in Hayward, California, sells a Pumpkin Ale, a spice beer made with with pumpkin, cinnamon, ginger, and cloves.

What percentage of beer is sold in cans/bottles/kegs?

Cans—58 percent
Bottles—31 percent (5 percent deposit bottles, 26 percent nonreturnables)
Kegs—11 percent

Do you really get a beer belly from drinking beer?

No, you get it from eating too much food with the beer.

Sources: Bill Owens, publisher/brewmaster, *American Brewer Magazine,* Hayward, CA; (800) 646-2701; www.ambrew.com.

Chocolate

What precisely is chocolate?

Chocolate is created by combining the cocoa bean, which is the seed of the tropical cacao tree, with other ingredients. The beans (about half cocoa solids, half cocoa butter) are dried, fermented, roasted, and processed into a liquid mass called *chocolate liquor* (nonalcoholic), which is further refined with additional cocoa butter, sugar, vanilla, and lecithin to create dark chocolate. Milk chocolate is created by adding condensed or powdered milk. When only the extracted cocoa butter (without the cocoa solids) is used, and sugar, milk solids, vanilla, and lecithin are added, you have white chocolate. Technically this is not real chocolate (and it does not taste like it, either) because of the omission of the cocoa solids that give chocolate its characteristic flavor and dark color.

What are the attributes of a truly great chocolate?

Just as wines and coffees have their degrees of excellence, so do cocoa beans. Great chocolate is a skillful blending of different varieties of top-quality beans of different geographical origins. A chocolate "grand cru" (also called "vintage" chocolate), like a great wine, should highlight the character of the particular cocoa beans used. The amount of sugar is an essential part of this process, as sugar should never mask or erase the character of the chocolate. A superb chocolate should have a relatively high cocoa content, with a proper balance between bitterness and sweetness; this process is risky and difficult to achieve. Godiva Chocolatier provides a list of ways to distinguish fine chocolate:

1. *Look at the chocolate.* It should have a satiny sheen. A soft shine is the result of a well-made chocolate that has been carefully handled.
2. *Break the chocolate.* It should crack evenly and without holes. A good "snap" indicates fine blending.
3. *Detect the fragrance.* Smell the fragrance of the fresh break. There should be a pleasant chocolate aroma.
4. *Feel the texture.* Melt the chocolate against the roof of your mouth with your tongue. A great chocolate will be velvety smooth. Any graininess indicates insufficient refining.
5. *Experience the flavor.* Chocolate should be tasted at room temperature in order to discern all the flavor. Roll the chocolate over your tongue, allowing the flavors to permeate your mouth. The initial taste would be a nutty, roasted chocolate flavor; sweetness mingled with this flavor should follow.

Additionally, like a great wine, the aroma of a grand cru chocolate (made from rare and "noble" beans) unfolds slowly in the mouth and lingers for a long time, as opposed to ordinary chocolate, whose aroma explodes immediately and disappears just as quickly.

Swiss, Belgian, French, or American chocolate—what's the difference?

Switzerland is usually considered to be unsurpassed in the quality of its milk chocolate, having invented it in 1875. The Swiss like their chocolate on the sweet side, and love milk chocolate and white chocolate. Belgium is best known for its medium-dark, relatively sweet chocolate, oriented to the popular taste and akin to the taste of chocolate in pastries. Belgians traditionally mold chocolates excessively, and use a lot of crème-fraiche interiors.

France generally takes a purist approach, offering the darkest chocolate with emphasis on a deep, less sweet, more complex chocolate flavor that lingers in the mouth.

America, the land of industrial mass production, has produced a wider proliferation of chocolate mixed with other ingredients (nuts, caramel, etc.) in the form of candy bars and confections than any other country in the world.

Who makes the most expensive chocolate in the world?

Chocolatier Ortrud Carstens says the most expensive is Valrhona from France It is found in fancy specialty food stores and costs from $3.00 to $6.50 per 100-gram bar. Valrhona makes exquisite dark chocolates of different blends using very rare cocoa beans from different provinces. The chocolate is stellar in quality and very multidimensional in taste. In professional circles, it is comparable to aged wines.

Is there a chocolate that's generally accepted as being the best to bake with?

Some experts recommend using *eating* chocolate in baked goods rather than cocoa powder or baking chocolate. This is because high-quality eating chocolate imparts a smoother, richer feeling, a more well-rounded and long-lingering chocolate flavor to the baked good. Baking chocolate is unsweetened chocolate liquor (about half cocoa solids and half cocoa butter as they occur naturally in the bean, minimally refined and therefore courser in texture). You can also buy baking chocolate with added ingredients such as vanilla, nuts, etc. If you do use baking chocolate, *Chocolatier* magazine generally recommends several brands in its recipe section:

Unsweetened: Baker's, Ghirardelli, Hershey's, or Nestlé
Swiss Dark/Bittersweet: Ghirardelli, Lindt Excellence, or Callebaut
Swiss Milk: Lindt

What's the explanation for the chocolate–sex–love connection?

According to Central American legend, chocolate came down from heaven as a gift from the god Quetzalcoatl. It has been imbued with strong ritual, alimentary, and sensual powers. Mayan priests drank it during religious ceremonies, and the Aztec emperor Montezuma is said to have drunk many potions daily. The claim was that chocolate sharpened perception, increased physical strength, and had intoxicating and aphrodisiac properties. In eighteenth-century Europe, chocolate was given to patients as a healing potion, and courtesans served it to their lovers as a sign of luxury and love.

These traditional claims have survived into today's lore: Chocolate between meals restores energy, and a box of chocolate at Valentine's Day still carries romantic significance. There is also a decade-old assertion tracing the romance of chocolate to one of its chemical components, phenylethylamine, that is identical to one released in the brain when people fall in love.

Can chocolate make you happier? Is there a physiological effect of chocolate on the brain? Why do we crave it?

Chocolate contains three constituents that could account for the "lift" it seems to provide: the alkaloids theobromine, caffeine, and sugar. The principal effect of theobromine is a diuretic one, and the concentration is not sufficient to account for much of the elation that we feel when eating chocolate. The concentration of caffeine, which is considerably less than coffee, could have a moderately stimulative effect. The relatively larger amount of sugar in eating chocolate, from a practical viewpoint, probably has more of a morale-boosting effect than either the theobromine and/or caffeine.

No one has come up with a reasonable scientific explanation of why we crave chocolate or why it makes us feel happy. One explanation is offered by Tim Moriarty, managing editor of *Chocolatier* magazine, is that chocolate is a food we associate with comfort and safety. As a part of all our childhoods, its flavors and aromas trigger strong and powerful sense memories. He points out, too, that chocolate is one of the few foods you can eat that has a very pleasant tactile sensation of melting in your mouth—it reaches melting point at 98.6°F.

How much caffeine does chocolate contain?

According to the American Dietetic Association and the FDA, caffeine levels are as follows:

Milk chocolate (1 oz.)	6 mg
Baking chocolate (1 oz.)	35 mg
By way of comparison:	
Coffee (1 cup)	93–153 mg
Tea (1 cup brewed)	44 mg
Soft drinks (12 oz.)	32–65 mg

Sources: Ortrud Carstens, artisan-chocolatier, Chocolates for the Connoisseur; Public Relations, Godiva Chocolatier; Tim Moriarty, Managing Editor, *Chocolatier* magazine.

Cigars

Should you take the band off before smoking a cigar?

The cigar band should never be removed unless, of course, the smoker is ashamed of the particular brand he is smoking. The band is sometimes glued on, and if removed there is a chance of damaging the delicate leaf of the cigar.

At what temperature should cigars be stored?

Some individuals prefer their cigars a little more moist, others like them drier. A good rule of thumb is to store cigars at 70/70, that is, humidity and temperature.

How much should one cut off the tip of a cigar before smoking it?

Only the thinnest membrane of the closed end, enough to get a sufficient draw. If too much is cut off, the cigar will unravel and fall apart.

Are hygrometers accurate in reading humidity level inside a humidor?

The only scientifically accurate hygrometer is a "hair" hygrometer, and the smallest ones are as big as a table humidor. Small-needle hygrometers should be calibrated and used as a secondary source. The proper way to check whether a humidor is humidifying properly is to feel the cigars stored inside. A properly humidified cigar should give a little when gentle pressure is applied with the thumb and forefinger, and then bounce back into shape.

Do humidors have to be lined with cedar wood?

The answer is no. Cedar is often used because of its ability to absorb humidity, helping to keep an environment of humidity more constant. There are other woods that perform as well, such as gaboon wood.

Why do cigars tend to fall apart when smoked in the wintertime?

To maintain constant humidity there must be constant temperature. When a properly moist cigar is placed in a cold, dry environment, the outer leaf—the wrapper—will quickly become dry, crack, and then fall apart.

What is Fidel Castro's favorite cigar?

The truth is that Fidel gave up smoking (publicly at least). When he did smoke, his favorite cigars were the Cohiba Lancero, Corona Especial, and the panatela sizes.

Why are Cuban cigars illegal in the United States?

The United States has had an embargo in place against Cuba since 1962, after Castro started to nationalize Cuban and foreign assets.

Do cigar smokers inhale the smoke?

No. Cigar smoke is meant to be savored in the mouth much as wine tasters take merely a sip of wine before expelling it.

Is cigar tobacco the same as cigarette tobacco?

Because of the longer fermentation process of the tobacco leaves, cigar tobacco is much lower in tar, nicotine, and acidity than cigarette tobacco.

Source: Jesse Jimenez, Davidoff of Geneva, 535 Madison Avenue, New York, NY 10022.

Coffee

How much caffeine does coffee contain?

Here is a chart that compares the caffeine content of coffee with other beverages, foods, and medications:

Beverages	Serving Size	Caffeine (mg)
Coffee, drip	5 oz.	110–150
Coffee, perk	5 oz.	60–125
Coffee, instant	5 oz.	40–105

Coffee, decaf	5 oz.	2–5
Tea, 5 min. steep	5 oz.	40–100
Tea, 3 min. steep	5 oz.	20–50
Hot cocoa	5 oz.	2–10

Foods	Serving Size	Caffeine (mg)
Milk chocolate	1 oz.	1–15
Bittersweet chocolate	1 oz.	5–35
Chocolate cake	1 oz.	20–30

Over-the-Counter Drugs	Dose	Caffeine (mg)
Anacin or Midol	2	64
Excedrin	2	130
Nō-Dōz	2	200
Aqua-Ban (diuretic)	2	200
Dexatrim (weight control aid)	1	100

Everyone reacts to caffeine differently, so the rule of thumb when drinking coffee should be "everything in moderation." Scientifically, caffeine increases physiological symptoms: You get a slight increase in heart rate, become alert, sweat a little more. If these symptoms become troublesome, you should cut down on your caffeine intake.

What's the best coffee in the world?

There is no single "best" coffee—the best coffee is the one you feel like drinking at the time. However, perhaps the world's most famous is Jamaica blue mountain, an extremely expensive and rare coffee from the Blue Mountains of Jamaica, which sells for $20 for half a pound. Other prized coffees include top Guatemala and Antigua coffees, certain Kenya coffees (prized for their acidity), and coffees from Papua New Guinea, which really have quite a broad flavor spectrum—lots of body, lots of flavor, and lots of acidity.

What's the worst coffee in the world?

Two species of coffee, *arabica,* used in 99.9 percent of speciality coffees, and *robusta,* a lower-growing coffee in terms of elevation, are used in commercial-grade coffees. Some commercial grades of robusta are pretty foul; for instance, Thai robusta is really bad coffee. However, robusta can be appropriately used in some commercial blends. Interestingly enough, the robusta contains twice as much caffeine as arabica coffee.

What's the best method of brewing coffee?

The direct infusion method, using what is known as a coffee press, is considered best. Put the coffee in the pot, pour just-boiled water (at a temperature between 195° and 205°F) over it, and let it steep for four minutes. Pressing the plunger removes the coffee from the water, screening out the grounds from the brewed coffee. The grounds are trapped on the bottom of the pot and infusion stops.

This method gives the fullest flavor and the best body and acidity. It also allows the coffee to sit in the water so the water can absorb its flavorful oils. The coffee press doesn't use a filter, which can transfer a paper flavor to your coffee.

Percolators tend to burn the coffee, because it cycles through again and again, and the boiling water causes bitterness. In addition, every time you hear the *bloop* noise, the water is cycling through the coffee, extracting more components (there are 800 components in coffee, only half of which have been identified) than are necessary. This also makes the coffee taste bitter. In a coffee press you use just-boiled water, not boiling water, so the coffee doesn't burn. And, after brewing, the water is separated from the coffee grounds so that it doesn't absorb the components that cause it to taste bitter.

Is coffee just ground beans, or can there be additives in coffee?

Coffee is not always 100 percent coffee. Some commercial coffee processors use fillers—e.g., coffee distributed in Eastern Europe or very low grade commercial coffee in the United States. A reputable speciality company only uses 100 percent coffee. Find a local roaster that you like and trust, and go by the taste.

Is it possible to make espresso at home as good as I get in a coffee shop?

Yes, you can get pretty close. Buy a good-quality electric pump espresso machine and a good-quality home espresso grinder. Make sure you have the correct grind for the coffee—not too fine or too coarse. This can affect how the machine pulls the espresso shot. Also make sure your machine is very clean, so that no dirt or soap affects the coffee taste. Another tip is to use filtered water. Sometimes water in different areas can have a distinct flavor which can affect the taste of the espresso. Finally, make espresso fresh and drink it fresh.

How should I store my coffee at home?

There is some debate on this issue. Most sources agree that coffee should be kept in an airtight container. They disagree, however, *where* coffee should be stored. According to Roger Scheumann of Quartermaine's, coffee should never be frozen because in the freezer water molecules crystalize and expand, shattering the cellular structure of the coffee bean, which increases oxidization. This means that the coffee goes stale faster. The refrigerator, on the other hand, is cold enough to inhibit oxidization but not cold enough to start the crystalization process.

Starbucks recommends: For coffee that will be consumed within two weeks, store in an airtight container, and keep it in a cool dark place. For coffee to be kept longer than two weeks, store in the smallest airtight container in your freezer. Do not return the coffee to the freezer once it has been removed since moisture from the condensation will hasten flavor loss. Maxwell House advocates refrigerating coffee for up to eight weeks, and freezing it for up to six months. They advise returning the coffee to the refrigerator or freezer immediately after use to prevent condensation, which makes the coffee stale.

To avoid the entire issue, the best thing to do is just to buy what you need for the week and keep it in an airtight container. The coffee then does not need to be refrigerated or frozen, simply kept in a cool dark place. Also keep in mind that whole-bean coffee retains its flavor much longer than ground, since less surface area is exposed to air. A home coffee grinder is inexpensive and will provide fresh coffee flavor every morning.

How is coffee decaffeinated?

According to Maxwell House, pure water is utilized to prepare the beans and draw out the caffeine. The beans are exposed to natural effervescence in the form of carbon dioxide (a naturally occurring gas that is present in the air). The effervescence gently draws the caffeine out of the beans, preserving the coffee flavor. No harsh chemicals are used in the decaffeination process.

At Starbucks, all decaffeination is done with green (unroasted) beans. The most commonly used method, direct contact, immerses the beans in warm-to-hot water, which raises their moisture content and brings the caffeine to their surfaces. A solvent is used to extract caffeine and wax from the beans, leaving maximum coffee flavor intact. The beans are then rinsed, dried, and shipped to the roaster. Starbucks also offers coffee decaffeinated with the Swiss Water Process, but they feel that its taste pales in comparison to direct contact decaf.

Can decaf taste as good as regular?

Caffeine is virtually tasteless and odorless, so the flavor differences between regular and decaf are primarily due to the decaffeination *process,* discussed above. Good decaf is easily obtainable, however, due to the combination of today's new decaf methods and the right blend of coffees.

Sources: Roger Scheumann, Vice President, Quartermaine coffee roasters; Maxwell House Customer Service; Starbucks Coffee contributed to questions 4, 6, 7, 8, and 9. Chart adapted from FDA data, published in the *University of California, Berkeley Wellness Letter,* © Health Letter Assoc. 1990.

Coca-Cola

What is the secret formula?

Only a few people in the company know the secret formula of Coca-Cola. It is closely guarded and kept in a vault, so as to maintain the valuable trademark.

Whatever happened to New Coke? Is it still available?

You can still buy New Coke in select places across the country where there is a demand for it. Its share, however, is small compared to Coca-Cola Classic. The company has no plans at this time to take it out of any of the current markets.

How much Coke is consumed per capita in the United States?

Per capita consumption for the United States is 363. (The number refers to an 8-oz. serving of company carbonated soft drinks per person per year.) One of every two colas and one of every three soft drinks consumed by the American public is a Coca-Cola branded product.

Does the United States consume the most Coke per capita in the world?

The United States consumes the most at 363 servings per person per year. Mexico is second, with 333 servings per person per year.

Is it true that the original formula for Coca-Cola contained cocaine? Has the formula changed from its original ingredients? If so, how many times has it changed since its beginnings?

Coca-Cola does not contain cocaine, and cocaine has never been an added ingredient for Coca-Cola. The company has indicated for years that decocainized coca-leaf flavor is one ingredient in a complex of flavors used in Coca-Cola, and the ingredient is approved by the U.S. Food and Drug Administration. The company does not discuss the formula, but rest assured, it has not changed.

Is there anywhere in the world where I *can't* find Coke?

Thanks to the world's largest distribution system, Coca-Cola can be found in nearly 200 countries (as of year-end 1996) at a rate of 889 million servings each day.

Source: George Barkley and Mary Butin, Public and Media Relations, The Coca-Cola Company.

Pipe Smoking

Which brand of pipe is best?

There isn't any one pipe brand that is the best, as this is subject to an individual's particular taste. Some people choose a pipe because of its looks, craftsmanship, or smokability.

Which pipe tobacco is the best?

This is also very subjective, due to the fact that some people like strong tobacco while others prefer mild or sweet tobacco. There are so many different types out on the market that it is very difficult to choose just one brand.

When did pipe smoking begin?

According to most recent research and documented facts, archeologists date the origins of pipe smoking to the pre-Columbian period in Central and South

America. In fact, in a temple in Chiapas, Mexico, relics and carvings were found which suggest that pipe smoking was used in Mayan rituals.

Which is the best material to use in making a pipe?

One of the finest materials used is briar, which comes from the root of the heath tree. This tree is found in France, Greece, Corsica, Sardinia, Algeria, and Turkey. Briar has heat-resistant properties that prevent the bowl of the pipe from burning.

How do you clean a pipe?

You first remove all tobacco that has been smoked, using a small knife. Then you run a pipe cleaner from the stem to the smoke chamber. You can use cognac or a little rum to clean out the residue that might be left in the bowl. Let it dry before using again.

What is the difference between a bent pipe and a straight one?

A bent pipe is easier to keep in your mouth for longer periods of time. The bent pipe hangs better, reducing the tension on the teeth due to biting the stem. A straight pipe is easier for a beginner to keep clean.

What type of pipe did Sherlock Holmes use?

He smoked a Calabash Petersen made in Ireland.

Which is the best way to light a bowl?

It is better to use either matches or a pipe lighter. Gas lighters are not recommended as they can cause damage to the bowl and may also affect the taste of the tobacco.

How long should a pipe last?

It depends upon the quality of the briar, the frequency of use of the pipe, and its maintenance. A high-quality pipe should last a lifetime.

Which style of pipe do most Americans purchase?

In general, Americans prefer freehand design pipes over the classic pipes that most Europeans like (save for the Scandinavian countries, which also have a more individualistic flair in choosing pipe design).

Source: De La Concha Tobacconist, 1390 Avenue of the Americas, New York, NY 10019; (212) 757-3167.

Wine

How important are vintages?

Less than you might think. Some years are better than others, but no wine maker will ever send poor wine into the market. Wine collectors fuss over vintages, but for most of us, wine in the shops is wine ready to drink. Most red wines can be drunk young; white wine and Beaujolais should be drunk young.

How long will a bottle of wine last once it's been opened?

Any red wine, except a very delicate old one, will last three or four days after the cork has been pulled. Simply replace the cork and put the half-empty bottle in a cool place. Often a little exposure to air will enhance a young red. An expensive white Burgundy may lose its charm, but who recorks great white Burgundy?

How does one choose the right wine for a meal?

There are books on this subject, but the basic rule still applies: red with meat and white with fish. Put it another way: the heavier the dish, the heavier the wine. Before you buy a book, find a serious wine shop; the experts there will know what you need.

There's one other rule, which supersedes the above. It says: The best wine with your meal is the one you feel like drinking.

How much wine is enough for a dinner party?

At least one bottle per person. That includes both red and white, if you plan to serve one wine with the appetizer and another with the main course. Seems like too much? Okay, get four bottles for your next dinner for eight—and be prepared to serve mineral water through the second half of the meal.

Should I open my bottle of wine before dinner to let it breathe?

If it makes you feel better. With rare exceptions, your wine will get all the fresh air it needs once you've poured it into a glass. Some powerful wines, like Barolo, which need several years in the bottle, can be softened up a bit by exposure to air, but that can be achieved by decanting. Very old wines have been known to fade and die when exposed to air; they should be opened only when they are about to be drunk.

Wine labels say, "Contains sulfites." Are sulfites harmful?

Sulphur compounds are added to wine to preserve it. U.S. government rules set the maximum amount of sulfites that can be used in wine at 350 parts per million. Modern wine-making techniques allow the use of less than half that amount.

About 5 percent of Americans suffer from chronic asthma; of that group about 5 percent, or a quarter of 1 percent of the total population, are affected by sulfites. They should not drink wine.

Are there any sulfite-free wines?

A few wineries claim to make wines without the use of sulfites as preservatives, but as a practical matter virtually every commercial wine contains some. In fact, sulfites occur naturally in all wines as a by-product of fermentation.

What about organic wines?

Wine-grape growers throughout the world have been leaders in the movement away from chemical pesticides, fungicides, and fertilizers. But only a few, in this country and in Europe, claim that their wines are made entirely from organically grown fruit. Fetzer Vineyards in California, which makes several organic wines, is one of the best-known names in the trend to organic farming. There are as yet no universally accepted standards for what constitutes an organic wine.

Will drinking red wine lengthen my life?

In moderate amounts, it probably won't shorten it. Researchers have known for years that moderate amounts of alcohol—not necessarily from wine—may lower "bad" cholesterol levels while raising "good" cholesterol levels. They may also slow the formation of blood clots. The public became acutely aware of these findings in 1991 when the CBS program *60 Minutes* cited them and implied that red wine might have something to do with the fact that the French have a lower rate of heart disease than Americans, despite the fatty French diet. In fact, 50 percent of the French never drink any wine. What's more, heart disease is France's number one killer, accounting for 30 percent of all deaths.

The best that can be said for wine—and it applies equally to red and to white—is that it's certainly not as bad as the anti-alcohol forces have painted it and that, taken in moderation, it may make life a little better.

One sees wines sold for $5,000 or more a bottle at auctions. Is the wine really worth that much?

To a wine collector, yes; to a wine drinker, no.

Is American wine as good as French and Italian wine?

Yes.

Source: Frank J. Prial, "Wine Talk," the *New York Times*.

INDEX

Bathrooms
  accessibility, 9
  painting, 42
Bee stings, 476
Beer, 638–39
Benenson, Peter, 200
Better Business Bureau, 383, 384
Bidding process (contractors), 4
Bidet, 8
Bipolar disorder, 521–23
Birds
  backyard, 56–57, 98
  protecting fruit from, 68
Birth certificates abroad, 346
Birth control, 426–30. *See also* Vasectomy
  abstinence, 426
  cervical cap, 428
  condoms, 427
  Depo-Provera, 429
  diaphragm, 428
  emergency contraception, 430
  fertility awareness methods, 426
  IUD, 428
  Norplant, 429
  outercourse, 426
  pill, 428–29
  spermicides, 427
  vaginal pouch, 427
  withdrawal, 427
Birth defects, 457
Birth records, 234–35
Blackheads, 606
Bleaches, 13
Blood, safety of abroad, 342, 343
Blood donation, 430–31
Blood pressure, 502–3, 625
  and strokes, 515
Blueberries, 66
Boilers, 20
Bonaparte, Charles J., 203
Bonds, 414
Bone density, 512
Bookmarking (Web browser), 132
Brain tumors, 482–83
Breast cancer, 484–85
  detecting, 484
  risk factors, 484
Brewpub, 639
Brushes, paint, 40
Budgets, 392–94
Builders, 4
Bulbs, planting, 58–59
Bulimia, 525–26
Bulletin board systems (BBSs), 123
Business, small, 378, 411–13
Business cards (abroad), 327, 333–34
Business plan, 411–12
Business travel, 325–27
  cultural differences, 332–34
Butterflies, 57

C

Caffeine, 642, 643–44
Calcium, 512–13
Calories, 617–18
Cancer, 479–82. *See also* Brain tumors; Breast cancer; Lymphoma; Prostate cancer
  racial differences, 480
  viral agents, 481
  warning signals, 482
Candling (eggs), 614
Canned food, storing, 615–16
Capital, raising, 412
Cardiopulmonary resuscitation (CPR), 579
Cardiovascular disease. *See* Heart attack; Heart disease
Caregivers, in-home, 168–71. *See also* Baby-sitters
  interviews, 169–70
  placement agencies, 168–69
  written agreements, 170
Carpet and Rug Institute Seal of Approval, 10
Carpets, 9–12
  barrier-free living, 6
  burns, 12
  cleaning, 11–12
  fibers, 10
  padding, 11
  piles, 9–10
  vacuuming, 11
  wall-to-wall installation, 10
Cars. *See* Automobiles
Ceilings
  painting, 40
  types, 53
Central processing unit (CPU), 110, 146
Cerebral palsy, 488–89
Certificates of deposit (CDs), 394
Certified public accountant (CPA), 377–79
Chair, office, 24
Challenger shuttle, 215–16
Chapter 11 bankruptcy, 358
Chervil, 80
Chicken. *See* Poultry
Chicken pox, 490–93
  complications, 491
  vaccine, 492–93
Child abuse, 153–55
  abusers, 154
  deaths, 154–55
  sexually abused children, 154, 180
  types, 154
Child Care Aware information hotline, 171
Child-care programs, 165–67
  costs, 167
  evaluating, 166
  licensing, 166
Child custody
  disputes, 176
  and sexual orientation of parent, 261
Childbirth
  preparation, 447–50
  water birth, 464–67
Children's television. *See* Television, children's
Children's Television Act, 162
Chiropractic, 542–44

diagnostic X-rays, 544
educational requirements, 543
Chlorofluorocarbons (CFCs), 22
Chocolate, 639–42
  baking, 641
  caffeine, 642
  grand cru, 640
  physiological effects, 641
Choice-in-Dying (CID), 581
Cholesterol, 618, 623, 624, 650
Chronic fatigue syndrome (CFS), 493–95
Cigars, 642–43
Cilantro, 80
Circumcision, 434–36
  foreskin function, 435
  risks, 435
Citizen's arrest, 209
Citizenship, U.S., 323–24
  dual nationality, 323–24
Civil Rights Act, 250, 260, 286
Cleansing (skin), 604
Clothing damage liability, 290
Coca-Cola, 646–47
Coffee, 643–46
  additives, 645
  brewing, 644–45
  caffeine, 643–44
  decaffeinated, 646
  storing, 645–46
Coffee press, 644–45
Cold cuts, 610
Coldframes, 72–74
College
  paying for, 401–4
  selecting, 197–98
College catalogs, 197–98
Colors and interior design, 32, 51
Comforter, drying, 14–15
Commodities market, 379–81
Comparison shopping, 392
Compensatory damages, 271
Compost, 60–61
Compulsions, 528
Computer viruses, 138–40
Computers
  backing up, 117–20, 143
  booting failures, 142–43
  buying, 110–16
  data recovery, 143
  hard disks, 146–47
  lighting, 36
  memory, 143, 146, 148
  multimedia, 111
  peripheral installation, 144
  RAM requirements, 143
  sources of information, 122–24
  upgrades, 110–11, 147–48
  used, 116
  video, 147
  warranties, 114
Concerned United Birthparents, 235
Concrete, painting, 41
Condensation problems, 31
Condominiums, 361
Condoms, 427, 461, 516

Congressional Research Service (CRS), 227
Contraceptives. *See* Birth control
Contractors, 4
  fences, 16, 17
  insulation, 30, 31
Cooperatives, 361
Copyright, 242–44
  fair use, 242
  public domain, 243, 244
  registration, 244
  sheet music, 244
Copyright Office, U.S., 229
Corticosteroids, 475
Cortisone injections, 475
Cosmetic labels, 588–90
  active ingredient, 590
  alcohol-free, 589
  fragrance-free, 589
  hypoallergenic, 589
  natural, 589
Cosmetics. *See also* Makeup application; Skin care
  shelf life, 586, 602
Cost-of-living adjustment (COLA), 226
Counters, kitchen, 34, 626
Cover crops, 100–101
Cover letters (employment application), 372–74
CPR, 579
Credit bureaus, 374–75
Credit cards
  annual percentage rates, 393
  secured, 359, 375
Credit reports, 374–76
Creeping phlox, 76
Cremation, 563, 571–74
Crime. *See also* Victims' rights
  sentencing, 282–85
Cruises, 328–31
  and children, 328
  contracts, 331
  insurance, 331
  medical services, 330–31
  tipping, 330
Cultivation, 63
Customs (U.S.) restrictions, 334–35, 350–52
Cutting boards, 626
Cystic fibrosis, 495–96

D

Dandruff, 593
Dating (food products), 612, 614–17
Deadheading (flowers), 63
Deafness (travelers), 338
Death penalty, 202, 285
Debt collection, 244–47
Deer (least favored plants), 68
Defendants' rights, 285
DEFRAG program, 146
Defrosting food, 626, 633–34
Deja news, 136
Delta hepatitis, 501
Delusions, 532
Dental hygiene, 436–38. *See also* Teeth
Dentistry, cosmetic, 587–88

testing, sex offenders, 298
HIV-positive physician, 264–65
Hives, 476
Hodgkin's disease, 485–86
Hoes, 70
Hollow-wall fasteners, 52–53
Home, buying, 360–62
Home equity loans, 394
Home insurance, 381–83, 394
  deductibles, 382
  discounts, 382
Home office, 24–27, 421–23
  arrangement, 27
  interruptions, avoiding, 25–26
  location, 25, 26
  supplies, storing, 26–27
Home shopping (television), 385
Homeopathy, 545–48
  ailments best used for, 545–46
  insurance coverage, 547–48
  medicines, 546
Hoover, J. Edgar, 204
Hormone replacement therapy (HRT), 454, 484,
  513
Hoses, 71–72
Hospice care, 574–76
Hospitals, choosing, 433–34
  accreditation, 434
  teaching hospitals, 433
Hot flashes, 451–52
Houseplants, 84–86
  and air conditioning, 85
  insect control, 85–86
  watering, 84–85
Human rights, 200–202
Humidifiers, 20
Humidity, indoor, 22
Humidors, 643
Humus, 101
Hung juries, 270
Hybrid plants, 77
Hydroponics, 81–83
Hydrosols, 539, 540
Hygrometer, 642
Hypertension, 502–3
  risk factors, 503
  and strokes, 515
Hysterectomy, 440–43
  risks, 441–42
  types, 440–41

I

Immune globulin, 340–41
Immunotherapy (allergies), 475
In vitro fertilization, 445–46
Incontinence, 452
Individual retirement account (IRA), 401, 558
Infertility, 443–46
  causes, 444
  insurance for treatment, 446
Inflation, 417
Information, freedom of access to, 205–8
Informed consent, 264

Ink stains, 14
Inkjet printers, 126, 127
Insect control
  biological methods, 69
  cultural control, 68–69
  houseplants, 85–86
Insomnia, 504–5
  causes, 504
  types, 504
Insulation, 30–32
  R-values, 30
  types, 30
Insulin-dependent diabetes (IDDM), 497, 498
Insulin injections, 498
Insurance. See Automobile insurance; Home insur-
  ance; Life insurance
Insurance agents, 391
Integrated pest management (IPM), 68
Interest rates and Federal Reserve System, 416, 417
Interior design, 32–33
International Concerns for Children (ICC), 234
Internet, 128–37
  and children, 163
  college catalogs, 197–98
  Library of Congress, 228
  newsgroups, 123, 134–37
  search engines, 128–29
Internet service provider (IPS), 131
Investment adviser, registered, 405
Investment clubs, 386–87
Irrigation systems, 107

J

Jeweler, choosing, 308, 309
Jewelry, 308–9
Job Accommodation Network, 248
Job interviews, 388–90
Jury duty, 269–71
  employer's responsibility, 258
Jury System Improvement Act, 258

K

Karmal, Marjorie, 447
Kevorkian, Jack, 266, 577
Kidney disease, 506–7
  types, 506
  warning signs, 506
Kidney stones, 506–7
Kitchen cabinets, 34
Kitchen sink drain, cleaning, 625
Kitchens, remodeling, 33–35
  costs, 33–34
  work triangle, 34–35
Kuhn, Maggie, 555

L

Labels, cosmetic. See Cosmetic labels
Lamaze, 447–50
Lambda Legal Defense and Education Fund, 263
Landscaping, 86–87
Lanolin, 586, 589

cost-of-living adjustment, 226
disability benefits, 224–25, 226
survivor benefits, 224–25, 226
taxes on benefits, 225
Social Security Administration (SSA), 224
Sodomy laws, 263
Sofa, 18
Soil, 98–102
  aeration, 101–2
  improving, 99–100
  red, 101
  testing, 99
  types, 98–99
Solution culture (plants), 81
Space station, 215, 216
Speculators (futures), 379–80
Spotlighting, 35, 37
Stafford Loan, 403
Sterilization, tubal, 429
Stockbrokers, 409, 415
Stocks, 409–11, 414–16
  accounts, cash or margin, 410
  brokerage firms, 409, 415
  dividends, 415
  over-the-counter, 414
  risks, 410–11
Strawberries, 66
Stroke, 513–15
  racial differences, 514
  risks, controlling, 515
  types, 513–14
  warning signs, 514
Sugars, 618–19
Suicide, physician-assisted, 266, 576, 577–78
Sulfites, 649–50
Sunscreens, 604, 607
Supplemental Security Income (SSI), 211
Survivor benefits, Social Security, 224–25, 226
Syphilis, 516–17

T

Tanning, 606–8
Tape drives, 118, 119
Tar paper, 45
Taxes
  extensions, 223
  forms, 223, 224
  household employees, 170–71
  itemizing, 224
  refunds, 223
  Social Security benefits, 225
Tea roses, 92
Teenagers, parenting, 193–97
Teeth
  bonding, 438, 587
  brushing, 436–37
  flossing, 437
  whitening, 437–38, 587
Telecommuting, 421–23
Telemarketers, 48, 385
Telephone calls, unwanted, 48
Television, avoiding glare, 35
Television, children's, 158–63

blocking technologies, 161–62
monitoring by parents, 160–62
negative influences, 159–60
time spent watching, 158–59, 162
Temper tantrums, 172
Term life insurance, 390
Thermometer, meat, 627, 630, 631, 633
Thermostats, 21, 23
THOMAS, congressional database, 228
Thomas Jefferson Building, Library of Congress, 229
Ticks, 344, 509–10
Tile roofs, 45
Timers, lighting, 46
Tobacco. See Smoking
Toilets
  cleaning, 7–8
  low-flow, 8
Tomatoes, heirloom, 78–79
Tools, 28–29
  garden, 69–72
Topsoil, 101
Track lighting, 37
Trade secrets, 259
Traffic tickets, 294–96
Trans Union Corporation, 375
Transient ischemic attacks, 514, 515
Travel warnings, 325
Traveler's diarrhea, 336–37
Treasury notes, 394
Tube feeding, 578–79
Turkey, cooking, 627, 628–31
  safety guidelines, 629
Typhoid fever, 349–50

U

Unemployment insurance, 418–20
  benefits, 251, 257, 260, 420
  eligibility, 419
Unidentified flying objects (UFOs), 204
Universal design, 5–6, 9
Universal life insurance, 391
Upholstery, 18
Urinary tract infections, 452
Used cars. See Automobiles
User groups, 115, 123–24

V

Vacation offers, free, 384
Vaccinations (for travel abroad), 326
Vapor retarders, 30–31
Vasectomy, 429–30, 462–64
  electrocautery, 463
  and sexual performance, 462–63
Vegetable oils, 624
Vegetables, 102–4
  fertilizing, 102
  root vegetables, storing, 104
  rotating, 103
  watering, 103
Vegetarian diets, 634–35
  types, 634